MW00577957

Restitution and Memory

RESTITUTION AND MEMORY

Material Restoration in Europe

Edited by

Dan Diner

and

Gotthart Wunberg

Berghahn Books
NEW YORK • OXFORD

Published in 2007 by
Berghahn Books

www.berghahnbooks.com

Library of Congress Cataloging-in-Publication Data

Restitution and memory: material restoration in Europe/edited by Dan Diner and Gotthart Wunberg.

p. cm.

Papers presented at an international conference held June 21–23, 2001 in Vienna.

Includes bibliographical references and index.

ISBN 1-84545-220-8 (alk. paper)

1. Holocaust, Jewish (1939–1945)—Reparations—Congresses. 2. Jews—Claims—Congresses. 3. Collective memory—Europe—Congresses. I. Diner, Dan.- II. Wunberg, Gotthart.

D819.E85R47 2006
940.53'18144—dc22

2006013938

British Library Cataloguing in Publication Data

A catalogue record for this book is available from the British Library.

Printed in the United States on acid-free paper.

ISBN 1-84545-220-8 hardback

Contents

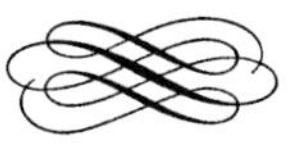

Tesselated European Histories of Memory

Resolutions

INTRODUCTION

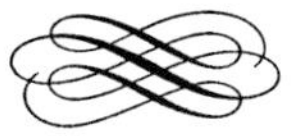

World War II never ended. It is still very much with us. At least that is how it may appear if one looks at the myriad debates on restitution and memory that have come to occupy discourse and debate within the national cultures of the old continent for more than a decade. Increasingly, a memory of World War II is emerging that remained hidden beneath the Cold War's taut surface. That memory is now resurgent, especially in the wake of the recent eastward expansion of the European Union. It is connected with the ever more intense transposing of constituents of the sovereignty of the nation-states onto the plane of European institutions. Paradoxically, this process is bolstered by a concomitant manifest rebounding of the nation-state in the very process of globalization. This pervasive tendency is bound up with complex and profound events basically flowing from the icon of 1989 and its watershed events. That led to a new phenomenon: with the reinstitution of *historical spaces* on the heels of the end of the Cold War, the *historical times* interwoven with these spaces were re-invoked once more in memory's chamber of consciousness. A concomitant phenomenon was that in the aftermath of communism's collapse in these areas, the changing collective order of economy went hand in hand specifically with an evocation of the complex of remembrance of World War II. Those were memories that appeared to have been under a lasting imposition of nonrecollection.

In particular, we can note that the mounting privatizations and reprivatizations in "Eastern Europe" are transporting something that might be called a *memory of materia*—an ensemble of remembrance that was long neutralized or silenced under the blanket of collectivization and nationalization of property after 1945. Private property redux and rehabilitated, the so-called memory of things, is proving to be a lever for prying open a recrystallizing memory of the period that went before—the prewar era, as well as and most precisely the catastrophe of World War II, when along with staggering losses in human life, there were also immense intrusions into the existing reticulation of property relations. It is thus justified to presume that the foreseeable future of Europe will be accompanied by the rush of memory of that foundational event par excellence—World War II—which drew all European peoples into its vortex. This is how best to comprehend the paradoxical thesis that is our terminus a quo: in the history of memory, the period of the war is still very much present and accounted for.

The chapters in this volume attempt to arrive at a kind of interim assessment of the problematic of restitution, closely interconnected with the discourses of memory that have emerged in the last decade of the twentieth century. The authors proceed from a shared view that the massive remembrance of the Holocaust, in keeping with shifts and fault-lines in concomitant phenomena in the constitution of culture and political identity, has expanded into a discourse on questions of restitution that is universalizing, reaching far beyond the paradigm of Jewish experience of catastrophe. Indeed, it appears that the paradigm of the Holocaust is being generalized as an expression of the ultimate experience of catastrophe, augmented to the point that the concrete historical event and icon we call "Auschwitz" is making increased use of a discourse of human rights. Such a conversion of particularistic Jewish experience into a universal moral and morality is most manifest materially in the question of restitution.

Ultimately it was an ensemble of Jewish organizations, linked together in the Claims Conference against Germany established in 1951, which raised demands for compensation, reparation and restitution. It did so in a manner that must indeed be regarded as an innovative departure against the backdrop of the historical experience of interstate agreements on damages after an international conflict, where one state confronts another. Formative as a matrix here was in particular the fact that the reality of the genocide and the resultant phenomenon of heirless property brought about a kind of transformation in the web of claims in civil law, raising these to a public level of quasi-international law—in this way enabling the "Jewish people" to constitute itself as the claimant putting forward a collective demand.

With the reinstitution of private property in ex-socialist Eastern Europe, the watershed year 1989 led to new demands. That was also bound up with a simultaneous opening of the archives long sealed there, and should be seen against the backdrop of the reconfiguring culture of memory that had already emerged earlier in the West. Initially these were largely Jewish demands, but soon, they extended to other groups of Nazi victims never before indemnified—including individuals, who as former citizens of the people's democracies and the Soviet Union, had previously been excluded from compensation. Interesting in this debate on restitution that began in the 1990s is likewise a new, more absolute attitude toward *private* property, driven by the modes of globalization and individualization: and this is in comparison with its understanding in the postwar period, when public claims had a more fundamental character. This debate also led to a readiness on the part of various German firms to try on their own to cast light into the dark recesses of their company histories during National Socialism through specially appointed commissions of historians, in certain circumstances also contributing materially to compensation for past injustices.

As a result of the deepening internationalization of law, juridical traditions that in the past were relatively separate strands are beginning to intertwine. Thus, the principles of American civil law differ from continental European usage in that they tend to privilege the restoration of previous titles of ownership even after a long period of lapse, while continental European law prefers to prioritize legal security and thus the concept of *Rechtsfriede*, "legal peace." Consequently, differing temporal conceptions of expectations of justice clash along with different traditions of law. In any event, such tensions were clearly operative in the 1990s in the clash between North American and European legal culture as debates raged regarding the restitution of former private property.

The strengthening of private property over the past decade springing both from the decline in collective forms of ownership in the former state-socialist societies and planetary tendencies toward globalization is one side in the bolstering of past claims to restitution that we can observe. The other side is rooted in an analogous tendency toward increased generalization of human rights and their scope, quite beyond the perimeter of all concrete historical circumstances and their circumscriptions. More and more, the resultant moral evaluation of suffering inflicted by human beings on their fellows transcends the confines of a historical assessment in the sense of the nexus between cause and effect, responsibility and guilt. Such an anthropologizing or universalizing of human suffering is ultimately situated in a realm beyond history. Increasingly, that is leading to a new evaluation of relevant events in World War II. If all violence inflicted by man on man is infused with a drastic moral stigma beyond the envelope of all historical circumstances, then the expulsion of the Germans in the final phase of the war, for instance, and the strategic bombing campaign of the Allies, should be weighed and assessed in terms of that "anthropological" perception, not the historical one. And if the historical image of the war is shifted in the direction of a prism of evaluation in which human suffering sui generis is highlighted, beyond the reticulations of cause and effect, responsibility and guilt, then claims for restitution may arise that would have been inconceivable in this form and focus in earlier decades—especially if international agreements can be undercut and relativized by claims moored in civil law, buttressed by European integration and the concomitant strengthening of private property vis-à-vis activity by the national government. It is in any case by no means agreed whether this could become relevant in the German-Czech and German-Polish relation, viewed against the backdrop of events in the final phase of the war and its immediate aftermath.

The papers collected in this volume originated in the main from a joint initiative of the International Research Center for the Cultural Sciences (Internationales Forschungszentrum Kulturwissenschaften, IFK) in Vienna and the Simon Dubnow Institute for Jewish History and Culture at Leipzig University, supported by the Fritz Thyssen Foundation, Cologne. Sociologists, anthropologists, historians, legal experts and scholars in literary studies here look from differing vantages and platforms of expertise at the connection between memory and property in their importance for the question of restitution as a reinstatement of justice after the fact in collective conflicts. World War II in Europe is the historical ambient for the present collection of studies. The perspective here centers not only on the past. Rather, it is committed to examining that question and the associated complex of practice in their significance for a common European memory.

The introductory article (Dan Diner) illuminates this vantage point, which views World War II as the foundational act of shared European memory. The section "Anthropologizing Restitution" (John Borneman, Natan Sznaider and Sigrid Weigel) deals with the question of the convertibility of suffering into money. It thematizes the problematic of compensation within the irresoluble tension between loss and material restitution. The section "Commissions of Inquiry and the Practice of Restitution" contains papers by a historian and a legal expert with hands-on experience in restitution practice, in which they became engaged in the 1990s beyond the perimeters of their own profession (Lutz Niethammer, Clemens Jabloner). A central section, entitled "Tesselated European Histories of Memory," seeks to explore the diverse facets of the development of restitution in Europe. Special micrological studies deal with the restitution claims of rural Jews in southern Germany (Ulrich Baumann); the discussion on Jedwabne, so traumatic today for Poles (François Guesnet); and the importance of plundered Jewish libraries and book collections as arsenals of collective memory (Markus Kirchhoff). The Central European context after 1989 is the focus of a comparative study (Catherine Horel), while the quite differing circumstances of restitution and national memory for recipients of restitution in Hungary and Austria is examined in companion papers (Béla Rásky, Heidemarie Uhl). An investigation of the question of the role of the Swiss banks centers not only on the situation of a neutral country not militarily involved in the conflict but also spotlights a case which has increasingly become a kind of paradigm for the 1990s (Elazar Barkan). There is a significant shift in perspective in a chapter centering on the expulsion of the Germans, viewed from the topical vantage of Poles and Czechs (Claudia Kraft). The open questions of the relations between Jews and Arabs are investigated in a micro-study on a Haifa neighborhood. Here the memories of Arabs who were expelled or fled in 1948 are contrasted and compared with those of Oriental Jews who settled in Haifa after 1948, as one burden of suffering is weighed against another in the scales of memory and the urban environment (Yfaat Weiss). The volume closes with a comprehensive study on the German practices of compensation given to Jews after World War II (Hans Günter Hockerts)—that paradigmatic case of *Wiedergutmachung*, which preceded all other restitution efforts and initiatives.

We would like to express our gratitude for the support provided by Dr. Eva Cescutti, Internationales Forschungszentrum Kulturwissenschaften Wien (IFK), as well as Dirk Sadowski and Sebastian Voigt, Simon Dubnow Institute for Jewish History and Culture at Leipzig University. Without the outstanding intellectual and organized skills of Philipp Graf, Simon Dubnow Institute, his dedicated involvement in the material and formal supervision at all stages of the preparation of the texts gathered in this anthology, the task of completing this project possibly would not have been fulfilled. For this we are extremely thankful.

Dan Diner / Gotthart Wunberg

Part I:
The Setting

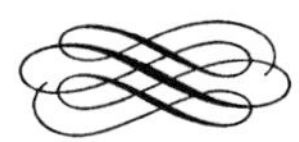

— *One* —

MEMORY AND RESTITUTION: WORLD WAR II AS A FOUNDATIONAL EVENT IN A UNITING EUROPE

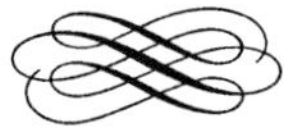

Dan Diner

Europe, on the track to enlarged integration, seems to be successively constructing a common, unifying canon of binding values. That canon is based on human rights and a powerful repudiation of genocide. It is rooted historically in the memory of the events of World War II and what is increasingly emerging a posteriori as its core event—the Holocaust. Such a commonly shared European memory is not only assuming the salience of an arsenal of remembrance. It is also being transformed into a seminal event—a foundational act, so to speak. To a certain extent, this grounding event is quite comparable with the impact of the Reformation or the French Revolution—watersheds to which historical memory, as it thickens into a catalogue of narratives and values, seems to lead back.

The conception of World War II as an act of political foundation for a future and united Europe is not novel. Immediately after 1945, statesmen such as the Frenchman Robert Schuman, the German Konrad Adenauer, and the Italian Alcide de Gasperi, propagated in due time the idea of Europe as a project for defusing antagonistic historical nationalisms on the continent. All three personalities were more or less deeply rooted in the nineteenth century, by dint alone of their age; they were also deeply attached to the peripheries of their respective nation-states. Schuman was born in Luxembourg and educated in German-annexed Alsace; he fought in the Imperial German Army during World War I.[1] Adenauer, the former mayor of Cologne, always stressed his distance from the Protestant and Prussian dominated German nation-state; after

1919, he was even blamed for the emergence of something like a pro-French Rhenish swell of separatism.[2] De Gasperi stemmed from Trento, an irredenta area, and up until World War I served as a member of the imperial parliament in Vienna, the old-Austrian *Reichsrat*.[3] All were conscious Catholics; their common language was German. As a former Central-European imperial language, German at the time functioned in Europe as a "universal" language of wider communication. The historical perceptions of these three figures were evidently molded by the strongly negative experience of World War I as a European civil war driven by excessive nationalism, while World War II was interpreted as its mere continuation. However, their intention to neutralize the historically established national antagonisms on the continent by creating a unified Europe—something we might term today (in the language of cultural studies) as "particular and solely collective memories institutionalized by territorialized state power"—was by and large the result of external circumstances. It was far less the making of the European statesmen themselves. Indeed, the Cold War's chemistry acted as the great neutralizer of the substrate of nationalism and the particularistic memories bound up with it—nationalist particularities that had been central in European history for far more than a century.[4]

The pivotal category for the following inquiry into the fundamental changes that occurred during the Cold War and in the European domain (though not exclusively in Europe) is the notion of "neutralization." The term encompasses a revocation of historically established national antagonisms as well the collective memories that go with them. The concept of neutralization is borrowed from a specific tradition in juridical and political thought that seeks to deal with the consequences of the New Order subsequent to the Peace of Westphalia and the nature of the absolutist state. This school of thought tended to neutralize, i.e. to internalize or privatize religious belonging as the dominant configuration of political partisanship and public truth. The tendency toward neutralizing religious partisanship in the public sphere—the obligation to pursue peace, not truth—was given its ultimate emblematic formula in Hobbes' dictum: "*auctoritas, non veritas facit legem.*"[5]

In political and legal theory as well as in international law, this Hobbesian tradition of the neutralization of "truth" in politics was appropriated and elaborated later on, in the twentieth century, by Carl Schmitt. He dubbed the era after the Westphalian peace an "epoch of neutralization." That would later be transformed by Reinhart Koselleck's work on the late absolutist era. He developed a fundamental historical paradigm of interpretation, especially in his path-breaking *Critique and Crisis*.[6]

In the beginning was the Cold War. It was formally launched by the Truman Doctrine in 1947. From that year on, the dominant academic and public discourse became one of ideological confrontation. This tendency contrasted with the formerly dominant layer upon layer of the various national interpretations of history in the European domain—interpretations bound up with past memories.[7] From that point on, an opposition in societal inspirations and values came to hold sway: freedom and democracy as espoused by the Western alliance contra the Soviet Union and the so-called people's republics of the East, championing a distorted ideal of literal social equality. Such a global confrontation in values, extending far beyond the former leading concepts of nations and nationality, characterized the conflict between East and West as a kind of *international civil war*.[8] Indeed—and this makes this phenomenon relevant for our focus here—this global dualism in values successively upstaged World War II and its prehistories, so to speak. Up until that point, these values had shaped all thought and action, ultimately seeking to master them judicially through the Nuremberg trials. From this juncture on, they receded ever more into the background, while the new context of international civil war—based on opposing albeit universal values—absorbed the seminal event of World War II, integrating it into its modes of interpretation, in the process distorting its very significance.[9]

These antagonisms in values were highly significant for the dualistic nature of the Cold War. But at the very core of the memory of World War II is the impact of the nuclear bomb and the universal threat of global destruction. And above all there is the arch-event in its shadow—Auschwitz, or more broadly what is called the Holocaust. Western consciousness was slow in comprehending its ontology as ultimate genocide, because the West had to confront the nuclear threat as well as the moral and the ethical questions it posed—most particularly the possibility of mutual annihilation, a kind of universal doom.[10] In the 1950s and 1960s, Auschwitz and Hiroshima were referred to almost universally in one and the same breath. Often they were invoked simultaneously, to point up the means and feasibility of mass destruction inherent in Western civilization—or even in the diabolical potential of modernity as such.[11] It might well seem that the emerging universal menace of nuclear destruction at the high point of the Cold War suppressed the event of Auschwitz as an ultimate genocide before humankind had grasped its very meaning. In this context, it is interesting to note that during the late 1970s and early 1980s, when public fear peaked under the impact of political debate over removing American medium-range missiles in Western Europe in general and in the Federal Republic in particular, the angst of a potential nuclear destruction of Germany was palpably illustrated by a constant barrage of photos and metaphors specifically connected to the Holocaust. By expressing possible German victimization, the memory of the past was verbalized in a trope of massive destruction—although paradoxically in a reversed manner, contraphobically.[12]

So the Cold War cast a cloak of forgetting over the meaning as well as the remembrance of World War II. That result was compounded by the fact that the epistemic of interpretation in the age of the confrontation of values was primarily geared to the paradigm of *society*.[13] The latter's power qua paradigm to neutralize memory, its unquestioned dominance, had become most evident where historiography shifted to focus on social history, increasingly oriented to a totally *societal* interpretation of past realities. That primacy of what was bound up with society in historical interpretation was evident particularly in states that were indeed by and large, by dint of division and the Cold War, simply "societies," like the Federal Republic of Germany. West Germany was an institutionalized society-based polity, not a nation-state. And simply by virtue of its class-oriented understanding of history, the German Democratic Republic—as the opposing polity of the Federal Republic in the antagonism of values in conflict—was, according to the principles of Marxism-Leninism, properly obliged to espouse hard-core materialist imaginaries of the social as its guiding *telos*. However, it was no surprise then that with the universal termination of the ideological validity of an all-embracing materialist perception of historical reality, the GDR, based so exclusively on social constructions, seemed to unravel and wither away.[14]

In respect to its political pedigree, Austria, the third successor state of the Nazi Reich, occupied a kind of middle position between the other two during the Cold War. Even at the time of the founding of the First Austrian Republic in 1918, it had been conceived as a republican nation-state that resembled Germany but was by no means identical to it. Austria's post–World War I leanings toward an enlarged German nation-state were propagated by its Vienna-centered Social Democracy, trying to attach itself to the more progressive developments in the Reich at the time. Ultimately, this objective was fulfilled negatively (when compared to the original demand) by National Socialism and the common German experience of World War II. In 1943, the status of the Austrian nation was ironically elevated by the Allies by giving it the cachet of victimhood. This was a crass reversal of historical reality and Austrian popular consciousness; its upshot was long-term collective amnesia.[15]

In 1955, this amnesia in Austrian collective memory was augmented with the restoration of the country's sovereignty, grounded on so-called permanent neutrality. In this way, Austria's neutrality, anchored constitutionally and in international accords, served to institutionalize the memory of the immediate Nazi past, even to neutralize it. That was a tendency strengthened by the fact that most Austrian politicians of the immediate post-war era and shortly thereafter were either political victims of Nazism, incarcerated in concentration camps, or political émigrés—communicating their narratives as Nazi victims to the ensemble of the post-war Austrian nation.[16]

When society, the previously dominant paradigm of interpretation, was rudely surprised at the end of the Cold War by the wholesale return of historical memory, the impact of its global and especially European transformation was almost pre-programmed to have a drastic impact on the Republic of Austria. This watershed spelled a dramatic awakening for the Austrian polity; up to now, it had led a sleepy, if comfortable existence, wedged between the ideological blocks of freedom on the one hand and the distorted ideal of basic equality on the other. Now the new reality acted to banish it from that Eden of neutered memory. And to complicate matters: the country found itself on the doorstep of the Balkans, with its welter of ethnic turmoil in the wake of rekindled memory there.[17]

The case of Austria can exemplify the broader transformation across Europe over the past decade. Everywhere one can sense the epistemic metamorphosis of narratives based on *society* into those of *memory*—particularly in connection with that foundational event on which more and more eyes in Europe now find their attention riveted, World War II, with its emerging core, the Holocaust. Such a reemergence, however, is not free from ambiguities. When memory is invoked, it contains the experiences of the different powers, nations, and ethnicities involved in the previous struggle. Although European values rely fundamentally on the arsenal of memory of World War II, the memory as such is separated, sectioned off in accordance with the different particular differences of the nations involved. A built-in tension appears. And the result of this inherent tension of memory becomes ever more obvious—the creeping sense that World War II is still not over.

There has been much speculation about the strengthening impact of the memory of the Holocaust—about this seemingly paradoxical fast rewind of recollection as it recedes in time. The intention is not to interpret the time-retarding effect of traumatic historical experiences, or the influence that the process of coming to judicial terms with the event has had on the constitution of memory. Those were indeed trials which had some impact on the old Federal Republic of Germany, and to a certain extent—although quite differently—in Israel as well.[18] Neither will this evaluation take a look at the debate that has recently flared regarding a real or imputed conscious cultivation of the Holocaust, especially in the United States, as an expression of the domestic discourses of ethnified identities. Those discourses were sparked in America in the late 1960s by an emerging rivalry in victimhood.[19] Through its treatment in the media, especially in the film industry in the 1970s, that manifestation is believed to have resulted in a veritable globalized phenomenon of Holocaust-centred remembrance—and this extending over and beyond the specific elements of the European domain of experience.[20]

As important as all these tendencies may have been for the enhancement of Holocaust memory, our interest here centers more on the specific conditions and factors in present-day Europe. Here lies the "old continent," where the Holocaust was, after all, perpetrated, and where its remembrance impacts factually on political discourse and future political realities.[21]

The growing awareness about the Holocaust evident in Europe particularly since 1989 seems to be largely moored in a basic anthropological assumption—the obvious, indeed, organic interconnection between the restitution of private property rights and the evocation of past memories, or vice versa: *restitution of property as the result of recovered memory.*[22] This intriguing conjunction between property and memory can help to explain why World War II and the Holocaust may well look forward to a long future in an emergent European common memory.[23]

Let us look at most recent German history, the unification of the two German states in 1989–90. The unification was not just a national event, although the reestablishing of the unified German nation-state was its immediate implication. Rather, it should be understood as the outcome of a far more sweeping development, namely the collapse of communism and the associated retraction or revocation of the socializations and nationalizations of *property* instituted in the second half of the 1940s in the "people's republics."

As is well known, a treaty was concluded between the yet existing two German states to oversee the process of merger—the so-called Unification Agreement signed August 31, 1990. One of its important paragraphs, Article 41, stipulates that prior ownership rights from 1949 onward are to be reinstated—the principle of *Rückgabe vor Entschädigung*, or "restitution before compensation."[24]

This seemingly modest formulation is in fact quite loaded. Its practical (not just metaphorical) consequence is that restored private property tends to seek its former legal owner. By restoring former private ownership rights, the social substratum inherent to the institution of property—and by covering a period far beyond the biological life span of the individual owner, the practice takes on a trans-generational dimension. As a result, re-privatization—not just privatization—re-invokes the trans-generational dimension of memory. By its very nature, restitution of private property acts as a means of remembrance, while the postwar nationalizations and socializations carried out by the communists in Central and East Central Europe had had just the opposite effect: they functioned to neutralize memory. Not just memory about the legal rights of private property, bound to mere objects—no, this went far further, to encompass memory of times past, tethered to *longue-durée* prewar events as well as *court-durée* traumatic events during the war.

In the meantime, most especially after 1989, restored property titles have come to function as a kind of fulcrum for memory, geared to reappropriating the past. More and more, the land register becomes an arsenal of a memory complex extending further back, beyond the postwar socializations, as these layers are successively pealed off. They disclose so-called Aryanizations of property carried out but a few years earlier, lying right beneath. Such an archaeology of legal claims reflects the layer-by-layer succession of violence and political coercion in the past. Anthropologically, property and memory are interrelated epistemically.[25]

This insight into the dynamic relation between memory and property strikes the mind as quite plausible. It is plausible in that it assists in better grasping why in the 1990s the question of restitution snowballed in Europe. Its point of departure was restored property in the East, formerly socialized and later restituted. Its momentum spread, soon pulling Aryanized possessions and hidden bank accounts into its dynamics. The property-memory nexus also helps to understand why it radiated out in a kind of universal wave, a surge from the former Eastern European people's democracies, sweeping over countries in the West. Its inundation reached countries that had been staunchly neutral during the war, like Switzerland. Precisely by dint of their neutrality, countries like Switzerland were allowed to proceed with a certain kind of normality, with a seeming fabric of continuity from the prewar to the postwar area. That was a normalcy pretty much inconceivable in the rest of war-torn Europe.[26]

Yet such restitution—and the concomitant reinstated validity of past times of memory—will obviously have a far-reaching, even universal, impact. And this beyond the extreme case, likewise so paradigmatic, of the Jewish experience in Europe. In principle, this subtends all unilateral changes by force in the sphere of property relations. In Europe, a line could be drawn from the Nazi Aryanizations and the exploitation of slave-labor to the later acts of expropriation and socialization by socialist regimes after 1945—actions of disowning and expropriation of previous nationalizations, precipitated by demographic expulsions after 1945 from the former German East, the Sudetenland, and the forced flight of ethnic Germans from other regions of eastern and southeastern Europe.[27] Moreover, some of these events fuse elements of politically oriented socialization and ethnic nationalization, a fact also true of conflicts elsewhere that were an immediate result of the European catastrophe of World War II and that likewise led to population movements.[28]

Thus, for instance, the establishment of the Jewish state in 1948—obviously not *in* Europe but most certainly *of* Europe—stems directly from the temporal icon of 1945, just as the flight and expulsion of the Palestinian Arabs found a certain subjective justification in Israeli consciousness against the parallel violent backdrop of the events in Europe—especially in the formerly German provinces in the East, now under Polish rule, and the Sudetenland.

The Palestinian "right to return," which ideally may involve restitution and monetary compensation rather than literal—that is physical—repatriation of refugees, becomes in this light an integral part of the discourse related to World War II and its aftermath.[29] Indeed, in terms of temporality—and in accord with the causal meaning of the time, the icons of 1945 and 1948—the demand for adjudication of past possessions in the Israeli-Palestinian case falls onto a distinctively *European* sounding-board that molds memory and restitution.

Although obviously to be settled by state action between the parties involved, the various claims and demands for restitution in Europe are such that one can somehow anticipate how they may will develop in the future, and how they will do so in the context of continuous restorations of private property rights across the continent—especially in light of the expansion of the European Union eastward, to include the Czech Republic, Poland, Hungary, and other post-socialist states. It is likely, however, that there will be an increasing qualitative extension of memory arising from the growing incorporation of the events of World War II, while the Holocaust will continue to impact and color ever more powerfully the various European national memories. In such a possible process, where the different collective memories in Europe may undergo a kind of settling of accounts among themselves, a common European canon of remembrance will be established. The tendencies presently dominant indicate that this will perforce play itself out against the backdrop of the memory of the Holocaust as the constituting—indeed inaugural—event of a commonly shared European memory. In such a process of equalizing and bottom-lining the various European memories of World War II, the differing experiences and histories of the various nations during the war and its aftermath will make themselves felt. Here, after all, were countries allied with the German Reich, some that collaborated, others that were overrun or conquered, and still others that concealed themselves behind a hedge of neutrality.

The specific image of that time cherished by each individual memory collective will contribute to the composite aggregate of European self-identity. There can be little doubt that in a reversal as well as elongation of its historical role as the ultimate perpetuator, Germany will likely become the center and focus of this negatively shared European memory. In respect to monuments, memorial sites and memory culture, the German initiatives are distinctly paradigmatic. Berlin, for example, is becoming both a German and a universal site of remembrance. By contrast, certain European states that suffered enormously under Nazi occupation—but which, like Poland, have developed their distinctive memory of victimhood, ultimately resulting in a dynamic rivalry with Jewish memory—may find it difficult to come to terms with accepting the Jewish Holocaust as a prime, all-embracing, foundational event. However, the recently evoked mass murder of the Jews of Jedwabne by their Polish neighbors in 1941 may painfully revise the Polish self-perception as a significantly victimized nation, and will allow for a more differentiated picture to crystallize.[30]

Up until now, there was a more martyrological self-representation. Just think of the notorious example of the 1940 Katyn massacre in the woods near Smolensk, where some 15,000 Polish officers were slaughtered by the Soviet NKVD. For the Poles, this slaughter is not some mere event that transpired during the war—it is infused with an almost iconic quality. Why? Because the liquidation of the Polish officers, as it filters through deep layers of Polish tradition and self-awareness, is wrapped around a sacred core: *corpus Christi* and the image of the crucifixion. In the Polish imaginary, those officers symbolically represent the corps of the Polish nobility as the living incarnation of the Polish nation. According to modes of interpretation of medieval political iconography, the Poles see themselves in the context of their tradition as "Christ among the nations."[31]

Strung between Nazi Germany and Soviet Russia, the ethnic component of the long-duration Polish memory is modulated into an ideological interpretation: the Polish nation's self-perception is infused with a unique kind of antitotalitarian identity. The elemental substance of such an identity, however, is less universal than it might seem, by virtue of the *national* equidistance the Poles as victims seek to establish in regard to the crimes of both of the perpetuators—those of Auschwitz and those of Katyn.

Yet the tensions of diametrically opposed perception within the national memories in Europe are not generated solely by the differing experiences that Jews and others went through during the Holocaust. World War II ultimately constituted the broader frame or drama within which highly diverse events unfolded. That includes the various stages of the war itself, fundamentally determined by the relation between the warring parties: Germany and its Axis partners and collaborators contra their adversaries. Within that seemingly clear reticulation of relations, differences and distinctions arise, including open and concealed civil wars. In addition, during the war's final stage and thereafter, circumstances arose that turned Germans ever more into victims.[32] These events of the war and immediate postwar period, penetrating public consciousness, have generated a discourse that seeks to revise the constellations in memory shaped by the war. It presses in a direction where it is not the constellation and circumstances of the war that determine judgment—but rather a heavily abstract morality of human rights. In Germany, part of this complex is the emergent memory of the Germans themselves as victims. This victim discourse, which was quite in evidence especially in the 1950s, is increasingly oriented today toward a critique of the conduct of the war by the Anglo-American forces and the strategic air war, such as the bombing of major cities like Dresden, along with the violence perpetrated against Germans in connection with mass expulsions. Indeed, that critique views these acts as incompatible with ethical principles and human rights.[33] The reinvigoration of nation-states and the transfer of sovereignty to European institutions, bound up with a pervasive tendency to (re)privatize property in the former people's democracies, has led to a powerful resurgence of World War II. So powerful indeed that it is conceivable that Germans may well sooner or later raise claims for restitution to Poles and Czechs. Such demands are no longer unimaginable. Although the will to forge a European union and a European basic agreement appear unshakable, the order of memory established after the war certainly is not vouchsafed unto all eternity—not even when Europe's memory of that war continues to be indelibly stamped by the destruction of European Jewry.

The Holocaust assumes an increasing importance as a foundational event for European collective memory; and as the historical foundation of a canon of human rights and powerful convictions against genocide. That perception cannot be taken for granted. After all, over many decades, and in view of the enormous military confrontation World War II entailed, the mass murder of the Jews tended to be treated more as peripheral, an *epi-event* of the broader cataclysm, so to speak.[34] Today a quite different view has emerged. The Holocaust has been shifted to the conflagration's center stage: it is now regarded as the *negative core event* of the twentieth century. It may rightfully be doubted whether such a view might have corresponded with the contemporaries' historical perspectives and perception. But the vantage of a mere historical reconstruction alone is hardly appropriate for a phenomenon like the Nazi Holocaust—whose real magnitude, paradoxically, seems to unfold only from a widening temporal distance.

The Holocaust is an event of *compressed time.* This metaphor of temporal condensation means that the Holocaust, as an ultimately radical happening of short duration, packs all preceding and subsequent time layers into its vortex. In length it embraced a compacted span of time: from the summer of 1941 to the end of the war in 1945, or more precisely and radically, from the summer 1942 to autumn 1944. That maelstrom of negative *telos* sucks not only the European and most especially the German past and pre-past into its whirl—rather, even the future appears contaminated by the event.

From this vantage, the Holocaust looms as epochal, especially since over and beyond its primarily but not exclusively Jewish victims it entailed a massive rupture with fundamental anthropological assumptions about what guides human action. From the perspective of the victims, the Nazis broke with the basic tenet of self-preservation that otherwise subtends all conflict, even the most radical. Ultimately, the entire body of modern political philosophy is founded on this guiding principle of self-preservation. Because Auschwitz lies beyond Machiavelli's *Principe* and Hobbes' *Leviathan*, and thus beyond the perimeters of all conceptions of conflict possible, no matter how radical, it seizes posterity's consciousness as a universal and negative elemental event. The artefacts of property, although seemingly trivial in their material meaning, function in daily life as signs and symbols of this event.

If the proper consequences are to be drawn from this radical finding, the Holocaust would be given, as suggested at the very beginning, the analogous weight of the Reformation or the French Revolution in periodizing European, Western history. There is, of course, the difference that Auschwitz was not a tangible watershed: it did not usher in any visible epochal change in life-worlds, any transformation in civilization. Auschwitz, like a kind of temporal black hole, is inscribed only with negativity. Because of that negativity, its victims, in the main the Jews, appear as the bearers of negative emblems of a universal denial of meaning. Such a negative semiotic conflates with the traditional discourses of Western (i.e., Christian secular) civilization, in which the Jews or their imagery have a substantial importance, even if today that role is increasingly dropping from awareness.

Today, more and more discourses of collective victimhood in history are being adapted in contemporary reconstruction to the paradigmatic narrative of the Holocaust. The ongoing assimilation of the Holocaust narrative gives rise to an unfortunate kind of rivalry—a contest unable to properly evaluate either the universal elemental character of Auschwitz, or the always legitimate ultimate quality of one's own suffering. Instead of accepting the consequences of such insight, a tournament of contending suffering begins, assuming features reminiscent of traditional and religiously anchored patterns of dispute about Jewish "election" and Christian universalty.

Notes

1. Gilbert Trausch, *Robert Schuman, Les racines et l'oeuvre d'un grand Européen* (Luxembourg, 1986).
2. Hans-Peter Schwarz, *Konrad Adenauer. A German Politician and Statesman in an Age of War, Revolution, and Reconstruction* (Providence, R.I., 1995).
3. Elisa A. Carrillo, *Alcide de Gasperi: The Long Apprenticeship* (Notre Dame, 1965).
4. Wilfried Loth, *The Division of the World: 1941–1955* (London, 1988); John L. Gaddis, *We Now Know: Rethinking Cold War History* (Oxford, 1997).
5. Thomas Hobbes, *Leviathan* [1651], chapter 26.
6. Carl Schmitt, "Das Zeitalter der Neutralisierung und Entpolitisierungen," in ibid., *Der Begriff des Politischen* (orig. 1932; Berlin, 1987), 79–95; Reinhart Koselleck, *Critique and Crisis. Enlightenment and the Pathogenesis of Modern Society* (Oxford, 1988).
7. John L. Gaddis, "Was the Truman Doctrine a Real Turning Point?," *Foreign Affairs* 52 (1974): 346–402; Howard Jones, *A New Kind of War: America's Global Strategy and the Truman Doctrine in Greece* (New York, 1989).
8. Dan Diner, *Das Jahrhundert verstehen. Eine universalhistorische Deutung* (Frankfurt a.M., 1999), esp. chap. 5, "Dualisms: Decolonization and Cold War," 251–315.
9. Hanno Kesting, *Geschichtsphilosophie und Weltbürgerkrieg* (Heidelberg, 1959). For a detailed depiction, see Gerhard L. Weinberg, *A World at Arms. A Global History of World War II* (New York, 1994).
10. Dan Diner, *Der Krieg der Erinnerungen und die Ordnung der Welt* (Berlin, 1991), 11–12.
11. Günther Anders, *Die Antiquiertheit des Menschen*, 2 vols. (Munich, 2002).
12. Dan Diner, "Kontraphobisch. Über Engführungen des Politischen," in ibid., *Kreisläufe. Nationalsozialismus und Gedächtnis* (Berlin, 1995), 95–111.
13. Gerhard Schulz, *Das Zeitalter der Gesellschaft. Aufsätze zur politischen Sozialgeschichte der Neuzeit* (Munich, 1969).
14. *Geschichte und Gesellschaft. Zeitschrift für Historische Sozialwissenschaft* 22, no. 2 (1996). Erweiterung der Sozialgeschichte; Jürgen Kocka, "Eine durchherrschte Gesellschaft," in *Sozialgeschichte der DDR*, ed. Hartmut Kaelble, et. al. (Stuttgart, 1994); Hartmut Zwahr, "Kontinuitätsbruch und mangelnde Lebensfähigkeit. Das Scheitern der DDR," in: ibid.
15. Heidemarie Uhl, *Zwischen Versöhnung und Verstörung. Eine Kontroverse um Österreichs historische Identität fünfzig Jahre nach dem "Anschluß"* (Cologne, Weimar, 1992).
16. *"Ich bin dafür, die Sache in die Länge zu ziehen:" Die Wortprotokolle der österreichischen Bundesregierung von 1945 bis 1952 über die Entschädigung der Juden*, ed. Robert Knight (Cologne, Weimar, 2000); ibid., "Restitution and Legitimacy in Post-war Austria: 1945–1953," *Leo Baeck Institute Yearbook* 36 (1991): 413–441.
17. Susan Woodward, *Balkan Tragedy: Chaos and Dissolution after the Cold War* (Washington, D.C., 1995).
18. Norbert Frei, *Adenauer's Germany and the Nazi Past. The Politics of Amnesty and Integration* (New York, 2002).
19. Peter Novick, *The Holocaust in American Life* (Boston, New York, 1999).
20. Daniel Levy and Natan Sznaider, *Erinnerung im globalen Zeitalter. Der Holocaust* (Frankfurt a.M., 2001).

21. *The Stockholm International Forum on the Holocaust. A Conference on Education, Remembrance and Research, Stockholm, Sweden, 26–28 January 2000: Proceedings* (Stockholm, 2000).
22. Martin Dean, "The Plundering of Jewish Property in Europe. Five Recent Publications Documenting Property Seizure and Restitution in Germany, Belgium Norway, and Belarus," *Holocaust and Genocide Studies 15* (2001): 86–97; Marilyn Henry, *The Restitution of Jewish Property in Central and Eastern Europe* (New York, 1997).
23. Franziska Becker, *Gewalt und Gedächtnis. Erinnerungen an die nationalsozialistische Verfolgung einer jüdischen Landgemeinde* (Göttingen, 1994). On the first and second stage of restitution, see *"Arisierung" und Restitution. Die Rückerstattung jüdischen Eigentums in Deutschland und Österreich nach 1945 und 1989*, ed. Constantin Goschler and Jürgen Lillteicher (Göttingen, 2002).
24. *Bundesgesetzblatt* 1990, II, 885. See *Einigungsvertrag mit amtlichen Erläuterungen*, 4th ed. (Baden-Baden, 1992), 33; John Torpey, "'Making Whole What Has Been Smashed'. Reflections on Reparations," *Journal of Modern History* 73, no. 2 (2001): 333–358. For a discussion on the meaning of property, see Hannes Siegrist and David Sugarman, "Geschichte als historisch-vergleichende Eigentumswissenschaft," in *Eigentum im internationalen Vergleich, 18.–20. Jahrhundert*, ed. ibid. (Göttingen, 1999), 9–30. For the historical dimension of questions of property see André Gain, *La restauration et les biens des emigrés. La législation concernant les biens nationaux de seconde origine et son application dans l'Est de la France: 1814–1832* (Nancy, 1928).
25. Peter Burke, "Geschichte als soziales Gedächtnis," in *Mnemosyne. Formen und Funktionen der kulturellen Erinnerung*, ed. Aleida Assmann and Dietrich Harth (Frankfurt a.M., 1991), 289–304.
26. John Authers and Richard Wolffe, *The Victim's Fortune: Inside the Epic Battle Over the Debts of the Holocaust* (New York, 2002). For a first discussion on Jewish restitutional claims, see Nehemiah Robinson, *Indemnification and Reparations* (New York, 1944); Ronald W. Zweig, *German Reparations and the Jewish World: A History of the Claims Conference* (London, 2001).
27. Norman M. Naimark, *Fires of Hatred: Ethnic Cleansing in Twentieth Century Europe* (Cambridge, 2001).
28. Joseph B. Schechtman, *Postwar Population Transfers in Europe 1945–1955* (Philadelphia, 1962); Jan Gross, "War as Revolution," in *The Establishment of Communist Regimes in Eastern Europe, 1944–1949*, ed. Leonid Gibianskii and Norman M. Naimark (Oxford, 1997), 17–42; *Bevölkerungstransfer und Systemwandel. Ostmitteleuropäische Grenzen nach dem Zweiten Weltkrieg*, ed. Helga Schulz (Berlin, 1998).
29. Jean-Marie Henckaerts, *Mass Expulsions in Modern International Law and Practice* (The Hague, 1995).
30. *My Brother's Keeper? Recent Polish Debates on the Holocaust*, ed. Antony Polonsky (London, 1990); Jan T. Gross, *Neighbors. The Destruction of the Jewish Community in Jedwabne* (Princeton, N.J, 2001); *Der Beginn der Vernichtung. Zum Mord an den Juden in Jedwabne und Umgebung im Sommer 1941. Neue Forschungsergebnisse polnischer Historiker*, ed. Edmund Dmitrow et al. (Osnabrück, 2004). See also the contribution by François Guesnet in this volume.
31. Magdalena Opalski and Israel Bartal, *Poles and Jews: A Failed Brotherhood* (Hanover, London, 1992).

32. *Redrawing Nations: Ethnic Cleansing in East-Central Europe, 1944–1948*, ed. Philip Ther and Ana Siljak (Lanham, M.D., 2001); *Documents on the Expulsion of the Germans from Eastern-Central-Europe. A Selection and Trcnslation from Dokumentation der Vertreibung der Deutschen aus Ost-Mitteleuropa*, ed. Theodor Schieder (Bonn, 1960–1961) and Joachim Nolywaika, *Flucht und Vertreibung der Deutschen. Die Tragödie im Osten und im Sudetenland* (Kiel, 1996).
33. Jörg Friedrich, *Der Brand. Deutschland im Bombenkrieg 1940–1945* (Munich, 2002).
34. Gordon A. Craig, *Europe Since 1815* (New York, 1971).

Part II: Anthropologizing Restitution

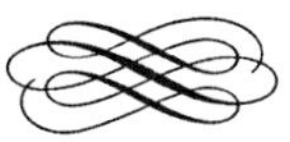

— *Two* —

MONEY AND MEMORY: TRANSVALUATING THE REDRESS OF LOSS

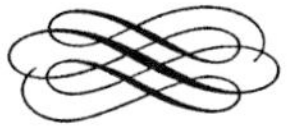

John Borneman

How do we explain the uncanny intransigence of our individual and collective ability to settle accounts following severe losses of life and property? Contrary to a popular wisdom, time does not heal all wounds. In fact, only with the passing of time is it possible to register some losses and to recognize the language of a wound. Healing the wound, the memory of loss, is a process about which we know little. Such memory appears to act like gravity, pulling us, indebted and guilty, toward an inescapable fault. We appear to have an obligation or duty to address the memory of loss and to seek redress. But while memory can often speak eloquently, it rarely listens well. Memory's instability and inflexibility makes it difficult to address directly. Hence we conjure up spirits, ghosts, djinns, therapists, even anthropologists—interlocutors who might provide access to memory's speech, a speech about our duty to address loss. We expect these mediators to talk with memory and absolve us of our individual and collective fault, debt, guilt—what is bundled together in the German concept *Schuld*. Even in those rare cases where legal remedy exists, where the apparatus of the state (or states) offers a fair legal accounting and an indemnity for the loss, the wound resists final "closure" and continues to speak from a seemingly inaccessible and secure position.

It is this insoluble problem, of addressing and redressing memory of loss, that I want to examine, specifically in its relation to money as a form of redress. Under what conditions does money contribute to the transvaluation of the memory of loss? My argument follows in three parts: a theoretical discussion checked against cases of acceptance and rejection of monetary compensation for loss; a historical sketch at the collective level of fault, guilt, and debt as it relates to money in Germany; and a comparison of the relation of money and memory in the lives of two German individuals.

Memory, Money, and Compensation for Loss

The offer of money to compensate for a loss, wound, or injury is widely practiced, but it is not always accepted. Because of its liquidity, money distinguishes itself as a form of indemnification from restitution of material goods, such as land. Often property called "land" is given a special value. Land that is stolen or lost cannot be replaced by a substitute object; it cannot be transvalued. An eye for an eye, so to speak, only land can replace land. This form of restitution is similar to what in anthropology is called "restricted exchange," a theory developed out of a consideration of wife exchange between two groups where only a woman can replace another woman. Valued goods of another order—such as pigs, or cowry shells, or even money—are never adequate recompense for giving up a "wife."

Restricted exchange is in fact rare, as is actual restitution. The more common form of recompense is called "generalized exchange," and the use of money as compensation or reparation, as a substitute for loss, is of this type. Most lost or stolen or confiscated objects change over time and therefore can never be returned in their original form; one must propose and accept a substitute, that is, compensation. Today, most transvaluation of loss involves the substitute of money. When is money an appropriate or adequate substitute for severe loss?

The possibility of restricted exchange was posed recently following the collapse of Communist governments in 1989–90. Should the successor states return property expropriated and redistributed after 1945, or should they compensate former owners? Only in Germany, with the policy of *Rückgabe vor Entschädigung* (return/restitution before monetary compensation), did the state make restricted exchange official policy in the former GDR. Other East-Central European states practiced generalized exchange: returning property only on a case-by-case basis, favoring compensation and taking into consideration the experiences and needs of present owners and users. In Germany, the guiding principle was that the original land and the original real estate should be returned to prior owners as if there had been no subsequent history of other occupations and ownerships since 1933. This did not of course prove workable, for practical and political reasons, and in most cases monetary compensation was instead paid as recompense in a generalized exchange. In what way here did "money talk" to this prior injury? Let us examine more closely exactly how and from where money speaks.

Two of the most recent highly public refusals to accept a monetary transvaluation of loss have been those of the "comfort girls," who were coerced into working as sex slaves for the Japanese in World War II; and of Argentinian "Mothers of the Plaza de Mayo," whose children and relatives were "disappeared" during the government's "dirty war" against its civilians suspected of opposition between 1976 and 1983. In both cases, the wounded refuse to let go of their memories of having been harmed. And they refuse to accept the monetary (in legal jargon, "punitive") damages from the perpetrators (represented by successor governments)—unless those damages are accompanied by other, qualitative forms of rectification, such as punishment, acts of atonement, apology, or memorialization. Sometimes victims may accept money only if it is camouflaged or hidden and not seen as a direct substitute for the loss. Other times victims desire to see the "punitive" aspect of damages, where the perpetrator is punished in some way, and where the source of the money is seen as coming directly from the perpetrator.

When money, as a substance, is offered to address the memory of injury, or when additional conditions are stipulated before agreeing to accept it as remedy for an injury, we often say that money "cheapens memory," and we disparage money's value even as we accept it by calling it "bitter money," "poison money," or "blood money." In this sense, money never really compensates adequately for loss but may instead devalue or trivialize the harm and actually increase the sense of injury. When confronted with this situation, we often say, "It's like adding insult to injury." In both of the "refusals" to accept money, of Japanese sex slaves and Argentianian "mothers" of the approximately 30,000 "disappeared," there is no possibility of restricted exchange or substitute redress. The losses are permanent and irrecoverable.[1] May it not be, then, that the money offered is not to compensate for the loss, but for the *memory* of the loss?

One of the major reasons why injured parties reject this monetary compensation is because they demand other, nonmaterial forms of redress of memory before accepting money. As the actual injured parties making demands for redress, memory of the loss seems to have a direct hold on them that money cannot address. Money appears inadequate to the task of absolution from guilt and release from debt. Memory's grip is too strong. Money cannot speak to this memory of loss directly or it would in fact "cheapen memory."

Alternatively, money often seems to possess curative powers that enable it to act as compensation and to transform one's past harm or loss into future opportunity. Here, it seems as if no demands are placed on the wrongdoer other than payment, and payment appears to substitute for the memory of the injury. There is the sense that loss can be adequately quantified and that memory itself can be redressed by money. Two of the most recent highly public "acceptances," both still not fully completed, are the $5 billion German reparations fund set up in 2001 to compensate the million or more people who were forced to work in concentration camps, ghettos, and German businesses in the Nazi era; the other a settlement reached on 12 April 2001 by New York Life, one of the largest life insurance companies in the United States, to pay up to $10 million to heirs of the victims of the Armenian genocide in Ottoman Turkey. Both of the "acceptances," of money for Nazi forced labor and of life insurance payments to Armenians, appear to be monetary substitutes for the injury or death. They appear to be examples of a monetization of the memory of loss. Let us examine this transvaluation more closely.

Many factors enter into explaining why the German government and industry settled the case of slave laborers under the Nazis now. Above all, the end of the Cold War made it possible to unify victims across borders, and in the face of reunification the German state had to re-legitimate itself internationally. Also, two recent precedents were decisive with regard to government restitution, leading also to a change in the private sector's sense of responsibility for past human rights violations: the Swiss government initiative establishing a $5 billion Holocaust fund,[2] and the willing and continuous intervention of U.S. American courts in hearing restitution claims against foreign governments and companies.[3]

Here I want to focus theoretically rather than historically on three factors that make a monetary substitute for loss acceptable, the conditions under which money can speak to memory. There were many previous efforts by the German state to rectify losses inflicted under the Nazi regime. These include historiographical work and apologies and memorials and commemorative events and treaties and, most prominently, the policy of *Wiedergutmachung* (a direct exchange of money for loss), which initially addressed Jews and the state of Israel but later was extended to other victim groups.[4] In short, more than a half-century after the war, most of the Nazi-era claims had already in fact been addressed if not adequately settled. Money, then, has not been asked to speak alone, but always as a supplement to other means of addressing memory of injury or loss. And this is the first factor: Money is acceptable as a supplement to other remedies.

For slave laborers, the critical element missing in the initial constitution of loss was in fact money; if the workers had been paid at the time of their labor, there would be at most a demand for nonmaterial indemnification for coerced labor as a foreign national under the conditions of war (a demand unlikely to be heard on a world stage). A second factor is temporal: the advanced age of those injured: the surviving forced laborers were nearing the end of their lives, meaning they had little to gain from holding out, and the delay in compensation has made the payments more affordable for German industry and government. A third factor is the growth and prominence of a primarily American legal industry, itself driven by profits, active in a type of indemnification called "class action" lawsuits where the remedy is money for loss.

In other words, the first factor is that of money as supplement: Other nonquantifiable measures were already taken to address the memory of injury or loss, which allows the payment of money to appear as a direct and restricted exchange, not as a substitute for memory; money is owed for past labor and money is paid.[5] The second factor is a temporal delay that makes the monetization of loss more acceptable. The third factor is the contemporary proliferation and power of institutions, like legal firms, that use the "cash nexus" and the idea of "more money," as well as the form of the class action lawsuit, as a logic and mode of response to problems generally. Some U.S. American law firms, for example, have created entire departments solely to investigate "war crimes practices," involving primarily restitution claims in countries wealthy enough to present the possibility of a monetization of loss.[6] I'll return to these factors later.

My second example, of life insurance to be paid to Armenian survivors of the Ottoman genocide, is an extreme case of the association of money with the ultimate loss, death. Life insurance establishes an equivalence between death and its monetary value. The insurance payment is a reimbursement to pre-specified survivors, which, according to the insurance industry's "indemnity principle," is "limited to losses actually sustained by the policyholder." The benefits must be "no larger than the loss sustained (though it may be smaller)."[7] Here, there is not a restricted but a generalized exchange, involving a substitution and transvalution, of money for death. Like the Nazi slave laborers, there is a temporal delay and reliance on an institutional mediator, life insurance, that is premised on the monetization of loss.[8] This settlement comes eighty-five years after the events, between 1915 and 1922, in which Turks slaughtered up to 1.5 million people. According to New York Life, 8,000 policies, including 3,600 by Armenians, had been sold in Turkey before the outbreak of World War I, when sales were stopped. New York Life settled 300 policies before the massacres, and another 1,100 after, leaving 2,200 unresolved. Integral to this deal was New York Life's agreement to a nonquantifiable form of rectification: to publish the names of the policyholders in major American as well as ethnic newspapers.[9]

On the surface, this case appears to be about money substituting for the memory of loss. A life insurance company agrees to pay monetary compensation for deaths that occurred in a genocide. The company pays designated heirs of the victims, most likely of a third generation removed. But given the rather large amount of money and time required to pursue the claims over eighty-five years, and the rather paltry sum in dispute (approximately $10,000 per person), the pursuit of money or profit cannot be the primary drive behind the desire for rectification. Rather, it appears that the primary reason for the persistence of the memory of death would be the desire for historical recognition, a fuller account and an accounting, of the injury—the massacre, the genocide—by others, any others, Americans, Europeans, or Turks. This was indeed part of the settlement, in the agreement to publish names of the victims in newspapers.

Here, as with Nazi slave labor, money is supplementary though also necessary to complete the indemnification of the memory of loss. The unwillingness of Turkey and the rest of the international community to recognize Armenian deaths is most probably the primary reason why several generations of survivors have vigorously held onto their memory of loss, or, put another way, why memory's obligation to the dead—the Schuld (debt and guilt)—seems to speak without listening.[10] Yet the monetary compensation promised in the life insurance contract also speaks in some way to this memory of loss.

How and from where does money speak to loss? Pierre Nora comments in his ambitious project on "Realms of Memory" that gold is the memory of money.[11] If that is so, and we have now eliminated the gold standard, then what is money the memory of? Now, we do attribute to money many social meanings—calling it old money, new money, allowance, wage, salary, and dole, for example—all suggesting the social origin of the initial transaction that created value, which creates a possible memory stored in specific "special monies."[12] But there is a way in which money can become cleansed of memory of its origin over time, as expressed in the distinction between "old money" and "new money." Old money is what the Fords and Rockefellers and Mellons give to us in grants, we no longer inquire into its origin; new money is what media moguls like Silvio Berlusconi or junk bond kings like Michael Milken or computer innovators like Bill Gates accumulate. Old money is more proper and acceptable than new money largely because we have "forgotten" its origin.

In the case of money as remedy for the memory of loss, I want to turn to the utilitarian argument of Marx and Simmel, and suggest that *money cannot transvalue memory but it can transvalue loss.* That is because money is the memory of nothing, it is an empty signifier free to be filled however one pleases. It is the means for a generalized exchange par excellence. No women for women, or land for land. Anything can substitute for money. Even a "savings account" made by accumulating some "special monies" secured through a specific sort of past labor or inheritance, is freed over time from its past and becomes open to any imagined future. As can be seen from the way in which fortunes are legitimated over time, the longer one has a savings account, the more divorced it becomes from any specific memory of accumulation, the more released it is from the actual moment of original deposit and accumulation. Money derives its link to freedom not as a negation, for with money one can, if one wishes, afford to cultivate or indulge in memory. Rather, by not being tied to the memory of anything, by being the memory of nothing, money can speak a language without specific content or relation to the past, one of virtuality and freedom.

It is well known that money offers the promise of universal exchangeability and translatability. I trust my contribution here is an explication of the connection of money to memory, specifically to contemporary memory. Not only did we just live through a decade, following the collapse of the Cold War, of a discourse on money and wealth that seemed to dominate if not colonize most other value domains, and not only in Europe and the U.S., but worldwide. But also, we are living through an explosion of interest in memory: Frederic Jameson decries the "colonization of the present by the nostalgic mode" leading to a new depthlessness, a "historicism that effaces history";[13] Pierre Nora talks of a "crisis of social memory" and the replacement of the memory-nation with "*lieux de memoire*";[14] Ian Hacking talks of a new "memoro-politics," where "the sciences of memory have become surrogates for the soul" and provide access to our most essential truths.[15]

Why, at this time, this parallel embrace of memory and money? My argument is that memory and money rely upon but have inverse relations to the same issue: accountability. Memory of loss is an account obtained through recall of something learned, experienced, or imagined in the past. Money is what Webster's defines as an "archaic" form of accounting: "to give or receive a financial account," involving "counting, remuneration, computation." Both speak the language of accounting, but while memory over time seeks accountability, money over time evades accountability. And since money is the memory of nothing, it speaks "orthogonally" to or *around* memory as does nothing else. Other symbolic means to address loss—rituals of mourning, commemoration, therapy, and legal justice—can, in fact, with proper mediation and under certain circumstances, affect memory by enabling a social displacement of the loss. But they are all themselves caught up within memory, establishing a relationship of accountability to it, trying to access and speak to something that rarely and only under the most unusual circumstance listens. Money, by contrast, does not rely on access to memory in order to relate to loss. It speaks to loss directly. But as to the memory of loss, money always enters into a relationship with this memory as supplementary, perhaps necessary for a full accounting as part of a generalized exchange, but secondary to the mediation of retribution and commemoration as forms of restricted exchange.

In the next part, I pursue the relationship between the modes of redress to loss (what I am calling "modes of accountability"): restitution and monetary compensation, legal retribution and restorative justice, and commemoration.[16] What is the specific way in which money speaks to loss but around memory of loss in Germany over the last half-century?

Relating the Collective to Money and Memory

First, one should note that Germany and the people who live in that country have been positioned not primarily to receive money as compensation for injuries suffered or for death, but to pay money to compensate for injuries inflicted. Internationally—and a nation make sense only as part of a community of nations—Germany and Germans have been on the perpetrator, not the victim, side of the question of Schuld. They are collectively positioned as guilty and in debt to the memory of loss.

One should undoubtedly begin not with 1945 but 1918 and the "war guilt clause" of the Versailles Treaty that Germans were forced to sign, and with the crippling reparations—calculated at $33 billion in gold-based exchange in 1921—that they were obligated to pay for losing the war.

Even though Germans were, arguably, the aggressors in World War I, the reason they had to pay reparations was merely because they had lost. My interest is precisely in how this "loss" has become a "memory of loss," a German memory of the issue of World War I reparations. Germans did collectively pay money to indemnify other nations, primarily the French, for losses they inflicted. It was not the French losses, however, that were assigned weight in memory, but the German losses during the war and the postwar reparations were locally emplotted as memory of loss. Immediately after the war, the issue of *Vergeltung* (revenge/retribution) for this unjust settlement was employed to identify internal traitors—Jews, Jewish capitalists, communists and the like—and by the Nazi era it contributed to a discourse of German innocence, or blamelessness, with respect to others as Germany pursued victory in World War II.

This narrative of national *ressentiment* following World War I contrasts starkly with the narrative of coming-to-terms with defeat following World War *II*. Two difficult-to-translate and awkward concepts were even coined for this new kind of reflexivity: *Aufarbeitung der Geschichte* ("working-off of history") and *Bewältigung der Vergangenheit* ("reckoning with history"). Within two decades of World War II, Germans had largely internalized the narrative of the victors (which also became a global narrative): that Germans collectively were responsible for the harm they had inflicted, which required active redress, and that Germany itself required an external remedy (the presence of Western Allies). Germany's brutal "war crimes" against its neighbors were the legal basis for initial retribution by the Allies, specifically in the Nuremberg trials, but later responsibility was extended to "human rights violations," specifically the Nazi crime of the "Final Solution" and the annihilation of European Jewry, including its own citizenry.[17]

Already in 1944, the Allied military authorities in Germany passed laws allowing them to seize and control property and assets of the Nazis, including that acquired wrongfully; and in 1947, they passed a law mandating restitution or compensation of property acquired under duress.[18] In 1952, the West German state, in an attempt to redress these wrongs, and in its search for international recognition and legitimation, signed an agreement with the state of Israel regarding the return of Jewish property and reparations, called *Wiedergutmachung*. This "making-good-again" was a reiteration of the assumption of collective responsibility and it functioned primarily by transforming claims of symbolic debt into *Entschädigung* (monetary compensation), *Schuld* (guilt/fault) into *Schulden* (monetary debt). Many Jewish groups in Israel vehemently opposed the transvaluation of loss into a numerical figure, calling it "blood money," "sacrilege," and "betrayal [of] the memory of six million Jews who had perished in the Holocaust by negotiating the forgiveness of their blood."[19] This payment from national collective to national collective was followed by other forms of redress (e.g., from state to harmed individuals or state to harmed groups such as Jewish organizations), most of which similarly turned moral rectification into monetary remuneration.[20]

Restitution and compensation did not, however, alleviate Germans from what they refer to as the *Last der Vergangenheit* (burden of history) or the *Last der Verantwortung* (burden of responsibility), for there is in fact no way to calculate the costs of a genocide. If we agree with Saul Friedländer, in a position first suggested by Hannah Arendt, that the Jewish Holocaust is an ungraspable event, an event that continually points to all limits of possibility, then any proposed understanding or remedy, for that matter, is always too little.[21] No restricted exchange of redress for memory of loss is possible, as there is always symbolic excess from the Holocaust, something that escapes all accounting, all calculations of injury and remedy. This symbolic excess complicates what Karl Jaspers in 1946 appropriately called the "*Schuldfrage.*"[22]

Over the course of the last fifty-five years, this *Schuldfrage*—the question of fault, guilt, and debt—has been addressed in all of the ways Jaspers defined guilt: criminal, political, moral, and metaphysical. The country was divided into two states. Fault was addressed in many nonmaterial ways, particularly through legal rites of retribution. Initially in the Nuremberg Trials, but followed by a series of trials of concentration camp administrators between 1963–65, many individuals were tried and executed or sentenced to long prison terms.[23] And the Allies, in their de-nazification efforts, disqualified large numbers of civil servants from working for the government, using a controversial index of individual fault: Nazi Party affiliation.[24] That is, they used a *sign of collective liability* to assess individual fault independent of the individual's actions vis-à-vis the crime.[25] Admittedly, all of this collective compensation, restitution, and retribution was *Schuld* not only for the Holocaust but for the war generally. Yet without the Holocaust as exceptional and unique crime, it is doubtful that the claims would have been so extensive and enduring.

Even after the fault and debt aspects of the *Schuldfrage* of individual Germans were addressed through monetary compensation and through the military and criminal courts, the question of guilt remains. To what extent were Germans individually responsible—guilty—for wrongdoing done in the name of the collective that was not or could not be addressed in criminal courts or through reparations? Since the 1960s, this dimension of guilt has been addressed in the civil or cultural domain, by public apologies, the setting aside of days of mourning, investigatory commissions, support for historiography, and constructing memorials (*Denkmäler* and *Mahnmahle*) and museums—sites of memory intended primarily as provocations to further thought or as admonitions.[26] Most of these cultural responses are what we call "rites of commemoration." Commemorations are public and they are collective. And unlike monetary compensation and legal trials, rites of commemoration are to operate *ad infinitum*, after the perpetrators are dead and the question of individual fault and debt are no longer relevant.

Commemorative acts initiate a repetition, they institutionalize the memory of loss by making visible and permanent a representation of that loss. Most of the commemorative sites in Germany are part of a memoro-politics that deal with the excess of the Holocaust. Many attempt a figurative representation of the horror, but others, perhaps the most disturbing, insist on the presence of the real thing—actual suitcases or cable cars used in transport, actual cannisters of cyclon B, actual clothing or shoes or hair of death camp victims. What was lost permits no substitution. Such commemorations attempt to speak directly to the memory of loss, to bring into the symbolic order that resists symbolization through a confrontation with the materiality of loss. They intend to go beyond rational understanding, to enter into the emotion, and they tend to provoke questions of collective guilt.

These commemorative sites are always conflictual, as the state and other social groups never fully agree on how to appropriate losses and the dead; each actor tends to have a different purpose in mind. The effect of commemorative sites is not to restrict the damage of loss, however, but to generalize its memory and make it permanent. And since no particular cultural form can enclose or contain or perfectly represent memory of loss, there is a dynamic of proliferating memorials and commemorative events, each intended to give expression to those inassimilable memory traces that speak the language of the memory of loss. This dynamic coincides with and is inseparable from a social process of generational differentiation and the transmission of generational accounting.

A first postwar generation addressed collective liability through restitution, monetary compensation, and, later, legal retribution. Or to be more specific, this address was done for them, with taxpayer's money, in the name of Germany. The generation presently in positions of power in Germany, a postwar generation called the "68ers" (*Achtundsechziger*), is the most active in pursuing commemoration (with differences among them in the degrees of moralism or pragmatism). I am trying to explain why the 68ers have been so active in redressing the memory of a loss inflicted by their parents in the name of Germany as a "restricted guilt" over the Holocaust. Along these lines, the sociologist Bernhard Giesen has even called the postwar Germans a "Holocaust-nation."[27]

Something remains of the *Schuldfrage* after restitution, monetary reparations, and the assessment of individual criminal liability. And what remains is something more ineffable than either individual fault or a numerically calculable debt. Many Germans draw on the distinction between *Schuld* (guilt) and *Scham* (shame) to address the fact that legal guilt (*Haftung*) cannot be inherited but shame can and usually is. But Schuld, of course, is not only produced by the legal system. One major difference is that Schuld (guilt) tends to be externally applied and projected onto Germans, whereas Scham (shame) tends to describe an inner psychological state. One says, "*Ich habe Schuld*" (I am guilty), or "*Ich habe Schuldgefühl*" (I feel guilty), but one speaks reflexively with shame: "*Ich schäme mich*" (I am ashamed of myself). Yet both shame and guilt share two problems inherent in representations: First, to what extent are they generalizable (i.e., do they hold for all Germans)? Second, to what extent are they mere projections or do they actually correspond to the internal states of the actors?

Of the two states, Schuld may in fact function foremost as an ascription. Therein also is the source of its significance and durability—it keeps returning to individual Germans, regardless of their inner state, as an external projection. Shame may come and go, but only through repression and denial may Germans free their inner states of a relation to Schuld. As part of the symbolic excess of the Holocaust, it continues to weigh heavily on the collective psychology for this first postwar generation of Germans. Much like we talk about language or culture, Schuld is a "social fact"—coercive, external, enduring—that cannot be chosen or rejected but is itself part of the conditions of articulation.

Ever since Willy Brandt fell to his knees and apologized in the Warsaw ghetto on 17 December 1970, every German head of state has confessed that crimes were committed "*im Namen Deutschlands*" (in Germany's name) for which the collective was responsible.[28] Even Chancellor of Unity Helmut Kohl, who had coined the clever phrase "*Gnade der späten Geburt*" (lucky to have been born late) to indicate his lack of individual fault by having been born too late to be complicitous with the Nazis, reiterated the phrase "*im Namen Deutschlands*" in a visit to Yad Vashem in Jerusalem on 6 June 1995. Is he not acknowledging that when he speaks in the name of the country, he is being interpellated as *schuldig* (guilty) for something he himself did not do? Fault for crimes can be assessed only individually, and monetary debt is calculable; payment releases one from the debt. But guilt speaks a collective or social language of memory of loss, from a seemingly inaccessible and secure position. Yet guilt is unstable and takes many forms. In the final section, I will briefly depict this historical instability, with a focus on the relation of money to memory in the lives of two individuals.

Individual Experience of Money and Memory

It may be dangerous but it is also much easier to talk about these matters at a collective rather than an individual level, easier to generalize about a group when one is not confined to the specificities of individual life histories which resist discipline and reduction to single issues. One might say that this article thus far has been anthropological but not very ethnographic. Permit me to remedy this by turning to the ethnographic present and to the experiential data on which I draw to construct a collective history, and to trace the relation of money to memory in the lives of two individuals that I know.

During my first full year of fieldwork in 1986–87 in East Berlin, I was paid in two currencies, a monthly stipend in East German "Mark der DDR" and a small sum of U.S. dollars, which I could use in the Inter-shops that sold imported Western (mostly West German) goods. The Inter-shops would only accept Western currency, not East German Marks. During my second and third year of fieldwork in 1987–89 in West Berlin, I was paid in West German Marks, which I could also use in the East. Whenever I visited the East, after a compulsory exchange of 1:1 for my first DM 25, I could exchange as many D-Mark or dollars as I wanted on the black market for 3: or 4:1. Whatever did not get spent was either thrown away or saved to give to friends as souvenirs of the Communist East. What I want to emphasize is the way East German money, lacking convertibility, was a "special money" (at the time often compared to the play money used in the game "Monopoly"). It was for restricted exchange only. It symbolized lack of freedom, and this lack dominated the unification process.

One winter day in 1988, I was walking with a friend along Friedrichstrasse in the center of East Berlin, and I saw a child of about age six discover a one-coin DM on the street. He was filled with pure joy and exuberance, and began to proclaim his finding—"Look mama, look mama"—in that loud, high-pitched voice of children his age. His embarrassed mother tried, unsuccessfully, to hush him. My friend commented, "If it goes so far, that is the end of us."

We all know what happened next. A year later, the Wall came down and the first thing most East Germans did was to cue in block-long lines to collect their *Begrüßungsgeld* ("welcome money") from the West German government. This welcome money was a Cold War propaganda ploy, viable only when a few East Germans were able to visit the West, not when the entire population could visit. Three months later, in March 1990, a near majority of citizens voted for a speedy dissolution of the GDR, and crowned Helmut Kohl "Chancellor of Unity," justifying this by saying, "*Kohl bringt die Kohle!*" (Kohl brings the bucks!)[29]

And what followed was the setting up of the *Treuhand*, a formally independent trust with the mandate to "*sanieren*" (manage and restructure) all collective—state- and (SED) Party-owned—property. *Sanieren* soon became "*privatisieren*." Under the operative principle of *Rückgabe vor Entschädigung* (return before compensation) determined by the German Constitutional Court, the Treuhand was to restore property to former owners and to privatize what remained. Its work rekindled memories of the East German state's expropriations and negated two other kinds of memory: the memory of accumulation and the memory of loss. One might even characterize the Treuhand's work, without exaggeration, as part of a general annihilation of "communist memory." Communist memory is a memory of the history of capitalism, of ownership, exploitation, and class relations. In the context of German unification, the restoration of property to its former owners and its distribution to new ones parallels what Marx dubbed the critical moment in capitalism of "primitive accumulation."

One of the major fears that the GDR used in its initial fight for legitimation was that, should East unite with West, West German industrialists would come in and gobble up their land and resources. I even have hanging in my office a poster to this effect, made in 1948, showing the hands of speculators reaching from uncolored territory into the colored land of the GDR, a large red and black hammer posed to crush the attempted land grab. And that is what, from 1990 to 1994, the West Germans and a few other Westerners did, through the Treuhand: obtain East German property often without paying anything—simply with the promise that they would invest and modernize and make it profitable.[30]

Profitability was only one, and not all that frequent, effect of privatization. Most privatization resulted in a "second privatization," as West German companies fired workers (called "rationalization"), sold off the most profitable parts, and dumped the larger parts that truly needed investment back onto the Treuhand. My West Berlin friend Claudio was hired to do a second privatization of the largest East German energy *Kombinat* (trust)—and he failed, too, for reasons that should be studied; but since all of the documents are under *Datenschutz*, the far-reaching law protecting data from public access, I doubt if any researcher will ever get close to them in my lifetime. Indeed, among West Germans there is no official support for and very little interest in the memory of either the first or second privatization—or more accurately, in this late twentieth-century moment of primitive accumulation. There is, on the other hand, widespread interest in the issues of restitution and compensation, to which I will return later.

My leftist West German friends were highly critical of the East German turn to Kohl in two successive elections to save them and lead their integration into the West. They attributed this to GDR naivete and stupidity, which the East Germans knew and resented, contributing to an alienation of groups that should have been working in alliance—East German socialists, leftists, and workers, and the small group of environmentalists and dissidents, from West German Greens and Social Democrats and "68ers." Nothing more pointedly symbolizes the one-sidedness of unification than *die Abwicklung*, the "bringing to completion" of East German institutions through "scientific" evaluation, meaning the firing of East Germans and closing of their institutions, all in the interest of renovation, renewal, modernization. Needless to say, there was no comparable evaluation of West German institutions. Some West Germans undoubtedly benefited from this, especially those in professions with replicas in the East, such as banking or academics or administration. But what most West Germans remember is the *Solidaritätsbeitrag*, the 7.5 percent monthly contribution to solidarity that is automatically deduced from and specially marked at the bottom of each paycheck. Ten years later, they are still paying. So went the first decade of "unification": two historical trajectories, unable to speak to each other, and now two fundamentally different histories of money and memory, of memories of loss and amnesia about accumulation.

I sat with my friend Arnim and watched the results of the first free election of March 1990, which led to the dissolution of the GDR, from the headquarters of the old Communist Party (renamed PDS: Party of

Democratic Socialism). Arnim told me he voted for the Social Democrats, but in 1995 he rejoined his old nemesis, the PDS. Feeling he must resist the dominance of the West and defend the interests of the dispossessed, he is now active in PDS public events, including anti-fascist and anti-xenophobic actions.

Now, what I want to say here—any life history takes us in many directions—is that Arnim is a citizen with a specific history of memory and money, which is then interpellated *im Namen Deutschlands.* Only through the history of this collective "Volk" can we understand Arnim's memory of loss and money in his life. But for his conscious, adult life Arnim was an East German for 51 years, and a German for only the last decade. And Arnim's own personal history is one of a sequence of dramatic losses, starting with the loss of his uncles in the First and Second World War, the loss of his home and flight with his mother and brother from the Soviets and his physical displacement, the attempt of his panicked mother to drown him in her fear of advancing Russian soldiers, and in 1950, the loss of his family's elite clothing manufacturing business. Nonetheless, Arnim had a stellar career in clothing sales, as the large Kombinat that absorbed his family business retained him and members of his family, even giving them high positions. He joined the SED in 1958, but in 1974, he was kicked out of the party. Arnim then withdrew from this career and became what in the GDR was called "*asozial.*" As rents were low, health care free, food and entertainment cheap, he could live well as long as he kept his monetary needs to a minimum. In short, Arnim has three competing sites of memories of loss—which we might designate as the (1) Holocaust and World War II, (2) the GDR, and (3) Unified Germany.

Although both states and societies engaged in legal retribution for the Holocaust and World War II during Arnim's childhood and youth, it was only the West German state that engaged in the monetary-compensation part of *Wiedergutmachung.* (The GDR did engage in restitution, and it began to negotiate compensation.) Hence this West German history of addressing memory of loss with money, of German money redressing losses committed *im Namen Deutschlands*, is not one that Arnim experienced but one he inherits.

Today Arnim speaks, awkwardly, the West German language of Schuld and Wiedergutmachung that he has recently inherited. Given the total dominance of West German concepts and speech in the unification process, this language is *the* mode of articulation for Germans of his generation, without which he would not be heard. Arnim grew up feeling absolved from guilt through the official GDR position of anti-fascism. As a child he had been part of the "Timur movement," based on a character in the novel *Timur and His Gang* by Soviet author Arkadi Gaidar. Timur stood for the best qualities of a young communist, a cross between a Bolshevik Boy Scout and an ideologically trained Hardy Boy, committed to selflessly serving others in the struggle to emancipate mankind. Unification processes worked relentlessly to smash whatever was left of Arnim's idealism, and the entire edifice of GDR ideology, including its commitment to anti-fascism, was delegitimated and declared myth. Arnim now assumes that he shares with other Germans a Schuld for past injuries inflicted, and that these require additional redress.

I asked him what precisely this Schuld entails, and what is its relation to money. Arnim says he is aware and in fact supportive of the legal retribution done by a first generation of postwar West Germans, and of a second generation's commemorative work—public apologies, days of mourning, critical historiography. At the same time, he is uncertain about whether this redress requires further monetary compensation, or the building of the large Holocaust Memorial near the Reichstag and Brandenburg Gate. Instead, he emphasizes the need to show solidarity with other contemporary victims of violence, which may also mean that Germans make a disproportionate monetary contribution to peace-keeping efforts, as they currently do in budget politics of the European Union. This does not mean, he emphasizes, following the dominant argument of his party, the PDS, that Germans should engage in military combat outside the country proper, even if its intent is to stop genocide.

In this way, Arnim works through and against the hegemony of the West German memoro-politics, but his opposition is not total. At a macro-level, he shares with West Germans the fact that the unconditional *defeat* and then the Allied *occupation* of nearly half a century were enabling losses, as these two conditions, defeat and occupation, enabled an individual accounting at the level of fault and debt, and some consciousness about guilt, the three dimensions of Schuld, and ultimately the transformation of Germany in its relation both with internal difference and with its neighbors. What he does not share with West Germans is the history of money.

These enabling losses were experienced as gains by another friend, Kolja, who worked with me from the summer of 1989 through 1995 on a project on Jewish repatriation to Germany. Kolja was born in 1954 in Kazakhstan in what his mother in 1989, before the GDR began dissolving, still called a "work camp" instead of a gulag. At the time, his father was in exile in Siberia, banned to a gulag there in 1937 in a Stalinist purge of German emigrants. Both parents, as Communists and Jews, left Germany for Paris in 1933, and then voluntarily left Paris for the Soviet Union in 1935, where they eventually picked up Soviet citizenship. They did not return to Germany until 1956, when Khrushchev released the last group of prisoners of war and German detainees. And as committed Communists, they of course returned to the East, as his mother explained to me, even though they could have gone to West Germany or to England, where Kolja's maternal grandparents lived.

German defeat and Soviet occupation were initially emancipatory for Kolja's family, because their experience of exile and loss meant that they were relieved of the kind of burden of *Schuld* that other Germans carried. And Kolja's family was subject to both German as well as Jewish fates. In East Germany, the family was even rewarded in small ways—a better apartment, political agreement with the ideology of the "Worker and Farmer State." His mother worked as translator of Russian and English newspapers for the Politburo. That Kolja's brother escaped to the West a week before the Wall was built, and the family did not see him for another eleven years, was a real blow, especially to him since he was emotionally closest to his brother. But the family explained it as a burden of the Cold War that many German families experienced, and hence not one for which they were personally singled out.

In 1988, after a long period of unemployment, Kolja began working for the Zentrum Judaicum, a document and cultural center for Jewish activities financed by money from the American Ronald Lauder, son and heir to the Estee Lauder cosmetics empire. Lauder was interested in supporting Jewish culture and the memory of Jewish life in East-Central Europe. By 1990, after the opening of the Wall, Kolja was heavily involved in memory work: helping Jews who lived outside Germany, nearly all from the West, reconstruct their histories in and around Berlin. By 1992, he was spending a large part of his time aiding in the research of claims for restitution of Jewish property, the majority of the claims being in the Prenzlauer Berg, the district where Kolja worked and lived. Several times, Kolja took me on walking tours of the old Scheunenviertel near Alexanderplatz, the poor and densely populated Jewish district before the war. Kolja was highly ambivalent about these restitutions.

Morally, of course it was important to return stolen property. But the legal firms often had to hunt hard to find legal heirs to much of the property, and then some of the distant relatives, once located, were unenthused about the restitution. Kolja found that it was not the loss of property with which they were primarily concerned, but the memory of this loss and the events surrounding it. Any attempt to transvalue this memory of loss threatened to "cheapen memory." Very few of the heirs had any memory of the actual property, and those that did had not seen it for half a century. In the meantime most of the property had indeed been transformed—with new buildings and new neighborhoods—and most of the claims involved not actual victims but the inheritors of the initial dispossessed. Nearly all cases invariably seemed headed toward a monetary compensation. At bottom, then, was the fact that compensation would end up speaking not to loss but to this memory of loss, as if such memory could be transvalued into money. This was precisely the turning of Schuld into Schulden, guilt into debt, that the actual injured parties had always wanted to avoid.

Kolja observed that in practice most restitution involved simply paying intermediates—law firms and distant relatives—a fee before taking the property out of the hands of its current renters and users. In the GDR, much of this property had been administered by municipal authorities and used by non-elites. Now, it was put back onto the open market at a much higher price than if it had been merely privatized, making it unaffordable to East Germans, like Kolja himself, to buy, since East Germans had very little individual savings. Restitution meant, in effect, dispossessing current tenants and users and turning this stolen or expropriated property over to West Berlin and West German speculators who then, together with legal firms from the United States, made a profit, some of which went to legal heirs of the injured parties. Not only was this a direct negation of communism, the very antithesis of what Kolja's family over several generations had fought and suffered for. It was also less about restitution—a form of restricted exchange where the original property is returned to the original owner—than about a form of class redistribution. That is, a generalized exchange occurs through a series of substitutions: the original stolen or expropriated property is taken out of circulation or use, turned into monetary value, and then resold in order to compensate legal firms and heirs of victims of the original theft.[31]

All the while I worked with Kolja, rumors circulated that he was involved with the Stasi, the State Security. It was always rumored that many East German Jews were involved with the Stasi, because, first, many were ideologically committed to the socialist state, and second, they were safe recruits, for who among the non-Jewish Germans would suspect them or could rightly accuse them of complicity? Unification changed this all, as the East and West Berlin Jewish communities had to reunite, and the personal histories of those in the East became public. By 1998, documents turned up that seemed to confirm Kolja had been a Stasi employee, part-time as had most of their employees, but this made no difference. He was fired from his job, and perhaps partly because of this, his non-Jewish wife subsequently left him. In short, Kolja's fate, like Arnim's, is linked to three particular sites of the memory of loss: the Holocaust and World War II, the GDR, and Unified Germany.

Unlike Kolja, however, Arnim seems to have adjusted well to claiming either East German or German identification when it suits either his pocketbook or his memory. Arnim's history is of course not merely of expropriations or losses. Several years ago, he became a beneficiary of the compensation policies of the new Germany. To make a long story short, in 1997, Arnim filed a legal claim for restitution of his family business, and he was successful, but not in receiving the original property as that property had been transformed into part of an East German trust, and then twice privatized by the Treuhand. He was successful in obtaining compensation: about $10,000, which he hopes to use as a supplement to his small pension, and to take yearly bus trips to Spain. "You wouldn't believe the beauty," he explained, "of the morning sun waking up on the bus and descent from the French mountains into Spain!"

What is clear is that Arnim understands this payment as compensation not for the memory of loss but directly for the loss itself. His parents might have had that memory, and this settlement may have been unacceptable to them. But the debt owed to Arnim by the GDR, or the Federal Republic acting in its name, is not about property loss but about an experience of confinement and lack of mobility, and money could transvalue this loss and repays this debt with freedom. Indeed, that is what this money offers Arnim, a transvaluation: not only freedom to indulge in memory but, more important, freedom from memory. By being the memory of nothing, money can speak a language without specific content or relation to the past.

As to the memory of loss of World War II and the Holocaust, both Arnim and Kolja are interpellated by the German Schuldfrage, though they are on opposite sides of this question. But since memory of loss cannot be addressed directly, the whole issue of monetary compensation is about something else, certainly about loss, but not about its memory.

Notes

1. There are, of course, strategic disagreements among the parties to both cases. The Argentinean group, for example, has consistently worked in the spirit of "truth, justice, and memory," claiming that to accept money would invalidate truth and destroy memory. Nonetheless, the group has recently split into two factions, with one working with forensic anthropologists who employ DNA evidence to uncover the actual identities of victims; the wish is to confirm deaths and enable them to "move beyond" the traumatic losses. The other faction has refused to cooperate in the search for such evidence, since it would close the books on their losses and force them to acknowledge that their children or loved ones were actually dead. A group of mostly grandchildren of "disappeared," called "HUJOS" (combining history and justice), works to keep memories alive by performing mock kidnappings and murders at or near the homes where they suspect the events had actually occurred, and informing neighbors of who had done what (conversation with Billie Jean Isbell, who has kindly provided me with this information).
2. See Elazar Barkan, *The Guilt of Nations* (New York, 2000), chap. 5.
3. See Michael Bazyler, "Holocaust Restitution Litigation in the United States: A Triumph of American Justice." Paper presented in conference "Confronting the Past: Memory, Identity, and Society," 4–5 February 2001, UCLA Center for Jewish Studies.
4. *Wiedergutmachung* was initially used by Nazi ideologues to justify their entitlement to Jewish assets because of their alleged suffering at the hands of the Jews. See Gerald Feldman, "Reparations, Restitution, and Compensation in the Aftermath of National Socialism, 1945–2000." Paper presented in conference "Confronting the Past: Memory, Identity, and Society," 4–5 February 2001, UCLA Center for Jewish Studies.
5. Bazyler, "Holocaust Restitution Litigation in the United States," 3, quotes an interview with Holocaust survivor and head of the Anti-Defamation League, Abraham Foxman: "But there's another reason that we didn't deal with this issue for 50 years—because the trauma of the human tragedy was so tremendous, so enormous, so gargantuan, that nobody wanted to talk about material loss for fear that it will lessen the human tragedy. Because when you begin talking about property, then what about life?"
6. Ibid. On the other hand, legal motive cannot be reduced to profit alone, for much legal work in this and other fields is done "pro bono."
7. Carol A. Heimer, *Reactive Risk and Rational Action: Managing Moral Hazard in Insurance Contracts* (Berkeley, 1985), 43.
8. Vivienne Zelizer, *Morals and Markets: The Development of Life Insurance in the United States* (New York, 1979), 33, has found that, while life insurance in early nineteenth century United States was condemned as a sacrilegious, speculative venture, by the end of the century, it had become acceptable and widespread. She attributes this to the fact that a voluntaristic religious outlook replaced an obligatory confessional standpoint, and to the rise of a dominant entrepreneurial economic morality. In Europe, life insurance was banned in the sixteenth and seventeenth century—Belgium in 1570, Amsterdam 1598, Rotterdam 1604, Sweden 1666, France 1681—and only fully legalized after 1860. In Japan, life insurance spread after 1881. Islamic law still prohibits "speculation on human life."

9. Coverage averaged less than $1,000 each, and heirs are now to receive ten times the amount stated on their policies. Interestingly, claims against European insurers remain unsettled, as they have yet to produce a list of policyholders. See Joseph B. Treaster, "Insurer to Pay Armenian Massacre Claims," *New York Times*, 12 April 2001, www.nytimes.com/20001/04/12/national/12ARME.html (17 August 2005).
10. On patterns of denial in reckoning with the Armenian genocide, see Robert Hovannisian, "The Armenian Genocide and Patterns of Denial," in *The Armenian Genocide in Perspective*, ed. R. Hovannisian (New Brunswick, N.J., 1986), 111–34.
11. Pierre Nora, "General Introduction. Between Memory and History," in: idem, *Realms of Memory: Rethinking the French Past*, vol. 1: Conflicts and Divisions (New York, 1996), 1–23.
12. Cf. Viviana Zelizer, "The Social Meaning of Money: 'Special Monies'," *American Journal of Sociology* 95 (1989): 342–77.
13. Frederic Jameson, "Postmodernism, or The Cultural Logic of Late Capitalism," *New Left Review* 146 (1984): 53–92, here 58, 65, 67.
14. Nora, *Realms of Memory*, 20f.
15. Ian Hacking, "Memory Sciences, Memory Politics," in *Tense Past: Cultural Essays in Trauma and Memory*, ed. Paul Antze and Michael Lambek (New York, 1996), 67–88, here 73.
16. I formally elaborate these modes in "Events of Closure, Rites of Repetition: Modes of Accountability," Unpublished manuscript, paper delivered at conference on "Settling Accounts: Truth, Justice and Redress in Post-Conflict Societies," 2–3 November 2004, Harvard University.
17. Richard Falk, "The Holocaust and the Emergence of International Human Rights." Paper presented in conference "Confronting the Past: Memory, Identity, and Society," 4–5 February 2001, UCLA Center for Jewish Studies, argues that political elites strongly resisted an international human rights regime after World War II, and that the "nominal regime" instituted came about only because of pressure from "civil society … reinforced by guilty consciences of governmental leaders about such official accommodations of the Hitler challenge as amicable participation in the Berlin Olympics of 1936, the diplomacy of appeasement, the rejection of refugees, and the failure to bomb the railroad tracks leading to Auschwitz during the latter stages of the war."
18. See Feldman, "Reparations, Restitution, and Compensation."
19. See Barkan, *The Guilt of Nations*, 24. Israeli claims for *Wiedergutmachung* were not calculated based on human loss, however, but based on the cost of absorbing 500,000 refugees. In addition, Germany payment was over twelve years, and not only in money but in "goods in kind" that contributed to the infrastructure of the Israeli state. The 1952 treaty had three provisions: reparations to the state of Israel in the form of "goods in kind"; financial compensation to the Claims Conference; and a commitment to pass domestic legislation on compensation and restitution.
20. By 1978, West Germany reparations totalled DM 56.5 billion; by 2000, DM 102.6 billion. See Christian Pross, *Paying for the Past: The Struggle over Reparations for Surviving Victims of Nazi Terror* (Baltimore, 1998), 40f.
21. In her correspondence with Karl Jaspers, Arendt argues, "For these crimes, no punishment is severe enough. It may well be essential to hang Göering, but it is totally inadequate. That is, this guilt, in contrast to all criminal guilt, oversteps and shatters any and all legal systems." See *Hannah Arendt. Karl Jaspers: Correspon-*

dence, 1926–1969, ed. Lotte Kohler and Hans Saner (New York, 1992), 121f. See also Saul Friedländer, *Memory, History, and the Extermination of the Jews of Europe* (Bloomington, 1993).

22. Jaspers distinguishes between four kinds of guilt: criminal, political, moral, and metaphysical. Criminal guilt (liability or "*Haftung*") refers to judgment and punishment in courts of justice. Political guilt ("*Schuld* ") applies to all citizens of a modern state insofar as they did not speak and act openly against that state's criminality. Moral guilt concerns those actions and defaults of the German citizen that implied his support of the criminal regime. Metaphysical guilt, the concept which has provoked the most debate, implies the failure of "solidarity among men as human beings that makes each co-responsible for every wrong and every injustice in the world, especially for crimes committed in his presence or with his knowledge". See Karl Jaspers, *The Question of German Guilt* (New York, 1947), 32 (first published Heidelberg, 1946). For Jaspers, all four kinds of guilt (criminal, political, moral and metaphysical) were restricted, individually and collectively, in a temporal sense, to those who were living at the time of the genocide.
23. Of the eighteen Nazi leaders indicted in the Nuremberg trials, sixteen were convicted. The Allies then prosecuted or oversaw German prosecution of other Nazi leaders in their respective zones. American courts were reported to be the most zealous, convicting hundreds of Nazi soldiers and officials. Individual European states conducted further trials in the 1950s (with several famous trials in the 1990s in France). See Steven Ratner and Jason Abrams, *Accountability for Human Rights Atrocities in International Law: Beyond the Nuremberg Legacy* (New York, 1997), 46f. West German courts ended up sentencing 5,288 people for Nazi crimes, and East German courts also a large number. See Ingo Müller, *Hitler's Justice: The Courts of the Third Reich* (Cambridge, 1991), 274.
24. Critics of "denazification" make the claim that it was extremely limited due to the growing Cold War threat, and the U.S. need to quickly rebuild Western Europe as a bulwark against communism. In West Germany, an estimated 1,600 persons were convicted as "major offenders," and 150,000 Nazis were disqualified from holding public office. See *Entnazifizierung. Politische Säuberung und Rehabilitierung in den vier Besatzungszonen, 1945–1949*, ed. Clemens Volnhalls (Munich, 1991), 227–236. Ultimately, both Germans and Israelis avoided any reference to "collective guilt," though, I am arguing, the concept is still implied with the formulation "Schuldfrage."
25. In 1948, Hannah Arendt, for one, harshly criticized the tendency by the Allies to abandon the distinction between Germans and Nazis, declaring these tactics "a victory for the Nazis." The "vast machine of administrative mass murder" worked to coopt ordinary Germans, she wrote, and thus compelled them to be complicitous in its criminality. This totalitarianism of the everyday made it became impossible to distinguish between the innocent and those to be held responsible. See Arendt, "Organized Guilt and Universal Responsibility," in *Collective Responsibility: Five Decades of Debate in Theoretical and Applied Ethics*, ed. Larry May and Stacey Hoffman (Savage, MD., 1991), 273–284, here 274, 277.
26. This second reckoning is sometimes even referred to colloquially as a "*zweite Schuld*," meaning collective responsibility for the debt or guilt that remains after monetary restitution. See Ralph Giordano, *Die zweite Schuld oder Von der Last Deutscher zu sein* (Köln, 1987).

27. Bernhard Giesen, *Die Intellektuellen und die Nation. Eine deutsche Achsenzeit* (Frankfurt a.M., 1993).
28. Cf. John Borneman, "Can public apologies contribute to peace? An argument for retribution," *The Anthropology of East Europe Review* 17 (1997): 7–20. – Although Brandt is credited for this apology for the collective, partly due to audience and place, already in 1951, the FRG's first Chancellor, Konrad Adenauer already stated, "In our name, unspeakable crimes have been committed and demand compensations and restitution." See German Information Center, http://www.germany-info.org/relaunch/info/archives/background/ns_crimes.html (14 August, 2005).
29. Much of this narrative is initially and more fully developed in John Borneman, *After the Wall: East Meets West in the New Berlin* (New York, 1991) and, idem., *Belonging in the Two Berlins: Kin, State, Nation* (New York, 1992).
30. For a balanced account of this process, see Charles Maier, *Dissolution: The Crisis of Communism and the End of East Germany* (Princeton, 1997).
31. The argument that the Holocaust has been instrumentalized for ideological and material gain has been widely asserted, most recently by Norman Finkelstein and his book *The Holocaust Industry* (2001), who claims that an American-Jewish elite is debasing the Holocaust for financial gain. The evidence for this instrumentalization and appropriation of the suffering of others deserves systematic research. Certainly, the U.S. legal industry is most active in the pursuit of restitution cases, and while this litigation is often represented publicly as rectifying Jewish memory of loss, the actual motive may be more banal: profit.

— *Three* —

PECUNIFYING RESPECTABILITY? ON THE IMPOSSIBILITY OF HONORABLE RESTITUTION

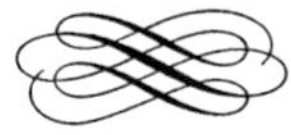

Natan Sznaider

Why is Restitution Considered Dishonorable?

Why is it so difficult to think about money in connection with restitution, justice, redress, suffering, forgiveness and morality? Why do romantics on both the left and the right agree in condemning money payments as a "dirty" business, as having a "bad smell" about them, or as "blood money?" Even those who are in favor of restitution payments seem to be defensive when it comes to the money.[1] We all seem to accept it as inevitable that every lawyer who seeks monetary compensation for his clients will find himself someday condemned for his low, ambulance-chasing morals, whether he does it on the small scale of personal injury or the grand scale of national reparations. There is a reason for this. Honor and money, like fire and water, cannot exist together. They are the circulatory media of two very different systems of behavior that are distinguished in both our historical memory and in social theory. Economic behavior is supposed to be self-regarding, rational, and calculative. Honorable behavior is supposed to be undertaken without thought of gain, to be based on intrinsic values, and to be other-regarding. In common parlance, to act honorably is to override one's personal interest and to act on principle. But restitution, by its very nature, must mix the two together. Does that mean that it is impossible to satisfy the demands of principle by means of money? In which case true restitution is a contradiction in terms. It is perfectly possible to satisfy justice by means of money. But in order to understand the widespread sentiments to the contrary, it is necessary to explore how inherited ways of thought that were appropriate to a previous social formation are still molding the way we think and feel today. These connections become especially striking when we think about the Holocaust and the ways to compensate its victims. The Holocaust constitutes a particular moment, an epoch-making event that, during the last three decades, has become a defining moment for the self-understanding of the Western world. The Holocaust has gained this symbolic stature not only because of the astounding number of people killed, but mainly because of its genocidal intentions and the use of industrialized modes of mass extermination. Shedding light on basic questions of morality, reason, and humanity, the Holocaust constitutes a paradigmatic case for the relation of modernity and social theory. Modernity, the primary analytic and normative framework for social theory, is itself questioned. On this view, the mass murder of European Jews by the Nazis is not considered solely as a German-Jewish tragedy but as a tragedy of modernity itself.[2] Hence, this essay explores not only how social theory can help explain the Holocaust, but also how it is related to compensation and to premodern notions of honor and its modern equivalent of dignity.

Honor and Dignity

Honor is appropriate to a world of social hierarchies that no longer exist. Its attraction lives on even though the world it once regulated is dead. But it is important to emphasize how the concept of honor is inextricably linked to inequality. Charles Taylor[3] makes this point quite clearly in his extended analysis. For some to have honor, it is necessary that others must not have it. And when the currency of social life was honor, Jews were among those were not allowed to have it. They were *unehrenhaft*, "not honorable," and therefore *satisfaktionsunfähig*, or "incapable of giving satisfaction"—that is, of demanding a duel to satisfy their honor.

The bourgeois concept that is analogous to honor is the concept of "dignity." Unlike honor, it applies to everyone. Everyone can have it, everyone can lose it, everyone can fight for it. It is an egalitarian concept, and it therefore compatible with democratic society. And it is a universalist concept that is therefore compatible with money. Money makes very different things equal. That's the whole point of it. But it is also exactly what romantics of the left and right hate about it.

Thomas Carlyle is a good example of a conservative for whom money, universality, and vulgarity were three sides of the same thing.[4] Many other conservatives felt the same way, and the source of their feelings is not mysterious. As aristocrats by birth or aspiration, their own value lay in distinguishing themselves from plebeians and the vulgar. This is what "honor" truly means in action. Universality is anathema to the conservative mind precisely because it obliterates distinction, which for conservatives is the ultimate social reality. In mundane terms, this meant an insistence that every individual is unique, and that therefore any attempt to generalize is doomed to eradicate precisely what is most important about people. But in political terms it meant that the distinctions that matter cannot be changed by human effort. The conservative and racist thinker Gobineau in the middle of the nineteenth century put it succinctly in his "Essay on the Inequality of the Human Races": "A man is great, noble or virtuous not by his actions but by his blood. Virtue is not a thing to be acquired. It is a gift from heaven or a gift from the race."

Statements like that give an entirely different meaning to the notion that "there are some things in this world that that are above money." The big conservative fear was that the upper social classes, who were the capstone of society's arch, were being infiltrated by outsiders whose only distinguishing characteristic was their possession of money. Incapable of understanding the laws of deference that held society together, these newcomers would thus undermine and destroy it from within. This is how Carlyle in his 1839 essay "Chartism" describes the loss of a meaningful relationship between masters and men, between the upper and lower classes. He recalls a feudal period in which

> the old Aristocracy were the governors of the Lower Classes, the guides of the Lower Classes; and even, at bottom ... they existed as an Aristocracy because they were found adequate for that. Not by Charity-Balls and Soup-Kitchens.... But it was their happiness that in struggling for their own objects, they had to govern the Lower Classes, even in this sense of governing. For, in one word, Cash Payment had not then grown to be the universal sole nexus of man to man; it was something other than money that the high then expected from the low, and could not live without getting from the low. Not as buyer and seller alone, of land or what else it might be, but in many senses still as soldier and captain, as clansman and head, as loyal subject and guiding king, was the low related to the high. With the supreme triumph of Cash, a changed time has entered.... Cash payment the sole nexus; and there are so many things which cash will not pay! Cash is a great miracle; yet it has not all power in Heaven, nor even in Earth. "Supply and demand" we will honour also; and yet how many "demands" are there, entirely indispensable, which have to go elsewhere than to the shops, and produce quite other than cash, before they can get their supply![5]

But the conservatives were not alone in their disdain for money. Four years later, the young Marx in his *Economic and Philosophical Manuscripts* expressed very similar thoughts and revealed a surprisingly similar romantic longing for a nobler past:

> Money, then, appears as this distorting power both against the individual and against the bonds of society, etc., which claim to be entities in themselves. It transforms fidelity into infidelity, love into hate, hate into love, virtue into vice, vice into virtue, servant into master, master into servant, idiocy into intelligence, and intelligence into idiocy.... Assume man to be man and his relationship to the world to be a human one: then you can exchange love only for love, trust for trust, etc. If you want to enjoy art, you must be an artistically cultivated person; if you want to exercise influence over other people, you must be a person with a stimulating and encouraging effect on other people. Every one of your relations to man and to nature must be a specific expression, corresponding to the object of your will, of your real individual life. If you love without evoking love in return—that is, if your loving as loving does not produce reciprocal love; if through a living expression of yourself as a loving person you do not make yourself a beloved one, then your love is impotent—a misfortune....[6]

This longing for a past when personal relations were more "authentic" makes the desire for money out to be inauthentic by contrast. If society is thought of as having once been held together by personal bonds, then money can only be cast in the role of a depersonalizing agent, and thus as an agent of de-humanization. But despite the seeming paradox, it was all too easy to personalize this supposed agent of depersonalization. Conservatives constantly railed against the social climbing of the bourgeoisie. And we all know about the identification of the Jews with money, which Marx himself mulled over in his essay "On the Jewish Question," written a few years before the manuscripts just quoted.

Money and Honor

Now, if this roughly lays out the relations between money, honor, and the Jews in a world of class privilege, what are the corresponding terms for thinking about these phenomena in a world without aristocracy? I would like to suggest that our thinking has yet to catch up with reality on these matters, and that the attitudes just outlined continue to exist, with very little consciousness of their roots, in contemporary attitudes toward cosmopolitanism and globalization. There is another tradition in social theory that tries to come to terms with money from a completely differerent angle. It was Georg Simmel who, in his *Philosophy of Money* (1900),[7] first elaborated without prejudice the deep connection between money and monotheism. Both are able to reconcile differences through abstraction, by separating themselves from every particular time and place. It was also Simmel who first made the heretical assertion that consumerism is a worthy replacement for religion. Many Jeremiahs have lamented that the people seem more concerned with commerce than with God. Simmel points out that the Jeremiahs are right that consumerism is something that you can get lost in, but in this way, like religion, it enacts a dream world, here with material objects. The cultivation of tastes expresses both our identity and our place in society—our status—just as the practice of religion used to do.[8] And it does it so through the objects of everyday life, just as religion once did. When left- and right-wing Jeremiahs cry out that "the people worship things," Simmel would have responded that the people worship *through* things, just as they always have.

Money is identified by Simmel as the means and expression of social abstraction. The abstraction of personal relations results in the much wider nexuses of impersonal relations. Historically, money has been a universal solvent that has replaced personal obligations with services purchased on the market, and thereby freed individuals from particular others by making them more dependent on the whole. This replacement of one large, unbreakable bond by a thousand little bonds is real freedom; it is the history of an increase in the individual's scope of action. At the same time, the extension of the money economy tends to erode inequality through the same process of making people substitutable. It is hard to maintain the ideal of inequality—that some people were born to rule, and others born to serve—when people are functionally interchangeable. Money therefore tends to extend the concept of equality, in so far as the legitimacy of inequality was based upon a perception of essential differences in the person.[9] The hatred of the bourgeoisie and its spirit was clear in the works of conservative and leftist thinkers, which often mixed with anti-Semitism as well. They denounced the modern world as a world of strangers. Simmel characteristically turned their idea on its head and defended strangerhood as one of the most positive features of the modern world. He thought indifference was a great cultural and historical achievement, and thought that strangership made a positive contribution to the social order. And this brings us straight to the modern global world. When people are strangers, each person gives signs to the others to let them know that he has recognized their existence, but signs that also make clear in the same instant that the other person is not a special target of curiosity or design. But we only need to add that concept of "civil society" to see what an epochal turning away this is from warrior society. Now we are in a world where people are constantly, without thinking about it, assuring each other of their nonhostile intentions. And this just might be the cultural and social underpinnings of the current reparations movement. This is also how the current movement differs from efforts to gain reparations in the 1950s. Those efforts were informed by national politics and the beginning of the Cold War.

Money and Globalization

The complaints raised against globalization—that it homogenizes; that it abolishes all precious distinctions; that it is a solvent of valuable traditions and irreplaceable social bonds—are very much like those once raised against money from the perspective of honor. And just as money culture was once thought to be embodied in the anti-culture of the bourgeoisie and the Jews, so globalization is often presumed to be synonymous with the spread of "mass" culture outwards from America. And there is more than a little overlap between the two views, insofar as attacks on Anglo-American culture—and on London, New York and Hollywood in particular—were often in the past a way of expressing anti-Semitic sentiments in a nobler-sounding tone.

But there is a more positive side to the drive of continental Europe to distinguish itself. The Europe of the twenty-first century is looking for a new self image. It is trying to transcend its identification as the Old World, as the birthplace of nationalism and the subsequent graveyard of hundreds of millions of people. It wants to refound itself, to reach over the twentieth and the nineteenth centuries back into the eighteenth, to the Age of Enlightenment. That was a brief and glorious and very European moment of intellectual cosmopolitanism. It was, however, completely ineffectual in diminishing war, and it arguably laid the essential groundwork for the horrors of the two centuries that followed. The brief dream of a world society that flourished in the Enlightenment was almost completely crushed by the nationalism that it gave birth to simultaneously.

Europe today would like to return to the cosmopolitan dream and to make it a reality, to make it the antidote to nationalism. But to do that it has to remember the horrors that nationalism and ethnocentricity gave rise to and encode that memory in its political structures. And the image that it has settled on as a synecdoche for those horrors is the Holocaust.

The Holocaust unites Europe in two ways. It unites it from within, as the crime that Europe committed, Europe suffered, and that Europe must expiate. And it unites it from without, against the only common enemy that is not another country, against the negation of civilization—in short, against all those who would commit "crimes against humanity."

On this understanding, the attack on globalization as Americanization is completely misguided. It is not America but Europe and the EU that provide the more developed image of globalization, of nation-states merging into a larger whole. And the attack on globalization as something that breaks down social structures without building new ones is also misguided. If there is one thing the EU does, it is building new structures. But most of all, and what concerns us most here, is that the idea that globalization eradicates historical memory is clearly false. The Holocaust is not just a collective memory, it is a global collective memory. It was created out of national memories in the same way that the EU was created out of nation-states. But in a similar manner, it has become independent of those national memories without shedding them completely, and it has begun to exert a shaping force upon them. It has the same relation to the EU as national collective memories have to nation-states: it provides a collective identity, a we-they relation in which all members of the polity can participate to become part of the We. It is the natural accompaniment of the constitution of a new collectivity.

The Globalization of Holocaust Memory

It is not an accident that the historiography and the memorialization of the Holocaust have exploded in the last two decades. It is global culture that has both created the need and supplied the means to satisfy it. The Holocaust has become a moral certainty on which action can be based, which is exactly what was felt to be needed. And it is a moral certainty that stretches across national borders and unites the West.[10] There is a heated debate among theorists about whether the Holocaust was a negative culmination of modernity or a reaction against it. But the simple fact that there can be people on both sides of this debate is the best indication that the Holocaust no longer fits into the framework of modernity. The scaffolding of modernity is the nation-state. But the Holocaust has become a phenomenon of cosmopolitanism: a transnational moral certainty that is the basis of transnational moral claims and moral action.

This was not originally so. It took decades for this phenomenon to develop into its present form. The Holocaust began to be publicly remembered decades after the reality itself had passed. It did not in any way spring naturally from those events. And it is curious and interesting how it came to public prominence in many Western countries at about the same time. But it originally emerged in each of them for very different reasons, in very different national contexts, and had very different meanings. Yet the important point here is that it is this worldwide memorialization of the Holocaust that led to the demand for restitution in the form of money. The memory of the Holocaust can now be a unifying and transformative power. The recent international reactions against "ethnic cleansing" and "violations of human rights" represent a qualitative change in political values, corresponding to a change in the structure of global politics. What was before a dream, or an oft-expressed wish, has become on several occasions a reality: the world has intervened simply to stop violations of human rights. Whether those efforts entirely succeeded is still an open question. My starting point is that the motives and underlying values were different from those that motivated such interventions in the past, and they were indispensably based on the memory of the Holocaust. To my mind, this represents a sea change in political values. These actions were motivated by global values, that is, values that make sense only when the actors involved accept that there is something higher that sovereign rights of territorial entities. And the goals of the actions were two-sided, aimed both at stopping the crime and at fostering global unity through the action. Taken together, they represent the emergence not only of different political objects, but also of a different political subject, a cosmopolitan political entity.

Now, while the sovereignty of states remains intact, their autonomy to determine the scope of solidarities in purely national terms has been progressively diminished. It is this that has produced the space, and the need, for the emergence of new transnational solidarities. And the deterritorialized memory of the Holocaust has filled this need. But what we need to underline is that it is only in its "universalized" and "Americanized" form that it was able to fill this need. Only in that form is it deterritorialized. And only in that form has it been able to provide Europeans with a new sense of "common memory."

The Intergovernmental Conference on the Holocaust, which took place in Stockholm in January 2000, provides a clear view of how this particular memory has been deterritorialized and cosmopolitanized while still remaining a collective memory. The conference was attended by high-ranking European politicians and was the site of a global debate over values. Here was an example of culture offering politics a template of how a unified Europe, the site of the historical Holocaust, could reimagine itself as a community of shared values. The final declaration of the Stockholm Forum displays the steps by which this emerging European cosmopolitan memory is being institutionalized.[11] Its first article states:

> The Holocaust (Shoah) fundamentally challenged the foundations of civilization. The unprecedented character of the Holocaust will always hold universal meaning. After half a century, it remains an event close enough in time that survivors can still bear witness to the horrors that engulfed the Jewish people. The terrible suffering of the many millions of other victims of the Nazis has left an indelible scar across Europe as well.

The Second Article emphasizes the "witness" perspective and calls for active intervention and compassion for the victims:[12]

> The magnitude of the Holocaust, planned and carried out by the Nazis, must be forever seared in our collective memory. The selfless sacrifices of those who defied the Nazis, and sometimes gave their own lives to protect or rescue the Holocaust's victims, must also be inscribed in our hearts. The depths of that horror, and the heights of their heroism, can be touchstones in our understanding of the human capacity for evil and for good.

But it goes further than that. Moral categories like "good" and "evil" are being connected to a new European duty to act:

> With humanity still scarred by genocide, ethnic cleansing, racism, antisemitism and xenophobia, the international community shares a solemn responsibility to fight those evils. Together we must uphold the terrible truth of the Holocaust against those who deny it. We must strengthen the moral commitment of our peoples, and the political commitment of our governments, to ensure that future generations can understand the causes of the Holocaust and reflect upon its consequences.

So by the end of the declaration, the prevention of another Holocaust has been declared the founding project of a new transnational civilization. The powerful symbolism of its victims has been used to override the privileges of the nation-state and smooth the way toward political cosmopolitanism. This conference provides an excellent example of how this new European collective memory is being institutionalized and encoded into the a new framework of politics. It is not simply a memory to do reverence to. It is intended, and will be used, to legitimate military and nonmilitary interventions on the now sacred ground of preventing future genocides.

The cosmopolitanization of the memory of the Holocaust was a necessary step before this last proposition became possible. In the national memories of the Holocaust that preceded it, the Nazis were a unique perpetrator, and the Jews were a unique victim. The political lessons that were first derived therefore were: never again to the Jews, and never again by the Germans. But when this new cosmopolitanized memory is projected onto the future, the next Holocaust is transformed into something that can happen anywhere to anyone, and for which all of Europe is responsible. It is only thus that it could be the basis for a transnational collective memory. And it is only thus that it could be the basis for either unity or action on the scale of Europe as a whole.This future-oriented dimension is a defining feature of cosmopolitan memory. It is not a memory that is looking solely toward the past to produce new formative myths. Discussions about post-national collectivities are usually focused on the future, because they arise in the first place from the impasses, from the need to cope with new risks. Post-national solidarity grows largely out of the desire to prevent or limit future disasters. Kyoto is a global attempt to avoid an ecological disaster. The war in the Balkans revealed a different risk: the risk of genocide resulting from the unmanaged disintegration of nation-states.

This future-oriented form of cosmopolitan memory can be distinguished from previous collective memories that were directed toward the past. Their main purpose was to preserve the feeling of national or ethnic continuity. Cosmopolitan memories, by contrast, grow up precisely where past ways of doing things seem to be leading toward disaster. So cosmopolitan collective memories are by nature self-reflexive. They emerge from attempts to forge new social forms adequate to new social tasks. Where national collective memories drew their strength from a desire to repeat the past, cosmopolitan memories draw their passion from the conviction that the past must *not* be repeated. The Stockholm Declaration makes a contribution to the supposedly impossible creation of a common European cultural memory precisely through its process of abstraction. The abstract nature of the "good and evil" that the Holocaust now symbolizes is what gives cosmopolitan memory the extra-territorial quality that it needs to be collective and transnational at the same time: in short, to be both European and substantial. And at the end of this conference (held on January 27th, the anniversary of the liberation of Auschwitz) the Holocaust became literally official memory. This conference was the first official European commemoration of the third millennium.

Market and Moral Cosmopolitanism

In its ideal form, "moral cosmopolitanism" is the view that all human beings are members of single moral community, and that they have moral obligations to all other human beings regardless of their nationality, language, religion, and/or customs. But like it or not, moral cosmopolitanism has historically been inextricably linked to "market cosmopolitanism." Market cosmopolitanism is the belief that the spread of markets will unite the world into a single market, and that this will promote prosperity and reduce the role of states. And both the increase in prosperity and the reduction of the role of states are supposed to foster peace and individual freedom. One can argue with aspects of this vision. But there is little doubt that it has interacted powerfully with moral cosmopolitanism. This interaction in fact is the prime reason why the latter has changed from a pious wish into an emerging reality. Moral cosmopolitanism is both the outgrowth and the legitimation of market cosmopolitanism. They are not opposed to each other. They are mutually reinforcing. And it is at the intersection of the two that we find moral restitution in terms of money.

Restitution: Dishonorable but Dignified

Why do groups and individuals demand restitution? For moral reasons. Why do countries and companies pay it? For market reasons. But it is a peculiar market reason. It is because *not* paying it would damage their moral standing, and that damage to their reputation would cost them money. And this latter case has only become true in a globalized world, when each nation's relation to its trading partners and its immigrant workforce has become essential to its economic well-being; when economic assets have been so widely distributed that they cannot be pulled back within the city walls of the nation-state; and when, as a consequence, legal suits have a new threatening power that they never had even fifteen years earlier when they would have been canceled due to a lack of jurisdiction. If "legal peace" was not something that could be disturbed, it could never be exchanged. What is exchanged when a nation makes restitution? At the level of states and ethnic collectivities, money is exchanged for forgiveness. Real forgiveness, legal forgiveness, politically consequential forgiveness, which is distinct from feelings of forgiveness. And at the level of individuals, the act is one of closure. Money symbolizes the irrevocable admission that a crime has been committed.

As Marcel Mauss laid out already in 1925 in his analysis of *The Gift*,[13] symbolic exchanges are relations between people as much as or more than they are relations between objects. In the case of restitution, the acceptance of the money symbolizes the acceptance of the giver. And that is an acceptance that would never be possible on the basis of personal relations. Who can forgive the murderer of his grandparents? But as the relation between whole states, it happens all the time. Every war in history has been eventually followed by a peace. Holocaust restitution is a way of producing peace in the age of globalization, not between nations but between Europe and its past, for the sake of its future. It is collective restitution individualized.

Restitution payments strengthen the project of cosmopolitanism by furthering the institutionalization of this key collective memory. The ironic thing is that this is true even though it was not the original motivation of the leading movers and shakers in the reparations movements, almost all of whom entered into it for reasons of political or economic gain—and if they entered into it idealistically, it was more to punish than to forgive. But in the same way as the pursuit of self-interest provides the greater abundance of the market; and the sins of ambition bring forth important inventions; and the sins of vanity bring forth magnificent performances—in the same ironic manner, these venial motivations have converged to produce a further institutionalization of the collective memory of the Holocaust, which is more universal, more globalized, and more institutionalized than ever before. In addition, money payments perform the following function: they furnish the whole operation with the patina of banal everydayness. In the end, reparations are paid out like insurance, like an insurance against evil, as if national barriers did not exist. And they are mostly paid to people who never fought for them, simply because they deserve them. This is precisely the image of what a just and peaceful world would look like. The transformation of horrible ethnic wars into mundane peace is exactly the moral alchemy that restitution is supposed to accomplish. It is the transformation of the strong (but opposed, and divisive) collective passions of ethnic and nationalistic war into the weak (but numerous, and unifying) forces of cosmopolitan peace.

But what does it mean for the Jews? And what about our original question, of honor? The two questions fit together like a hand in a glove. It is true that money payments and honor are incompatible. And that is a good thing. Honor, in this sense is something to be stamped out, something to be transcended, something to be proud of overcoming. When the Jews were called dishonorable, it was the same as calling them democrats. When they were called cosmopolitans—well, who would consider that an insult today? It is exactly what modern Europe is presently striving toward: to be as cosmopolitan, as deterritorialized, and as comfortable in all the cultures of its various countries as the Jews that it killed off in the Holocaust. And what of that older world that the Jews were accused of undermining? It was precisely its undemocratic aspects that they were accused of dissolving, which in retrospect is something to be proud of. And the same goes for the corrosive modernity of which the Jews were supposed to be the premier agents. The world today has entirely embraced it.

And finally, what about the money that represents all those forces in motion? There could be no better symbol of the inner connection between the Jews of the past, the cosmopolitanism of the future, and the memory of the Holocaust that unites them. The framework of the Holocaust simultaneously allows evil back into a secularized world and presents it with a solution. There is no evil so great that it is beyond the human ability to understand and heal, and no crime so great or complicated that it cannot theoretically be dealt with by human justice.

In short, all the elements that once constituted dishonor now constitute our newest and most cherished cosmopolitan values. It is true that restitution cannot be honorable. But this may actually be a good thing. The appropriate concept in the age of cosmopolitanism is not honor, which privileges one group at the expense of the other, but human dignity, which treats all individuals as equally valuable. Human dignity is one of the most fundamental of human rights. And it is no more incompatible with money than cosmopolitanism is.

Notes

1. See for example: Elazar Barkan, *The Guilt of Nations: Restitution and Negotiating Historical Injustices* (New York, 2000); Roy L. Brooks, ed., *When Sorry Isn't Enough: The Controversy over Apologies and Reparations for Human Injustice* (New York, 1999); Martha Minow, *Between Vengeance and Forgiveness: Facing History after Genocide and Mass Violence* (Boston, 1998); John Torpey, "'Making Whole What Has Been Smashed': Reflections on Reparations," *Journal of Modern History* 73, no. 2 (2001): 333–358, as representative for a burgeoning literature.
2. See for example: Theodor Adorno and Max Horkheimer, *Dialectic of Enlightenment* [1944] (New York, 1999); Zygmunt Bauman, *Holocaust and Modernity* (Cambridge, 1989).
3. Charles Taylor, *The Politics of Recognition* (Princeton, 1992).
4. Thomas Carlyle, "Chartism," in *Selected Writings* (Harmondsworth, 1971), originally published in 1839.
5. Ibid.
6. Karl Marx, "The Economic and Philosophical Manuscripts of 1844," in *The Marx-Engels Reader* (New York, 1978).
7. Georg Simmel, *Philosophie des Geldes* (Berlin, 1900).
8. For the sociological process of consumption as civilizing process, see Natan Sznaider, "Consumerism as Civilizing Process: Israel and Judaism in the Second Age of Modernity," *International Journal for Politics, Culture and Society* 14, no. 2 (2000): 297–314.
9. See Gianfranco Poggi, *Money and the Modern Mind: Georg Simmel's Philosophy of Money* (Berkeley, 1993).
10. For more a detailed account, see Daniel Levy and Natan Sznaider, *Die Globalisierung der Erinnerung. Der Holocaust* (Frankfurt a.M., 2001) and Daniel Levy and Natan Sznaider, "Memory Unbound: The Holocaust and the Formation of Cosmopolitan Memory," *European Journal of Social Theory* 5, no. 1 (2002): 87–106.
11. For the entire text see: http://www.holocaustforum.gov.se/ (30 August 2005).
12. For the historical and intellectual context of the emergence of compassion in modern society, see Natan Sznaider, *The Compassionate Temperament: Care and Cruelty in Modern Society* (Boulder, Colo., 2000).
13. Marcel Mauss, *The Gift: The Form and Reason for Exchange in Archaic Societies* (New York, 2000), originally published in 1925.

— *Four* —

Conversion, Exchange, and Replacement: Reflecting Cultural Legacies of Indemnity

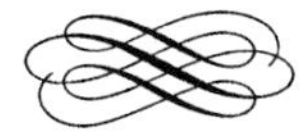

Sigrid Weigel

Money, as a pure equivalent and universal means of exchange, can remain indifferent toward historical and national differences. It thus seems especially suited for use as a means of international agreements and more generally for any policy tethered to a global perspective, such as international restitution policy. In the monetary sphere, conversion seems neutral vis-à-vis criteria other than the quantitative, since numbers are surrounded by an aura of the purely measurable and calculable. This attribute of neutrality may help explain why a country like Switzerland, which has defined itself and its position within the international arena via money and neutrality, has been so shaken by the affair over Nazi gold. Apparently in this specific context, it became more evident that even money is affected and sullied by the spheres through which it circulates. The images of politicians with suitcases in hand loaded with money, occurring during the latest "payoff affairs" have stoked the fires of further scandalizing money. Even money, seemingly free from other values as a medium of pure value, is prone to contamination by impurity, echoed in part in our notion of money "laundering." What is such laundering? It tries to clean money of the spots and traces of its past, its former history. So it is an attempt to restore pure money, that is, money devoid of memory, the pristine form that lies at the very basis of the concept of money.

So if on the phenomenological level there is a clear connection between money and memory, the epistemological frame constituting the foundation for an investigation of historical memory and material indemnification in Europe is far more complex. For that reason, it is useful to begin by discussing this epistemological bond between memory and money by looking at the foundational myth of *ars memoriae.* The current emphatic reference in memory theory to the foundational legend of the art of memory bears in itself marks of forgetting, including the thorny problem of (currency) conversion.

The Foundational Myth of the Art of Memory

In rhetoric, the *ars memoriae* is derived from the legend, which tells of the singer Simonides of Keos. It is narrated that at a banquet given by a nobleman, Scopas, Simonides who was commissioned to chant an encomium in front of Scopas' guests and in honor of his host included, as usual, praise of the twin gods, Castor and Pollux. Scopas responded by telling Simonides that he would pay him only half of what had been agreed; the other half he should obtain from Castor and Pollux! A bit later Simonides received a message that two young men were waiting to see him outside Scopas' house, and so he left to find out what they wanted. While he was away the roof collapsed, crushing Scopas and all of his guests. So violent was the collapse that the corpses were severely mangled and could no longer be easily identified for burial. Simonides alone was able to identify them by reference to his memory of precisely the places where the dead persons had been sitting in the hall. Now this reconstruction according to the distribution of the seats in the hall became a paradigm for the program of *ars memoriae* or mnemonics as part of traditional classical rhetoric. For example, in Cicero's *De Oratore* (Book II, 354):

> He inferred that persons desiring to train this faculty must select places and form mental images of the things they wish to remember and store these images in the places, so that the order of the places will preserve the order of the things, and the images of the things will denote the things themselves, and we shall employ the places and images respectively as a wax writing-tablet and the letters written on it.[1]

In this much-quoted passage, the legend is translated into a form of mnemonics, or instructions for the practice of proper remembering. Aside from the fact that this rhetorical art involves a technique of noticing, as distinct from memory or the remembrance of what had passed, this translation itself is inscribed with a kind of multiple forgetting. In a subtle analysis, Stefan Goldmann has reconstructed the cultural-historical context from which the legend was removed in order to reduce it to a textual basis for a technique of mind, pointing in particular to the repressed origin of mnemonics in the cult of the dead, which this legend contains.[2] In addition, the current popularity of the legend as the foundational myth of memory contains a multiple problem of translation or conversion "buried away," as it were. Despite its popularity this aspect has to date been given scant attention.

Thus, the analogy between Simonides' identification of the dead after the catastrophe and the technique of remembering points to a problematic semiotic transformation. When Cicero compares the mental images, which are to be used in mnemonics like letters with the dead identified by the poet, then these corpses are treated as though they were themselves semiotic signs. But it was Simonides' actual task to assign to the destroyed bodies the names of persons whom he had seen before the catastrophe. The forgotten heterogeneity between the corporeal remains and the names is thus a prerequisite for the entry of the dead as signs into the comparison, the deletion thus of *différance* as a possible condition for their entry into the circulation of language in rhetoric.

By contrast, the role of money in the foundation myth points to another type of conversion. While the legend of the singer springs from a cultural system of the art of commissioning, which functions by providing a reward for an encomium, in the miraculous salvation of Simonides, the worldly reward denied him is replaced and surpassed by another value: namely the divine gift of life, here in a literal sense. Within the narrative, the heterogeneity of reward and life thus corresponds to that of corporeal remains and identified individuals. Only when this mythical scenario is translated into a technique of signs is this heterogeneity lost. Thus, the complex interplay between sign and money, gift and life, as the narrative recalls it, has found as little entry into the rhetorical art of memory as into current theories on memory.

So in canonized tradition, memory was cleansed of the traces of the problems of comparison, conversion and transposition triggered by a conflict over money. These problems form the epistemological horizon serving as the backdrop against which the policy of restitution in the field of tension between memory and material restoration must also be discussed.

Observations on the "Modern" Concept of Restitution

In his comparative study on state policies of reparation payments to individual groups, Elazar Barkan links the perspective of a new potentially global morality with the concept of restitution. This is based principally on the difference between reparations and restitution. Reparations paid to a group, based on the recognition of national guilt or the acceptance of responsibility for injustice perpetrated by one's predecessors is the core of the "modern concept of restitution." The author regards "German reparations to the Jews" as embodied in German payments to Israel as the paradigm and first case example here: "In 1952 the Germans began to pay compensation, but instead of paying the winners, they paid those they had victimized the worst—primarily the Jews.... This was the moment at which the modern notion of restitution for historical injustices was born."[3] In his study, Barkan develops a comprehensive concept of restitution, ranging from forms of reparation to compensation to symbolic gestures such as apology. But there is a problem here: precisely the decisive difference that distinguishes the restitution of historical injustice from the older conventional notion of restitution, centered on compensation for material damages as a result of war, threatens to be submerged and disappears once again within this more general concept. That will be examined below in connection with the historical primal scene.

In fact, the political struggle over "reparations" (*Wiedergutmachung*) in Germany in the early 1950s revolved precisely around this difference, and thus the entire question of restitution. The difference between war and crime, which marks the conflicts over memory down to the present day, became very pointed in the question of reparations. A key, even emblematic, year was 1952 and the conflict between The Hague and London, between the Luxembourg Agreement involving Germany and Israel and the Claims Conference[4] on the one hand, and the London Debts Conference, on the other. Here in the one case was the attempt by the head of the German delegation in London, H. J. Abs, to avoid "special negotiations" with Israel, and to integrate the "Israeli claims" into a total settlement of the "postwar debts." In the other, we can note the initiative by the delegates in The Hague, Franz Böhm and Otto Küster, who struggled to achieve recognition for a German obligation to provide compensation for past injustice and for a German Reparations Law[5]: the consciousness of a war lost counterposed to a debate over historical injustice and crimes.

Yet in the cultural memory of the Federal Republic, these controversies have remained largely in the shadow of the concept of *Wiedergutmachung*. Within its frame, the concrete facts of restitution[6] blur in a diffuse amalgam in public consciousness where material and psychological elements are fused, in accordance with that pathos formula enunciated by Adenauer as a new dictate of conscience in his famous declaration of 1951: "Yet unspeakable crimes were committed in the name of the

German people which obligate us to *moral* and *material* reparations."[7] So at the very beginning of German obligation to provide compensation stands an emphatic emphasis on the specifically moral dimension.

Barkan is primarily interested in the fact that "the idea of compensation, the rhetoric of guilt, and limited recognition-forgiveness were *translated*, through the legal medium of restitution, into new possibilities in international relations."[8] Here I would like to focus once more on the prerequisites for that translation, looking at another previous transformation in this process inherent in restitution. It involves Adenauer's use of "and" and the hidden relation between moral and material reparations—that is, the transformation of historical injustice into the form of material compensation and the associated conversion of guilt into debts.[9]

The Transformation of Guilt into Debts (*Schuld* into *Schulden*): Asymmetries in Reparations in the Federal Republic[10]

Beginning with the early postwar period, there was talk about German guilt within the discourse of debts, balancing of accounts and payments, a monetary discursive field. In this context such concepts as guilt and suffering, victims and crime, become measurable, quantifiable entities in the medium of rhetoric of comparison and counter-calculation. Thus the deaths in bombing raids and expulsion of Germans are interpreted as some form of recompense for the crimes committed by Hitler's Germany. It is striking that in talk about one's own sufferings as Germans, there is also often a note of fear of punishment and retribution. This discourse, involving a kind of balance sheet of blame and suffering, formed the mental prerequisite for a politics in which the consciousness of an unsettled balance—one in which the crimes done to others outweigh the suffering inflicted by others on Germans—is articulated in the image of an abiding and constant guilt. This then forms the basis of an obligation to pay reparations, making the project of *Wiedergutmachung* possible in the first place; no matter how half-heartedly and reluctantly it was and still is implemented. In this frame, compensation or indemnification gets at the same time the meaning of a mode of discharging of indebtedness, of *Entschuldung*, not *Entschuld-ig-ung*, to apologize. This moral rehabilitation corresponds to the political reentry of the Federal Republic as a sovereign state onto the stage of the international community. The Federal Compensation Law (*Bundesentschädigungsgesetz, BEG*) was the precondition for this rehabilitation of the nation.

But in the complementarity and simultaneity of compensation and the discharging of debts inscribed in the modern concept of restitution we can find non-simultaneities and asymmetries in respect to restoration. These point to the complex problems of symbolic exchange and conversion, which are operative in the interplay between moral and material reparations. My earlier remarks on the asymmetry of reparations[11] revolved primarily around the fact that the symbolic exchange of guilt into debts in German restitution policy corresponds to the wish for the restoration of the self in a psychoanalytic sense: the overcoming of a depressive position when stabilizing the ego by identifying with the better object.[12] So the detour via money leads back to the moral motif, on the German side. For them the transformation of guilt into debts corresponds with a reverse transformation of payment into rehabilitation. But when it comes to the victims, where "damage to life and limb, health, freedom, property and economic and professional advancement," as the Federal Compensation Law puts it, is supposed to be compensated in the main by financial payment of some kind, the traces of the problematic of all material compensation for nonmaterial, suffering or damage are inscribed in the intended restitution. A restoration in the sense of a reimbursement, a return to the status quo ante or a substitution can only function in the sphere of what is measurable. Inherent in the concept of indemnification in the literal sense, i.e., the removal or cancellation of the damage, is always the heterogeneity of money and what was suffered.

Therefore it is not surprising that the practice of reparations of the damage to "property and economic and professional advancement," viewed in the framework of the extremely restrictive regulations, appeared to be functioning relatively smoothly, while "damage to life and limb" and deprivation of freedom first had to become normalized in terms of the laws on insurance, so to speak, before they could be treated as a case of arranging provisions for family members and claims for damages by those who were falsely imprisoned. These went hand in hand with all precarious accompanying phenomena of such a normalization, such as disregard for the specific forms of violence in the context of Nazi policies of annihilation, that had, of course, not been considered when formulating possible types of insurance, since they were indeed not imaginable in any actuarial sense. The most lasting and tenacious conflicts arose around "damage to limb and health." Here the problem of conversion came into play as an endless dispute over questions of the measurability of damage (in terms of percentage) and over the definition of a "causal relation" with persecution.

However, in what follows it is not intended to examine the conflicts in the practice of reparations or to address the sense and value of the

German *Wiedergutmachungs* project altogether. Rather, the focus is on the cultural-historical prerequisites from which those problems of conversion, symbolic exchange, and asymmetry derive, and that are operative in restitution, by outlining a sketch of the problems as illuminated by a few scenes on the stage of cultural history.

Legacies and Estates

With increasing distance to the historical events themselves, or, to put it differently, to the degree that the cases involving questions of restitution and their settlement are passed on to the second and third generation, restitution appears to become more and more a question of purely material restoration, or a question of money. This may be explained partly by the fact that the protagonists of those events, perpetrators and survivors—and with them, naturally, the embodied presence of guilt and suffering—are gradually disappearing from the contemporary historical stages. One effect of time passing is that the two parts that are involved in the conversion move further apart during the transferal between generations, because the inheritance of guilt on one side, and the genealogy of damage and sufferance on the other, differ enormously. So there is an increasing and continuing asymmetry.

On the German side, it is evident that in the imaginary of the second generation, historical inheritance has assumed the form of an interest on debt: the debts are recognized but the responsibility for them is separated from a person's origin as part of the nation of the perpetrators. Thus, the later generations in Germany tend to view reparations payments largely as the interest on a debt, which has nothing to do with one's own. One symptom, or memory symbol, of the degree to which reparations and personal guilt can separate in the consciousness of the second generation was the political scandal around money and capital in the 1968 movements. The critique of capitalism then was dominated by the phantasm of a fundamental impurity intrinsic to money. An apt formulation for the specific socialism of 1968, as for no analogous historical constellation before or since, was Benjamin's comment in his essay "Capitalism as Religion," in which he combines Freud and Marx: "What has been repressed, the idea of sin, is capital itself, which pays interest on the hell of the unconscious ... the capitalism that refuses to change course becomes socialism by means of the simple and compound interest that are functions of *Schuld* (consider the demonic ambiguity of this word)."[13]

If political discourse in the decades following was marked by a shift of the desire for purity into the channels of the ecological movement, in the private sphere inherited property increasingly was infused with feelings of the uncanny, a product of the blind spots in knowledge regarding the real origin of inheritance in the *Society of the Heirs*—as an issue of *Kursbuch* 1999 aptly labeled the contemporaries.[14] In taking care over inheritance, the knowledge returns that a community of heirs is always at the same time a community of guilt/debt. By contrast, in Germany of the third generation there has been almost a total rupture in the link to blame as a result of the crimes of the forefathers. So that in their eyes all that remains is the settlement of outstanding debts, which people are again quite prepared to negotiate over in the form of "Jewish claims"—a return of the repressed rhetoric from the first generation.

By contrast, with increasing distance to the immediacy of suffering, the survivors and their descendants gradually also remember the material assets they were robbed of and that were withheld from them. In part, this is a reaction to the remarkable fact that in the project of reparations—that grand enterprise of *Wiedergutmachung*, which was heavily marked by moral rhetoric and the discharging of blame by means of reparations—a major dimension went largely forgotten, namely, restitution in the *actual* sense of the term, that is, the repayment of the concrete monetary or material debts such as property, real estate, companies, art objects, wages, insurance benefits, and the like.

Inherited Sin vs. the Passing On of Guilt and Debt in History

The increasing legalization and monetarization of the process of *Vergangenheitsbewältigung*, "coming to terms with the past" as events fade into history, points to the fact that the current project of restitution is already responding to the history of a partially failed reparation. There is a split in it between the relations of the generations and the conception of inheritance, bifurcated into a privatized concept of inheritance and a political-cultural heritage, which also subsumes the debates about compensation for forced laborers in World War II. Guilt and debts have separated here, in a sense uncoupled: while there was never any debate about the need for the descendants of Hitler's Germany to accept the material inheritance, the transgenerational responsibility for the consequences of the crimes tends to be rejected, interpreted as the false attribution of a hereditary guilt of some kind or even a hereditary or "original" sin, an *Erbsünde*.

The association with *Erbsünde* is symptomatic in that it in Christianity means *peccatum originale*, which stands in opposition to *peccatum actuale*, or sin that springs from an actual deed: so that in the concept of original sin, the connection with deeds perpetrated associated with reparations again fails to be taken into consideration. Because original sin as systematically formulated by St. Augustine does not signify a sin inherited from one's fathers but rather the sinful nature of humankind since the Fall, including the fall from man's similitude to God (which in Augustine is only considered as a phenomenon of the soul). In other words: the sin, which emerges in the same moment when mankind falls into history. Since the descendants of the perpetrators grasp the historical legacy in the image of an inherited original sin, the crimes of Nazi Germany take on the status of a sinful Fall from Grace—one from whose inheritance there can be only one exit; via redemption. Against the backdrop of such a mythization of history, we can interpret many rituals in contemporary German culture as substitutes or surrogates for the ritual of baptism, which for Augustine promises a ritual cleansing from original sin.

The fact that Germany was reconstructed after the war as a capitalist system must perforce be viewed by the descendants as disturbing in the context of the desire to purify oneself from guilt inherited from the fathers and the associated search for corresponding rituals. To quote Benjamin's analysis of "capitalism as religion" once again, which stresses the cultic nature of the system but sees this cult, in contrast with the conventional function of cults, as one that produces blame: "Capitalism is probably the first instance of a cult that creates guilt, not atonement."[15] This phenomenon may explain why anticapitalist rhetoric runs like a recurrent leitmotif through German discourse on guilt since the early postwar period.

To present an alternative concept of inheritance from cultural history, one that does not engage in a splitting into economic and moral components, it is useful to recall a scene from Heinrich Heine's *Memoirs*. In this scene the narrator reflects on the afterlife of that "dream time" in which he lived in the writings from his ancestors. Both the possibility of dealing in a relaxed manner with the relation between guilt and debts by means of a word play and the following chain of associations—on another person's account, to demand the debts of a bond, debt and guilt—are based in Heine on a natural recognition of the indivisibility of a debt register handed down from previous generations.

In Heine's *Memoirs*[16], the narrator tells us that he is accustomed to count certain baffling mistakes on the account of his oriental double. He explains this hypothesis to his father in order to gloss over one of his own failures. The roguish answer of his father is: "He hopes, that my granduncle has not signed bonds which I would once have to pay for."

By taking the phrase "on account of" literally and by translating this into the monetary equivalent of an account from the past—i.e., a bond—the father turns his son's attempt to get rid of blame (*Schuld*) back into the possibility of debts (*Schulden*). Through the detour of the wit transforming guilt into debts, the word play has turned into a serious reflection, leading to the quotation of a biblical sense of guilt. Heine notes:

> But there are certainly worse debts than debts of money, which our ancestors leave us to settle and discharge. Each generation is the continuation of the one preceding and is responsible for its acts. The Bible says: "the fathers have eaten unripe grapes, and the children's teeth will be set on edge" (Jeremiah 31:28).

Through this reference to the Bible the transformation from guilt to debts has been returned and we end up again with guilt—this time, however, in a reverse perspective: "There is a solidarity of the generations which follow one another, yes even of the peoples which follow each other upon history's stage take over such a solidarity, and in the end all of humankind liquidates the great bequest of the past." The author names two competing solutions for this liquidation: "In the Valley of Josaphat, the Great Registry of Debts will be destroyed. Or maybe before hand by a universal bankruptcy."

The life of the descendants is described here as an action, interpretable as a kind of coming to terms with a generational heritage.[17] Inheritance in this sense is not suitable for a process of individual discharging of debts, as often used today in explanations based on pop psychology. Rather, it entails a burden of responsibility for blame, which is not placed on the shoulders of the individual as moral guilt but rather shapes the law of action in history. Historical action—that is, acting in that field opening up within the Valley of Josaphat, the Last Judgment on the one side and a universal bankruptcy (rejection of responsibility, the casting off of inheritance and debts, or, in Heine's view, revolution as well) on the other—this means acting in the wake of the debt registry handed down from the past. The acceptance of responsibility here is not a voluntary act derived from a universal morality. Rather, it springs from what Heine calls the "solidarity of the generations," or, put more simply, from genealogy, from history manifested as a sequence of generations.

Incommensurability of Compensation and Punishment

With the complementarity of compensation and discharge of blame in the project of restitution, a mixture of punishment and indemnification returns that extends back beyond the history of modern insurance systems and the separation of civil and penal law insofar as money there takes on the meaning of both substitution (*Ersatz*) and penalty.

But while in the modern system of law indemnification is oriented to the consequences of the act for the injured party and seeks to restore his or her rights, punishment is a means to an end: rehabilitation of the perpetrator. If compensation is oriented to the victim, the idea of punishment is centered on the perpetrator. It is the prerequisite for his other reintegration into the social community. And it serves this function even when it assumes the form of a monetary penalty, which today is regarded as a less discriminating form of punishment than imprisonment. So a monetary penalty is strongly and strictly distinguished in law from compensation. Both are associated with different problems in conversion and the compatibility of yardsticks and amounts. In the context of the history of insurance, compensation is subsumed under a monetary concept in which compensation never means restoration; rather, damage to limb, life, or property that damages the biography of a person is recalculated as money-value. By contrast, meting out punishment is confronted with historically alterable evaluations of different types of crime. The task is to translate these changes in concepts of criminality, rooted in cultural mentality, into a form of penalty that is obtrusive and interferes in the biography of the perpetrator, demanding from him or her lifetime or a monetary penalty. Money is only indirectly involved here, via imprisonment, as its equivalent in the sense of provoking in the perpetrator a sense of repentance or penance.

In his *The Philosophy of Money* (1900), Georg Simmel reminds us in the chapter on the "money equivalent of personal values" of an old variant of a monetary penalty, "penance for the act of murder by payment of money." He discusses in this connection past cultural norms in which "the connection between the value of the individual and money-value" often dominated "legal conceptions."[18] Simmel links this with the archaic phenomenon of blood money, demanded for compensating the debt of a death. In Simmel's evolutionary model of history, this monetary penalty replaced blood feud: "The tribe, the clan, the family demanded compensation for the economic loss which the death of a member entailed."[19] This archaic form of indemnification was related to the claim for settlement of a personal, concrete loss.

But quite independent of how one views Simmel's evolutionary image of history, his description of a broad, cultural-historical phenomenology of monetary equivalents—equivalence relations between money-value and the value of life and limb; from blood money to slavery and bride price to monetary penalty—presents us with an uneasy question. Simmel emphasizes that the conception of a fundamental incommensurability between material values and the absolute value of the human being is a genuinely Christian concept, linked to the concept of the soul (and thus the body-soul dualism). "When Christianity declared the human soul to be the vessel of divine grace, it became totally incommensurable for all mundane criteria, and so it has remained."[20] This conception is predominant in the European history of philosophy and discourse about human rights:

> But the value of the personality, which by this means removes it from any possibility to be compared with the purely quantitative criterion of money, can have two meanings that must be kept quite separate. It may concern the human being qua human being as such, and it may concern the human being as this definite individual.... In the first perspective, on whose soil "human dignity" and "human rights" have grown, we see the most decisive contours of that development which renders inwardly impossible any sale of a human being or penance for his killing by means of money.[21]

In regard to the connection asserted by Simmel, the modern conception of restitution, insofar as it relates to a universal moral condition, should be interrogated regarding its inherent central contradiction: anchored in the idea of human rights (the absolute worth of every single individual, "man as man"), restitution introduces at the same time a policy of compensation into the discourse on human rights based on older, pre-Christian or non-Christian conceptions of the equivalence between money and human value.

At the same time, more light should be shed on the paradigm of incommensurability from a perspective grounded in the history of comparative religions. The Christian principle discussed by Simmel has to be viewed in connection with a contrast between the soul and all mundane earthly values, a contrast derived from the uniqueness of the Christian concept of sacrifice. As distinct from the cultic concept of sacrifice dominant in most ancient religious cultures—sacrifice in the sense of a gift addressed to God or the gods[22]—Christianity, in the death of Jesus as expiatory sacrifice, has introduced the concept of a unique, one-time sacrifice. This sacrifice can be adequately approached by means of an ideal form of devotion:

> This idea is in the service of paranesis (moral exhortation): through his sacrificial death, Christ has opened the path to a new life for Christians in "purity and truth" (1 Cor 5:8). This has brought into view the "ethical" or better paranetic turn and application of the idea of sacrifice. The true sacrifice of the Christians, pleasing to God, is that they present their bodies to God as a "living" sacrifice pleasing to God (Romans 12:1). This sacrifice is not an achievement of some kind nor is it the presentation of an object or *gift* external to the person. Rather it is the *devotion* of one's entire human existence. That has been made possible by God's mercy shown to the sinner, which opens for him the door to a new freedom. The self-sacrifice of the individual is the true sacrifice in keeping with God's will and wish.[23]

Compared to this, the cultic sacrificial rituals of many other religions know no conflict with money. Temple money, rather, is an example of the sacred origin of money.[24] In addition, there are repeated reports that coins could be used instead of sacrificial animals, which themselves were substitutes for human beings. Money thus was able, in the cult and long before it was secularized into a universal means of exchange, to assume the status of a gift or a substitution for animals or even human beings. This would mean that in restitution, the function of money reconnects with such cultic conceptions.

Money as an Equivalent or Substitute: Observations on the Prohibition on Usury

So the conversion problem in restitution is situated within the context of a complex cultural history of money and its function as substitute, equivalent, and means of exchange. The conflicts over the relation between the value of life and value of money were also involved in debates on the prohibition of interest. Particularly in the myriad arguments for prohibiting interest, we find a recurrent comparison between interest and natural procreation. "*Nummus nummum non gerit*" ("money cannot create money")—there was a similar dictum voiced by Aristotle, Thomas Aquinas, and many of their successors. However, the thesis that money is not fruitful, is "infertile" has generated a whole repertoire of images and narratives about "money procreating money" (*das Geld heckende Geld*[25]) that engage in subtle play with the analogy between monetary and sexual reproduction.[26] In political economy, Marx was the first in a critical analysis of the transformation of money into capital to ascribe to money itself the ability to reproduce itself. In his view, only as capital does money acquire the power to reproduce itself, though here by means of a detour via the investment of human life through the use of labor power.

By contrast, in the *Merchant of Venice*, in the correspondences between the story of Shylock and Portia, there is a specific reflection of the asymmetries between money lending and pawn on the one hand and family economy and bride-price on the other. Both stories or narratives come together before the bench of the law, or rather collide in court: while Shylock's pound of flesh from the body of his adversary marks an absolute limit in the exchange between bodily pawn and money, Portia's position as a bride tends to illuminate the interplay between general circulation and the power of family genealogy.[27] The detour via the family or private sphere conceals the role of physical procreation in general circulation and in the reproduction of wealth, while the dogma of the incommensurability between human beings and money is at the same time bolstered by the Christian ban on interest and usury. By contrast, the restriction of the ban on interest in the Hebrew Bible to the circle of relatives proceeds from a clear separation of the two spheres: internally it is a matter of physical, natural reproduction: externally, an increase and reproduction of wealth. This is expressed in the *Merchant of Venice* in the metaphor of treasure. While Portia's treasure chest regulates the ritual of looking for a bride, Shylock, when he loses his daughter, bemoans the loss of his treasure.

But there is no intention here to maintain a strict contrast between Jewish and Christian tradition. Thus, for example, the notion of the incomparability between the "infertile value of money" and the potential of natural procreation is also expressed in the regulations in ancient Israel on compensation for stolen domestic animals, which Simmel cites in the context mentioned: namely that "stolen domestic animals must be replaced by a double measure. But when they were no longer present naturally, and the payment of money came in their stead, the value of that payment had to be four or five times their worth."[28] This means that compensation in the sense of a restoration or restitution, with an eye to the potential of procreation and reproduction, was conceivable only as compensation in the same form, *in natura*, while the monetary equivalent was denied this quality. This is why, in the case of compensation in the form of money, the potential value of natural procreation, of offspring, had to be taken into account when figuring out the amount. Four or five times the amount of compensation is the provision for the virtual life of the offspring of the stolen domestic animals. This idea can be interpreted as a kind of *natural interest*, which far exceeds the criteria of monetary interest, since body and money are incommensurate. Precisely because of the fact that life and money cannot be compared, compensation cannot be geared to the norm of the equivalent. Rather it has to be oriented to compensating the stolen possibility for life, the expropriated potentiality of life, or that virtuality of life that is inherent in all bodies.

These differences between money functioning as an equivalent and money as substitute, surrogate, or compensation should also be taken into account in terms of the consequences for that concept of reparation that is at the core of modern restitution: compensation for the sacrifice of life and limb. In terms of the cited logic of a destroyed or stolen *potential* life, compensation would have to grow greater rather than smaller in proportion to the temporal distance from the events, regarded as an equivalent for lost *virtual* life, for life that never came into being, life that was unlived.

Translated from the German by Bill Templer

Notes

1. Cicero, *De Oratore/Über den Redner* (Stuttgart, 1976); here Liber Secundus, 354. Engl. transl. quoted from F. Yates, *The Art of Memory* (London, 1966), 17f.
2. On the analysis of this forgotten origin and the reading of mnemonics as a *Deckerinnerung*, a "concealing memory," see Stefan Goldmann, "Statt Totenklage Gedächtnis," *Poetica* 21 (1989): 43–66.
3. Elazar Barkan, *The Guilt of Nations: Restitution and Negotiating Historical Injustice* (New York/London, 2000), XXIIIf. In Barkan's view, several elements constitute the new structure of this altered concept of restitution: the form of negotiation and agreement, the national dimension of the agreements, the declaration of intent by the perpetrators or their descendants to compensate the victims, and the associated self-rehabilitation of the perpetrators.
4. The agreement approved payment of DM 3 billion to Israel for the absorption of refugees and survivors and DM 500 million to the Claims Conference, and entailed a formal obligation on the part of the Federal Republic to draft a Federal Compensation Law (*Bundesentschädigungsgesetz*).
5. On the analysis of the political debate, see Christian Pross, *Wiedergutmachung. Der Kleinkrieg gegen die Opfer* (Hamburg, 1988). See also Hans Günter Hockerts, "Wiedergutmachung in Deutschland. Eine historische Bilanz 1945–2000," *Vierteljahreshefte für Zeitgeschichte* 49, no. 2 (2001), in English translation in the present volume.
6. Such as compensation in accordance with the Bundesentschädigungsgesetz, which regulates individual compensation and entitlements for application, as well as payments on the basis of bilateral agreements of the Federal Republic, especially with Israel and several West European countries.

7. Bundestag, 27 September 1951, quoted in Pross, *Wiedergutmachung*, 57, emphasis added.
8. Barkan, *Guilt of Nations*, XXIII, emphasis added.
9. The conversion of "Schuld" into "Schulden." The ambiguity of the German word Schuld and its double sense in terms of a moral and a monetary meaning is the basis of the whole analysis presented here.
10. Here I refer to ideas in my essay "Shylocks Wiederkehr. Die Verwandlung von Schuld in Schulden oder: Zum symbolischen Tausch der Wiedergutmachung," in *Fünfzig Jahre danach. Zur Nachgeschichte des Nationalsozialismus*, ed. Sigrid Weigel and Birgit R. Erdle (Zurich, 1996), 165–192.
11. Ibid.
12. See Melanie Klein's concept of restoration, localized in the phase of infantile sadism and related to the childhood phantasies of restoration as a beloved object vis-à-vis the mother.
13. Walter Benjamin, "Capitalism as Religion" (1921), in *Selected Writings*, ed. Marcus Bullock and Michael W. Jennings, vol. I, 1913–1926 (Harvard, 1996), 289.
14. *Kursbuch*, Heft 135, 1999.
15. Benjamin, ibid., 288.
16. See Heinrich Heine, "Memoiren," in *Sämtliche Schriften*, ed. Klaus Briegleb, vol. 6/1 (Munich, 1976), 574 ff.
17. It was precisely in this sense that Sigmund Freud later in his *Der Mann Moses und die monotheistische Religion* developed his concept of phylogenesis—as dealing with of an archaic inheritance passed on as it were in the (collective) unconscious over many generations, which creates in this way a memory that goes beyond the boundary between generations.
18. Georg Simmel, "*Philosophie des Geldes"* (1900/1907), in *Gesamtausgabe*, ed. v. Rammstedt, vol. 6 (Frankfurt a.M., 1989), 482.
19. Ibid., 485.
20. Ibid., 492.
21. Ibid., 493.
22. See Gene Girard, *Das Heilige und die Gewalt* (Frankfurt a.M., 1992), first published in 1972.
23. A. Schimmel, "Opfer," in *Die Religion in Geschichte und Gegenwart. Handwörterbuch für Religionsgeschichte und Religionswissenschaft*, ed. Kurt Galling (Tübingen, 1956–63), vol. 4, 1648.
24. See inter alia Horst Kurnitzky, *Ödipus. Ein Held der westlichen Welt. Über die zerstörerischen Grundlagen der Zivilisation* (Berlin, 1978).
25. See Karl Marx, *Das Kapital*, vol. 3, Marx-Engels-Werke 25 (Berlin, 1971), 404 ff.
26. See inter alia Jochen Hörisch, *Kopf und Zahl. Die Poesie des Geldes* (Frankfurt a.M., 1996), chap. II. 4.
27. For a more exact analysis, see Sigrid Weigel, "'Das Motiv der Kästchenwahl' und 'Shylock'. Zur Differenz von Gabe, Tausch und Konversion in der allgemeinen Zirkulation von 'The Merchant of Venice'," in Sigrid Weigel, *Literatur als Voraussetzung der Kulturgeschichte. Schauplätze von Shakespeare bis Benjamin* (Munich, 2004).
28. Simmel, *Philosophie*, 499.

Part III: Commissions of Inquiry and the Practice of Restitution

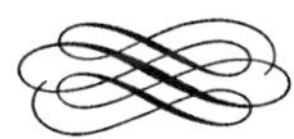

— *Five* —

CONVERTING WRONGS TO RIGHTS? COMPENSATING NAZI FORCED LABOR AS PARADIGM

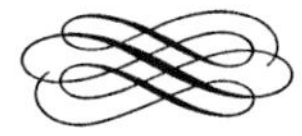

Lutz Niethammer

I.

At the end of 1998, a small working group, with members from a number of ministries and parliamentary parties forming the new red-green coalition in Bonn, sat together conferring with two academic advisers in a closed meeting. This working group had completed a staff study concerning the question of compensation of Nazi forced laborers. In this study information was compiled about forced labor during the Second World War and about the contradictions of reparations during the Cold War. We hoped to explain why there had been no compensation for forced labor. In addition, our recommendation was that compensation be allowed to be given to those who suffered the most among the former forced laborers, namely, the prisoners in concentration camps and those civilian workers who were deported from Eastern Europe to the German Reich and deployed in private industry under prison-like conditions. The exact provisions of the compensation were to be negotiated by representatives of the victims.[1]

The governing partners of the new red-green coalition had been calling for compensation for Nazi forced laborers for a decade, while they were still in opposition—and doing so without external pressure.[2] In this way, they represented the evolved result of the "crabwalk" of much of West German public memory since the 1970s.[3] This movement of recollection was increasingly driven by the experience and memory of those who were born during and after World War II. With full respect for the primacy of the Holocaust and the related legislation on *Wiedergutmachung* of the 1950s, it increasingly extended its perception to encompass ever more groups of individuals victimized by the Nazi crimes against humanity, persons now generally included among the potential recipients of compensation.[4] But such recollection failed to perceive the largest relevant group—namely, those who from the beginning of 1940 or 1942 were completely deprived of their civil and human rights by the decrees regulating workers from Poland and the occupied areas of the Soviet Union (the so-called "Ostarbeiter"), along with their exploitation in the German war economy.[5]

Next to the Jews and the Gypsies of mixed blood, the Slavs were classified as on the lowest rungs in the Nazi hierarchy of European peoples. This racist discrimination of the Slavs permitted and naturalized their deportation into the Reich and their complete separation from the German population and from other West European foreign workers as well, often in guarded camps, and under the threat of arrest. Racist discrimination regulated their exploitation through low pay rates, while they were also given totally substandard accommodation and minimal nutrition. In cases of resistance or undisciplined behavior, it authorized their committal by police order—i.e., without legal due process—to corrective labor camps ("Arbeitserziehungslager")[6] and concentration camps.[7] They might even be sentenced to execution, in the event, for example, of having had sexual intercourse with Germans. Many workers from the East did not survive this labor deployment in the German Reich. In addition, the majority of the Soviet POWs starved to death in German prison camps (more than three million), even prior to their removal to the Reich.[8]

After the historic opening up of the Soviet bloc, an awareness developed in a growing section of the public that many of the surviving former Nazi forced laborers within the Soviet empire had never been recognized as victims. On the contrary, they had been additionally discriminated against in their homeland, accused of being potential traitors. New research in Russia showed that upon "liberation," almost a tenth of them had been transported into the Gulag camps. In their old age, they were now living for the most part under conditions of extreme misery and in great poverty. In the light of their exploitation in the German war economy, this final round of compensation was to be implemented by means of contributions from civil society; that is, with participation by business and industrial firms in covering the costs.[9]

Following global indemnification to Eastern European states in the first part of the 1990s, which had reached recipients in amounts usually less than $500,[10] the prior conservative head of the Federal administration had not even considered the possibility that commercial firms might supplement state reparation. Instead, he had responded to corresponding proposals with the announcement that the coffers of the state would from now on remain tightly closed. However, fully justified negotiations to include Jewish survivors of the Holocaust in Eastern Germany and Eastern Europe in the state-financed scheme of *Wiedergutmachung* continued, with little publicity, and came to a successful conclusion and settlement at the end of the Kohl government.

As a result of the first class-action lawsuits on behalf of Jewish forced laborers—above all, from those now living in the United States and Israel—the managements of top German companies involved in business in America were put under pressure, this time with a lot of publicity. They, in turn, requested the new administration in Bonn to mediate. This created the possibility for the Left to raise the issue of participation by industry in symbolic compensation for Nazi forced labor. Their effort was initially a project aimed mainly at fairness for Eastern Europe. Now it was possible to implement it in such a as to reduce the damage done to the image of the companies facing litigation in the United States.

In order to raise the funds—at that time, it was assumed that at least DM 2 billion would be needed, though the final sum remained open—industry set up a foundation initiative for German enterprises named "Remembrance, Responsibility and the Future." Half of the funds were to be distributed to deserving survivors before the turn of the millennium, starting with the 60th anniversary of the outbreak of the Second World War, on September 1, 1999. The other half would be placed in a foundation, "Remembrance and Future"; its capital yield, over the long term, was to promote international cultural and social projects for historical remembrance and international understanding, as well as initiatives in the interest of human rights and social justice. The double definition of aims for the use of the funds—half for compensating wrongs from the past, half for the promotion of a culture of remembrance and human rights in the future—originated from a suggestion by the American ambassador in Bonn, John Kornblum, who raised the prospect that the pending class-action lawsuits against German companies in the United States might (in view of the size and scope of the fund) eventually be dismissed by American courts. He did not elaborate on the dimension of such a foundation, but explained that the judicial sphere in the United States was much more political than in Europe, and collective lawsuits of this type were often intended only to initiate a negotiating process, reaching out for a compromise with or without the help of the courts.

At the time of the initial lawsuits, the only class actions were in the interest of former Jewish forced or slave laborers, mostly living in the United States; and there were parties prepared to settle a deal within this framework. That would have affected approximately 5 percent of the problem of Nazi forced labor, an issue that since the time of the London dept agreement of 1952 had been deferred to a later date. To be more precise, those affected were in the main victims who had already received compensation payments from *Wiedergutmachung* that had been set up in parallel at that time, though this had not been in recognition of their forced labor and its ordeal.

The majority of our working group was fully aware of the special experience of Jewish survivors, most of whom were completely deprived of any rights and forced to work not only under the worst possible conditions and treatment, but also under the threat of extermination. Often they had survived only because to the Nazis it appeared possible to continue to exploit their labor power. But we felt that an exclusive regulation of their compensation claims would be extremely unfair for a great majority of others also forced to labor under onerous conditions, and who had also been deprived of their human and civil rights. Within our working group, many feared that such a process would add oil to the fires of Eastern European anti-Semitism, poisoning the new European web of neighborly relations. Consequently, the working group pressed for the inclusion and compensation of *all* surviving forced laborers, who were among the most severely exploited and deprived of their rights. That is, most of the funds were to go to Eastern Europe, where the compensation of the victims had been blocked not only by the Cold War and its constraints, but also by the general suspicion of the Soviet leadership that these forced laborers deported into the Reich were possible traitors.

From the outset, however, there was a general consensus that a significant, pragmatic exception to the goal of justice was imperative: prisoners of war who were also deployed as forced laborers would have to be excluded from compensation. The reason for this was twofold: first, to include them would have linked their personal fate with the general question of reparations between states. All German administrations in Bonn regarded this issue as a nonstarter in light of the staggering reparations extracted by the Soviet Union from East Germany, the loss of the Eastern provinces and the expulsion of their population to the West, and the deployment of German POWs as forced labor in the Soviet Union. Reopening this question would have most likely doomed any agreement to failure. Moreover, any inclusion of Soviet POWs in a compensation settlement would doubtless have spurred latent questions within the German public about the fate, acknowledgement, and compensation of German prisoners of war in the Soviet Union. This could have blocked and stalled the growing consensus regarding compensation policy within German politics and the aim of reconciliation with Eastern Europe. Seen from the perspective of a general human desire for justice, this exception seemed intolerable, especially because the Soviet POWs had been among the worst treated and experienced the highest mortality rates. On the other hand, it was only possible to achieve more justice in relation to civilian workers by decoupling the question of prisoners of war from compensation for civilian forced laborers.

We in the working group knew from the initial confidential discussions that Manfred Gentz, one of the most important spokespersons for the foundation initiative launched by the companies facing litigation—an effort then only on the drawing boards—was aware that the potential injustice adhering to any compensation settlement rested largely with the question of Eastern Europe. Counter to the interests of his company group, which was very active in the United States, Gentz stressed—for purely moral, humanitarian, and general political reasons of fairness—that further injustice to East Europeans was to be avoided. On this issue, it was possible to reach an early agreement with the minister responsible in the Federal chancellery and the foreign minister, both of whom stemmed from expellee families. Then and there the chancellor's decision was taken, prior to the international negotiation process, and even before the formal establishment of the Foundation Initiative of German Industry early in 1999.[11] That, in my view, was the most important decision, one to which our working group in its advisory capacity contributed.

Yet the weakness of our position was that neither we nor anyone else actually knew at the time how many of the forced laborers who had suffered most were still alive. Over the next several months, my responsibility working backstage to the negotiations was to discover more about this. I worked in close contact with numerous representatives of the victims and with historians specializing in the field. In fact, for some time I became a kind of informal go-between for all of the delegations in the background of these complex (and at times rather conflict-ridden) international negotiations.

After various trips to Israel, Eastern Europe, and America and two improvised international workshops—one at the memorial site of Buchenwald at Weimar in the summer of 1999 and another at the European University Institute in Florence in the early fall of that year—we ended up with a database of informed guesses about the size, characteristics, and distribution of the population concerned. All sides were able to agree on this.[12] It was only thereafter that the international negotiations turned to the question of money. And it surely was of great help that we already had a consensual basis for its international distribution, if not for its overall amount.

A second fundamental decision was predefined politically, but we in the working group had no argument against it. With payment recipients restricted to individuals in *industrial* forced labor, a quick and generous initiative from civil society, concentrating only on forced laborers employed in private industry, should produce a breakthrough for a more general compensation solution. The remaining problems would be dealt with later by the government or by a separate federal foundation. Obscured in the public debate was the fact that the majority of concentration camp prisoners and almost a third of those forced workers deployed outside farming had not been employed by private enterprises but by *public* agencies and organizations. And slightly less than half of all the forced and other laborers from abroad—most living under more favorable circumstances, even when suffering the same deprivation of rights—were deployed in agriculture. No one was under the illusion that the farmers, themselves highly dependent on subsidies, could be induced to make a substantial contribution, even if symbolic, to compensation.

Of course, problems arose in the implementation of our recommendations since the best laid plans of mice and men often do not work out in real life.[13] In fact, a few weeks later, companies in the private sector facing litigation in the United States established the foundation initiative. Other firms joined them, first hesitatingly, later in greater numbers, and they accepted most of our recommendations, including the name of the foundation and the inclusion of Eastern Europe. But the companies were wary of the factor of risk. They wished, first of all, to see the American lawsuits quashed before they would pay funds into the foundation. Subsequently, as a result of complex international negotiations, the management was essentially handed over to the U.S. government—and more particularly to the mediating energy and intelligence of Stuart E. Eizenstat. This cost a further DM 8 billion (by far the largest portion paid by the taxpayers), and necessitated two more years of waiting for the elderly affected by the settlement.

During the negotiations, the number of surviving forced laborers became clear in its basic outlines. Depending on the definitions of the groups entitled to receive compensation, between 800,000 and 2.4 million people qualified. This meant that the extension of the funds was fully justified, if this material form of recognition was not to result in extremely small payments to the individuals entitled to them. The final outcome was that the "slave laborers" (largely Jewish ghetto workers and prisoners in concentration camps from numerous nations) were to receive three times as much compensation per person as the other qualifying forced laborers in industry, who had been exploited under prison-like conditions. The number of the latter was estimated to be at least three times as large. This differential also ensured that Jewish survivors in America still received an amount, which in their case could be taken seriously as a symbolic gesture. This compensation scheme was a matter of especial dispute and controversy among the representatives of the interests of the various groups of victims: most representatives of Jewish interests initially wanted a much higher differential, whereas Eastern European representatives tried right down to the last moment to reduce this to a ratio of 2:1. Nevertheless, the vast majority of the Slavic forced laborers were ultimately taken care of, and more than two-thirds of the total funds allocated went to them.

Formulae were even worked out for the forced laborers from Eastern Europe deployed in farming who, because of their generally more favorable living conditions, had been formally excluded. These new formulae allowed for their compensation at substantially lower rates. However, this in turn meant a reduction in the respective national rates for those deployed in industry. In this way, the principle of internationally identical entitlement to claims had to be revised again in terms of actual application. By unanimous vote of all victim representatives, this principle had won out over an alternative principle in the German proposal—namely, payment of higher rates only to those in need, and adapting the payments to the living standards of the countries concerned.[14] Moreover, the attempt to bring class-action lawsuits into force in Europe failed, as did in the end similar attempts to use legal suit to solve this complex international problem of justice, fairness, and recognition. The courts were useful only for legal closure.[15]

After the global negotiations were underway, because of the need to provide a safeguard for the companies sued it likewise seemed sensible to abandon the previous pioneering role of the private sector. Now, all negotiations were carried out essentially by the states involved. The German side, now represented by Graf Lambsdorff as commissioner of the chancellor, a highly experienced elder statesman with close ties to industry, formally accepted half of the costs to be paid by the state, after taxes amounting de facto to three-quarters. The commercial company partners retained a kind of veto power over procedure. But since they made substantial use of this and repeatedly pressured for legal closure, likewise utilizing public statements, they harmed their public image.[16] Originally they had been concerned to improve that very image. In any case, over a period of two years, even the most willing German managers succeeded in presenting an extremely negative image in the press as far as the morals of German commerce went. At some stage, Jewish organizations had even begun an advertising campaign in the United States against certain German companies singled out as representative. They soon had to terminate this, however, when the companies threatened to leave the negotiating table. In the end, there was hardly any large German town or city that lacked a citizen's action committee (*Bürgerinitiative*) for remembrance of the local experience of forced labor and for outing companies responsible for such labor but unwilling to pay compensation.[17] The international negotiations of compensation were thus of huge importance as a public process of remembrance and a symbolic reminder of recognition and responsibility. They did not, however, result in any significant legal advances.

Toward the end of the negotiations, a particularly disturbing factor arose. It was the impression of some East European (and more particularly Polish and Czech representatives) that at the very beginning, a devious deal had been struck in the back rooms. It involved accusations that Jewish pressure groups had garnered something like a social reserve fund as a reward for retaining their silence about a major corporate takeover in the United States by a large German bank that had been particularly compromised during the Nazi regime.[18] This reserve fund, which amounted to DM 1 billion, would release German industry from all future claims based on its involvement in the injustices of the Nazi regime (extending well beyond the issue of forced labor). As these rumors spread, the negotiators undertook separate, supplementary discussions to identify rationalizing formulae. These enabled East Europeans as well to formally register insurance claims and specify property losses under carefully formulated clauses that in practice did not significantly impair the claims of Jews.

Let me now return to the start of this tale, to the editorial work of our policy study for the German Federal Chancellery. In the first days of 1999, we had almost come to the end of our work. An experienced diplomat, Social Democrat, and lawyer then asked with a sigh: "Should we really let that happen to us? What we have written down here is not unjustified. It is wellintentioned, but it will bring about the collapse of legal barriers which have been guarded for decades, which have produced reassurance; and we will let loose a process which is bound to shake up everything, and the result surely will then be that nobody is satisfied." I was, at that time, the chairman of this advisory group, and I had supported its propositions even against this friendly dissenting opinion. But I have often thought subsequently about this most experienced skepticism. It intensified the vexing question at the back of my mind: "Should we strive to achieve justice in situations and matters in which this goal cannot be achieved?"

II.

The historian Dan Diner once remarked that all things turn trivial if they are examined in too great a detail. Let me therefore attempt to step back in my imagination and view this vista from a more historical perspective. Drawing on the example of Carl Schmitt, one can readily recognize the predominant attitude toward law and justice that made its way into interwar Germany.[19]

As viewed within the international context, modern law has different roots and has been subject to correspondingly different shaping influences. In essence, one can trace this back to the long prehistories of Roman law and common law; and one can locate the most precarious problems of the transnational validity and fragility of law in radically modern form exactly where both traditions are confronted and where law is least institutionally anchored in international law (including private law). After a guilty verdict was handed down on Germany in the Treaty of Versailles, with wide-ranging consequences regarding German sovereignty, German national territory and German obligations to pay reparations, the basis of this verdict in international law, and subsequently the international culture of law in general, was called into question. It became a matter of vehement debate in Central and Eastern Europe.

For more than two decades, Carl Schmitt was the most articulate spokesman of a movement within legal thought that tried to expose and denounce this "liberal" international and constitutional law, branding it an Anglo-French instrument of institutionalized interests. In Schmitt's view, it had to be historicized, sociologized, ontologized as an illegitimate instrument of the victor against the vanquished. In his battle against "Weimar, Geneva and Versailles," this law was to be delegitimated. Gradually, step-by-step, a spatially bound, anti-universal, historical and existentialist law of an eventually triumphant vanquished people was to be propagated. It would be modeled on the dictates of national interest and constitutional traditions. Schmitt sought to denounce liberal law as the mask of English and French interests and traditions. With the establishment of a plurality of such legal systems, with their own roots and spaces (and the establishment of the Soviet system was just the most prominent proof of the time that it was feasible), the precarious transnational and international legal community that was just developing would be deconstructed. International politics would then be restored to its proper right and place. Here Schmitt's political concepts entered the picture: he viewed politics as a sovereign decision between friends and foes, thus undermining human rights. He regarded the Nazi seizure of power and the expulsion of the Jews as actions constituting political identity by an authoritarian democracy. He later would justify continental imperialism as a legally autonomous *Großraum* ("macro-area"), calling for a "ban on interventions by outside powers" into Europe and its realm, just as the United States had done in the ease of the Monroe Doctrine.

During the time of the Hitler-Stalin Pact, Schmitt conceptualized the Greater German Reich and the Soviet Union as models of a continental Monroe doctrine. These extended areas of influence of leading nations over their neighbors were based on a fictional ontology of people of unequal value. In terms of the racist power politics of Germany in the areas it occupied, this opened the door to abrogating all vestiges of autonomy and human rights in the case of conquered and subjugated populations. Schmitt halted before reaching this final conclusion, but the leading jurist of the SS, Werner Best, took it over—and, after all, most of the SS police elite were young lawyers educated in the Weimar Republic. When the Wehrmacht invaded Russia, Schmitt's theory was shelved, even though it had paved the way to abolishing liberal democracy, to distinguishing between people of unequal rights, and to constructing a legal framework for a plurality of empires beyond the nation-state. All the same, in terms of world history, the total deprivation of rights of what the Nazis termed "racial enemies" (*Rassenfeinde*) and the legitimacy of the Reich to conscript peoples subjected to forced labor and slave labor, along with its creation of racial hierarchies of exploitation, was a concrete result of such new departures in legal thought. It signified a profound hiatus in the process of the trans- and international legal civilization of Europe, theretofore not consolidated.

This new departure had been prompted by the political instrumentalization of international law at the end of World War I, but it went far further than mere instrumentalization of preexisting legal forms. The more radical departure became more persuasive in times of crisis. It called for an end to the internationally unconsolidated process of legal universalism, and for a belated restoration of claims in the international sphere that would allow the "leading peoples" (*die Führungsvölker*, equivalent, perhaps, to today's "superpowers") to define their extended areas of influence, to abandon universal human rights, and to build up legal structures within these empires in keeping with the interests and ideologies of the Führungsvolk. The rupture in the process of civilization marked by Auschwitz as a metaphor of human annihilation, that *Zivilisationsbruch* (Diner), had begun long before as a legal strategy. It responded to the political abuse of law by challenging its universal validity altogether. This strategy, in another form already established in the Soviet Union, had gained hegemony in Germany when the Nazis came to power. They were to implement it to the extreme. In its original design, it had styled itself as a defensive move by victims; most certainly it had not originally aimed at the Holocaust. But it also had no basis for resistance and restraint after SS jurists took over and radicalized it to legitimate crimes against humanity on a scale of monstrosity previously unknown.[20]

III.

German legal thought concerning the macro-areas rationalized in public the expulsions of the Jews; but the industrialized extermination of human beings, and more particularly of the Jewish people from all over Europe, was a covert implication. By contrast, the imperial regulations for forced conscripted labor were publicly visible—regulations that affected the life and the context of over ten million people in the Reich during the Second World War, and present in almost every German enterprise and corporation, town and village, and in many German households. Ulrich Herbert has determined that the German war economy depended on these deported workers, that their arrival in the Reich represented, however, at the same time, a central challenge to the racial homogenization or (in contemporary parlance) *national identity* project of the Nazis in Germany. This inconsistency in a strategy of radicalized repression was resolved as follows: if we need these foreigners in the Reich, then they should at least be discriminated against by means of a drastic apartheid regime—or, to be more specific, in a negative ethnic hierarchy with dramatic legal consequences for human rights.

The resulting regulations are proof not only of the perversion of the Nazi mind but also of the abandonment of all civilizing legal traditions. These regulations found their expression in the Nazi notions about *Großräume*, manifest in carefully ordered stages of deprivation of the rights of the different groups of foreign workers and in a repressive casuistry regarding sexual intercourse. Decrees for those deported to the Reich regulated in detail who could sleep with whom and in which cases having sexual intercourse would be punished by internment in a concentration camp—and, indeed, in which instances this would eventuate in public execution.[21] Rarely was public law in modern times so intimate, and never has its intimacy in practice become brutal to such a degree.

IV.

Following the Second World War, the world was terrified to learn of the magnitude of the Holocaust and its crimes, and many in Germany also were appalled by its enormity—even if it did take more time before its reality and significance began to sink in and be truly comprehended. In the case of the forced laborers, this was different. The idea of a racist apartheid within a greater German empire, wherever it could be provided with a pragmatic impulse to exploitation, was normalized. It became naturalized by realignment into the context of imperialist war, and its obscene rejection of human rights was repressed. In particular, new macro-areas or Großräume, each with its own nonracist norms, now reigned over Europe, which indeed laid claim to universal validity for their principles. In practice, however, they were bent on the integration of rival blocs. Far be it from me to equate the significance of these Cold War blocs either with one another or with Nazi apartheid doctrine and practice; but one cannot overlook the fact that these Großräume of specific legal systems did exist and, possibly selectively and within their own sphere of influence, brought conflicting notions of justice to bear.

At the same time, the liberal approaches of the Atlantic Community, in contrast to the egalitarian dictatorship of the Soviet empire, proved itself capable of evolving. With the demise of the Soviet Union, we currently find ourselves in a spatially extended phase of this evolution, in which efforts to achieve a universal validity of human rights are confronted by significant challenges. These challenges lie in the areas of social justice, cultural independence, political self-determination and, quite significantly, the availability of military instruments of power. Their combination and differentiation in space—despite technical, financial, economic and cultural globalization tendencies—favor existing and emerging political power structures and regional structures, including different legal systems and cultural notions of law and right. Processes of cultural understanding—and efforts to achieve social justice cannot be separated from this—are at least as important for their diffusion as the extension of the competences of international courts and marshals. That can be welcomed, provided that the principles they safeguard can be enforced, in cases of conflict, against great powers and their interests as well.

To appreciate just how precarious is actual progress in international legal culture related to universalization, social justice, and intercultural understanding, it is useful to learn from the chronicle of early *Wiedergutmachung* and the belated compensation of forced laborers. I cannot develop this theme extensively here but shall only refer to some of its weak points and internal inconsistencies.[22] At the peak of the Cold War, a balancing of interests was mediated, in part as a result of support from the United States, which in a parallel fashion regulated Germany's foreign debts in a way highly favorable for the Federal Republic. West Germany began the payment of reparations for the benefit of Jewish and German survivors of Nazi brutality (and global reparations to the state of Israel as goods in kind amounting to the equivalent of DM 3 billion). But it deferred the regulation of compensation for forced laborers, translated as interstate claims to reparation, to a future peace treaty. Since the United States at the time was primarily interested in the mobilization and binding of the (West) German potential within the framework of the East-West confrontation, it supported this postponement. Almost at the same time, the Soviet Union and Poland renounced the claim to additional reparations from Germany, whose sum total (likewise because of the cession of territory) is difficult to estimate. For example, the removals from the Soviet Zone of Occupation and the GDR (including costs of occupation) had, up until 1953, a value between DM 30 billion and DM 53 billion ($15 billion to $26.5 billion). Down to 1960, there were additional equivalent payments amounting to DM 10 billion at present prices. However, such payments in our context are important only for the donor side, because the recipient states did not pass on the funds to the true victims of Nazi rule (and, to an even lesser extent, to those deported to Germany). Subsequently, right up until 1988, the GDR did indeed provide for Nazi victims among its citizenry, privileging supporters of state socialism among them, but it consistently refused individual compensation extending across borders.

Following the establishment of the European Economic Community, the Federal Republic had to pay moderate global payments to the Western European partner states at the beginning of the 1960s as compensation for their Nazi victims. This amounted altogether to a little less than DM 1 billion, whose distribution to date in the individual countries is little documented and researched. Later, after the demise of the Soviet Union—and in accordance with the 2+4 Agreement, which in 1990 replaced a peace treaty—global funds were transferred to five Eastern European countries for the establishment of reconciliation foundations for the compensation of Nazi victims there. In total, a little more than DM 2.1 billion was distributed in payments of between DM 700 and DM 1,500 per person. In the same decade, the accumulated state expenditure of the Federal Republic for the reparations of Jewish and German Nazi victims, as well as the payment obligations for the future, reached a total of DM 130 billion—the greater part of which was spent on pensions for surviving Jews for physical and mental injury and for impediments to occupational advancement. Between 1945 and 2000, private German companies spent the sum of DM 134 million (or a little more than a quarter of a DM 1 billion in terms of current cash value) for the compensation of forced laborers and other Nazi victims.

A first glance at such a rough balance sheet suffices to show that the postwar German compensation payments could not achieve justice or even reasonable fairness at the level of the individual—they were structured by large-scale political factors and international dependencies in their benefits and deficiencies. On the one hand, the payments of *Wiedergutmachung* are both remarkable and unparalleled, both in terms of their extent and the greatly increased readiness to make them over a period of decades. They are also remarkable, of course, because of their reason. On the other hand, even when they reached the surviving Nazi victims in reasonable amounts (and that was only the case for a greater part of surviving Jewish and German Nazi victims), they were only a stopgap measure, which cannot compensate in any meaningful way for the actual loss.

Third, and this is a point worth underscoring, the payments differed to such an extent that the differentials hardly corresponded with the losses actually experienced. Rather, they were congruent with the power relationships in the politically extended areas and the diverse power blocs that had come into being in the meantime. Just to give an example (albeit an extreme one): after German government agencies learned at the end of the 1990s how their global payments to Nazi victims in Eastern Europe were being distributed among tens of thousands of former concentration camp prisoners—in single payments of around DM 1,000, and less—they acquiesced to a demand, following protracted negotiations, for a special German-American agreement. In this agreement, a few former U.S. soldiers and other U.S. citizens who were taken prisoner by the Germans and confined in concentration camps were to be compensated for their hardship—in some cases at a rate 200 times higher than their East European counterparts.

V.

History is complex, but money is not. In historical memory, even well intentionend impotence within constellations of power and blatant injustice can be recognized and may be acknowledgeable. By these means the core of a desire for responsibility, peace, and solidarity can develop for the future. But the language of money has the opposite effect. It is the medium of a reductionist comparison, one that abstracts from concrete experience and establishes an estimated value that can be traded in markets. This was described by Karl Marx with bitter irony in chapter 24 of *Das Kapital*, still unsurpassed on the subject of the transformation of use value into exchange value. But no one can or wishes to barter with the victims of crimes against humanity; neither a rusty American used car for a traumatized life, nor a small motorcycle for a Ukrainian grandchild, serves as materialization of a recognition, denied until death, of grandma's mortal fear and degradation during the war, and her silence ever since. Against this background, what can be termed the "monetarization of memory" emerges as an inhuman outrage. Mindful of the exchange value and comparative function of money and of political frameworks tending toward very different compensation rates, the outcome is bound by dint of its very selectiveness to offend the majority of victims of violence—instead of acknowledging their suffering and making a contribution to its alleviation. So should there be no compensation for the innumerable forgotten victims and those cast into the shadows by the Cold War, often entangled in the inextricable new international power relationships, half a century after the events? Are there viable alternatives?

Certainly there are. The undesirable secondary effects of compensation fought for in a complex international poker game of interests is foreseeable. They could become widespread. The question from the experienced diplomat in the working group at the government chancellery, "Should we really let that happen to us? No one will be satisfied!," was not unwarranted. On the contrary, it was very much to the point. Invariably, mere symbolic compensation does not constitute justice. Often it is not even fair by comparison with other victims, and it can reinforce the feeling of injustice. But it also harbors redeeming elements of solidarity (however attenuated) and an attempt, however inadequate, at recognition. Symbolic compensation can gain recognition only when the medium of money remains a point of departure rather than an attempt at "coining" the results of experience. And the money can be recognized as a powerless means of expressing earnestness and solidarity, leading the way to a fuller understanding of what transpired then and more recently in the complex perception of history.

The other alternative is the justice of the constitutional state. This has shown itself completely unable to provide an adequate response to the challenges of the crimes against humanity of the twentieth century in general, and those under the rule of the Nazis in particular. That holds whether under criminal law, civil law, or international law. Under Nazi rule, Germany left the playing field of this civilization under the rule of law; reestablishing this resulted in obvious contradictions between the sense of justice and procedural rules and other positive legal regulations that in practice, however, form part of this culture (and that for good reason). In Germany, it was not possible for compensation suits for Nazi conscripted labor to succeed before the courts during the lifetime of the surviving perpetrators and victims except in the case of one individual: in 1965, when the claim of a single forced laborer to obtain his back pay was successful. But his actual back pay then, owing to monetary reforms in 1948, had been reduced to a paltry DM 178, something on the order of $80. The class-action lawsuits brought against particular German companies operating in the United States have in the main not come to a final ruling because of their international complexity. In two cases in which a decision was reached before the political compensation settlement, they were turned down awaiting a political solution. If the lawyers in these lawsuits had seen a real chance for their clients in court, they would never have entered into international negotiations for politically symbolic compensation for forced laborers, and ultimately accepted the result. They looked for a political compromise in a cause that was politically and morally well substantiated, but one having few legal prospects for success. Above all, from the very beginning, this was an approach bound to lead to unfair results with regard to all who could not use this legal instrument, because the ability to bring a German company before an American court has hardly anything to do with the extent of its involvement in the Third Reich half a century before. It has even less to do with the experience of the majority of forced laborers excluded from such a procedure. But class actions opened a political process structured by power relations rather than by law, and by the insight into a more just solution of the problem than that offered by law.

Consequently, it is evident that neither the route of politics nor the path through legal institutions leads to a satisfactory result. And that is true no matter whether they close their eyes to further compensation, as was the case in Germany up until 1998, or whether they follow the course that has been subsequently practiced. In the wake of the rupture in civilization, fairness and justice are unobtainable in the world in which we all live. Should compensation be granted nevertheless? Compensation too late, too little, and too unjust? Should this be an aim, given the historical complexity of a half century of Cold War and the legal inaccessibility of an equitable solution? Does situation compounded by the danger of the monetarization of memory—i.e., the danger that results from an international poker game of diverse interests—now shape the historical perception of a hierarchy of victims? I think that the general aim is defensible, because a step towards justice, fairness, and recognition is better than its idealization or negation. But such a decision can be appreciated only if symbolic compensation is pursued not as a final gesture of some sort, but as the reestablishment of relationships meaningful to the subjects involved—in the form of a material sign, which is not the most essential thing, but certainly a prerequisite for it.[23]

VI.

To conclude, there seems to be no direct way leading from wrongs of such magnitude to rights; nor can crimes against humanity be compensated with money. Rights spring from culture and consent. Wrongs have to be disclosed, admitted; and victims have to be recognized. Compensation is a credible sign of recognition for surviving victims. Now, when only a small minority of victims still survive awaiting recognition, the sign of compensation is all the more imperative for reasons of credibility. But it also harbors a danger, lest cultural memory in the end be structured by the pragmatism and shortcomings of the power politics of compensation. Observers of the collective infringements of rights in the twentieth century are increasingly coming to realize that, under the impress of neoliberal globalization, we have hardly any language at our disposal other than that of money to articulate recognition and make it credible. Since such settlements are almost necessarily unjust, especially when immediate solidarity with the victims has been offset by a long and complex intervening international history, we have to make use of this "language." And we must also overcome this language. The final result is not a material settlement of the wrongs committed, but rather a move to enable cultural discourse about what has happened. That hopefully serves to free recollection from the unavoidable gateway of monetarization. The language of money is only useful in so far as it paves the way to overcome it, and enable reentry into a civilized legal and cultural community, bound up with a prolonged and still insecure process. We will not erase the remembrance that this community and process collapsed in Europe, but perhaps we will become more conscious of its fragility.

Notes

1. The paper is the result of an informal working committee composed of specialists of the Federal Chancellery, the Ministries of Foreign Affairs, Finance, and Labor, the parliamentary parties in government, the Social Democrats and the Greens, under the supervision of two scientific advisors to the Chief of the Federal Chancellery, Ulrich von Alemann (Political Science, Düsseldorf) and Lutz Niethammer (History, Jena). After approval by the Federal Ministers of the Chancellery and for Foreign Affairs, it became, in late January 1999 and under a changed heading, the political paper of the German government at the beginning of national and international negotiations on the question of compensation of Nazi forced labor. It was distributed to the Foundation Initiative of German Industry, and—in a somewhat shortened translation—to American partners in February 1999 (Ulrich von Alemann and Lutz Niethammer, *Policy Paper for the Head of the Federal Chancellery on topical issues concerning compensation for the victims of forced labour,* 14 January 1999).
2. For pertinent essays and legislative materials prior to class-action lawsuits in the U.S. and subsequent international negotiations, see Klaus Barwig, Günter Saathoff, and Nicole Weyde, eds., *Entschädigung für NS-Zwangsarbeit. Rechtliche, historische und politische Aspekte* (Baden-Baden, 1998); for a short sketch, see Lutz

Niethammer, "How to Address the Injustices of the Nazi Era from a Historical Perspective," in *The German Remembrance Fund and the Issue of Forced and Slave Labour: Contributions to a Seminar of the Washington Office of the Friedrich Ebert Foundation held in Washington, D.C. on November 1*, ed. Friedrich Ebert Foundation (Washington, D.C.,1999), 55–68, 83–89; a shorter version is "Schuld und Schulden," *Zeitschrift für KulturAustausch* 49, no. 4 (1999): 48–52.

3. The crab walk is an allusion to Günter Grass's recent novel *Crabwalk* (*Im Krebsgang*, 2002), where the central metaphor is of history zigzagging back and forth, like a crab that walks backwards to move forward. A comprehensive survey of these many debates is given in Peter Reichel, *Vergangenheitsbewältigung in Deutschland. Die Auseinandersetzung mit der NS-Diktatur von 1945 bis heute* (Munich, 2001).
4. On the origins, enlargement, practice, and deficiencies of "Wiedergutmachung," see Nicholas Balabkins, *West German Reparations to Israel* (New Brunswick, 1971); Nana Sagi, *German Reparations: A History of the Negotiations* (Jerusalem, 1980); Ludolf Herbst and Constantin Goschler, eds., *Wiedergutmachung in der Bundesrepublik Deutschland* (Munich, 1989); Herrmann-Josef Brodesser et. al., *Wiedergutmachung und Kriegsfolgenliquidation. Geschichte, Regelungen, Zahlungen* (Munich, 2000); Christian Pross, *Wiedergutmachung. Der Kleinkrieg gegen die Opfer* (Berlin, 2001); Constantin Goschler and Philipp Ther, eds., *Raub und Restitution. "Arisierung" und Rückerstattung des jüdischen Eigentums in Europa* (Frankfurt a.M., 2003); Constantin Goschler, *Schuld und Schulden. Die Politik der Wiedergutmachung für NS-Verfolgte seit 1945* (Goettingen 2005). For Austrian and comparative perspectives, see Dieter Stiefel, ed., *Die politische Ökonomie des Holocaust. Zur wirtschaftlichen Logik von Verfolgung und 'Wiedergutmachung'* (Vienna/Munich, 2001); Oliver Rathkolb, ed., *Revisiting the National Socialist Legacy: Coming to Terms with Forced Labor, Expropriation, Compensation, and Restitution* (Innsbruck, 2002).
5. Earlier attempts at a historical reconstruction of forced labor in Nazi Germany were superseded by Ulrich Herbert's dissertation "Fremdarbeiter." It employed in-depth archival research and caused wide public discussion in Germany after its first publication in 1985. For an English version, see Ulrich Herbert, *Hitler's Foreign Workers: Enforced Foreign Labor in Germany Under the Third Reich* (London, 1997); for international and intertemporal perspectives, see Ulrich Herbert, ed., *Europa und der "Reichseinsatz". Ausländische Zivilarbeiter, Kriegsgefangene und KZ-Häftlinge in Deutschland 1938–1945* (Essen, 1991); idem, *Geschichte der Ausländerpolitik in Deutschland. Saisonarbeiter, Zwangsarbeiter, Gastarbeiter, Flüchtlinge* (Munich, 2001); and idem, *A History of Foreign Labor in Germany, 1880–1980* (Ann Arbor, 1990). A recent survey with useful quantitative data, chapters on responsibility and compensation, and a good bibliography is Mark Spoerer, *Zwangsarbeit unter dem Hakenkreuz. Ausländische Zivilarbeiter, Kriegsgefangene und Häftlinge im Deutschen Reich und im besetzten Europa 1939–1945* (Stuttgart/Munich, 2001).
6. On these camps, far too long neglected, see Gabriele Lotfi, *KZ der Gestapo. Arbeitserziehungslager im Dritten Reich* (Stuttgart/Munich, 2000).
7. A comprehensive survey of recent German and much of the wider international research was assembled in a Buchenwald conference and published in Ulrich Herbert, Karin Orth and Christoph Dieckmann, eds., *Die nationalsozialistischen Konzentrationslager. Entwicklung und Struktur*, 2 vols. (Göttingen, 1998) (for labor in the camps, vol. 2, 533–754). A sociology of the camps—after a first blueprint

by one of the survivors of Buchenwald, Eugen Kogon, *Der SS-Staat* (1946); English: *The Theory and Practice of Hell: The German Concentration Camps and the System behind Them* (London/New York, 1950)—is the widely discussed study by Wolfgang Sofsky, *Die Ordnung des Terrors. Das Konzentrationslager* (Frankfurt a.M., 1993); English: *The Order of Terror: A Sociology of the Concentration Camp* (Princeton, 1997).

8. Christian Streit, *Keine Kameraden. Die Wehrmacht und die sowjetischen Kriegsgefangenen 1941–1945* (Stuttgart, 1978).
9. The great innovation among established compensation policies for the Nazi era by the state this time was the acknowledgement of civil society, i.e. industrial responsibility for the damages to be compensated, if on a voluntary basis.
10. In 1993, some $750 million went to Eastern Europe (Russia, Belarus, Ukrainia, Poland and Czechoslovakia) as lump sums to compensate victims of Nazism that had not been recognized during the Cold War period. It is interesting that at this time, compensation for forced labor was expressly excluded by the German government; however, the money was passed on to a substantial extent by the national distributing agencies precisely to this category of victims.
11. Stuart E. Eizenstat, *Imperfect Justice: Looted Assets, Slave Labor, and the Unfinished Business of World War II* (New York, 2003), gives his account of the negotiations with the same care and thoughtful judgment with which he moderated the negotiations and kept, on his yellow sheets, his own minutes of the discussions. I found astonishing and somewhat biased, however, that he reports from the outset (205ff., esp. 217) that it was his persuasion if not pressure that won the German side over to include non-Jewish Eastern European slave and forced laborers into the compensation process. This may have been his impression from his initial talks with Bodo Hombach (we persuaded him simultaneously from the inside), but I was present in earlier talks when Manfred Gentz, the later president of the Foundation Initiative of German Business, strongly advocated in a meeting of business leaders in the chancellery that the real task lay in Eastern Europe, or when, on a different occasion, Foreign Minister Joschka Fischer, questioned by the chancellery, decided, as we in our advisory comittee had hoped, that Eastern Europe was to be integrated in the then evolving compensation policy. This decision was one of the cornerstones on which our Policy Paper of January 1999 was built. Hombach accepted the decision and the paper, which became a blueprint for the announcement of the 'foundation initiative' by the chancellor and Gentz on February 16, 1999. In the following weeks, I toured Israel and Eastern European capitals in search of information and possible partners, many of whom were invited to Bonn long before the international negotiations began in Washington. For reasons of truth and European neighborliness, it seems to me to be noteworthy that it was German initiative, and not (or at least not primarily) American pressure, that brought our Eastern European neighbors to the table and into this compensation process.
12. The outcome of the first international scholarly conference at Weimar on July 8–10, 1999, was announced publicly; see *International Workshop at Buchenwald on Nazi Forced Labor—Historical Concepts and Data.* The second fact-finding meeting at the European University Institute in Florence on September 2–4, 1999, was confidential and brought together, among other specialists, representatives of the Jewish Claims Conference, of American Jewish Lawyers, and of the Reconcilation and similar foundations of Belarus, the Czech Republic, Poland, Russia, and

Ukraine. Based on data from previous compensation payments to survivors, we accumulated there by consent a database of possible survivors of slave and forced labor in various categories (the statistics were also translated into English as *Living Survivors of Nazi Forced Labor, 1999*), and discussed, with the help of the expertise of Mark Spoerer, the complicated question of private vs. public responsibility: the majority of slave laborers had been employed by public agencies and the vast majority of forced laborers in the private sector. I sent our findings together with my evaluation to Count Lambsdorff on September 5, 1999, and they had two results. The following week, on advice from Graf Lambsdorff, the chancellor and German business leaders agreed that the funds of the foundation initiative be doubled by state funds, and (after some discussions with less scrutinized American statistics) the proportions of victims from various nations from our findings became in the long run the basic ratio of distribution of compensation.

13. The best critical account of the negotiations in German is Matthias Arning, *Späte Abrechnung. Über Zwangsarbeiter, Schlussstriche und Berliner Verständigungen* (Frankfurt a.M., 2001), 64. For an even better informed report by American journalists, see footnote 18.
14. A major part of the German side, including industry, favoured such a model at the beginning, and I had even explained its implications in public hoping for a larger share for those in need (cf. *Die Welt*, 2 June 1999, 5). But the idea was torpedoed when, at the very first round of negotiations in Washington, a Jewish delegate from the Czech Republic announced the unanimous resolution of all delegates representing victims' interests against it. Not without cause, they felt it could impair their negotiating position in regard to the overall sum to be distributed. When that sum had eventually been fixed, the principle of equal compensation across nations vanished again quickly and was buried in complicated detail of the foundation law.
15. Various aspects of the legal process are discussed in Peer Zumbansen, ed., *Zwangsarbeit im Dritten Reich. Erinnerung und Verantwortung. Juristische und zeithistorische Betrachtungen* (Baden-Baden, 2002). In the final evaluation, Libby Adler and Peer Zumbansen, *The Forgetfulness of Noblesse: A Critique of the German Foundation Law Compensating Slave and Forced Laborers of the Third Reich*, lament the circumvention of the courts by international agreement, because this "enabled the culprits to evade accepting any real responsibility for the enslavement of millions," but acknowledge the fact that otherwise the victims "might have lost. They might also have died before the verdicts were delivered. This article is not an hommage to the promise of litigation to bring justice to the wronged" (392).
16. Their view of the negotiations, and their reiteration and somewhat less than wise public pressure for legal closure, are well documented in the official history of the business part of the foundation initiative "Remembrance, Responsibility and Future." See Susanne-Sophia Spiliotis, *Verantwortung und Rechtsfrieden. Die Stiftungsinitiative der deutschen Wirtschaft* (Frankfurt a.M., 2003).
17. There are far too many publications resulting from this memory boom to be documented here. Let me just say that even in my small hometown, Schalksmühle, North Rhine-Westphalia, a well-documented exhibition on forced labor in the county, enriched by local documents, was opened by the mayor in the presence of all local notables and an equally well documented book from the nearby county town was distributed: Matthias Wagner, *"Arbeit macht frei". Zwangsarbeit in Lüden-*

scheid 1939–1945 (Lüdenscheid, 1997), that had been produced even prior to the negotiations; and for the exhibition after them a catalog in book form was issued. Such a local example was not in the least unusual. Some of the most renowned enterprises had teams of historians research into their dubious past well before the negotiations, such as, notably, Barbara Hopmann and Mark Spoerer, *Zwangsarbeit bei Daimler Benz* (Stuttgart, 1994)—provoked by independent research such as *Das Daimler-Benz-Buch. Ein Rüstungskonzern im "Tausendjährigen Reich,"* ed. Hamburger Stiftung für Sozialgeschichte des 20. Jahrhunderts (Nördlingen, 1987), or unprovoked: Hans Mommsen and Manfred Grieger, *Das Volkswagenwerk und seine Arbeiter im Dritten Reich* (Düsseldorf, 1996), and others like major banks and insurance companies followed suit, if sometimes more reluctantly. One of the outstanding examples is Gerald D. Feldman, *Die Allianz und die deutsche Versicherungswirtschaft 1933–1945* (Munich, 2001). On the occasion of the launching of a major research initiative into forced labor in the mining industry in the Third Reich and its occupied areas, I dealt with the accomplishments and deficiencies of this research boom in Lutz Niethammer, "Klärung und Aufklärung. Aufgaben und Lücken der Zwangsarbeiterforschung," in *Zwangsarbeiterforschung als gesellschaftlicher Auftrag*, ed. Klaus Tenfelde (Bochum, 2001), 13–22.

18. Correspondents of the *Financial Times* report a similar story, as it then was rumoured, in their rather well informed account of the negotiations. John Authers and Richard Wolffe, *The Victim's Fortune: Inside the Epic Battle over the Debts of the Holocaust* (New York, 2002), 200. The more general problem of the competition of victims for recognition has been dealt with, before these negotiations, by the Belgian philosopher and sociologist Jean-Michel Chaumont, *Die Konkurrenz der Opfer. Genozid, Identität und Anerkennung* (Lüneburg, 2001), first published in Paris 1997.
19. His work and the interpretations of it are much too vast and complicated to be documented here. For my reading and broader documentation of the literature, see Lutz Niethammer, *Kollektive Identität. Heimliche Quellen einer unheimlichen Konjunktur* (Reinbek b. Hamburg, 2000), 77–122, and my essay "Die polemische Anstrengung des Begriffs. Über die andauernde Faszination Carl Schmitts," in a forthcoming volume on Kulturwissenschaften und Nationalsozialismus, ed. by Hartmut Lehmann and Otto Gerhard Oexle.
20. Ulrich Herbert, *Best. Biographische Studien über Radikalismus. Weltanschauung und Vernunft 1903–1989*, 3rd ed., (Bonn, 1996), 225, 271.
21. See Herbert, *Hitler's Foreign Workers*.
22. For broader discussion of the following issues, see the literature quoted above in footnotes 2 and 4.
23. This was the reason for setting aside, during the negotiations on compensation of Nazi forced labor, a substantial fund "Remembrance and Future" for social and cultural projects among the nations concerned in the future. After consultations in Eastern Europe, Israel, the United States, and Germany, I outlined suggestions on how it should be spent in "Der Schlussstein soll ein Grundstein werden," *Frankfurter Allgemeine Zeitung*, 19 July 2000, reprinted in *Ego-Histoire? Und andere Erinnerungs-Versuche* (Vienna, 2002), 253–259.

— *Six* —

Scholarly Investigation and Material Compensation: The Austrian Historical Commission at Work

Clemens Jabloner

After more than four years of research, the Austrian Historical Commission presented its final reports to the public in February 2003. This series of about 50 reports[1] contains the results of separate research projects and expert reports involving 160 researchers working on a total of 47 projects. The culmination is the Final Report,[2] which comprises the findings, evaluations and summaries of the Historical Commission and its permanent experts. Contents of such a work cannot be summarized in a few sentences or pages. This paper intends to provide basic information about the path leading to the setting up of the Historical Commission and the structure of its work, mentioning several particularly illustrative results. The central topic of the Historical Commission were the economic aspects of National Socialism in Austria, including the expropriation of assets (*Vermögensentzug*), and attempts for restitution or compensation after 1945.

Motives for Establishing the Historical Commission

There were various underlying motives behind the creation of the commission in the autumn of 1998. First of all, in postwar Austria up until the 1980s, there was a predominant notion of the so-called "thesis of the victim." According to that thesis, the Republic of Austria had been invaded in 1938 and had ceased to exist until the end of the war, so that it could not be held responsible for any of the crimes perpetrated by the

Nazi regime. In terms of the terminology of international law, this is known as the "theory of occupation." The espousal of this view was correct in terms of international law and meaningful in terms of Austrian foreign policy, because it parried any attacks on German property and territorial claims and, on an ideal level, contributed to solidifying Austrian national identity. Yet this thesis of the victim was not only mobilized in the arena of international politics. It was also utilized against the actual victims of National Socialism. That was a questionable conclusion. As purposive as the juridical construction was in foreign policy, it was inadmissible in terms of domestic policy and, more important, in terms of morality. It soon proved very suitable for rejecting any claims for restitution brought against the Austrian state or to lessen their efficiency. Ultimately, the Moscow Declaration of 1 November 1943 had not only mentioned Austria as the first victim of the "typical policy of attack by Hitler," but also underscored Austrian responsibility for "participation in the war at the side of Hitler's Germany."[3]

Only with the emergence of the discussion regarding Kurt Waldheim and the 50th anniversary of the *Anschluß* in 1988 was there the beginning of a stepwise departure from and revision of the thesis of victimization. In Waldheim's television address on 10 March 1988, and most especially in the statements by Chancellor Vranitzky before the National Parliament in Vienna on 8 July 1991 and by President Klestil before the Israeli Knesset on 15 November 1994, was there an ever more clear enunciation of the principle of Austrian moral shared responsibility for events in World War II.

If talk about Austria as a "victim" of National Socialism seems so offensive, this is principally as such talk serves to exonerate and excuse Austrian complicity in and sympathy for the Nazi cause, or at least its tacit acceptance of it. After all, the label "victim" can properly be applied to those who suffered after 13 March 1938 under the crimes condoned or even committed by a large proportion of the Austrian people.[4]

So it is important to stress that after the "annexation" of Austria by the Reich in March 1938, many Austrians became victims. The Jews and Roma, and the numerous others who were persecuted, were also Austrians. But if one follows this simple dichotomy, many Austrians also became perpetrators and profiteers. Discourse on Austria as the first victim ultimately served to help integrate all groups at a lowest common denominator into postwar Austria. There were the victims of February 1934 and the period of the authoritarian *Ständestaat,* the victims at the hands of the illegal Nazis before 1938, the victims of Nazi terror after 1938, the victims during the war, the victims of the Allied Occupation, the "de-Nazified" Austrians as victims, and so on. Those persons, encompassing almost all in the Second Republic, individually and in keeping with their subjective feeling, were able to join the ranks of the "victimized." Individual acceptance went hand in hand with the political implementation of a collective role of victim for the state—a kind of generalized victim identity. It thus masked and negated the situation of the real victims of National Socialism.

The extreme right seldom espoused the thesis of the "victim" with any conviction. As their worldview saw it then, and probably still does today, the struggle against Jews, Bolsheviks, and other groups was a common struggle of the "decent" (*die Anständigen*) against society's dregs. In this schematic view, the fact that this battle was lost and Austria had to accept a position dictated by the victorious powers leads to the notion that the price for that defeat was and is the payment of "protection money."

The broader social-psychological frame is also part of the picture, where injustice is placed on the scales and weighed, as if in the market. That is understandable in that on the individual level, the sacrifices and pain of this period were experienced as existential torment and loss. But viewed in political terms, the key question is responsibility. The Austrian Republic bears responsibility today for events in the Nazi period, accepting that responsibility not only politically but in regard to it legal consequences as well.

But this paradigm shift would not in itself have led to the creation of the Historical Commission. It was supplemented by another factor, namely, a change in the attitudes inside the groups of victims themselves. They now emerged onto the public stage as more self-confident, bolstered by progress in research on contemporary history and the opening of the archives in the former communist countries.

Finally, it is undeniable that "international pressure" and the special features of U.S. law—including the institution of "class action litigation" and the extension of the territory where law could apply—forced Austria into a kind of legal and ethical corner. The creation of the Bergier Commission in Switzerland, in some respects in a similar situation, pointed the way.[5]

The Results of the Historical Commission

In keeping with its mandate,[6] the Final Report is divided into two parts. The first deals with various aspects of the expropriation of property, focusing on the groups affected, primarily Jews, as well as on the categories of property expropriated. The second part deals with the period after 1945 and presents political, economic and legal aspects of restitution and compensation in their historical context.

The reports on expropriation of property from the various victim groups and the techniques of that expropriation and fleecing convey the harrowing picture of a huge enterprise of what today one would call "organized crime." This process of plunder extended from clever "take-overs" by corporations to pure acts of unadulterated force. It was the first step on the road to destruction. The so-called *Vermögensentzug* accompanied the victims up until the removal of their last few possessions before entering the gas chamber.

The commission did not concentrate on "Aryanizations," though quantitatively they were probably of the greatest import. To rob some 200,000 Jews is quite an undertaking, something like the entire population of the city of Graz. But, to mention one further example, the victims of euthanasia were also robbed of their possessions. The murder of the mentally or physically disabled was carried out in the name of saving the nursing and accommodation costs as well as associated social expenditures. The valuables and clothing of those murdered were distributed among the workers in the institutions where the murders were carried out, and among relevant Nazi welfare organizations, such as the National Socialist People's Welfare (NSV). The doctors whose expertise decided the fate of the patients gained a considerable extra income from their activity as "experts." Members of the family of those murdered and their local councils continued to be charged nursing fees even after the victims had been killed.

Restitution and compensation are extraordinarily complex topics. Expectations at the time the Historical Commission was launched were confirmed: it is not true that Austria restituted everything stolen and compensated all who had been exploited. But it is likewise not true, as has been repeatedly alleged, that Austria avoided any and all responsibility. The truth lies somewhere in between. A system of restitution and reparation was built up, but hesitatingly, slow-moving, full of gaps and traps. Basically, all of that goes back to the problematic matrix of the beginnings of the Second Republic and the above-mentioned thesis of "victimization."

From the huge abundance of material, two elements will be looked at here in greater detail. They can serve to point up the differing facets of the fundamental problems Austria encountered in dealing with the victims of National Socialism up until the most recent period: the law on citizenship and the system of social insurance.

The transfer of citizenship in 1945 carried on from 13 March 1938; it simulated the fiction of the continued validity of the 1925 Austrian Citizenship Law. This meant that only expellees who were Austrian citizens on 13 March 1938 and who had not adopted foreign citizenship between 1938 and 1945 were Austrian citizens on 27 April 1945. Anyone who had been a citizen on 13 March 1938 was now a citizen again—as long as he or she had not adopted foreign citizenship. Thus, although a formal restitution of citizenship was achieved, the actual consequences of the expatriation were overlooked—since expatriated Austrians whose only chance had often been to apply for a foreign citizenship were now *unable to regain* Austrian citizenship. The 1945 Austrian citizenship law thus attempted to turn back the wheels of history.

A series of amendments to the citizenship law were admittedly intended to improve the legal situation; but owing to their faulty construction, they did not in fact succeed or succeeded only partly in doing so. It was not until 1993 that a situation was established that can to some extent be regarded as satisfactory. Since then former Austrians have no longer been obliged to give up foreign citizenship, and the residency condition—that is, actually living in Austria—has also been dropped. And only in 1993 were the expellees exempted from the relatively high naturalization fees. The completely inadequate regulation of citizenship provisions had its principle effect "above" where Austrian citizenship was a precondition for compensation measures, such as victims' welfare.

The development of social insurance law after 1945 in Austria presents a mixed picture riddled with contradictions: For most victims of Nazism, persecution by the regime also meant social security disadvantages. The loss of livelihood and/or a job, a forced break in education, arrest, escape and deportation, but also living a life in hiding, involved the loss of social security benefits or pension entitlements. It made it impossible to acquire the credits needed based on periods of insurance contributions. The Jews constituted the largest persecuted group and thus also those most affected by disadvantages in social security rights.

The social security legislation of the Second Republic had to react to these damages. It did so within the framework of a *Begünstigungsrecht*, a so-called "right to preferential treatment." The core of this right had been created in the transfer of law of 1945, codified and anchored since 1956 primarily in section 9 of the Social Security Law (ASVG, paras. 500–506). Typical of this area of law, a concentration of the material on a few regulations raised many questions of interpretation. These made numerous amendments necessary and led to a widely ramified dispensation of justice. These amendments brought a gradual extension of the system of preferential treatment and ultimately, albeit only after several attempts, led to a legal situation that can largely be seen as satisfactory. Primarily, this applies to those who are now given favorable treatment under social security legislation, persons who in the early stages of the law were dealt with in an extremely restrictive manner. The various extensions, the result of a better understanding of the historical background, were implemented in the end. But that implementation often came late, sometimes too late.

The Historical Commission has interpreted its mandate in a broad frame while at the same time assuring that a project is drafted that can be completed within the scope of the means allotted and the time deemed reasonable and proper. Despite this self-restriction, the endeavor has become the most extensive single project of research in the human sciences in the history of the Second Republic. It is a persuasive proof of the quality of both the historical sciences and jurisprudence.

The many studies required, and whose details cannot be examined here, included estimating the total assets of Jewish Austrians in 1938; research on the "Aryanization" of Jewish real estate; "Aryanization" in the federal states; expropriation of Roma, Sinti, and other ethnic minorities; estimates on the number and whereabouts of still living former forced laborers; questions of tax law in connection with restitution; citizenship law questions; aspects of the law on equities; and the role of the legal representative for financial matters (*Finanzprokuratur*), the state finance offices, and the courts in restitution proceedings.

Impact of the Historical Commission

After concluding so many extensive studies, the general question worth asking is what impact the Historical Commission's report has had or should have had. This question is relevant on a number of quite different levels. Let us look at a few of these.

It was important for the commission to ensure that its creation not be regarded as yet another instrument for "dragging matters out indefinitely," as the familiar formulation went. It was thus clarified already in 1998 that in several areas, there could be political and legal measures instituted immediately. In order to accelerate this process, the commission quickly presented partial reports on questions of the expropriation of tenure rights and the probable number of still-living former forced laborers. In both spheres, there were rapid developments. One the one hand, a "reconciliation fund"[7] was set up to compensate former forced laborers. On the other, as a consequence of the Washington Agreement[8] of 17 January 2001 on various measures in federal law, there was a general settlement for renting rights.[9]

If one looks at the total results of the historic Washington Agreement in the light of the Final Report of the commission, it is justifiable to ask whether on the whole a satisfactory legal situation was created. Two problems still remained by the end of 2003: first, it was and is still necessary to reach an agreement with the Austrian Jewish Communities on expropriated communal properties and assets. That agreement should express the basic interest of the Republic of Austria in the continued existence of Jewish institutions on Austrian soil. Second, it remains unfortunately true that owing to the still-unresolved and outstanding class-action suits in the United States, the requisite "legal peace" has not yet been achieved, so that an amicable agreement and end to litigation is not yet in sight. One can in this instance only appeal to the good will of all those involved to come to a satisfactory and speedy solution.

As a scientific document, the report of the Historical Commission is valuable in itself, that is, by dint of its scientific treatment of the area of expropriation of assets, restitution, and compensation. Of course this is somewhat unwieldy and complex material that does not readily lend itself to popularization. The commission's Final Report stresses that it is the coming task of the schools and the media to present its basic contents in a suitable form to a large audience. That is a suggestion by the authors that has already been made concrete reality in a number of spheres. The most diverse aspects of the results of comprehensive research have been presented and discussed in numerous lectures at universities, in schools, at institutions for adult education, before professional associations, and elsewhere. Teaching materials, such as those on the topic of forced labor in agriculture, have been assembled. Special in-service training for teachers is in the planning stages, along with focused conferences. Political representatives have been given relevant instruction. Follow-up projects such as the listing of the names of all murdered Sinti and Roma have been initiated, and TV documentaries have been filmed and telecast. The impact can also be observed where groups are confronted with this thematic complex on the basis of their own profession and occupational involvements. Thus, for example, experts on citizenship legislation have begun an initiative through which the children and grandchildren of Jews expelled from Austria will automatically be able to acquire Austrian citizenship.

In this context, however, there is repeated talk in Austria about the need to "draw a line" and reach some kind of "closure" on these matters. The discourse connected with this central, ambiguous term here—"*Schlußstrich*," "or final line"—can in the final analysis only be misleading. For scientific reasons alone there can be no "final line" drawn, because science presumes that all findings are subject to further revision, correction, and interpretation. There is no "closure" when it comes to inquiry and its epistemology. In serious scientific terms, there can be no final "balance sheet" of expropriated, restituted, or compensated values. But there is also a classic dilemma in terms of social psychology here: as long as demands continue to be voiced for "drawing the line" and closing the files, there can in fact be no such "closure." Only when the findings of such inquiry no longer generate a *call* for "closure" will it be possible to draw that "final line.' But then no one will any longer want to call it that.

Translated from the German by Bill Templer

Notes

1. All reports (49 books) have been published as *Veröffentlichung der Österreichischen Historikerkommission. Vermögensentzug während der NS-Zeit sowie Rückstellungen und Entschädigungen seit 1945 in Österreich* in the Oldenbourg Verlag, 2002–2004.
2. Clemens Jabloner, Brigitte Bailer-Galanda, Eva Blimlinger, Georg Graf, Robert Knight, Lorenz Mikoletzky, Bertrand Perz, Roman Sandgruber, Karl Stuhlpfarrer, Alice Teichova, *Schlussbericht der Historikerkommission der Republik Österreich. Vermögensentzug während der NS-Zeit sowie Rückstellungen und Entschädigungen seit 1945 in Österreich. Zusammenfassungen und Einschätzungen*, vol. 1 (Vienna/Munich, 2003).
3. On the meaning of shared responsibility, see Ludwig Adamovich, "Das Unbehagen in der Zweiten Republik," in *querela iuris. Gedächtnisschrift für Eduard Rabofsky* (Vienna/New York, 1996), 3; and Roman Sandgruber, "Opfer, Pflicht, Schuld," *Die Presse. Spectrum*, 5 January 2001. On the question of the co-responsibility of Austria and the Austrians, there is a copious literature. See, for example, the representative studies: Gerhard Botz and Gerald Sprengnagel, eds., *Kontroversen um Österreichs Zeitgeschichte. Verdrängte Vergangenheit, Österreich-Identität, Waldheim und die Historiker* (Frankfurt a.M./New York, 1994). On the Moscow Declara-

tion, see Gerald Stourzh, *Um Einheit und Freiheit. Staatsvertrag, Neutralität und das Ende der Ost-West-Besetzung Österreichs 1945-1955* (Vienna, 1998).

4. See in general Heidemarie Uhl, "Das 'erste Opfer.' Der österreichische Opfermythos und seine Transformation in der Zweiten Republik," *ÖZP*, no. 1 (2001): 19–34; Siegfried Mattl and Karl Stuhlpfarrer, "Auf deinem Altar ist Österreich. Österreichische Selbstbespiegelungen und Opferphantasien seit 1945," *Zukunft*, no. 4 (1985): 19–23; Karl Stuhlpfarrer, "Österreich, das erste Opfer Hitlerdeutschlands. Die Geschichte einer Sage und ihre Bedeutung," in *Die Mauern der Geschichte. Historiographie in Europa zwischen Diktatur und Demokratie*, ed. Gustavo Corni and Martin Sabrow (Leipzig, 1996), 233–244.
5. *Die Schweiz, der Nationalsozialismus und der Zweite Weltkrieg. Schlussbericht*, ed. Unabhängige Expertenkommission Schweiz-Zweiter Weltkrieg (Zurich, 2002).
6. See Working Program of the Historical Commission, Vienna 1999, http://www.historikerkommission.gv.at (1 August 2005).
7. "Versöhnungsfondsgesetz. Bundesgesetz über den Fonds für freiwillige Leistungen der Republik Österreich an ehemalige Sklaven- und Zwangsarbeiter des nationalsozialistischen Regimes," *Bundesgesetzblatt* I (BGBl), 2000/74.
8. "Bundesgesetz über die Einrichtung eines Allgemeinen Entschädigungsfonds für Opfer des Nationalsozialismus und über Restitutionsmaßnahmen," *BGBl* I, 2001/12; on the historic Washington Agreement, see http://www.austria.org/press/236.html (1 August 2005).
9. "Novellierung des Nationalfondsgesetzes. Bundesgesetz über den Nationalfonds der Republik Österreich für Opfer des Nationalsozialismus," *BGBl* 1995/432.

Part IV: Tesselated European Histories of memory

— *Seven* —

The Object's Memory: Remembering Rural Jews in Southern Germany

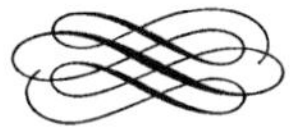

Ulrich Baumann

On 11 December 1940, there was a public auction in Ihringen, a vintners' village in Baden on the southern fringe of the Kaiserstuhl hills. Auctions in the countryside were nothing unusual. As a rule, they involved land or chattels of debtors to satisfy the claims of their creditors. However, the auction on this day differed from all others that had taken place in this small locality. This was a measure by the National Socialist bureaucracy that violated all principles of civil law, even if special laws and ordinances had been issued to lend such auctions the semblance of legality. The objects of the auction were the possessions of the Jewish inhabitants of the village. Less than two months before, on 22 October 1940, the Ihringen Jews had been deported along with almost all the other Jews in Baden and the Palatinate in special trains across the German-French border. They were transported to the Gurs concentration camp at the foot of the Pyrenees. Their houses had been sealed after 22 October, and were now emptied. The contents, insofar as they had not already been stolen by thieves, were brought to be auctioned off to the local public. The only exception were the household effects of Ihringen Jews who at the time were not "abroad" but rather located in other areas on the territory of the German Reich.

At the request of the chief of the Freiburg police, care was to be taken in the public announcement of the auction not to reveal the true circumstances behind it, that is, no mention was to be made of the fact that it involved the possessions of Jewish residents of the village.[1] Did the authorities fear that few people would attend the auction if it was public knowledge whose property was to be auctioned off? That most probably was already common knowledge in the village, where everything immediately made the grapevine rounds. Apparently the auction was well attended, for immediately after its conclusion an Ihringen resident complained to the municipality about an "empty bed frame" she had acquired: she had not been able to properly see what the bed looked like "since it had already turned dark and there was such a big crowd of people."[2] The typewritten list of the bidders confirms this statement. It indicates that there were sixty-seven buyers for the ninety-three items or groups of items from that single household from which the bedstead mentioned stemmed.

The events in Ihringen were repeated in dozens of other villages in Baden and, with the commencement of systematic deportation to the East (autumn 1941), across the length and breadth of the German Reich as well. The auctions marked the final culmination in the policy of systematic plundering of the German Jews. This process subsumed the policy of displacement of the Jewish merchants and businessmen from economic life, the forced transfers of ownership of firms in the framework of what the National Socialists termed "Aryanization," and the open and unvarnished fleecing of the Jews by special levies after the pogroms on 9/10 November 1938.

Historians have analyzed the first step in this policy with increasing depth and acuity in recent years. The present paper will concentrate less on the interplay of Nazi party, communal, and national government authorities in these actions than on the event's "post-history." The focus will in particular be on what the non-Jewish buyers who acquired these plundered household objects and properties did with them, what significance they accorded these material *things*, and what dimensions of *memory* were attached to these objects.

To spotlight this (hi)story after the fact of a rural auction is an attempt to illuminate these events in the context of a compact and close-knit social milieu. The analysis deals with rural areas, small towns, and villages where Jews and non-Jews lived together as neighbors in relatively close proximity and a maintained web of mutual contacts. The regional focus here is southwestern Germany, where prior to 1940–41 there were numerous rural communities with populations of mixed religious affiliation, most especially on the Upper Rhine, in Swabia, Franconia, and Hesse. These regions formed the historical geographic core of rural Jewry in Germany.

The History of Relations between Christians and Jews in the Countryside

What was the aftermath of these events of plunder in light of the fact of neighborly familiarity, that is, given that the families of the former owners and new owners had known each other for generations and were in regular social contact? In order to answer this question, it is useful initially to sketch a general picture of the relations between Jews and non-Jews in rural Germany. The history of most Jewish communities in the countryside dated back to the seventeenth and eighteenth centuries. Petty princes in the territories granted Jewish families the right to settle in exchange for corresponding special taxes, and provided these families with letters of protection. Up until the mid-nineteenth century, these rural Jewish communities in the small towns and villages increased in demographic strength. In several localities in southern Germany and Hesse, the Jewish population was even in the majority in the period 1830–70. Once Jews were granted civil equality around 1865, coupled with a free right to settle where they pleased, a wave of out-migration commenced. It gained momentum as ever more Jews relocated to the larger cities. This weakened the rural communities demographically. At the same time, the social situation of those remaining in the countryside stabilized. Most Jewish families now no longer lived as peddlers or trafficked in any items that could be sold (so-called *Nothandel*). They established more viable economic relations within their regions, especially in the cattle trade. With respect to religion, the rural Jews were characterized by a traditional piety that cannot be fully grasped by the labels "Orthodox" or "liberal."[3] Life alongside the Christian rural population, which for a long time was problematic and repeatedly disrupted by violent excesses (especially during the Revolution 1848–49), solidified after the Jews gained civil equality, developing into a form of close cooperation, though not without occasional frictions. In many localities, Jews were also on the town councils and were actively involved in shaping the fate of their towns and villages. The highly vocal and radical anti-Semitism of the 1880s and 1890s proved unable to destroy the solid foundations of cooperation between Jews and non-Jews. In most rural communities around 1900, there was a predominant attitude of *common sense*: people believed that "religious peace" was a boon, and in cases of local anti-Jewish violence, officials did not hesitate to call in the police to restore order. The period 1900–14 probably marked the era of the highest levels of integration between rural Christians and Jews. The various voluntary associations constituted an important forum. The veterans' associations or voluntary firemen provided opportunities for everyday encounters between Jewish and Christian males. Yet the boundaries between the groups persisted. Jews continued to marry primarily inside their faith, a tendency also true of Catholics and Protestants.[4]

After World War I, the labile balance in Christian-Jewish consociation lost some of its stability. The demographic importance of the Jewish population within the broader population in these towns and villages declined owing to the constant out-migration to the larger cities. The integrating, albeit authoritarian, influence of the previously dominant village notables was in the decline. The lack of political orientation among the rural Christian population, especially in Protestant areas, led to a strengthening of folkish-nationalist groupings, whose political legacy was ultimately inherited after 1928 by the rise of a new political movement: the National Socialists. In many rural localities, there were landslide victories at the ballot box even before 1933 for the NSDAP. In 1932, for example, the party garnered 77 percent of the vote in the predominantly Protestant village of Ihringen, and in several neighboring villages chalked up victories of more than 80 and even 90 percent.[5] In most Roman Catholic country towns and villages, though not all, the NSDAP had a far more modest showing at the polls.

The differences in the political atmosphere between the individual localities leveled out within a few short months after the Nazis seized power. In many rural communities, the Jewish population was buffeted by violent outrages at the hands of the National Socialists and their sympathizers. A number of deaths were reported as a result of these attacks. The pogrom of November 1938 brought relations between Jews and non-Jews in rural Germany to a sudden and violent end. Many families previously unsuccessful in relocating to the larger urban areas now moved to bigger towns. Ultimately, the violent end of the Jewish country communities came with the beginning of the deportations. In Baden and the Palatinate, Jews had already been deported in October 1940 to southern France. In the other areas of southern and southwestern Germany, deportations commenced in October 1941, as Jews were channeled to the occupied or annexed territories in the East (Poland, the Baltic, White Russia). While a small number of Jews from Baden and the Palatinate managed to emigrate from the internment camps in southern France overseas, deportation to the East for the rest meant certain death in the ghettos, the sites of mass execution or in the extermination camps.

Among the few who survived the mass murder were some individuals who returned again to their native towns and villages after the war. They were usually the sole survivors, had lost all family members, and resettled in localities where there was no longer any Jewish community. The history of rural Jewry in Germany had come to a violent end as a result of the Nazi policy of mass murder.

For decades it then appeared as if public memory of the former lifeworld of rural Jewry would remain alive only among the ranks of the minute number who had survived the devastation. In any event, historiography on the German-Jewish past long chose to neglect the topic. The pioneer in inquiry here was the critically oriented Tübingen School of folklife and folklore studies established by Hermann Bausinger. Of greatest importance was the work of Utz Jeggle, whose path-breaking dissertation on the Jewish villages in Württemberg was published in 1969.[6]

To a certain extent, a conference organized in 1974 at the Leo Baeck Institute in New York served as the scholarly prelude to intensified interest in this thematic complex within historiography. In the 1980s, studies on rural Jewry enjoyed something of a boom as interest in small-scale, local dimensions grew in the broader context of a flowering of regional research in history and new approaches in the history of everyday life. In the huge corpus of regional and local studies of rural Jewish life, the topic of memory and remembrance of the history of persecution of Jewish neighbors after 1945 was repeatedly broached, though generally somewhat marginally.

The most striking treatment of this topic is in the work of a pupil of Jeggle, the ethnologist and cultural studies scholar Franziska Becker. She conducted interviews over many months in the Württemberg village of Baisingen, today incorporated as a neighborhood within the town of Rottenburg am Neckar. Her study based on these field interviews, *Gewalt und Gedächtnis,* explores the techniques used by local village memory "in order to privilege and promote forgetting."[7] Becker was also the first to deal critically with the "power of memory of material objects." In the present study, I make use of Becker's paradigms and her armature of argumentation and presentation, supplementing it here and there with my own material. On the one hand, Becker oriented her investigation to the data given by her interview partners, to whom she presented a "space of memory" as a buttress for their own recollections. That space consisted of the various stations of escalating force against Jews in the village and, as she determined, reflected the points of orientation of her interviewees. At the same time, she relied on contemporary sources, especially the files of the finance office responsible for the auctions, and the files of the reparations office set up after 1945.

The Social Structure of the Village and Its Material Manifestations

Before looking in detail at memories of Jewish persecution and the power of memory of material objects, it is useful to turn once more to a more precise look at patterns of consociation between Jews and non-Jews in the nineteenth and twentieth centuries. In what way were the possession or nonpossession of various goods and objects and the associated lifestyle inscribed in the social web of village life? How were confrontations and struggle over the always scarce resources in the village engraved within the contours of social interaction?

On the one hand, this question requires a better understanding of village peasant mentalities. On the other, it necessitates a deeper analysis of the social relations between Jews and Christians in the rural areas. The present study attempts a preliminary foray into this terrain of inquiry. Large areas of southern Germany were regions where small farmers dominated the rural topography of settlement. Driven by a custom of inheritance whereby farmland was divided among several heirs, the average acreage of a homestead declined as the population grew. Frequently, farming families owned less than two hectares (ca. five acres) of cultivated land, and as industrialization spread the number of part-time farmers rose who cultivated a plot as a secondary source of income alongside their primary job in industry. The scarce resources impacted mentality in the farming communities. People were preoccupied with survival and its associated questions, even in a region (state) like Baden, celebrated in popular parlance as the "garden of Germany." Social relations in the village mirrored this situation. Thus, the neighborhood had for centuries been a social network oriented to cooperation and mutual aid. In some rural communities, this was reflected in codified local law. On the other hand, there were also disputes with neighbors involving the use of scarce resources. People were quite prepared to file a formal complaint against a neighbor when they noticed, for example, that she was mowing and gathering grass that did not belong to her. Protection of property and its rights were a supreme value. It also acted as a brake on upward mobility. If poorer families had attempted to "escape" socially, they would have felt the full brunt of disdain of the village community. In this sense, as empirical cultural studies have shown, apathy was a public virtue in the village.[8]

Within the family as well, social relations were oriented to economic factors. Both spouses brought their inheritance of land into the marriage, in the ideal instance approximately equal shares, because families did not wish to worsen their situation by marriage. To marry above one's status was thus practically impossible, and unions of rich and poor were genuine misalliances: they violated the iron laws of the social system and the time-honored techniques for survival of village society. The material basis of the marriage also stamped the emotionality of the nuptial bond. As Jeggle and Ilien formulated it in their village study of Württemberg, "love [in the village] is something totally different from the bourgeois middle-class hope to be loved for one's own self."[9] It is hardly surprising, then, that relations among brothers and sisters in a household, and the relations between children and their parents, were not saturated by the same warmth of family sentiment that the urban Bürgertum demonstrated for its web of familial consanguinity, or at least was wont to postulate. Brothers and sisters on the farmstead were both needed helpers and more mouths to feed at the generally modest dinner table. Ambivalence was a dominant emotional tone in the village. If a member decided to leave the homestead, the consequences could be devastating, because organization was still based on the principle of the "family farm," where social and economic units were closely intertwined.

Despite the grinding poverty that beset most Jewish families up until the middle of the nineteenth century, their circumstances and living conditions were significantly different. Very few Jewish families had their own plot of land for cultivation, aside from a small garden, since they had for centuries been effectively banned from land ownership. Their orientation to trade and commerce generated rhythms in daily life that differed from those among the small farmers. As a cattle, wine or produce merchant, a Jewish head of household was often away for five or six days on exhausting business trips within his area of regional customers, what was termed in local Jewish parlance his *medineh*. The poorer merchants traveled on foot, the wealthier traders went by train or even their own automobile. Most of their customers were small farmers who often had been doing business with the same traders for decades. Monika Richarz, who was one of the first to investigate the social history of Jewish cattle dealers, called these commercial relations a "symbolic economic tie."[10] Helmut Walser Smith has stressed those "rural commoralities," that is, the similarities in the economic morality of Jews and Christians.[11] But it should be recalled that this occupational dichotomy of merchant versus farmer was heavily impregnated by pronounced stereotypes in the mentality of the peasants. The farmers did not regard commerce as real "work"; it had a pejorative connotation. Utz Jeggle has shown that the underlying reasons for this probably lay in the peasant worldview that counterposed the social estate of "food providers" with that of "commercial travelers" (*Nährstand* versus *Zährstand*).[12] In retrospect, Christian informants described this gulf in occupational involvement as an essential ingredient in a residual element of distance between the two groups in the village.

In view of the fact that Jewish families placed less importance on self-sufficiency moored on their own homestead, the Jews had greater need of cash for their own maintenance in the countryside than was the case among their Christian farming neighbors. The Jewish families had to purchase most of the food they consumed. As a result of their network of commercial dealings, most (though not all) Jewish families had the necessary financial means. An analysis of tax revenues in several rural localities in Baden shows that the average per capita income of Jews was greater than that for Christians.[13] A study of communal tax records in the Rhön Mts. in Bavaria indicated that a larger-than-average number of Jews were among those paying the highest taxes.[14] But the economic and conjunct social situation of the Jewish rural population differed from village to village, and Jews were not able everywhere to contribute to communal taxes in proportion to their percentage in the local population.

Despite great differences within and between Jewish communities, the overall picture shows that the economic and social profile of the Jews as a demographic group underwent enormous change in the period from the beginning of legislation on emancipation and civil rights until 1914. It is now an established fact in the historical literature that a process of bourgeoisification (*Verbürgerlichung*) arose among rural Jews. This shift was manifested in efforts for improved education and changes in lifestyle. As a consequence, country Jews were also categorized as "agents of modernity" (Monika Richarz). Even if more recent research has revised this view, since processes of cultural transfer in small towns and villages were initiated not only by Jews but also by strata of Christian burghers, the role of Jews as forerunners in this regard is evident. Christian women in the countryside regarded their Jewish neighbors as a tone-setting avant-garde in matters of fashion, since they often got their clothes from town or went shopping for clothing there when they visited their relatives in the urban areas.[15] In their descriptions of Saturday afternoon strolls by Jewish neighbors in the village, a Christian informant from the village of Eichstetten in the Kaiserstuhl hills noted that people used to wait in great anticipation for the Jewish families to come walking by: "it was like a fashion show.... [It] was really interesting!"[16] The young Jewish women were the first in the village to sport bobbed hair and stiletto heels.

Interviews with Christian informants do not indicate any special envy of those Jewish families whose lifestyle was more "modern" than that of most of the local farming families. An evaluation of a contemporaneous source, an analysis of several hundred reconciliation negotiations in cases of slander (which in Germany were handled by the mayor's office before taking the matter to court), did not indicate evidence of a confrontation between Jews and Christians driven by their differing lifestyles.[17] With the exception of pogroms during the nineteenth century, forms of illegal encroachment on property or robbery were not specifically directed against Jews. Due to its fundamental scarcity, property in the village was considered an extremely valuable good. Whoever violated it could expect to be punished by village society.

Was It Only a Matter of "Too Bad about All the Material Damage"?

The events after 1933 represented a radical departure from the past as neighbors were attacked and their homes were damaged. Step by step, more and more obstacles were placed in the way of social coexistence between Jews and Christians. Finally, the violence of 9/10 November 1938 constituted the last stage in the intentional ravaging of the web of social relations between Christians and Jews. The picture of destruction in the wake of the pogrom was possibly even more harrowing in the village than in the city. Furniture thrown into the street, broken dishes, and swirling bed feathers were part of the picture of devastation in the villages and small towns. The synagogues of the Jewish population had been destroyed or vandalized, frequently including the Jewish cemeteries as well.

The violence of the National Socialists and their sympathizers on 9/10 November 1938 was met by a reaction of ambivalence—such, if generalizations are possible—in the non-Jewish population. Ian Kershaw was one of the first to systematically investigate the threads connecting anti-Semitism and popular opinion and the reactions of the population to the measures of persecution and Jewish harassment. He deals in detail with the situation in the countryside after 10 November 1938. One of Kershaw's most important sources were the reports by local police on popular reaction, which he evaluated with the critical caution necessary in dealing with such documents. His summary conclusion: "Widespread hostile anti-Jewish attitudes, non-critical approval for the anti-Semitic laws, yet a strong condemnation of the pogrom, due to the senseless destruction of property and the mob-like character of the violence, marked the reactions of a substantial proportion of the population."[18]

How was this destruction recalled later on? Franziska Becker devotes several central chapters in her study to memories of the "Reichskristallnacht." The typical pattern of the village "narrative report," as she terms the narratives given by her informants, was mention to the fact that the perpetrators of the pogrom came from outside the village, followed by a description of the lack of participation by village residents. Becker stresses a further important aspect, namely, the unemotional and dry discursive façade of the reports on the excesses of the violence. Violence appears to be unfortunate only because it resulted in material damage. Becker wonders: "Is it merely a question of 'too bad about all the material damage' that was involved, or is there an unarticulated sense here that what mattered was the loss suffered by the Jews?"[19] She extends this question in various directions, exploring several examples. It is instructive to look at one of her interview analyses verbatim:

> The residents of Baisingen were shocked by the huge "material destruction" of that night, most particularly because of the economic way they tended to look at events.... This perception, rather than some moral abhorrence of violence, is what triggered a sense of outrage in Frau Schaller: "It wasn't right what happened back then. They should have taken their money. Instead of destroying all that stuff." In the case of Frau Schaller, one can sense her empathy when she declares that the smaller variant of damage against the Jews would have been sufficient. The thin expression of empathy is simultaneously relativized in the reduced frame of a traditional anti-Semitic way of thinking.... In other opinions expressed, both are echoed: criticism of the extent of the violence, as well as a certain degree of agreement on her part.[20]

After the excess of 9/10 November 1938, the situation of the Jews in the countryside was no longer tenable. A large number of Jewish men were taken into custody and interned for weeks—in a number of cases for several months—in three concentration camps in the Reich: Dachau, Buchenwald, and Sachsenhausen. Encounters between the Jewish women remaining in the villages and their neighbors frequently took place out of sight and under cover of darkness. Further economic activity had been prohibited by the ordinances that followed the pogrom. Many Jewish families now attempted to obtain papers for emigration abroad.

Auctioning Off Homes and Their Contents

The outbreak of World War II cut off most of the paths of possible escape. At the same time, the German leadership changed the ends and means of their policy of persecution of the Jews.

Step by step, the leadership now abandoned the policy of pressuring Jews to emigrate and set about developing plans for the mass deportation of the Jewish population of Central Europe to the margins of German-controlled territory. This included the transport of several thousand Jews from Baden and the Palatinate to southern France. These deportations were the prelude to the systematic deportations to the occupied territories in East Central and Eastern Europe that began in the fall of 1941—the beginning of the mass murder of the German Jews in the framework of the genocide of European Jewry. The deportees were forced to leave almost everything behind. They were allowed to take only a small amount of hand luggage. Before their departure, the finance administration had forced most Jews to make a "declaration of assets." It gave information on any possessions, and immediately after the deportations, the finance authorities began to evaluate these assets. The "legal" basis for this was the 11th Ordinance to the Reich Citizenship Law, according to which the property of Jews "resident abroad" was confiscated by the Reich.[21] Real estate and household goods were now placed under state administration. Frequently, only a few weeks after the deportation of the legal owners, these household effects were then released for auction.

As in case of the ravages of the November 1938 pogrom, one cannot reduce the reactions of the non-Jewish population to a single common denominator. There can be no doubt about the large number of potential interested buyers. The "crowd" in Ihringen mentioned above was probably not the exception. Many now believed the hour had come to acquire desirable household items at bargain prices. The finance offices or municipalities received letters of request, which often made specific mention of objects that the writers desired to acquire. As so frequently in the history of Nazi Germany, measures by the government and actions by of segments of the population went hand in hand, leading to an escalation of the injustices.

Of course, there are also reports about behavior that was just the opposite. In the village of Michelbach an der Lücke in Württemberg, people still tell the story of a farmer from a neighboring village who went off to attend a finance office auction in Michelbach. At the edge of the village, an opponent of the regime explained to him what kind of an auction it was. The farmer was told that these objects were stained with blood, and for that reason decided to return to his village.[22] Naturally, it is now impossible to determine whether this tale is a true story or a later legend. But it names the core aspect of the event, the question which Becker formulated as follows: "How did people protect themselves from feelings of guilt which the possession of these objects might keep alive? Where was the fear of the uncanny power of memory of these material things?"[23] She sees here a "self-protective mechanism" of repression at work, supported in the main by two elements. One was that mentality of "too bad about the destruction of all that stuff," which had marked attitudes among some regarding the extent of the damage in the pogrom. This was the unemotional and objective way of dealing with household effects that was customary in the village. It prevented these items from being infused with emotional memories. But at least just as important was the fact that the auction was organized by a state authority (the finance office). The official character of the auction acted to "cleanse" the items of any residue of criminality.

The Immediate Postwar Situation

With liberation by the Allied armies, the extent of German crimes throughout Europe became visible for the Christian rural population as well. At the same time, it was now finally clear what the relation was between the measures of persecution against the Jewish population in one's own village and the total picture of massive criminal policy. It was recognized as certain that most of the neighbors who had been deported were murdered.

Individual survivors returned to a small number of localities, and some stayed on. How were they received back into the rural community? What action did they themselves take? General answers to these questions remain open at present, if indeed one can generalize at all given the relatively small number of those who returned. These questions have not as yet been the focus of a comparative study.

The survivors encountered a situation that externally had changed. In most of the rural localities, those with no incriminating political past had taken over the leading positions, and most of the Nazi party officials were confined in Allied internment camps. The Christian population endeavored to avoid anything that might suggest a tie to the old regime, and tended to style itself as a victim. No matter how problematic that behavior was, it assured an absence of overt anti-Semitism and a wall of protection against new pogroms. The returnees confronted a kind of vacuum: their families and most Jewish neighbors had been murdered or were now living abroad. In order to rebuild their lives once again, those returning were forced to overcome a series of bureaucratic hurdles.

The Auschwitz survivors Hans Frankenthal and his brother Ernst also found themselves confronted by a typical mixture of official mulishness and bureaucratic nitpicking when they returned to their native Schmallenberg, a small town in the Sauerland (British Zone of Occupation). The two brothers did not respond to an oral directive to go and re-register officially at the municipality. Not until they were threatened with a withdrawal of ration coupons did they decide to go down to the town hall. At first they refused to enter the building. A small group of curious onlookers formed to watch what was happening. Finally they went in and were asked to give their personal data. After they continued to refuse to provide any information, the officials decided to pull their birth certificates from the files and write down all the data from these documents, as Hans Frankenthal had demanded. He ultimately succeeded, again in the face of resistance by the officials, in obtaining a license as a cattle dealer, which his father had also possessed. In 1946 he learned that an automobile that had belonged to the family was still in the possession of a local resident, a former Nazi. A first direct attempt to get it back proved abortive. Frankenthal was also unsuccessful in regaining possession of the car when he went to the new owner armed with a document from the Allied municipal commander ordering that the automobile be surrendered. Only when Frankenthal appeared accompanied by the police did he have success. Only then, with a car at his disposal, was he in a position to build up the cattle business in earnest and with the necessary geographical radius.[24]

Becker reports from Baisingen that the bailiff had gone through the village ringing a bell after the return of a former Jewish resident from Theresienstadt, calling on the population to "return Haarburger his things." No one responded.[25] Many survivors were unable to build on such official assistance like a document from the military government or the bell of the bailiff. Frequently they were forced to go about pressing their initial claims by themselves, without any help from the Allied or German authorities. Becker provides another example from Baisingen, that of the cattle dealer Harry Kahn returning from Theresienstadt. Kahn's son in a later interview with Becker stated that his father had "taken care of his own reparations": he demanded back his property personally. He went to the homes of his Christian neighbors and checked directly whether they had anything from the property of his family. Becker quotes a later letter that Kahn wrote to a friend that noted how he "had not needed any finance office" to get his furniture returned: "If I had waited for that kindness, I wouldn't have a plate to eat from, let alone a chair to sit on."[26]

Undervaluing and Its Opposite

It should of course be noted that the Allies and the administrations operating under their supervision did not sit with folded hands. But the wheels of bureaucracy moved more slowly. The German authorities acting in accord with Allied ordinances initially tried to put together a picture of the extent of the expropriations and plunder during the Nazi period. In the French Zone of Occupation (Rhineland-Palatinate, South Baden, Württemberg/Hohenzollern), there had been an order from 8 December 1945 "concerning measures of plunder against individuals, including Germans as well, due to their belonging to a race or because of their beliefs."[27]

A year and a half later, in May 1947, the residents of the wine-making village of Eichstetten in the Kaiserstuhl hills were ordered to account for any objects they had acquired at auctions or elsewhere. Once again lists were drawn up, information was recorded on cards, objects were enumerated and described, just as happened six years earlier. But not all could recall the full extent of those earlier events. The farmer Wilhelm Schulze (real name altered) wrote to the office conducting the inquiry:

> Of the objects in my possession, my relatives were able to say more or less where they had been acquired. I cannot recall anything about the items I was appointed to auction off. 1. As a result of the great many things which I had to take care of in five years of service, I can no longer remember any details. 2. As a consequence of the injury to the head I suffered on 25 January 1944, my memory has been so impaired that the auctions would, had I not been reminded of them, have seemed to me like something I had dreamt.[28]

The new owners would soon awaken from that "dream." That same year, in November 1947, the French Occupational Authority issued Ordinance No. 120 on the Return of Stolen Items of Property. Here for the first time was a clear regulation. It went further than regulations in the other zones of occupation in that it called for a return of the property under any and all circumstances. Any person who wished to retain these objects or real estate would have to formally acquire them once more, purchasing them for their real value. The price at the time could be taken into account, but had declined due to devaluation by a ratio of 10:1.[29]

Then began the difficult process of restitution, which extended down into the era of the Federal Republic. The procedures became a bureaucratic battle among the parties involved, their attorneys and other offices. Thus, the political municipalities had also been drawn into the proceedings. The files of the municipalities, along with the papers in the restitution offices, reflect the complexity and ponderous character of the entire procedure, as well as its enormous scope, even for small village communities. After all, what was at issue in the villages was not just the homes and household effects of the individuals expropriated but also the businesses of the dealers, the extent of their business and circle of clients, as well as the ownership of gardens and plots of agricultural land.

Thus, for example, several of the mayors of the community of Eichstetten in the Kaiserstuhl hills were successively involved in the proceedings of restitution. In April 1946, a little less than a year after liberation, the head of the community received a letter from an emigrant relating to property expropriated after 1940. By 1949, two more letters had been received in which the family attempted, directly or through an attorney, to gain some clarity about their possessions. This restitution matter then appears to have remained in abeyance another four years, until July 1953. At that point, within the span of two days, the attorneys of the family and the State Restitution Office contacted the Eichstetten municipality. The state office demanded that the mayor's office provide information on the type and quality of household effects. The claimant (the mother of the emigrant who had initially begun the inquiry) indicated that objects with a total value of RM 70,000 had been lost as a result of deportation. These were household effects supposedly located in their six-room apartment.

The mayor did not reply to the letter of the attorneys. He notified the State Office for Restitution that "nothing officially or private is known here" about the furnishings, but then also added this comment: "I find the amount of RM 70,000 far too high an estimate. Nor do I know where the six rooms are located that Frau X. is supposed to have occupied." The son learned about this letter and wrote in anger to the mayor. He pointed to the high value of the furnishings, and especially to an antique from the seventeenth century that was present up until the time of deportation, adding; "I will not allow the circumstances my grandmother and mother lived in before the war to be depreciated. Eichstetten was rendered 'free of Jews' by Hitlerism, but thank God those days are over and done with."[30]

He then threatened the mayor with an immediate complaint filed with the district attorney accusing him of "presenting facts under false pretenses." Only when faced with this letter did the mayor see reason to reply to the attorneys of the family. He noted that the communal archive had no list detailing the assets of the deportees. On the basis of the "very impolite letter" of the emigrant, he could see no reason to provide any further information in this matter.

In this case too, the present analysis here follows the paradigms and sections as laid out by Franziska Becker. She devotes a special chapter of her book to the problem of the "devaluations," that is, the subsequent monetary devaluing of the property acquired in the framework of "Aryanization" or through auctions, by the non-Jewish population. Her analysis shows that these efforts to devalue the expropriated objects were a central component in the projections and distortions that formed the basis of historical interpretation in the village. Becker can identify both psychological and practical implications in the strategies utilized for devaluation. Thus, it served to reduce feelings of guilt if a person could convince him- or herself that the possessions of the Jews had not been anything special, while the events of the auction were themselves depicted as a form of familiar compulsory auctions of property.[31] The material utility of depreciating the value of these objects is obvious: it was an attempt to reduce the amount of extra payment to be made in the restitution proceedings.

For the new Christian owners of these goods, the devaluations were also an important prerequisite for constructing themselves as victims—that is, for attempting to reverse the consciousness of injustice. One of Becker's interviewees typified this view when she admitted that after extra payment in the framework of restitution arrangements she had been quite "upset," even though the house had been "an old pile of junk." In her interview with Becker, she summed up with the remark: "That Jew was not cheap."[32] To pay a fair price once again for that "old pile of junk," the supposedly neglected and rundown houses of the Jews in the village, for which only a few years before so much ink had been laboriously expended in requests to finance and Nazi party offices, now seemed an intolerable and onerous demand.

Complex Memories and Ambivalent Associations

So is that the end of this affair? Were the memories of those murdered and those who managed to escape in time actually lost and buried once their property was taken over? Were those objects newly acquired and "assimilated," to be militantly defended against any possible claim by their former owners? Did people manage in this way to repress their bad conscience? Were there no intermediate zones between black and white, no perturbations of sentiment and conscience, no secrets of safekeeping, whether lovingly or full of fear? These questions cannot be clearly answered in the affirmative. Both Franziska Becker and Utz Jeggle found touching attempts at remembrance, efforts to hold these objects in a gentle, loving and sometimes silent storage for the future. In Oberdorf on the Ipf, a cabinet contained the nicely folded sheets and pillow cases of the former Jewish owners. "Well, maybe someone will come some day and want them," an informant told Jeggle in his fieldwork at the time. In Baisingen Becker made the acquaintance of a man who had relocated the sukkah of a Jewish family, beautifully decorated inside, to a meadow near the village. He kept brushwood stored there, branches and twigs that he did not need, as Becker later learned. The practical utility of this, wrote Becker, was more "to hide from the public sphere in the village, and perhaps also from himself, the fact that the expulsion and murder of the Jews had been a painful loss, which one might mourn through objects containing and conserving the past."[33]

A rather disturbing experience I had in a village community suggests further associations regarding the problematic meaning of these objects acquired from former Jewish villagers. In an interview with a Christian contemporary, whose daughter was also present, mention was made of a small pamphlet, the annual report of a Jewish foundation for the year 1905, which the family had found in the house after they had moved in and taken it over.

> *Interviewer:* This pamphlet, I wonder, I wanted to ask if maybe I could make a copy of it. Or get a copy somehow; I don't know if there's any possibility here in X to make a photocopy somewhere ... *Daughter* (after she had explained that there was a photocopy shop in the village)*:* Well, uh, I don't want to let you have it. *Interviewer:* Oh, of course, that's clear, no no. *Daughter:* Yes, well, I mean, it belongs in the house, and it has to stay here. *Interviewer:* It belongs in the house. *Mother:* She won't let people have anything. *Daughter* (probably)*:* Laughter *Interviewer:* No, right, that's the way it should be. *Mother:* She won't let anybody have anything that belongs to the Jews ... Not even a spool of thread ... *Daughter* (defensive)*:* No, c'mon, that's ... *Mother:* Like not even a spool of thread, she won't let people have anything. *Daughter:* Listen, it's, uh ... *Mother:* She just says: "Nothing doing, it belongs here in the house." *Interviewer:* Really? *Daughter:* Those are things in the house, they belong to the ... former owners.

> *Interviewer:* Of X (Jewish family)? *Daughter:* Right, they belong to X, right, and (emphatically) they have to stay here in the house ... (voice more quiet) stay here. *Interviewer:* I think that's the right thing. *Mother:* We are afraid of Jews. *Daughter:* No, not true, I'm not afraid, it's simply that, well ... *Mother:* Earlier on, earlier when, uh, when ... *Daughter* (simultaneously)*:* ... It just belongs in the house here. (less distinctly) It belongs here. *Mother:* Before, when we'd have a thunderstorm, well then dad used to say ... *Daughter* (simultaneously)*:* You can ... *Mother:* You're afraid of Jews! *Daughter:* So then let's go over (and get a copy made).[34]

Why does the pamphlet have to stay in the house? Why does the spool of thread have to be kept there? In the discussion, it is the mother who guides the discourse to the topic of the former Jewish owners and Jews more generally. Perhaps she was also motivated by the interview situation, where she was ultimately asked as a contemporary to tell me something about the history of the Jews in the village. In this situation, the mother starts talking about her daughter, not herself. She says that such small and perhaps insignificant things as a spool of thread are objects her daughter does not let anyone take out of the house. And the mother tries to emphasize how strict her daughter is about this. Her daughter doesn't talk about the Jews, just about the "former owners." She does not see any connection with the second topic her mother raises, the question of fear (*Judenangst*). She even is defensive ("no, not true").

Her tone is somewhat jocular vis-à-vis the criticisms her mother voices, she is objective and distanced. What her mother attributes to her is apparently also a bit embarrassing. It is impossible to properly interpret her behavior from what her mother ascribes to her. Her mother's statements likewise reveal very little about what she assumes or fears. For that reason, her use of the expression "afraid of Jews" (*Judenangst*) is difficult to understand. Is it a fear that Jews might demand to have something returned? Is it a fear of the criticism of the survivors? Is it a fear of being cursed by the dead Jews? There may be some evidence for that interpretation, because at another point in the conversation she talks about such a curse. The use once again of the expression "afraid of Jews" ("*Du hast Judenängste!*") in connection with talk about a thunderstorm allows for several interpretations, especially since the recording at this point is not completely audible. Even if we follow the transcription as indicated, it is not clear whether before they used to be afraid of Jews or be afraid "like Jews." The second reading would follow a possible anti-Jewish stereotype in the village,[35] but deviate from the actual topic. In short, there are various interpretations for the statements in this interview. Perhaps the objects that belong to the history of the house should be stored safely and not be lost by accident. Perhaps they should be stored away and kept ready for the possible return of the former owners. Another interpretation would be that these small things have taken on a kind of fetish value, that they help protect the house. Perhaps, it is felt that they somehow extend or prolong or embody the physical presence of the original expelled Jewish owners, symbolically or even magically. Or maybe to lose the objects or give them away to a third party could provoke the revenge of the dead Jews.

Dealing with Sacred Architecture: The Fate of the Former Synagogue Buildings

The sukkah relocated to the meadow, the pamphlet of a Jewish foundation that should be kept in the house—the safekeeping and storage of these objects points to a further topic, not yet broached here, namely, how to deal with the remainders of Jewish religious life in the village. Aside from the cemeteries, in many of the approximately 700 Jewish rural communities in Germany, the synagogue, the Jewish school, the cantor's and rabbi's homes, and the ritual bathhouse were preserved after 10 November 1938. The National Socialists and their accomplices often did not dare to set these structures ablaze because they feared the flames might then spread to other nearby buildings in the village.

There was no other visible relict of Jewish life (except perhaps the cemeteries) where the question of remembrance or repression crystallized more palpably than in the synagogue buildings. They often stood in the very center of the village. Their architecture, at the beginning of the nineteenth century still in the form of neo-classicist temples, later in Moorish or neo-Romanesque style, characterized them as sacred buildings. Jeggle noted that "extreme historical experiences have infused their ruins and remnants, and have been burned into their sites."[36] At the end of the 1990s, thirty years after his pioneering study on the "Jews' villages" in Württemberg, Jeggle once more took up the topic. He was now able to include in his observations the vital development of a decentralized and local culture of memorializing, which had come to encompass the rural communities as well as the cities. The fate of the synagogue buildings appeared as a suitable yardstick for gauging the forms of memorializing applied to the murdered Jewish neighbors. Jeggle defines several different phases in dealing with these buildings, which at times ran parallel to one another.

Initially he notes a continuation of the work of destruction of the years 1938 to 1945 in the immediate postwar period. That destruction was masked by a utilitarian approach that was socially acceptable, especially in the 1950s—simple pragmatism: a parking lot seemed more useful than an empty synagogue. Jeggle provides the corresponding figures for destruction from the relevant documentation: of the 151 synagogues and prayer halls in existence in Baden, Württemberg, and Hohenzollern in 1938, 60 had burned down after the pogrom, while a further 77 had been badly vandalized or plundered. Twenty-eight of the damaged buildings still standing were torn down after 1945. Of the 363 synagogues and prayer halls in Hesse, 145 were destroyed during or as a result of the pogrom. After the end of the war, 59 more synagogues were torn down.[37]

At the same time, a new phase began for the still numerous buildings that had not been torn down: alteration of their function. This phase has largely continued in numerous instances up until today. Jeggle regards the actions of the residents in these villages and small towns as a "program of banishment or eclipsing [of memory], generally unconscious," and recognizes a symbolic level of meaning in such actions. The new "functions" for which these structures were converted were quite diverse; in some cases, former Jewish sacred buildings were "Christianized," as Joachim Hahn termed this in his study on Baden-Württemberg. Jewish synagogues and prayer halls became churches, and Jeggle recognizes a certain "logic of tradition" in the utilization of the structures for religious purposes; "but in a specific sense: the ecclesia is now victorious over the synagogue, a popular motif in Gothic cathedral architecture."[38] Thus, the synagogue in Merchingen in Baden was "Christianized" by the addition of a large cross and a bell tower. The cross was mounted on the eastern façade, precisely at the place where formerly the apse had stood with the shrine of the scrolls of the Torah. "A further bit of evidence that the accidental choosing of precisely this scene of the crime was following certain unconscious rules" was the new attitude manifest in memorial plaques set up in the 1980s. These underscored "our own mistaken behavior" by including Paul's warning to the Romans to deal with the Jews with respect. Speaking to Gentile believers, Paul says, "it is not you who supports the root, but the root supports you" (Rom. 11:18b).[39]

Other new functions for the buildings often served to provide dwellings or premises for purposes of business and commerce or other utilitarian ends. Such conversions to new "functions" had taken place openly and brazenly in the Nazi period. As Jeggle notes, there was a conscious idea of utilizing a synagogue as a home for Hitler Youth, as a factory for making rifles, or as a POW camp to "teach a lesson in forgetting." After 1945, these converted functions were given a new meaning. It was disputed in the villages that destruction or alteration of the buildings' function—conversion to a parking lot, gas station, or fire house—had some sort of symbolic meaning. This utilization had simply come about for pragmatic reasons, nothing else. This was a logic that corresponded to the notion of "too bad about all the material damage" analyzed by Becker. As Jeggle noted, village memory had accorded the former synagogues a kind of right to remain in town over many decades after the war, converted to a "useful" new function. The village admixture of memorializing and practicality had nonetheless made it possible to preserve these buildings as objects of local memory—though without having to deal inwardly with history. The village residents closed their minds to any elaborated form of discourse on history, even in the form of commemorative plaques.[40] In this connection, Jeggle recalls Assmann's systematics of collective memory. A communicative memory, whose competence lay in the "situations of everyday life," assumed the form of silencing and trivialization in the villages in respect to Jewish history. Ritualized forms of memorializing, forms of cultural expression, such as a commemorative plaque or monument—forms that otherwise had a certain resonance in the village—encountered resistance among the local population.

Perhaps, Jeggle suggests, ritualized forms of memorializing also led to fossilizing of emotions. Memories, he stresses, should not just be cultivated—they are best given a new and vital shape. In his view, the numerous new decentralized institutions, museums in former synagogues or Jewish schools, can become the beginning of a process of transformation from a communicative rural memory (one that is trivializing and ultimately silencing) to a cultural memory, in this way paving the path to a conscious acceptance of one's own complex history.

Translated from the German by Bill Templer

Notes

1. Communal Archive Ihringen, IV, 3, 56, letter, Police Chief, Freiburg im Breisgau, Section Jewish Property, 12 November 1940.
2. Letter, E.M. to Municipality Ihringen, 12 December 1940, Communal Archive Ihringen, IV, 3, 56.

3. Lowenstein, "Jüdisches religiöses Leben in deutschen Dörfern. Regionale Unterschiede im 19. und frühen 20. Jahrhundert," in *Jüdisches Leben auf dem Lande. Studien zur deutsch-jüdischen Geschichte*, ed. Monika Richarz and Reinhard Rürup (Tübingen, 1997), 219–230, here 220.
4. On the Grand Duchy of Baden, see Ulrich Baumann, *Zerstörte Nachbarschaften. Christen und Juden in badischen Landgemeinden 1862–1940* (Hamburg, 2000), 246ff.
5. See Baumann, *Zerstörte Nachbarschaften*, 203.
6. Utz Jeggle, *Judendörfer in Württemberg* (Tübingen, 1969); a revised version was published in 1999.
7. Franziska Becker, *Gewalt und Gedächtnis. Erinnerungen an die nationalsozialistische Verfolgung einer jüdischen Landgemeinde* (Göttingen 1994).
8. Vgl. Utz Jeggle and Albert Ilien, "Die Dorfgemeinschaft als Not- und Terrorzusammenhang. Ein Beitrag zur Sozialgeschichte des Dorfes und zur Sozialpsychologie seiner Bewohner," in *Dorfpolitik. Sozialwissenschaftliche Analyse. Didaktische Hilfen*, ed. Hans Georg Wehling (Opladen, 1980), 38–53, here 47.
9. Ibid.
10. Monika Richarz, "Viehhandel und Landjuden im 19. Jahrhundert. Eine symbiotische Wirtschaftsbeziehung in Südwestdeutschland," *Menora. Jahrbuch für deutsch-jüdische Geschichte* 1 (1990): 66–88.
11. Helmut Walser Smith, "The Discourse of Usury: Relations Between Christians and Jews in the German Countryside, 1880–1914," *Central European History* 32, no. 3 (1999): 255–276, here 276.
12. Jeggle, *Judendörfer*, 158. The term *Zährstand* has a connotation of those who live off the work of others.
13. Baumann, *Zerstörte Nachbarschaften*, 131 (communities of Gailingen, Eichstetten, Sulzburg, Kirchen).
14. Richard Mehler, "Die Entstehung eines Bürgertums unter den Landjuden in der bayerischen Rhön vor dem Ersten Weltkrieg," in *Juden, Bürger, Deutsche. Zur Geschichte von Vielfalt und Differenz 1800–1933*, ed. Andreas Gotzmann, Rainer Liedtke and Till van Rahden (Tübingen, 2001), 193–216, here 204.
15. Beate Bechtold-Comforty, "Jüdische Frauen auf dem Dorf—zwischen Eigenständigkeit und Integration," *Sozialwissenschaftliche Informationen* 18, no. 3 (1989): 157–169, here 160–62; and Marion Kaplan, *Jüdisches Bürgertum. Frau, Familie, Identität im Kaiserreich* (Hamburg, 1991), 49.
16. Interview by Cristina Weiblen and Ulrich Baumann with K.R., 28 November 1992 in Eichstetten.
17. Solely in Schmieheim, a village whose Jewish population numbered about 15 percent of the total, there is a trial from the 1920s involving an insult on this topic. A Christian villager had accused a Jewish woman of being "generally wasteful. She went to Freiburg twice a week to have her hair bobbed, had run up debts in the shops all over the place, had spent 150 marks on chocolate, which she ate, and did not keep a kosher kitchen, just full of tref." The man had uttered this slander, which contained a few other points as well, in the presence of the mother of the woman, and in doing so had, notably so, also expressed some internal Jewish views on the matter. But this case appears to have been an exception. See Communal Archive Schmieheim, B, 1a, Sühneverhandlungen in Beleidigungsfällen, 1927–1950.

18. Ian Kershaw, “Antisemitismus und Volksmeinung,” in *Bayern in der NS-Zeit*, ed. Martin Broszat and Elke Fröhlich, 6 vols. (Munich, 1979ff.), vol. 2: “Herrschaft und Gesellschaft im Konflikt,” Teil A, 281–348, here 332f.
19. Becker, *Gewalt und Gedächtnis*, 37.
20. Ibid., 38.
21. “11. Verordnung zum Reichsbürgergesetz vom 25.11.1941,” *Reichsgesetzblatt* 1941 I, 722–724. The term “abroad” also referred to territories occupied by Germany, see circular letter, minister of the interior, 3 December 1941, reprinted in *Einige Dokumente zur Rechtsstellung der Juden und zur Entziehung ihres Vermögens 1933–1945*, ed. George Weiss (Berlin, 1954), 53. The Law on the Confiscation of Property Hostile to the People and the State of 14 July 1933 was also applied to expropriate those deported to the territories annexed by Germany in the East, with the same consequences, *Reichsgesetzblatt* 1933 I, 479 f.
22. Otto Ströbel, *Juden und Christen in dörflicher Gemeinschaft. Geschichte der Judengemeinde Michelbach-Lücke* (Crailsheim, 2000), 248.
23. Becker, *Gewalt und Gedächtnis*, 80.
24. Hans Frankenthal, *Verweigerte Rückkehr. Erfahrungen nach dem Judenmord* (Frankfurt a.M., 1999), 101f.
25. Becker, *Gewalt und Gedächtnis*, 87.
26. Ibid., 89.
27. State Archive Freiburg F 202/32, Nr. 2407 (Vorbemerkung zur Verordnung Nr. 120 über die Rückerstattung geraubter Vermögensobjekte).
28. State Archive Freiburg F 202/32, Nr. 5274.
29. Becker, *Gewalt und Gedächtnis*, 127.
30. I would like to thank Christina Weiblen for pointing out this source. Communal Archive Eichstetten GA II, H 395 a-m., letter 3 April 1946. On the history of the Jewish community there, see Christina Weiblen and Ulrich Baumann, “Die jüdische Gemeinde Eichstetten im 19. und 20. Jahrhundert,” in *Eichstetten. Die Geschichte des Dorfes*, ed. Thomas Steffens, 3 vols. (Eichstetten, 2000), vol. 2, 109–160.
31. Becker, *Gewalt und Gedächtnis*, 87f.
32. Ibid., 136.
33. Ibid., 91.
34. Interview by Ulrich Baumann with an informant (name withheld on request).
35. Baumann, *Zerstörte Nachbarschaften*, 97f.
36. Utz Jeggle, “Nachrede. Erinnerungen an die Dorfjuden heute,” in Rürup and Richarz, *Jüdisches Leben*, 399–411.
37. Jeggle refers here to Thea Altaras, *Synagogen in Hessen. Was geschah seit 1945? Eine Dokumentation und Analyse aus allen 221 hessischen Orten, deren Synagogenbauten die Pogromnacht 1938 und den 2. Weltkrieg überstanden. 223 architektonische Beschreibungen und Bauhistorien* (Königstein i. Taunus, 1988) and Joachim Hahn, *Synagogen in Baden-Württemberg* (Stuttgart 1987).
38. Jeggle, *Nachrede*, 406.
39. Ibid.
40. Ibid., 410.

— *Eight* —

"These Are German Houses": Polish Memory Confronting Jedwabne

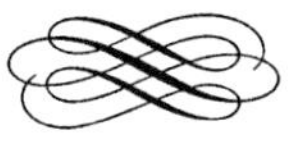

François Guesnet

The discussion of the massacre on 10 July 1941 of hundreds of Jewish residents of the town of Jedwabne in eastern Poland, on the heels of the withdrawal of Soviet troops following the German attack on the Soviet Union, can properly be reckoned among the most comprehensive and intensive debates on Polish postwar history in recent memory. It began immediately after the publication of the book *Sasiedzi* (Eng. trans., *Neighbors*) by Jan Tomasz Gross in the spring of 2000 describing and interpreting the events in Jedwabne. That debate did not subside in heat and intensity until after the 60th anniversary of the massacre in July 2001.[1] It still continues.

There were several hundred newspaper and magazine articles locally and nationally, radio broadcasts, TV discussions, lectures and talks by experts, thousands of postings in Internet listservs and chat rooms—it is virtually impossible to gauge the full scope of this debate. The extraordinary importance for civil society of the Jedwabne debate in Poland, and its far more extensive significance for evaluating the relation between the German occupation, genocide, and Jewish-local relations in the occupied countries during World War II, is reflected in the intensity of scholarly reflection, in Poland and internationally, on this discussion.[2]

Among its principal consequences, the book and ensuing dispute about its historical background led to a renewed legal inquiry into the events by an institution responsible for information and enlightenment on the crimes committed against the Polish population during the war and the period of the people's democracy, the Instytut Pamieci Narodowej (IPN; Institute of National Remembrance).[3] In the course of these inquiries, documentation from an investigation conducted in the 1960s was reviewed once again. That original investigation had not resulted in the intended preferment of charges against possible German accomplices. New testimony was now taken, along with a renewed search for documentation in the Federal Archive Koblenz and the Military History Research Office (MGFA) in Freiburg.[4] In the meantime, the IPN has published a two-volume study with scientific analysis of and documentation on the events.[5]

Neighbors **and Its Consequences**

The important debate was triggered by a core thesis suggested in Gross's book, formulated in the final sentences of the study in reference to a memorial plaque that had previously been mounted at the scene of the massacre: namely, that the "1,600 victims of this heinous act were not murdered by Hitlerists [i.e., Germans], members of the Soviet political police or secret service, but by the society." By "society" Gross means the Polish Catholic population of Jedwabne. On the basis of statements by Jewish and Polish witnesses from the immediate postwar period (contained in the archive of the Jewish Historical Institute, the files of a court case from the late 1940s and his own interviews with witnesses to the slaughter), Gross concluded that the principal persons responsible for the massacre were the Polish residents of Jedwabne. In so doing, Gross radically questioned the previously accepted historical picture. It postulated that there were a small number of culprits who had betrayed the Jews, as well as many indifferent individuals who refrained from giving assistance—an act bound up with great personal danger—and who were even impervious to sympathy. Yet, the story went, there were also a large number of Poles who, at great personal risk, had rescued Jews.[6]

The new inquiries of the IPN were unable to answer all the questions that arose from Gross's study, questions that had sparked exceptionally intensive discussion and controversy. Initially, it proved possible to locate the remains of the victims of the massacre in two mass graves.[7] Weighing the historical and juridical interest in facts over against the stipulations of Jewish ritual law regarding the remains of the dead, a partial exhumation was carried out in which two rabbis from Poland and Israel participated.[8] On the basis of the exhumation, the number of victims in the mass graves investigated was estimated at a minimum of 300 and maximum of 500. This was far below the figures given by the eye-witnesses cited by Gross.[9] Neither archival work, investigations on the spot, nor questioning of new witnesses who previously had not given testimony were able to provide investigators with conclusive evidence regarding the role of German Gestapo units operating in the region around Jedwabne at the time of the massacre. However, it now appears unlikely that German police or army units played any important role in the events beyond encouragement of the pogrom. But that does not rule out possible assistance, as evidenced by other mass murders of Jews by Poles in the immediate temporal context of the massacre at Jedwabne.[10] Yet it is also evident for Jan Tomasz Gross that the precondition for these events was the German occupation, after the June 1941 attack on the Soviet Union, of the areas of eastern Poland that had been under Soviet occupation since September 1939.[11]

The present paper initially attempts to place the debate on Gross's book within the context of previous discussions of Polish-Jewish relations during World War II.[12] It then tries to illuminate differing layers and fields of collective remembrance that can be read in the paradigmatic example of Jedwabne. The focus in academic and media discussions on the political-historical evaluation and categorization of the events will be contrasted with local collective memory and its own life and dynamics.

Bands of Violence: The Kresy in July 1941

The murderous events in Jedwabne were first reported to the Jewish Historical Commission headed by Szymon Datner in Bialystok immediately after the end of the war—and thus four years after their occurrence—by a Jewish survivor, Shmuel Wasserstein. This testimony was one narrative within several thousand in which Jewish survivors of the genocide described their experiences after the German invasion of Poland on September 1, 1939. These were preserved in the archive of the Jewish Historical Institute in Warsaw and were basically accessible for historical research from that point on. The massacre in Jedwabne is not the only massacre where the guilt is attributable in the main to the Polish neighbors of the Jews murdered. Rather, one can accurately speak of a monstrous "band of violence" that extended from Lithuania across districts in eastern Poland down into eastern Galicia (and the western Ukraine). In the vicinity of Jedwabne, immediately following the withdrawal of the Red Army, massacres and violent plunder of the Jewish population took place in a number of localities, including Radzilów, Wasosz, Zareby Koscielne, Wizny, Kolno, Tykocin and other towns and villages in the region.

One of the best experts on this material, Andrzej Zbikowski, pointed out in an essay in 1992 that there were a large number of similar massacres of the Jews by the Christian Lithuanian, Polish, and Ukrainian population after the withdrawal of the Red Army and occupation by the Germans.[13] He estimates at least sixty such massacres, but considers it possible that the figure was closer to one hundred.[14] They resembled one another in their exceptional brutality, their duration (extending in some instances to several days), the large number of victims, and the extent of the plunder of the real estate and household effects of the victims (both during the course of the massacres and in their aftermath). This plunder points up an especially striking motive for action.[15] That is the picture resulting from the concurring testimonies of Jewish survivors and their Christian neighbors. In the case of the mass murder in Radziłów, a Polish witness describes the haste with which the neighbors occupied the houses of the murdered victims and the conflicts that erupted regarding the divvying up of their looted possessions.[16] The diverse forms of this plunder by the local non-Jewish population, in part spontaneous and in part consciously planned, have been given insufficient attention by historical research to date. As Dieter Pohl has correctly noted, they remained more or less in the shadow of the enormous events of the genocide.[17]

The description of the events in Jedwabne, which can be compared with similar events in Radziłów[18] described by the journalist Anna Bikont on the basis of interviews with Polish eye-witnesses, triggered a shockwave across Poland. That was manifest in the numerous reviews of the book and in a veritable deluge of letters and postings on the Internet.[19] The effect of this shock was intensified by the publication of a series of articles in *Rzeczpospolita* by Andrzej Kaczynski, whose position was in basic agreement with that of Gross.[20] Naturally, this shock wave was generated primarily by the already mentioned core thesis put forward by Gross; namely, that the main culprits responsible for the events in Jedwabne had been the Catholic Polish neighbors of the slaughtered Jews.[21] It did not take long before doubts were voiced regarding individual elements of Gross's argument.[22] But his central thesis was rejected by only a few nationalistic publications, as well as by certain segments of the Catholic clergy. Thus, the *Nasza Polska* denounced the book, deeming it an "anti-Polish diversion," and the bishop of Lomza (the district capital not far from Jedwabne), Stanislaw Stefanek, spoke of a "provocation" and "mendacious campaign of lies."[23]

The reaction of the Catholic hierarchy was marked by a new departure when it chose to deal with the murders in Jedwabne in a church service of repentance on 27 May 2001 in Warsaw. Here it went beyond the well-known smaller circle of a few individual personalities concerned to achieve reconciliation with Jews from Poland. The joint prayer of the bishops on this solemn occasion was introduced by a declaration from Bishop Stanislaw Gadecki, who noted that "there had also been Poles and Catholics, baptized Christians, among the perpetrators." This statement "also" expressed the hope—at the time of the service not yet completely illusory—that evidence might be found, beyond the incontrovertible responsibility the Polish Catholic population bore for the events in Jedwabne, for the involvement of German armed units in the killing.[24] However, it should be noted that this prayer itself represented a kind of high point in clerical casuistry. Along with a prayer for the welfare of the fatherland and other honorable wishes, it associated the hope that Jews would never again be the victims of violence and destruction with a request: that Jews should not forget the commandment to love thy neighbor. Moreover, the prayer did not combine supplication for the murdered Jews with supplication for the Polish perpetrators. Rather, it mentioned only the "criminals and murderers, especially in Jedwabne and Poland, who were guilty of heinous acts and wicked crimes." Thus, it did not combine explicit reference to the Jewish victims with an equally explicit reference to the Polish-Catholic perpetrators. This non-explicit recognition of guilt, tempered with certain reservations, was correctly criticized. It was contrasted with the position taken by the Polish bishops in 1965, when their correspondence with German bishops was far in advance of the thinking of the time and the mood in the general population.[25] Nevertheless, it should be noted that there has to date never been a public demonstration of Polish remorse where Polish bishops have fallen to their knees in contrition, asking forgiveness for the crimes of Christians against the Jews.

Debates over a Common Polish-Jewish History

The debate surrounding the events in Jedwabne is not the first public discussion on Polish-Jewish relations during World War II, though it is indeed the most extensive.[26] In the first few years after war, there was a quite intensive examination by surviving Jewish historians of the fate of Polish Jewry during the war. It proceeded basically unimpeded, since it limited itself to the mass crimes committed by the German occupiers, without reflecting on or assessing Polish attitudes on this. Among the leading researchers at the time were Filip Friedman, Arie Tartakower, Szymon Datner, and Artur Eisenbach. This research had little public impact, especially since it was published in part in Yiddish (in the Warsaw *Bleter far geshikhte*). The power struggle within the Polish Workers' Party (PZPR) in 1968 triggered the last extensive wave of anti-Semitic repression in the Polish People's Republic. In the course of that repression, the majority of the small number of remaining Jews in Poland were forced to leave the country. This forced emigration ultimately led to the first more intensive internal oppositional discussion on the relation between Poles and Jews during the war.[27]

Opposition circles such as the Committee for Defense of the Workers (KOR) and the Clubs of the Catholic Intelligentsia (KIK) began to debate the question of the relation between Poles and Jews posed anew by the 1968 campaign. However, a decisive qualitative and quantitative change did not appear until the first success of the independent trade union Solidarity, when public discussion turned with special intensity to an examination of previously taboo questions of history.[28] The history of the Jews in Poland was accorded the function of a key element in the Polish interrogation of the past. That history had been distorted by persistent anti-Semitic prejudices, and had additionally been covered up by party censorship or shunted onto sidetracks of irrelevancy: "This search for the Jews was deeply Polish since it was an integral component within a larger movement to regain the Polish past.... Jews appeared more and more as the legitimate and particularly respected representatives of this new image of Polish history."[29]

The recognition of the specific fate suffered by the Jews under German occupation—a fate that had been repressed in the official culture of memory of the Republic, as in other people's democracies in Eastern Europe—played a key role here. The children of survivors who were part of the opposition movement turned at the same time to the rich traditions and history of Polish Jewry.[30] A special expression of the close link between the opposition and a new approach to a common shared history was the call by Marek Edelman, a participant in the Warsaw Ghetto uprising of 1943, to boycott the official commemoration by the regime of the fortieth anniversary of the revolt in 1983. Edelman argued that these festivities made cynical use of the uprising in order to refurbish the largely delegitimated rule of the party.[31] Growing interest in Jewish history in Poland was also reflected in the great success of books by Julian Stryjkowski, Henryk Grynberg, and Hanna Krall.[32]

Several debates that were exceptionally controversial for a public sphere under the impress of state censorship[33] marked the tenor of confrontation on the historical background of Polish-Jewish relations in the ensuing years of the 1980s. Thus, the Polish public perceived those sections of Claude Lanzmann's film *Shoah* in which Christian Poles were interviewed as being anti-Polish. It was argued that by means of this selectivity—Lanzmann had spoken mainly with rural farmers who made no secret of their glee in the fact that Jewish neighbors had "disappeared" during the war—a distorted picture of the Christian Polish attitude toward the mass murder of Polish Jews had arisen.[34] An accurate critique of the documentary noted that there was no mention of assistance by the Poles for persecuted Jews.[35] However, Lanzmann had neither invented nor falsified the documented statements, so the film functioned more as a one-sided correction to the Polish self-perception than an inadmissible interpretation of history.

If the greater portion of the Polish public sphere, including research in Polish at the time of the war, remained largely immune to these significant additions to historical perception, there were also examples reflecting a more differentiated perception. Thus, in the fall of 1986, Aleksander Smolar published an extensive essay dealing with Jewish-Polish relations in the journal *Aneks*, a London-based quarterly of the political opposition. In the essay, Smolar noted that those "righteous" persons who had given assistance not only were subjected after the war to anti-Semitic repression—they also still feared that this might become public knowledge.[36] He also quoted the shattering appeal entitled "Protest" by Zofia Kossak from the Polish underground movement in August 1942, a leaflet in which Kossak pointed to the murder taking place at the time and to the unbearable indifference of the Poles who had become witnesses of this slaughter: "Whoever remains silent in the face of this murder becomes an accomplice. Whoever does not condemn that murderer allows these things to happen." As one of the first, Smolar also criticized the attitude of many Polish intellectuals in the country who had covered over or played down the persistence of anti-Semitic prejudices there. It should be recalled that Adam Michnik, in his remarks on Jedwabne published in the spring of 2001,[37] likewise quoted Zofia Kossak, whose views are included in the recent volume of documentation on the discussion in Poland.[38]

A short time after the publication of Smolar's article, Jan Blonski triggered an even more vehement debate with his piece published in *Tygodnik Powszechny*, an opposition journal closely allied with the Church.[39] Proceeding from an interpretation of two poems by Czeslaw Milosz, he warned his contemporaries that they should engage in an unstinting examination of the guilt the Poles incurred during the war vis-à-vis their fellow Polish Jews. He accused them of not dealing honestly with the past: "We wished to see ourselves free of any possible accusation of blame," wrote Blonski, "we want to be *totally* pure. And ultimately we wish ourselves to be victims." In his view, that strategy could have no future. Blonski demanded: "We have to face the question of our complicit responsibility with total openness, with total sincerity."[40] By "complicity," Blonski meant the moral responsibility of the Poles for the crimes they had committed in the temporal and spatial context of the German occupation, involving forms of collaboration as well as acts of injustice perpetrated by Poles—and not induced by the German occupiers. For example, the handing over of Jews who had fled and were in hiding, the refusal of assistance or even the passive act of quiet satisfaction if not glee in the face of Jewish persecution.

In the poem "*Biedny chrzescijanin patrzy na getto*," Czeslaw Milosz had captured this complex of feeling and sentiment after the murder of the Polish Jews in the image of fear for the warder advancing below the ground like a mole, a red lamp attached to his forehead, counting the buried dead and weighing the burden of guilt associated with them: "And my shattered body exposes me to his glance / and counts me among the helpers of death, the uncircumcised." At the time of their publication in Poland, Blonski's views were clearly repudiated. The general rejection was due largely to a circumstance external to this discourse on the moral evaluation of past actions.

Within a heavily censored and extensively manipulated public sphere, the fundamental prerequisite for an unprejudiced interrogation of history was lacking. There was an absence of the approximate equality of rights in the formulation and publication of differing opinions that might lead to the formation of opinion among the private individuals gathered together as a public, according to Habermas's definition of a civil public sphere as the realm of such a debate.[41] There could of course be no such open interrogation of history as long as discussion of one's own history consisted of an officially sanctioned version of historical reality that followed the permutations of party rule—and its knee-jerk negation by the opposition. That was a version of history that compensated for its lack of access to the mass media by means of collective forms of symbolic commemoration: of special significance here was the memorialization of the murder by the Soviets of thousands of Polish officers in Katyn in 1942.

Too many accounts that had to be settled with one's own history, especially in regard to the hegemonic Soviet Union, remained open, unresolved. This impeded the possibility of simple insight into the reprehensible character of certain ways of behavior and action. The Polish-Jewish reticulation of historical relations was all the more impenetrable due to the fact that party propaganda, prohibitions on publication and discussion, traditions of anti-Jewish animosity and stereotypy nurtured by the Church over centuries—and accusations of guilt hurled at surviving Jews in regard to their prominent role in the party and security apparatus of the postwar period—intermingled in a complex amalgam. That convoluted admixture can be illustrated by reference to a propaganda initiative of the workers' party from the early postwar period in which the Jews active in the ghetto uprising of 1943 are styled as heroes, whereas the Polish resistance fighters of the Armja Krajowa, who had fought against the German occupiers, are declared to be "bandits."[42] But even after these conditions changed fundamentally with the demise of the one-party system of rule, large segments of the Polish public remained beholden to the received attitudes grounded on collective attributions and sensitivities. The conflict over the Carmelite monastery on the grounds of the former concentration camp at Auschwitz, which stirred international controversy in 1989 (and continued up until 1990, when the first free elections of Polish postwar history were held); the polemical debate regarding the murder of Jews perpetrated by units of the patriotic resistance during the Warsaw Uprising of 1944 (1994); the debates on the victim status of Poles and Jews under the German occupation, as they erupted in connection with the 50th anniversary of the liberation of Auschwitz (1995)—all bore features of a dialogue of the deaf. Its existence had been anticipated in the conflict that raged over Blonski's article.[43]

Local Collective Memory and Historical Guilt

The essay by Gross constitutes a watershed in this discussion. One factor, as already suggested, lay in the drastic contours of the event's depiction and the shock it generated.[44] But that is not a sufficient explanation for the readiness among so many to confront and deal with the events at Jedwabne and to test collective conscience in their light. Rather, we are confronted here with a highly complex happening in memory, where the latent memory of the events themselves, the circumscription to a local collective memory and an extraordinarily subtle, undirected transmission of knowledge about historical guilt to the later generations within the community of the perpetrators are being fused with each other. Yet to get from that point to a public discussion and on to a national and finally international discussion, a few more steps had necessarily to follow. To move forward from a locally kept secret, though one passed on within that circumscribed collective, to a broader platform of discussion, one simple fact had enormous importance: the testimony of Shmuel Wasserstein and numerous other sources consulted left no doubt about the *actual substance* of the murders as described. They led directly to that barn in which several dozen Catholic male residents of Jedwabne, after an entire day spent tormenting and murdering—witnessed by the other residents of the village—then proceeded to burn several hundred of their Jewish neighbors alive. Even the still unresolved question as to when and to what extent a German Gestapo unit was involved in this massacre, and how that participation should be interpreted, does not lead past this burning barn. Even if for this last step in the development of the public discussion, freedom of expression and a highly differentiated landscape of media as exists today in Poland—which for the first time makes possible a historically differentiating dynamic complex of reflection in the form of many hundreds of articles, letters, radio programs, TV programs, scholarly discussions, and the involvement of the Internet and its myriad postings—played an important role, these remain secondary for the original movement of memory. It unfolded in the framework of local collective memory and before the huge public debate took place.

As Dan Diner, building on Halbwachs and others has pointed out, collective memory is no mere random collection of fragments and shards of remembrance. The constitutive element in collective memory is a moral dimension that systematically stores in particular all forms of violent injustice and its consequences. If this injustice involves the collective memory itself, then a kind of amnesia can be generated that permanently obstructs actualization of this memory, repressing it. But if a deed of injustice was directed to the outside, then conscience counts this, its own collective, "among the helpers of death" (Milosz). Morality does not allow memory any respite.[45]

In this context, it is necessary to point to the social distance between Jewish and Polish life-worlds even on the eve of World War II. Despite the accelerated acculturation among Jewish youth, especially as a result of attendance at common schools, as has been demonstrated for the Second Republic, Catholic and Jewish milieus in rural Poland remained separate worlds.

> One cannot comprehend the events in Jedwabne or the general indifference toward the fate of the Jews at the time of the occupation without taking into account the enormous gulf between the respective milieus that separated Polish from Jewish society before the war. This was marked by the differing

> religion, economic competition and the fact that people lived more separated, side by side, than in symbiosis with one another.[46]

To that extent, the massacre was an action that in the eyes of the perpetrators was directed to the outside, not against members of one's own milieu.

Jan Tomasz Gross received initial stimulus for investigating these events in Jedwabne on 10 July 1941 from the film director Agnieszka Arnold. While doing research on the archive of the ghetto historian Emanuel Ringelblum, Arnold became aware of the massacre and went with a film team to the village several times in the late 1990s.[47]

> I asked myself: how to continue, what's the next step? You can't just go up to someone on the street and ask: "Excuse me, did you murder 1,600 Jews during the time of the German occupation?" My cameraman helped me out at the time. He suggested going to a bar. And there in a few minutes I had confirmation of the testimony of Wasserstein. Without asking where we were from or where we were headed, we strangers were addressed with questions like: "Hey, you know what happened here in town? Like what happened during the war here?" ... The people in the bar told me that if I wanted to find out more, I should go to talk with the daughter of the owner of the barn where they had burned the Jews.

Memory presses forward up against the mass of unprocessed and unforgiven guilt. This process is ubiquitous. An anthropologist from Jedwabne who even before the publication of Gross's book had conducted a series of interviews on the events, recently explained: "When I was a kid of seven or eight, my best girlfriend confided to me a Big Secret. She said: 'Hey, you know, the Poles burned a lot of Jews once, in a barn, right here in Jedwabne.'"[48] Most of those interviewed for this field study stated that the Poles were clearly the perpetrators. "I asked: 'Who did it?' The answer was always: 'Poles' or 'we did it.' Or: 'Listen, Germans too.' But in personal narratives, the Poles were always the ones in the foreground."[49]

In one case, parents told their children about the massacre. In another, a child overheard a conversation about this between adults. Such memories are uniformly related by all postwar generations in Jedwabne.[50] The intimacy of this exclusively local, generally even family discourse on the massacre was able to lead to a situation where "the murder was common knowledge for 60 years, and nonetheless remained a big secret."[51] This memory of a huge burden of guilt was imparted to the younger generation in a kind of inadvertent manner, almost casually. This general picture is confirmed by the investigation behind one of the first and most influential press articles triggering the huge debate of the years 2000 and 2001, written by Andrzej Kaczynski: "A lot of the inhabitants of Jedwabne refused to talk, but it was without much trouble that I could confirm most of the elements in the Jewish reports about the massacre. Not only those older people, who lived through the events of the war in Jedwabne, knew and talked about the fact that above all Poles had cruelly killed the Jews, but also the younger who knew the truth only through the account of their parents."[52] The descriptions of how bad conscience among those directly involved took control of them in the course of time contain striking similarities: "As they were themselves dying, a number of those who had taken part in the pogrom called out the names of those they had murdered, asking for forgiveness."[53] In an interview, the Catholic husband of a Jewish woman who had survived from the neighboring village of Radzilów stated:

> But the murderers did not die an easy death later on. One of my fellow workers who had been in hospital next to one of those men told me that he started to call out the names of the Jews he had murdered. As death approached everything returned to him, visible to his mind's eye. His relatives tried to keep him from opening his mouth, but he shouted: "The hall is full of them. Please have them leave."[54]

The fate of the neighbor perpetrators was given a kind of moral evaluation by means of a quasi-religious rationalization in the local community of Jedwabne:

> God's punishment lies at the center of all local narratives in Jedwabne. The local talk about the murderers is usually connected with some inexplicable cases of sickness and death in their families. People then talked about "God's punishment" or a "curse." Or about the "curse of the Jews." That perception was also related to Jedwabne as a whole: "Evil has descended upon this town."[55]

So local collective memory passed on one of its constituents, the bad conscience due to the murder of Jewish neighbors, in a form that was spontaneous, and, as it would appear, almost undirected. In the context of memory and restitution, a further aspect of the continuity of memory of the injustice perpetrated in Jedwabne is of especial importance. If the murder of the Jews of the locality is foregrounded in memory, the plunder of their homes and household effects is likewise a solid component of the remembered past. It hounds the descendants due to its moral ambiguity and irresolution: "I can't recall I ever heard earlier that our people here murdered the Jews. That although I've been living here for more than 50 years.... But I can remember from my childhood someone pointing to another person and saying: 'He got rich stealing from the Jews.'"[56] That is what was told to the Polish journalist Anna Bikont, who pursued the events of July 1941 armed with a Jedwabne land register from the time before 1939. This is also a confirmation of the assumption that "property seeks its owner" and that the illegal character of the appropriation of that property becomes part of collective memory and of collective bad conscience. This mechanism is further illustrated by the almost naïve attempt to control this collective memory, which is the destruction of those pages of the parish protocols pertaining to the days of the massacre.[57]

In one of his responses to criticism of his book, Jan Tomasz Gross refers to the work of Saul Friedländer. After a lecture, one of those in the audience told Friedländer that his "Aryan" grandmother had taken a pillow for herself from the household effects of a deported Jewish family. An upwelling following the theft, which turned this benefactor of Jewish persecution into an accomplice, led to her putting the pillow "at the bottom of a cabinet" for safekeeping. By hiding it away and out of sight, she also in a sense made the associated guilt invisible.[58] That was likewise the case in Jedwabne: "Don't frighten me that way," said another woman to the journalist. "Whoever took the possessions of someone else has to live now in fear and trembling. But my house was built after the war. I don't know who lived here before, that doesn't interest me. Who murdered whom is not my business." This quote points to the immediate connection between action and property and the right of ownership. A further quote confirms this assumption ex negativo. Another passer-by the journalist speaks with refuses to give any information: "I could already tell from your accent that you're Jewish. You have no business being here. These houses belonged to Germans." In three short sentences,[59] the mere possibility of formulating a claim to ownership of the houses is connected with the presumed Jewish background of the journalist. This potential moral claim is rejected by the fact that ownership was taken over by those whose historical moral guilt is beyond any doubt: by the Germans (who did not live in Jedwabne before 1941). By defining Germans as the purported earlier owners, the speaker regards the appropriation of these houses as being morally justified.

The acquisition of property through theft from the murdered by the murderer,[60] as often occurred in Jedwabne, must be viewed as a prevalent pattern of the transition from Jewish to non-Jewish property. World War II and its consequences led particularly in the case of Poland to an almost unsurpassed complexity in the shifts of relations of property ownership. Although Polish Jews were by far the most adversely affected, they were not the only ones. First there was the expropriation by the German occupiers, then destruction as a result of the ravages of the war, then the changes in borders and sovereignty directly after the war's end—and then came the nationalization of previously private property, both land and houses.[61] Against the backdrop of this complexity, there is also ownership of formerly Jewish property that is not connected with a moral responsibility of the new owner in the manner described for Jedwabne. Nonetheless, and also quite apart from the immediate and direct link between murder and plunder in the case of Jedwabne, an irresolvable reservation lies like a heavy burden upon former Jewish property, both real estate and household possessions—namely, that "this property did not come into the possession of the new owners through the customary chain of transaction or inheritance. A horrible and monstrous crime is woven into its history."[62]

It seems appropriate to consider the historical turn that brought about the end of communist rule in East-Central Europe as the decisive factor in stimulating this debate about guilt, memory, and restitution. It served as the precondition for a public debate by creating a public debate without censorship restriction. What is more, the specters of the past were ressucitated by the fear that regime change would also lead to a revision of property and ownership. As a recent analysis by Tomasz Szarota has shown, the fact of the murder of the Jews in Jedwabne had been discussed much more frequently than anybody, including Jan Tomasz Gross, knew. Since the early 1980s, for example, a regional state prosecutor, Waldemar Monkiewicz, had written and publicly discussed the massacre in Jedwabne, ascribing it to the German occupier and taking an apologetic stance.[63] *The New York Times* dealt with the massacre for the first time in 1996 by publishing the letter of a relative of Holocaust survivors in the context of similar events in Eishyshok, prompting the official protest of the Polish embassy in the United States. However, no public debate of significant scope followed, either in the United States, or in Poland.[64] The intensity of the reaction of the Polish public in the year 2000 seems closely linked to the discussion about restitution, and the eventuality that historical guilt might lead to questions about property rights. This fear already appears in Andrzej Kaczynski's article in May 2000, when his interviewees inquire if the Jews now want their property back.[65]

A proper weighing and assessment of the relation in which the differing forms of the acquisition of formerly Jewish property stand to one another is a task that historical research is only now beginning to address. Doubtless the example of Jedwabne broaches the fundamental moral questions conjunct with this. In addition, that example points up a further desideratum: initially, research must probably traverse the path of local monographic studies.

Within lightning time, Jedwabne has become an emblem subsuming massacres of Jewish neighbors in World War II perpetrated principally by the local population. In a comparable moral context, in the coming years there will undoubtedly be discussion of the many hundreds if not indeed thousands of murders of returning Jews. The direct background of these killings in many cases was undoubtly the elimination of those who could possibly claim their houses and their belongings. Here too, the background and circumstances of the passing on or taking over of property will become a "gateway to memory" (Dan Diner). Here too, morality, ownership and collective memory interweave in a complex knot. The systemically fixated memory of what was morally repugnant is torn from the sphere of the spontaneous and locally limited *mémoire involontaire*, becoming in turn a constituent of a newly defined, systematically fixed collective memory.

Translated from the German by Bill Templer

Notes

1. The book initially was published in Polish as *Sasiedzi* (Sejny, 2000). Other editions soon followed: *Neighbors* (Princeton, 2001), *Nachbarn* (Munich, 2001), and in Hebrew as *Shkhenim* (Jerusalem 2001). There are now translations into French (*Fayard* – Paris, 2002), Dutch (*De Bezige Bij* – Amsterdam, 2002) and several other languages.
2. Jan Tomasz Gross has dealt with a number of aspects of the discussion in his *Wokól ‚Sasiadów'. Polemiki i wyjasnienia* [On 'Neighbors.' Polemics and Explanations] (Sejny, 2003). Other publications include *Thou shalt not kill. Poles on Jedwabne* (Warsaw, 2001); "Die 'Jedwabne-Debatte' in polnischen Zeitungen und Zeitschriften," in *Transodra. Deutsch-polnisches Informationsbulletin* 23 (December

2001), ed. Ruth Henning. See also Joshua D. Zimmerman, ed., *Contested Memories: Poles and Jews during the Holocaust and its Aftermath* (New Brunswick, N.J., 2003); and Antony Polonsky and Joanna Michlic, eds., *The Neighbors Respond: The Controversy over the Jedwabne Massacre in Poland* (Princeton, 2004). In addition of interest: Robert Jankowski, ed., *Jedwabne. Spór historyków wokól ksiazki Jana T. Grossa "Sasiedzi"* [Jedwabne: The Historians' Debate on the Book by Jan Tomasz Gross "Neighbors"] (Warsaw 2002).

3. *Rzeczpospolita,* 1 September 2000.
4. The president of the IPN, Leon Kieres, describes the resumption of inquiries in a detailed interview with Teresa Toranska: "Najgorszych listów mi nie daja" [The Worst Letters They Don't Even Give Me], *Gazeta Wyborcza,* 4 July 2001.
5. *Wokól Jedwabnego* [On Jedwabne], ed. Pawel Machcewicz and Krzysztof Persak, vol. 1: "Studia", vol. 2: "Dokumenty" (Warsaw 2002). See also *Frankfurter Allgemeine Zeitung* (hereafter *FAZ*), 4 February 2003.
6. Most recently for example in this form in Piotr Wandycz, "Odrodzenie narodowe i nacjonalizm (XIX–XX wiek)" [National Rebirth and Nationalism. 19th and 20th Century], in *Historia Europy Srodkowo-Wschodniej* [History of Central-Eastern Europe], ed. Jerzy Kloczowski, 3 vols. (Lublin, 2000), vol. 2, 168.
7. *Gazeta Wyborcza,* 1 September 2000.
8. *Rzeczpospolita,* 21, 23 and 25 May 2001; *Gazeta Wyborcza,* 23 May 2001; *Haaretz,* 23 May 2001 and *FAZ,* 23 May 2001.
9. On the basis of substantial differences between eye-witness reports and the results of the exhumation, Jan Tomasz Gross argued for a complete exhumation of the mass graves, despite the associated unavoidable violation of the prescriptions of Jewish religious law (*Gazeta Wyborcza,* 8 June 2001). See also "Report," *Polska Agencja Prasowa* [Polish Press Agency], 9 July 2003.
10. Thus, Jewish and Polish eye-witnesses of the massacre of the Jewish population that occurred three days earlier in Radzilów, following an astonishingly similar pattern, talked about a Gestapo unit providing the Polish population with handguns. See *Rzeczpospolita,* 6 April 2001; *FAZ,* 6 April 2001 and *Gazeta Wyborcza,* 25 June 2001.
11. Interview with Jan Tomasz Gross in *The New Yorker On-Line,* 9 March 2001.
12. The equally relevant reception of Gross's book in the United States and Israel cannot be dealt with in the confines of the present essay.
13. "Lokalne pogromy Zydow w czerwcu i lipcu 1941 roku na wschodnich rubiezach II Rzeczypospolitej" [Local pogroms against Jews in the Eastern borderlands of the Second Republic in June and July 1941], in *Biuletyn Zydowskiego Instytutu Historycznego* 162/163 (1992): 2–18, English: "Local Anti-Jewish Pogroms in the Occupied Territories of Eastern Poland, June–July 1941," in *The Holocaust in the Soviet Union: Studies and Sources on the Destruction of the Jews in the Nazi-Occupied Territories of the USSR, 1941–1945,* ed. Lucjan Dobroszycki and Geoffrey Gurock (New York, 1993).
14. *Rzeczpospolita,* 25 June 2001.
15. Ibid., 4 January 2001.
16. Ibid., 23 June 2001; *Gazeta Wyborcza,* 25 June 2001. Likewise in the case of the massacre in Radzilów, the IPN began a legal inquiry at the level of district attorney into the events; it was still in progress in the summer of 2003: see "Report," *PAP,* 9 July 2003.

17. Dieter Pohl, "Der Raub an den Juden im besetzten Osteuropa 1939–1942," in *Raub und Restitution. "Arisierung" und Rückerstattung des jüdischen Eigentums in Europa*, ed. Constantin Goschler and Philipp Ther (Frankfurt a.M., 2003), 58–72, here 58. Pohl's article deals basically with the acts of plunder for which the German occupation authorities were responsible. See also Laurence Weinbaum, "Defrosting History: The Restitution of Jewish Property in Eastern Europe," in *The Plunder of Jewish Property during the Holocaust*, ed. Avi Beker (Basingstoke, Eng., 2001), 83–110, here 84, giving solely a brief description of the robbery.
18. *Rzeczpospolita*, 25 June 2001.
19. A comprehensive impression of this reaction can be gained on the basis of the reactions to newspaper reports and book reviews accessible via the homepage of the publishing house Pogranicze: http://pogranicze.sejny.pl/menu.htm (26 August 2004).
20. *Rzeczpospolita*, 5 and 19 May, 10/11 July and 1 August 2000.
21. Here inter alia: *Gazeta Wspolczesna/Bialystok*, 30 April, 11 July 2000; *Midrasz*, June 2000; *Gazeta Wyborcza*, 12 July 2000; *Krajobrazy*, 25 August 2000; *Slowo Zydowskie*, 25 August 2000; *Rzeczpospolita*, 9/10 December 2000; *Gazeta Wyborcza*, 16/17 December 2000 and *FAZ*, 23 April, 2 May 2001.
22. *Gazeta Wyborcza*, 29/30 July 2000. Gross accepted some of these corrections: *Rzeczpospolita*, 23 June 2001.
23. *Nasza Polska*, 1 September 2000; *Gazeta Wyborcza*, 12 March 2001. Two volumes of essays also now argue from this vantage, attempting to refute Gross: *Operacja "Jedwabne": mity i fakty* [Operation 'Jedwabne'. Myths and Facts], ed. Lech Zdzislaw Niekrasz (Wroclaw, 2001) and Jerzy Robert Nowak, *Sto klamstw J.T. Grossa o Jedwabnem i zydowskich sasiadach* [The 100 Lies of Jan Tomasz Gross about Jedwabne and the Jewish Neighbors] (Warsaw 2001) and several polemic essays.
24. *Gazeta Wyborcza*, 29 May 2001. The following quotes are taken from there. On the disputes on the eve of the religious service, see *FAZ*, 18 May 2001.
25. Roman Graczyk, "Zabraklo proroctwa," *Gazeta Wyborcza*, 12 June 2001.
26. I rely here principally on the comprehensive studies by Iwona Irwin-Zarecka, *Neutralizing Memory: The Jew in Contemporary Poland* (New Brunswick, N.J., 1990) and Michael Steinlauf, *Bondage to the Dead: Poland and the Memory of the Holocaust* (Syracuse, N.Y., 1995).
27. Steinlauf, *Bondage to the Dead*, 89–94.
28. A forum for these discussions were, up until the introduction of military law, the numerous new media and other publications, and in the period after the imposition of military law on 13 December 1981, the "second run," the Polish form of samizdat.
29. Steinlauf, *Bondage to the Dead*, 94.
30. They appropriated these in the framework of the "Jewish mobile university," modeled on the opposition's "mobile university," a forum for discussion and education in the underground, itself a tradition of the Polish independence movement from the time of Russian hegemony and German occupation during World War II, see Steinlauf, *Bondage to the Dead*, 93f.
31. Steinlauf, *Bondage to the Dead*, 107–09.
32. At the same time, both in Poland and internationally, there was a marked upsurge in research. Regular international conferences and the establishment of specialized publications (*Gal-Ed* in Israel, *Polin* in England) opened up much utilized forums for scholarly exchange and communication.

33. The present paper cannot deal with the nature of the media in Poland in the 1980s. These were characterized by a reduced but still effective censorship and an exceptionally broad array of illegal media after the liberating phase of legal Solidarity and the period of repression under military law (13 December 1981 to the spring of 1983).
34. The Paris daily *Libération* termed it in the spring of 1985 "La Pologne sur le banc d'accusé" [Poland stands accused].
35. Steinlauf, *Bondage to the Dead,* 110–113.
36. Aleksander Smolar, "Tabu i niewinnosc" [Taboo and Innocence], *Aneks* 41/42 (1986). Reprinted in *Gazeta Wyborcza,* 12 and 19 May 2001, published in German in *Babylon. Beiträge zur jüdischen Gegenwart* 2 (1987).
37. *Gazeta Wyborcza,* 17 March 2001; published the same day with minimal changes in the text in English in the *New York Times.*
38. Polonsky and Michlic, *The Neighbors Respond.*
39. Jan Blonski, "Biedni Polacy patrza na Getto" [The Poor Poles Look at the Ghetto], *Tygodnik Powszechny* 2 (1987). The article was translated several times and reprinted. It appeared in German in *epd-Dokumentation des Evangelischen Pressedienstes* 41 (1988) and in English in *Polin* 2 (1987) as well as in *My Brother's Keeper? Recent Polish Debates on the Holocaust,* ed. Anthony Polonsky (London/New York, 1990). Reprinted with other articles in Polish in *Biedni Polacy patrza na getto,* ed. Jan Blonski (Cracow, 1994), 9–29.
40. Blonski, *Biedni Polacy,* 19, based on the 1994 edition, emphasis in original.
41. Jürgen Habermas, *Strukturwandel der Öffentlichkeit. Untersuchungen zu einer Kategorie der bürgerlichen Gesellschaft* (Frankfurt a.M., 1990; first published 1962), 84. On the constitution of the Polish political public sphere in the period of the people's republic and in particular on the integration of nationalistic perspectives within this sphere, see Marek Jan Chodakiewicz, *Zydzi i Polacy 1918–1955. Wspólistnienie, Zaglada, Komunizm* [Jews and Poles 1918–1955. Coexistence, Destruction, Communism] (Warsaw, 2000), 448–518.
42. Steinlauf, "Poland," in *The World Reacts to the Holocaust,* ed. David S. Wyman and Charles H. Rosenzweig (Baltimore, London, 1996), 111 and Chodakiewicz, *Zydzi i Polacy,* 463.
43. Steinlauf, *Bondage to the Dead,* 122–144.
44. New descriptions of the course of the massacres a few days earlier in other cities in this same region also provide much gruesome detail; see esp. Andrzej Zbikowski, "Nie bylo rozkazu" [There Was no Order], *Rzeczpospolita,* 4 January 2001 and Anna Bikont, "Przed Jedwabnem. Mord na Zydach w Radzilowie" [Before Jedwabne. The Murder of the Jews in Radzilów], *Gazeta Wyborcza,* 15 June 2001.
45. Dan Diner, "Der Holocaust als europäisches Gründungsereignis" (ms., 15 February 2001, Berlin). I am grateful to Prof. Diner for providing me with this text.
46. Interview by Anna Jarmusiewicz with Feliks Tych, "Historia musi polegac na prawdzie" [History Must Be Based on Truth], *Rzeczpospolita,* 16 June 2001.
47. Interview of Piotr Litka with Agnieszka Arnold, "Film o pamieci, od której nie mozna uciec" [A Film on a Memory You Cannot Run Away From], *Film-Magazin Kino* 4 (2001). The following quotes are taken from there.
48. Marta Kurkowska-Budzan, "My Jedwabne," *Polin* 15 (2002): 401–407, here 402.
49. Ibid., 404.

50. "Jestesmy innymi ludzmi. Dyskusja o Jedwabnem w Jedwabnem" [We Are no Longer the Same. A discussion about Jedwabne in Jedwabne], *Wiez* 4 (2001). In their articles, Stanislaw Michalowski (head, City Council, Jedwabne) and Stanislaw Przechodzki (Public Health Office Lomza) report about conversations with a similar content which they heard as children.
51. Kurkowska-Budzan, "My Jedwabne," 405.
52. Andrzej Kaczynski, "Calopalenie. W Jedwabnem zaglady Zydow Niemcy dokonali polskimi rekami" [Holocaust. In Jedwabne, the Germans Annihilated the Jews with Polish Hands], *Rzeczpospolita* May 5, 2000.
53. Interview of Piotr Litka with Agnieszka Arnold, see note 47.
54. Interview, Anna Bikont with Stanislaw Ramotowski, "Nieporzadnych bylo wiecej" [There Were more Perpetrators], *Gazeta Wyborcza*, 15 June 2001.
55. Kurkowska-Budzan, "My Jedwabne," 405.
56. Anna Bikont, "Prosze tu wiecej nie przychodzic" [And Please Don't Come Back], *Gazeta Wyborcza*, 31 March 2001. The following quote from this article as well. See also Bikont's article "My z Jedwabnego", *Gazeta Wyborcza*, March 10, 2001.
57. Stanislaw Musial, "Prosimy, pomozcie nam byc lepszymi" [We Ask You to Help Us to Be Better], *Gazeta Wyborcza*, May 21, 2001.
58. *Tygodnik Powszechny*, 11 February 2001; see also *Transodra* 23 (2001): 138.
59. It must be emphasized that the only source for these statements are the press articles by Bikont cited above.
60. Already in Kings it is pointed out that such actions lead to divine punishment (1. Kings 21:19): "Hast thou killed, and also taken possession? And thou shalt speak unto him, saying, Thus saith the Lord, In the place where dogs licked the blood of Naboth shall dogs lick thy blood, even thine."
61. Dariusz Stola, "Die polnische Debatte um den Holocaust und die Rückerstattung von Eigentum," in Goschler and Ther, *Raub und Restitution*, 205–224.
62. See the persuasive systematic presentation in Stola, "Die polnische Debatte", quote 219.
63. Tomasz Szarota, "Mord w Jedwabnem. Dokumenty, publikacje i interpretacje z lat 1941–2000. Kalendarium," [Murder in Jedwabne. Documents, Publications and Interpretations from the Years 1941–2000. Chronology] in *Wokól Jedwabnego. Studia*, ed. Machcewicz and Persak, 353–488, especially 477–481.
64. Ibid., 483.
65. Kaczynski, "Calopalenie".

— *Nine* —

LOOTED TEXTS: RESTITUTING JEWISH LIBRARIES

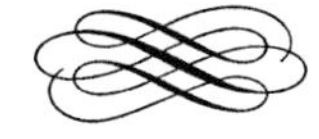

Markus Kirchhoff

Introduction: Jewish Lost Books in Search of Their Owners

Jewish private and institutional libraries, secular and religious, with rich or modest holdings in general literature, Judaica or Hebraica, adored by their users or criticized, were of course among the ubiquitous cultural institutions of Jewish life-worlds and everyday life across Europe. In many localities, these libraries experienced a veritable flowering, particularly in the decades prior to the great catastrophe. National Socialism also destroyed this dimension of Jewish culture in Europe.[1]

Alongside ravaged libraries and the millions of books burned and converted to pulp, numerous stolen and "relocated" books of Jewish readers survived the Shoa, silent witnesses to the ravages. At war's end, the surviving holdings were nowhere any longer in their original location. Thus, one can rightly speak of "displaced books" or, analoguous to the more common term "lost art," of "lost books." Some of the holdings that survived in Europe were restituted after the war to private Jewish individuals and institutions. But for most books, this was not the case, including hundreds of thousands of volumes that had found their way into German libraries during the war.

Such stolen property remaining in German libraries is no longer open to litigation. It is true that the restitution regulations of the Allies and the subsequent laws of the Federal Republic were also valid in the case of restitution and compensation for "Aryanized" Jewish cultural objects. But these laws have long since expired. As legislation lapsed, the return of stolen books to their former Jewish owners, their private heirs, or the successor organizations had by no means been fully accomplished. Yet since the late 1990s, after decades of forgetting or disinterest, this fact is no longer considered morally acceptable. Increasingly, German public libraries are now agreeing to open up access to such holdings in question on their shelves and in their storerooms.

That is reflected, for example, in the German professional library science journal *Der Bibliotheksdienst.* In 2003, the Nuremberg Municipal Library published a report significantly titled "*Lost Art-Bücher suchen ihre Eigentümer*" (Lost Art Books in Search of their Owners), dealing with attempts by the library to restitute books of Jewish provenience.[2] Another article in the same journal in 2003 examined the question of books formerly owned by Jews that during the Third Reich had been on the shelves of the "*Forschungsabteilung Judenfrage*" (National Socialist Research Department for the Jewish Question) in Munich. The library of the University of Munich, the responsible successor in this matter, reported it had identified the holdings in question and passed this information on to the Coordination Office for Lost Cultural Assets in Magdeburg.[3] Since 1998, this coordination body, an institution of the German states and federal government, has augmented its efforts to contribute to the restitution of lost or stolen Jewish cultural objects. For this purpose, the office maintains a special website—www.lostart.de. This website provides access to a database in which any private person or institution can publish information on cultural items found or sought.[4] Dependent solely on the participation of those it addresses, this platform provides for a high degree of transparency and democratization in the restitution process.

Yet such efforts for the restitution of Jewish lost books in Germany come late. Nonetheless, for their part, they are an expression of a new or renewing consciousness now gaining ground since the 1990s regarding the question of the Aryanization and restitution of Jewish property more generally. In the case of most of these books, they are neither extremely rare nor do they have any large financial worth. Indeed, one might well argue that the belated restitution of the lost books does not involve any appreciable monetary loss, so that this is a proper gesture, albeit a relatively cheap and feeble one. In fact, most of these books have little market value. Only a few are so rare that they cannot be readily replaced on the used book market or by reproduction. If German libraries agree to the demand to open up these holdings to public scrutiny, the ensuing costs for historical research on library history, the careful perusal of acquisitions lists, and the examination of holdings will probably be greater than the market value of the identified books. Even then it is not certain that claimants for the volumes will appear. All this makes clear that although simple old books are involved, the matter is not quite so simple. The impetus increasingly accepted as an obligation to find and make such holdings known is an ample demonstration that these volumes are anything but books in the ordinary sense.

Rather, the crucial aspect here is the specific external and highly *material* feature of these volumes as vessels of memory. Of course, in the case of any older book, one may wonder who the original reader may have been or in what library it once stood. An observer today then deals, along with its content, with the nostalgic element inscribed in the volume, or its antiquarian materiality, so to speak, its former readers and presence in specific places at specific times: its roots and routes. Information on that is provided by external features such as private rubber stamps, exlibris, written entries of names, dates or localities, dedications or library stamps and markings. Such external indications reflect the civil course of affairs, so to speak: regular acquisition by a library, private sale, or inheritance. Yet if books have become the object of expropriation, theft, and expulsion of their owners, which has happened repeatedly throughout history and most especially during World War II, they certainly give us some idea of their original legal owners, correspondingly contextualized. They take on a fateful itinerary. In the case of the Jewish lost books, the rubber-stamped markings and other external features point to forced emigration and flight, even deportation and mass murder—the Shoa. Here we are dealing in both a literal and metaphorical sense with inscriptions of the persecution, if not indeed the annihilation of the former owners and readers.

In many cases, additionally there are indications pointing to the history of restitution or its failure. One example can illuminate this: on the open shelves of a departmental library at the University of Bochum stands an almost complete set of all volumes of the famed *Zeitschrift der Deutschen Morgenländischen Gesellschaft*, which has appeared since the late 1840s. The early volumes 4 and 5 (1850/1851, here bound together) have four features that point to earlier ownership: on the inner side of the front binding, which is in need of restoration, there is a pasted note with the printed information: "Schenkung der Frau Professor Lazarus. Berlin, 9. Februar 1873. (M. A. Levy'sche Bibliothek)" (Donated by Madame Prof. Lazarus. Berlin, 9 February 1873. [M. A. Levy Library]). On the back of the title page there are three stamps: "Bibliothek der Hochschule für die Wissenschaft des Judentums Berlin" (Library of the College for the Science of Judaism, Berlin), and above it the angular stamp "Der Chef d. SP. u. d. SD. Bücherei der Führerschule. Unter Nr. 4953 der Zugangsliste eingetragen. Berlin, den 20. 3. 1943" (Chief of the Security Police and Security Service. Library of the Leaders' Candidate School. Acquisitions No. 4953. Berlin, 20 March 1943). This is then followed by the round stamp "Evang.-theol. Seminar Univ. Bochum" (Department of Protestant Theology, Univ. of Bochum).[5] Aside from the fact that this indeed is a very valuable edition, it is rare for the history and fate of a book to be so graphically documented by means of a series of rubber stampings. Here one can trace the donation from a private library, to the Jewish Hochschule in Berlin opened in 1872, via a Nazi library of "confiscated" books, on to a departmental library at a major university in the Federal Republic.

Often, however, all that one finds are individual single stamps. But these are sufficient to give some indication of the persecution and murder of their original readers. That can be a rubber-stamped notation "Sichergestellt durch den Einsatzstab RR" (Taken into possession by the Operations Staff Reichsleiter Rosenberg) or the "Zentralbibliothek Theresienstadt" (Central Library, Theresienstadt), a library that served as a source of a certain cynical delight to the local SS camp command. Some stamps indicate the restitution of the volume as a lost book, that is, as expelled, relocated, and often heirless property. That is the case, for example, in connection with the Archival Depot Offenbach a. M., an important institution of the American occupation forces active in the early postwar years.

Only by means of stamps of this kind, but frequently also through far less obvious features, such as certain abbreviations or acquisition dates stamped in the book by libraries, do such histories of the books become manifest or at least open to inquiry. This facilitates the discovery of the specific inscribed memory of the lost books.

The present essay deals with this kind of discovery, which can be increasingly noted since the 1990s, not only in Germany but in Austria.[6] But the prehistories of these books are necessarily at issue and under focus here: initially, significant features of National Socialist violence and force vis-à-vis books of Jewish origin are identified. A further layer in inquiry is the era of restitution efforts in the postwar period. From that period we have a number of observations by Jewish contemporaries on so-called "Jewish Cultural Reconstruction" (as it was termed at the time). Among them were Jewish authors who on the spot in Germany attempted to have stolen books restituted to Jewish readers worldwide, including Hannah Arendt, Gershom Scholem, and Lucy Dawidowicz. These contemporaries and their analyses are utilized for the historical underpinning of the more recent consciousness of the memory imprinted in the lost books. Thus, the present essay looks not only at the important and necessary efforts by German libraries to identify and restitute books of Jewish origin. It is also concerned more generally with the memory inscribed in these books.

Theft, Destruction, and Nazi Control of Jewish Memory

We have only an approximate notion of the actual number of Jewish books subjected to National Socialist violence. According to estimates by the Israeli library historian Dov Schidorsky, there were some four million volumes of Judaica and Hebraica throughout Europe affected by the war. Half of these, some two million books, are today considered destroyed or lost. The other half, likewise about two million volumes, were still in existence at the end of the war but dispersed over a wide area.[7] His estimate is based primarily on a list published in 1946 in *Jewish Social Studies* and put together by the Commission on Jewish Cultural Reconstruction.[8] The activities of this commission will be discussed below. The list covers holdings in Judaica and Hebraica for twenty countries in Europe in public libraries (state, municipal, and university) as well as in important private Jewish libraries with a minimum of a thousand books or more. The addition of their holdings (not always fully amenable to reconstruction) led to a figure in excess of 3.3 million volumes. It is of course clear that this figure does not take account of many Jewish items that were not subsumable under Judaica or Hebraica. In his "The Fate of the Jewish Book during the Nazi Era," an article of central importance for the presentation here, Philip Friedmann notes: "It may be assumed that of the approximately 1,500,000 Jewish families comprising the 6,000,000 Jews killed during the Nazi period, at least several books, religious or profane, in Hebrew, Yiddish and other languages were treasured in every home. There is, however, no way of making an accurate estimate of those stupendous cultural losses."[9] If Schidorsky adds an unknown quantity of smaller holdings to the known larger libraries, increasing his total estimate to four million books affected by the war, this figure can still be considered a low estimate.

Fundamentally speaking, two types of Nazi violence can be distinguished in this stocktaking of the book shelves: Jewish-owned books were either (a) stolen or (b) willfully destroyed. In respect to stolen books and their later restitution, it is useful to differentiate whether books were "confiscated," "seized," or "taken into possession by the authorities" (to quote the wording of that time) for either material or ideological reasons. Those taken for material reasons were, for the most part, destined for the shelves of German public libraries. The others landed in special Nazi collections that, in fact, would help to identify these items at the time of restitution: The upshot of this is that many lost books survived and acquired a certain stratum or imprint of memory precisely because the Nazis pilfered them for their special collections. In her *Eichmann in Jerusalem*, Hannah Arendt recalled this process in a striking formulation: "An eagerness to establish museums commemorating their enemies was very characteristic of the Nazis. During the war, several services competed bitterly for the honor of establishing anti-Jewish museums and libraries. We owe to this strange craze the salvage of many great cultural treasures of European Jewry."[10]

But the destroyed books must not be overlooked in this context. Certainly, only those books that survived National Socialism are today repositories of reminiscence of their former owners. Those that were burned or turned to pulp cannot be. But recollection of the fate of the surviving books would be incomplete without recalling the lot of those destroyed. Both ideologically motivated theft and destruction point up the nature of the National Socialist attitude toward the memory of its Jewish victims: in all cases it was paramount to control this memory. Since the Nazi intention was to preserve the memory of their victims solely in their way, for their own ends, the prerequisite was the need simultaneously to extinguish any trace of Jewish memory itself.[11] So from this perspective, the fate of superfluous material neither of ideological nor material value was sealed: it was doomed to destruction. With respect to the categories of both theft and destruction, each relevant to the theory of memory, a pattern emerged in Germany after January 1933 and in "annexed" Austria from 1938 that in a radicalized form would later be extended, applied in practically all the occupied territories.

Significantly, the first attack on the books of the "enemy" was launched right at the beginning of National Socialist rule. The pyres of burning books in May 1933, officially instigated and implemented in many German university towns by organized student mobs, were meant to provide a first sign of things to come. The new regime demonstrated its grip on power over the printed word, extending all the way to willful extinction.[12] These were still actions driven by a semiotics of power: the new regime wished to draw a clear line between itself and the recent past. Goebbels called the burning of books by Jewish authors and any others somehow associated with the previous Weimar Republic on 10 May 1933 in Berlin a "symbolic act ... meant to document before the eyes of all the world that the intellectual foundations of the November Republic had here been razed. But from these ruins will rise victorious the phoenix of a new spirit."[13] This "symbolic act" was already sufficiently barbaric to evoke the gesture of a coming totality. Book bonfires in which nothing remains but ashes are an effective instrument for extinguishing history or competing memories of the (recent) past.

In the "*Reichskristallnacht*" pogrom of 9/10 November 1938, huge numbers of Jewish books were destroyed in Germany and Austria. In some cases, the libraries attached to synagogues also fell victim to the flames. In addition, targeted violence was directed against a number of Jewish libraries. Numerous Jewish publishing houses were also ransacked and compelled soon thereafter to completely cease all operations. As the war expanded, there was systematic destruction particularly of Jewish *religious* books practically everywhere in the wake of German occupation, most especially and in an extreme form throughout Eastern Europe. Almost everywhere, synagogues were destroyed. In addition, so-called "*Brenn-Kommandos*" (arson squads) set systematic fire in particular to Torah scrolls and religious books. One illustrative example is the destruction of the library of the Yeshiva in Lublin, the largest Talmudic academy in Poland at the time. Many months later a German who had been directly involved gloated in a report in the German press that the Talmudic library had burned on, smoldering for 20 hours. The loud lamentations of the Jews had been drowned out by a military band and the shouts of glee of the Germans.[14] It is estimated that some 70 percent of all Jewish libraries in Poland were destroyed in World War II.[15] Wherever important libraries of the "ideological enemies" beckoned in occupied Europe, "experts" were assigned to decide on their fate. The standard options were to send the contents of book shelves regarded as uninteresting to the local paper mills, or to confiscate and transport the books to libraries, in particular to the National Socialist "research institutes" in Germany.

Ideologically motivated theft of Jewish books can be documented back to the very beginning of Nazi rule. In 1933, "the Jewish book" was declared an "enemy of the people." "Forbidden" Jewish literature on the Nazi index had to be removed from German book stores and the lists of German publishing houses, and placed under lock and key in non-Jewish libraries.[16] This also extended to the reading public: Jews now were not permitted to use general public and scientific libraries. "Permitted" Jewish literature, by contrast, was allowed to appear, published by presses such as the Schocken Verlag, founded in Berlin in 1931. Jewish libraries were allowed to operate up until 1938. This policy aimed at segregating and isolating Jewish readers[17] while "protecting" and warning "Aryan" readers to be wary about "Jewish books" and their contagion.

At the same time, the authorities began to reconnoiter the library landscape, searching for specific Jewish holdings in synagogues, book shops, and private residences. These were of especial interest for the research institutes and libraries that National Socialism had been setting up since the mid-1930s. These institutions, competing among themselves, were meant to pursue "research on the Jewish Question." Among the most prominent were the *Reichsinstitut für Geschichte des Neuen Deutschlands* (Reich Institute for the History of the New Germany) in Munich, founded in 1935 and headed by historian Walter Frank. In 1936, it set up a special department for the "Judenfrage." Another key center, long in preparation, was the *Institut zur Erforschung der Judenfrage* (IEJ; Institute for Research on the Jewish Question), officially inaugurated in Frankfurt am Main in 1941. Operating almost everywhere on the heels of the advance of the Wehrmacht as a kind of chief executive arm of the National Socialist plunder of books was the *Einsatzstab Reichsleiter Rosenberg* (ERR; Operations Staff Reichsleiter Rosenberg).

Quite separate from this were the activities of the *Reichssicherheitshauptamt* (RSHA; Reich Central Security Office), which was independently involved in plundering Jewish books from Germany and Austria. Additional institutes that all wished to acquire books of ideological interest and import for their shelves joined during the war. Pointing to this opaque machinery, Hannah Arendt illustrated one thesis of her *Origins of Totalitarism*, namely, the buraeucratic organization of "scientific anti-Semitism," so important for the Nazis, reflected a kind of "planned shapelessness," or general absence of stability, under the authoritarian rule of Hitler. This stratagem made it possible, hidden behind an array of facades, to strip one institute after another of power.[18] Behind these facades, formed by the established and still existing history departments and the new research centers as well, lay something hidden that was virtually unknown to the public, namely, that the actual center of power, where decisions were made both about the historical role of the Jews and the solution to the Jewish Question, was the RSHA in Berlin.[19] As Arendt notes, that none of these old or new institutes were ever shut down can be viewed in a broader perspective: in this manner, a rivalry immanent to the system was promoted. That intense rivalry rendered the basic activity that accompanied this "research," the destruction of Jews and their culture, seemingly appear irrelevant or secondary.

A 1940 article entitled "Eine Fachbibliothek zur Judenfrage" (A Specialized Library on the Jewish Question) published in the *Historische Zeitschrift* makes clear what criteria were actually relevant for such institutes. The topic is the "acquisitions policy" of the library of the abovementioned *Reichsinstitut für Geschichte des Neuen Deutschlands.* The librarian and author of the article, Günter Schlichting, stressed that new paths had been blazed in Munich.[20] It was important to exclude "internal Jewish materials" that had no relevance for the "Jewish Question." By contrast, it was important "to discover the traces of Jewish influence in non-Jewish intellectual life everywhere." This included Aryan followers of Freud as well as the works of Mischlinge ("half" and "quarter" Jews) "such as Klaus and Erika Mann," etc. A "genealogical research project by the Institute" was to determine whether an author, editor, or associate working on a book was "a Jew, of Jewish descent or had Jewish relatives." Precisely by means of the building up of the library, it proved possible to work out a systematic scheme on the "Jewish Question" for the first time. This was the reason for interest in editions of the Babylonian and Jerusalem Talmud and the Mishna, Tosefta, Midrashim, Targumim and Responsa, "which were often of far-reaching political importance."[21] Apparently there was hardly any subject area that was not of some import. What was significant was the new "method." Although the author was mistaken when he talked about the "largest library in Europe on the Jewish Question" in the future, the library did receive hundreds of thousands of books, in the main pilfered.

This apparently also included the holdings of the library of the Jewish Theological Seminary in Vienna, confiscated in 1938.[22] In the wake of the "Anschluss," there was a radicalization of Nazi policy on books as well. Numerous private holdings and the book shops owned by Austrian Jews were "seized," "emptied," and passed on to interested institutions in Germany and Austria. In July 1938, Eichmann personally paid a visit to the library (closed since March 1938) of the Israelitische Kultusgemeinde in Vienna in order to declare the facility the property of the German state.

A Book Utilization Office was set up in Vienna in 1938, and it is estimated that up until July 1939 in Austria, more than two million books of Jewish and other origin were stolen, sold, or destroyed by the new rulers.[23] In Germany itself, the radicalization in book policy came in conjunction with the November 1938 pogrom. Although it had been anticipated and intended that there would be substantial damage to and loss of cultural assets in the pogrom, Reinhard Heydrich, head of the State Police and the Security Service, had also issued instructions to spare the archives of the Jewish communities from destruction. Important for him was material regarded as "of historical value." In several cities, based on this order, the archives and even libraries of the Gemeinden were protected from the flames and seized by the state.[24] This measure was congruent with the ideologically motivated interest in such collections, which was now followed by action seemingly unbridled. In Berlin, for example, the important library of the Jewish community and its branches was confiscated, in so far as those branches had not been demolished in the pogrom.

Among the new institutes, a fierce rivalry for leadership developed between the IEJ in Frankfurt and the institute in Munich.[25] A significant factor behind this was Alfred Rosenberg, "Deputy of the Führer for the Supervision and Oversight of the Entire Spiritual and Philosophical Schooling and Training of the NSDAP." Rosenberg had had a falling out with Walter Frank. With Hitler's authorization, Rosenberg had plans to establish a Nazi party university called *Hohe Schule*, centred at Chiemsee in Bavaria. Its branches would focus on individual areas of special interest to Nazi ideology, such as communism, freemasonry, racial biology and the like. The *Hohe Schule* itself was never built, but one branch did take shape in 1939: the IEJ. That same year, the central library of the *Hohe Schule* was founded, though in Berlin.

The conquests in the war then made possible a veritable campaign of book plunder of an unknown scope, along with the picture of willful destruction as sketched. In October and November 1939, the RSHA in Berlin directed a commando operation that seized complete libraries and shipped them to Germany, such as the Warsaw libraries of the Sejm and Senate as well as the Jewish library of the Great Synagogue. This involved a total of some 200,000 volumes.[26] Soon thereafter, the Frankfurt IEJ, in close cooperation with the ERR, also entered the field of action. The occupation of the Netherlands, Belgium, and France in May and June 1940 provided an opportunity, covered by a decree from the "Führer," to seize and ship off "written materials suitable for Germany" as well as "ownerless Jewish property" and "cultural assets of manifest value." Rosenberg's operations staffs eagerly grabbed the most famous collections in Amsterdam[27] and Paris, where they plundered the library of the Alliance Israélite Universelle (40,000 volumes) and the book collection of the Rothschild family (28,000 volumes); it was subsequently transported along with the family archives to Frankfurt am Main, packed in 760 crates. After Rosenberg was appointed "Reich Minister for the Occupied Territories" in November 1941, Hitler's above-mentioned order, was now, from March 1942, also applied to the "Eastern territories under civil administration."[28] In southern Europe, German control reached into Greece, in the East to the banks of the Don. An estimate after the war surmised that in Eastern Europe, 375 archives, 957 libraries, 402 museums, and 531 research and educational institutions were affected by these German raids.[29]

On instructions from IEJ "experts," the inspected holdings were to be prepared, usually by Jewish forced laborers, for shipment to Germany or for transfer to paper mills. This was true for example for Vilna, where there were four important Jewish libraries, and Saloniki with its unique Sephardic book culture. There are agonized reports by Jewish forced laborers from Vilna and Saloniki. These individuals were plunged into deep despair, compelled to ready their own cultural items for shipment. Or they engaged in small-scale resistance by smuggling a portion of the books from the collection points.[30]

Up to 1944, the Frankfurt institute was, according to its own reports, sent more than a half million volumes. But other institutes had in the meantime also expressed their "needs," such as the Innsbruck-based *Institut für Rassenkunde* (Institute for Racial Science) or the *Hochschule für Rassenschutz* (Academy for Racial Protection) in Budapest. In 1940, the *Institut für deutsche Ostarbeit* (Institute for German Work in the East) was established in Cracow. In 1941 a branch of the IEJ was opened in Łodz. That same year, a department for Jewish History and Languages was set up at the *Reichsuniversität Posen*, which had a special collection of an estimated 400,000 volumes pilfered from confiscated Jewish libraries.[31]

In regard to the total amount of loot, Rosenberg's units were actually bested by the RSHA: the library of the "Cultural Department" VII in the RSHA, not to be confused with the central library of the *Hohe Schule* in Berlin, grew to an estimated two to three million volumes. Last housed in a synagogue in Berlin-Schöneberg, this library was subdivided into four "adversary libraries": on the "Church," "Freemasonry," "Marxism," and "Judaism."[32] The holdings of the latter comprised the libraries of the Jewish Communities in Berlin, Breslau, Gleiwitz, Hamburg, Königsberg, Warsaw, and Vienna, along with the famous collections of the *Jüdisch-Theologisches Seminar* in Breslau and the *Hochschule für die Wissenschaft des Judentums* in Berlin, as well as private collections. A team of twenty-four Jewish scholars, whose working conditions resembled those in concentration camps, were assigned the job of sorting the books. After the

Allied bombing raids of 1943, which also destroyed hundreds of thousands of the pilfered volumes hoarded here, these scholars were deployed in preparations for transport of the books to safer locations.[33]

Another chapter in the history of libraries under National Socialist occupation worth brief mention here is that of the Jewish ghetto libraries in Kaunas (Kovno), Łodz, Warsaw, Vilna, and other cities. Such improvised libraries had an immensely important function for their readers during the brief span up until the liquidation of the ghetto.[34] One ghetto library was even official, namely, the *Zentralbibliothek Theresienstadt*. It had been set up by the Nazis for propaganda reasons, was run by Jewish librarians, and had its own special official stamp. Its holdings contained an estimated 200,000 books pilfered from across half of Europe from Jewish libraries, including, from 1943 on tens of thousands of Hebrew and Yiddish volumes from the evacuated library of the RSHA.[35] This institution, due to the efforts of its Jewish librarians, in fact did serve the reading needs of the inmates of the Theresienstadt camp. But the cynical dimension is that the SS camp command was especially pleased with and proud of the most illustrious volumes in this collection. They presented the library as a special "exhibit" and proof of the "normalcy" of everyday life in Theresienstadt—while at the same time tens of thousands of prisoners were dying in this very same "model" ghetto, or were deported to the extermination camps.[36] The fate of the users of ghetto libraries was thus also inscribed into hundreds of thousands of books, clearly manifest or only to be surmised.

In the meantime, the "everyday" looting of books from Jewish owners had also taken its course—"everyday" to distinguish it from the ideologically motivated pilfering machinery described above. One purely material motive behind this theft was that for valuable editions, as for works of art, interested buyers could be found in Germany and abroad.[37] As long as it was still possible, emigrating Jews had tried to take along their books.[38] But in many instances it was not possible to transfer the books to their countries of destination. Like other possessions, books and other printed material, such as musical scores, had to be left behind. These were then auctioned off or given away as gifts by the Gestapo or other offices. Buyers for these cultural assets in Germany, generally offered for sale at prices far below their real market value, were non-Jewish Germans or German state libraries. The libraries were often either given the material as a "gift" or specifically requested, that they be accorded such "donations" to supplement their regular shelf holdings. This also was dramatically intensified with the policy shift on Jewish persecution: from emigration to expulsion and on to deportation. Millions of books formerly owned by Jews were now open for acquisition by private interested parties and especially by public state libraries. During the war, the state libraries had an additional material motive: the desire to replace losses suffered in bombing raids. German public libraries were to receive stolen Jewish books indirectly, whether "allotted" or requested. Due to their inclusion into the general holdings, they in effect soon had almost "vanished" from sight.

Restitution Efforts in the Postwar Period

Gershom Scholem is an important contemporary witness of early efforts to restitute stolen books in the years immediately after the war's end. He was among the small number of Jewish contemporaries who now traveled through the ruins of Europe on a sad mission: the question arose in what way at least the surviving books could be saved. Scholem aptly formulated what an appropriate rescue of such books could mean, in a phrasing still valid today. In 1946 in a letter to Leo Baeck he remarked: "We believe, to put it succinctly, that where Jews go to is where their books should go too." („Wir glauben, mit einem Wort, daß dorthin, wo die Juden hinwandern, auch ihre Bücher mitgehen sollen.")[39] The letters and other writings by Scholem in this period are filled with a profound concern about the books of the annihiliated Jewries in Europe. These were books that were no longer in their original localities yet could be found in the space of the destroyed Jewries of Europe. Their former readers were gone. He was deeply concerned to prevent the books from being lost a second time; rather, they should be preserved for a Jewish readership.[40]

On an institutional level, three bodies were especially concerned with such a rescue initiative: the Hebrew University in Jerusalem; the Commission on European Jewish Cultural Reconstruction (CEJCR), established in the summer of 1944 in New York; and the Jewish Cultural Reconstruction, Inc. (JCR), founded in 1947. The two American bodies were based on the cooperation of several already existing Jewish organizations,[41] and both were headed by the historian Salo Wittmayer Baron. Hannah Arendt, who herself was very active in Europe in this matter, had an important function in both bodies.[42] While the CEJCR worked in terms of a program, researching the books to be rescued, the JCR was active as an executive body.

Within the CEJCR, the Research Staff conducted important spadework. It utilized a list prepared by members of the Jewish National and University Library Jerusalem.[43] Supplemented by a number of additions, especially by Jews who had emigrated or fled from Germany and the occupied countries and who had been active in cultural institutions there, a "Tentative List on Jewish Cultural Treasures in Axis-Occupied Countries" was put together, published in 1946 as a supplement to *Jewish Social Studies.* This consciously "tentative" list mentions 430 Jewish libraries, archives, and museums. That is preceded by a listing of fifteen anti-Semitic research institutes that had profited through acquisitions from these holdings. An appendix lists Jewish books in more than 270 larger state and public libraries, museums, and archives. By contrast, synagogues and Jewish cemeteries, "though indubitably among the most characteristic Jewish communal and cultural institutions in all ages," were not included in the list, "for their locations and present fate are easily ascertainable on the spot."[44] This initial list was followed up until 1948 by various addenda and corrigenda and further surveys of former Jewish schools, periodicals, and publishers of Judaica and Hebraica, likewise published as supplements to *Jewish Social Studies.*[45] These form a unique overview of an irretrievably lost culture, and as such constitute a historical document in their own right.

Along with this initial necessary task of listing, the commission right from the start raised the demand for restitution in the broadest sense. The aims were as follows:

> 1. To constitute, together with similar bodies, an Advisory Council to the United Nations in the restoration and/or reconstruction of the cultural aspects of European Jewish life and in the rehabilitation and the redistribution of such Jewish cultural institutions (libraries, museums, schools, archives, etc.) as have been destroyed or confiscated.
> 2. To serve, in collaboration with governmental or intergovernmental agencies, as a Board of Trustees to take charge of and administer Jewish cultural institutions and properties formerly owned by communities now dispersed or by agencies now liquidated.[46]

Here there was a parallel with the problematical nature of the claim to restitution for persecuted Jews more generally. As various Jewish authors, politicians, and institutions stated, existing international law was not adequate for the singular case of the Holocaust in respect to reparations and indemnifications.[47] Established international law privileged nation-states. One consequence was that Jews could not raise their valid claims *as a collective,* although they had been persecuted preciseley as such a transnational collective. As a consequence, they were unable to demand restitution as a recognized subject of international law, analogous to a state. This meant that the still existing possessions of Jews in Europe whose legal owners were no longer living and for whom their were no private heirs or communal successors would fall to the possession of their countries of origin. The demand was now raised that the power to decide about Jewish property where no heirs were present should be given to Jewish institutions under a kind of trusteeship.

In regard to the restitution of books, the CEJCR located its most important partner for discussion in an institution of the occupying American forces, the Offenbach Archival Depot (OAD). In 1945, the American Monuments, Fine Arts & Archives Section had discovered, especially in southern Germany and Thuringia, some 2,000 depots with stolen cultural objects cached in salt mines, castles, and other buildings. In view of the fact that many of the stolen books had been destroyed by Allied bombing raids, the Nazi authorities had ordered the holdings transferred to what were deemed safer locations. The central library of the *Hohe Schule* was evacuated in 1942 from Berlin to the monastery Tanzenberg and other localities in Austria. Rosenberg's *Ostbibliothek* was evacuated to Ratibor, and hundreds of thousands of other books were transferred to depots presumed safe in Silesia and Czechoslovakia. In Frankfurt am Main, portions of the famous collection of Hebraica and Judaica in the Municipal Library had been lost in the flames. The IEJ then secured its holdings by evacuation to localities in rural Hesse.

The discovery of these objects led in May 1946 to the creation of the most important body for the redistribution of stolen books, whether from Jewish or non-Jewish previous ownership. Housed in a former building of I.G. Farben, the OAD gathered together objects from the raids of the Nazis that had been discovered stashed away in the American Zone of Occupation, including portions of the RSHA library in Berlin. The depot employed at times up to 200 personnel, including German workers. It had its own special rubber stamp. The first directors of the institution, the American-Jewish officers Seymour J. Pomrenze, followed by Isaac Bencowitz, reportedly had a good sense for identifying the origin of the books. They had long lists made of library stampings and other markings of possession, according to which the books were then sorted. About half were of Jewish origin. A total of more than 4,000 library stamps were registered, more than 2,000 of which stemmed from Eastern Europe. The OAD saw itself as the exact antipode of the ERR: "reversing the flow started by the Einsatzstab Reichsleiter Rosenberg," as was noted on a map listing the return to the end of 1946 of some 2.5 million books to various cities in Europe.[48]

Up to the final days of the depot, more than 3.2 million volumes were identified and restituted. Most were returned to France and the Netherlands, with the Soviet Union in third place. Even the Prussian State Library received back 700,000 of its volumes evacuated during the war.

An impressive achievement of the OAD was the return of Jewish books: while no Jewish owners or heirs could be located in the case of about half a million books, the OAD did succeed in restituting a number of complete institutional collections. The IEJ in Frankfurt had in many cases not even opened and unpacked the crates sent by the ERR. Thus, for example, the holdings of the *Bibliotheca Rosenthaliana* from Amsterdam were completely restituted, and returned unpacked to their origin. That is also the case for the stolen library holdings of the *Yidisher Visenschaftlicher Institut* (YIVO) in Vilna. The American historian Lucy Dawidowicz was among those who helped to identify these holdings. In the process of that work in Offenbach in 1947, she rediscovered a part of Vilna, the city she had visited shortly before the war:

> I stayed there until June, when my work was successfully completed and I witnessed the removal from the depot of some 420 cases of books and archives to the YIVO Institute in New York. That experience was for me like a dream come true. All through the war years I had been obsessed by recurring fantasies that I might find, even rescue, some of my lost Vilna friends. Finally, I had, in a very tangible way, rescued a part of Vilna, even if it consisted just of inanimate objects—books, mere pieces of paper, the tatters and shards of civilization. But in the course of my melancholy work, I also learned that one could not restore the murdered past to life. One could never put Vilna together again.[49]

In so far as these could be located in Offenbach, they were sent to New York, once a branch but now the main center of YIVO. Along with large-scale transfers, there were also small shipments of books for immediate use, to camps for displaced persons,[50] or a kibbutz where young survivors of the Holocaust had settled. They received the collection of stolen Hebrew books assembled by the arch anti-Semite Julius Streicher.[51]

As exemplary as the policy of restitution practiced by the OAD was, Jewish observers perceived as especially painful the primary principle in accord with existing standards in international law—namely, to return rediscovered cultural assets (including archival holdings, objects of art, and religious objects, along with books) from one *state* to another, that is, exclusively to the countries of origin. Though an application of complaint in accord with international law, this geographic-territorial principle did not guarantee that such restituted books would find any Jewish readers whatsoever, or that they would be made accessible to the small numbers of Jews still living there. The CEJCR thus reiterated its view that the still existing important books and cultural objects should be sent to the centers of Jewish life and learning, doubtless at the time in the United States and mandatory Palestine (and subsequently Israel). Already in 1944, the British-Jewish historian Cecil Roth had proposed that Jewish property without any identifiable heirs should be transferred to the custody of the Hebrew University of Jerusalem.[52] Gershom Scholem, as representative of the Hebrew University in Europe, took a similar position. He himself identified various Hebrew manuscripts in the Offenbach depot. Writing in the paper *Ha'aretz* in October 1947, he noted that the return to the countries of origin had "severely damaged the interests of the Jewish people, whose authority as an organized body which can demand return of its stolen treasures was not recognized."[53] In one of his letters he pointed out that on the basis of this procedure, "large holdings will disappear into Russia and Poland, books about whose future fate we should have no illusions."[54]

But the OAD complied to a large extent with the Jewish demands for recognition of a successor organization. The Americans were initially concerned to arrive at a consensus view with the British, French, and Soviet Allied authorities and with the German Länderrat in the American Zone.[55] But it was soon clear that the Soviets were not prepared to accept either international or internal restitution. For their part, Washington refused to recognize the Soviet annexation of the Baltic countries. In consistent fashion, cultural assets from these countries were excluded from immediate restitution. This related to the above mentioned holdings of YIVO; additionally, until a final decision could be reached, a Baltic Collection was set up in Wiesbaden.

One important initiative was American Military Government Law No. 59, November 1947, issued by General Lucius Clay. It regulated the restitution of identifiable property. In June 1948, Regulation 3 to this law was issued. It recognized the Jewish Restitution Successor Organization (JRSO) established a year earlier as formal claimant in the case of all Jewish property without identifiable heirs.[56] Similar organizations were also recognized in the British and French Zones of Occupation, but not in the Soviet Zone. The JCR was active as part of the JRSO from 1948 to 1951 in Germany. Its main office was initially located in Offenbach, close to the OAD, and then, with regard to the Jewish holdings in the Baltic Collection, moved to Wiesbaden.

In view of the looming closure of the OAD, the efforts of the JCR concentrated initially on the hundreds of thousands of Jewish books for which there were no claimants. They were sent on to numerous Jewish institutions where today there are accessible for the use of generations of readers to come. The JCR distributed 85 percent of these books to Jewish educational institutions in Israel and the United States, 8 percent went to countries in Western Europe (half to England), and the remaining 7 percent to countries such as South Africa, Argentina, Brazil, Austria, and West Germany, including West Berlin. Up until the end, it apparently remained difficult to decide how many of the books should remain for the use of the small Jewish communities left in Germany and Austria, and how many should be redirected to the centers of Jewish life in the United States and Israel.[57] After the OAD closed its doors at the end of August 1949, the JCR concluded its activities in Europe in March 1952.

In Austria the situation was far more complex. At the end of the war, British forces discovered 500,00 to 700,000 volumes cached in the monastery Tanzenberg near St. Veit in Carinthia. These were the holdings of the central library of the *Hohe Schule*, which, beginning in 1942, had been evacuated to Kloster Tanzenberg to escape the bombing raids in Berlin. These books initially had been purchased legally, but probably some 400,000 volumes had been stolen, pilfered from non-Jewish collections such as Soviet university libraries or the Czar's Palace, or taken from confiscated Jewish private libraries. British policy was also to restore the books to their original owners. German office personnel in custody were deployed to sort the books and prepare them for restitution. Up to May 1948, some 450,000 volumes were restituted in this way to European countries.[58]

The Persistence of Pointers to Memory

It was precisely those Jewish books stolen for ideological reasons, destined to be included in the collections of National Socialist research centers and libraries, that proved easiest to locate. These were thus relatively easy to restitute. In many other instances, such a reconstruction was difficult. While National Socialism seized in effect the entire library of European Jewries, the state libraries in the German Reich acquired books formerly owned by Jews, books from Gestapo holdings, and books from the libraries of occupied enemy countries. Thus, Scholem was correct when he wrote with foresight in 1947: "Most of these larger libraries were scattered to the four winds. It is also possible that in part they were integrated into German public libraries, and it will not be easy to identify their presence there."[59]

That is true both for Germany and Austria. The Austrian National Library and the libraries of the University of Vienna had received an immense number of stolen books. A complex legal situation contributed to rendering their return more difficult: the State Treaty signed with the Allies in 1955 specified that German property found in Austria was to be passed on to the Austrian state. But the books pilfered by the Nazis were also subsumed under this category of "German property." Here the Jewish National and University Library (JNUL), in cooperation with the Israelitische Kultusgemeinde Vienna, managed at least to arrange the following compromise with the Austrian government: according to the agreement, part of the books were sent to the JNUL; part from Jewish ownership was given to the National Library in Vienna and to the libraries of the University of Vienna.[60] According to various statements from 1998 and 2000, there were still between 100,000 and 180,000 books formerly owned by Jews housed in Austrian libraries.[61]

In Germany, restitution of lost books had virtually come to a halt after the 1960s. In 1950, the JCR had sent an open appeal to all state libraries in West Germany to attempt to locate and identify possible book holdings that had formerly belonged to Jewish owners. Now the restitution legislation became law in West Germany, but the JCR at this juncture apparently saw few ways to influence actual practice and thus terminated its activities.[62] The search initiated by the JNUL librarian Shlomo Shunami represented a lonely quest and mission, pursued with dedication over a number of years. According to a newspaper report in the *Jerusalem Post* in 1959, Shunami managed to bring some 400,000 volumes to Israel, half of which stemmed from West Germany. Of these, some 100,000 were presented to the JNUL, and the remaining 300,000 were distributed to other libraries in Israel.[63]

If after the expiration of the various legal deadlines hundreds of thousands of lost books apparently still remained in German libraries, there are various reasons for such gaps in restitution. These include intentional cover-up and concealment, a lack of readiness on the part of the libraries, or a lack of adequate knowledge, as well as insufficient information among the surviving former owners or their descendants and heirs, which led to an absence of claimants for the books. When this question resurfaced in the early 1990s, particularly as a result of the work of the *Arbeitsgemeinschaft Kritischer Bibliothekarinnen* (in short: Akribie, the Association of Critical Librarians),[64] various persons determined that from a purely legal standpoint, there was no basis for raising this topic anew.[65] Even for the reunited Germany, there is no clear legal and binding obligation in this regard.[66]

Thus initially it was primarily reports in the press, particularly on initiatives by the critical librarians in Akribie, that informed a broader public about the topic. Thus the weekly newsmagazine *Der Spiegel* carried an article with the sensational title "Bombs in the Basement," which pointed out that a portion of the stolen books, some 250,000, had been handed over to Jewish organizations after the end of the war. "But hundreds of thousands of books, whose owners were scattered across the entire planet, soon vanished from sight."[67] An initiative by the State and University Library Bremen was a thrust in the opposite direction. The specific background in Bremen was that many Jews who fled from the Third Reich or prepared to emigrate had consigned containers with their belongings to shipping companies in the Bremerhaven port. But their possessions had not been sent. In 1942, the Gestapo confiscated the containers and then proceeded to auction off their contents. The State Library Bremen bought 1,500 books at auction, popular cheap novels and valuable first editions alike. On the basis of miniscule markings, such as a hardly legible "JA" in pencil, the abbreviation for "Judenauktion" (Jewish auction), it proved possible to identify a portion of these items. This was largely thanks to the meticulous and painstaking work of a retired school inspector, Elfriede Bannas.

People continued to work with persistence in Bremen, and up until 1997 they were able to return 330 books to their former owners. One illustrative example is the story of the books belonging to Martin Moritz Mayer, who had lived in Berlin and fled with his family in 1939. In his container were editions of Schiller, Heine, and Grillparzer. When his son Henry Mayer learned in Bridgeport, Connecticut, that these books had indeed been identified, he wrote a letter. A half century before he had left Germany together with his family. Now he requested, writing in German in a touching style, for the return of these books.

Yet this exemplary initiative by the State and University Library Bremen long remained an isolated instance. Apparently one reason it was not imitated was the fact that at the very same time, the debate on "looted art" was reaching its high point—a debate that involved especially valuable *German* lost art located *abroad.* In the wake of the political changes after 1990, with the opening up of states formerly controlled by the Soviets, it appeared the time was ripe to demand a return of German cultural objects removed from Germany at the end of the war as well. But under President Boris Yeltsin, the Russian parliament was not prepared to authorize such steps, and other East European states did not rush to satisfy German wishes for restitution. The discourse of "loot" and "trophies" (mobilized especially in relation to Russia) appeared ever more short-sighted and insensitive, the more the German side overlooked the fact that the Third Reich had destroyed vast quanities of cultural treasures specifically in the countries of Eastern Europe. In October 1997, the weekly *Die Zeit* cited the example of the Bremen initiative as an argument against the one-sided character of the debate.[68] In addition, members of the Akribie group joined in the fray, confronting representatives of the debate on German "looted art" with new research on the destruction of Polish libraries in World War II.[69]

But a genuine breakthrough in official German cultural policy regarding any and all forms of lost art did not appear until the international conference in Washington on "Holocaust Era Assets" in 1998. Initiated by the Clinton administration, more than forty countries and numerous NGOs voluntarily agreed to make public unrestituted Jewish assets confiscated by the Nazis, including art and cultural objects. They also agreed to provide financial means for such identification. This step then led in Germany to a clear change in the official position. Thus, a short time later the director of the Prussian State Library expressed the view that it was a moral obligation to check and determine whether German libraries contained books that had been illegally acquired.[70] The new approach was institutionalized in the above-mentioned *Koordinierungsstelle für Kulturgutverluste* (Coordination Office for Lost Cultural Assets). Earlier this office, under a slightly different name, had been set up to deal solely with *German* cultural assets abroad.

In the meantime, a sensitivity for "problematic origins" has been accepted as a moral obligation binding on the German libraries.[71] In April 2003, the *Frankfurter Allgemeine Zeitung* published an article entitled "It was the Attempt to Confiscate an Entire Culture," by Klaus-Dieter Lehmann, director of the foundation Preußischer Kulturbesitz. This new quasi-official and historically broad-ranging viewpoint regards an "offensive stand on the issue"—that is, a pro-active initiative on the part of the libraries—not only as desirable but as absolutely necessary. Lehmann's statement serves as an expression of a new awareness of the nexus between restitution and memory in the view here that the legitimacy of the libraries addressed "as objective repositories of knowledge and cultural memory" is dependent on an open and candid explanation of their illegally acquired holdings.[72]

As indicated above, German libraries are increasingly aware of this task. There is today a vigorous exchange of information on the moral obligation and the appropriate approaches for identifying and restituting lost books.[73] But what if the lost books once again seek their owners, yet cannot find any? The Bremen initiative thus asked: "Should they be treated as icons, archived separately—or simply left in circulation for use by the public?"[74]

Apart from whether these lost books change their location again or not, this problematic is grounded on the persistence of the pointers to memory. Indeed, such pointers persist in massive numbers. In so far as they are in public libraries, restituted or not, the lost books remain potentially accessible to all. In most cases, these are not unique works but technically reproducible objects in the famous sense of Walter Benjamin. Far more than in the case of "looted art," which ultimately is the concern primarily of experts and negotiators, an encounter with a lost book is an everyday occurrence: it can happen unexpectedly, at any time. To that extent, such books are especially democratic media that contain and preserve, beyond their actual content, references and pointers to a specific collective historical fate.

In addition, questions can be raised regarding the original use of the books as well as the nature of the private or institutional collections in which they once were housed. These are questions that lead to a revitalization of a once living culture of the library. So in many respects the lost books are impregnated with a certain "aura" of remembrance.

In the meantime, American libraries that acquired lost books from the JCR after the war are in the forefront of those institutions that have now discovered the dimension of inscribed memory in these books. According to the records of the JCR, the library of Baltimore Hebrew College (now University) received 4,552 items, including books, brochures, and periodicals. All bear stampings that point to their unique origin. The library itself strengthens this awareness by reference to this fact in its online database.[75] A similar case is the University of Iowa Libraries. They have introduced a rubber stamp to honor the history of those books in their holdings that were stolen during the Holocaust and presented to the libraries by the JCR.[76] So it is not just a question of restitution. At stake here more generally is the memory of a catastrophe. The German libraries must also find a suitable form to deal with this reality even in cases where no new owner can be found.

The circumstance that it is actually possible in many places to have an encounter with a "lost book" points to a further aspect—that of a special history of migration: theft and restitution have led to transfers of the lost books themselves in the same measure as these books are now inscribed with the recent history of Jewish migration.[77]

Michel Foucault regarded the "materiality" of books as quasi-museum pieces and the markings and markers of their origin, such as stamps, dedications or ex libris, as an expression of that *heterotopy* that he saw embodied in libraries and museums as sites of a "time that accumulates endlessly."[78] Not only the *times* of the contents described in the books but also the *topoi* with which they are infused appear as pointers to the places of the former readers—as traces, externally readable in books, of "other spaces."

Translated from the German by Bill Templer

Notes

1. David Shavit, "The Emergence of Jewish Public Libraries in Tsarist Russia," *Journal of Library History* 20, no. 3 (1985): 239–252; idem, *Hunger for the Printed Word: Books and Libraries in the Jewish Ghettos of Nazi-Occupied Europe* (Jefferson, N.C./London, 1997), for the flowering in the inter-war period, ibid., chap. 1, 3–40; more generally also Markus Kirchhoff, *Häuser des Buches. Bilder jüdischer Bibliotheken* (Leipzig, 2002).
2. Stadtbibliothek Nürnberg, "Lost Art-Bücher suchen ihre Eigentümer," *Der Bibliotheksdienst* 37, no. 4 (2003): 501–502.
3. Sven Kuttner, "Geraubte Bücher. Jüdische Provenienzen im Restbestand der Bibliothek der 'Forschungsabteilung Judenfrage' in der Bibliothek des Historicums der UB München," *Bibliotheksdienst* 37, no. 8/9 (2003): 1059–1065.
4. Koordinierungsstelle für Kulturgutverluste, Lost Art Internet Database, http://www.lostart.de (28 January 2004).
5. Universitätsbibliothek Bochum/Bibliothek der evangelischen Theologie, Signature: ZI 25.
6. This article can deal only marginally with the question of the restitution of books formerly owned by Jews in Austria. See here Evelyn Adunka, *Der Raub der Bücher—Plünderung in der NS-Zeit und Restitution nach 1945* (Vienna, 2002).
7. Dov Schidorsky, "Das Schicksal jüdischer Bibliotheken im Dritten Reich," in *Bibliotheken während des Nationalsozialismus,* ed. Peter Vodosek and Manfred Komorowsky, part II (Wiesbaden, 1992), 189–222, here 190–191 and 210.
8. "Tentative List of Jewish Cultural Treasures in Axis-Occupied Countries," by The Research Staff of the Commission on European Jewish Cultural Reconstruction, *Jewish Social Studies* 8 (1946), Supplement: 1–103.
9. Philip Friedman, "The Fate of the Jewish Book during the Nazi Era," in *Essays on Jewish Booklore: Articles Selected by Philip Goodman* (New York, 1972), 112–122, 113. Likewise in *Jewish Book Annual* 13 (1957/58); reprinted in *Jewish Book*

Annual 54 (1996/97): 81–94. An important early study is Joshua Starr, "Jewish Cultural Property under Nazi Control," *Jewish Social Studies* 12 (1950): 27–48.

10. Hannah Arendt, *Eichmann in Jerusalem: A Report on the Banality of Evil* (New York, 1994; orig. 1963), 37. The paradox mentioned evidently generates a negative fascination; the disconcerting fact of "rescue" on the basis of the theft is addressed by several library historians, see Schidorsky, "Das Schicksal jüdischer Bibliotheken"; Jacqueline Borin, "Embers of the Soul: The Destruction of Jewish Books and Libraries in Poland during World War II," *Libraries & Culture* 28, no. 4 (1993): 445–460. This idea was formulated very early on by Starr, "Jewish Cultural Property," 28 and 48. Joshua Starr, as editor of *Jewish Social Studies*, was actively involved in early Jewish efforts for restitution. He committed suicide in 1949.
11. This becomes strikingly clear in a related case of the planned museum "einer untergegangenen Rasse" (for a "race gone down to its destruction"), see Dirk Rupnow, *Täter, Opfer, Gedächtnis. Das "jüdische Zentralmuseum" in Prag 1942–1945* (Vienna, 2000), as well as literature cited there in the epilogue, 200–210.
12. See Leo Löwenthal, "Calibans Erbe. Bücherverbrennungen und kulturelle Verdrängungsmechanismen," in *Kanon und Zensur. Archäologie der literarischen Kommunikation II*, ed. Aleida and Jan Assmann (Munich, 1987), 227–236.
13. Quoted ibid., 230.
14. Friedman, "The Fate of the Jewish Book," 114–115; on Poland, see the general overview in Borin, *Embers of the Soul.*
15. Friedman, "The Fate of the Jewish Book," 120.
16. See Volker Dahm, *Das Jüdische Buch im Dritten Reich*, 2nd rev. ed. (Munich, 1993); Manfred Komorowski, "Die wissenschaftlichen Bibliotheken während des Nationalsozialismus," in *Bibliotheken während des Nationalsozialismus*, part I (Wiesbaden, 1989), 1–23.
17. As intended by the Nazis, the libraries of the Jewish Gemeinden had a marked increase in readers. The profile of those readers seems to have shifted though. In the case of the Gemeinde library in Berlin, for example, it was noted in 1934 that Jews from Eastern Europe had made up the largest single group in library users before, but that now "physicians, lawyers, and dismissed public prosecutors were a major contingent." The Nazi measures appeared to be sparking a greater interest among Jews in Palestine: "Assimilated Jews who wished to learn more … about Zionism accounted for a large number of readers. But a huge contingent were young people who were preparing to go to Palestine.… While earlier only the rabbis or Talmudically trained Jews used the library, now everyone was going there." T[heodor] Simon, "Plaudereien in der jüdischen Bibliothek," *Jüdische Rundschau* 39, no. 67 (1934), 21 August 1934, 9.
18. Hannah Arendt, *The Origins of Totalitarianism* (New York, 1951), 383f.
19. Ibid.
20. Günter Schlichting, "Eine Fachbibliothek zur Judenfrage. Die Münchener Bibliothek des Reichsinstituts für Geschichte des Neuen Deutschlands," *Historische Zeitschrift* 162 (1940): 567–572, quotes 567.
21. Ibid., 568, 569, 571.
22. Presumably parts of the Grand Synagogue in ul. Tłomackie in Warsaw plundered in 1939. Portions of the holdings evacuated in 1943 are stored today in several American university libraries and in the Historicum of the University of Munich.

On this also: "Antisemitica. 'Forschungsabteilung Judenfrage:' Eine Münchener Bibliothek," *Süddeutsche Zeitung*, 13 November 2001.

23. Adunka, *Der Raub der Bücher*, 72f. and 86–89.
24. Friedman, "The Fate of the Jewish Book," 116; Starr, "Jewish Cultural Property under Nazi Control," 29–30; Schidorsky, "Das Schicksal jüdischer Bibliotheken," 193.
25. Dieter Schiefelbein, *Das "Institut zur Erforschung der Judenfrage Frankfurt am Main." Vorgeschichte und Gründung 1935–1939* (Frankfurt a.M., 1993) and idem, "Das 'Institut zur Erforschung der Judenfrage Frankfurt am Main.' Antisemitismus als Karrieresprungbrett im NS-Staat," in *Jahrbuch 1998/99 zur Geschichte und Wirkung des Holocaust*, ed. Fritz Bauer Institut (Frankfurt a.M., New York, 1999), 43–71.
26. The library for Jewish Studies of the Great Synagogue of Tłomackie contained 40,000 volumes. After its plunder, the teacher Chaim A. Kaplan noted in his famous Warsaw diary: "This is a burning of the soul of Polish Jewry, for this library was our spiritual sanctuary where we found respite when troubles came to us. Now the fountain which slaked our thirst for Torah knowledge is dried up." Chaim A. Kaplan, *Scroll of Agony: The Warsaw Diary of Chaim A. Kaplan*, ed. and trans. Abraham I. Katsh (New York, 1965), 105. Original Hebrew: C. A. Kaplan, *Megilat Yissurin – Yoman Getto Varsha, September 1, 1939–August 4, 1942* (Tel Aviv/Jerusalem, 1966).
27. In Amsterdam, for example, the library of the Portuguese Jewish seminary Ets Haim, going back to the seventeenth century, and two theological libraries were confiscated; just from the Bibliotheca Rosenthaliana alone, 153 crates were put together and prepared for shipment to the IEJ, containing a total of 60,000 books.
28. Reinhard Bollums, Art. "Einsatzstab Reichsleiter Rosenberg," in *Enzyklopädie des Nationalsozialismus*, ed. Wolfgang Benz, Hermann Graml and Hermann Weiß, Digital Library Vol. 25, CD-ROM (Berlin, 1999), 1237–1277.
29. Friedman, "The Fate of the Jewish Book," 117.
30. Ibid., 118f.; Starr, "Jewish Cultural Property under Nazi Control"; Maria Kühn-Ludewig, *Johannes Pohl (1904–1960). Judaist und Bibliothekar im Dienste Rosenbergs. Eine biographische Dokumentation* (Hannover, 2000), 153–161, 184–196, 230–234.
31. "Tentative List of Jewish Cultural Treasures," 9–11.
32. Schidorsky, "Das Schicksal jüdischer Bibliotheken," 193–197. Commenting on the Department for Judaism, it notes: "A Jewish library was assembled in the RSHA so large and complete as probably could not be found anywhere else." Ibid., 194.
33. Ibid., 212–214; idem, "Confiscation of Libraries and Assignments to Forced Labour: Two Documents of the Holocaust," *Libraries & Culture* 33 (1998): 347–388.
34. The most important study on this: Shavit, *Hunger for the Printed Word*; see also *Bücher und Bibliotheken in Ghettos und Lagern (1933–1945)*, ed. Raimund Dehmlow (Hannover, 1991).
35. Adunka, *Der Raub der Bücher*, 82.
36. Karl Braun, "Die Bibliothek in Theresienstadt 1942–1945. Zur Rolle einer Leseinstitution in der 'Endlösung der Judenfrage'," *Bohemia* 40, no. 2 (1999): 367–386; Kornelia Richter, "Lesen im Ghetto Theresienstadt," in: *Bücher und Bibliotheken in Ghettos und Lagern*, 43–56.
37. Art and rare books owned by Jews were sent abroad by agents in return for foreign currency. Even before the war, the contents of the Jewish Museum Berlin were

dealt with in this manner on the instructions of the Reich finance minister; Friedman, "The Fate of the Jewish Book," 115.

38. This for example is the reason for the many editions of the German classics or modern Jewish authors that made their way to Palestine; Dov Schidorsky, "Germany in the Holy Land. Its Involvement and Impact on Library Development in Palestine and Israel," *Libri* 49 (1999): 26–42, here 35–39.
39. Gershom Scholem, *Briefe* I, 1914–1947, ed. Itta Shedletzky (Munich, 1994), 314–317, quote 316.
40. Ibid., see the letters nos. 132–137, 139 and 141.
41. Organizationally the Commission was part of the Conference on Jewish Relations based in New York.
42. Arendt was initially coordinator of the Research Staff of the CEJCR, and from 1949 to 1952 Executive Secretary of the JCR, on whose behalf she traveled to Europe six times. As seen, the knowledge and insight she gained on these trips regarding cultural theft by the Nazis is reflected in her publications. See Elisabeth Young-Bruehl, *Hannah Arendt: For Love of the World* (New Haven/London, 1982), 187f.
43. Participants were Gershom Scholem and the librarians Gotthold Weil und Daniel Goldschmidt, who emigrated after 1933 from Germany. See Schidorski, "Das Schicksal jüdischer Bibliotheken im Dritten Reich," 190.
44. Here once more full bibliographical data: "Tentative List of Jewish Cultural Treasures in Axis-Occupied Countries, [by] The Research Staff of the Commission on European Jewish Cultural Reconstruction," *Jewish Social Studies* 8 (1946), Supplement: 1–103. See there also Introductory Statement, 5–9, quote ibid., 7.
45. The further overviews which all appeared as supplements to *Jewish Social Studies* (JSS) are: "Tentative List of Jewish Educational Institutions in Axis-Occupied Countries," *JSS* 8 (1946); "Tentative List of Jewish Periodicals," *JSS* 9 (1947); "Addenda and Corrigenda to the Tentative List of Jewish Cultural Treasures," *JSS* 10 (1948); "Tentative List of Jewish Publishers of Judaica and Hebraica," *JSS* 10 (1948).
46. "Tentative List of Jewish Cultural Treasures," 5–6.
47. This is the title of the book by Nehemiah Robinson, *Indemnification and Reparations: Jewish Aspects*, ed. Institute of Jewish Affairs of the American Jewish Congress and World Jewish Congress (New York, 1944). That book played an important role inter alia in the reparations agreements between West Germany on the one hand and Israel and the Claims Conference on the other; a good overview is provided in Nana Sagi, *German Reparations: A History of the Negotiations* (Jerusalem, 1980).
48. F. J. Hoogewoud, "The Nazi Looting of Books and its American 'Antithesis': Selected Pictures from the Offenbach Archival Depot's Photographic History and Its Supplement," *Studia Rosenthaliana* 26 (1992): 158–192, here 167–173, map 192.
49. Lucy S. Dawidowicz, *What is the Use of Jewish History: Essays*, ed. Neal Kozodoy (New York, 1992), 37.
50. Hoogewoud, "The Nazi Looting," 170.
51. Friedman, "The Fate of the Jewish Book," 122.
52. Cecil Roth, "The Restoration of Jewish Libraries, Archives and Museums," *Contemporary Jewish Record* 8 (June 1944), 253–257.
53. Gershom Scholem, "Zur Frage der geplünderten jüdischen Bibliotheken, aus dem hebr. Typoskript in dt. Übers.," in: Scholem, *Briefe* I, appendix, 472–478, quote 476.

54. Scholem, *Briefe* I, 315. In Czechoslovakia, where he observed salvage operations from the book caches the Nazi authorities had hidden, he did not presume to address the question of the fate of books formerly owned by Jews when Hebraica or Judaica were not clearly involved. His hope was that the Hebrew University would be appointed trustee for the Hebraica rescued from the Theresienstadt ghetto library, some 30,000 volumes. Ibid., 318, 328. In the event, most of the volumes from Theresienstadt were passed on to the State Library of the Jewish Museum in Prague. Nonetheless, 30,000 volumes from the books found in Czechoslovakia were transferred to the Jewish National and University Library, see Adunka, *Der Raub der Bücher*, 83f.
55. For a detailed treatment, see Michael J. Kurtz, *Nazi Contraband: American Policy on the Return of European Cultural Treasures, 1945–1955* (New York and London, 1985), chap. 7, 198–225.
56. Jewish Restitution Successor Organizations are organizations for searching out and restituting Jewish property without identifiable heirs. Their goal is to use these assets in particular to assist surviving Jewish victims of the Nazis.
57. Kurtz, *Nazi Contraband*, 218–220.
58. To France 217,000, to the Soviet Union 64,000, to the Netherlands 90,000 volumes. A detailed account of this in Adunka, *Der Raub der Bücher*, chap. 1, 15–70.
59. Scholem, "Zur Frage der geplünderten jüdischen Bibliotheken," 476.
60. Adunka, *Raub der Bücher*, passim.
61. Ibid., 206.
62. Kurtz, *Nazi Contraband*, 224–5.
63. Adunka, *Der Raub der Bücher*, 165.
64. See the important documentation *Displaced Books. Bücherrückgabe aus zweierlei Sicht. Beiträge und Materialien in Zusammenhang von NS-Zeit und Krieg*, Laurentius Sonderheft, ed. Maria Kühn-Ludewig für den Arbeitskreis kritischer BibliothekarInnen (Akribie), 2nd ed. (Hannover, 1999).
65. The federal finance minister wrote in 1991: "There is no longer any legal obligation ... to restitute property.... Where property items formerly owned by Jews could not be returned, the victims or successor organizations have received compensation on the basis of regulations on restitution." If further stolen property should be found, then "the decision for the return of former Jewish property is in the power of the respective institution itself." See *Displaced Books*, 77.
66. This can be derived from the generally rather complex legal situation regarding restitution in reunited Germany. In the German-German Unification Treaty of 1990, West German restitution legislation from the 1950s and 1960s was taken over, but de facto "it was a transfer of dead law." Christian Meyer-Seitz, "Die Entwicklung der Rückerstattung in den neuen Bundesländern seit 1989. Eine juristische Perspektive," in *"Arisierung" und Restitution. Die Rückerstattung jüdischen Eigentums in Deutschland und Österreich nach 1945 und 1989*, ed. Constantin Goschler and Jürgen Lillteicher (Göttingen, 2002), 265–279, quote 269. That same year, a united Germany, under the 2 + 4 Agreement, was confronted with a demand of the former Western Allies to guarantee reparations for victims of Nazi persecution in the territory covered by the agreement. In principle, this meant that the Federal Republic was obligated to apply Western restitution in the territory of the former GDR. After numerous improvements, the Vermögensgesetz (Law on Assets) and its interpretation can be

regarded as a fair basis for restitution of Jewish assets confiscated after 1933; this is the conclusion of the legal expert Meyer-Seitz, ibid., 276–279.

67. "Bomben im Keller. Die Bremer Staatsbibliothek will von Nazis geraubte Kunstgegenstände den jüdischen Eigentümern zurückgeben," *Der Spiegel* 46, 1992, Heft 34, 59–65, quote 61.
68. Rolf Michaelis, "Worüber kein Gras wächst. Beutekunst—andersrum. Eine Tagung in Bremen über den Skandal geraubter Bücher aus jüdischem Besitz in deutschen Bibliotheken," *Die Zeit*, 10 October 1997.
69. According to what is now known, two thirds of the Polish library holdings, which amounted in 1939 to 60 million volumes, were destroyed, principally by intentional theft and conscious destruction operations. Andrzej Mezynski, "Die Verluste der polnischen Bibliotheken während des Zweiten Weltkrieges im Lichte neuer Archivforschungen," in *Displaced Books*, 34–39.
70. "Pressemitteilung des Laurentius-Verlages Hannover," 2 September 1999, in *Displaced Books*, 88f. The director was regarded earlier as the principal spokesperson in the German debate on "looted art." See ibid., 32f.
71. Ulrich Schmidt, "'Problematische Provenienzen'. Wieviele geraubte jüdische Bücher stehen in deutschen Bibliotheken?," *Jüdische Allgemeine. Wochenzeitschrift für Politik, Religion und jüdisches Leben*, no. 2 (2003), 16 January 2003.
72. Klaus-Dieter Lehmann, "Es war der Versuch, eine ganze Kultur zu beschlagnahmen. Beuteschriften: Zur Diskussion um Bücher aus jüdischem Eigentum in deutschen Bibliotheken," *Frankfurter Allgemeine Zeitung*, 1 April 2003, 38.
73. See, for example, Ragnhild Rabius, "Kombination und Kriminalistik. Die Niedersächsische Landesbibliothek lud ein zum Workshop 'NS-Raubgut und Restitution in Bibliotheken'," *Der Bibliotheksdienst* 38, no. 1 (2004): 66–70.
74. Thus the sense of helplessness presented in the following article "Displaced books. Über Rückgabe enteigneter Bücher wird gestritten," *taz Bremen*, 11/12 October 1997, reprinted in: *Displaced books*, 75.
75. Baltimore Hebrew University, The Joseph Meyerhoff Library/Jewish Cultural Reconstruction Books, http://www.bhu.edu/meyerhoff/#JewCult (16 January 2004). To view JCR records in the BHU Library online catalogue: Select Advanced Search from the drop-down menu, choose Notes in the Search box, type Jewish Cultural Reconstruction, click on Search, scroll down to browse the listing of titles.
76. The bookplate reads: "This book was one of millions of books and documents confiscated from their owners by the German National Socialist (NAZI) Government. At the end of World War II, it passed through a U.S. Army processing center in Offenbach, Germany, which was unable to determine its prior owner or country of origin and became one of 500,000 books placed in the hands of the Jewish Cultural Reconstruction, Inc. for distribution to American colleges and universities. In this way, it came into the collection of the University of Iowa Libraries in 1951." See University of Iowa News Service, http://www.uiowa.edu/~ournews/2001/april/0424holocaust.html (16 January 2004).
77. See Kirchhoff, *Häuser des Buches*, chap. 7.
78. Michel Foucault, "Andere Räume," in *AISTHESIS. Wahrnehmung heute oder Perspektiven einer anderen Ästhetik. Essays* (Leipzig, 1990), 34–46, here 43.

— *Ten* —

RESTITUTION AND RECONSTRUCTED IDENTITY: JEWISH PROPERTY AND COLLECTIVE SELF-AWARENESS IN CENTRAL EUROPE

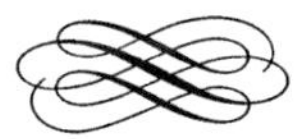

Catherine Horel

Since the fall of communism in East Central Europe, the question of the restitution of confiscated property in general, and more precisely of Jewish property, has been pointedly raised in the three countries considered in this article.[1] Nowadays, the process of restitution or compensation is still ongoing in the Czech and Slovak Republics, while it seems to be almost nearing its conclusion in Hungary. In the three countries, the restitution of the property confiscated by the Nazis and then by the communist regimes has raised many problems, even sparking polemics. This was compounded by another question: the compensation for the sufferings endured by the Jews under Nazism as well as under communist rule. Thus, the terms of restitution and compensation refer to two different processes: the first being restitution, generally to the communities, of real estate properties lost, and the compensation granted to the individuals or their descendants for stolen property and assets; and second, the matter of moral compensation for the persecution and hardship endured.

So Czech, Slovak, and Hungarian society are rediscovering the existence of the Jews in their midst. But of course their number is now far less than it was before 1945. After the Second World War, Hungary had the largest Jewish population in East Central and Eastern Europe, second only to Soviet Russia, and this is still the case today. The Hungarian community is estimated to be nearly 100,000, a large number compared with the 10,000 Czech Jews and 1,500 to 3,000 Jews in Slovakia, for example.

The problem of restitution and compensation of confiscated property involves questions concerning politics, economy, law, sociology, culture, and religion. In the three societies under focus here, the debate gave rise to an array of polemics and resistance, not only critical of the Jews, but formed in more general terms. The confiscations were carried out with two categories of benefactor in mind, the state (i.e., national government) and the municipalities. If the national government restitutes or compensates in keeping with the laws of the land, it is sometimes difficult to compel the municipalities to return buildings they use as common good. The restitution or compensation then principally benefits the communities, and only partially trickles down to the individuals.

In order to investigate the process of restitution, it is necessary to look back at the different confiscations before and during the Second World War and at the beginning of the communist period. Here, of particular interest is the fact that numerous Jews who had survived the Holocaust were unable to regain possession of their property, which was immediately seized by the communists. In this way, they were twice victimized, and thus subjected to what can be called *double discrimination.* The first confiscations carried out in Hungary by the Hungarian government were between 1938 and 1944. The Slovak regime of Monsignor Jozef Tiso, authoritarian ruler of Slovakia and a quisling backed by the Nazis, began expropriating Jewish property already in 1939. The German authorities seized Jewish property in the Czech Lands immediately after invading the country in 1939. The feeble attempts at restitution undertaken after the war were quickly repealed by the establishment of the newly installed communist regimes. These new rulers perpetrated further expropriations of property and using the pretext of nationalization and elimination of all "remnants of the capitalist system." Later on, they used the disappearance of Jewish communities in many towns as a pretext for razing the synagogues there for purposes of "urban renewal."

Slovakia: A Slow and Conflict-Ridden Process

Two essential dates need to be recalled to understand the Slovak case. First of all, the particular conditions of application of the Restitution Law 255/1946 Col., which sought to create a basis for compensation legislation. Following the difficult enactment of this law by the Slovak authorities, some individuals were legally able to assert their rights. Thus, the dwellings owned and inhabited by Jews before their displacement and deportation were for the most part restituted, on condition that the claimant prove himself or herself rightful original owner, as well as having been in continuous occupancy of the residence in the years previous to the war. Last but by no means least, the claimant had to prove his/her allegiance to Slovakia and not be suspected of harboring pro-Magyar or pro-German feelings. In spite of these constraining restrictions, the restitution of the properties intended for permanent habitation was apparently well handled.[2] By contrast, the properties left heirless and not claimed in a short period after the war, or belonging to Jews who had settled abroad, were not subject to any process of restitution.

Second, during the regime of Jozef Tiso, although almost all Jewish private property was seized, the Slovak state did not confiscate the properties of the communities, except in very rare exceptions.[3] Thus, the Jewish communities were able to reoccupy their buildings already in 1945. The problem was dealt with within the communities themselves, decimated by the deportations: they were unable to make full use of this possibility for extra space. The existence of empty and deteriorated buildings offered an excellent pretext for the communist regime later on to seize or to destroy them in the course of "urban renewal" (*asanácia*) operations.

The restitution claims should be examined on two levels: (1) in connection with the confiscations of private property carried out in 1939–45 by the Tiso-dominated Slovak state; and (2) in connection with the expropriation of private and community properties carried out by the communist regime from 1948 to 1989. The first step was grounded on Czechoslovak federal laws. It concerned the assets expropriated or taken under communist rule from 25 February 1948 on: confiscations, forced sales, or bestowals. Enacted in 1990 and 1991, the two texts 403/90 and 87/91 did not apply solely to Jewish properties. Nevertheless, they provide a sound legal basis for further claims from individual Jews. However, these laws apply to private persons as well as to legal entities; the first did not require that claimants be citizens of the Czechoslovak Republic or permanent residents of the country, while this was specified in the second law. The period for registering restitution claims was fixed as valid up until 1994 for the first law, but it was then extended to 1995 after approval of the second text.[4]

These two laws enacted before the breakup of the Czechoslovak Federation have been taken over, with all their faults, by the two independent countries. The specific Slovak feature is the enactment of a new law by the National Council of the Slovak Republic. On 27 October 1993 the Slovak Parliament passed Bill 282/1993 on the restitution of properties to the religious communities. The general frame of the law mentions the period covered as 8 May 1945 to 31 December 1989, which means it is relevant for the confiscations perpetrated by the communist regime against the Jewish communities as well as against the Christian churches. But in the case of the Jewish communities, a special clause extends this period back to the years of fascist rule, stipulating that valid claims begin on 2 November 1938.[5] The requests should then be put forward by representatives empowered by the communities and submitted before 31 December 1994 to the competent authorities.[6] Only at the end of this process does the Slovak national government intend to promulgate the separation of church and state. But the paradox lies in the fact that the state is at the same time judge and party for a significant proportion of the properties claimed by the different churches that happen to be in state possession.

The other main owner of the properties belonging to the religious communities are the municipalities. Just like the national government, the city councils are obliged to restitute properties claimed by the churches. If a municipality refuses to proceed with restitution of one or several buildings, the law allows the possibility of suing the recalcitrant councils within a period of 15 months after the closing date for the registration of the claims, in this case 31 March 1996.[7] This disposition indicates that the legislators were well aware of the problems that could arise at the end of the registration of the claims. But if Slovakia actually has a unique law on this matter when contrasted with the two other countries, it differs in respect to the difficulties and the slowness of its application process.

The conflicts appear on two levels. On the one hand, they emerge in the restitution process concerning private property according to the Czechoslovak federal law from 1991. It is very easy to realize that it remains almost impossible to restitute private property owing to a loophole in the law: if the present owner of the assets or his heirs is able to prove property rights by a permanent occupancy and possession over a period of at least 50 years, then restitution is impossible. Thus even if documents still showing the name of the former Jewish owner can be found, the law assigns rights to the present resident, since in effect possession is nine-tenths of the law. This disposition completely ravages the restitution process for private property. Indeed, according to František Alexander, it appears that we are observing a kind of Aryanization "twice legalized."[8] Besides, in most cases it is impossible to advance the suit so far, since private individuals are unable to prove that the property they possessed was the subject of a forced sale or bestowal (i.e., expropriation). Such a process could be set in motion only in the case of assets that had remained without a rightful heir in 1948. But these properties are not mentioned in the legislation, so it is impossible for the Central Union of the Jewish communities of Slovakia to claim them.

In the field of the community properties, the results differ. It is not surprising to learn that the Jewish community of Bratislava was able to recover a certain number of buildings. While the restitution process developed smoothly and rapidly in Bratislava, several Jewish communities in the provinces experienced serious difficulties with the local administration. Thus, the second largest community in the country, Košice, which was the main center of the Jewish life in eastern Slovakia before the war, has not yet succeeded in obtaining restitution of its buildings, while some smaller communities have by contrast managed to achieve their goals.[9] In Košice, only the Orthodox synagogue is used as a place of worship and congregation, while the two other synagogues still remain in the hands of the town's administration.[10]

The estimate is that 80 percent of the Slovak synagogues were destroyed, which is all the more lamentable because this destruction was equally at the hands of the communist regime.[11] The synagogues were then razed under several pretexts; the one invoked most frequently was "urban renewal" in the case of dilapidated buildings that could not be claimed by communities that no longer existed. Almost eighty synagogues still stand, but most of them are devastated, when they are not used for purposes far removed from their original aims. The municipalities are happy to restitute the derelict synagogues; the problem arises when the municipality uses one or several buildings for purposes it considers essential for municipal services, such as schools, gymnasia, dispensaries, and so on.

The case of the cemeteries is more simple. They have been razed, or are situated in desolate areas of no interest for the immediate town, and thus have been preserved. Or they owe their preservation to the fact that they are more or less part of a Christian entity, like the two cemeteries of Bratislava, the Orthodox and the Neolog, which are next to the large cemetery of Žižkova Street, not far from the Mausoleum of the great Rabbi Moses Sofer, which the communist authorities did not dare to violate. Thus it is estimated that about 600 cemeteries still exist, placed under the responsibility of the Central Union of Jewish Communities. However, the Union has little money to take care of them.[12] A lack of money is in fact the essential problem created by successful restitution.

The revival, even simply to keep Jewish memory alive, often exceeds the financial possibilities of the communities. These find themselves dependent on external support if they wish to preserve their restituted properties and avoid irreversible dilapidation.

The Czech Republic: A Seemingly Positive Situation

In the Czech Republic, the solution of the restitution problem in general quickly became a political issue that went far beyond the national frame, and emerged long before the breakup of Czechoslovakia into the Czech and Slovak states. Like elsewhere, the democratic transition required the need for acknowledging the harm done to private persons during the communist era and needed reparations. But in the case of the Jews, the confiscations and *a fortiori* the crimes were also actions perpetrated by the authorities of the Protectorate and the Nazis. The choice of the dates considered for the validity of the restitution claims appears to be very problematic: by including the period prior to 1948, the government exposes itself to the potential claims of German expellees, a highly sensitive issue. Initially then, the first restitutions dealt only with the communist period. The dispute about the dates became a real bone of contention between the Czech and Slovak Federative Republic, and later the Czech Republic on one side, and the Federal Republic of Germany as well as Austria on the other. Slovakia did not experience these kinds of problems with Hungary, for the measures of expulsion concerned less than 100,000 Hungarians.[13] The Slovak-Hungarian dispute today is centered on the situation of the Hungarian minority living in Slovakia. Nevertheless, an agreement was signed between Germany and the Czech Republic renouncing the restitution of property belonging to the Germans expelled from the Sudeten.

The compensations granted by Germany since the middle of the 1950s were awarded only to Holocaust survivors in the West. They were distributed by the Federal Republic of Germany on the condition that the German Democratic Republic should provide the same type of possibilities as regards Nazi victims in the Eastern bloc. But that did not occur. Following the Luxembourg Agreement of 1952, the *Bundesentschädigungsgesetz* (BEG) was passed in the years 1953–57.

At the beginning of the compensation process, most of the international Jewish organizations played an important role in creating an institution in charge of receiving and handing the claims, the Conference on Jewish Material Claims against Germany, abbreviated later as the Claims Conference, which was party to the 1952 agreement. After the closing of the term for the claims in 1965 (extended to 1969), the Claims Conference was entitled to distribute the sums. In 1980, the Federal Republic of Germany signed bilateral agreements with twelve countries, which led to a new assignment of sums, the Hardship Fund, again distributed by the Claims Conference.[14]

Following the breakup of Czechoslovakia, the Czech authorities resumed their talks with their German counterparts in order to achieve an agreement on the Holocaust issue. The first round of talks ended in 1992 with no results. After a second negotiation, a Czech-German declaration was signed, but this too proved unable to lead to individual compensation. The other problem was that once again, no mention was made of the specific fate of the Jews: all victims of the Nazi era were considered on an equal footing before the eyes of the law. And last but not least, the declaration stated that only the needy and disabled could be eligible to help. The Fund for the Future (*Fond budouctnosti*) established by the declaration is meant to provide indirect help in the form of shelter, nursing homes, medical or social care. It was criticized by the Czech Federation of Jewish Communities and by the foundation *Terezínská Iniciativa.* They stated on the one hand that most of those affected would die waiting for hospitals to be constructed, and on the other that it is somehow unjust to help only the poor, sick, and disabled. It was argued that compensation should not be granted in recognition of the present condition of the claimants but rather with regard to their suffering endured in the past. The Federation of Jewish Communities is still trying to convince the authorities to adopt a system of individual compensation for the Jewish victims.[15] Since then, the Fund for the Future has established that about 9,000 survivors of the Nazi persecutions live in Czechoslovakia, among them some 2,000 to 2,500 Jews. To date, approximately 6,200 persons have applied for assistance from the Fund, but not all are going to receive help. The recipients are registered in three categories: the first takes into account people who have suffered up to 9 months of deportation, awarding them 17,000 Czech crowns a year (US$450); the second category extends up to 30 months, with 40,000 Czech crowns ($1,000); and the last one include individuals deported more than 31 months. They are entitled to receive 60,000 Czech crowns ($1,600) annuity.[16] After 1989, Czechoslovakia finally decided to indemnify the Czech victims of the Nazis and of communism on the basis of two laws enacted in 1990 and 1991, already mentioned for Slovakia. These laws concern all private persons, with no particular reference introduced in the texts to single out the Jews. Well aware of the near impossibility of restitution of the properties of private persons, the Jewish Community of Czechoslovakia and later of the Czech Republic concentrated its efforts on community assets. By contrast in Hungary, as we will see, the struggle dealt far more with individual private property and moral compensation.

In 1992, the community elaborated a list of common properties potentially subject to restitution. From the 1,000 records of communal Jewish property assembled by the Federation of Communities, 130 buildings were registered.[17] The Czech government then prepared a very simple law stipulating the direct transfer of public properties to the community. But the project, drawn up under the responsibility of the leader of the Czech government at this time, Petr Pithart, coincided with the campaign for the parliamentary elections of June 1992. Already then, efforts were under way to block the system of the Federation from within. Actually, in order to see a law enacted, the text first had to be approved by the Czech Parliament before being introduced in the Federal Parliament. The Federation was then composed of three legislative bodies: the two parliaments, Czech and Slovak, and the Federal Parliament. Thus, the law brought in by the Pithart government was quickly buried. Parallel with the renunciation to this project, another law was drafted to help deal with the expense of the dysfunctional federation. This was the law on church properties, which could have enabled the Jewish communities to recover a portion of their communal assets and property. But the text included only the communist period; finally, it was defeated and died on the floor due to the negative vote of a few Slovak representatives.[18]

In the period following the breakup of the Federation, the problem of restitution seemed to disappear from the front pages, because the various political parties as a whole were hostile in principle to the restitution process. The leading party in the government coalition, the Civic Democratic Party (*Obcanská Demokratická Strana*, ODS) of Prime Minister Václav Klaus, declared itself against the restitution of property. It put forward as pretext the danger of causing new injustices, especially to the municipalities, which would then be obliged to return buildings they use for the benefit of the entire collectivity. The ODS believed the towns should restitute only the buildings directly claimed from them, which implies that in localities where there is no Jewish population (most localities in the country, in fact), there would be no reason to restitute. This argument paid scant attention to the Federation of Jewish Communities, a body that acts on behalf of the Jewish community as a whole, raising claims more broadly and not case by case. Yet, this approach was to become ever more the prevailing rule.

The other parties, namely the Social Democratic Party and the former communists, are also opposed to the restitution principle, in this loyal to their attitude in the postwar period. Finally, it was the small party of the Civic Democratic Alliance (*Obcanská Demokratická Aliance*, ODA), a member of the government coalition, that made restitution a favorite issue, since after the failure of the Pithart project nothing had been settled in this matter. The laws regarding private persons had come into force, but there was a necessity to legislate on the question of communal properties because the towns did not spontaneously return the buildings. Theoretically, a majority of three-fifths of the city council should be enough for returning a building. The leaders of the Jewish community were then eager to put forward their claims to the government coalition, and they gained the favorable attention of several members of the ODA. The representative of the district of Plzeň in western Bohemia, Viktor Dobal, began to ponder a new bill that would reenact the essential elements of Pithart's project.The text elaborated by Viktor Dobal consisted of three topical sections: properties of private persons, landed properties, and other real estate. The last two paragraphs concerned communal property and were directly inspired by the Pithart project. The new contribution is seen in the introduction of clauses relative to private persons. The law was prepared by lawyers hired by the Jewish community as well as by the leaders of the Federation of Jewish Communities. Its elaboration was the result of two years of work by the community and the representatives who chose to take part. According to the Constitution of the Czech Republic, every member of the Parliament is authorized to introduce a bill. The government then must express its opinion. The problem arises when the text comes from a party belonging to the government coalition and the government, after having studied the bill, rejects the project.

While waiting for the decision of the government, the ODA launched its campaign of public information and collected support for the project. Viktor Dobal gathered the signatures of the Parliament members in favor of the law, then gaining the endorsement of his entire party, together with several other voices belonging to the ODS, and one or two members of the Social Democratic Party, despite the global hostility of this party toward all forms of restitution. The former communists and the far-right movements remained of course outside the perimeter of these endorsements and solicitations of support.[19]

But this entire undertaking had in fact been undermined from the inside since its very inception, because the government had decided not to support this initiative, even though it came from the ranks of one of its own constituents. At the end of the fall 1993, displeased to see the Parliament agitated by this discussion, Prime Minister Václav Klaus wrote to the president of the Parliament in order to let him know that the situation in the country was alarming. He noted that his duties demanded he focus the attention of representatives on questions more essential for the existence of the republic. It was necessary, he argued, to postpone *sine die* the debates concerning the restitution of the Jewish property.

Later on, the government finally expressed its negative view about the bill. This obvious repudiation considerably weakened the position of the partisans of the project, all the more so because the few ODS representatives who supported it began gradually to disband. In a bid to comprehend this snub, several reasons were invoked in the press and in well-informed circles. The Czech government and its prime minister cannot be suspected of anti-Semitism or even of being lukewarm toward the persecutions inflicted on the Jews. For that reason, it is necessary to look for other explanations. The principal one, according to different sources, was the fear the government had of seeing the Catholic Church stand up to claim the restitution of its properties expropriated by the communist regime. The question of church property surfaces regularly in Czech public opinion and among policy makers. In the summer of 1996, some divergences came to light in the Czech Catholic Church itself regarding restitution. Some leaders of the Church are not favorably inclined toward this development. They foresaw financial difficulties that may occur in order to retain such an enormous patrimony, from which the Church moreover would receive lower income compared to the present dispensation, where it is sponsored by the state.[20] Because of the difficulties that could arise from this process, the government remained hesitant.

In February 1994, after the negative vote on the Dobal law, an ODS representative, M. Trojan, proposed to amend it in order to reintroduce it in another form; this sensational development had obviously been prepared in advance, since the text was already available. One of the arguments put forward by the opponents to the project was the injustice that would be committed against the towns obliged to restitute buildings they use for the common welfare. The proposed amendment intended then to authorize them to refuse to give back this kind of building, the state then being authorized to grant a financial compensation to the Jewish community in return. This motion provoked the anger of the members of the ODA and of the two Christian Democratic Parties. As a result, the law was enacted with a comfortable majority,[21] albeit disguised and no longer a law, because it could be easily denounced.

Following this, the government decided to restitute on its own authority all the Jewish properties it still retained, that is, about 20 buildings. For the most part, they were located in Prague, like the structures constituting the Jewish Museum. For its part, the Jewish Museum was officially declared an independent structure from 1 October 1994. This initiative gave the community a platform of autonomy vis-à-vis the national government, but deprived it of proper support to negotiate the restitution of other properties still in the hands of the towns.[22] The state shifted its responsibility to them in "advising" them to restitute the Jewish properties they possess.[23]

Finally, on 29 April 1994 the Parliament promulgated a new law regarding the properties of private persons. That replaces the federal law of 1991; the text does not explicitly mention Jewish assets and the paragraph devoted to landed properties was suppressed. These new restitution proceedings concern the properties of private individuals still retained by the national government or the municipalities. However, in 1994 a considerable quantity of these assets, Jewish and non-Jewish, such as shops, houses, etc., had already been subject to privatization. Yet the law cannot reconsider these transactions, they are regarded as having been consummated and are purely and simply confirmed. This law is nevertheless the only effective element remaining of the so-called Dobal law. It enables persons to enter into negotiations.

For the moment, the Jewish community has succeeded in recovering a large portion of the properties that were in the hands of the state. The difficulties now consist principally in the at times recalcitrant attitude on the part of the municipalities. If one takes into account the efforts of the national government in restituting Jewish properties, the results are satisfying. It is, however, true that the ministeries did not always apply the decisions from above with efficiency and even less so with dispatch, especially the ministry of justice. There a certain ignorance of the laws passed in the postwar period seems to have spread through the bureaucracy. It is then very difficult for the national government to dispossess institutions such as the police or the army, more or less legitimate "purchasers" of Jewish properties after their nationalization by the communist authorities. But on the whole, the national government seems to have made the necessary effort and is also listening with relative goodwill to the Federation of Jewish Communities.

Matters tend to proceed very differently in the provinces where the Jews are in most cases absent from the immediate stage. This puts them at a decided disadvantage in negotiations with the local authorities. The latter obviously drag the matter out and the process appears to be prolonged and difficult. Certain financial factors are not extraneous to this attitude. In Karlovy Vary (Karlsbad), for example, since 1945 the town has rented the Villa Lauretta to the Jewish community as a compensation for the loss of the synagogue burned down by the Nazis. The municipality is reluctant to renounce its property rights to a building from which it gains a clear profit.

In several cities, the municipality has made lucrative use of buildings belonging lawfully to the community and refuses to part with it as a source of income. Thus, in order not to deprive the towns, the Federation has to commit itself to maintaining the activities considered essential to the public good over a period of ten years in the restituted buildings. Such activities involve in the main the spheres of health care and education.[24] Even derelict buildings are not an exception to this. Often we note that when towns experience serious financial difficulties, their secret hope is for the building to completely deteriorate or burn down—so that they may be able to sell the ground in order to realize an attractive profit. This is of course an extreme case; generally the municipalities prefer to get rid of these buildings and restitute them without any problem. Like in the two other countries, the community finds itself entrusted with a real estate patrimony whose upkeep, let alone restoration, seriously taxes its budgetary means. The support of the state can only be occasional and modest, considering the independence granted to the Federation of Communities; and even then, the national government is already overburdened with a lot of classified buildings that it can hardly maintain. The autonomy conceded to the Jewish communities was therefore also a way of providing for their maintenance. The Federation of Jewish Communities has made a list of the 44 cities that still retain Jewish properties, spread throughout all of Czechia, from Prague to the former centers of Jewish life in the provinces.[25] The leaders of the community estimate that of the 202 buildings claimed by the Federation of Jewish Communities, about half have not yet been recovered.[26] Only 14 claims have been withdrawn from the list by the Federation, three from properties owned by the state, nine from municipalities, and two from private owners. The remaining cases give rise to some problems, whether because of the difficulties encountered with the municipalities, or because some of them happen to be properties that were privatized before the beginning of the process and then theoretically excluded from the restitution. In this last case, the Federation attempts to negotiate in order to obtain a financial compensation or the restitution of another building.[27] The private companies that still own and use Jewish communal properties and refuse to negotiate their return have also been listed by the Federation of the Communities. In such cases, too, the most famous Czech enterprises side with small firms.[28]

In Prague, three groups of buildings are under consideration: the synagogues that are part of the buildings of the Jewish Museum, and thus directly managed by that institution since October 1994. Two of them, the Old-New synagogue (*Altneuschule*) and the Jubilee synagogue in Jerusalem Street, are used for worship. The second ensemble of buildings consists of communal structures that remained in the possession of the community even during the communist era. The third group consists of the buildings restituted to the community. In order to administer the latter, the Federation has set up a joint-stock company that represents it: the buildings are then restored and later rented for a commercial purpose, or directly rented to a company and renovated by the new tenant. The Federation obtains an income that is used, along with revenue coming from the entrance fees to the Museum, to provide for the needs of the community, however precarious this arrangement.[29] Though restitution proved rather successful in Prague, the process has remained slow and insufficient in the provinces.

Yet there have been marked changes since the elections in 1998, which saw the Social Democratic Party of Miloš Zeman form the new government. The Social Democrats were initially reluctant to raise the question of restitution, and in the first several years after the transition were even opposed to it. Since coming to power, there has been a change in their position, and the topic has been broached in the government program. The Federation of Jewish Communities has seized the opportunity to reenter into negotiations on the restitution process. Since January 1999, the government has established a commission to deal with the restitution problem, concerning both properties and assets. The head of the commission is Vice-Prime Minister Pavel Rychetský, who presides over three subcommittees: the first deals with unresolved individual restitution, the second with communal properties, and the third is a search committee for stolen art, bank accounts, insurance policies, and other valuables. The commission is composed of representatives of different ministries and appointed members of the Federation of Jewish Communities. Following the agreement between the Federation and international Jewish organizations, foreign Jewish delegates are also invited to cooperate with the commission, such as Rabbi Andrew Baker from the American Jewish Committee; participation by the World Jewish Restitution Organization is also planned. The work of the commission was financed by the Czech government with a grant of two million Crowns (US$53,000), funded until the end of 2000.

Since the establishment of the commission, the Federation has devoted its work primarily to maintaining restituted buildings and to publicity about the cases still not resolved. Progress is of course less spectacular now than at the beginning of the transition. On occasion one has the impression that the process is slowing down, but there are nonetheless concrete results.

Hungary: A Far-Reaching Process

Three laws have been enacted by the democratically elected Hungarian Parliament in 1990 in order to institute a partial compensation of private persons for the properties confiscated by the national government. First, Law XXV/1991, aiming at the partial compensation for the discrimination and persecution suffered by private individuals between May 1939 and 8 June 1949. This law was enacted on 26 June 1991. It was later complemented and strengthened by Law XXIV/1992 on the Compensation of Unjust Persecution Caused by the State and Affecting the Private Property of the Hungarian Citizens, passed on 7 April 1992.[30] At the beginning of the process, the law was limited to the period 1945–63, and later extended following pressure from the Jewish community, in order to consider the persecution against the Jews that had begun in 1938. In contrast with the Czech Republic, plagued by the German question, Hungary takes into account not only present Hungarian citizens but also persons of Hungarian origin who had Hungarian nationality at the time of expropriation. It also includes persons who had forfeited their Hungarian citizenship at the time of their persecution and persons of Hungarian origin living in Hungary since 31 December 1990, in other words, emigrants who returned to the country since liberal reforms were introduced after November 1989.[31]

The time frame considered by the law thus enabled the Jews to claim reparations for the losses occasioned by the Horthy regime and then by the Nazi occupiers, but also under communist rule. Yet these two laws, as in the two other countries, concern all the victims of expropriations. However, as in Slovakia, the time frame was extended all the same in order to comprehend the Jewish persecution. Whereas in Slovakia the text of the law made no clear mention of the Jews, the Hungarian law is much more explicit. The first appendix to the law was devoted to the chronological listing of the various laws of confiscation enacted by the Hungarian national government between 1939 and 1949.[32] In that respect, the second law of 1992 was more precise on the matter of Jewish property, but the latter is still considered in a more general manner. However, the first rider to this new bill was entirely devoted to the Jewish properties. It enumerated in eight parts the different properties for which restitution had been considered subsequent to the executive orders of 1945, 1946, and 1947, but which were then reconfiscated by the communist regime. These properties can be considered the basis for compensation.

The Hungarian laws alluded simply to a system of compensations, not to the restitution of lost property. The compensation rates are very precisely defined in the two laws, but in practice matters seemed to have been less simple. Once accepted by the National Office of Compensation (*Országos Kárrendezési és Kárpótlási Hivatal*), the claims were associated with a compensation voucher, proportionately calculated for the cost of the property on the present-day market. It was necessary to have registered the claims before 15 March 1994.[33] This process concerned real estate as well as other assets, such as gold and silver.[34] It was then possible to obtain a compensation of 1,000 to 2,000 forints (between US$3.50 and $7) for each square meter of real estate located in Budapest.[35]

The compensation vouchers were utilized in a variety of ways.[36] In some cases, it has been shown that they were used to buy back the properties for which they had been issued. But the voucher holders were also able to convert them into equity shares after they had been introduced on the Budapest Stock Exchange in December 1992.[37] One of the uses preferred by the voucher holders was the purchase of privatized goods sold by the national government. In this way, the state was able to recoup money while realizing a profit, which means that the money came back in the pockets of the state.

An estimated two million claims reached the National Office of Compensation during the three years from 1991 to 1994. The national government was able to satisfy the greater proportion of them by granting compensation vouchers for a total amount of 141 billion Hungarian forints (US$500 million).[38] The campaign of compensation following the enactment of the laws of 1991 and 1992 concluded in 1994.[39]

In the meantime, the Hungarian national government was able to promulgate a third compensation law. It dealt with individuals. This answered the claims of the Jewish community, which had demanded indemnification for the sufferings during the war. Yet once again the text was unsatisfactory and overly general, concerning "persons illegally executed or deprived of their freedom for political reasons." Law XXXII/1992 thus enabled the victims and their spouses or direct descendants to benefit from the system of compensation vouchers. This new dispensation involved some 360,000 persons, also granted vouchers. For example, in the case of an imprisonment that had lasted beyond thirty days, the person received a voucher corresponding to a basic asset of 10,000 forints (US$35), this amount then eventually was multiplied by the number of months spent in jail.[40] This cold calculation led inevitably to injustices toward the victims if one considers that six months behind bars are not necessarily equivalent to six months spent in a forced labor battalion or in a concentration camp.[41] This maladjustment was one of the reasons why the Alliance of Jewish Communities was not fully satisfied: to reduce the persecutions suffered by the Jews to an act of purely political prejudice is shocking. In the wake of this law's enactment, the Alliance chose to struggle on to obtain a genuine text from the national government: it would deal with the person and the property of the Jews persecuted and expropriated both by fascism and by communism. Following the first three compensation laws, an estimated number slightly more than 30,000 persons were able to benefit from the granting of compensation vouchers. Besides, 40,000 other persons living abroad and having filed claims would also have been indemnified. However, for Westerners, the sums granted by the Hungarian government often appear absurdly low. As a result, many do not make use of their vouchers. Thus, it is probably far more in the interest of persons of East European origin living in the West to file their claims directly to the World Jewish Congress (WJC). Through the medium of the Claims Conference, it seeks to recover funds that are then applied to compensation.[42]

One of the financial problems raised by compensation lies in its ceiling, assessed at five million forints (US$17,500). This limitation was determined by Law XXV/1992 and was not revised later despite the galloping inflation that affected Hungary, and was most especially evident in the real estate market.[43] The leaders of the community consider this ceiling much too low for the market and the quality of the properties. Indeed, such a paltry sum seems rather ridiculous with respect to a factory or entire large buildings. Moreover, this is a ruling that applies to all beneficiaries, Jewish and not.

The Alliance of Jewish Communities then began a real struggle in order to obtain an acknowledgement from the national government of the specificity of the persecutions imposed on the Jews, which would lead to the enactment of a special law. At the beginning of this fight, the claims were based on the third compensation law. It sought to add a text to the law regarding financial compensation for elderly concentration camp survivors living in financially difficult circumstances, worsened by the transition from state socialism to a market economy, and in great physical distress.

The Alliance was critical of the obvious unwillingness of the government of József Antall, which believed it had done enough for compensation, and was very reluctant to recognize the responsibility and the collaboration of the Hungarian state in the persecutions. That reluctance was reflected, for example, in the government's decision to return the remains of the wartime profascist and anti-Semitic Hungarian ruler, Admiral Horthy, to his native town of Kenderes in September 1993 from Portugal, where he had died in exile in 1953. The atmosphere was not very favorable for historical revaluations, but the Jewish community pressed its case and won the support of individuals both in Hungary and abroad. This was assisted in particular by certain international organizations that had returned to Hungary and publicized the debate in the media, much to the discomfort of the government.

The World Jewish Congress, which had returned to Hungary in 1993, was soon involved in a campaign for compensating persons for the mental anguish they had suffered, and also broached again the question of the restitution of confiscated property.[44] Earlier that same year, the Constitutional Court had ruled that the Parliament had to fulfil the implementation of the 1947 Peace Treaty concerning questions of restitution and compensation. The Alliance then organized a census of the persons entitled to compensation, as well as an inventory of private and community properties.[45] On 8 February 1995, the Hungarian Constitutional Court issued a favorable judgment on a new law concerning compensation for detriment losses suffered by the Jews.[46] The Court ruled that the text of Law XXXII/1992 was discriminatory regarding the Jews. It stated that in particular, the discussion on the terms "deprivation of liberty" led to an acknowledgment of the responsibility of the Hungarian national government for the fate suffered by the Jews, recognizing that it was a sovereign nation that had delivered its citizens into the hands of another country. Even after the arrival of the Germans on 19 March 1944, Regent Horthy continued to administer Hungary as a sovereign state. It was his police that organized the deportation of the Jews.[47]

This statement by the Constitutional Court was one of the great moments of the Hungarian transition period. It marked a point of no return in the evolution of the question of Hungarian responsibility. From this date on, the project was repeatedly discussed by this institution and the government, and finally by the Alliance of Communities supported by the WJC.

An agreement was reached in July 1995 between the new government coalition, formed after the second parliamentary elections of the post-communist era which took place in May 1994, and the representatives of the Alliance of Jewish Communities of Hungary, seconded by the WJC and the International Committee for the Restitution and the Indemnification of the Jewish Property.[48] Following this first agreement, the parties approved the creation of two mixed commissions in charge of defining the ways and means of the compensation.[49] The negotiations were resumed in September 1995 and they materialized in the preparation of the Law XXV/1996, which was submitted for approval to the Constitutional Court. The discussions continued during this time between the different members of the commissions and some tensions appeared now and then among the leaders of the Community and the delegates of the WJC, easily accused of being more interested in the American emigrants and their families than in the Hungarian Jews themselves. This criticism was also levelled at the American ambassador to the European Union, likewise very active in Jewish matters, Stuart E. Eizenstat.[50] The Hungarian Constitutional Court, in a ruling handed down on 21 June 1996, recommended to extend the scope of the intended beneficiaries to include compensation for survivors of the forced labor battalions as well as prisoners in the Soviet gulags. The spouses and descendants of the persons who died as a result of political persecution are considered possible beneficiaries, while in the case of the deportations and forced labor, only the spouses are entitled to benefits. In other words, the Court confirmed and upheld the distinction between the victims of the communist regime and victims of fascist political persecution. In the case of the former, such accusations dogged the entire family for generations. Its members were often banned from working and their children from education, and subjected to permanent surveillance by the political police. However, the then president of the Constitutional Court, László Sólyom, stressed the moral repugnancy of introducing any distinction between victims who had perished in the concentration camps, in the prisons of the Hungarian political police *AVH*, or the Soviet gulags.[51]

In the absence of descendants or other potential beneficiaries, compensation claims were now put forward by the Jewish community. The funds thus obtained were utilized to assist Holocaust survivors. Since individuals most of the time were too old or too ill to initiate proceedings themselves, a census was taken in order to register all beneficiaries. Thus, the number of Jewish survivors of the persecutions is estimated at between 18,000 and 19,000 persons,[52] and the sum of the funds allocated by the national government for this new phase of the compensation amounts to four billion forints (US$14 million), always in the form of compensation vouchers.[53] The compensation was revised in March 1997, and 1.4 billion forints (US$4.9 million) were added to the original amount. This was changed into life insurance, which made it possible to increase by 10 percent the amount allotted to 38,200 former victims of the deportation, and to the soldiers and inmates of the forced labor battalions who were taken prisoners by the Soviets and sent to the gulag.[54] For example, the compensation for twelve months in a deportation camp, 132,000 forints, was increased to 145,200 (US$500).[55] Up to December 1997, the 18,600 survivors received their first payment, totaling 130 million forints (US$460,000).[56]

The law was finally passed by the Hungarian government on July 3, 1996. Hungary thus became the first among the former communist states to promulgate a law devoted specifically to the compensation of Jewish property losses as well as to the indemnification of the sufferings of Second World War. Israel Singer, general secretary of the WJC, declared that "the last chapter of Second World War has finally been written," and the Western press did not hesitate to talk of an example that was paradigmatic, to be followed by the other countries of the region.[57] The day before, the government and the Jewish organizations had come to an agreement that, far from being perfect in the eyes of the Jews, enabled them to close the discussions on a satisfactory basis. Moreover, the law created a Public Foundation on the Jewish Heritage (*Magyarországi Zsidó Örökség Közalapítvány, MaZsÖK*), in charge of managing the distribution of the funds paid out by the government to the survivors. This institution will also have to ensure the management of the properties restituted by the national government or by the local authorities.[58] The foundation is composed of a board of directors,[59] headed by Ronald S. Lauder, whose activities in Hungary are already manifold. The foundation is also entitled to try to recover the works of art belonging to the Jews of Hungary seized by the Germans during the occupation of the country. Lauder is also the president of the Commission for Stolen Art inside the WJC.Coming to power after the elections of 1998, the government of Viktor Orbán has promised to end the compensation process,[60] by granting a new amount of 30,000 to 35,000 Hungarian forints (US$120) for the benefit of the direct descendants of the victims. The brothers and sisters will receive 15,000 Forints (US$50).[61] The sums have already been calculated for the next budget, but their paltry amount has provoked the indignation of both the Hungarian Jewish community and various international organizations. It also means that the survivors will have to turn exclusively to international help to obtain complementary aid. After a first allocation of 80 million deutsche Marks (US$35,200,000), which was distributed in the ratio of DM 500 per person, the Federal Republic of Germany has then promised to grant a second compensation for the benefit of the concentration camps survivors—in Hungary about 3,000 persons—amounting to DM 500 (US$220) per person. The Swiss government did the same in acknowledgement of the money frozen in its banks, and granted a sum of $200 million, to be administered by the World Jewish Restitution Organization. It will amount to US$500 or US$1,000 per person.[62] The federal government also proposed a project according to which persons who were turned back from the Swiss border or arrested in Switzerland and later deported could claim up to US$2,500. In 2000, Austria has also adopted a law under which the Hungarian Jewish forced workers are eligible to a compensation of a maximum of 105,000 Schillings (US$7,000).[63] Last but not least, the Claims Conference has received funds from the Federal Republic of Germany funds to grant an annuity for life of DM 250 (US$110) to the concentration camps survivors. The Frankfurt Office of the Claims Conference has recently opened a branch office in Budapest, and the latest estimate shows that about one thousand persons have already received their annuity.[64]

The juridical structure of the compensation was finalized by Law XXXII/1991 regarding the restitution of the properties of the country's various churches. In this case, it was really a matter of restitution of the buildings. The text intended to return the buildings used by the recognized churches, namely Catholic, Lutheran, Calvinist, and Jewish, within ten years. These were structures formerly used for their religious, cultural, social, and health activities, and which are still in the possession of the national government and local administrations (towns and regional authorities). Unlike in the Czech Republic, the Jewish community is relieved from ensuring continuity in their former activity.[65] But, as in the two other countries, the authorities sometimes seem dilatory and unwilling. Yet this appears to be more a manifestation of bureaucratic carelessness than any sign of hostility on the part of the government. In the towns, the same problems as in Slovakia or the Czech Republic are present. Synagogues have indeed often been restituted but are at the point of collapse compared to the well-kept buildings that the municipalities do not agree to part with under the pretext that they are state property. As in the Czech Republic, the Jewish community is completely autonomous and thus can only expect occasional support from the national government for the restoration of classified buildings. One such example is the Great Synagogue of Budapest, successfully renovated and reopened in September 1996. In contrast with the Czech Republic, in Hungary the separation of church and state is now in effect, involving all denominations. Nevertheless, the national government does not hesitate in sometimes showing proof of bad faith, as exemplifiedby the synagogue on Rumbach Street, an early work of the great Viennese architect Otto Wagner. The synagogue was first sold in 1988 by the Jewish community to a state construction firme for 2.5 million forints (US$8,600). Following this, the building was partially restored; but the interior is still in disastrous repair, since it was used in 1941 as a detention camp for foreign Jews whom Hungary was about to hand over to the Germans. After the national government decided to liquidate this unproductive construction firm, the synagogue was put up for auction. Then, after two fruitless attempts to sell it in 1991 and 1992, the national Hungarian government intended to sell back the synagogue to the Jewish community for 800 million forints (US$2,700,000), while according to the law it should restitute it immediately. Of course, the Alliance of Communities does not have this sum at its disposal and thus is trying to prevent the sale of the building before the national government privatizes it, which could turn the structure into some business not in keeping with its former sacred status.[66]

Nevertheless, the restitution and compensation have enabled the Jews of Hungary to have a certain number of buildings recovered or, with the help of the funds obtained from the Office of Compensation, to purchase or even to build new properties when unable to buy back formerly owned real estate.The restitution of stolen works of art constitutes another sphere of its own.[67] In most cases, these works of art were later taken by the Soviets, whether on Hungarian soil itself or in Germany. Other works were sealed as enemy treasures by the Allied Forces in Austria and in Germany, and were sometimes restituted to the Hungarian state, but not to their lawful owners or interested parties. A certain number are still stored in warehouses, notably in Austria.[68] An estimate by Lajos Ungár suggests that 15,000 to 20,000 Jewish-owned pieces were taken from their owners by the Hungarian national government; some were later confiscated by the Germans, and a sizeable amount finally ended up in Soviet hands.[69] On the whole, the value of the items seized and taken to Germany reaches a hundred million forints (US$350,000).[70]

The Soviets took possession of the collections of art objects, including in particular the paintings that the Germans had systematically confiscated from the wealthiest and most prominent Jewish families, such as Hatvany, Herzog,[71] Kornfeld, and Weisz, after their arrival in the country, even at that time organizing a private exhibition.[72] No list was found of these items, but according to Lajos Ungár, "it is improbable that the Germans, as precise as they were in everything, did not inventory them."[73] A Hungarian-Russian Committee of Restitution (*Magyar-orosz restituciós munkabizottság*) was established that includes representatives of the Alliance of Communities.[74] This question was discussed at length on the occasion of the state visit by President Boris Yeltsin to Budapest in 1992. At the time, Yeltsin brought with him a picture from the famous collection of Baron Ferenc Hatvany that the Soviets had stolen at the end of the siege of Budapest. The collection contains more than sixty paintings. The Hatvany family was among the pioneers of Hungarian industry. The father of Baron Ferenc Hatvany, Sándor Hatvany-Deutsch, founded the Hungarian Association of the Sugar Industrialists in 1894, and participated with other great Jewish capitalists in the creation of the National Association of Hungarian Industrialists in 1902. His brother, Baron Lajos Hatvany, was also a benefactor, a connoisseur of the arts and an art collector.[75] Ferenc Hatvany assembled a collection of 750 paintings and other works of art.[76] When Hungary entered the war, he stored his collection for safekeeping in three Budapest banks under the names of Christian employees in his firm; the rest was hidden away or given to relatives. But a large number of masterpieces stayed in the Baron's villa, where they were subsequently seized by the Nazis. When they finally agreed to let the Commission for the Registration and Safeguarding of Art Treasures Confiscated from the Jews enter the house, only sixty paintings were found, but the Nazis had refused to transfer them to a museum. That is why these works, which the commission was nevertheless able to inventory, were later taken away by the Soviets. The collections of other members of the family suffered similar fates. After the liberation, a Ministerial Committee for Displaced Art Works was established. But it could determine only that the bank safes had been robbed by the Red Army. Although lists of the missing items were drawn up, after 1948 it was impossible to continue work on these questions—this, despite the fact that the archive funds exist and are being searched.

The Russians thus probably retain possession of other works of art as well. The total number is practically impossible to estimate. It falls within the competence of the committee to locate and make an inventory of these items, of which nearly 90 percent belonged to Jewish owners.[77] Since the foundation of the committee, only 130 objects have been given back subsequent to joint agreements. But then a decision of the Russian Duma gives very little hope. The Duma does not want to consider items taken as war booty from the enemy. The law has to be examined by the Russian Constitutional Court, which could decide that the "religious" items have to be restituted.[78] Since then, the Russian authorities seem to have considered the problem in a more positive manner and some officials, among them the Russian Ambassador in Budapest, Valeri Mussatov, declared that restitution may now be a possibility. But the Hungarian specialists have not yet gained access to the inventories and were not permitted to undertake any research in the Russian museums.[79]

On the other hand, negotiations are now under way with Austria in order to reach an agreement on the restitution of the Hungarian works of art, most formerly owned by Jews and still in federal depositories, their ultimate fate still undetermined. These objects had been seized by the Western Allies at the time of their entry into Austria, were then sealed and transferred to the supervision of the Austrian authorities. About 6,000 items have thus been stored in Austria, but with one advantage, namely, that they were registered: therefore one can find more than 600 paintings, gold and silver plates, as well as an important number of diverse objects, tapestries, sculptures, and so on, in these lists.[80] The Jewish communities may try to get some help from the institutions that have recently shown an interest in this question: in August 1997, the National Jewish Museum in Washington, D.C., launched the "Holocaust Art Restitution Project." A similar objective is being pursued by the Commission for Stolen Art within the WJC. The main task is not only to identify the items but to return them to their legitimate owners. For the first time in fifty years in former Eastern Europe, an auction of Judaica was held in the Atrium Hyatt Hotel in Budapest on 28 November 1999 for the express benefit of the Hungarian Jews.

Conclusion

The restitution is part of a larger process of re-appropriation by the Jews of their stolen past, however painful it may be. To file a compensation claim is one move among various gestures of rediscovering an identity that has long been repressed. Therefore, restitution and compensation were in a way the first step toward acknowledging the rights of the Jews. This is a considerable achievement. It must now be regarded as nearly settled, even if the three countries are far from equal when it comes to its final completion. Thanks to the democratic transition, the Jews have partially succeeded in restoring their status as full citizens in the bosom of societies that today are themselves experiencing huge transformations and whose values are sometimes in rapid flux. After the disappearance of a system based on lies and dissimulation, the Jews were at the same time able to call the government to account, reappearing openly in the society. From the national government they deserve acknowledgement of their great suffering, from society recognition of their reestablished identity. Now, their aim is to preserve and energize the memory of the persecutions, but also to shape a future for the younger generations in which they will be able to live their Judaism fully, without having to bear the burden of the tragic past.

Notes

1. The article is part of the author's habilitation thesis, *La restitution des biens juifs et le renouveau juif en Europe centrale (Hongrie, Slovaquie, République Tchèque)*, published in the series Wiener Osteuropa Studien (Bern, 2002).
2. František Alexander, *Short Report on the Restitution Process in the Slovak Republic.* A one-sided document presented by its author, who is executive chairman of the Central Union of the Jewish Communities of Slovakia.
3. Ibid.
4. Ibid.
5. Martin Plichta, "Le Parlement approuve la restitution des biens des Églises et de la communauté juive," *Le Monde*, 29 October 1993.
6. Alexander, *Short report.*
7. Interview with František Alexander on 29 April 1996.
8. Ibid.
9. Ibid.
10. Eugen Bárkány and Ľudovít Dojč, *Židovské náboženské obce na Slovensku* [The Jewish Religious Communities in Slovakia] (Bratislava, 1991), 375–378.
11. Interview with Pavol Mešťan on 29 April 1996.
12. Interview with Jozef Weiss on 23 April 1996.

13. Štefan Šutaj, "Ungarische Minderheit in der Slowakei während der Nachkriegsentwicklung," in *Nationale Frage und Vertreibung in der Tschechoslowakei und Ungarn 1938–1945. Aktuelle Forschungen*, ed. Richard G. Plaschka (Vienna, 1997), 85.
14. *Compensation for Holocaust Survivors*, document elaborated by Tomáš Kraus, General Secretary of the Federation of Jewish Communities in the Czech Republic, 1 June 1997.
15. Interview with Tomáš Kraus on 24 June 1999.
16. Interview with Oldrich Stránský (Fond budouctnosti) on 24 June 1999.
17. In 1994, the Federation of the Communities made a re-evaluation of the number of the properties open to possible claim, amounting to 202, including a variety of assets: synagogues, cemeteries, communities buildings, houses, and other types of real estate. Interview with Tomáš Kraus, General Secretary of the Federation of Jewish Communities on 10 July 1996.
18. Interview with Viktor Dobal, former representative (Western Bohemia), member of O.D.A. (Civic Democratic Alliance), on 9 July 1996.
19. Interview with Viktor Dobal on 9 July 1996.
20. Martin Plichta, "La restitution de forêts à l'Église divise le clergé tchèque," *Le Monde*, 6 August 1996.
21. Interview with Viktor Dobal on 9 July 1996.
22. Interview with Leo Pavlát, director of the Jewish Museum, on 4 July 1996.
23. Interview with Viktor Dobal on 9 July 1996.
24. Interview with Tomáš Kraus on 10 July 1996.
25. "Restitution of Jewish Property," document elaborated by the Federation of Jewish Communities in the Czech Republic, 2.
26. Interview with Leo Pavlát on 4 July 1996.
27. Interview with Tomáš Kraus on 10 July 1996.
28. See the list in "Restitution of Jewish Property", 3.
29. Interview with Tomáš Kraus on 10 July 1996.
30. Edit Petri, *Kárpótlás és kárrendezés Magyarországon 1989–1998* [Compensation and Compensative Legislation in Hungary 1989–1988] (Budapest, 1998), 97–102.
31. *Magyar Törvény Tár* [Corpus of Hungarian Laws] 1991, 116–121; 1992, 110–111.
32. Ibid., 1991, 119–120.
33. The Law II/1994 was enacted in order to officially end the period of registration of the claims. *A Magyar Országgyülés Jogalkotása* [The Legislation of the Hungarian National Assembly], 1994, 136.
34. Ibid., 111.
35. *Magyar Törvény Tár* 1991, 121.
36. "End of the campaign of financial and political indemnification," *Weekly Report of MTI*, 10 March 1994, 11–12.
37. "Tözsdei adatok" [Stock Market Data], see Petri, *Compensation*, 738–741.
38. "Two million persons are concerned by the compensation," *Weekly Report of MTI*, 17 June 1994, 17.
39. See the complete statistical data in Petri, *Compensation*, 699–700.
40. "Compensation vouchers for an amount of 50 billion Forints are already on the market," *Weekly Report of MTI*, 18 June 1993, 12.
41. Interview with Lajos Ungár, Alliance of the Jewish Communities of Hungary, on 17 June 1996.

42. Ibid.
43. *Magyar Törvény Tár* 1991, 116.
44. Interview with Lajos Bakos, Vice-President of the Eastern Europe Commission of the WJC, on 18 June 1996.
45. Interview with Lajos Ungár on 17 June 1996.
46. Petri, *Compensation*, 490–511.
47. Stephen J. Roth, "Indemnification of Hungarian Victims of Nazism," in *The Holocaust in Hungary Fifty Years Later*, ed. Randolph Braham and Attila Pók (New York, 1997), 753f.
48. Interview with Lajos Bakos on 18 June 1996.
49. "Agreement on the restitution of the confiscated Jewish properties in Hungary," Telegram A.F.P., 20 July 1995.
50. See interviews with Lajos Ungár on 17 June and with Lajos Bakos on 18 June 1996.
51. "Bövíteni kell a kárpótlásra jogosultak körét" [The Circle of the Recipients of the Compensation Has to Be Extended], *Magyar Hirlap*, 22 June 1996; András Sereg, "Alkotmánybíróság: életek ertéke között nem lehet különbséget tenni" [The Constitutional Court: It Is not Possible to Establish a Scale of Values to Judge Between Human Lives], *Népszabadság*, 22 June 1996.
52. Document on the latest developments of the restitution process elaborated by Lajos Ungár, July 26, 1999. *Összefoglaló tanulmány. Az 1997/X törvény alapján a Mazsök kuratóriuma által megitélt életjáradék* [Summarized Study. The Attribution of Life Annuities by the Head of the Public Foundation for the Hungarian Jewish Heritage under the Law 1997/X], 15.
53. Interview with Lajos Bakos on 18 June 1996.
54. "Deportálás: plusz 10 százalék" [Deportation: Plus 10 Percents], *Héti Világgazdaság*, 1 March 1997.
55. Document on the latest developments of the restitution process elaborated by Lajos Ungár, 26 July 1999.
56. Ibid., "Összefoglaló tanulmány," 15.
57. "Gov't approves 'model' plan for Holocaust Jews," *New Europe*, 7–13 July 1996 and *The Economist*, 6 July 1996, 24.
58. Government decision 1035/1997, on the creation of the Public Foundation for the Jewish Heritage (*Magyarországi Zsidó Örökség Közalapítvány*), see Petri, *Compensation*, 644f.
59. See the members' list in Petri, *Compensation*, 646f.
60. "Orbán jövöre ígér megoldást a zsidókárpótlás ügyére" [Orbán Promises the Settlement of the Jewish Compensation for Next Year], *Magyar Hirlap*, 2 July 1999.
61. "Document on the Latest Developments of the Restitution Process," elaborated by Lajos Ungár, 26 July 1999.
62. The first list made public in July 1997 by the Swiss Bankers Association contained 27 accounts registered in Hungary, 19 in Czech Republik and 7 in Slovakia, presumably owned by Jews. Later the Association opened contact offices to identify the applicants, one of these based in Budapest, see *Time Magazine*, 20 November 1999.
63. "Kárpótlási tájékoztató. Magyarországi Zsidó Örökség Közalapítvány" [Information on the Compensation. Public Foundation on the Jewish Heritage], *Szombat*, October 2000, 7.
64. "Document on the Latest Developments of the Restitution Process," elaborated by Lajos Ungár, 26 July 1999.

65. "1200 Buildings Given Back to the Churches," *Weekly Report of MTI,* 10 June 1994, 3–5.
66. Interview with Robert Turán, director of the Jewish Museum on 13 June 1996.
67. In the Czech Republic, the director of the Jewish Museum, Leo Pavlát, negotiated with the Czech National Gallery regarding the stolen works of art that this institution had held since the end of the war. Most of them were seized by the communists before 1951. Among the 80 pictures inventoried then, only 67 have now been found in the deposits of the National Gallery; the missing items have probably disappeared in the apartments of former apparatchiks, in the embassies, ministeries, etc. The works of art will be juridically restituted, but the National Gallery will still keep them on the condition that they will be exhibited to the public (some are already part of the permanent collection).
68. Interview with Lajos Ungár on 17 June 1996.
69. Miklós Hernádi, "Hiányzó adalékok a nemzeti kulturális örökséghez. Nagy zsidó mügyüteményék sorsa" [Missing Pieces from the National Cultural Heritage. The Fate of the Great Jewish Art Collections], *Múlt és Jövö,* no. 4, 1998, 93–98.
70. Letter of Lajos Ungár, 9 August 1999.
71. Mravik, "Hungary's Pillaged Art Heritage," 98.
72. *A zsidó Budapest* [The Jewish Budapest], ed. Géza Komoróczy (Budapest, 1995); English translation: *Jewish Budapest* (Budapest, 1998), 515.
73. Letter of Lajos Ungár, 9 August 1999.
74. Interview with Lajos Ungár on 17 June 1996.
75. László Mravik, "Hungary's Pillaged Art," *The Hungarian Quarterly* 39, no. 150 (1998) (printed from the web site of the review).
76. *Magyar-Zsidó Lexikon* [Hungarian-Jewish Encyclopedia] (Budapest, 1929), 346–347.
77. *Weekly Report of the MTI,* 16 December 1994.
78. Letter of Lajos Ungár, 9 August 1999.
79. "'Elvi lehetöség' az orosz restitúció" [The Russian Restitution, a "Provisional Possibility"], *Népszabadság,* 10 February 2001.
80. Interview with Lajos Ungár on 17 June 1996.

— *Eleven* —

ELOQUENT SILENCE: INSCRIBING HUNGARIAN MEMORIES

Béla Rásky

Hungary generally is regarded as a society with a tradition of thinking along pronounced historical lines, a social body endowed with a marked and complex historical memory.[1] The legitimation of virtually every political system in Hungary has always been via the agency of history. The concept of cultural memory was never just a slogan but an ever-present practice in politics and the media. In Hungarian political culture, the politics of past history always played a substantial if not central role, though the tendency was to style oneself more as a martyr and far less (in this, very unlike Austria, for example) as a victim.[2] No matter what political position one espouses, reference to history provides the undergirding, although the historical reference points or axes with which one operates may differ. For this reason too, the West European debate on remembrance, on cultural and communicative memory, awakens keen interest in Hungary. As something Western and decidedly en vogue, it is also politically legitimated. That discourse is received and absorbed in Hungary, while its central concepts are adapted at the same time to Hungarian inscriptions.[3]

But when it comes to the country's history in the twentieth century, there are evidently various types of memory and memories circulating in the public sphere that should be discussed and explained differently. Classical historiography, which traditionally played an important role in Hungarian discourse (and which can claim both the aura of an authoritative arena for lateral thinkers and a platform for assertion and collaboration), is only one part of this cultural complex. Another is the politics of memory. As a kind of "cultural engineering," it always had central importance in constructing the Hungarian nation, or at least in forming the two approaches for constructing the traditions of a Hungarian nation;[4] and, as a state-controlled policy, it played a role in legitimizing any political system. And finally there is private memory, which is split between memorialization and "*damnatio memoriae,*" in the rites of forgetting or in collective reluctance to speak about the past. Predisposed by official (and often totalitarian) memory cults, private biographical lies often became "discursive truths," while the private politics of forgetting and resistant memorialization often became antagonistic strategies of survival. "Since the private biography and CV [curriculum vitae] was of decisive importance for evaluating an individual's status, people who wanted to stay in the Big Social Game had to create a past which seemed to be readily adjustable into the collective history of the society, and therefore in narrowest sense of the term, they had to eliminate the inadequate elements of their past."[5] These types of memory and memories are hard to separate, since they are intertwined, entangled, and often have reciprocally influenced each other. For that reason, they will be addressed here simultaneously.

Within broad sections of Hungarian society, the public historical demonstration of memory repeatedly demanded by the political, social, and cultural elites in Hungary also leads to a dehistoricizing and loss of sensitivity vis-à-vis the key critical issues in national history. Ultimately, that serves to block any debate in contemporary history regarding guilt and restitution, collaboration with and resistance to fascism and Stalinism (and the "soft" Kádár dictatorship as well).

A First Glance: Hungary and Its Historical Mentality

The historicity of Hungarian political culture is only a pillar of the "deformed character of Hungarian history in a dead-end street," as István Bibó put it.[6] And much in current political development suggests that the short-term attempt initiated in 1989 to break with this tradition and find legitimation via a constitution, democratic institutions, and a functioning public sphere may be little more than an episode. Before people in Hungary look into the future, they pause to derive—or, better, construct—their legitimating narrative out of the past.[7] But this bizarre obsession of the country with its own historical shadow is relatively recent. Even the nineteenth century was not necessarily an era in which large segments of Hungarian society thought so historically that, fixated on the past, they lost sight of the future. The celebration of a millennium of Hungarian history or the architectural shaping of Budapest serve to historically anchor a nation somewhat belatedly born yet seeking to claim a place for itself in the concert of European nation-states. The rupture in continuity can be dated to the Trianon Peace Treaty of 4 June 1920, signed in Versailles in the Trianon Castle, where the "Entente" implemented a decision by which historic Hungary was in effect dismembered, forcing 3.2 million Hungarians to live beyond the newly drawn borders of the state. Only from that catastrophic watershed is the construction of history likewise a process of generating legitimacy that dominates all. And how else could the demand for revision of this treaty have been justified except based on history?[8]

Looking Again: Is Perhaps Everything Totally Different?

Often, and in part because of the quite concrete sanctions of state power and its topical conception of history, communicative historical memory in Hungary in the twentieth century was significantly impeded, although not totally blocked: the occupation of private remembrance was, after all, a favorite pastime of the Hungarian state over the course of the past century. Frequently, not even in the bosom of the family was there any talk about the persecutions of the Jews, the years of Stalinism, or the 1956 uprising. And that tabooed history ultimately was manifest in a definite and mangled form of cultural memory.

Literature, theater, and most especially the cinema were the few media in which this memory could articulate itself, albeit cautiously and in a circumscribed discursive veil: the language of forms was indirect, symbolic, a method to skirt the censors. As a rule, direct personal historical memories and fragments of memory were cached away in shoe boxes on hidden bookshelves, to be dug out only in a certain and highly trusting temporal milieu: 1944–45, 1956, the years of Kádár's terror up to 1963, 1968—those time frames and segments ultimately survived in memory only in this clandestine way. But this was not an emotional form of remembrance as demanded in a more free and open political constellation. Rather, in dealing with its own history on a communicative level, Hungary had retained a distanced, self-reflective, melancholic element, indeed something self-ironic. Hungarian society approaches its own history less pedantically and emotionally than its elites might well desire.

1848 is perhaps the only historical memory that is actually also deeply etched into the cultural memory of the entire country, a national inscription. About 1848 consensus reigns. It apparently is so important to Hungarian society that no government, system of rule, or regime was able to avoid enunciating a position on 1848: not the dual monarchy in all its mendacity, strung between a rotten compromise and national dreams of independence, not the Council Republic nor the counter-revolutionary Horthy system. Not the short-lived Hungarian democracy between 1945 and 1948. Not the Rákosi regime, not the Kádár regime. And of course not the new Hungarian democracy after 1990.

The main interest of the custodians of the power of definition is generally not in the spoken or written word, but in "statutes, names and images, because icons are more important than texts."[9] That is not true in the case of Hungary. Hungarian historical memory is heavily geared to texts; memory as a rule remains inscribed in essays, words, not things. The hyper-historicizing of political culture is little reflected in Budapest's buildings. The city gives the same impression as Europe's other large metropolitan centers. Probably it is experience with history itself that can serve to explain this reticence when it comes to historicizing as embodied in architecture: there are few cities in Europe where so much was reinterpreted, constructed and reconstructed as in Budapest. These architectural cultural memories were often destroyed in the twentieth century, stormed and demolished: the Council Republic, the Horthy era, the short-lived democracy, Stalinism and Kádárism mark the stations. Architecture is too rigid, concrete and stone too solid to be able to elude such reconstruction, reconfiguration, and demolition. What is nonmaterial is far less endangered. And perhaps this helps explain the nonmateriality of Hungarian historical discourse. Essay and feuilleton are ephemeral, but a monument can stand, be razed, reinterpreted, misinterpreted. So it would seem it is precisely history with its myriad reinterpretations that is the reason why Hungarian publics and elites remain so apprehensive about erecting new, large, representative monuments, even if they can spark heated emotional debate on the necessity of such measures.

Only the early Kádár era was able to vault the historical orientation of Hungarian political culture and move beyond it. And indeed had to do so. Because in its case, any historical remembrance would have washed to the surface the circumstances of its own genesis, the bloody suppression of the 1956 Revolution. Conservatives as a rule still condemn that regime the most for this particular dimension of its birth. Namely, that it stole from Hungarian society its own history, intentionally of course, in order to "break the back of the nation." Naturally however, de-historicizing was only part of the basis of legitimacy of the regime. And Hungarian society also participated in these events, gaining certain benefits as recompense. Never was Hungarian society more ahistorical than in the prime of Kádárism. Nonetheless, perhaps paradoxically, precisely because of the taboo, it also facilitated an ironic (even if uncritical) confrontation with the Stalinist past of the country.[10]

After the Great Turn: History and Cult—Two Examples

Since 1989/90, the traditional and controversial images of history have resurfaced in public discourse. The politics of past history has experienced a powerful comeback. The nation, its elites are wont to aver, has to remember. Pathos is once more de rigueur, irony out of style. This element in the new Hungary that has regained cultural hegemony was able to reweave the political culture from the warp of historical fabric, since the marginal radical democratic opposition found itself unable to create any generally acknowledged traditions. The hullabaloo over the festivities to mark the new millennium with the transfer of traditional banners to every tiny market town and hamlet, the display of the "holy" Hungarian crown of Stephan in the Parliament, the "crown guard" with its phantasy-rich uniforms, the state-subsidized historical pageant films, the mediatizing of Hungarian politics—all these naturally are powerful images of neoconservative Hungary and its politics of memory.

The declared aim of the producer of the film "Sacra Corona" (directed by G. Koltay, 2001) needs no commentary: the audience was to leave the theater with their "heads held high."[11] Only the future will show if this way to deal with the past has any durability. Yet more than fifteen years after the "annus mirabilis," it is still not yet clear which of the two available alternatives the young democracy has opted for: a critical confrontation with the past or a return to the old national myths. It is likely that the two directions will remain locked in a kind of conflict-laden love-hate relationship. And thus will have to coexist side by side, with an impact on intellectual life at times paralytic, at times energizing.

A key element in the reburial on 16 June 1989 of the Hungarian prime minister Imre Nagy, executed in the aftermath of the 1956 Revolution, was the pronouncement before a crowd of 300,000 of the phrase "*emlékezzünk!*"—"let us remember!"

This reburial of Nagy's remains was an attempt to create new lines of tradition by rehabilitating the memory of the anti-Stalinist revolution: as so often in its history, Heroes Square in Budapest was quickly remodeled.[12] In this way, it became the locus for the staging of the Great Turn in Budapest.[13] "The funeral took place in a time which could be called a 'revolutionary situation'.... More precisely, at that time none of the existing political-ideological groups in Hungary were in a position to shape the ceremony and exterior of the funeral in their own image.... Therefore, vacant space—'empty space' was created for art and this is indeed exceptional."[14] The deconstructivist design has been described and analyzed several times. It was the "cult of [remembrance] and forgiveness."[15] And perhaps the cult of symbolic restitution at the core of the commemoration[16]—even if this act, properly so, was ruffled to some extent by the superb speech of the then prime minister Viktor Orbán (1998–2002).

The attempt to restore historical continuity beyond 1956, to restitute remembrance, failed. Sites, rituals, symbols, and monuments related to 1956 became topics charged with conflict and controversy. More and more, it was the extreme right that appropriated this memory—and this despite the fact that analysis of the 1956 monuments from this phase reveals a quite intriguing picture of innovative artistic statements.[17] In view of these trends, Hungarian society appears to be banning the memory of 1956 once again to its gray zones of abeyance. Once again, the question of the extent and manner in which Hungarian society has preserved the memory of 1956 below the chronicled surface is undecided. The media specialist Péter György[18] contends that this memory was initially repressed, then forced into private channels. Today it has been allowed to atrophy into a kind of limbo as the result of an intentional politics of selective memory. No sooner had that thesis been advanced than it was vehemently challenged by historians.[19]

For a short time after 1990, it appeared as if it might be possible to bring to a close a tragic period in the country's history soberly and without excessive pathos. After an emotional debate about how to remove the physical presence of socialist structures and monuments from the cityscape, a decision was finally made to create a monument park at the edge of Budapest.[20] This memorial meadow can also be read as a "monumental" illustration of Hayden White's thesis about alternative readings of historical events, including their ironization. Now after more than a decade, the still unfinished park made it possible for such irony to gain the upper hand:

> The realization of the embodiments of the past constantly accessible for purposes of memory, in the form of a park or open-air museum meant, over and beyond the removal of the statutes and "clean up" of public places, a kind of localizing of this past. Fenced in, the evil spirits petrified in stone, coupled with a rearrangement of the statues chronologically and thematically, a new narrative about socialism came into being. This was facilitated by the exploitation of the park for purposes of tourism—sic transit gloria mundi—as a marketing of the past.[21]

The more the memory of Stalinism and Kádárism becomes a part of the politics of memory of a state policy on culture and the past, the more irony is driven out, replaced by pure and unadulterated cynicism.[22] The motto of the new Momento Park set up by the ministry for the national cultural heritage is: "not irony, momento."[23] Yet it has a cynical ring, because what emerges is the very opposite of genuine memory. The remembrance of the relatively soft Kádár dictatorship, with its little loopholes, tiny special privileges and pervasive mendacity—where you could build your cozy private little world if you kept your public mouth shut—is now to be supplanted by the image of the "regime of communist terror." But Hungarian society has a different memory of the days of "goulash communism," and so this engenders precisely the opposite effect. More and more, if one can believe the opinion surveys, János Kádár is becoming a positive symbolic figure of the twentieth century.

Beginning with the school year 2000–01, three historic days of memorial were introduced at all Hungarian schools: the commemoration of the martyrs of Arad 1849,[24] the victims of communism, and the Holocaust. These became an obligatory ritual in the schools. The historian András Ger has commented that it probably would have been better "if the memorial day had centered on legal equality, still so easily infringed in Hungary, on human dignity, and then to show what happens when the principle of equal rights is violated. The Holocaust was the final point in a long process—an eternal memento of that path which simply portends the destruction of human dignity."[25]

Memory and the Holocaust

What role does the Shoah play in this special Hungarian discourse of memory? How is the Holocaust inscribed in the specific texture of memory and the politics of the Hungarian past? "In every country's memorials, in every national museum and archive, I found a different Holocaust; and at times, I found no Holocaust at all."[26] In any event, it is striking that in a country otherwise so heavy with history, there are no larger-scale debates about a memorial for the Holocaust. And that a debate over restitution and reparations similar to that in the German-speaking countries is barely audible, or in any event has little of the vehemence that characterizes it there. It is maybe still that the prerequisites are missing for the discussion of material restitution since the country still has not clarified its own responsibility. And it is also striking that Hungarians such as György Konrád and Imre Kertész are so centrally involved in this debate in the German-language press.

It should not be forgotten that the mass deportations and murders in 1944 were "Hungary's 20th-century Mohács. And there is nothing to gloss over. Hungary was the perpetrator, we Hungarians":[27] Auschwitz, together with Mauthausen, are the greatest mass grave of Hungarian history: 400,000 Hungarians, or more precisely 400,000 Hungarians declared by the Hungarian state to be Jews, were murdered here within the span of less than three months. The main point in the entire debate is that "we Hungarians" did this to "us Hungarians."

A book appeared in 1948 in which a political scientist described the historical situation of Jewish Hungarians and Hungarian anti-Semitism in a definitive way[28]—and in his view it actually was even then already too late. István Bibó's contribution to confronting and grappling with the past was banned immediately after the communist takeover, not to be republished until shortly before the overthrow of the Kádár regime. The Stalinist system simply had no need for an uncompromising analysis of Hungarian anti-Semitism, the moral neglect of Hungarian society, all its classes. The confrontation with this era became part of a cynical politics of the past; the guilty party were those who were to be excluded from the Stalinist project of a "new Hungary."

In the early 1980s, Bibó and his work became a kind of mentor voice of the democratic opposition, the integrating figure of a new and promising democratic political culture. At the end of the 1980s, many politicians prominent today lived as students in the István Bibó Home, a student dormitory that was run along the lines of radical democratic management—and therefore in many respects reflective of the political ideas of Bibó.[29] Today you only need to open a paper or turn on state-controlled television, which is one and the same no matter what party happens to be in power, in order to see that Bibó has been forgotten. Or was perhaps never taken all that seriously. That radical democrat has generally vanished from public political discourse: in a Hungary awash with remembrance, there is not a single bridge, street, or park named after him; maybe you can find a school somewhere.[30]

Bibó's book today stands in no need of revision. It remains a clear and surprisingly still-topical analysis, an uncompromising reckoning with Hungarian anti-Semitism, with clear suggestions on how to overcome and clarify the situation: "The demands for restitution and moral reparations for the persecutions of the Jews in Hungary were, from their inception, marked by nebulous circumstances and insincere preconditions."[31]

It was precisely this cynicism of the young Hungarian democracy after 1945, and most especially of the communist regime after 1948, that blocked any coming to terms with and working through of the Holocaust in Hungary, in an ironic vein as well. By contrast, and on the other side, the unbracketing of Stalinism and its taboo status had at least prepared the path or even facilitated its ironic "overcoming" already in the Kádár era. In Hungary, though differently than in Austria, everything was done to block a memory of World War II, and thus to "come to terms" with it. The topic after 1948 was not merely taboo but forbidden, or part of a specific politics of past history. The memory of those many Hungarian soldiers, non-Jews, who were simply fed into the jaws of the senseless slaughter was suppressed, deflected to an individual level. Any public declaration about personal suffering on the eastern front was obliterated, while surviving Hungarian Jews were allowed to recall their suffering only as a collective. As martyrs for the whole of Hungarian society, they were permitted to remember the horrors of Mauthausen or Auschwitz.

Here too it was the medium of film, with its relative measure of free space, that at least facilitated a kind of memory work. Censorship forced filmmakers to adopt a strange and distinctive language of imagery and narration (which rendered it impossible for broad segments of the population to decode it, this encrypting likewise part of its free space). But we owe to this conjunction numerous sensitive, explosive films on the Holocaust that are still valid and powerful today. Think of the work of Zoltán Fábri, whose "Utószezon" (Off-Season) was the great scandalous movie of 1967: it deals masterfully with the questions of Aryanization, restitution, guilt and expiation, here through the prism of a druggist's assistant and fellow-traveler. A powerful mode of cynicism is likewise present, because the film's main star was a well-known ex-Arrow Cross activist who had returned to Hungary after 1956:[32] a kind of Paula Wessely of the Hungarian cinema.[33]

As mentioned, only films about Stalinism were allowed a modicum of irony. Not until after 1990 did the films on this topic take on a recurrent pathos or schematic quality. They acquired the didactic textbook character of an exact film version of standard works in social science, where the main characters represent some tendency or direction that can be demonstrated empirically, sociologically, or in terms of political theory and science. History on a grand scale dominates the intimate strands of narrative. These films solidify a form of a history in theory, and therefore present an opportunistic past.[34] István Szabó's "A Taste of Sunshine" is similar in this regard: the central question of the film, which attempts to trace the fate of a Hungarian-Jewish family in the twentieth century in three episodes, is whether or not Jewish assimilation in Hungary failed.

At the end we see that this process was mistaken, senseless: the final descendant of the family chooses to readopt his original name.[35]

Immediately after the Great Turn, there was a short-term interesting development in Hungary: numerous villages and small towns spontaneously erected memorials in memory of the victims of World War II. Soldiers, victims of the bombing raids, and Jews were all remembered; the various classes of victims were not clearly distinguished.

Naturally, a "politically correct memory" should have differentiated more distinctively among the losses, but this was a spontaneous process without ulterior motives, simply the expression of a need to honor and commemorate the dead. Only in the course of the phase of consolidation of Hungarian democracy was this memorialization politicized, reformed according to political and racist categories. In the meanwhile, a genuine struggle over memory is being waged in Hungarian politics, frequently percolating into anti-Semitic undertones. It weighs victims in the scales, once again permitting only a selective memory.[36] Precisely in the discourse of memory, in scholarly debate, or the acceptance of certain rules regarding the Holocaust, there still seems to be a kind of boundary or barrier inside Europe. Many rules, codes, texts, images, and tacit compromises and agreements of postwar Western Europe are not (yet) valid in this part of Europe. But at the same time, memory of the Holocaust in Eastern and Central Europe still retains a democratic potential reminiscent of and nourished by the anti-fascist traditions in the region.

As an East-Central European country, Hungary will always be confronted with the problem of the necessity or ability to remember both the victims of National Socialism and Stalinism. As long as the mass victims of the German occupation and Hungarian collaboration remain in Hungarian memory as an ethnified collective, culturally and historically distinct, it will be impossible to really come to genuine terms with the Hungarian past. There will only be weighing in contrastive scales. And in such argumentation, a flaw will always be found in the reasoning of the other.

Of course, one must also be concerned here with the question of the singularity and comparability of the mass murders by the National Socialists and the communists. István Lovas, a well-known journalist of the right, sparked and stoked the debate in early 1999,[37] and it was continued in mid-November of that same year by the historian Mária Schmidt: "She compared the Holocaust and Gulag as parallels, failing to find the necessary expiation for the crimes committed by communism." Her dictum that in the perspective of the combatants, the Holocaust was a "secondary aspect of the world war," that neither the mass murder nor its prevention had been among the war aims neither of the Germans nor the Allies, led to a scandal and protests by the Association of Jewish Communities.[38]

But the fact remains: the memory of the Holocaust is not important either for Hungarian society or for the state-managed politics of past history. In a country so saturated with the substance of history, the question 'why?' is naturally justified. One answer is that Hungarian society, in contrast with Germany and Austria, still maintains that it bears no guilt in the Holocaust, which in Hungary was basically the doing of the Nazi occupiers. For that reason, a process of grieving was not necessary. But the fact is that the Budapest cityscape contains many memories of the persecutions of the Jews in the 1940s. A provocative thesis on why the debate on restitution is non-functional in Hungary is because the Jewish communities ("Jewish Hungarians") are chary of discussing the whole matter—because too much is at stake for them. Questioning of the process of assimilation of 150 years in Hungary is currently, after all, a dubious hot button in the Hungarian media. But naturally that too is only the result of persecution. As a rule, discussion is oriented to individual cases, such as the "gold train"[39] or the papers of the Herzog family.[40]

But it would "only" need one clarification: namely that Hungarian non-Jews persecuted that segment of Hungarian society that the state had declared to be "Jewish." That is still a long path ahead. Probably, the crux in the denial of memory work lies in the unparalleled state of neglect of Hungarian society in the 1940s.

> There were too many "skeletons in the closet." And unfortunately, to my mind this image rings partially true: 25 to 30 percent of Hungarian national wealth was concentrated at the time in the hands of the Hungarian Jews (five percent of the total population). That wealth was not lost or transformed, but rather was largely transferred to "Aryan" non-Jewish ownership. And this by means of a stealing of corpses in the most narrow sense of the term. Private property is not necessarily sacred: that was the common experience of hundreds of thousands, indeed on millions of Hungarians after 1938. Up to 1945, only the Jews had been the victims of this view.... After 1945, all plundered each other. Before 1945, the Jews were the sole victims. Almost all of "Christian" civil society participated in their plundering.[41]

Sixty years later, 2004, the memory of the Shoah has become something in Hungary that is virtually ubiquitous, but only if you really wish to see it. The townscape is now marked by innumerable small, quite impressive, honest and therefore moving memorials. All accessories of European forms of commemoration exist in Budapest, and in 2002, to an extent as a conclusion to crown this development, a Hungarian Holocaust museum opened its doors. But a deeper glance shows that this memory, or better this staging of a memory, remains very superficial. Sometimes, though not always, it resembles the "working off" of a kind of debt, of an almost burdensome duty, in order to prove one belongs in the ordered ranks of the European Union.

Architectural critics are unanimous in bemoaning the fact that the new Holocaust Museum, closed inwardly in its architectonics, is almost a building in hiding, located in a less than representative suburban area of the city, turning its back on the hustle and bustle of the metropolis. In actual fact, the architecturally closed quality of this ensemble in the Páva-utca is striking, contrasted with the great projects of Jewish memory at the beginning of the twentieth century, actually built or only on the drawing boards of utopian fantasy. Those structures or blueprints were replete with openness, edifices exuding the self-confidence of an ever more encompassing middle-class consciousness and process of Jewish assimilation.[42] It appears as if the museum is almost ashamed, as the memorial and documentation center for the 400,000 murdered Hungarian Jews, to have to document this fact, seemingly turning its gaze away from the city in which it stands.

Other great museums, such as the recently opened "House of Terror," devoted to the most recent contemporary history of the country, do not deal at all with this dark chapter in the Hungarian chronicle. As if they wished to relegate the entire topic to a Holocaust museum, as though the Shoah were not an integral part of Hungarian history:

> The museum has attracted controversy and should concern historians because of the exclusions on which the interpretations of history it presents is based. It concentrates in large part upon the crimes against humanity committed during the Stalinist years and minimises those committed prior to 1945. This "museum" presents an argument that implies that "terror" began with the Arrow Cross in October 1944. This effectively ensures that the deportation of Hungary's Jews to Auschwitz in the summer is given no coverage.... Furthermore the "museum" seeks to whitewash the issues of domestic collaboration and responsibility. Few historians would disagree that the understanding of Hungary's mid-twentieth century tragedies is impossible without consideration of the anti-semitic measures of the inter-war and early wartime years.[43]

Moreover, the form in which the awarding of the Nobel Prize to Imre Kertész in 2002 was celebrated in Hungary is more than a bit depressing in its implications. It was precisely the conservatives who repeatedly stressed their cultural traditions. Approaching the boundaries of what was detestable, they were in part not prepared to share the euphoria of a liberal and left-liberal public.[44] "The day after the announcement of the award, the Hungarian liberal daily *Magyar Hírlap* carried the ironic headline: "Imre Kertész, Hungarian author, is a Nobel laureate. Jew." The article predicted that the decision in Stockholm would "tear open a wound that would run straight through Hungarian culture, history and society."[45] And that is what indeed has come to pass.

But Hungarian civil society did raise its voice in the spring of 2004, as the 60th anniversary of the deportation of Hungarian Jews neared. The reason was that the Cultural Committee of the Budapest Municipality decided to erect a monument to the former prime minister Pál Teleki, a leading protagonist of anti-Semitic legislation in Hungary in the interwar period, who committed suicide in 1941 in the wake of Hungary's attack on Yugoslavia (with which it had signed a nonaggression pact). While recognizing Teleki's act as an important symbolic gesture, these citizens opposed putting up a public monument to a former Hungarian prime minister who had never dissociated himself from his own anti-Semitism. And the mayor of Budapest has called on the Cultural Committee to review its decision. This is a hopeful sign.

In 1998, commenting in a respected German weekly long before he became Nobel laureate, Imre Kertész wondered whether it was permissible to laugh about the Holocaust.[46] His answer was unequivocal: if the rules of the game are unambiguous and everything is clear, of course you can. But memory of the Holocaust in Hungary has been mendacious since the beginning, murky, cynical. State politics of past history, Stalinist, Kádárist and nationalist, and "Christian" civil society had always been in agreement on that. That is why neither Hungarian society nor state politics of memory dared broach the topic, and certainly not by the means of irony. And up until today, memory of the Holocaust, despite all the historical eloquence and the hysterical drivel, has remained cloaked in silence.

Translated from the German by Bill Templer

Notes

1. Hilde Weiss and Christoph Reinprecht, *Demokratischer Patriotismus oder ethnischer Nationalismus in Ostmitteleuropa. Empirische Analysen zur nationalen Identität in Ungarn, Tschechien, Slowakei und Polen* (Vienna, 1998), 139f.
2. Béla Rásky and Karin Liebhart, Hösök áldozatok, vértanúk / Helden, Opfer, Märtyrer. Versuch einer Genealogie in ungarischen und österreichischen nationalen Mythen und historischen Erzählungen, in *Zeitreise Heldenberg. Lauter Helden. Katalog zur Niederösterreichischen Landesausstellung 2005*, ed. Wolfgang Müller Funk and Georg Kugler (Vienna, 2005), 77–84.
3. It is also striking that the debate in Western Europe pays attention to Central and Eastern European discourse only in exceptional cases, see T.G. Ashplant, Graham Dawson, and Michael Roper, eds., *The Politics of War Memory and Commemoration* (London/New York, 2000).
4. Árpád von Klimó, *Nation, Konfession, Geschichte. Zur nationalen Geschichtskultur Ungarns im europäischen Kontext (1860–1948)* (Munich, 2003).
5. Zsolt K. Horváth, "Önarcképcsarnok. A személyes emlékezés mint történeti probléma" [The Hall of Self-Portraits. Personal Memory As a Historical Problem], in *A történész szerszámosládája* [The Tool-Kit of the Historian], ed. András Szekeres (Budapest 2002), 81–102, here 93.
6. Bibó István, "Eltorzult magyar alkat, zsákutcás magyar történelem" [Hungarian Character Deformed, Hungary's History in a Dead-End Street], in *Összegyűjtött munkái*, ed. Európai Protestáns Magyar Szabadegyetem [European Academy of Protestant Hungarians], vol. 1 (Bern, 1982), 255–286.
7. See Imre Kertész, "Zeit der Entscheidung. Wird es auferstehen?! Europa von Osten betrachtet," *Neue Zürcher Zeitung*, 20/21 January 2001, 51f.: "In Hungary ... we've already seen how the self-pitying cultivation of historical traumata and frustrations in a nation can release the worst powers, exclusively minded of catastrophe, exploiting catastrophe."
8. Ferenc Glatz, "Der Zusammenbruch der Habsburger-Monarchie und die ungarische Geschichtswissenschaft," *Studia Historica* 180 (Budapest, 1980).
9. Dieter Simon, "Verordnetes Vergessen," in *Amnestie oder die Politik der Erinnerung in der Demokratie*, ed. Gary Smith and Avishai Margalit (Frankfurt a.M., 1997), 21–36, 31; quote in: Günther Sandner, "Hegemonie und Erinnerung. Zur Konzeption von Geschichts- und Vergangenheitspolitik," *Österreichische Zeitschrift für Politikwissenschaft* 30, no. 1 (2001): 5–19, here 11.
10. The best and best-known example for this is the film "The Witness" by Péter Bacsó, see: http://us.imdb.com/title/tt0065067 (14 September 2004).
11. The script is based on true events of eleventh-century Hungarian history: the story of King László I. His coronation closed the long chaotic interregnum after István's death and consolidated Hungary's position as a strong Christian Kingdom in medieval Europe, see http://us.imdb.com/title/tt0281154 (14 September 2004).
12. See András Gerő, *Der Heldenplatz Budapest als Spiegel ungarischer Geschichte* (Budapest, 1990).
13. "Nagy Imre temetése, és az 56-os emlékmű születése. Mihancsik Zsófia interjúja Rajk Lászlóval és Jovánovics Györggyel" ["The Funeral of Imre Nagy and the Birth of the 1956 Memorial. Zsófia Mihancsik's Interview with László Rajk and György Jovánovics"], *budapesti negyed* 2, no. 1 (1994): 122–145.

14. Gábor Bachman, László Rajk and Miklós Peternák, *Ravatal. Catafalque* [Laying Out] (Budapest, 1989), 31.
15. Éva Kovács, "Mythen und Rituale des ungarischen Systemwechsels," *Österreichische Zeitschrift für Geschichtswissenschaften* 10, no. 2 (1999): 210–237, here 220.
16. Another reading is that this staging was a self-deception of Hungarian society, akin to the Havel phenomenon in the Czech Republic. Hungary made itself believe after 1989 that it had preserved the values of the 1956 Revolution. And in the cultic act of reburial, it had more or less wished to prove this to itself.
17. See Boros Géza, *Emlékmüvek '56-nak* [Monuments for 1956] (Budapest, 1997).
18. György Péter, *Néma Hagyomány. Kollektív felejtés és a kései múltértelmezés 1956 1989-ben. A régmúltól az örökségig* [Silent Tradition. Collective Forgetting and Belated Interpretation of the 1956 Revolution in 1989. From the Past to Heritage] (Budapest, 2000).
19. Gyáni Gábor, "1956 elfelejtésének régi-új mítosza" ["Old-New Myth about Forgetting in '56"], *Élet és Irodalom*, 9 February 2001; Rainer M. János, "1956 változó emlékezete" ["Changeable memory of 1956"], *Magyar Hírlap*, 21 October 2000 and Litván György, "Az elnémult hagyomány," *Élet és irodalom*, 13 April 2001.
20. György Szücs, "A 'zsarnokság' szoborparkja" ["The Monument Meadow of Tyranny"], *budapesti negyed* 2, no. 1 (1994), 151–165.
21. Kovács, *Mythen und Rituale des ungarischen Systemwechsels*, 234f.
22. I owe thanks to Éva Kovács for pointing this out.
23. "Memento Park—Budapest avagy az emlékezés mementója" ["Memento Park Budapest or the Momento of Memory"], see www.szoborpark.hu/mementopark/emlekezes.htm (1 May 2001) and interview with the designer Ákos Eleőd in *Magyar Narancs*, no. 22 (2001), 28f.
24. The fortress of Arad (in Transylvania, now Romania) played a great role in the Hungarian struggle for independence in 1849. Defended by the Austrian general Berger until the end of July 1849, it was then captured by the Hungarian rebels; they made it their headquarters during the latter part of the insurrection. It was from this fortress that Kossuth issued his famous proclamation on 11 August 1849, and it was here that he handed over supreme military and civil power to Görgei. Arad became the capital of Hungary for a very short time, 2–9 August 1849. It was soon captured by the Russians on August 17, shortly after the surrender of Görgei to the Russians at Világos. Thirteen Hungarian rebel generals were executed at Arad on 6 October 1849.
25. András Gerő, "2000. október vége—Egy polgár naplója" ["End of October 2000—A Citizen's Diary"], *Magyar Hírlap*, 28 October 2000.
26. James E. Young, *Writing and Rewriting the Holocaust: Narrative and Consequences of Interpretation* (Bloomington, 1988), 172.
27. Komoróczy Géza, "Magyar Jorcajt," in *Holocaust. A pernye beleég a bőrünkbe* [Holocaust. The Ashes are Burning into our Skin], ed. Géza Komoróczy (Budapest, 2000), 72–79, here 74.
28. István Bibó, *Zur Judenfrage. Am Beispiel Ungarns nach 1944* (Frankfurt a.M., 1990).
29. "Szeplőletlen fogantatás" [Immaculate conception], *Népszabadság*, 2 June 2001.
30. Finally, at the end of May 2005 a monument for him was inaugurated in Central Budapest; see "Bibó-szobrot avattak" ["Bibo monument inaugurated"], *Népszabadság*, 21 May 2005.

31. István Bibó, *Zur Judenfrage*, 144f. The word "account" (*Rechenschaft*) in my 1990 translation was replaced here by "restitution," since it seems more applicable in the context of the present debate. See also Emery George, "István Bibó, 'The Jewish Question in Hungary'—A Review Essay," *Cross Currents* 4 (1985): 47—57.
32. Bikácsy Gergely, "Mítoszok és parabolák" [Myths and parables], *Beszélő Évek* (Budapest, 2001), 531–535, here 532.
33. See Maria Steiner, *(Un)gebrochene Kontinuitäten. Paula Wessely—Eine "österreichische Institution"* (Vienna/Innsbruck, 2000).
34. Éva Kovács, "A hinta szédülete. A 'Glamour' és közhelyei" ["Rocking Phantasmata, Rocking Dizziness. The Movie 'Glamour' and its Platitudes"], *Magyar Narancs*, no. 48 (2000).
35. See review, http://www.indiewire.com/people/int_Szabo_Istvan_000612.html (14 September 2004).
36. Géza, *Holocaust.*
37. See on this also: Sándor Révész, "Egy plagizátor" ["A Plagiarist"] and László Karsai, "Holokauszt: eygediség, tények, hazugságok" ["Holocaust: Singularity, Facts and Lies"], *Élet és irodalom*, 6 April 2001, 4f.
38. A.O. [Andreas Oplatka], "Politisierter Historikerstreit in Ungarn. Holocaust und Gulag—Umstrittene Meinungen und Deutungen," *Neue Zürcher Zeitung*, 24 November 1999.
39. Kádár Gábor and Vági Zoltán, *Aranyvonat* [The Gold Train] (Budapest, 2001). See also Ronald W. Zweig, *The Gold Train—The Destruction of Jews and the Looting of Hungary* (New York, 2002); likewise "The Mystery of the Hungarian 'Gold Train,'" http://www.holocaustassets.gov/goldtrainfinaltoconvert.html (14 September 2004).
40. On this battle over looted Nazi art in Hungary and the recent lawsuit to regain objects from the stolen Herzog collection, see www.ontheglobe.com/notes/notes62.htm (14 September 2004). The Herzog Collection was formed by the banker Baron Mor Lipot Herzog, and originally contained 1,500 to 2,500 objects. Following the Nazi occupation of Hungary in 1944, a large portion of the collection was taken from its hiding place outside Budapest. Later the Hungarian State Security Police found the works and delivered them to SS Commander Adolf Eichmann. Eichmann evidently made his personal selection, which was subsequently shipped to Germany. The remaining works, including those involved in the lawsuit, were eventually handed over to the Museum of Fine Arts for safekeeping.
41. Ungváry Krisztián, "Kerülve kellemetlen kérdéseket. Gyurgyák János: a zsidókérdés Magyarországon" ["Avoiding Unpleasant Questions: On János Gyurgyák's New Publication on the Jewish Question in Hungary"], *Magyar Narancs*, no. 22 (2001): 24–26, here 26.
42. See Kinga Frojimovics, et al., eds., *Jewish Budapest: Monuments, Rites, History* (Budapest, 1999).
43. See Mark Pittaway, comments on the House of Terror, http://h-net.msu.edu/cgi-bin/logbrowse.pl (14 September 2004).
44. See Kóczián Péter, "Kertész Imre és a jobboldal" ["Imre Kertész and the Right"], *Népszabadság*, 24 October 2002, 12, especially the headlines in the leading Hungarian dailies on 11 October 2002.
45. Nicolas Pethes, "Nobel-Dilemma. Ist Imre Kertész falsch? Ein Blick in die ungarischen Feuilletons" (Ms., in the possession of the author).
46. *Die Zeit*, 19 November 1998; Hungarian translation in: *Népszabadság*, 28 November 1998.

— *Twelve* —

Recovering Austrian Memory: Stratifying Restitution Debates

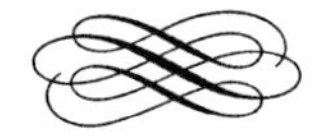

Heidemarie Uhl

The debates on restitution of property stolen during the Nazi period rank among the principal transnational emblems of a European process of wrestling with the past and coming to terms with it. That process has been a powerful factor in dislodging and supplanting the "political myths in postwar Europe"[1] and the associated denial and suppression of National Socialist crimes from collective memory. Since the mid-1980s, in fundamental debates on the place of National Socialism in the national image of history and the interpretations and representations of the Holocaust, there has been a kind of renegotiation of that historical image. In that new stocktaking, dominant views regarding the supposed resistance of one's "own" people when it came to Nazi crimes, or the nation's basic innocence, have forfeited a certain degree of their legitimacy.

Not just in Germany and Austria, the "successor states of the Great German Empire,"[2] is discourse on guilt now emerging as a "motif of collective self-assurance of eminent importance for the shaping of culture."[3] In numerous countries in Europe, the question of collective and individual entanglement in the Holocaust has led to a series of public debates.[4] Symbolic acts requesting forgiveness from the victims of Nazism and official declarations of shared responsibility for National Socialist crimes have become indicators for the respective degree of transformation of the social culture of memory in its orientation to the Holocaust as a central historical reference point. In this same vein, within cultural memory new days of commemoration and monuments have been engineered, and there has been struggle over how these forms of remembrance should be implemented. In this process of renegotiated history, the question of restitution has taken on a special function with respect to the "guilt of nations."[5] Specifically in this realm, the abstract political declaration of guilt has been transformed into new concrete forms of communication between groups whose past was in effect spliced and interlinked by a "historical crime."

In the ensemble of social forms of action in the area of the politics of memory and culture, the question of restitution would appear to be on a level of realistic politics describable in the categories of economic-political and legislative-juridical procedures. However, Sigrid Weigel has pointed to the complex interlinkage between economic and symbolic dimensions of the *dispositiv* (Foucault) or "apparatus" of restitution: measures of material reparations emerge against the backdrop of the "desire to cleanse oneself of the guilt inherited from the fathers" and the quest for corresponding rituals.[6] In the "logic of compensation" (Weigel), material restitution payments are not "neutral." Rather, they are bound up with projections of "compensating" for guilt, its *Wiedergutmachung*, and reconciliation with the collective of victims. Its recipients are drawn into a "scenario of reconciliation." But the fear is that the "conversion of guilt into debts and the associated possibility of repayment" and thus erasure of those debts is now reopening that final chapter in the working through and settlement of the past—a culmination that had been vehemently demanded in the decades of the denial of possible guilt, to no avail.[7]

The present paper analyzes the interlocking of economic-political and symbolic forms of action in the question of restitution as illustrated in the example of Austria. Two aspects are highlighted. First, I look at the connection between the new debate on restitution and the paradigm shift in dealing with Nazi rule. It can be termed a paradigm shift of sorts, because placement of the issue of restitution on the agenda of public communication was possible only after authorities and the public mood began to distance themselves, at least partially, from the thesis of Austria as Nazism's first national "victim," and came to recognize Austrian guilt or shared responsibility for and complicity in the Holocaust. Second, I examine the intentions and symbolic forms in the policy on history and the culture of memory associated with restitution measures since 1995 in the Republic of Austria.

The Shift in Perspective on the National Socialist Past and the Reemergence of the Debate on Restitution in Austria

In the Austrian context, the first discernable beginnings of a reemergence of the question of restitution were at the end of the 1980s. Here a topic gained new relevance that otherwise had come to be viewed as a closed chapter in postwar history. After the Austrian government had initially rejected reparations payments, citing the "victim status" of the country between 1938 and 1945, the "great Austrian reparations" in 1961 were largely based on adoption of the guidelines of the indemnification laws in West Germany.[8] This appeared to bring to a close debate on compensation for the victims of Nazism.

Not until the end of the twentieth century did a new sensibility arise about the fact that those groups of victims not easily subsumed under the category of politically persecuted individuals had not received adequate compensation after 1945, and that there was a lingering continuity in anti-Semitic bias and resentment in regard to the claims of Jewish victims. The awareness of an existing injustice was promoted by research on the inadequate indemnification paid. In addition, the "disturbing remains"[9] began to make their presence felt. Questions of guilt and responsibility for the Holocaust and for nonpayment of restitution or only insufficient compensation are inscribed in the material estates left behind by the victims of National Socialism. Former Jewish property now appeared contaminated by a dimension of guilt which extended beyond the concrete responsibility of the "generation of perpetrators" of Nazi crimes, casting its shadow on the behavior of the second and third generation.

Since the shift in looking at the Austrian Nazi past, driven in part by the Waldheim debate (1986), the question of restitution had become one of the central topics in a critical confrontation with the "repressed" National Socialist past, not just in scholarly and intellectual discourse. In 1987, the Documentation Archives of the Austrian Resistance, together with the ministry of education in Vienna, the Jewish community, the Jewish Welcome Service, and other cultural and educational organizations organized a competition for best essay on the topic "Austrians and Persecution of the Jews." This was conceived as a contribution by the Documentation Archives to the 50th anniversary of the year 1938. The winning essay was the "History of the Piano" by a Vienna high school student aged 12. Sandra Melloni had heard about this project from a German language teacher and she was certain she had to be involved even before she had considered "what I could actually write about." An associate at the Archives suggested she write about émigré Jews, but Sandra decided that topic was "too broad and difficult." At the same time, she got the "great news" from her mother that she would soon be receiving a special gift, the piano of her grandmother. The history of that piano became the point of departure for the transgenerational narrative about Nazi persecution. "Munching vanilla cookies and drinking tea, we looked through all kinds of old documents," learned about "Aryanization" ("That's how they used to call it then when they ripped the Jews off, stole something") and failure to restitute: because this piano had belonged to a friend of her great-grandmother who had emigrated. Sandra's grandmother herself had been racially persecuted, and after the *Anschluss* in 1938, "when she was as old as I am today," she had been forced to leave school.[10]

Sandra Melloni's text itself documents the fact that over and beyond all the controversy, political and scholarly, about the "thesis of Austria as a victim," which dominated discourse in the commemorative year 1988,[11] the "memory of things"[12] generated a lasting source of perturbation. The inscription into the material estates of the victims of the Nazi crimes and the continuing injustice after 1945 of the failure to provide any or any adequate compensation began to contaminate family narratives and local, institutional, and company tales. The real or symbolic acceptance by the third generation of a contaminated legacy—namely, the possessions of the Jews which had been Aryanized—transformed the question of guilt from an abstract historical guilt related to the collective or the state into an "embodied" guilt immersed in facts and circumstances that were concrete and real.

The unease generated by the "topography of theft"[13] of the property of some 130,000 emigrated and 65,000 murdered Jewish Austrians evidently demanded reactions. Since the mid-1990s, there have been numerous activities in Austria connected with a symbolic and material reparation. These opened up various forms of communication by the "society of perpetrators" with the "collectivity of victims." The associated "possibilities for reconciliation"[14] mobilized social energies and imagination that transformed restitution into a complex field for action situated between strategy in the official policy on history on the one hand and desires for reconciliation on the other. As mentioned, it had only been possible in Austria to open the gate to this field of activity after the thesis of Austria as Hitler's victim and the associated "externalization" of National Socialism and its removal from the historical system of reference had lost validity during the course of the heated debate on Waldheim.

This sense of unease was thematized ambivalently in the new "negotiations" of the Austrian historical narrative in the late 1980s. For one thing, in the commemorative year 1988, the question of some acceptance of guilt in Nazi crimes was placed on the official agenda in Austria. Two years earlier, the doctrine of Austria qua victim that had guided action since 1945 had been drained of its core legitimacy. Kurt Waldheim's attempt to justify his own actions by referring to the "fulfillment of duty" in the German Wehrmacht was incompatible with Austrian self-identity as the "first free country to fall victim to Nazi aggression." A country whose people had supposedly been "led into a senseless and hopeless war of conquest ... which no Austrian had ever desired," as the Declaration of Independence, the foundational document of the Second Republic, had stated on 27 April 1945.[15]

The erosion of the thesis of National Socialism's "first victim," which since 1945 had dominated Austrian self-description and the position of the government regarding "reparations," now demanded the reconstruction of a valid official standpoint on how to deal with the Nazi past by representatives of the Austrian state. The commemoration of the 1938 *Anschluss* thus opened up a kind of performative setting in which it was then possible to express the new position on events from 1938 to 1945. Though the thesis of Austria as victim was not totally discarded, it was largely limited to the level of Austria's status in international law ("As a state, Austria was indeed the first victim of National Socialist Germany," said foreign minister Alois Mock [Austrian People's Party] at an official commemorative ceremony on 11 March 1988 in the Hofburg in Vienna). By contrast, the behavior of Austrian citizens was given a more differentiated assessment. There was talk for the first time by government leaders of a constellation of perpetrators and victims, explicitly mentioned in the television address by President Kurt Waldheim on 10 March 1988: "We must never forget that many of the worst Nazi thugs were Austrians. There were Austrians who were victims and others who were perpetrators." Although there could be no collective guilt, Waldheim wished to "apologize as president of Austria for the crimes of National Socialism committed by Austrians."[16]

The political declarations of March 1988 contained the first formulation of that new narrative in political rhetoric on dealing with the Nazi past, which Oliver Marchart has called the "discourse of confession."[17] This was the recognition of the victims and their descendants as part of Austria's history and the associated generally unarticulated expectation that confessing guilt and repentance would induce victims and their families to forgive Austria and come to a reconciliation with Austrians and their past. But the official positions voiced in 1988 also contain models of explanation still explicitly beholden to the policy on history shaped by the thesis of Austria as a Nazi victim. That also includes the presentation of the official position of the Austrian government on the question of restitution. Apparently criticism of the policy of reparations of the Second Republic was so virulent that an "official reaction" appeared necessary.

The Question of Reparations in the Context of Austria as Nazi's First Victim

The official presentation of the question of restitution by the Austrian Press Service on the occasion of the commemorative year 1988 gives concentrated expression to the official rhetoric of justification that had dominated the question of material reparations and indemnification since the 1950s. In 1988, the series "Austria Documentation" published a brochure on "Measures by the Republic of Austria since 1945 for the Benefit of Certain Individuals Persecuted for Political, Religious or Racial Reasons." This brochure was distributed by the government in translation, most vigorously abroad. It begins by stating: "Austria was invaded by heavily armed German troops on 12 March 1938, thus becoming the first victim of Hitler's aggression. By this action, the country was stripped of its ability to act on the stage of international law or domestic affairs." The Moscow Declaration on Austria's status as "first victim" had been made in "clear recognition of the historical facts," (and not, as Robert Keyserlingk and Günter Bischof have shown, as an instrument of psychological warfare[18]). The Nuremberg Military Tribunal stated in its decision on 1 October 1946 that the "violent nature of the Anschluss had been recently conclusively proven on the basis of historical fact." The four signatory powers also dropped the so-called paragraph on co-responsibility in the final phase of negotiations on Austrian sovereignty.

For that reason, the official presentation of restitution measures by the Republic of Austria concluded that the Republic "was not basically obligated to reparations for injustices against those politically persecuted for reasons of politics, religion or their origin," because "according to the principles of international law, an injustice should be compensated by the guilty party. But Austria is in no way a legal successor state of the former German Reich." Nonetheless, "in consideration of the terrible injustice and suffering perpetrated against those persecuted by National Socialism," Austria regarded it as "a moral obligation, beyond the restitution of property confiscated by the National Socialist rulers, to assume responsibility for the payment of financial reparations, and to take other legal measures in order to ameliorate the fate of individuals who have suffered from previous persecution."[19] This statement precedes the documentation of the "measures of assistance, laws of compensation and reparation" and "further compensation by the Republic of Austria" and "other benefits for those who have suffered persecution," as well as "benefits in the area of social insurance" (these are the section headings). These are meant to show that "since 1945, the Republic of Austria had introduced and implemented numerous laws and measures to benefit individuals persecuted for reasons of politics, religion and origin."

The documentation of the Press Office presents a strict formulation of that pattern of argumentation that had been developed since 1945 in the framework of the conception of Austria as Nazism's first victim. This concept, arguing that the *Anschluss* had been a military occupation and the subsequent period had been a foreign dictatorship imposed upon the Austrian people, had been used to dismiss responsibility for the crimes of the Nazi regime and any material claims by its victims. The function of this thesis as the foundational narrative of the Second Republic was largely limited to externalizing the years 1938–45, in effect bracketing or removing them from the context of Austrian history. Its positive meaning, the notion of Austria as an "anti-Nazi" country and the broad popular identification with the "Austrian liberation struggle" against the Nazi regime was limited, aside from a short "anti-fascist" phase in the early postwar period, to Austria's self-presentation on the international stage.

By contrast, on the domestic political front, new strategies were pursued in the politics of integration toward former Nazis and in the context of the Cold War. They were geared to a symbolic rehabilitation of those strata in the population that had not opposed the Nazi regime. One such indicator of this policy was the way the landscape of memorialization for the victims of the war and the Nazi crimes was configured in the postwar period. The memory of the resistance and the victims of the Nazi regime was increasingly marginalized, while remembrance of the soldiers who had died in World War II "faithfully performing their duty" became the predominant factor shaping the Austrian landscape of memory in the Second Republic.[20]

But there was consensus regarding the potential for foreign policy and image-building abroad of the conception of Austria as a victim. That conception went hand in hand with a kind of natural reflex of resistance to accepting any responsibility for the crimes of the Nazi regime. A comparison between the "documentation" mentioned and the rejection of reparations payments by the Austrian government in the 1950s points up the continuity in this line of argument and the strategies regarding the proper policy toward history derived from such argumentation. When the Jewish Claims Conference, after concluding an agreement with Bonn, leading in 1953 to the Federal Law on Compensation, made similar demands on Austria, the government retreated to the position that Austria had been a country occupied by the Germans. Therefore, in terms of international law, it had no obligation for financial reparation, nor did it have any moral obligation, since crimes against the Austrian Jews had been perpetrated by Germans. Members of the Committee for Jewish Claims on Austria were told that "all the sufferings by the Jews during this time were inflicted upon them by Germans, not by Austrians. Austria had no blame for these terrible acts, and where there was no guilt there could be no obligation for compensation."[21] Only after world public opinion and the Allied Council exerted pressure did the government back down and decide to provide indemnification, though without recognition of the basic principle of responsibility.[22]

The Concept of Shared Responsibility and the New Direction in Austrian Restitution Policy

Under the impact of the shift in perspective as result of the Waldheim debate, the effects of the master narrative of the concept of Austria as victim on dealing with the actual victims of the National Socialist regime became a key topic in public and scholarly critique of the failings of Austrian policy on national history. In 1988, the British historian Robert Knight created a veritable sensation with his publication of the minutes of official meetings of the cabinet and Ministerial Council on the question of reparations for Jewish victims of Nazism. These protocols showed a "surprising discrepancy between the way the government presented itself in public at the time and what was actually said among the ministers in private discussion."[23] For example, a meeting of the Ministerial Council on November 9, 1948, the 10th anniversary of the pogrom, discussed the miserable situation of the 9,000 Jews living in Vienna. A member of the government advanced the argument that was apparently already common soon after the end of the war: "the injustice suffered by the Jews was not caused by Austria." Minister Helmer (Socialist Party) responded: "what was taken away from the Jews was not on the level of the Great German Reich. A large proportion of that is connected with a segment of our own countrymen." He went on to say, thereby formulating an anti-Jewish ressentiment, that the "Jews were prominently represented everywhere among doctors and in commerce, especially in Vienna." And "in 1945, the Nazis were also stripped of everything." So in his view compensation for the Jews should be "dragged out indefinitely."[24]

In her research on reparations policy, Brigitte Bailer-Galanda in particular has pointed up the injustices and paradoxes in respect to legal measures for victims of Nazism. In the logic of the theory of Austria as victim, the status of victim was associated with the struggle for a free and independent Austria. So initially only those in the political resistance were given the status of a victim of the regime. Characteristic of social welfare for victims, especially in the early postwar period was that Jews and other categories of victims, such as Roma and Sinti, homosexuals, euthanasia victims, "asocial individuals," army deserters and others were at a decided disadvantage when compared to political victims. The victims of the "Austrian freedom struggle" served to legitimate the concept of Austria as a victim. Immediately after the end of the war, they were granted a privileged status as victim. Corresponding benefits were not granted those who had been racially persecuted until changes were introduced in the law on social welfare for victims, since the former had not been "actively engaged" in the struggle for an independent Austria. They had not "fought with a weapon in their hand or in total commitment in word and deed" for that new Austria.[25] For example, this was the argument mustered to reject the claim of the heirs of the conscientious objector Franz Jägerstätter. It was argued that his opposition to the Nazi regime had not been due to "his active struggle for a free, democratic Austria," but rather was the product of his religious convictions.[26]

On the whole, however, measures for the benefit of victims of the Nazi regime were increasingly placed side by side with compensation for Wehrmacht soldiers and even for former National Socialists. The linking of improvements in legislation for victims with laws for the benefit of former Nazis or Aryanizers and former soldiers (including members of the Waffen-SS) implied a "formal equation of victims and perpetrators."[27] In efforts to win the votes of former Nazis, the National Socialists who had been subject to de-Nazification measures were in many cases even portrayed as the "real" victims.

In 1961–62, the restitution question was viewed by the Austrian government as having been brought largely to a satisfactory conclusion as a result of the "large-scale Austrian compensation package," which included the Compensation Fund Act (*Abgeltungsfondsgesetz*), the 12th supplement to the Law on Social Welfare for Victims, the arrangements for West German payments to Austria in respect to the period of National Socialism within the framework of the Kreuznach Agreement, and the establishment of the New Assistance Fund.[28] The lines of conflict in relation to the complex of restitution of property and compensation for Nazi persecution began to fade and blur. The topic largely vanished from the public stage or remained restricted to discourse inside the Jewish communities and the victims' organizations.

In this way, it was possible for the impression to arise that Austria had been rather successful in dealing with its past, including the question of indemnification and restitution. This was the view expressed by the official 1988 brochure mentioned above, which summed up by observing: "All in all, it would appear that the compensation measures introduced by the Republic of Austria for alleviating the material losses of those persecuted for racist reasons are quite substantial in the light of the numerous obligations on Austria as a result of the State Treaty, the need to provide relief for the damage arising from the war and postwar period, and in consideration of Austrian non-responsibility for all such damages and claims." So the Republic should not blame itself in this regard. Rather, the victims of racist persecution were in fact a privileged group in comparison with other groups in the population: "In any event, compensation paid to persons who suffered political persecution, the overwhelming proportion of whom were persecuted for reasons of race, is far greater than compensation accorded to other persons who suffered injury and damage as a result of events during and after the war."[29] This passage creates the impression that the Jewish victims received more than they had actually been accorded. The "boundaries of what could be stated in public" in regard to allusions that might be interpreted as anti-Semitic were evidently not marked, even in the commemorative year of 1988, by that degree of linguistic sensitivity which became determinant for the official "discourse of confession" in subsequent years.

In the narrative economy of the Austrian memory, however, the argument for Austria as a victim receded into the background, and this despite repeated efforts to reactivate it, especially by the government of the People's Party and Freedom Party. The historical image of the postwar myths and mythologems, and their associated strategies of justification and denial, found little support in the key bodies of interpretation in Austrian society, especially in scholarship and science. What gained ground instead? A new broaching of the question of guilt and the quest for forms of symbolic and concrete reparations. The most lasting resonance in respect to a new political positioning in dealing with the past has been generated by the avowal of a "shared responsibility for the suffering inflicted on other human beings and peoples, not by Austria as a state, but by individual Austrians"—a confession of faith uttered by Chancellor Franz Vranitzky on 8 July 1991 before the Austrian National Parliament.[30] This declaration continues to be regarded, even beyond the political turning point of 2000, as a valid new definition of official policy on history and national memory.

Symbolic and Material Restitution since 1995

The official avowal of shared responsibility, already anticipated by the expression of guilt in March 1988, opened up a performative frame that provided the prerequisite for forms of action within a new culture of memory. The commemorative year 1988 saw several first acts of symbolic reparations on an official plane. The monument by Alfred Hrdlicka against war and fascism erected on the Albertinaplatz in Vienna, but also many initiatives in smaller towns and cities in memory of the night of the great pogrom (monuments, solemn commemorations), signified a kind of "sign of repentance" for the historical guilt and complicity in the Nazi crimes. When in November 1988 in Graz a monument for the destroyed synagogue was unveiled, officials from the municipality spoke about a "memorial to our shameful deeds."[31] In November 1997, one year after declaration of January 27, the day the Red Army liberated Auschwitz, as the official memorial day for the victims of fascism in Germany, the leadership of the Austrian Parliament decided to declare a national memorial day on May 5, the day the concentration camp Mauthausen was liberated, as a "clear and unmistakable sign" of solidarity with the "European year against racism and xenophobia."[32]

In the mid-1990s, the first steps for reparations were also taken. In 1995, on the occasion of the 50th anniversary of the Second Republic, the National Fund of the Republic of Austria for the Victims of National Socialism was established. Its very name makes clear that it is an enterprise of national importance, to a certain extent a material expression of the "acknowledgement of our own guilt" and the associated "recognition of the victims."[33] This intention was also reflected in the text of the law: the goal of the National Fund and the reparations to be paid to the victims of the Nazi regime was to "express the special responsibility we have toward the victims of National Socialism."[34] The task of the National Fund was to "distribute the symbolic amount of 70,000 shillings ($5,087) to all victims of National Socialism, designed as a gesture to communicate to them the special responsibility of the

Republic of Austria for the injustices suffered."[35] With this one-time "symbolic payment," "all victims of National Socialism, including for the first time groups not taken into account before," were to be given symbolic recognition.[36] The relevance of the symbolic aims for the agenda of the National Fund may also have influenced the makeup of its executive board. A dedicated team around its general secretary, Hannah M. Lessing, assisted the board in moving beyond its function as a center for information and service to become a node for non-bureaucratic encounter, inquiry, and communication, especially for Jews expelled from Austria.[37] In personal dialog and in written correspondence with emigrants, an attempt was made "to build a human bridge to the victims still alive." At the same time, a letter of response to applicants admitted that "we are well aware that neither the immeasurable human suffering nor impairment to personal health nor the loss of one's homeland can be compensated for and 'made good again' in any way."[38] Excerpts from letters of thanks shed light on the reactions of the surviving victims to this "symbolic gesture." These are often moving documents expressing an emotional bond with the countries from which they were driven. But they also contain expressions of rage, anger, and sadness. Yet the majority of the reactions to this "gesture of apology, consolation and respect" (President of the Parliament Heinz Fischer) by the Republic of Austria showed that the "desire for reconciliation" on the part of the descendants of the "society of perpetrators" was viewed positively.[39]

But the situation in Austria changed fundamentally in 1995 as debate flared over "dormant" bank accounts of Holocaust victims and the "stolen gold" in Switzerland[40] and subsequent legal steps taken by Holocaust survivors (class-action suits). Now it was no longer symbolic gestures for the victims but rather the legal demands by the victims, in the courts, that shaped the further debate on restitution.

Demands for the return of "Aryanized" property became a topic of national interest with the eruption of the "debate on art theft" in January 1998. The seizure of two paintings, "Portrait of Wally" and "Dead City" by Egon Schiele, from the Leopold Collection by a Manhattan attorney during an extensive Schiele exhibition in 1998 at the Museum of Modern Art in New York "aroused the emotions of the entire nation."[41] Further suits followed. The case of Bloch-Bauer became a matter that assumed national significance in Austria. It involved the demand by the granddaughter of Adele Bloch-Bauer for return of six paintings by Gustav Klimt from the Austrian Gallery in the Belvedere in Vienna, and revolved around a question involving veritable icons of the Austrian "cultural heritage."[42] In view of the demands and under pressure from public opinion, a commission of historians was appointed in the fall of 1998 charged with investigating the entire complex of the expropriation of property on the territory of the Republic of Austria during the Nazi period as well as restitution, indemnification, or compensation by the Republic of Austria after 1945.[43]

Up to February 2000, the Austrian path of "coming to terms with the past" could thus appear as a kind of "success story" in the mainstream of European confrontations with the "guilt of nations" in the Nazi crimes and Holocaust. The efforts by official Austria to rectify the national image damaged by the Waldheim debate was received quite positively in the international arena. The "remarks" by Jörg Haider on the "well-ordered employment policy" of the Third Reich (1991) and on the "decency" and faithfulness of former members of the Waffen-SS made at a veterans' get-together in Krumpendorf in 1995,[44] were interpreted as right-wing populist actions for which there was no place under the constitution of the Second Republic. But then politics took a special turn: with the formation of the coalition government between the Freedom Party and the People's Party in February 2000, this self-identity, and especially the laboriously refurbished image of Austria as an "antithesis to National Socialism" (Chancellor Franz Vranitzky), came to a sudden and abrupt end.

Restitution and the Policy on History and Memory of the Government of the People's Party/Freedom Party

The Austrian "relapse into sin" resulted in a further fillip for self-reflection by the EU as a community of values defining itself as the "antithesis of National Socialism."[45] In the formulation of a European canon of values, which crystallized in part under the impact of the Austrian "breach of taboo" involving the inclusion of Haider in a governing national coalition, the declaration against xenophobia, racism, and anti-Semitism, and the memory of the historical reference point for these basic values—that "rupture in civilization, Auschwitz" (Dan Diner)—occupy a central place.

However, the political shift in Austria also provided a new framework for the ongoing negotiations on restitution. Precisely in regard to a rehabilitation in international public opinion, negotiations on material compensation took on an important political function for the new government. The establishment of the Reconciliation Fund for the Compensation of Forced Laborers (2000),[46] the successful conclusion of the treaty on restitution of "Aryanized" property (2001),[47] and the subsequent creation of the General Fund for Compensation (2001)[48] became, together, a kind of emblem in policy on history of the new government with respect to attempts to remedy and eliminate previous failings in compensation policy.

The official strategies of argumentation in connection with concluding negotiations on compensation for property stolen during the Nazi period were instructive precisely because the difficult choices pursued by this coalition government in the question of "coming to terms with the past." The accomplishments of the new government in regard to measures for compensation, previously lacking, were publicly singled out with pride and pointed to as one of the few political successes of this government that also had a positive echo abroad. The media celebrated the conclusion of the negotiations on reparations and compensation in headlines proclaiming a "historical discharge of debts."[49] The front page of the *Kurier* for 11 January 2001 carried a banner headline: "Historical Breakthrough for Jewish Victims of the Nazis. Copious Praise from Washington for 7.2 Billion in Compensation." This also articulated the symbolic capital that the government gained: U.S. Under-Secretary Stuart E. Eizenstat spoke about a "success of the Austrian government, the Austrian parliament and the Austrian people," and an "enormous historical accomplishment" that "could speak volumes to the world about where Austria stands at the beginning of the 21st century."[50]

The federal government reaped unanimous praise regarding this question on the occasion of its first year in office, not only from the foreign press but also from critical Austrian publications. Thus, an editorial in the *Standard* on 11 January 2001 noted that Austria was getting off comparatively cheaply—five billion shillings for the victims of Aryanization represented only a small part of the total assets stolen from the Jews. It also emphasized that the Austrian government, although forced by demonstrations at home and protests abroad to take action, had acted properly. "Thus, precisely a party which is criticized for having a problematic relation to the past bears co-responsibility here for the solution to a highly sensitive complex of problems."[51]

Although there were scarcely any critical voices raised in public opinion, and even the populist *Kronen-Zeitung* was reserved in its pronouncements, the polls showed a tendency that was more negative in its view of restitution: 38 percent endorsed the compensations for Jewish victims, but 45 percent were against and 17 percent had no opinion. A large majority favored symbolic gestures: 59 percent thought it necessary to keep the memory of the Jewish Holocaust alive, while 73 percent supported the idea of the Holocaust as a topic in the classroom. A majority of 45 percent believed Austria bore co-responsibility for the events during the Nazi period in Austria, while 34 percent endorsed the view that Austria had been Nazi Germany's first victim.[52]

Is the Past Now Something Settled and Done With or Is the Question of Guilt Still an Issue?

Given the measures of restitution by the Austrian government since 1995, can one speak of a lasting collective recognition of guilt for the Nazi crimes? Or has a semantics of the "discharge of debt" taken hold? The idea of a "conclusion" to the matter, a kind of "closure" and "exoneration" by the paying off of material "debts," was also expressed by Chancellor Wolfgang Schüssel, who noted on the occasion of the announcement of the successful agreement: "well, now we're free to deal with other matters."[53] He added: "only someone who's come to terms with the past can be free to address the future."[54]

But it is worth noting just how contradictory and multifarious the strategies in the policy on history and memory are that have served in differing contexts to legitimate indemnification or to make it more acceptable to various interested parties and stakeholders. In a section on "Arguments on Questions of Restitution" on the Website of the People's Party (bearing the caption "Wrestling and Coping with the Past" ["*Vergangenheitsbewältigung*"]), the criticism was initially rejected: Austria had done "a lot," yes, "more than many other countries in Europe."[55] At the same time, the question of compensation for Nazi victims is connected with a new POW indemnification allotted to former Wehrmacht soldiers. People point to the POW Compensation Law (*Kriegsgefangenenentschädigungsgesetz*) of 1 January 2001, which grants former prisoners of war in Central European and Eastern European countries a monthly supplementary pension of 500 Austrian schillings ($36.34).[56] The law for compensating POWs, passed at almost the same time as the restitution payments, can be seen as a subtle signal sent to an electorate that rejects a self-critical exploration of the past. Simultaneously, however, there is an associated and highly problematic symbolic equating of the victims of the Nazi regime with the German Wehrmacht soldiers in the "war of destruction" in the East.

In the People's Party, the range of contextualizing of the positive conclusion of restitution negotiations ranges from reactivating the theory of the victim, metaphors about drawing a final line of closure, and the declaration of the need to engage in a critical encounter with history.[57] On the People's Party home page, you could also read (under "Coping with the Past") that the solutions for compensating forced laborers and restituting "Aryanized" property were not some kind of "conclusion." They did not signify "the end of attempts to confront and work through the problems posed by Austrian history." Rather, the People's Party espouses a "continuation of steering a sensible course and engaging in critical confrontation with the Nazi past."[58]

But fears are being voiced that the chapter of the theft of assets can now be considered "closed" and may soon begin to be forgotten—three years after agreement was reached in the restitution negotiations, in view of the concrete measures taken on the material restitution of stolen property and the completion of the Historian's Commission's investigation into the complex of the expropriation of assets during the Nazi period, as described in the commission's final report, a work of some 14,000 pages scheduled to be published in 49 volumes.[59] The question of how to keep alive memory of the shared guilt in Nazi crimes even after material compensation and in-depth scholarly study have brought about a certain framework of possible closure, has sparked a number of initiatives, such as the preparing of the results of the Historians' Commission to be utilized in materials and units for the classroom.[60]

Yet precisely because of its daily presence in people's lives, the abiding matrix that generates the disconcerting remembrance of expulsion and the Holocaust would appear to be the "memory of things." Sigrid Weigel has referred to the need to be cleansed of inherited guilt. That need can be found in numerous cultural symbolic representations in connection with the expropriation, expulsion, and murder of the Jewish population. Thus, for example, the Federal Furniture Depository initiated a project dealing with its items of furniture formerly owned by Jews but "Aryanized" under the Nazis. This led to an exhibition of the "Aryanized" objects, a photo show, and a catalog documenting the events surrounding the expropriation and transfer of material to the Furniture Depository (one can see, for example, a photo of the folder cover for the main files on "Aryanized" furniture, with the heading "Confiscated Furniture Owned by Jews").[61]

The contamination of objects by Nazi crimes is especially evident in connection with the apartment buildings where Jewish families rented apartments before their expulsion and murder.[62] The mounting of a commemorative plaque for the former Jewish inhabitants of a building, such as the initiative by the architect Friedrich Achleitner in his building in the 1st District in Vienna, can become an initiative and form that others might emulate. It states: "In Memory of / Erwin Abeles / Sissel Berkovicz / Pauline Ekstein / Rudolf Ekstein / Alois Löwy / who until their deportation in 1939/1942 lived here in this building." As a publicly visible sign of remembrance and commemoration, such plaques can serve to drive out "negative memory,"[63] rendering a residential building "livable" once again in a symbolic sense.

Yet contamination as a result of shared responsibility for the theft of property from Nazi victims also affects, as mentioned, central icons of Austrian identity. Not until the Schiele paintings were seized and impounded in New York, and the demand raised to restitute six paintings by Klimt, was a disturbing fact propelled into public consciousness: namely, that these works of art in national Austrian collections had been illegally acquired, at least in a moral sense, and were somehow artistic contraband.

In this way, the question of guilt was irreversibly inscribed into the art of Fin-de-siècle Vienna, a body of artistic creation that since the mid-1980s had increasingly become an internationally marketed component of the national Austrian cultural heritage. This also involves icons of popular culture as well. Once it was learned in 2003 that Matthias Sindelar, the famed soccer idol and center of the Austrian "wonder team" in the 1930s, who died mysteriously in January 1939 and was later venerated as an anti-fascist, had acquired an "Aryanized" coffee house, the myth surrounding this still popular Austrian athlete of the Wiener Austria team was permanently damaged.[64]

The "memory of things," the material legacies left behind in public space by the victims of the Holocaust, as documented for Vienna by Tina Walzer und Stephan Templ in their *Topographie des Raubes*, has evidently still not forfeited any of its primary perturbing force.

Translated from the German by Bill Templer

Notes

1. Tony Judt, "Die Vergangenheit ist ein anderes Land. Politische Mythen im Nachkriegseuropa," *Transit* 6 (1993): 87–120, published in English as "The Past is Another Country: Myth and Memory in Postwar Europe," *Daedalus* 4 (1992): 83–118.
2. M. Rainer Lepsius, "Das Erbe des Nationalsozialismus und die politische Kultur der Nachfolgestaaten des 'Großdeutschen Reiches'," in *Kultur und Gesellschaft. Verhandlungen des 24. Deutschen Soziologentags, des 11. Österreichischen Soziologentags und des 8. Kongresses der Schweizerischen Gesellschaft für Soziologie in Zürich 1988*, ed. Max Haller, Hans-Joachim Hoffmann-Nowotny and Wolfgang Zapf (Frankfurt a.M./New York, 1989), 247–264.
3. Dan Diner, "Über Schulddiskurse und andere Narrative. Epistemologisches zum Holocaust," in *Bruchlinien. Tendenzen der Holocaustforschung*, ed. Gertrud Koch (Cologne/Weimar/Vienna, 1999), 62.
4. See István Deák, Jan T. Gross, and Tony Judt, eds., *The Politics of Retribution in Europe: World War II and its Aftermath* (Princeton 2003); Oliver Rathkolb, ed., *Revisiting the National Socialist Legacy: Coming to Terms with Forced Labor, Expropriation, Compensation, and Restitution* (Innsbruck, 2002); Constantin Goschler and Philipp Ther, eds., *Raub und Restitution. Arisierung und Rückerstattung des jüdischen Eigentums in Europa* (Frankfurt a.M., 2003); Berthold Unfried, "Restitution und Entschädigung von entzogenem Vermögen im internationalen Vergleich. Entschädigungsdebatte als Problem der Geschichtswissenschaft," *Zeitgeschichte* 30, no. 5 (2003): 243–267.
5. Elazar Barkan, *The Guilt of Nations: Restitution and Negotiating Historical Injustices* (New York, 2000).
6. See Sigrid Weigel, "Conversion, Exchange, and Replacement: Reflecting Cultural Legacies of Indemnity" in this volume.
7. Sigrid Weigel, "Shylocks Wiederkehr. Die Verwandlung von Schuld in Schulden oder: Zum symbolischen Tausch der Wiedermachung," in *Fünfzig Jahre danach. Zur Nachgeschichte des Nationalsozialismus*, ed. Sigrid Weigel and Birgit Erdle (Zurich, 1996), 165–192, esp. 178f.
8. See the comparative studies by Agnes Blänsdorf, "Zur Konfrontation mit der NS-Vergangenheit in der Bundesrepublik, der DDR und in Österreich: Entnazifizierung und Wiedergutmachungsleistungen," *Aus Politik und Zeitgeschichte. Beilage zur Wochenzeitung Das Parlament*, no. 16/17 (1987): 3–18; David Forster, *"Wiedergutmachung" in Österreich und in der BRD im Vergleich* (Innsbruck/Vienna/Munich, 2001).
9. On the concept of "disturbing remains," see Michael S. Roth and Charkles G. Salas, eds., *Disturbing Remains: Memory, History, and Crisis in the Twentieth Century* (Los Angeles, 2001).
10. Sandra Melloni, "Die Geschichte des Klaviers. Warum ich über das Klavier schreibe, und was dieses Klavier schon hinter sich hat," in *Dokumentationsarchiv des österreichischen Widerstandes. Jahrbuch 1989* (Vienna, 1989), 173–177.
11. See Heidemarie Uhl, *Zwischen Versöhnung und Verstörung. Eine Kontroverse um Österreichs historische Identität fünfzig Jahre nach dem Anschluß* (Vienna/Cologne/Weimar, 1992).

12. See Detlef Hoffmann, *Das Gedächtnis der Dinge. KZ-Relikte und KZ-Denkmäler 1945–1995* (Frankfurt a.M./New York, 1998).
13. See Tina Walzer and Stephan Templ, *Unser Wien. "Arisierung" auf österreichisch* (Berlin, 2001), esp. the chapter "Topographie des Raubes," 109–226.
14. Weigel, "Shylocks Wiederkehr," 173.
15. "Proklamation vom 27. April 1945," in: *Staatsgesetzblatt für die Republik Österreich*, 1 May 1945.
16. Quoted in Uhl, *Zwischen Versöhnung und Verstörung*, 103.
17. Oliver Marchart, "Das historisch-politische Gedächtnis. Für eine politische Theorie des kulturellen Gedächtnisses," in *Transformationen gesellschaftlicher Erinnerung. Studien zur Gedächtnisgeschichte der Zweiten Republik*, ed. Christian Gerbel et. al. (Vienna, forthcoming).
18. Robert H. Keyserlingk, *Austria in World War II: An Anglo-American Dilemma* (Kingston/Montreal, 1988) and Günter Bischof, *Austria and the First Cold War, 1945–55: The Leverage of the Weak* (Basingstoke, 1999).
19. *Maßnahmen der Republik Österreich zugunsten bestimmter politisch, religiös oder abstammungsmäßig Verfolgter seit 1945*, ed. Bundespressedienst (Österreich Dokumentationen) (Vienna, 1988), 5f.
20. Heidemarie Uhl, "Transformationen des österreichischen Gedächtnisses. Geschichtspolitik und Denkmalkultur in der Zweiten Republik," *Tel Aviver Jahrbuch für deutsche Geschichte* 29 (2000): 317–341.
21. Gustav Jellinek, "Die Geschichte der österreichischen Wiedergutmachung," in: *The Jews of Austria*, ed. Josef Fraenkel (London, 1967), 398, cited from Hans Safrian and Hans Witek, *Und keiner war dabei. Dokumente des alltäglichen Antisemitismus in Wien 1938* (Vienna, 1988), 12.
22. See Helga Embacher, *Die Restitutionsverhandlungen mit Österreich aus der Sicht jüdischer Organisationen und der Israelitischen Kultusgemeinde*, ed. Historikerkommission der Republik Österreich (Vienna, 2002), 73–154 and Brigitte Bailer, *Wiedergutmachung kein Thema. Österreich und die Opfer des Nationalsozialismus* (Vienna, 1993), 77–98.
23. See Robert Knight, ed., *"Ich bin dafür, die Sache in die Länge zu ziehen". Die Wortprotokolle der österreichischen Bundesregierung von 1945 bis 1952 über die Entschädigung der Juden* (Vienna/Cologne/Weimar, 1988), 196 f. (sec. ed. 2000).
24. Ibid., 197.
25. Only subsequently, beginning in 1949, were victims of National Socialist persecution also included in the group of those entitled to pensions. However, up until the 1960s, one requirement was that they had to have suffered serious damage to their health as resistance fighters in order to qualify. Up to 1995 three groups of victims—victims of forced sterilization and euthanasia, so called social misfits and homosexuals—have been excluded from any compensation or assistance. See Brigitte Bailer-Galanda, "Die Opfer des Nationalsozialismus und die so genannte Wiedergutmachung," in *NS-Herrschaft in Österreich. Ein Handbuch*, ed. Emmerich Tálos, Ernst Hanisch, Wolfgang Neugebauer and Reinhard Sieder (Vienna, 2000), 892–894. On reparations in Austria, see in general the publications of the Historians' Commission of the Republic of Austria, esp. Brigitte Bailer, *Die Entstehung der Rückstellungs- und Entschädigungsgesetzgebung. Die Republik Österreich und das in der NS-Zeit entzogene Vermögen* (Vienna/Munich, 2003).

26. Applications for pensions by Jägerstätter's widow Franziska and his mother Rosalia were repeatedly rejected after the war. A decision by the State Government of Upper Austria, 10 August 1948, Zl. F-1491/10-1948, notes: "The Ministry for Social Administration has decided the following in Zl. 84.199-OF/48, 3 August 1948: 'It is clear from the report of the Police HQ Ostermiething of 21 March 1948 that the son of the plaintiff was an opponent of National Socialism. But his action cannot be seen as an act on behalf of a free and democratic Austria in the sense of § 1, OFG/1947. He was considered melancholic and stated before being drafted into the Wehrmacht that he would not fight for Hitler. However, this conviction was not rooted in an attitude opposed to National Socialism and for a free Austria. Rather, it was based on motives connected with his religious beliefs.'" See Erna Putz, "'Zuviel der Mahnung'. Das Gedenken an den Kriegsdienstverweigerer Franz Jägerstätter," in *Steinernes Bewusstsein II. Die öffentliche Repräsentation staatlicher und nationaler Identität Österreichs in seinen Denkmälern*, ed. Heidemarie Uhl, vol. 2 (Vienna/Cologne/Weimar, forthcoming).
27. See Brigitte Bailer, "Alle waren Opfer. Der selektive Umgang mit den Folgen des Nationalsozialismus," in: *Inventur 45/55. Österreich im ersten Jahrzehnt der Zweiten Republik*, ed. Wolfgang Kos and Georg Rigele (Vienna, 1996), 190f.
28. Forster, "Wiedergutmachung," 156–160.
29. *Maßnahmen der Republik Österreich zugunsten bestimmter politisch, religiös oder abstammungsmäßig Verfolgter seit 1945*, 23.
30. Cited from Gerhard Botz and Gerald Sprengnagel, eds., *Kontroversen um Österreichs Zeitgeschichte. Verdrängte Vergangenheit, Österreich-Identität, Waldheim und die Historiker* (Frankfurt a.M./New York, 1994), 575f.
31. See Heidemarie Uhl, "Gedächtnisraum Graz. Zeitgeschichtliche Erinnerungszeichen im öffentlichen Raum von 1945 bis zur Gegenwart," in *Erinnerung als Gegenwart. Jüdische Gedenkkulturen*, ed. Sabine Hödl and Eleonore Lappin (Berlin/Vienna, 2000), 211–232.
32. "Bundesrat beschließt Gedenktag gegen Gewalt und Rassismus am 5. Mai," *Parlamentskorrespondenz*, no. 785, 20 November 1997.
33. Hannah M. Lessing, "Der Nationalfonds. Die Arbeit des Nationalfonds der Republik Österreich und Österreichs Umgang mit der Vergangenheit," in *Nationalfonds der Republik Österreich für Opfer des Nationalsozialismus*, ed. Nationalfonds der Republik Österreich für Opfer des Nationalsozialismus, 2nd ed. (Vienna, 2003), 54.
34. *Bundesgesetzblatt*, no. 432/2995 STO136, quoted in ibid., 9.
35. Ibid., 11.
36. Hannah M. Lessing and Renate Meissner, "'Möglichst rasch, flexibel und unbürokratisch zu helfen'. Die Arbeit des Nationalfonds und des Allgemeinen Entschädigungsfonds," in *Gedächtnis und Gegenwart. HistorikerInnenkommissionen, Politik und Gesellschaft. Sonderheft der Informationen zur Politischen Bildung* 20 (2003): 91.
37. See Heinz Fischer, "Vorwort," in: *In die Tiefe geblickt. Lebensgeschichten*, ed. Nationalfonds der Republik Österreich für Opfer des Nationalsozialismus (Vienna, 2000), 2.—In the brochure issued on the occasion of the 5th anniversary of the National Fund, twelve biographies of Austrian victims of National Socialism were published.
38. Nationalfonds der Republik Österreich für Opfer des Nationalsozialismus, "Auszug aus den Briefvorlagen des Nationalfonds an die AntragstellerInnen," Vienna, made available to the author by Renate Meissner.

39. "NS-Opferfonds konstituiert," *Der Standard*, 7 July 1995.
40. See Jakob Tanner, "Geschichtswissenschaft und moralische Ökonomie der Restitution: Die Schweiz im internationalen Kontext," *Zeitgeschichte* 30, no. 5 (2003): 268–280.
41. Oliver Rathkolb, "NS-Kunstraub und Diversion in den Erinnerungen über den Holocaust in Europa," in *Kunst —Kommunikation—Macht. 6. Österreichischer Zeitgeschichtetag 2003*, ed. Ingrid Bauer et. al. (Innsbruck, 2004), 443–448.
42. See Verena Ringler, "Der Fall 03-13. Kunstraub. Der oberste US-Gerichtshof entscheidet, ob Österreich in den USA geklagt werden kann," *Profil*, no. 10, 1 March 2004: 36f. On the theft of art, see Sophie Lillie, *Was einmal war. Handbuch der enteigneten Kunstsammlungen Wiens* (Vienna, 2003) and Sophie Lillie, "Thema: Kunstraub in Österreich," *Gedächtnis und Gegenwart*: 79–83.
43. See Clemens Jabloner, "Die Historikerkommission der Republik Österreich," in ibid., 15–21. See also Clemens Jabloner, Brigitte Bailer-Galanda and Eva Blimlinger, *Schlussbericht der Historikerkommission der Republik Österreich: Vermögensentzug während der NS-Zeit sowie Rückstellungen und Entschädigungen seit 1945 in Österreich. Zusammenfassungen und Einschätzungen* (Vienna/Munich, 2003) and the paper by Clemens Jabloner in this volume.
44. Hubertus Czernin, "Die Folgen von Krumpendorf," *Profil*, 30 December 1995, 11. On the historical image in the mind of Jörg Haider, see Brigitte Bailer-Galanda, *Haider wörtlich. Führer in die Dritte Republik* (Vienna, 1995) as well as Hans-Henning Scharsach and Kurt Kuch, *Haider. Schatten über Europa* (Cologne, 2000).
45. Anton Pelinka, "Die geänderte Funktionalität von Vergangenheit und Vergangenheitspolitik. Das Ende der Konkordanzdemokratie und die Verschiebung der Feindbilder," *Österreichische Zeitschrift für Politikwissenschaft* 30, no. 1 (2001): 44.—In regard to transnational activity, see esp. "Task Force for International Cooperation on Holocaust Education, Remembrance and Research" (http://taskforce.ushmm.gov), which was formed in January 2000 at the International Holocaust Conference in Stockholm.
46. The law on the Fund of Reconciliation was passed on 7 July 2000 with approval by all the parties represented in the Austrian Parliament. See *Bundesgesetzblatt* I, no. 74/2000.
47. See the speech by the Chancellor on restitution in the Parliament, 31 January 2001, http://www.austria.gv.at.
48. The General Fund for Reparations was established in 2001 (*Bundesgesetzblatt* 12/2001) with the aim to recognize by means of voluntary compensation the "moral responsibility for losses and damage caused to Jewish citizens and other victims by the Nazi regime." See Lessing and Meissner, "Die Arbeit des Nationalfonds und des Allgemeinen Entschädigungsfonds," 93.
49. A so-called "Schuldentilgung." *Kurier*, 11 January 2001.
50. Ibid. On the restitution negotiations, see Stuart E. Eizenstat, *Unvollkommene Gerechtigkeit. Der Streit um die Entschädigungen der Opfer von Zwangsarbeit und Enteignung* (Munich, 2003) (originally published as *Imperfect Justice: Lootet Assets, Slave Labour, and the Unfinished Business of World War II* [New York, 2003]).
51. Peter Mayr, "Erfolg trotz Tempo," *Der Standard*, 11 January 2001. The author is of course referring here to the Freedom Party.
52. "45 Prozent lehnen Restitutionslösung ab," *Die Presse*, 6 June 2001, 9.

53. Cited from Christian Thonke, "NS-Raubgut: Verhandelt wird in Wien und Washington parallel," *Kurier*, 16 January 2001, 2.
54. Cited from Christian Thonke, "Historische Schuldentilgung," *Kurier*, 11 January 2001, 3.
55. "Zwangsarbeiter & Kriegsgefangene. Zur Restitution: Österreich hat bereits viel getan!" http://www.oevp.at/etopics (2 February 2001).
56. See NS-Vergangenheit. Kriegsgefangenenentschädigung, http://www.oevp.at/etopics (2 February 2001).
57. Cited from Thonke, "Historische Schuldentilgung."
58. See "NS-Vergangenheit. Vergangenheitsbewältigung: Zwangsarbeiter, Restitution, Kriegsgefangene." http://www.oevp.at/etopics (2 February 2001).
59. See, for example, the statement by the Jewish Community Vienna on the occasion of the publication of the Final Report of the Historians' Commission in a press conference on 27 February 2003. There it stresses that even with the present report in hand, "there can be no final closing of the chapter. On the contrary: this report constitutes the prelude to sustained research and public treatment of this topic." The establishment of the commission was an "act of substitution for the lack of a scholarly-scientific culture. This deficiency cannot be remedied in the span of four years, even by 14,000 pages." See "Der Bericht der Historikerkommission. IKG zum Schlussbericht," *Die Gemeinde. Offizielles Organ der Israelitischen Kultusgemeinde Wien*, no. 548, March 2003/Adar II 5763, 12.
60. See the special issue "Gedächtnis und Gegenwart. HistorikerInnenkommissionen, Politik und Gesellschaft," *Informationen zur Politischen Bildung* (Nr. 20, 2003), which would like to apply the research findings of the Austrian Historians' Commission to "relevant arenas for action and implementation," especially in the classroom, as Gertraud Diendorfer spells out in the foreword there (4).
61. Ilsebill Barta-Fliedl and Herbert Posch, *inventARISIERT. Enteignung von Möbeln aus jüdischem Besitz* (Vienna, 2000). The exhibition was entitled "inventoried," playing on the partial morpheme in German "—arisiert," (i.e. "Aryanized").
62. Brigitte Bailer-Galanda, Eva Blimlinger and Susanne Kowarc, *"Arisierung" und Rückstellung von Wohnungen in Wien. Die Vertreibung der jüdischen Mieter und MieterInnen aus ihren Wohnungen und das verhinderte Wohnungsrückstellungsgesetz*, ed. Österreichische Historikerkommission (Vienna, 2000).
63. See Reinhard Koselleck, "Formen und Traditionen des negativen Gedächtnisses," in *Verbrechen erinnern. Die Auseinandersetzung mit Holocaust und Völkermord*, ed. Volkhard Knigge and Norbert Frei (Munich, 2002), 21–32.
64. See Emil Bobi, "Sindelars List. Zeitgeschichte. Der Wunderteam-Fußballer Matthias Sindelar galt bislang als Antifaschist. Dokumente belegen jedoch, dass er 1938 ein 'arisiertes' Kaffeehaus erwarb," *Profil*, no. 52, 22 December 2003: 24–26. For an official appreciation of Sindelar, see the online article in *Austrian Information* (vol. 51, no. 4, April 1998), "Matthias Sindelar. The Magic of Soccer, Politics and Death," http://www.austria.org/oldsite/apr98/sindelar.html (14 September 2004).

— *Thirteen* —

HISTORICAL INJUSTICES AND INTERNATIONAL MORALITY: EASTERN EUROPEAN AND SWISS CASES

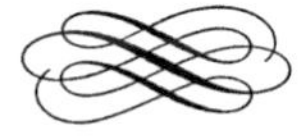

Elazar Barkan

History as Identity

Since the end of the Cold War, there has been a sudden rush of restitution cases all over the world. The pattern formed by these cases potentially provides for our understanding of a new international morality. These cases testify to a new globalism that pays greater attention to human rights. Critics of these trends often refer to the spread of a "victims culture." Instead, I would like to underscore the increasing way in which our histories shape our identities. This truism is particularly applicable in the postmodern and post-Cold War world, where an increasing number of groups and nations recognize the malleable nature of their own history, based in part upon perceived historical rights negotiated over shared political space. Both realism and tentativeness in historical identity have become part of the growing liberal political space that no longer includes only Western countries, for it is becoming attractive to numerous diverse groups and nations globally.

This is most apparent in a world that shares vague liberal political and moral commitments to individual rights as well as to group human rights. This universe is studded with abundant contradictions, but increasingly subscribes to a shared political culture, which pays greater attention to history as a formative political force.

In the past, history supposedly provided "objective" knowledge of past events that were largely immune from reinterpretation; history was the past and little could be done about it. In subsequent decades, history was differently construed, as a largely factual (and relatively uninspiring) winners' history. More recently, however, there has been recognition of the growing elasticity of history, and an awareness that history is anything but fixed. As history has become increasingly malleable, it has simultaneously become more central to political discussion. History informs identity more intimately today; and, being subject to reinterpretation, it has also become a space for contesting perspectives. The new "we" of history are both winners and losers. History changes who we were, not only who we are. In this sense, history has become a crucial field for political struggle. Yet the politics of memory, as it is often referred to, operate according to particular rules and its own tempo. For a "new" history to become more than a partisan "extremist" story, the narrative often has to persuade not only the members of the in-group who will "benefit" from the new interpretation, but also their "others": those whose own history will presumably be "diminished" or "tainted" by the new narratives.

Although the new morality is global, its implementation is specific to each case. History is idiographic and abhors rules. The following cases help illustrate how difficult it is to generalize about injustices with adequate specificity. Nor do we know how to evaluate the degree to which the notions of "victims" and "crimes" is shaped by the context. We have no theoretical framework to think about context distinct from the moral approach applied to those actions/injustices, for our morality is itself informed by politics. The following comments are meant to illustrate the dialectics of morality and politics in the context of historical injustices.

An Overview of Restitution

How do victims and perpetrators negotiate restitution and historical injustices? Restitution for historical injustices is a new phenomenon. It began after World War II with the agreement between Germany and Jewish organizations, including Israel, for reparations for the Holocaust. This was an unprecedented agreement, in which for the first time perpetrators compensated their victims without being forced to do so by the victorious powers. This was an agreement based, in addition to politics, on moral considerations, where victims and perpetrators came face to face to barter their suffering and responsibility for the past and create a future that both sides could subscribe to. While Konrad Adenauer considered political issues, and his decision was not idealistically based, I believe there is little doubt that he could have chosen a different route of not compensating the Jews. His decision to place reconciliation with the Jews high on the German agenda was driven in part by moral considerations, which no doubt influenced also his *Realpolitik*. Germany's political history after 1950 would probably have been only marginally different, largely defined by the Cold War. Historical analyses might differ, but the Allies did not pressure Germany on this score in any sustained way, and did not see this as a high priority by the early 1950s. World politics had moved on, and Adenauer could have chosen to do the same. He did not. This moral commitment was sustained in the following decades, and remains unchanged to a large degree today. The situation would have been more dramatic for Israel, particularly for the survivors of the Holocaust, had there not been a reparations agreement.

A different source for restitution has emerged in the case of indigenous peoples in modern democracies, primarily ex-British colonies (including the United States, Australia, New Zealand, and Canada). In these countries, beginning in the 1960s, indigenous peoples won elementary civil rights that expanded over time. These include various forms of restitution of property, land, economic resources like fishing rights, casino rights in the United States, and variations of affirmative action. The legal system had to change and accommodate more explicitly group rights. Over time, political shifts in each country led to changes of pace and even, at times, of direction in the attitudes of the state toward the indigenous peoples. While the achievements are notable, there has been frustration and disappointment among activists. Today the struggle continues, and restitution remains the major form of enabling indigenous peoples to achieve greater equality.

The third force underscoring the centrality of moral considerations in politics and the need to make amends for historical crimes was the Civil Rights movement in the United States. Affirmative action, never precisely articulated as a form of reparation, was at least in part viewed as compensation for historical injustices. It included a welfare component as well as a gesture to minimally compensate for past discrimination. The language of restitution, however, was not used. The dissonance is most evident in the current conversation over reparation for slavery in the United States.

Efforts to atone for historical injustices bore perhaps unexpected fruit in the case of the Japanese Americans, who were compensated in the late 1980s for being subjected to internment during World War II. The success of this reparation campaign was very implausible. It was done under a Republican administration that did not pursue prominorities policies, and at a time of large budgetary deficits when nobody was in the mood to spend unnecessarily. Japanese Americans were not an important voting block. Especially surprising, perhaps, was that it took place at the height of Japan bashing as an American national pastime. Despite these unfavorable circumstances, compensation was presented as a moral policy and as the right thing to do. Domestically, the legislation had an immediate impact on African Americans, who asked that similar considerations be extended to them; after all, who is more deserving of acknowledgment from the United States for historical crimes perpetrated against them than African Americans?

These modest beginnings were followed by the end of the Cold War and the explosion of a new history of restitution as a component of international morality.

Eastern Europe

There were largely two focal points in the post-1989 period for the politics of restitution in East-Central Europe: those that stemmed directly from unresolved World War II issues, and those that resulted from communist rule. The first category included the ex-communist countries' attempts to address the complexities of a cascade of historical crimes. Poland, the Czech Republic, and Hungary have struggled with these issues perhaps more than have other countries. The second category involved such disputes as between Russia and Germany over plundered cultural objects, the Swiss handling of Nazi gold, various insurance claims, German compensation and restitution for plundered art, and slave labor.

Sorting out *deserving* and *undeserving* victims was a major challenge, one that was and is continuously under tension. Furthermore, developments since 2000 suggest that even when moral and political solutions are reached, they tend to be temporary, final only until the next round of political struggle. The historical malleability is continuous, as each party to a debate, each side in a conflict, continues to pursue its claims.

Adjudicating deserving from undeserving victims has only increased in complexity since September 11. The widespread controversy over the high moral justification by the United States for its war on terror and over the role of "Islam" in perpetrating terror, not to mention the vexing attitudes toward political violence globally, has made demarcating the guilty from the innocent all but impossible. Afghanistan, Iraq, the Palestinians, Israeli settlers, Tamils—one only has to pick a region to recognize the impossibility of determining the just force from illegal violence. As I write this, there are indications that even the UN might be able to reach a convention on terror, after Muslim countries have come to see themselves as victims of terror. But even in earlier eras, delineating justified force from criminal behavior was not an easy task. Before we can explicate this, we must pose the question of whether there is such thing as justified political violence?

Under extreme war suffering and severe national destruction, politicians and public opinion seem to accept types of actions that would otherwise be rejected as horrendous crimes against humanity. Such, for example, were the strategic bombing during World War II, or the ethnic cleansing at the end of the war. In such cases, inflicting extraordinary suffering and victimizing populations is seen as justified by the doers as a way of achieving higher aims, specifically to stop anticipated *worse* violence and crimes. The policies of the Allies at the end of World War II are the best candidates for such classification. The belief that multiethnic countries are bound to fall into violence led to justification of the turning Eastern Europe into a region that was largely ethnically homogenous after the war. It also informed the modest actions taken by the United States and Europe to stop the violence in the former Yugoslavia—which, after all, was thought to be doomed to the destruction of age-old hatreds. Thus, the victims of such actions are "collateral" victims: that is, those who are not directly implicated as responsible, or participants in the crimes that are reputedly being stopped or averted through this extraordinary violence, but the ones in any case who are paying the price.

How are we to think of these "collateral" victims? Who are these "undeserving victims" whose suffering has to be accepted as part of the historical process? Morally, the very category of "undeserving victims" ought to be offensive to the victims and their descendants. Or perhaps not. But historical context helps sort these things out, and suggests a moral yardstick that may be applicable to contemporary conflicts as well.

I would like to briefly touch upon these issues in the context of Central Europe and the legacy of World War II. In 1910, East-Central Europe was the embodiment of European multiculturalism. Nationalism was a powerful force, but so was the mosaic of ethnicities. Over the next eighty years, the region was subjected to genocide, ethnic cleansing, revolutions, fascist and communist dictatorships, and two world wars. While the earlier period was hardly a Garden of Eden, it surely seems so in hindsight.

With the fall of communism, each country sought to establish its own new, post-communist identity. Restitution became a focal point for these domestic debates. The dilemma was in determining which aspects of historical infliction should be reversed: personal suffering—such as loss of freedom and other human rights abuses—or property loss? Which of the historical constituencies should be privileged and become the future identity of a country? Which, if any, ethnic or other groups decimated by the war should be revived; for example: Jewish, German, the aristocracy, or the church?

The "Real" Foreigners

The big losers in Eastern Europe were the ethnic minorities. In the immediate drives by post-communist governments to construct priorities and strengthen cohesion in East-Central Europe, present and past minorities were largely ignored. Across the region, German, Jewish, and Roma minorities had existed in different numbers, together with other minorities in specific countries (for example Hungarians in Romania and Slovakia). The attitudes toward these minorities underscored the moral economy of restitution. Historical, moral, and pragmatic considerations led to dissimilar outcomes in the case of each minority.

The legal questions turned out to be the easiest to untangle and served to manipulate political ends. At one end of the spectrum were the Roma, who are perhaps the clearest example that in East-Central Europe, perceived injustice without economic interest or political power does not lead to restitution. At the other end of the spectrum were the ethnic Germans, who were exiled from Eastern Europe after the war. Millions were driven to Germany. Those from the East spread throughout West Germany, while those from the Sudetenland settled in Bavaria. The former largely ceased to exist as a political force, while the Sudeten Germans remain a significant political pressure group. In the 1990s, they reemerged in the international arena, shaping the internal politics of the Czech Republic and its relationship with Germany. They became the clearest example of "undeserving victims."

The Sudeten Germans—Undeserving Victims?

The suffering of German refugees in the aftermath of World War II may appear indistinguishable from any other refugees of the period. Yet, it aroused the least compassion and created minimal sympathy as political capital. In responding to the outcry of the suffering of the Sudeten refugees, the Czechs argued in the UN debate fifty years ago: "We have suffered more than many delegates in this room can imagine." This quantification of suffering explained, if not justified, the horrors of the war's aftermath and the refusal to recognize the German refugees as victims.[1] Of all of the World War II victims, it was, and remains, hardest to weep publicly for German suffering. Notwithstanding the number of German refugees and fatalities (and both are highly controversial topics subject to intense political manipulation), they were viewed by the Central European nations not as victims but as perpetrators. Before and during World War II, the German minorities in Central Europe often supported the Nazi invasion; and after the war large number of Germans were expelled by Czechoslovakia (2.5–3.5 million), Poland (1.5 million), and Hungary (500,000). They were part of the more than 20 million refugees of postwar Europe. The refugees were often the lucky ones; many others did not survive the war's onslaught.

In 1989, when the Sudeten Germans again raised their case, Czechoslovakia largely shrugged it off. More than forty years after the fact, nobody was eager to explicitly justify the expulsion, and certainly not the individual victimization. But the Czechs viewed the Sudeten Germans as responsible for their own fate. Public opinion decried that, as representatives of the German atrocities, these victims deserved neither restitution nor sympathy. Was the expulsion in the late 1940s an appropriate and legitimate retribution? Against their better judgment, Germany and the Czech Republic were to feud over the fate of the Sudeten Germans for the next decade. [2] Following a lull of few years, the conflict was reignited before the 2002 election. Exploring the legacy of the Sudeten expulsion underscores the primacy of moral economy over legal considerations in the politics of restitution. It also represents a clear case of contemporary political considerations shaping the construction of history. The demand in 2000 by Sudeten Germans for a Center for the Remembrance of Expulsion to underscore their removal, and the controversial debate that followed, shows that the issue is not over but is simply going through another phase.

At issue is the juxtaposition of the Sudeten German's claim for restitution, and the Czech counter-claim regarding the lack of German compensation to Czechoslovakia. The Sudeten Germans demanded that the Czechs recognize their right to a homeland, namely Bohemia and other regions, and that they be allowed to build a community having minority rights. This, they claimed, would restore the pre-war situation. The Sudeten Germans continue to emphasize their demand for a restored community and not just individual rights. The rights of free movement and equal citizenship, which were forthcoming as part of the anticipated Czech membership in the EU, would not have been enough. Rather, their demand was that Germans returning to the Czech Republic be treated as an old minority instead of merely as recently arrived immigrants.

The Sudeten Germans view the repeal of the Munich Agreement of 1938 and the return of the Sudetenlands to Bohemia as accomplishing a return to the *status quo ante*, which cannot be completed without restitution. This is a limited view of what constitutes a revocation of the Munich Agreement and the return to the status quo. This view is not shared by the victims of the war, who focus instead on the war as the major catastrophe that resulted from that disastrous agreement. The Sudeten German emphasis is that only by achieving restitution of national minority rights would the moral and psychological stigma of the collective punishment inflicted by the Czechs in 1946 be alleviated. In the meantime, property demands lurk in the background, left for a later stage in the negotiations.[3]

German officials tried to evade formally recognizing the German Sudeten responsibilities in cooperating with the Nazi regime, and to establish a parity of victimization between the Czechs and the Sudeten Germans. When apologizing to the Czechs, both German President Roman Herzog and Chancellor Helmut Kohl said that Germans ask for forgiveness and want to forgive. The equivalency was most evident in Kohl's reluctance to alienate his political allies, the Sudenten Germans. His most consistent comments during the 1990s were to emphasize the Sudenten German claims and their right to participate in the negotiations. His apology was most evident as he signed the Czech-German agreement, which was supposedly final.[4]

The Czech response to the Sudeten German demands has been ambivalent. While refusing restitution as such, Czech leaders have, at certain moments, acknowledged the injustice of the mass expulsion and recognized it as Czechoslovakia's moral responsibility to correct. Vaćlev Havel accepted in principle the notion of the collective guilt, and condemned the expulsions. He called this injustice the "greatest immoral deed," adding that the expulsions "caused not only the Germans but possibly to an even greater degree also the Czechs themselves moral and material damage."[5] By recognizing that the perpetrator's integrity is injured, Havel both validated the victimization and claimed to be a part of it.

Yet in the calculus of moral economy, even the most liberal and conciliatory Czechs view their nation as a victim of the upheaval, worse off than the expelled Germans. Because of Czech ambivalence, as well as the German economic power and the political potency of the demands by the Sudeten Germans in Germany, the diplomatic maneuvers by the Czechs have been precarious, and the official exchanges between the two countries have been far more constricted than one might have expected. The Sudeten Germans' continuous intervention in the Czech privatization process, calling it a "provocation" and a "hostile act," coupled with their rejection of compensation for Czech victims of Nazism and their pressure to reject the German-Czech friendship treaty, did not make negotiations easier. Nor did it endear their case to the Czechs. By 1993, the German government was implying that a resolution of the Sudeten issue would be a precondition for Czech integration into Europe. Restitution became a potential showdown.

The rhetoric testified to the nature of the negotiations; it was not intended to persuade the adversary of the justification of one's claim, and hardly to advance compromise. Rather, it was directed at domestic political gains. In the meantime, the Czechs embarrassed the German government by restituting 20,000 victims of the Nazis, including 3,000 Jews who, because they were not refugees and therefore did not fall within the international definition of victims, were never eligible for German reparations. (For the same reason, the surviving Czech Jews were ineligible for reparations under various German-Jewish agreements.)

The Sudeten German self-perception as victims led them to ignore any role they may have had in contributing to World War II, either by supporting the Nazi regime or by standing to benefit from the occupation. Comparing the war's effects in the Czech Republic to the damages inflicted upon Germany and the German people, the Sudeten Germans argue that the Czechs have suffered less. They claim not only that the Czechs suffered very little material damage but that the Nazi policy of building up Bohemian industry actually benefited the Czechs.

Reciprocal calculation, say the Sudeten Germans, would only benefit them. This unrepentant position, which views the Sudeten Germans solely as victims and ignores their role in supporting the Nazis and profiteering from the 1938 expulsion of Jews, is clearly targeted for internal Sudeten consumption and could never amount to a serious effort to find a common ground internationally. For the Sudeten Germans, the only just restitution would be German self-determination in Bohemia and the return of property.

Political changes in Germany largely brought the dispute to a seeming end with the election of Gerhard Schröder as chancellor in 1998. Yet the rhetorical insistence on both sides suggests that nothing of the conflict's poignancy has abated. The conflict reignited briefly in the spring and summer of 2002, as part of the German election campaign. This time the conflict encompassed a larger constituency. The ethnic cleansing at the end of the war included other minorities and countries; and the dispute has spread to Hungary, where the right-wing prime minister, Viktor Orbán, took the Sudeten German position as part of his own political campaign. This was against the background of Miloš Zeman, the Czech prime minister, rallying his own political support by reminding his voters that the ethnic Germans living in Czech lands had been Hitler's "fifth column," helping him to annex the Sudetenland in 1938 and overrun democratic Czechoslovakia.

This is a prime issue for political exploitation. In this case, both sides have to be interested in inflaming the dispute. Schröder had very little to gain and much to lose, and he was clearly not eager to enter the debate, canceling a scheduled visit to the Czech Republic. Political stability might prove a strong obstacle to those interested in increased tension, and the anticipated enlargement of the EU to the East and the dying off of the victims of ethnic cleansing more than a half century ago might well bring an end to the dispute. But as the 2002 election cycle suggested, the case is primed for ethnic xenophobia and political exploitation. There is widespread political interest on both sides among those who see themselves as victims and are adamant in rejecting their protagonist's position. The details of the negotiation, which cannot be examined here, were a fascinating illustration of how the moral frame trumps legal and even pragmatic political considerations. The most salient point was "Who was the victim?" The Czech public, aside from Havel and a small minority, could find very little sympathy for the affluent ex-refugees in Bavaria.

Russian Plunder of Art

If the Sudeten Germans were viewed as undeserving victims, the moral fuzziness increases when we consider the question of the Soviet plunder of art. Following Russia's 1992 disclosure of the trophy art in its possession, including numerous masterpieces, hundred of thousands of art objects, and a couple of million books, the image of a new Ali Baba's cave arose in the public eye. By 1995, with major exhibits mounted in Leningrad and Moscow, the (re)discovery of the looted art became, perhaps, the most important cultural event of the decade.

The discovered treasures raised the question of who owns the art. The intense politicking in this regard, in Russia and to a lesser degree in Germany, captured the public imagination. Initially, a moral resolution to the ownership question seemed desirable and feasible, but the window of opportunity quickly disappeared under political pressure—and with it, the moral certitude.

The general story has become well known. While liberating Eastern Europe from the Nazis at the end of World War II, the Soviet army engaged in retribution against Germans and Germany. And there was much to avenge. Today it is hard to regard the transfer and relocation of trainloads of treasures under horrendous conditions (which sometimes caused a great deal of damage) as involving any of the heroism that was widely depicted by those in the Soviet Union who performed it. How are we to think of the pillage? Should the Soviet plunder be understood and legitimized in retrospect?

Understandably, observers are queasy when faced with the demand to arbitrate ethically between validating either Soviet injustices or German claims. The German-Russian dispute is constructed as a national rivalry over national art treasures. The national essentialism imposed upon this trophy art is especially noteworthy because most of the art is actually European in origin and lacks any explicit national symbols particular to either country. Germany, for example, demanded the return of art objects taken by the Soviets regardless of their origin, including art that was previously seized by the Nazis from other locations in Europe, particularly Dutch and privately owned art. Conversely, from the Russian perspective, there is little that can be called Russian by any definition because much of the Russian art was destroyed. Yet in both countries, national pride is projected onto these treasures as though they were are imbued with national identity.

The Soviet army's atrocities against the occupied civil populations at the end of the war have been the subject of criticism for many years. The question is whether the 1945 plunder ought to be condemned as part of those atrocities or construed as a legitimate form of restitution. This raises a larger question: are there, or ought there to be certain instances in which ordinary moral considerations are suspended in favor of a "locally moral, legitimate" revenge? There are excellent reasons to assert that no revenge can ever be considered legitimate. Those who hold such an honorable position would find it hard to empathize with any of the parameters of this debate. For those who privilege a more contextual approach to morality, the debate could present a significant challenge. Even those who entertain the possibility of a legitimate, limited revenge under national pain—and if any people is allowed to claim suffering as an excuse for revenge, certainly the Russians from 1944–45 could—face the perplexing dilemma of choosing a criterion by which to evaluate such actions, either at the time or in hindsight. How are such relative historical (in)justices to be evaluated? Should actions that happened a generation ago be judged wrong or immoral with the passage of time? If so, how are we to compare and evaluate historical crimes, and according to what criteria are we to judge them? The answers may depend on the context chosen.

The Debate in the 1990s

The West, as well as the Russian public, first learned of the existence of the plundered art in 1991. The initial enlightened impetus, both in Russia and the West, was to return the art. Indeed, naming all of it "plundered" left little room for moral questioning. After all, how could plunder be moral? In those early post-Communist "euphoric" days, even unofficial and "private" restitution was attempted. Several librarians even volunteered to send back collections that were kept under their supervision.

Yet opposition in Russia to the return of the art led to debate and a reassessment of the controversy. The only way one can give serious credence to the notion of plunder-as-justice is by recognizing the dissonance between historical and contemporary justice. This predicament is shaped by 1) the role of national cultural politics; 2) the historical memory in both countries; and 3) the relative wealth and potential of German reparations to Russia.

The Russian response initially split along the liberal reformist and the conservative nationalist line. On one side stood the reformists, who, in the Russian tradition, are "Westerners" because they appeal to Western values. On the opposite side stood the nationalists, the Slavophiles, who reject those standards. Russian history informed both camps: the first impulse of the reformers was to restitute the art. For Russians who advocate stronger connections to the West, returning the art would provide a golden opportunity to support Russia's emerging role in the West. For the Slavophiles, retaining the art was restitution for the lost Russian art. The West's initial response followed predictable lines. There was little doubt as to which Russians should be supported: on one side were the liberal reformers; on the other were the xenophobic, anti-Semitic nationalists.

The implicit context was: "If the Russians had behaved in Germany the same way the Germans behaved in Russia, the problem of restitution would not exist." This disparity, where Germany has nothing to restitute, placed Russia at a seeming disadvantage.

To the degree that Germany has come to terms with its responsibility for the Nazi war crimes, it has done so gradually and under pressure. The most generous attempts were directed at the Jews. Its continuous negotiations with Jewish representatives introduced a culture of national repentance, but even this recognition was slow and partial. Because of the Cold War, however, Germany has had neither reason nor opportunity to participate in a similar public discussion regarding its obligations to Russia. The art dispute could have provided such an opportunity if Germany had rethought its obligations to Russia rather than merely isolate the art dispute and hide behind national self-righteousness. Today, the raw pain and anger directed at Germany has largely subsided, which makes it hard to sympathize, in hindsight, with the actions by the Allies— actions that challenge our current moral convictions. Toward the end of the war, procedural justice in Eastern and Central Europe was either set aside or reshaped to suit the international community's embrace of a higher, if inexplicable, justice. The actions of "moral" retribution included international agreements to expel millions of peoples across borders because of their ethnicity. The expulsion of ethnic Germans from Eastern Europe, for example, was inflicted upon many Third Reich collaborators, but equally so upon millions of innocent individuals. At that time, this form of "ethnic cleansing"—as similar ethnic expulsions have become known—was not considered a crime. Rather, it was done according to an international agreement and with little or no protest, as was the case of the Sudeten Germans and other millions of refugees. This was retribution under the guise of justice. It is a type of justice to which nations over generations have succumbed, but which can hardly be justified in hindsight. Nonetheless, it was hard to oppose it at the time, especially when faced with the millions of survivors and the painful memories of those who were subjected to the military brutality, the genocidal policies, and the general ravages of the war.

Switzerland and Nazi Gold

Switzerland's neutrality during World War II made it attractive to Jewish refugees as a country in Central Europe in which victims fleeing the

Nazi regime's gas chambers and reign of terror could find safe haven. Over 20,000 Jews found refuge in Switzerland in the years just prior to, and just after, the beginning of the war. Others managed to deposit their hopes and savings in Swiss banks. After the war, agreements led to certain financial transactions that supposedly took care of balancing the books and gave whatever money there was to the Allies and the survivors. Switzerland remained a beacon of civility in the midst of savaged Europe. This picture remained throughout the Cold War as Switzerland maintained its allure as neutral ground for unsavory politicians, illegal political acts, and dirty money. In polite company this was the face of morality. And, most important, this is how the Swiss viewed themselves. The dispute has shaken the Swiss self-image, which is founded on the self-perceived "humanitarian traditions of Switzerland."

The fact that while accepting Jewish refugees, over 30,000 other Jews were turned away, often only to find themselves on their way to the extermination camps, was hidden from memory. Similarly hidden was the Swiss profit from handling German money and gold and the crucial services they provided to the Nazis. Swiss banks also became the repositories for the victims' property through Nazi confiscation. All that and much more remained repressed.

Switzerland was not alone in this; other countries were implicated in similar acts. Especially since 1996, questions regarding the precise knowledge and action of other neutral, conquered, and even Allied countries during the war have become central issues for domestic policies. Several have set up special commissions to internally examine their own history and conscience. The Swiss, however, have become the focus.

The dispute over the Nazi gold, as these treasures have come to be known, addresses issues of guilt and morality by questioning Swiss behavior during and after the war, as well as the specter of anti-Semitism raised by the country's response during the crisis of 1996–97. The Swiss were taken aback by the negative international publicity, and while internally debating their own national morality, they mounted a defense of the virtue of neutrality that they claimed guided their war policies. Yet it was significant that although much of the criticism was focused on the postwar policies and actions of the banks, there was little defense of these postwar activities. The Swiss did not defend the specific accusations but broadened the dispute into a question of national defense and pride. Both external critics and defenders have accentuated the dispute as it became a struggle for historical identity. The dispute was exacerbated by the magnitude of the treasure in contrast to the fate of the small number of surviving victims. Personal stories were juxtaposed with the allure of fantastic sums, the existence of which was asserted, investigated, and fueled by the banks' slow and piecemeal admission of "discovering" a few more millions here and there, as well as by their questionable practice of not responding to individual inquiries over the years. According to this revisionist history, Switzerland is viewed by its critics as a Nazi accomplice, guilty of prolonging both the war and the Holocaust itself.

At a certain level, the demand for justice has been long-standing, but Swiss banks had successfully fielded this demand in an orderly and official, if obstructionist, manner. In the mid-1990s, however, Jewish demands for justice were taken seriously and were exceptionally productive, initiating an unprecedented global exposure of an embattled national conscience regarding historical (almost temporally remote) issues.

Why did such a historical catharsis/witch-hunt erupt in the 1990s? Where did the Swiss go wrong? How could a country that had rarely been in the news suddenly be propelled onto the front page and receive an intense public relations scolding for doing what it has always done best: keep information about its banking industry inaccessible to the public? All politics is local, and the answer to these questions must be investigated in the Swiss context. But beyond the local looms international morality. As was exposed a short while later, many other nations had acted similarly and the Swiss investigations reverberated to those other countries in what became an international historical self-investigation, a litmus test of each contemporary society's view of its own history and morality during and after the war.

There were several important reasons for the timing of the dispute. The foremost was the end of the Cold War and the decline of Switzerland's role as a theme park for international corruption. Second was internal American and Jewish politics, both of which facilitated politicians who aimed at exploiting the situation. The increased visibility of restitution made it an attractive proposition for opportunistic politicians and lawyers. While such ambulance chasers were a minority among the activists, they dramatically impacted the debate. The interesting variable is that such opportunism always exists; but only rarely does it succeed. It is the context that matters. This time the opportunists' focus was directed to Switzerland because it became vulnerable. This was particularly true as the Swiss bungled their responses; the dissonance between the Swiss self-perception as a moral nation, and their actions, left them susceptible to such pressures. Eventually the Swiss chose to attempt to match their actions to their public moral reputation and not to give up on the humanitarian legacy. This is basically the domestic dispute in Switzerland: to claim that this is business as usual and deny the moral claims of the victims, or try and address these concerns.

For a time, it looked as though the guilt and the legacy of moral behavior would shape Swiss politics. This initial response included not only increased political anti-Semitism, but perhaps more important the promise to establish a Solidarity Fund, the value of which would be in the billions. The anticipated fund, it was promised, would devote its work to improved humanitarian work globally. This was meant to revive the Swiss moral standing, to realign the Swiss national identity with the high-minded spirit and legacy we associate with the Red Cross, and distance Switzerland from the sleazy bankers. Here was a wonderful example of the importance of sympathy to the other, of altruism if you will, that is concurrently part of the political realism. However, the benevolence did not last long. The political power play led to a stalemate. A Swiss national referendum (2002) defeated the proposal to establish the Solidarity Fund, and instead left the interest accumulated on the billions of Swiss Francs in the same banks that profiteered from robbing the victims of the Nazis—the very banks that brought the crisis to a head in the first place.

We know that many Swiss citizens may have learned from the history of their complicity with the Nazis, and yet more Swiss continue to value their own selfish interests. On the other hand, not all Germans favor responsibility to the victims. The politics of responsibility are often decided at the ballot box. While the margin of support between the pro- and anti-responsibility policies may be small within and between Germany and Switzerland, small margins can make all the difference in democracies.

Conclusion

Drawing on the discussion of restitution, I attempt to outline even broader conclusions regarding the role of morality in international relations. War and conquest have always led to crimes and injustices by one group against another. Yet, while international morality is an ancient topic, the discussion of international moral commitments has assumed new vigor in the post-Cold War world. In this context, public awareness of crimes against humanity committed by governments is increasingly translated into a political force. The abhorrence of such violations of human rights has even become an acceptable motive for national and international intervention in "domestic" politics, and a rationale for war waged by regional and international organizations. No longer does the brute and immediate existential security need of the country form the sole legitimate justification or motive in formulating a foreign policy. Instead, opposition to genocide, support for human rights, and the fear of being implicated in crimes against humanity (even by inaction), have become practical, not merely lofty ideals. These ideals increasingly shape political decisions, and the international scene.

Although restitution is spreading globally, it is not a catchall solution to every conflict. In many cases it is not part of the political agenda, and in other cases the parties have failed to reach an agreement. Restitution is successful as far as it goes, and has possible appeal for other cases, but it is not a panacea. Restitution played a secondary role in cases of transitional justice where the ruling and victorious power determined the fate of the perpetrators (whether through a war crime tribunal or a commission of reconciliation). Indeed it is an increasing point of contention in places like South Africa and Latin America.

In addition, it is important to recall that negotiations over restitution at times fail. While the potential of restitution is underscored here, we also must underline cases where restitution fails to barter memory, identity, and reparation. Such are the cases between Germany and Russia, between Japan and China (Nanking and more), and the very partial successes in Eastern Europe.

Notes

1. Michael R. Marrus, *The Unwanted: European Refugees in the Twentieth Century* (Oxford, 1985), 330. Alfred-Maurice De Zayas and Charles M. Barber, *A Terrible Revenge: The Ethnic Cleansing of the East European Germans, 1944–1950* (New York, 1994).
2. Bradley F. Abrams, "Morality, Wisdom and Revision: The Czech Opposition of the 1970s and the Expulsion of the Sudeten Germans," *East European Politics and Societies* 9 (1995): 234–55.
3. The Sudeten German Landsmannschaft was quoted as demanding 160 billion marks in compensation, *CTK National News Wire*, 23 January 1996.
4. President Herzog, who had displayed a favorable attitude to the Czech position for a number of years, was praised by the Czechs for being frank when he acknowledged "the suffering that Germans caused to millions of people." This mostly suggests how normalized Nazi Germany had become. In the 1990s it

was the exception rather than the rule for the German side to acknowledge that the actions of the Sudeten Germans, as allied with the Nazis, were the cause behind the expulsions (*The Prague Post*, 7 May 1997).

5. German President Richard von Weizsaecker in his Christmas speech (22 December 1989) quoting from a letter from Vaćlav Havel from the beginning of November, cf. CTK National News Wire, *Profile of the Sudeten German Problem* (Prague, 1995).

— *Fourteen* —

RECOLLECTING EXPULSION: LOCATING GERMAN REFUGEES IN POLISH AND CZECH MEMORIES

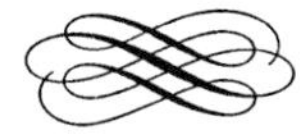

Claudia Kraft

This paper explores in depth the perception of the expulsion of the Germans in the historical memory of Czechs and Poles. What role did and does this topic play in their respective societies? The analysis probes how people dealt with the problematic of the expulsion during the socialist period, and how it has been viewed since 1989. Important in any such investigation is also the question of the nexus between memory of the German expulsion after the war and the renewed debates that have recently flared on the restitution of German property and/or possible material or symbolic gestures of compensation. These two cases are comparable owing in part to the significant fact that in contrast with other countries in East-Central Europe, here a large number of Germans were forced to leave their homes and homeland. This led to a profound demographic change on the ground, with perceptible consequences in virtually all spheres of social life.[1] Alongside such parallel phenomena, however, it is necessary to examine the extent to which differing initial historical conditions impacted on the way these respective societies have dealt with the entire complex. Take the fact that the majority of the Germans expelled by the Poles were German citizens who had to leave former territories of the German Reich, and were frequently supplanted by Poles expelled from the former Polish Eastern territories (*Kresy*, "borderlands") and settled in their stead. That marks a key difference with expulsion in the Czech lands, where there was no redrawing of borders and the expellees were Czech citizens of German ethnic nationality. Another major difference in these two spaces is the fact that in the case of Poland, a large number of Germans had already fled from their homeland at the war's end to escape the advancing Red Army, while the overwhelming majority of Sudeten Germans were still living in their ancestral localities when hostilities ceased. Certain specific political, legal, and even moral yardsticks for evaluation sprang from the matrix of these differing historical contexts.

The present cursory look at the period since 1945 is guided by several core questions. How was and is the expulsion of the Germans after World War II integrated into the respective national self-image? What is its function? What parts are played by the moral, political-juridical, and scholarly-historical dimensions of this issue? What importance is ascribed to the topic of expulsion for shaping dynamic development of an identity in civil society in Poland and the Czech Republic since 1989? And, finally, the question so significant for the history of cross-border relations: what underlies the perception of the purportedly excellent German-Polish relationship, and the still tension-ridden complex of German-Czech relations? This last question also entails the respective reception of these discussions in Germany, which can only be touched on briefly here. Yet the impact of that reception on debates among Poles and Czechs should not be underestimated. Particularly when it comes to discussion of possible restitution of German property, the influence and perception of domestic internal German discourses is of critical importance for the character of argumentation in Poland and the Czech Republic. This study is based primarily on elite discourses, that is, the treatment of the topic in political commentary, largely in the press, and in historiography. One upshot of political liberalization since 1989 is that the topic at hand has become a focus for discussion in ever larger circles in society. For that reason, the final section of this paper looks more closely at the forms reception assumes across the entire society.

War's End: The Establishment of Communist Power and Expulsion (1945–48)

It is necessary to view the expulsion of the Germans from East-Central Europe after World War II in the total context of National Socialist policies of conquest and destruction. So it is also important to examine the genesis of the plans for expulsion/resettlement within the occupied territories and the exile. In both the Polish and Czech cases, the plans for ethnic separation developed in stages. As the war progressed, they were radicalized. These ideas were espoused initially by middle-class political formations in the prewar era, before the left parties also jumped on the bandwagon.[2] Even if the left formations made use of a supplementary social-revolutionary rhetoric to justify the expulsion of the Germans, these events, as Dan Diner has correctly noted, impacted on the collective memory of the peoples as a form of what is called today "ethnic cleansing"—and not social revolutions symbolizing the victory of the communist worldview over that of the fascists.[3] But it should be borne in mind that long before World War II, "ethnic cleansing" had been seen as an instrument for terminating conflicts between nationalities. Since the war's beginning, the concept of separation or "demixing" had played an important role in Allied projections for the postwar period.[4] The belief that it was possible to implement *social engineering* in demographic policy had spread across borders and blocs in the first half of the twentieth century. That belief had been manifested in its most extreme and perverse form in the brutal instrumentalization of human beings within the framework of Nazi policies of conquest and destruction. Yet the communist-planned scenarios for the settlement of postwar Poland, espoused by nonsocialist demographers in the prewar era, confirm this observation.[5]

As a consequence of the suffering endured by Poles and Czechs during the war under German rule, at war's end there was a predominant mood of the need for retaliation, revenge. People were convinced that it was no longer possible to live together with the German community in a single state. This charged atmosphere went hand in hand with an accusation of German collective guilt. That perception was common to Poles and Czechs, and the more drastic German measures toward the Polish population in comparison with measures in the "Protectorate of Bohemia and Moravia" played a very subordinate role in the overall equation, if indeed any at all. The overwhelming majority of the population and all political parties across the board had no doubts about the legality of the expulsion of the Germans.[6] Given this ambience, there were repeated violent acts against the Germans in the months immediately following the end of the war. The "wildcat expulsions" in the summer of 1945 were characterized by brutal and ruthless action on the part of those who implemented them, in the main units of the army. Parallel developments in Poland and Czechoslovakia are evident in the introduction of discriminatory measures such as the requirement to wear a special identifying badge and the rhetoric of the authorities, who wished to end the "German problem" quickly by means of forced mass expulsion.[7] There was no social protest against the comprehensive scenarios of "resettlement." Only a few voices were raised in criticism of the manner in which it was implemented. Thus, the Catholic bishop Stanisław Adamski criticized the "methods of expulsion" in the summer of 1945; he believed they would compromise Poland's image abroad, but was careful beforehand to express his basic agreement with the removal.[8] In Czechoslovakia, Přemysl Pitter, an educator active in the Health Commission of the National Committee, criticized the treatment of Germans (especially German children) in Czech internment camps. The newspaper *Obzory* (Horizons), which was closely allied with the Catholic People's Party, was also critical of the "wildcat expulsions."[9]

Alongside this social mood tilted toward removal of the Germans, the topic of expulsions was likewise instrumentalized politically by the various parties vying for social influence and political power. It was specifically the Communists, who only later joined the choir of those calling for ethnic demixing, who functionalized expulsion as an issue for political debate. Initially, the Czech Communists wished to exclude German anti-fascists from mandatory expulsion. Only later, when it became clear that the Soviet Union was in favor of massive expulsion, did this attitude change. Like all other political forces, the CP also tried to gain capital for its own political program by using the issue of expulsion, forging a nexus between social and national revolution.[10] In the case of Poland as well, the communist camp sought to construct a genuine link between return to the "ancient Polish lands" (*prastare ziemie polskie*) and socioeconomic reconfiguration. The historical justification of a Polish right to the German eastern territories had previously not necessarily been part of the standard ideological repertoire of the Polish Workers' Party, so that agitators fell back on nationalist-democratic rhetoric from the interwar period.[11] But the attempts to fuse national and social argumentation tended to be more fumbling: the statement by Władysław Gomułka, minister for the new western territories, to the effect that these territories would strengthen the bond between the people and the regime,[12] was unadulterated wishful thinking in the early postwar period. Rejection of the Communist government was particularly strong precisely in these new Polish territories. One reason was that the general presence on the ground ("*ingérence*") of the Soviet Union as a result of the long stationing there of the Red Army was especially palpable. Another factor was that the Poles who had been expelled from the Polish eastern territories and resettled in these new areas were as a rule very anti-communist as a consequence of their experiences with the direct Soviet occupation in 1939–41.[13] On the other hand, it was evident that there was less opposition in these new territories to the establishment of Communist power, since society there was less consolidated in its political and social structure as a result of the constant swirl of movements of migration and the lack of stability.[14]

However, despite all similarity in the rhetoric of ethnic demixing and the collective guilt of the Germans, the respective historical context of these events in the two countries differed substantially. While Czechoslovak territory retained its integrity and the expelled Germans were Czech citizens, in the case of Poland it was primarily German citizens who had to leave areas that had long since ceased to belong to Poland, or in fact never belonged. These differing starting conditions impacted on the perception of the expulsions and the concrete political and legal problems that sprang from them, a legacy palpable up until the present. While in the case of Czechoslovakia, the expulsion of the Germans was viewed largely against the backdrop of the Czech-German conflicts over nationality, in Poland it was the large-scale territorial restructuring after World War II that played a central role. Two still-dominant historical discourses have evolved from this matrix, and are still quite vital despite the fact that historians have sought to oppose them. In the Czech case, there is a tendency to view German-Czech relations solely against the backdrop of integral nationalistic antagonisms whose more or less necessary and unavoidable product (or solution) had to be expulsion of the Germans after 1945.[15] Almost like a mirror image, the German side long clung to the myth that Czechoslovak politics, and particularly the politics of the man whom the Germans deemed to be principally responsible in this connection, Edvard Beneš, had, even in the interwar years, regarded the expulsion of the Germans as the only possible variant to resolve the nationalities conflict.[16] By contrast, in Poland the expulsion is integrated into contexts that extend over and beyond bilateral German-Polish relations. The shift westward of the Polish borders as a whole and Allied planning for postwar Poland turned the Poles in their own self-perception into disempowered spectators of unfolding historical events. In a nutshell: while in the Czech case there is a danger of adhering to and being misled by a teleological image of history that sees national separation/demixing as the only viable solution, the Polish example invites the assumption that the sole important factor was the historical context of the war years and the postwar period, that is, that German-Polish relations were a dependent variable in this equation.[17] There is another fact that has influenced this less exclusive concentration on the bilateral German-Polish relationship: despite all the propaganda about Polish-Soviet friendship, the Soviet Union continued even after World War II to be basically viewed by large segments of the Polish population as Poland's second great antipode and historical adversary.

The Two People's Democracies up until 1989

When the Communist Party enjoyed sole power in Poland and the Czech Republic, confrontation with the problematic of expulsion differed considerably in terms of content and institutional framework. The greatest similarity was in the way the topic was treated in the official historiographies, marked by a long-standing taboo and a subsequent approach to events that sought to present them in a more favorable light. The latter was reflected in compendia of source materials published in Czechoslovakia in the 1960s, though in Poland such volumes did not begin to appear until the early 1980s.[18] In the Czech case, the topic was more or less taboo beyond these official presentations.[19]

However, already in the late 1940s, there were statements articulated in exile abroad that condemned the expulsion as the result of an assumed and unwarranted collective German guilt.[20] In the second half of the 1960s, an attempt was made in Czechoslovakia to raise the topic of expulsion in historiography beyond the perimeters of the customary applications of propaganda.[21] But in the wake of the end of the Prague Spring in 1968, it was no longer possible to engage in any serious research on the expulsion of the Germans. The upshot was that the entire complex of German-Czech relations was relegated to discussion solely in the byways of samizdat or in literature published in exile.

In the Polish People's Republic, the factual treatment of "expulsion" (*wysiedlenie*), "repatriation," or "transfers" of the Germans, as it was commonly termed in official parlance, was far less of a taboo than it was in the Czech lands to the south. One important pillar of contemporary historical research was the examination of the economic and social integration of the Western territories into the Polish state. In the course of these studies, the treatment meted out to the German population also played a role. The result was that since the late 1960s, there were studies on the course of the expulsion of the German population for all of the so-called "recovered territories" and, to a lesser extent, on the living conditions of this population group in the Polish state.[22] These studies had to adhere to the guidelines of party-guided official historiography and were subject to censorship.[23] Nonetheless, to a certain extent they contributed to empirical treatment of the topic. One characteristic of this work was that it viewed the Germans and their expulsion as only one problem, and by no means the most important, connected with the newly "recovered" territories in the West. As a result of this work on the question of the German population after 1945, however limited thematically, this aspect of Polish postwar history was no longer a major taboo topic. Yet such a taboo still lingered, enveloping all questions of Soviet occupational policy after 1939 and the associated repression against the Polish people. For this reason among others, the Polish exile, which represented non-Communist Poland, generated a strong impulse for reflection and analysis of Polish-Soviet relations. In contrast with the Czechoslovak emigrés, the German-Polish relation played a very secondary role for the Poles in London or Paris in the early postwar period.

Due to the domestic political developments in the wake of 1968, historians in the Czechoslovak Socialist Republic were subject, far more than their Polish counterparts were, to political repression. Yet reflection on and analysis of the expulsion of the Germans, or more generally of the German-Czech relationship up until the Velvet Revolution in Czechoslovakia, would play an important role in exile circles and in the underground. Striking here was the tendency to view all of Czech history, as well as several pivotal events such as the establishment of Communist rule after World War II, through the prism of relations with the Germans, and to evaluate this complex most especially in terms of morality. At the end of the 1970s and in the 1980s, the result of this was the emergence of a sophisticated and differentiated discussion on German-Czech relations. In this discourse, there was a constant fusing of moral and historiographic yardsticks, which was also the focus of critical reflection. The point of departure for this discussion were the theses on the expulsion of the Germans published by the Slovak historian Ján Mlynárik under the alias of Danubius in 1978 in the Paris-based exile periodical *Svedectví* (Testimony).[24] He condemned this expulsion as a fundamental crime against the human right to a home and argued that it could not be justified even by its approximate historical contextualization in relation to the crimes of the National Socialist occupation. Mlynárik triggered some bitter and vehement responses by his position, and was accused of playing into the hands of German revisionist aims and efforts.[25] Alongside Mlynárik, voices were also raised that rejected viewing the expulsion solely in terms of moral criteria. They called for a more careful look at the *historical* genesis of the German-Czech relationship. In their eyes, Czech and German linguistic nationalism, which had reared its head with an increasing absolutist claim since the nineteenth century, was the main culprit, principally responsible for the failure of any shared community. They believed that the democratic foundations of the postwar republic had been severely undermined by the accusation of German collective guilt and the implementation of the mass expulsion: just like the Germans, other social groups had also been "deported" from political influence by the regime in power.[26] Other Czech historians also joined this discussion. They opposed a purely moralizing view of matters and likewise rejected a perspective of historical determinism that suggested it was necessarily impossible for Germans and Czechs to live together. They also repudiated the notion that there was any causal connection between the expulsions and the erosion of democracy at the hands of the Communists.[27] Jan Křen and Václav Kural called for a solid empirical analysis of relations between Czechs and Germans as a necessary prelude to any moral evaluation or historical classification of the events of the postwar period.[28]

After being revived as a focus among professional historians, the topic of the expulsion also was taken up by the political opposition. For them, the attitude toward their German neighbor became an important barometer of democratic awareness. In historical retrospect, a line is now drawn connecting the interest among historians, especially keyed to moral issues, in the topic of expulsion at the end of the 1970s and the genesis of the civil rights movement Charta 77. In its principled universal rhetoric on human rights, Charta 77, whose founding architects were Václav Havel, Zdenek Mlynar, Jiri Hajek, and Pavel Kohout, likewise responded to a "political and moral need" in Czechoslovak society.[29] Referring to the CSCE process, the movement demanded more than just political rights for the Czechoslovak people. It also denounced the division of Germany, which was in contradiction with the principle of the right to self-determination.[30] Probing reflection on German-Czech history in the discussions in the 1970s and 1980s also always touched on the question of the democratic and humanistic traditions of the Czechoslovak republic.[31] On the German side, there was virtually no echo of this multifaceted confrontation with German-Czech relations, although there had been translations of various statements and viewpoints since the 1980s, if not before. Yet even in Czechoslovakia, these debates remained confined to a narrow circle of intellectuals and dissidents, so that after 1989, there was despite everything a palpable lack of information on both sides of the divide.

In Poland developments took a different direction. The intensive engagement with the diverse waves of migration after World War II and the integration of the new territories anchored these increasingly in the commonly shared national Polish image of history. If the Western territories after 1945 were initially more of a burden for the Polish Communists, struggling for social recognition, due to the difficult living conditions there, twenty years later the Communists had managed, in large measure by means of their historiographic integration, to incorporate this terrain in public perception as an integral component of the Polish state.[32] Proceeding from this vantage, the expulsion had thus been unavoidable. The letter sent in 1965 by the Polish bishops to bishops in Germany asking forgiveness for the expulsion of the Germans triggered vehement criticism by the Polish authorities and met with a profound lack of sympathy among the Polish public, although in all other matters the Catholic Church remained the most important moral arbiter in the land.[33] Historians publishing in the underground did not have any particular interest in the topic of expulsion. They were closely aligned with the Polish opposition movement. It saw the Russians as the greatest adversary of the Polish people. So they focused particularly on aspects of Polish-Russian and Polish-Soviet relations which had been excluded by official historiography.[34] In a traditional mode, they continued to work on the Polish messianic image of national history. It cast the Polish people principally in the role of victim.

A fundamental moral judgment similar to that contained in the theses by Danubius for Czechoslovakia was made by the Polish journalist Jan Józef Lipski in 1981 in the Paris-based exile periodical *Kultura*. He criticized this view of the Poles qua victim as a kind of "national megalomania," suggesting that lurking behind it lay a hidden xenophobia. Lipski rejected attempts to make the expulsion of the Germans appear as a just act based on the historical context, decrying it as an evil, even if a "lesser evil" in the situation of the postwar period.[35] But in contrast with the Czechoslovak intellectuals, the Poles did not engage in any broader debate about this viewpoint.[36] In the mid-1980s, when the Polish journalist Adam Krzemiński began to write about the historical German legacy in the new Western territories, this sparked sharp reactions. Commentators warned of the danger that national assets could be foolishly abandoned.[37] However, the 1980s in Poland saw a revival of interest in the exceedingly problematic area of Polish-Jewish relations.[38] In this connection, a fresh sensitivity was achieved regarding the old question of "minorities,"[39] while there was a fundamental interrogation for the very first time of the Polish role of historical victim, laying the possible foundation for an eventual transformation in attitudes toward the Germans.

Since 1989

Developments since 1989 indicate that even in a climate of free speech and growing international communication, the task of dealing with controversial historical topics has not necessarily gotten any easier. In

Czechoslovakia, Václav Havel opened a new stage in discussion of the topic toward the end of 1989. He voiced his regret over the expulsion of the Germans: in his formulation, it was "something evil that had come to pass as retaliation for an earlier evil."[40] For the very first time, a broader public participated in this debate. It soon had broader access to an array of information. Publications appeared presenting underground debates as well as translations of viewpoints put forward by German historians.[41] This public discussion in part repeated earlier debates between adherents of a more moral approach and those who emphasized the need for a better calibrated historical analysis. In the meanwhile, instrumentalizing of this question in partisan political debate in West Germany and the raising of legal questions by the government in Bonn—or more specifically and pointedly by the Sudeten German Landsmannschaft—led to a situation where the topic and issue of expulsion grew into a major impediment for the normalization of Czech-German relations and rapprochement.[42] For many Czech intellectuals, the definition of the national self-image is still strongly shaped by the tenor of relations with the Germans. Václav Havel formulated this in 1995 as follows: "It is fair to say that the Czechs define themselves both politically and philosophically via their attitude to Germany and the Germans. By means of the character of this attitude, they determine not only their relation to their own history but also the actual type of their national self-image and the image of the Czech nation-state."[43] Both Czech and German historians take note of this depth dimension in the Czech confrontation with their relation to the Germans. Thus, Jaroslav Kučera writes that the question of the expulsion has a bearing not only on the Czech relations to the Germans but also on the place of the Czech nation in Europe.[44] Manfred Alexander notes that revisions in the Czech image of history always likewise have an immediate impact of the way they view their relation to the Germans.[45]

In sharp contrast with the implications for morality, instrumentalizing of the German-Czech relation evolved in the framework of the tactical politics of history. The sole reaction of the Sudeten German Landsmannschaft was a barrage of demands to counter the regret expressed by Havel. It linked the Czech "return into Europe" with a settlement and resolution of long-standing Sudeten German property claims. When for the first time the Czech side used the expression "expulsion" (*vyhnání*) instead of "deportation" (*odsun*) in the language of the Treaty of 27 February 1992 on Good-Neighborliness and Friendly Cooperation between the Federal Republic of Germany and the Czech and Slovak Federal Republic, the Czech opponents of this terminology argued that it implied a Czech admission of guilt, and thus provided a legal basis for Sudeten German demands for reparations.[46] In a bid to liberate Czech discourse on the past from the defensive reactions toward political and legal demands raised by the Germans, President Havel argued in 1995 against deriving such demands from historical events.[47] In some segments of the German public, such an approach was rejected: it was argued that after a short phase of opening up after 1989 in Czechoslovakia, nationalism had gained the upper hand once more even in the case of Havel.[48] Czechs criticized this view by noting that the admixture of historical and political-juridical demands specifically propagated by the Sudeten German Landsmannschaft was responsible for the fact that even as late as 1993, some 75 percent of the Czechs still considered the expulsion to have been correct.[49]

If you look generally at Czech public opinion regarding the expulsion of the Germans, it becomes clear that a growing percentage of Czechs share the view that German-Czech relations are burdened particularly by historical events. In 1993, 40 percent shared that view; in 1996 this had risen to 57 percent. The percentage who considered the expulsion to have been just, with several key reservations, also rose slightly in the 1990s. Striking here is the especially high percentage in border areas. People living in those locales feel the highest levels of insecurity regarding possible reparations for the Sudeten Germans or the possibility of their physical return.[50] One of the underlying reasons for this apprehension was Sudeten German efforts to establish a linkage between future Czech membership in the EU and questions of property rights in the German-Czech relations. Especially in contrast with Poland, the question arises as to whether the internal Czech debate does not likewise impact on public opinion. Numerous descriptions of the border areas published after 1989 give the picture of an economically depressed region where the new inhabitants still do not feel rooted in and part of the environment, and where the traces of the old regime are most palpably and deeply inscribed. People often mention a supposed sense that everything here is temporary; it is this provisional character that apparently still imbues these territories.[51] Under Communist rule, the thesis was formulated in underground debate on the expulsion of the Germans that there had been a close connection between the expropriation of German rights and the Communist takeover of power that had led to further groups in the society being stripped of their rights. The idea that the state had been oriented more "eastward" politically and culturally conjunct with the expulsion of the Germans played a role here. The expulsion of the

Germans had made Czech society not only "ethnically more simple" but also easier to regard in terms of social structure.[52]

By contrast, the public image in the new Polish territories in the North and West differs. The pervasive sense of alienation, abundantly evident in Polish sources from directly after World War II,[53] has largely been supplanted by a view that the Polish state here actually did "recover" ancient Polish areas. If initially Communist propaganda in the postwar period failed in its rhetoric regarding "recovered territories" to convince the new inhabitants or even cement their bond with the regime, public opinion altered over the forty years of the existence of the socialist system. The extensive historiographical output during the socialist regime doubtless contributed to this change in perception. The numerous studies that appeared on the new settlement in these areas in the decades before 1989 solidly inscribed these territories into the national image of history. In the light of this success, the expulsion of the Germans would appear to shrink to a relatively insignificant interlude. The expulsion had been a necessary prerequisite for the final integration of the new territories into the Polish state. In response to the question why Poland was allotted these territories after the war, 77 percent answered that these were old Polish territories that had now been "recovered." Some 57 percent argued that they should be seen as compensation for the lost Polish territories in the East. Far fewer, only 38 percent, stated that this was an act of historical retaliation, in order to punish the Germans.[54]

In connection with the specific perception of the new Polish territories in the North and West, the tendency dominant in Polish public opinion up to today is to incorporate the expulsion of the Germans into a total context of the territorial and ethnic restructuring of Europe after World War II. In 1996, some two-thirds of the Poles surveyed viewed the expulsion of the Germans as unavoidable, necessitated by to the westward shift in the territory of the Polish state and the resettlement of the Poles from Eastern Poland. Far few respondents, only some 50 percent, were of the view that the expulsion was a just punishment for crimes committed by the Germans during World War II.[55] The recognition of the western border of Poland in the German-Polish treaty of 1991 greatly reduced the potential for conflict in inter-state relations. This potential had been generated by Polish fears regarding German revisionist territorial ambitions. After this historic stabilization, a debate began in Poland, now for the first time moored on a broad social basis, about whether and to what extent the expulsion of the Germans was a bona fide separate historical topic and how it was best evaluated, including consideration of its moral dimensions.[56]

Commencing in the early 1990s, that debate soon took on an astonishing dynamism of its own. This turn was accompanied and promoted in part by institutions such as the Cultural Association Borussia, founded in Olstzyn (Allenstein) in 1990, with its concept of "open regionalism," geared to (re)discovering and fostering the multiethnic traditions of the region.[57] Not only in East Prussia but in other parts of the former German Eastern territories, it is young people who are asking questions about the German cultural heritage in their homeland, growing more aware of regional roots.[58] But there is also a clear shift in perception of the problem of the expulsion among the older generation, the generation that actually experienced these events. Several competitions have gathered together and published personal memoirs by Polish and German expellees.[59] Nonetheless, a German-Polish "community of memory" has not yet arisen. Rather, it would seem that there are two "discourses about the East." These recall the respective memories of expulsion in different terms and contexts, tending to make absolute their own experience of suffering.[60] The simultaneous experience of a historical event from the perspective of the perpetrators or the victims does not bring those who recollect closer together. Rather, it creates greater distance. Such a "damaged memory" will only be able to yield slowly to a relation of mutual understanding.[61] Direct dialogue between the groups involved thus seems all the more important.

Memory and Restitution in the Twenty-First Century

Even if the Great Turn in Central and East-Central Europe occurred only some fifteen years ago, opening up fresh perspectives and windows on the recent past, today we are confronted with a new paradigm shift in dealing with the traumatic history of the twentieth century in Europe. This impacts both on the German-Polish and German-Czech relationship. But characteristic is that this paradigm shift also includes these bilateral relations in a global debate on historical memory. The trans-nationalization of historical memory[62] against the backdrop of the Holocaust, which with the passage of time appears to be becoming an ever more central and powerful point of reference for European identity,[63] forms the system of reference and amplified space in view of which debates and disputes between the Germans and their Eastern neighbors about the history of World War II, its prehistory and consequences, are taking place. There has been repeated reference to the fact that in these dialogues, political-juridical, moral, and historical yardsticks overlap. With this new paradigm of global memory, which includes in its horizon in particular the victims of totalitarianism in the twentieth century across the planet, configurations of emphasis in the three yardsticks also shifted within the emergence of "cosmopolitan memory."[64]

Striking in these shifts is the fact that there appears to have been for some time now a much stronger nexus between legal-juridical and moral evaluations. The basis for that is a change in perception: international legal norms such as universal and European human rights conventions are now viewed much more seriously as a material foundation for a prosperous development of the international community. Closely connected with this is the perception of the European Union as a community founded on law and values. Entry into the Union for the countries of East-Central Europe is made dependent in part on their efforts to enhance civil society, a kind of test for admission. Yet one should not forget that since the 1970s, it was East-Central European intellectuals who were indeed the ones who introduced the discourse on basic civil rights into the international debate. Their reference to multilateral human rights conventions helped to strengthen the authority of such agreements in international relations.

This view of the European Union as a community moored on the rule of law and oriented to a set of guiding values has had far-reaching consequences for how disputed questions of property and ownership and restitution between the Germans and their eastern neighbors have been dealt with. German politicians, not only during election campaigns, forged a link between Polish and Czech entry into the EU and the restitution of German property. Candidates for membership were expected to annul legislation discriminatory of Germans after 1945, in keeping with the "spirit of the twenty-first century" and the conception of the union as a community of values. That is how the Bavarian chief minister Edmund Stoiber formulated this requirement in his June 2002 speech to the Association of East Prussians. Bernd Posselt, head of the Sudeten German Landsmannschaft and a member of the European Parliament, advanced similar arguments in connection with various legal documents on the Beneš decrees, examining their compatability with EU law. There was a decidedly critical reaction to such patterns of argumentation in Poland and the Czech Republic, where they were viewed as an inadmissible attempt to block out the historical framework underlying the laws under criticism. The Polish cleric Stanisław Musiał, who cannot be suspected of anti-German xenophobia, responded pointedly to well-meaning German declarations to the effect that Germany was not trying to win the Second World War after the fact, so to speak, and only wished to point out that this legislation was incompatible with contemporary thinking: "It is fully incompatible. And not only with the spirit of the 21st century, but with the 31st and all the rest. In relations between states, you cannot have a situation where the aggressor looses nothing after attacking another country—say, in accordance with the principle: 'if it works, great, if it doesn't, we haven't lost a thing. Because we'll just pull back to our old borders protected and guaranteed under international law' (or under the 'spirit' of the centuries to come)."[65]

In Poland and the Czech Republic, the German entry into a new universal discourse on victims—the "reconstructing of the society of perpetrators as a society of victims"[66]—is viewed with some discontent if not alarm. All the more so, since this shift entails more than a feared and improper new weighting of events during and after World War II. There is also apprehension that the reevaluation of the protection of individual human rights apparent in recent international judgments would seem to provide a basis recognized in the international community for pressing German claims to property and its restitution.[67] This is an unfortunate turn at a juncture when, specifically in Poland, one can note a recent significant shift in views on the matter of German victims of World War II and its aftermath. In a survey conducted in the summer of 2003, 57 percent of Polish respondents agreed that the Germans, like the Jews, Poles, and Roma, had also been victims of World War II.[68] It is particularly the younger generation that is critical of adhering to the notion of German collective guilt. They call for a perspective in which Germans are also seen as victims of National Socialist totalitarianism.[69]

Even the Czechs have provided space for the memory of the German victims within recent symbolic gestures. In September 2002, in Teplice nad Metují (Wekelsdorf), thanks to an initiative by several organizations, a "cross of reconciliation" was dedicated as a conciliatory gesture. It expressly commemorates all victims of disputes over nationality and ethnic origin in the region, including the Germans, especially the women, children and elderly persons murdered there in June 1945.[70] Critique of this initiative was rejected in internal Czech debate.[71] However, the Czechs were also quite aware that what was important in discourse in Germany was not the recognition of individual suffering; rather, these events and their memory were being instrumentalized in debates on current affairs, history, and the politics of history.[72] For this reason among others, there were no official symbolic gestures of compensation. By contrast, Polish President Kwaśniewski had contemplated such plans in the spring of 2002.[73] In the Czech case, though, there was a mitigating element: the German-Czech Fund for the Future had since 1999 been discussing the possibility of compensation for Sudeten German forced laborers and those imprisoned illegally. Ultimately nothing came of this.[74]

But there were other factors that served to torpedo the at least symbolic gestures of reparations. The reformulation of the memory of World War II and the Holocaust is a universal phenomenon. Yet in Poland, the Czech Republic, and elsewhere, it comes up against landscapes of memory with very specific configurations of reference to these historical events.[75] Here too one can see a new appraisal and reweighting between the various political-juridical, moral, and especially historical approaches to the topic. It is striking that the historical sciences view with some discontent and alarm these manifestations of historical events and contexts in debates on current political questions prompted by the discussions on restitution. In the age of truth commissions and class-action cases, it is not unusual for the individual memory of contemporaries on the one hand and judges and politicians on the other to become the final arbiters of interpretation. In relation to the expulsion of the Germans, whose course has been intensively researched by professional historians in Poland and the Czech Republic, historians view themselves under constraint as a result of the way in which the topic has been instrumentalized in political discussion on questions of the hour.[76] In 2001, Eagle Glassheim commented: "Comparison, contextualization, and a consideration of the structural prerequisites of expulsion are all part of a broader project to 'historicize' the forced migrations in postwar East-Central Europe.... I use the term 'historicization' in the spirit of Martin Broszat's call for a reevaluation of the history of Nazi Germany. More precisely, this refers to 'the normalization of our historical consciousness', the use of 'applied historical method' rather than a 'political-moral perspective'."[77] Such contextualization and historicizing stand in clear contradiction with the immense significance accorded the events in and after World War II for present-day politics of identity in East-Central Europe. Even if the perspective of victimization is dominant in keeping with the global trend, it is useful to examine more carefully just how the individual victims are differentiated.

Precisely in connection with the complex of restitution of property that lost and changed its owners during World War II, a striking element is the extent to which discourses of national and social homogenization have been inscribed in the collective memory of the Czechs and Poles. In these two instances, the Cold War and division of Europe did not function so powerfully as a "neutralizer of the soil fertile for nationalist conceptions."[78] Rather, it created a framework of conditions in which older elements of tradition survived and were further developed. Especially in the example of the Polish practice of restitution, it becomes clear that the concept of property has long had powerful ethnic connotations in Polish thinking. The Polish constitution of March 1921 describes the ownership of land as "one of the important basic pillars of the nation and state."[79] Nothing has altered in this attribution up to the present except for the fact that nation and state have become ever more a solely ethnic Polish matter, and this for several reasons: on the plane of discourse and debate, the political development of the Second Republic, the Nazi murder of the Jews, and the later expulsion of the Germans and other Eastern Slavic ethnic elements in the population in the aftermath of World War II. In the struggle for a restitution law in a state that is no longer socialist, the character of the "right of property as a national, non-personal matter" is becoming abundantly manifest once more.[80] In 2001, a new law on restitution was blocked by the Polish president's veto. It stipulated that only those individuals were entitled to indemnification who both at the time of expropriation *and* on 31 December 1999 were Polish citizens.[81]

In Poland, the majority of Germans are not entitled to benefits under the law of reprivatization in any case since they were citizens of the German Reich. But with the comment that in their case this involved the seizure of "property of the enemy,"[82] whose restitution if at all was a matter of internal German law,[83] one can note a renewed bid to externalize this entire problem. In the case of the Polish-Jewish victims of expropriation, and the Germans and Jews expropriated in the Czech lands, that externalization is not possible. The connection between the right to property, which is now highly valued in former socialist states on the way to a liberal economic order and functioning civil society, integrated into and bound to the nation-state,[84] generates complex problems. This is amply demonstrated by disputes over the restitution of Jewish property in Poland and the Czech Republic.[85]

In Sum

There will doubtless never be congruent "historical memories" among the Germans and their eastern neighbors in regard to World War II and its aftermath. The respective memory strands are too strongly shaped and stamped by the social contexts in which recollection takes place. Consequently, the demand for a "gesture of reconciliation in law," which at least de jure would rescind the expropriation of the Germans, even without a factual material compensation (and thus without the burden of material consequences for Poland and the Czech Republic),[86] overlooks an important aspect of the problem. Intertwined with the question of symbolic or material restitution is another salient factor: the representation of World War II in collective memory. The reception of the universal discourse of the victim must be viewed against this backdrop and the consequences for Poland and the Czech nation. Even if, as has been shown, there is now a penetrating confrontation underway with the attitudes and actions of Poles and Czechs in and after World War II, it must not be forgotten that certain patterns of memory persist.

The more problematic German-Czech relation appears to be grounded on a far closer linkage between historical, political, and moral arguments than in the case of Poland.[87] Another significant factor is that Czech confrontation with the historical fact of the expulsion of the Germans is far more tightly interwoven with conceptions of national identity and their salience, while among the Poles there is more of an attempt to externalize these elements. Even while recognizing German suffering during the expulsion, it is possible for the Poles to maintain their national myth of victimization. The shift westward of the territory of the Polish state as a result of an agreement between the Soviet Union and the Allies, turned Poles into passive, powerless observers of historical events and their consequences. This "over-contextualization" of the events serves as an exonerating element. The German-Czech case is more complex. Here is a shared history that is not simply reconstructed as a common history of victimization after the fact. The contextualization of the events functions less to exonerate and more to enlighten. It also extends far beyond the events of the war and postwar period proper, as the research of Jan Křen on German-Czech relations shows.[88]

In Poland, the new universal discourse of victimization encounters a landscape of memory that has begun to change in recent years but remains, and even in a reinvigorated way, marked by a "national-martyrological canon of socialization."[89] Already in socialist Poland, one could observe that victims of World War II who were not ethnic Poles were blocked out of collective memory.[90] And even today this specific view of the past, which finds it difficult to recognize that Poles were also perpetrators, is still quite manifest and palpable.[91] The increasing importance of the Holocaust in memory of World War II, and the debate on the German expellees that has recently dominated the Polish media, represent a challenge to the collective memory of the Poles. Polish debates would appear to blend effortlessly into universal memory of the victims. The call for a "European Center for the Victims of the Totalitarian Regimes of the Twentieth Century" advanced by Paweł Machcewicz can be viewed not only as a counterweight to the planned German "Center Against Expulsions." It also seeks to make the memory of communism and fascism into a kind of duplex foundation myth for a democratic European identity. He considers Warsaw as a privileged space, most appropriate for the memorialization of suffering under both of these dictatorships.[92] This initiative contains a renewed glimmer of the belief in Polish exceptionalism: that Polish experience of victimization is historically unique, and thus must collide perforce with the collective remembrance of the Holocaust as the foundational event for a future European identity.[93] A politics of mutual recognition of suffering can best counter any "rivalry in the status of victims."[94] Thus, the erection of a monument in the camp at Potulitz (Potulice), which commemorates both German and Polish victims, incorporates a bridging between German and Polish remembrance that even today recalls and commemorates World War II in quite different ways.[95] Such bridgings and attempts at recollective rapprochement appear to be more promising than attempts to level and homogenize differing memories by (re)activating the old theory of totalitarianism. Moreover, that theory distorts the view of scope and possibilities for action in the respective historical contexts.

Translated from the German by Bill Templer

Notes

1. Of the estimated 12.5 million German refugees and expellees, some 3 million came from Czechoslovakia. About 7 million stemmed from former German territories in the East which were incorporated into Poland after World War II, as well as from Poland and the Free City of Danzig. See Gerhard Reichling, *Die deutschen Vertriebenen in Zahlen. Teil 1: Umsiedler, Verschleppte, Vertriebene, Aussiedler 1940–1985* (Bonn, 1986), 26.
2. Detlef Brandes, *Der Weg zur Vertreibung 1938–1945. Pläne und Entscheidungen zum "Transfer" der Deutschen aus der Tschechoslowakei und Polen. Mit einem Vorwort von Hans Lemberg* (Munich, 2001).

3. Dan Diner, *Das Jahrhundert verstehen. Eine universalhistorische Deutung* (Frankfurt a.M., 2000), 245. In the Polish case, however, it is useful to ask whether discourse about the "pioneers" who ventured forth to establish the Communist system in the "recovered territories" was not in keeping with actual self-perception of some of these individuals, at least in the early years of the Polish People's Republic. On this, see for example Philipp Ther, *Deutsche und polnische Vertriebene. Gesellschaft und Vertriebenenpolitik in der SBZ/DDR und Polen 1945–1956* (Göttingen, 1998), 293–295. The anthology *Difficult Days* also reflects such a self-identity among the settlers: *Trudne dni. Wrocław 1945 r. we wspomnieniach pionierów* [Difficult Days. Wrocław 1945 in the Memories of Pioneers], ed. Mieczysław Markowski, 3 vols. (Wrocław, 1960–1962). Contained here are reports by officials in politics and administration. To what extent such a "pioneering" image was also present among more average, "simple" settlers in the new northern and western areas of Poland would have to be examined by a more precise analysis of the rich memoir literature from the era of socialist Poland. For example, the manuscripts of the memoir competitions organized by the authorities can be perused in the archive of the Institute of the West in Posen (Archiwum Instytutu Zachodniego w Poznaniu) or the archive of the Silesian Institute in Oppeln (Archiwum Instytutu Śląskiego w Opolu).
4. Hans Lemberg, "'Ethnische Säuberungen:' Ein Mittel zur Lösung von Nationalitätenproblemen?," *Aus Politik und Zeitgeschichte*, B 46/92, 6 November 1992: 27–38. The term "demixing" is used here for the German *Entmischung.*
5. On the at least partial comparability of the paradigm "demographic policy" in German National Socialist and Polish Communist policy planning, see Michael G. Esch, *"Gesunde Verhältnisse." Deutsche und polnische Bevölkerungspolitik in Ostmitteleuropa 1939–1950* (Marburg/Lahn, 1998).
6. See for the Polish case: Edward Dmitrów, *Niemcy i okupacja hitlerowska w oczach Polaków. Poglądy i opinie z lat 1945–1948* [The Germans and the Hitler Occupation in the Eyes of the Poles. Views and Opinions from the Years 1945–1948] (Warsaw, 1987); Bernadetta Nitschke, "Polacy wobec Niemców—odpowiedzialność Niemców za zbrodnie wojenne [The Germans vis-à-vis the Poles. German Responsibility for War Crimes]," *Zeszyty Historyczne* 1998, no. 123: 3–26. For the Czech case: Tomáš Staněk, "Politischer Hintergrund und Organisation der Aussiedlung der Deutschen aus den böhmischen Ländern von Mai bis August 1945," in *Odsun. Die Vertreibung der Sudetendeutschen. Begleitband zur Ausstellung* (Munich, 1995), 113–152.
7. In summary form for Czechoslovakia, see Tomáš Staněk, "1945—Das Jahr der Verfolgung. Zur Problematik der außergerichtlichen Nachkriegsverfolgung in den böhmischen Ländern," in: *Erzwungene Trennung. Vertreibungen und Aussiedlungen in und aus der Tschechoslowakei 1938–1947 im Vergleich mit Polen, Ungarn und Jugoslawien*, ed. Detlef Brandes, Edita Ivaničková and Jiří Pešek (Essen, 1999), 123–152. See also idem: *Perzekuce 1945. Perzekuce tzv. státně nespolehlivého obyvatelstva v českiých zemích (mimo tábory a věznice) v květnu—srpnu 1945* [Persecution 1945. The Persecution of the So-Called Politically Unreliable Population in the Bohemian Lands (except in Camps and Jails) from May to August 1945] (Prague, 1996). For Poland now: Włodzimierz Borodziej, "Einleitung," in: *'Unsere Heimat ist uns ein fremdes Land geworden...' Die Deutschen östlich von Oder und Neiße 1945–1950. Dokumente aus polnischen Archiven*, ed. Włodzimierz Borodziej and Hans Lemberg (Marburg/Lahn, 2000), 37–114; Bernadetta Nitschke,

Wysiedlenie czy wypędzenie? Ludność niemiecka w Polsce 1945–1949 [Resettlement or Expulsion? The German Population in Poland 1945–1949] (Toruń, 2001), esp. 134–164. There is a recent German translation: *Vertreibung und Aussiedlung der deutschen Bevölkerung aus Polen 1945 bis 1949* (Munich, 2003).

8. See for example the correspondence between Adamski and the minister for public administration in the summer of 1945, in: *Wysiedlenia Niemców i osadnictwo ludności polskiej na obszarze Krzyżowa-Swidnica (Kreisau-Schweidnitz) w latach 1945–1948. Wybór dokumentów* [The Expulsion of the Germans and Resettlement of the Poles in the Area Krzyzowa-Swidnica (Kreisau-Schweidnitz) 1945–1948. Documentation], ed. Karol Jonca (Wrocław, 1997), 116–119.
9. On Pitter see Tomáš Pasák, "Přemysl Pitters Initiative bei der Rettung deutscher Kinder im Jahre 1945 und seine ablehnende Haltung gegenüber der inhumanen Behandlung der Deutschen in tschechischen Internierungslagern," in *Der Weg in die Katastrophe. Deutsch-tschechoslowakische Beziehungen 1938–1947*, ed. Detlef Brandes and Václav Kural (Essen, 1994), 201–213. On the protests voiced in *Obzory*, see Jaroslav Kučera, "Die Vertreibung. Die Debatte um die Aussiedlung der deutschen Bevölkerung in der Tschechoslowakei und ihre politische Bedeutung," *Österreichische Zeitschrift für Geschichtswissenschaft* 3 (1992): 238–248, here 242.
10. Staněk, *1945—Das Jahr der Verfolgung*, 127 and Kučera, *Die Vertreibung*, 241f.
11. In this connection, cooperation between scholars formerly allied with the national democracy and the new Polish rulers was of great importance, as illustrated by the prominent example of the historian Zygmunt Wojciechowski, see Markus Krzoska, *Für ein Polen an Oder und Ostsee. Zygmunt Wojciechowski als Historiker und Publizist* (Osnabrück, 2003). Urszula Jakubowska, "Zygmunt Wojciechowski: O powrót Polski nad Odrę" [Zygmunt Wojciechowski: On Poland's Return to the Oder], in *Polska-Kresy-Polacy. Studia Historyczne* [Poland—Border Areas—Poles. Historical Studies], ed. Stanisław Ciesielski, Teresa Kulak and Krystyna Matwijowska (Wrocław, 1994), 215–223.
12. His statement at a meeting of the Central Commission of the Polish Workers' Party, see *Protokół obrad KC PPR w maju 1945 roku* [Minutes, Central Commission, PPR, May 1945], ed. Aleksander Kochański (Warsaw, 1992), 11.
13. Władysław Mochocki, "Polnisch-sowjetische Freundschaft 'auf Banditentum und Raub reduziert?' Die Rote Armee in Polens wiedergewonnenen Gebieten 1945–1947," *Osteuropa* 48 (1998): 286–299; Stanisław Łach, "Społeczno-gospodarcze aspekty stacjonowania Armii Czerwonej na ziemiach odzyskanych po II wojnie światowej" [Social and Economic Aspects of the Stationing of the Red Army in the Recovered Territories after 1945], in *Władze komunistyczne wobec Ziem Odzyskanych po II wojnie światowej* [The Communist Authorities vis-à-vis the Territories Recovered after WWII], ed. Stanisław Łach (Słupsk, 1997), 255–277.
14. Research comes to this conclusion for example in the analysis of the results of the first elections to the parliament, see Czesław Osękowski, "Wybory do sejmu 19 stycznia 1947 r. w zachodniej i północnej Polsce" [The Parliamentary Poll on 19 January 1947 in Western and Northern Poland], in: Łach, *Władze komunistyczne*, 99–112.
15. As early as 1980, there was criticism of this approach in description voiced by Jan Křen: "Tschechen und Deutsche. Kritische Bemerkungen," in: *Zur Geschichte der deutsch-tschechischen Beziehungen. Eine Sammelschrift tschechischer Historiker aus dem Jahr 1980* (Berlin, 1985), 5–57. This anthology published in samizdat

provides an overview of the lively debates on the expulsion of the Germans in the Czech Socialist Republic and among dissident Czechs in exile.

16. On this myth, see Hans Lemberg, "Die Entwicklung der Pläne für die Aussiedlung der Deutschen aus der Tschechoslowakei," in Brandes and Kural, *Der Weg in die Katastrophe*, 77–91, here 77.
17. Włodzimierz Borodziej, "Historiografia polska o 'wypędzeniu' Niemców" [Polish Historiography on the "Expulsion" of the Germans], in *Przegląd Badań. Polska 1944/45–1989. Studia i Materiały II/1996* [Survey of Research on Poland 1944/45–1989. Studies and Documents II/1996], 249–269, 256. The author describes the focus on international developments using the concept "*interpretacja poczdamska*" ("Potsdam Interpretation"). Robert Traba warns about an approach which views the expulsion of the Germans as an exclusive consequence of National Socialist policies or the decisions of the victorious powers. He argues for an approach that examines to what extent these decisions were in keeping with and reflected genuinely Polish traditions, idem: "'Każdemu należy się jego korona'. Wokół dyskusji o wysiedleniach Niemców z Polski" ["Each Deserves his Own Crown." Remarks on the Discussion Regarding the Expulsion of the Germans from Poland], *Odra* 37 (1997): 25–29, here 26.
18. *Die Deutschen in der Tschechoslowakei 1933–1947. Dokumentensammlung*, ed. Václav Král (Prague, 1964), 534–631 ("Der Transfer"); Piotr Lippóczy and Tadeusz Walichnowski, *Przesiedlenie ludności niemieckiej z Polski po II wojnie światowej w świetle dokumentów* [The Resettlement of the German Population from Poland after WWII in the Light of Documentation] (Warsaw/Łódź, 1982).
19. The dissertation by the later reform-minded Communist Milan Hübl appeared in 1968; he also dealt there with the expulsion of the Germans, characterizing measures against the Germans as severe but necessary. See idem: "Glossen zu den Danubius-Thesen über die Aussiedlung der Deutschen," *Deutschland-Archiv* 12 (1979): 737–735, here 728.
20. Susann Bethke, "Die Entwicklung der tschechoslowakischen Diskussion um die Vertreibung der Deutschen," *Deutsche Ostkunde*, no. 3 (1992): 95–108, here 96.
21. Jan Křen, "Odsun Němců ve světle nových pramenů" [The Deportation of the Germans in the Light of New Sources], *Dialog. Měsíčník pro politiku, hospodářství a kultury* [Dialogue. Monthly for Politics, the Economy and Culture], no. 4–6 (1967): 1–10. The article had little echo.
22. On terminology and bibliographical references, see Borodziej, "Historiografia polska o 'wypędzeniu' Niemców," 251–253.
23. Thus, for example, the dissertation by Bronisław Pasierb on the expulsion of the Germans from Lower Silesia was initially blocked for publication because he had explicitly pointed out that prior to the expulsions by the military in the summer of 1945, attempts had been made to incite the units to animosity against the Germans, see: Hieronim Szczegóła, "Przedpoczdamskie wysiedlenia Niemców z Polski (czerwiec-lipiec 1945)" [The Expulsion of the Germans from Poland Before Potsdam (June–July 1945)], in *Ludność niemiecka na ziemiach polskich w latach 1939–1945 i jej powojenne losy* [The German Population on Polish Territory 1939–1945 and Their Post-War Fate], ed. Włodzimierz Jastrzębski (Bydgoszcz, 1995), 47–55, here 49.

24. Danubius, "Tézy o vysidleni československých Němců" [Theses on the Expulsion of the Czechoslovak Germans], *Svědectví* 15 (1978): 105–122. The German text is reproduced in *Odsun*, 470–493.
25. On the echo and impact of the theses, see Eva Schmidt-Hartmann, "Menschen oder Nationen? Die Vertreibung der Deutschen aus tschechischer Sicht," in *Die Vertreibung der Deutschen aus dem Osten*, ed. Wolfgang Benz (Frankfurt a.M., 1995), 178–198, here esp. 186–194.
26. Using the pseudonym Bohemus, a group of Prague-based historians published "Slovo o odsunu" [A Word on the Deportation], in *Právo Lidu* [The People's Law], no. 1 (1980). The German text in *Sudetendeutsche—Opfer und Täter. Verletzungen des Selbstbestimmungsrechtes und ihre Folgen*, ed. Leopold Grünwald (Vienna, 1983), 89–110.
27. Thus, for example, Jaroslav Opat, "Zur der Arbeit von Bohemus 'Ein Wort zur Aussiedlung'," in *Zur Geschichte der deutsch-tschechischen Beziehungen*, 195–236, here 233–235.
28. See their articles there. The historians banned from working in Czechoslovakia published their views abroad, see Jan Křen, Václav Kural and Detlef Brandes, *Integration oder Ausgrenzung. Deutsche und Tschechen 1890–1945* (Bremen, 1986).
29. See Milan Otáhal, "Úvod" [Introduction], in *Češi, Němci, Odsun. Diskuse nezávislých historiků* [Czechs, Germans, Deportation. The Discussion among Independent Historians], ed. Bohumil Cerný et. al. (Prague, 1990), 3–5, here 4.
30. See Andreas Götze, "Verständnisprobleme auf dem Weg zur Partnerschaft nach 1989," in *Tschechen, Slowaken und Deutsche. Nachbarn in Europa*, ed. Niedersächsische Landeszentrale für politische Bildung (Hannover, 1995), 85–117, here 89; Bethke, *Die Entwicklung der tschechoslowakischen Diskussion*, 99.
31. See Kučera, *Die Vertreibung*, 243f. For a summary of the discussions, see also Bradley F. Adams, "Die Vertreibung der Sudetendeutschen und die tschechische Opposition in den siebziger Jahren," *Transit*, no. 10 (1995): 174–193.
32. Discourse on the "monolithic nation-state," which contrasted positively with the Second Polish Republic of the inter-war period, so bedeviled by minority problems, belonged to the standard repertory of the Polish Communists after 1945. It seems this propagandistic expression actually was absorbed into the collective image of history and was scarcely interrogated, at least up until 1989, see Zbigniew R. Wilkiewicz, "Die großen nationalen Mythen Polens," in *Nationale Mythen und Rituale in Deutschland, Frankreich und Polen*, ed. Yves Bizeul (Berlin, 2000), 59–72, here 66.
33. Włodzimierz Borodziej and Artur Hajnicz, "Raport końcowy" [Final Report], in *Kompleks wypędzenia* [The Complex of Expulsion], ed. Włodzimierz Borodziej (Kraków, 1998), 373–429, here 418f.
34. See for example Rafał Stobiecki, "Between Continuity and Discontinuity: A Few Comments on the Post-War Development of Polish Historical Research," *Zeitschrift für Ostmitteleuropa-Forschung* 50, no. 21 (2001): 214–229, here 224.
35. Jan Józef Lipski, "Dwie ojczyzny-dwa patriotyzmy. Uwagi o megalomanii narodowej i ksenofobii Polaków" [Two Fatherlands—Two Patriotisms. Comments on National Megalomania and Xenophobia in Poland], *Kultura*, no. 10 (1981): 3–29, here 8.
36. Borodziej, "Historiografia polska o 'wypędzeniu' Niemców", 254.
37. See the 1985 article by Adam Krzemiński and reactions to it in *Verlorene Heimat. Die Vertreibungsdebatte in Polen*, ed. Klaus Bachmann and Jerzy Kranz (Bonn, 1998), 37–44.

38. See the debate on the Polish attitude toward the Holocaust, triggered by Jan Błoński, "Biedni Polacy patrzą na getto" [The Poor Poles Look at the Ghetto], *Tygodnik Powszechny*, no. 2 (1987). Most recently, the study by Jan Tomasz Gross, *Sąsiedzi. Historia zagłady żydowskiego miasteczka* [Neighbors. The Destruction of the Jewish Community of Jedwabne] (Sejny, 2000), has sparked the most intensive debate on history and its politics in regard to the relation between Jewish and non-Jewish Poles under the Nazi occupation. There is now an extensive investigative report by the Institute for National Memory (Instytut Pamięci Narodowej, IPN) on the events in Jedwabne, though this is certainly not the end of the discussion: *Wokół Jedwabnego* [Around Jedwabne], ed. Paweł Machcewicz and Krzysztof Persak, 2 vols. (Warsaw, 2002); see also the URL minderheiten.orf.at/bin/at/en/news/200211/20021103004832kle.html; cf. the article by François Guesnet in the present volume.
39. See Borodziej, "Historiografia polska o 'wypędzeniu' Niemców," 262.
40. On Havel's position and the subsequent discussions, see "Die Diskussion über die Vertreibung der Deutschen in der CSFR," bearb. v. Rainer Beushausen, *Dokumentation Ostmitteleuropa* 17 (41), no. 5/6 (1991); Manfred Alexander, "Die tschechische Diskussion über die Vertreibung der Deutschen und deren Folgen," *Bohemia* 34 (1993): 390–409, here 401–408; Miroslav Kunštat, "Deutsch-tschechische Beziehungen—deutsch-tschechischer Dialog?", *Transodra* 12/13 (1996): 20–29.
41. See the anthology Cerný et. al., *Češi, Němci, Odsun.*
42. The website of the Sudetendeutsche Landsmannschaft is http://www.sudeten.de.
43. Václav Havel, "Die Tschechen und die Deutschen auf dem Weg zur guten Nachbarschaft (17 February 1995)," in *Rozhovory o sousedství: cyklus projevů přednesených v Karolinu v roce 1995* [Conversations on Being Good Neighbors: Lecture Series, Karolinum 1995] (Prague, 1997), 42–54, here 43.
44. Kučera, *Die Vertreibung*, 238.
45. Alexander, *Die tschechische Diskussion*, 390f.
46. On the discussions regarding the treaty and the relation to the Sudeten Germans, see Götze, *Verständnisprobleme*, 91–103.
47. Havel, "Die Tschechen und die Deutschen auf dem Weg zur guten Nachbarschaft," 49.
48. See Friedrich Prinz, "'Odsun Němců', die Vertreibung der Sudetendeutschen 1945: Ein kritischer Rückblick, *Odsun*, 71–84, here 71. For critical commentary, see Jaroslav Šabata, "Tschechen und die (sudeten-)deutsche Frage oder die Beneš-Dekrete und die europäische Frage," *Transodra* 12/13 (1996): 36–39, here 37.
49. Jaroslav Kučera, "Zwischen Geschichte und Politik. Die aktuelle Diskussion über die Vertreibung der Deutschen in der tschechischen Gesellschaft und Politik," in *Flucht und Vertreibung. Zwischen Aufrechnung und Verdrängung*, ed. Robert Streibel (Vienna, 1994), 174–187, here 183.
50. See Václav Houžvička, "Das gegenwärtige Niveau der Beziehungen zwischen der CR und Deutschland," in *Tschechen und Deutsche—Zeit nach der Erklärung*, ed. Ackermann-Gemeinde and Bernard-Bolzano-Stiftung (Prague, 1997), 154–160. At the beginning of the 1990s, the attitude toward the Germans was clearly more positive, see Václav Houžvička, "Vorsichtige Freundschaft," in *Tschechen und Deutsche—Historische Tabus*, ed. Ackermann-Gemeinde and Bernard-Bolzano-Stiftung (Prague, 1995), 282–285. See also idem, *Reflexe sudetoněmecké otázky a postoje obyvatelstva ceského pohraničí k Německu* [The Echo of the Sudeten German

Question and Attitudes among the Czech Population in the Border Area Near Germany] (Prague, 1997).

51. See, for example, Milan Augustin, "Die Vertreibung der Deutschen aus tschechischer Sicht," *Sudetenland* 40 (1998): 206–208 and 237–241; František Jedermann, *Verlorene Geschichte. Bilder und Texte aus dem heutigen Sudetenland* (Cologne, 1985). The pseudonym here is for three Czech authors. They note that Sudetenland, stripped of its traditions, was easily able to be transformed into a veritable bastion of the new Communist regime.
52. See, for example, Jaroslav Kučera, "Das Auseinandergehen mit den Deutschen. Ein Blick von tschechischer Seite," in: *Böhmen*, ed. Peter Becher and Hubert Ettl (Vietach, 1992), 99–108, here 102.
53. For former East Prussia, see for example Claudia Kraft, "Wojewodschaft Allenstein," in Borodziej and Lemberg, *'Unsere Heimat ist uns ein fremdes Land geworden...'*, 459 and 465. On the situation in the new Polish areas in the North and West after 1945, see also the numerous documents, some published over the last few years in *Karta.*
54. "Problem 'wypędzenia' w świadomości społecznej Polaków. Raport z badań CBOS, Warszawa, maj 1996" [The Problem of the "Expulsion" in the Social Consciousness of the Poles. A Report on Surveys by the CBOS, Warsaw, May 1996], in Borodziej, *Kompleks wypędzenia*, 439–451, here 443.
55. Ibid., 447.
56. The most important contributions in the debate are documented in Bachmann and Kranz, *Verlorene Heimat.* In the course of this debate, a body of texts appeared in Polish translation, taken from the documentation of the expulsion by Theodor Schieder, see Maria Podlasek, *Wypędzenie Niemców z terenów na wschód od Odry i Nysy Łużyckiej. Relacje świadków* [The Expulsion of the Germans from the Areas East of the Oder and Lausitz Neisse. Reports by Eyewitnesses] (Warsaw, 1995). In historiographic terms, the topic was first dealt with comprehensively at a conference in Posen in 1993, where German and Polish experiences of expulsion were compared and contrasted, see *Utracona ojczyzna. Przymusowe wysiedlenia, deportacje i przesiedlenia jako wspólne doświadczenie* [Lost Homeland. Forced Expulsions, Deportation and Resettlement as a Shared Experience], ed. Hubert Orłowski and Andrzej Sakson (Poznan, 1997).
57. Hubert Orłowski, "10 lat Wspólnoty Kultury 'Borussia'. Uczniowie historii i krajobrazu" [10 Years Cultural Association "Borussia". Pupils of History and the Landscape], *Rzeczpospolita*, 2 September 2000. See its homepage at: http://www.borussia.pl.
58. For Lower Silesia, see Krzysztof Ruchniewicz, *Kształtowanie się dolnośląskiej świadomości regionalnej w ostatnim dziesięcioleciu* [The Genesis of a Lower Silesian Regional Consciousness Over the Last Decade], manuscript in the author's possession.
59. *Vertreibung aus dem Osten. Deutsche und Polen erinnern sich*, ed. Hans-Jürgen Bömelburg, Renate Stößinger and Robert Traba (Olsztyn, 2000). In the 1990s in the area of the German Polish border, the sociologist Wanja Wronge organized conversation groups among German and Polish expellees who live there on both sides of the border, see idem, *Und dann mußten wir raus. I wtedy nas wywieźli. Wanderungen durch das Gedächtnis. Von Vertreibungen der Polen und Deutschen 1939–1949. Wędrówki po obszarze pamięci. O wypędzeniach Polaków i Niemców* (Berlin, 2000).

60. Hubert Orłowski, "O asymetrii deprywacji. Ucieczka, deportacja i wysiedlenie w niemieckiej i polskiej literaturze po 1939 r." [On the Asymmetry of Loss. Flight, Deportation and Expulsion in German and Polish Literature after 1939], in Orłowski and Sakson, *Utracona ojczyzna*, 189–207. On the treatment of expulsion experiences in literary form, see also *Konferencja literacka: Polsko-niemiecka wspólnota losów: uciekinierzy, wysiedleni, wypędzeni w niemieckiej "literaturze wypędzenia" i polskiej literaturze kresowej / Literarische Konferenz: Deutsch-polnische Schicksalsgemeinschaft: Aus der Heimat vertrieben, geflüchtet, ausgesiedelt in der deutschen Vertreibungsliteratur und der polnischen "literatura kresowa"* (Gliwice/Gleiwitz, 1996).
61. Hans-Jürgen Bömelburg and Robert Traba, "Einführung: Erinnerung und Gedächtniskultur," in *Vertrieben aus dem Osten*, 7–21, here 7.
62. Daniel Lewy and Natan Sznaider, *Erinnerung im globalen Zeitalter. Der Holocaust* (Frankfurt a.M., 2001). They note: "Der Umgang mit dem Holocaust ... öffnet exemplarisch unser Verständnis für neue Erinnerungskulturen in der Zweiten Moderne. Weiterhin behaupten wir, daß Erinnerungen an den Holocaust in einer Epoche ideologischer Ungewißheiten zu einem Maßstab für humanistische und universalistische Identifikationen werden" (9). While in the era of the "first modernity," nation-states had priority, the new era of the "second modernity" is marked by an "Entortung" (delocalizing, despatializing) of politics and culture (ibid.).
63. Dan Diner, "Der Holocaust in den politischen Kulturen Europas. Erinnerung und Eigentum," in *Auschwitz. Sechs Essays zu Geschehen und Vergegenwärtigung*, ed. Klaus-Dietmar Henke (Dresden, 2001), 65–73.
64. Levy and Sznaider, *Erinnerung im globalen Zeitalter*, 149.
65. Ks. Stanisław Musiał, "Więcej pokory, Niemcy" [More Humility, Germany], quoted in *Gazeta Wyborcza*, 27 June 2002.
66. See Harald Welzer, "Zurück zur Opfergesellschaft," *Neue Zürcher Zeitung*, 3 April 2002. See also Constantin Goschler and Philipp Ther, "Nach jüdischem Vorbild. Die Vertriebenen nutzen die Konjunktur der Opferdiskurse," *Süddeutsche Zeitung*, 1 Dezember 2003.
67. See Mariusz Muszyński, *Przejęcie majątków niemieckich przez Polskę po II wojnie światowej. Studium prawnomiędzynarodowe i porównawcze* [Poles Take Possession of German Property after WWII. A Study in International and Comparative Law] (Bielsko-Biała, 2003), 328–335 and 340. See also Niels v. Redecker, *Die polnischen Vertreibungsdekrete und die offenen Vermögensfragen zwischen Deutschland und Polen* (Frankfurt a.M., 2003), 50.
68. "Kim są ofiary drugiej wojny?" [Who are the Victims of WWII?], *Rzeczpospolita*, Special supplement, 28 August 2003.
69. See, for example, Krzysztof Kosiński, "Rozumiem wypędzonych" [I Understand the Expellees], *Gazeta Wyborcza*, 7 October 2003.
70. See the URL www.radio.cz/en/article/42405/limit (14 September 2004).
71. Jiří Dienstbier, "Mravní rozpaky české polityki" [The Moral Diffidence of Czech Politics], *Právo*, 21 September 2002.
72. There was also German critique of this view, such as that by Eva Hahn and Hans Henning Hahn, "Eine zerklüftete Erinnerungslandschaft wird planiert. Die Deutschen, 'ihre' Vertreibung und die sog. Beneš-Dekrete," *Transit. Europäische Revue*, no. 23 (2002): 103–116.

73. Gerhard Gnauck, "Polen üben heftige Kritik an Stoibers Vertriebenen-Rede," *Die Welt*, 28 June 2002.
74. Gernot Facius, "Prager Fonds lehnt Antrag auf Zahlung an Vertriebene ab," *Die Welt*, 15 October 2003.
75. On restitution debates in specific countries in regard to Jewish property, see also *Raub und Restitution. "Arisierung" und Rückerstattung des jüdischen Eigentums in Europa*, ed. Constantin Goschler and Philipp Ther (Frankfurt a.M., 2003).
76. See "Historikové proti znásilnování dějin. Stanovisko Sdružení historiků Ceské republiky" (Historians Against the Rape of History. Viewpoint of the Historians' Association, Czech Republic), in *Příloha ke Zpravodaji Historického klubu* [Appendix. Report of the Historians' Club], Vol. XII, 2001, no. 2 (Prague, 2002), 3–7. See also the declaration by the German-Czech Commission of Historians, 16 March 2002: "Deutsch-Tschechische Historikerkommission gegen Verkürzung der deutsch-tschechischen Beziehungen auf 'Beneš-Dekrete'." The Polish political scientist Piotr Buras also speaks about a "marginalization of history" (as a science), echoing Pierre Nora: "Powrót wypędzonych, czyli (nie tylko) niemieckiego sporu o pamięć ciąg dalszy" [The Return of the Expellees or the Continuation of the Struggle, Not Only German, Over Memory], in *Pamięć wypędzonych. Grass, Beneš i środkowoeuropejskie rozrachunki* [The Memory of the Expellees. Grass, Beneš and Central European Statements], ed. Piotr Buras and Piotr Majewski (Warsaw, 2003), 5–20, here 15ff.
77. Eagle Glassheim, "The Mechanics of Ethnic Cleansing: The Expulsion of Germans from Czechoslovakia, 1945–1947," in *Redrawing Nations. Ethnic Cleansing in East-Central Europe, 1944–1948*, ed. Philipp Ther and Ana Siljak (Lanham, 2001), 197–219, here 214. For a critique of the paradigm of historicizing without empathy in West German historiography on National Socialism, see Nicolas Berg, *Der Holocaust und die westdeutschen Historiker. Erforschung und Erinnerung* (Göttingen, 2003).
78. Diner, *Der Holocaust*, 66.
79. Grażyna Skąpska, "Zwischen Kollektivismus und Individualismus. Staatsbürgerschaft in der polnischen Verfassungsgeschichte," in *Staatsbürgerschaft in Europa. Historische Erfahrungen und aktuelle Debatten*, ed. Christoph Conrad and Jürgen Kocka (Hamburg, 2001), 255–278, here 267. A law of 1920 limiting the purchase of land by foreigners (persons not Polish citizens) is today still in force, though with various additions over the years, see v. Redecker, *Die polnischen Vertreibungsdekrete*, 41f.
80. Skąpska, *Zwischen Kollektivismus und Individualismus*, 274.
81. Muszyński, *Przejęcie majątków*, 115.
82. Ibid., 391–394.
83. Ibid., 396f. See also Marek Wielgo, "Strachy na Lachy" [Empty Threats], *Gazeta Wyborcza*, 31 October/2 November 2003.
84. Constantin Goschler and Philipp Ther, "Eine entgrenzte Geschichte. Raub und Rückerstattung jüdischen Eigentums in Europa," in Goschler and Ther, *Raub und Restitution*, 9–25, here 14f. and 20f.
85. Eduard Kubů and Jan Kuklík, "Ungewollte Restitution. Die Rückerstattung jüdischen Eigentums in den böhmischen Ländern nach dem Zweiten Weltkrieg," in Goschler and Ther, *Raub und Restitution*, 184–204. Dariusz Stoła, "Die polnische Debatte um den Holocaust und die Rückerstattung von Eigentum," in ibid., 205–224.

86. See v. Redecker, *Die polnischen Vertreibungsdekrete*, 19f.
87. Kučera, *Zwischen Geschichte und Politik*, 184f. The author describes the close link made by Sudeten Germans between coming to terms with the past ("*Vergangenheitsbewältigung*") and material restitution. This renders a reevaluation of the expulsion in Czech society more difficult.
88. See, for example, Jan Křen, *Konfliktní společenství. Češi a Němci 1780–1918* [Communities in Conflict. Czechs and Germans 1780–1918] (Prague, 1990). A German translation appeared in 1996.
89. Robert Traba, "Symboli pamięci: II wojna światowa w świadomości zbiorowej Polaków. Szkic do tematu" [Symbols of Memory: WWII in Polish Collective Consciousness. Sketch of a Problem], in idem, *Kraina tysiąca granic. Szkice o historii i pamięci* [Country of the Thousand Borders. Studies on History and Memory] (Olsztyn, 2003), 179–197, here 195.
90. Ibid., 190.
91. Marek Ziółkowski, "Pamięć i zapominanie: trupy w szafie polskiej zbiorowej pamięci" [Memory and Forgetting: Dead Bodies in the Closet of Polish Collective Memory], *Kultura i Społeczeństwo* 45, no. 3–4 (2001): 3–22.
92. Paweł Machcewicz, "Pamięć nie tylko o wypędzonych" [Memory Not Only of the Expellees], *Rzeczpospolita*, 1 August 2003.
93. On this see also Diner, *Der Holocaust*, 71f.
94. Ibid., 73.
95. See Helga Hirsch, "Rache ist eine Krankheit," *Die Zeit*, 3 September 1998.

— *Fifteen* —

CONFLICTING MEMORIES, UNRESTITUTED: WADI SALIB AS AN ISRAELI POLITICAL METAPHOR

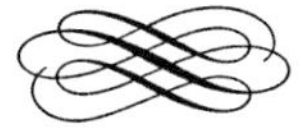

Yfaat Weiss

"You can get to Dasfina in two different ways—by boat or on the back of a camel. The city presents a different face to someone who approaches it from land or from the sea."

—Italo Calvino, *Invisible Cities*

Jewish and Palestinian communities share the same urban space, and the property transferred during the course of the 1948 war from the losers to victors is an enduring reminder of the event. Haifa in this regard is a compacted metaphor for the Israeli situation as a whole. I will focus in this paper on one particular neighborhood in Haifa, Wadi Salib, which will make it possible to examine the picture in greater detail and accuracy. The specific instance of Wadi Salib reveals the full force of the drama, as destitute Jewish refugees took possession of the property abandoned by Arabs fleeing into exile as Palestinian refugees. But the connection between property and memory is not restricted to the various aspects of the national dispute. The Wadi Salib neighborhood, populated at the end of the 1940s and in the early 1950s by Jewish refugees and immigrants, became in 1959 the arena of the first violent protests and struggle for social justice in Israel. In so-called intercommunal relations, there is also a powerful nexus among memory, property, entitlement, and rights.

Arabs and Jews

Since the 50th anniversary of Israeli independence in 1948, there has been a growing trend among Israeli Palestinians to mark their own memorial day as a parallel to and substitute for the Israeli Independence Day: the *nakba*, the Palestinian Catastrophe of 1948, commemorating the expulsion from and destruction of villages that Palestinians had called their home. This new tendency has sparked strong emotional reactions among Israeli Jews, and initiatives have recently surfaced calling for institutional sanctions against proponents of this new Palestinian movement. Such critics refuse to face the fact that the Palestinian community in Israel cannot celebrate the Israeli national holiday of independence as their own. Rather they see in Palestinian mourning of the *nakba* the firebrand of civil resistance. Such anger over Israeli Palestinian sentiment does not derive, for the most part, from denial of the historical facts. The historiographic debate and the existence of substantive disagreement about the character of some of the events notwithstanding,[1] over the past decade Jews too have in fact become well aware of the scope of the 1948 Palestinian catastrophe.

The tension over the term *an-nakba* does not spring from any disagreement over the details of the events themselves but rather from the memory of the event—that is, from the moral derivatives flowing from the demand to recognize responsibility and to question accountability and guilt. Much of the Jewish public sphere in Israel probably acknowledges what occurred but continues to place the blame on Arab leaders, thus stubbornly refusing to accept their own responsibility. The density of the historical events, with the founding of Israel following the heels of the Holocaust and the concomitant "revival" in the Israeli-Jewish experience, do not allow room for a parallel narrative on the Palestinian victims.[2]

Though not viewed as a key arena, Haifa, the classic city of "coexistence," is also involved in the debate on the Jewish-Arab past. In Haifa a public struggle over the control of memory is taking place, centering on the renaming of a main street in the Arab section of the city. The disputed street, now Zionism Boulevard (Sderot ha-Tsiyonut), used to bear the Arab name Shar'a al Jabal (Mountain Street). After the 1948 war, the name was changed with great ceremony to United Nations Boulevard to honor the international organization in the city's toponymy after it had recognized the state of Israel. In 1976, in protest against the UN resolution equating Zionism with racism, the street's name was changed once again, this time to Zionism Boulevard. Now the residents who live along the boulevard, mainly Arabs, are demanding that its original Arabic name be restored, thus clearly voicing their opposition to living along an avenue that bears the name of the national Jewish movement—an enterprise whose main achievement, the creation of the Israeli state, fails to stir in them feelings of identification.

Despite this episode, popular imagination perceives Haifa as one of the so-called "mixed cities,"[3] a model for coexistence, with Arabs making up some 8.5 percent of the total urban population of around 268,000. Living together does not spark open conflict, and this sense of calm creates a semblance of interethnic harmony—one that has helped Haifa's Jewish residents to forget the true dimensions of the historical tragedy that befell their Arab co-citizens in 1948.[4] The point of departure for the present essay is the alienation between the divergent memories of groups who live side by side in the present. To examine this present alienation, we first have to turn our discussion to the past.

Haifa and Wadi Salib

On the eve of the British withdrawal from mandatory Palestine in 1948, some 70,000 Jews lived side by side with 70,000 Arabs in Haifa.[5] Despite the clear pattern of residential segregation, there was a high degree of cooperation between Jews and Arabs based on common professional and economic interests.[6] In this city endowed with a thriving port and developing industrial base, the importance of capital, knowledge, and connections often outweighed nationalistic communal interests. Though intercommunal tensions existed, a kind of civil society evolved, in whose framework business ties were forged and labor struggles waged, while a joint municipality based on parity strove for the welfare of all residents of the city. A certain liberalism prevailed, likely the product of the distinctive geography and demography of the town: its geographic location as a seaport promoted industrial growth, while the weakness of the religious authorities in the town blunted the force of many tensions. In any case, a substantial proportion of its inhabitants, both Arab and Jewish, had settled there only a short time earlier. About half the Arab residents and nearly 80 percent of the Jews had arrived in Haifa in the 1930s and 40s, a town known among the Palestinian population before World War I by the Arabic name of Um al Amal. Along with the Arab economic elite, there were Arab villagers who had migrated to the city as a result of the rapid growth in the Arab population in the countryside and the consequent serious decline in the Arab village economy.[7] The expansion of the Wadi Salib neighborhood was also influenced by this influx from the rural areas: its cityscape was characterized by a conglomeration of hastily constructed tiny houses alongside spacious stone mansions with tile roofs and large balconies.[8] The Jews who began arriving in Haifa in the 1930s were largely refugees from Europe. They moved into the neighborhoods above those of the Arabs in residential patterns shaped by the national and religious segregation common in housing in Haifa.[9] Both communities were thus made up mostly of new arrivals.[10]

The delicate balance between Jews and Arabs was to change fundamentally between April and July of 1948. After the British pullout and the outbreak of the war, the number of Arabs in the city dropped precipitously from 70,000 to some 3,500.[11] Those who fled or were expelled from Haifa amounted to about 10 percent of the total number of Palestinian refugees.[12] Whether the Palestinians fled of their own volition or were expelled by force, still central questions in themselves, the state of Israel did not permit them to return. During the course of those same dramatic months, the number of Jews in the city rose considerably. Between May 1948 and April 1949, a total of some 190,000 immigrants arrived in Israel. Of these, approximately 110,000 (some 58 percent) were housed in abandoned Arab dwellings.[13] The reasons for housing immigrants in Arab houses were elemental: while hostilities were still raging, Israel was not prepared to absorb such an enormous influx of immigrants. However, by occupying the dwellings of those who had been uprooted, the state also strove to prevent Palestinian refugees from returning.[14] "Jaffa and Haifa," wrote Benny Morris, "had the largest and also most modern concentrations of abandoned Arab dwellings, and so it was only natural that the first mass channeling of new immigrants was into those two towns. This project was facilitated by the close proximity to the abandoned neighborhoods in these cities of Jewish urban infrastructure and services that had gone unscathed during the fighting."[15] Between May 1948 and March 1949, some 24,000 of all immigrants arriving in Israel through the port of Haifa were provided with living quarters in the city.[16] Seen from this perspective, the story was simple: many of these Jewish immigrants were simply housed in the dwellings that Arabs had abandoned.

From the outset, Wadi Salib, an Arab-Muslim neighborhood at the eastern entrance to the city, was destined to have a unique fate. Initially, the Israeli political and military authorities designated this quarter for Arabs who had remained in the city. Already at the time of David Ben-Gurion's visit to Haifa in early May 1948, plans were announced to concentrate the Christians in Wadi Nisnas and Haifa's Muslim population in Wadi Salib, in keeping with the character of the neighborhoods before the war.[17] These ideas were not implemented; instead, all Haifa's Arab residents were concentrated in Wadi Nisnas and a few other streets. It is doubtful whether it was thought that the small number of Muslims remaining in the city did not warrant their concentration in a separate quarter. Perhaps the location of Wadi Salib at the eastern edges of town, perceived as a possible threat as long as fighting continued, led to scrapping of the original plan.

During the months after the Arabs' flight and expulsion, Jewish Holocaust survivors occupied the homes abandoned by the Palestinians. In various neighborhoods, though it is doubtful whether in Wadi Salib itself, the process of moving Jews into Arab dwellings was implemented in part on a street-by-street basis while the fighting raged. Testimony from this period indicates that this housing operation was carried out using maps and special marking of living quarters to be allocated to the new immigrants. This testimony furthermore suggests that the close proximity of such dwellings to areas where fighting was still in progress terrified these camp survivors.[18] The scholarly literature has not investigated this topic in any detail, and references remain spare. It is unclear whether this silence is due to the naked simplicity of the given situation or whether it perhaps derives from the sense of some sort of taboo being violated when refugees moved into the property of other refugees.

It was only in 1969 that the Palestinian writer Ghassan Kanafani offered one of the rare references to the event with that of refugees welding together the fate of the exiled Palestinians on one side with that of the Jewish immigrants on the other, in a novel. He was himself exiled as a twelve-year-old boy from Acre to Lebanon in 1948. His novel, *Return to Haifa,* set immediately after the 1967 war, tells of the journey by Said S. and his wife Safiyya from Ramallah back to Haifa, from which they had been expelled in 1948. In the course of the uprooting and the panic of flight in 1948, Safiyya had lost her infant son. All these years, the couple had assumed he had been killed in the course of hostilities. Their trip to their house in the Muslim quarter of Halisa in Haifa put them into a situation both improbable and intolerable: against all expectations, their son Hulud had survived. He had been given to Holocaust survivors from Poland, Miryam Goshen and her husband Iphrat, as part of a package deal and agreement for their gaining occupancy of Said and Safiyya's abandoned house, where the infant had been left laying. Kanafani's tale touches on a raw nerve:

> Thus the day was Thursday, the 29th of April, 1948, the day when Iphrat Koshen and his wife Miriam, accompanied by the chicken-faced man from the Jewish Agency carrying a five-month-old baby, entered the house of Said S. in Halisa.
>
> As for Said and Safiyya, on that same day they were weeping together after Said had returned from the last of his endless attempts to get back into Haifa.[19]

It is likely that Kanafani's own fate as a refugee sharpened his vision, helping him to identify clearly the stark reality: the property of many Palestinian refugees had in fact been passed on to Jewish refugees.[20]

In 1948, Haifa, formerly a multinational city, was transformed in the span of a few weeks into a primarily Jewish town. In addition to the 65,000 Arabs who fled, the last of the British also left the city; the previous massive presence of both of these groups had left its distinctive stamp on the town's character. Over subsequent years, Haifa underwent a forgetting process, as it erased the memory of its multicultural past. But can one really claim that "cities" remember or forget? How can a city, composed not only of houses and squares but also of people undergo such processes? In order to answer this question, I will examine the development of Wadi Salib in its relation to other Arab quarters and neighborhoods in the city before 1948.

Wadi Salib and Other Neighborhoods

First, let us compare Wadi Salib and Wadi Nisnas. While Wadi Salib was emptied of its original inhabitants, Wadi Nisnas became more densely populated as the remaining Arabs of Haifa were concentrated there. To a large degree, this forced settlement destroyed its religious-communal features, since it introduced Muslims into a previously Christian area and to a substantial degree removed the Muslim population from its religious-cultural infrastructure, including its mosques and the Muslim cemetery. Carried out at the end of July 1948, the forced relocation was viewed by the Arab population at the time as a cruel and unjustified measure.[21] Some even denounced it as "ghettoization."[22] Yet this measure, originally implemented in part for military reasons, helped to create a vital Arab milieu. Over the years, Wadi Nisnas expanded and evolved into the preferred middle-class Arab residential neighborhood in Haifa.[23] This development was to have different meanings for Arabs and Jews. From the Arab perspective—in marked contrast to their anger and rage in 1948—their shared quarters in Wadi Nisnas made it possible to preserve a national identity firmly grounded on historical consciousness. It is arguable that the campaign to restore the name of Shar'a al Jabal on the Wadi's slopes would never had come about today had Israel prevented the concentration of the Arab populations remaining after 1948. In the eyes of the Jewish residents of Haifa, Wadi Nisnas' buzzing, integrated commercial life became an emblem of Jewish-Arab coexistence. As that coexistence was commercialized and given a folkloristic patina, an "Arab flavor," it helped most Israeli Jews to forget the real magnitude of the Palestinian tragedy.

An additional example of official Israeli treatment of Arab sites comparable with the story of Wadi Salib and Wadi Nisnas is that of Haifa's Old City, which, built at the end of the Ottoman period, connects the city's western and eastern districts. On the eve of the war, it was an Arab residential quarter.[24] Even during the mandate period in the 1920s, there were residential plans for urban renewal. The old neglected district was to be redeveloped and brought up to modern urban standards. But Israel's actions in the course of 1948 were hardly a direct continuation of those plans for urban renewal. In the shadow of the war's events, the Israeli army carried out extensive demolitions in the Old City, which although rationalized by the supposedly dilapidated state of the property, were designed to prevent the return of the Arab inhabitants of the city. Already in the course of demolitions, misunderstandings cropped up among municipality, government, and military authorities regarding financial responsibilities and the question of compensation of the former owners of the property. Despite proposals to turn Haifa's Old Town into the gentrified "city" of the future, nothing was done until the end of the 1960s, aside from improving the main traffic artery. For decades, the Old Town was left derelict and abandoned. The lack of construction and redevelopment in the years following the hasty destruction point to a clear fact: the motivation to prevent Arabs from living there was stronger than the desire for urban renewal for the benefit of all the city's inhabitants.[25]

Wadi Salib, in contrast to the other two neighborhoods, constitutes an intermediate example: unlike the Old City, it was not demolished, nor was an Arab population forcibly concentrated there, as in Wadi Nisnas. For these reasons, it did not revert to being an Arab quarter after 1948. The presence of some ten Arab families in Wadi Salib in 1948 and several hundred Arab residents in 1950 was unable to block the slow and profound process of forgetting who the original owners of the buildings had been.[26] A population of Jewish immigrants and refugees gradually settled in Wadi Salib. In the early 1950s, on the heels of the Holocaust survivors, came Jews from Romanía and North Africa, particularly from Morocco. While tolerating a very limited presence of Arab residents, the municipality attempted to limit the Arab character of the Wadi. However, they did not change the appearance of the houses, nor did they make repairs to the already run-down and rickety infrastructure.

Rather than altering the appearance of Wadi Salib, the municipality erased the original Arab character of the quarter in the most economical way available, namely, by changing the names of streets.[27] This revision had been designed to erase the toponymic heritage of the mandate period, which had been based on compromise and local authority. Before 1948, decisions on how to name streets had been left up to the individual neighborhoods; the procedure decided on by the neighborhood councils helped preserve the national and religious character of every neighborhood and quarter. Thus, the street names in Wadi Salib had been Arab names commemorating famous persons and places in the Arab and Muslim world. The changing of the Arab names of Haifa's streets began subsequent to the 1951 municipal elections; the newly elected mayor, Abba Houshi, chose not to continue the spirit of his predecessor, Shabtai Levy, whose composite tenure had bridged the period of parity and the Israeli era. There had been a legendary partnership between mayor Hassan Shukri and his deputy Shabtai Levy during the British Mandate, based primarily on the ability to focus on municipal issues without trying to resolve the wider Jewish-Arab conflict—a kind of functional division of authority in a very goal-oriented city that wanted to flourish. But Houshi, on this and other questions, had a decidedly aggressive view. He turned to the veteran leadership in the city, the liberators of Haifa, asking *them* to propose new names. They prepared a list containing names, which memorialized the 1948 war and defended the ethos of Israeli heroism and bravery.

Memory, Property, and Rights

Just as the question of ownership of property loomed like a cloud over the ruins of the Old City, preventing its metamorphosis into the center of modern Haifa, that same question loomed over the streets and alleyways of Wadi Salib, blocking its path forward to becoming a prosperous residential quarter. From the hour Israel resolved not to permit the Palestinian refugees to return to their native places, it was forced to use legal means to take possession of the abandoned Palestinian property for the state.[28] Thus, it is necessary to look at these legal arrangements in order to comprehend the legal status accorded to the abandoned property.[29] As early as 23 June 1948, only five weeks after independence was declared, emergency regulations were passed requiring individuals in the possession of abandoned property to register it with the police.[30] In 1950, the Knesset passed the Absentees' Property Law. This law is to some extent similar to legislation passed under similar circumstances in Turkey, Greece, Bulgaria, Czechoslovakia,[31] and Pakistan. Its purpose was the seizure of abandoned property for the benefit of refugees.[32] An "absentee" was defined under the law as a person who was a citizen of Palestine, was the legal owner of property within the territory of the state of Israel during the period from the UN decision on partition at the end of November 1947 to the declaration of the State of Israel in May 1948, and had departed from that territory before 1 September 1948 to another country or to an area controlled by forces that had attempted to prevent the establishment of the state of Israel. The law empowered a custodian to manage absentees' property and to expel occupants who, in the custodian's opinion, had no right to occupy it. The law did not give an absentee the right to return to his property.[33] In addition, the Absentees' Property Law transferred absentees' property to the Development Authority, a high governmental agency to be established by the Knesset, which, inter alia, would deal with abandoned property that had belonged to absentees and the German Templers. In 1953, an agreement was signed transferring absentees' property from the custodian to the Development Authority. Under this agreement, 69,000 apartments, houses, and businesses were transferred to the Development Authority. From that juncture, the original owners of the property were denied any possibility of return except for "settling an account." Such "accounts," however, were settled with only a small number of all absentees, those who were paradoxically termed "present absentees" (*nokhahim nifkadim*), that is, absentees who were legally living in Israel in 1953.[34] The 1953 regulation stipulated that the absentees' property be sold at its "official value," a function of the net annual value of the property for property tax purposes in the year 1947–48, taking into consideration reductions in price due to damage that reduced its possible use. However, owing to the inflation in the value of the Israeli pound between 1947 and the transfer agreement with the Development Authority in 1953, the amounts due under the original law were considerably lower than the real value of the property. A law passed in 1973 replaced the principle of "settling accounts" with that of compensation, but applied only to "absentees" then living in Israel. Compensation was granted in government bonds redeemable after fifteen years and indexed to the cost of living.

Most of the dwellings in Wadi Salib belonged to the Development Authority; the tenants rented their apartments from the Authority, paying a monthly rent. In the course of the years following the 1953 regulation, the demographics in the Wadi changed. Following the improvement in their economic situation, Holocaust survivors and the other immigrants from Europe began to buy apartments located on the slopes of the more prestigious Hadar ha-Carmel neighborhood. Beginning in the early 1950s, new tenants began to pour into the Wadi, new penniless immigrants from Romania and, later, Morocco. The latter arrived in the city by themselves on their own initiative and, for a time, moved into abandoned Arab property of their own accord. In reality, as part of the state's security strategy, the state directed Moroccan Jews into agricultural settlements or provincial "development" towns, many of which were located on the borders.[35] However, such settlement was far removed from the previous experience of some of these immigrants before their emigration, and was not in keeping with their desires and abilities.[36] These were poor refugees and were not agents of the historical process that gave them possession of the property of others.[37]

The "Wadi Salib Riots"

In the consciousness of the Israeli public, they and their history, and not the original Arab inhabitants, are associated with Wadi Salib. The "riots of Wadi Salib," as they are called in popular parlance, those stormy days in 1959 when the neighborhood of Wadi Salib became the scene of a violent struggle against ethnic discrimination, awakened for the first time public awareness in Israel of the economic distress suffered by Jewish immigrants from the Arab countries. Although the riots occurred in the same urban area in which the war had been fought eleven years earlier, they were inscribed in Israeli public consciousness and treated in the sociological literature as completely separate from previous events.[38] In mainstream Israeli consciousness, 1948 emblematizes a national dispute, while 1959 and the violent "riots of Wadi Salib" symbolize ethnic and social protest in Israel.

Concentrating on the link between property and memory within the physical space of Wadi Salib, I will try to examine briefly whether there is an immanent connection between these events in time apart from the accidental character of their presence in the same geographical space. I would argue that the relationship is not necessarily causal; it exists in symbolic spheres, but, as I will point out below, there is continuity, both institutional and in terms of actors.

In 1959, the Israeli government appointed a commission headed by the judge Moshe Etzioni to investigate the reasons for the violent riots, which led to injuries suffered by many demonstrators and police and damage to property. The minutes of the commission's deliberations and its conclusions are instructive documents regarding the topic at hand. The commission went beyond its assignment, expanding its deliberations to include the question of ethnic discrimination and communal deprivation as reflected in the Wadi Salib riots.[39] I will concentrate on the few references to questions of property, because they allow us to focus attention on the link in the eyes of government authorities between the original Palestinian residents of the Wadi and the new Jewish residents, who had immigrated from Morocco.

The minutes contain instructive testimony by Haifa mayor Abba Houshi, which offers a window into the nature of the Zionist utopia.[40] Houshi stated before the commission:

> Regarding the very existence of Wadi Salib, I put forward a proposal at the time of the War of Liberation in 1948 to raze the quarter. I suggested a plan for its urban rehabilitation, though with the proviso that it could only be implemented after all its residents had been relocated. (To remove the 3,144 families living there, 32 million pounds were needed. And anyone who claimed he could do that in a few days was talking nonsense.) Over the course of five to six years, it may be possible to effect removal of the majority of the residents and not allow others to move in. Then you can bring in the bulldozers, level the ground and construct other buildings. The municipality has a plan for comprehensive public housing. We want to carry that out, but recommended a method for distributing the population in the city, avoiding the development of special neighborhoods for any specific ethnic community. This is an excellent tool for the mixing of different immigrant groups, encouraging them to merge together and forget their origins.[41]

Houshi cited the example of new public housing developed elsewhere in Haifa (Kiryat Eliazar) "where members of all the [ethnic] communities live. In the course of time, they'll forget and will come to see that whoever lives here is Jewish."[42] But the argument that Houshi raised to justify destruction of the Wadi, namely the need to mix (ethnic) communities, contradicts the beginning of his testimony, where he insisted that only 20 percent of the inhabitants of Wadi Salib were from North Africa.[43] Thus, a mixture of communities appears to have indeed existed in the Wadi; Houshi's statement of his intent to "vacate the apartments in Wadi Salib, and as soon as they have been vacated, to demolish the buildings"[44] reflected a different agenda, that of modernization.

The Development Authority controlled almost all of the apartments in Wadi Salib. The tenants paid rent, which was passed on to the Authority, whose task was to maintain the property. The other housing option that the municipality offered tenants involved purchasing an apartment in public housing estates. People turned down this option in part because of difficulties in coming up with the necessary cash. The Development Authority, indirectly rationalizing their problems in proper maintenance, complained that roughly a third of the families living in the Wadi had moved in illegally and were not paying the rent.[45] Yet it can be argued that when the state put Wadi Salib, as part of the "absentees' properties," under its safekeeping and control, it actually took possession of the property without compensating the former owners. Thus the state's moral-economic defence of its own negligence in managing the property was built on shaky ground. The deputy mayor Zvi Barzilai grumbled about this to the commission:

> The Development Authority, the agency appointed by the Custodian to watch over the absentee property for the state, is gathering rent to pass on to the absent owners once peace is achieved. From the time of the state's creation until the present, the Development Authority has collected a total sum in the vicinity of 10 million pounds.... The Authority is required to invest these monies in redeveloping downtown. The agency should not bear the name "development" in vain.[46]

Although the solutions proposed by Barzilai initially did not differ from those put forward by Houshi, Barzilai was the only one during the deliberations who made specific reference to the Development Authority's source of funds.

In their testimony, the officials repeatedly claimed that there had been no interest in settling the immigrants in Wadi Salib, since housing there was so run-down.[47] It is difficult to evaluate this charge, but it appears too sweeping in light of the fact that during the mandate period, there were also middle-class families living in Wadi Salib. David Ben-Haroush, leader of the 1959 riots, testified that the Development Authority had been discriminatory in their allotment of housing:[48]

> When the immigrants came in 1948 and there was a massive influx, the most beautiful buildings were in the hands of the Haganah, and when they

> vacated the premises they passed them on to persons from a European background, who still have possession or have transferred them to others.[49]

This and other claims of discrimination sparked an angry response by Judge Etzioni and other members of the government commission, who decided to conduct a comprehensive investigation. One of them asked Ben-Haroush: "Where did you live in Morocco?" To which Ben-Haroush answered: "In Casablanca." The member of the commission went on: "In what kind of a house?" "In one that was more or less OK," Ben-Haroush replied. The investigator continued to press him: "How many rooms were there?" "One and a half" was the reply, "there were four of us living there, my father and mother, sister and myself. But a room there is a room. I didn't say I was rich in Morocco." To which the member of the commission responded: "Imagine that among those from Europe, some had lived in luxurious apartments."

While the member of the commission drew a direct line between Ben-Haroush's living quarters in Casablanca and his apartment in Israel—in a bid to put him in his place in the list of those entitled to housing—the commission's report pursued a more complex tactical approach. The report praised North African Jewry, according it a place of honor in the history of the Jewish people and Zionism. The commission attributed their economic hardship to the external circumstances, blaming, for example, the educational system and the structure of Israeli industry. Among other things, the report linked their distress to the "Arab character" of the architecture in Wadi Salib.[50] In conclusion, it noted:

> The Wadi Salib neighborhood in Haifa is a poor and overcrowded neighborhood, located at the bottom of the slopes. Buildings are jammed together, pressing one on the other. Some are even built one on top of the next, along narrow winding back streets, most with steep steps—in keeping with the tradition of crowded residential areas in the Arab Old City. Crammed together in dark and narrow quarters, among them tiny alcoves not fit for human habitation, live families with many children. Not every such "apartment" has even minimal sanitary conditions.... In sum, such a neighborhood has no right to exist in a modern city like Haifa. In any case, given the fact of its existence, the area requires an excessive amount of repair, maintenance, and care.

Such a course was logical and consistent: it was clear from the commission's deliberations that it disdained Oriental ways of life. Sitting in cafes in the Oriental context of the Wadi was associated with unemployment and idleness, having a drink with one's friends with alcoholism.

The Wadi was doomed. In the years following the committee's investigation, the Wadi's residents were removed and relocated to new neighborhoods; these in time deteriorated, becoming themselves impoverished areas. In the dilapidated housing into which they were relocated, the former residents of the Wadi were dubbed *mefunim*, or "evacuees," in the local slang. The buildings they were forced to leave were boarded up, and the Shikmona company took over the job of demolition. "Shikmona" is indeed a rather ironic name—based on the Hebrew root for "rehabilitate," "rebuild"—for an agency whose main task was the razing of buildings and leveling of the soil. Shikmona was the organization that in 1948 had razed the old city in Haifa to the ground.

Now the ruins of the Old City and Wadi Salib stood side by side on the perimeter of a metropolis with pretensions to modernity.[51] A modern city in this sense was "not Oriental."[52] To be Jewish now meant "not Arab."[53] And in the words of Amnon Raz-Krakotzkin, the Orientalist approach to Zionism was to "deny the culture in whose conception Jewish identity was previously defined: to surrender one's identity and memory became a condition for 'integration.'"[54] The fate of Wadi Salib was sealed when the Arab Oriental architecture occupied by Jews who represented the heritage of Arab Jewry had become an insufferable challenge to East European Zionism. That brand of Zionism preferred public housing projects, which, as Abba Houshi maintained, were a "marvelous instrument for the mixing of diverse Diasporas, fusing them together and obliterating their origins."[55]

Conclusions

In his insightful analysis of the role of reparations in regard to dealing with historical injustices, John Torpey introduces a model of reparations politics.[56] According to this model, reparation is a part of a series of concentric circles starting with transitional justice, followed by reparations and apologies, and ending with what he calls "communicative History." Torpey claims that reparations and restitution for Holocaust survivors and the state of Israel served as a standard and model for reparations for historical injustice in general. "The background of 'reparations politics' has been the emergence of a broader 'consciousness of catastrophe' that is rooted in but goes well beyond Holocaust awareness."[57] The meaning of the compensations of Holocaust survivors in the context of Israel in general and Wadi Salib in particular is above all an economic one. For many of the survivors, who accepted compensations, the money provided them with a new economic starting point in their lives, making it possible for them to move into better neighborhoods. Even more important was the psychological or symbolical meaning; Charles Maier points out that "the projects of reparation, remembering, and reconciliation involve the right to tell histories and have them listened to respectfully."[58] Holocaust survivors in Israeli society definitely enjoyed these intangible benefits of reparations. These processes of recognition and reparation did not go so far as to "fuse polarized antagonistic histories into a core of shared history to which both sides can subscribe,"[59] but they did help to integrate the fate of the survivors into the fabric of Israeli history.

The two other actors of our story—the Palestinians refugees and the Oriental Jews—have not yet taken part in this dynamic of reconciliation. The unforgivable memories of the inhabitants of Wadi Salib might result from the fact that neither the Palestinian refugees nor the Moroccan Jews were ever considered for reparations. Torpey analyzes three basic sources of claims for reparations: first, cases arising from acts of injustice perpetrated during World War II; second, claims ensuing from "state terrorism" and other authoritarian practices in the aftermath of a "transition to democracy"; and third, campaigns for reparations stemming from colonialism.[60] As to the types of reparations, Torpey argues that the claims arising from World War II are typically rooted in commemorative projects "that call attention to the acute barbarity or humiliation associated with past mistreatment of individual members of the group." In these cases, he writes, "reparations are largely symbolic attempts to recognize the recipients' past victimization."[61] This is not true for the third source of claims—colonialism. The "antisystemic" reparations, as Torpey calls them, are "more forward looking … as a means of transforming the current conditions of deprivation suffered by the groups in question, and are more frequently connected to broader projects of social transformation than are commemorative projects."[62]

This distinction among the types of reparations is very useful for our case. If we accept the fact that the Palestinians refugees are victims of the Israeli internal colonization of the country, and that the Jews from Arab countries in Israel are actually refugees of the de-colonization processes in the newly established Arab countries, then the compensations claims of the two groups, despite all their differences, all result from the same evil: colonialism. If Torpey is right, and I do believe he is, then reparations claims in this context are not the end of the matter. Rather, they are probably connected to broader movements demanding egalitarian social change. This is definitely the case for Oriental Jews in

Israel. First came the apologies: in 1999, Prime Minister Ehud Barak apologized for what the European establishment in Israel had done to the Oriental newcomers in the 1940s and 1950s. Then came demands for more distributive justice. The case of the Palestinians, however, is much more complicated, since it is not a domestic affair. Nevertheless, there is good reason to believe that "the property/memory nexus," this "kind of universal wave, a swell from the former Eastern European people's democracies to swamp countries in the West," might in "the best of all cases" come to replace the Palestinian claim to a right to return.[63] If this is the scenario to follow, than the simple fact of the "consolidation of the Holocaust as a standard and its 'globalization' as a model for [the reparations] demand"[64] will take on a painful, ironical meaning.

Notes

1. Ilan Pappe, "The Tantura Case in Israel; the Katz Research and Trial," *Journal of Palestine Studies* 30, no. 3 (2001): 19–39 and idem., "The Katz and the Tantura Affairs: History, Historiography, the Court and the Israeli Academia," *Theory and Criticism* 20 (2002): 191–218 [Hebrew].
2. Ilan Gur-Ze'ev, "The Morality of Acknowledging/not-Acknowledging the other's Holocaust/Genocide," *Journal of Moral Education* 27, no. 2 (1998): 161–177; idem., "Defeating the Enemy Within; Exploring the Link between Holocaust Education and the Arab-Israeli Conflict," *Religious Education* 95, no. 4 (2000): 373–401; idem., "The Production of Self and the Destruction of the Other's Memory and Identity in Israeli-Palestinian Education on the Holocaust/ 'Nakbah,'" *Studies in Philosophy and Education* 20, no. 3 (2001): 255–266 and idem. with Ruth Linn, "Holocaust as Metaphor; Arab and Israeli Use of the Same Symbol," *Metaphor and Symbolic Activity* 11, no. 3 (1996): 195–206.
3. A British term; see Tamir Goren, "The History of the Disappearance of the 'Old City' from the Perspective of Haifa, 1948–1951," *Horizons in Geography* 40–41 (1994): 57–81, here 57 [Hebrew].
4. For a much more radical interpretation, see Ghazi Falah, "Living Together Apart. Residential Segregation in Mixed Arab-Jewish Cities in Israel," *Urban Studies* 33, no. 6 (1996): 823–857.
5. Benny Morris, *1948 And After: Israel And The Palestinians* (Oxford, 1990), 49.
6. Joseph Washitz, *Social Changes in Haifa's Arab Society Under the British Mandate*, Ph.D. diss., Hebrew University (Jerusalem, 1993) [Hebrew], 10–21.
7. May Seikaly, *Haifa—Transformation of an Arab Society, 1918–1939* (New York, 1995), 66; Mahmoud Yazbak, "Ha-Hagira ha-Arawit le-Haifa bein ha-Shanim 1933–1948" ["The Arab Immigration to Haifa Between the Years 1933–1948"], *Cathedra* 45 (1987): 131–146.

8. Yossef Ben-Artzi, *Residential Patterns and Intra Urban Migration of Arabs in Haifa* (Haifa, 1980), 19–23 [Hebrew].
9. Seikaly, *Haifa*, 61–65.
10. Ibid., *Haifa*, 47–51.
11. Ben-Artzi, *Residential Patterns*, 19–23.
12. Benny Morris, *The Birth of the Palestinian Refugee Problem Revisited* (Cambridge, 2004), 186.
13. Ibid., 395.
14. Ibid., 394; Dvora Hacohen, *Immigrants in Turmoil: The Great Wave of Immigration to Israel and its Absorption, 1948–1953* (Jerusalem, 1994), 16–18 [Hebrew].
15. Ibid., 384, and Yossef Ben-Artzi and Tamir Goren, "Molding the Urban Space Of Haifa: Arabs in 1948," *Studies in the Geography Of Israel* 15 (1998): 7–27, here 19–23 [Hebrew].
16. Ibid., 21.
17. Morris, *1948*, 150.
18. Hanna Yablonka, *Foreign Brethren: Holocaust Survivors in the State of Israel 1948–1952* (Jerusalem, 1994), 19–20 [Hebrew].
19. Ghassan Kanafani, *Palestine's Children: Returning to Haifa and Other Stories* (London, 2000), 170.
20. In any event, 1967 marked a turning point in the consciousness of numerous Palestinians: for many who had been living in areas occupied by Israel in the 1967 war, the opportunity was opened up, for the first time after twenty years, to revisit their former towns and villages, abandoned in 1948. These forsaken homes and localities, to the extent they had not been destroyed and obliterated, returned from remembrance to reality.
21. Charles S. Kamen, "After the Catastrophe II: The Arabs in Israel, 1948–51," *Middle Eastern Studies* 24 (1988): 68–109, here 71–77.
22. Morris, *1948*, 160 and Falah, "Living Together Apart," 837.
23. Ben-Artzi, *Residential Patterns*.
24. Goren, "The History of the Disappearance".
25. Ghazi Falah, "The 1948 Israeli-Palestinian War and its Aftermath. The Transformation and De-Signification of Palestine's Cultural Landscape," *Annals of the Association of American Geographers* 86, no. 2 (1996): 256–258.
26. Ben-Artzi and Goren, "Molding the Urban Space Of Haifa," 18.
27. Maoz Azaryahu, "A Tale Of Two Cities: Commemorating The Israeli War Of Independence in Tel Aviv and Haifa," *Cathedra* 68 (1993): 98–125, here 102–104 [Hebrew] and Miron Benvenisti, "The Hebrew Map," *Theory and Criticism* 11 (1997): 7–29 [Hebrew].
28. Alexandre (Sandy) Kedar, "On the Legal Geography of Ethnocratic Settler States: Notes Towards A Research Agenda," *Current Legal Issues* 5 (2003): 401–441.
29. Kedar, *Israeli Law and the Redemption of Arab Land, 1948–1969*, Ph.D. diss., Harvard University (Cambridge, Massachusetts, 1996), 55–110.
30. Aharon Liskovsky, "The 'present absentees' in Israel," *The New Orient* 6 (1960): 186–192, here 187 [Hebrew].
31. Eduard Kubů and Jan Kuklík, "Ungewollte Restitutionen. Die Rückerstattung jüdischen Eigentums in den böhmischen Ländern nach dem zweiten Weltkrieg," in: *Raub und Restitution. "Arisierung" und Rückerstattung jüdischen Eigentums in Europa*, ed. Constantin Goschler and Philipp Ther (Frankfurt a.M., 2003), 184–

204 and Helmut Slapnicka, "Die rechtlichen Grundlagen für die Behandlung der Deutschen und der Magyaren in der Tschechoslowakei 1945–1948," in: *Nationale Frage und Vertreibung in der Tschechoslowakei und Ungarn 1938–1948,* ed. Richard G. Plaschka, Horst Haselsteiner, Arnold Suppan and Anna M. Drabek (Vienna, 1997), 153–192.

32. Liskovsky, "The 'present absentees' in Israel," 188.
33. David Kretzmer, *The Legal Status of the Arabs in Israel* (Boulder, 1990), 55–60 and Uzi Benziman and Atallah Mansour, *Subtenants* (Jerusalem, 1992), 157–71.
34. David Grossman, *Der geteilte Israeli. Über den Zwang, den Nachbarn nicht zu verstehen* (München, 1994).
35. Adriana Kemp, "Borders, Space and National Identity in Israel," *Theory and Criticism* 16 (2000): 13–43 [Hebrew].
36. Kemp, "State Control Resistance in the Israeli Borderlands," in *Mizrachim in Israel: A Critical Observation into Israel's Ethnicity,* ed. Hannan Hever, Yehouda Shenhav and Pnina Motzafi-Haller (Tel Aviv, 2002), 36–67 [Hebrew] and State of Israel Archives, Testimonies at the Etzioni commission for the investigation of the Wadi-Salib riots, testimony of Dr. Ra'anan Weiz, (general director of the department of settlement of the Jewish Agency), morning session 9 August 1959, testimonies before the commission (vol. 3), folder G, 17253, file 3, 12–17.
37. Yehouda Shenhav, "What Palestinians and Jews from Arab Lands Have in Common? Nationalism and Ethnicity Examined Through the Compensation Question," *Hagar International Social Science Review* 1, no. 1 (2000): 71–110, and Kedar, "The Legal Transformation of Ethnic Geography: Israeli Law and the Palestinian Landholder 1948–1967," *New York University Journal of International Law and Politics* 33, no. 4 (2001): 923–1000, here 944–945.
38. E.g. Henriette Dahan-Kalev, *Self Organizing Systems. Wadi Salib and 'The Black Panthers'—Implications for Israeli Society,* Ph.D. diss. (Jerusalem, 1991) [Hebrew].
39. Ibid., 110, 117.
40. For a general critic of Zionist utopia and public housing, see Rachel Kallus and Hubert Law-Yone, "National Home/Personal Home: The Role of Public Housing in the Shaping of Space," *Theory and Criticism* 16 (2000): 153–180 [Hebrew].
41. State of Israel Archives, Abba Houshi, morning session 5 August 1959, testimonies before the Etzioni commission (vol. 3), folder G, 17253, file 3.
42. On public housing as a Zionist project for ethnic standardization see Kallus and Law-Yone, "National Home/Personal Home," 168–170.
43. State of Israel Archives, Abba Houshi, morning session 5 August 1959, testimonies before the Etzioni commission (vol. 3), folder G, 17253, file 3, 2.
44. Ibid., 6.
45. State of Israel Archives, Yizhak Ponti, head of the housing department of the Development Authority, morning session 5 August 1959, testimonies before the commission (vol. 3), folder G, 17253, file 3, 15–18.
46. State of Israel Archives, memorandum of lawyer Barzilai, deputy mayor of the City of Haifa, 29 July 1959, testimonies before the commission (vol. 3), folder G 17252, file 3, 6.
47. State of Israel Archives, Kalman Levi (head of the department of Absorption of the Jewish Agency in Haifa and the northern province), morning session 4 August 1959, testimonies before the commission (vol. 3), folder G, 17252, file 3, 1; Avigdor Eshet (member of the secretary of the worker's council of Haifa), ibid.

48. State of Israel Archives, memorandum of lawyer Barzilai, deputy mayor of the City of Haifa, 29 July 1959, testimonies before the commission (vol. 3), folder G, 17252, file 3, 16–18.
49. State of Israel Archives, David Ben-Haroush, session that took place on Sunday 26 July 1959, testimonies before the commission (vol. 3), folder G, 17253, file 1, 16.
50. State of Israel Archives, Report of the official commission investigating the events of 9 July 1959 in Wadi Salib, presented to the government on 17 August 1959, 13, 15.
51. For the general notion of modernity in urban planning and architecture and for its popularity in the 1950s as well as for the revision up to the 1980s, see Thomas Deckker, *The Modern City Revisited* (London, 2000). How the image of inevitability and modernity is being constructed in the Israeli land regime, see Ronen Shamir, "Suspended in Space: Bedouins Under the Law of Israel," *Law and Society Review* 30, no. 2 (1996): 231–257, here 234–237.
52. Kallus and Law-Yone, "National Home/Personal Home," 156–158.
53. Ella Shohat, "Sepharadim in Israel: Zionism from the Standpoint of its Jewish Victims," *Social Text* 19/20 (1988): 1–35.
54. Amnon Raz-Krakotzkin, "A Few Comments on Orientalism, Jewish Studies and Israeli Society," *Jama'a* 3, no. 2 (1998): 34–61, here 54 [Hebrew].
55. State of Israel Archives, Abba Houshi, morning session 5 August 1959, testimonies before the commission (vol. 3), folder G, 17253, file 3, 5.
56. John Torpey, "Introduction, Politics and the Past," in *Politics and the Past: Repairing Historical Injustice*, ed. John Torpey (Boulder, 2003), 1–34.
57. Torpey, "'Making Whole What Has Been Smashed': Reflections on Reparations," *The Journal of Modern History* 73 (2001): 333–358, here 334.
58. Charles S. Maier, "Overcoming the Past? Narrative and Negotiation, Remembering, and Reparation: Issues at the Interface of History and the Law," in Torpey, *Politics and the Past*, 295–304.
59. Elazar Barkan, *The Guilt of Nations: Restitution and Amending Historical Injustice* (New York, 2000), xxii.
60. Torpey, "'Making Whole What Has Been Smashed'," 336.
61. Ibid., 337.
62. Ibid., 336.
63. Dan Diner, "Memory and Restitution: World War II as a Foundational Event in a Uniting Europe," in this volume.
64. Torpey, "'Making Whole What Has Been Smashed'," 334.

Part V:
Resolutions

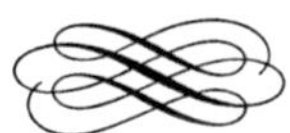

— *Sixteen* —

WIEDERGUTMACHUNG IN GERMANY: BALANCING HISTORICAL ACCOUNTS 1945–2000

Hans Günter Hockerts

What is Meant by *Wiedergutmachung*?

As one generation of contemporary historians has replaced another, the term *Wiedergutmachung* ("to make good again" damages caused by the Nazi-persecution) has been discredited. It is considered a notion that is "intolerable, tending to make light of matters that are most serious." Some of its critics contend that "in the way it relativizes matters and exonerates the guilty, it is virtually unsurpassed."[1] An angry Jewish journalist upped the critical ante: "I think the word Wiedergutmachung should have been taken to court, immediately. Its use should have been outlawed in connection with the persecution of the Jews."[2] To a certain extent, such criticism is understandable. It is obvious that it is impossible to reverse Nazism's legacy: the unraveling of law into fear and terror, the persecution and destruction of millions. That can never be "made good again," as the German expression *Wiedergutmachung* so patently might seem to suggest. And it may be that for some, what this means is the transformation of guilt, *Schuld*, into something monetary, a debt, *Schulden*. They then come to view the guilt as erased when the monetary debt has been paid—a kind of settling of accounts that does not necessitate further examination or concern.

But let us examine this German phraseology more carefully. The principal historical dictionary of the language, *Grimms Wörterbuch*, informs us that the verb *gutmachen* has a time-honored older meaning of "indemnify, pay for, expiate."[3] Perhaps such layering of meaning helps to explain why German-Jewish emigrants have for the most part embraced the word *Wiedergutmachung*—an expression difficult to render in English. The emigrés even decided, while the war still raged, to popularize the term.[4] In the founding years of the Federal Republic, the idea of *Wiedergutmachung* was pressed into service and used precisely by those individuals who understood better than most that the Germans had a huge legacy of historical debt: much to indemnify, pay for, and expiate. Among opposition circles, this was a widespread notion, and it was particularly the most resolute champions of assistance for the victims of National Socialist persecution who held *Wiedergutmachung* in high regard. One of them, Franz Böhm, a Bundestag member from the Christian Democrats, deciphered contemporary connotations in a very precise way in 1954: "Any person who was appalled by the cruelties and abominations of the Hitler period when they were perpetrated, who empathized with the victims and helped when he was able, is passionately committed to *Wiedergutmachung.* But those who identified with Hitler back then, who considered everyone the Gestapo arrested to be an enemy, a criminal or someone socially undesirable, or who, if confronted with the sight of all the cruelty and brutality, consoled himself with the old saw: 'you can't make an omelette without breaking eggs'—that person will view *Wiedergutmachung* today basically as some kind of nuisance."[5] At the time, the concept was mobilized as an appeal to conscience: a lever in order to overcome lethargy and apathy. Because the protagonists of reparations suffered from a sense of moral and political guilt, they wanted debts that were quantifiable, arranged in some manner—settled and paid off in the best possible way. Naturally they were well aware that there could be no literal *Wiedergutmachung* of past injustice: that "in any case, it is only possible to make good again a tiny bit" of what was really lost and suffered.[6] In addition, some wished to set an example for what "pro-active repentance" could mean, and a "symbolic reenactment of the law of morality."[7] For that reason, an emphatic, even metaphoric concept was preferred, one that was morally binding in its very semantics over a discourse that limited itself to anemic, colorless technical/legal terms, such as "compensation" (*Entschädigung*).

Today *Wiedergutmachung* serves to polarize people in a quite different way. Whoever uses it nowadays most likely wants to stress agreement with the fact of success: that much has been achieved in this realm. Thus, a report from the federal finance ministry states that, as of December 2000, the government had provided DM 136,5 billion ($69,790 billion) in reparations. This "covers almost all injuries stemming from Nazi injustice" in a "balanced relation in accordance with the reason for and scope of the damages incurred."[8] Yet the concept has become vexing to people who regard it as the epitome of an attempt to make light of the gravity of these events. This is often now done in a ritualistic manner, lacking any authentic differentiation. The upshot is that the very champions of *Wiedergutmachung* are caught up in an anachronistic false conclusion—as though they had only been concerned to achieve a "way of diminishing the damage and settling accounts."[9]

No matter how the semantic debate is waged, in terminological terms we are dependent on the concept of *Wiedergutmachung*. It is the only available inclusive term for a multitude of events and areas of law that decide whether, and if so how, the victims of persecution are entitled to compensation.[10] The collective concept subsumes at least five sub-spheres or dimensions. These can be briefly characterized as follows: (1) restitution of assets stolen or expropriated from the individual; (2) compensation for injury in the course of one's personal life, such as the loss of freedom, health, professional advancement, and other matters; (3) special regulations, particularly in the areas of public service and social security; (4) juridical rehabilitation, aimed at nullifying unjust verdicts, especially in criminal law[11]—but also in cases, for example, where individuals were deprived of their citizenship or had their academic degrees revoked.[12]

Initially, these four points were geared to the home front of German domestic law. But the Nazi persecutors also tore down international boundaries, exporting terror and bringing millions of foreigners by force to the German Reich. Consequently, the issue of "making good" takes on broad transnational dimensions. Hence the fifth aspect of *Wiedergutmachung*: (5) consideration of international treaties that were or remain in force. *Wiedergutmachung* could be conceived in far broader terms if separated from the constraining frame of law and politics and opened up for the multitude of forms and modes of independent social initiatives[13] and the whole process of "working through," on the plane of thought and the culture of memory, of the history of the persecutors and their victims.

Thus, here we encounter a very ramified field, particularly since prospects have in effect been tripled through the unification of Germany—that is, the content and form of reparations differ markedly depending on whether you look at West Germany, East Germany, or unified Germany since 1990. The present overview concentrates on the three main elements: restitution, compensation (*Entschädigung*, indemnification), and international agreements. The first and most detailed section examines developments in West Germany up to the reunification.[14] There are two guiding questions here: what traces did the respective conjuncture of time inscribe into the face of *Wiedergutmachung*? What are the underlying reasons behind the fact that compensation in the 1990s could become such a major political topic once more? The paper then looks at the German Democratic Republic, primarily as a basis for contrastive comparison. In conclusion, the study sketches the contemporary history of the question of *Wiedergutmachung* since the watershed year of 1989–90.

Restitution and Compensation in West Germany

Our point of departure is the locus where the early directions for developments were established, the American Zone of Occupation. The U.S. military government there initially prioritized restitution (*Rückerstattung*), working out with the prime ministers of the German states Law No. 59, The Restitution of Identifiable Assets, effective from November 1947.[15] All those who were in the possession of assets that had been surrendered under the pressure and threat of persecution or had been taken by force from their owner, were now obliged to return them, or in specific cases to compensate the owner. In most cases, this involved Jewish assets, because the Jewish Germans had been plundered more than any other group.[16] There was another legal basis for the return of the so-called "organizational assets and property" that had been pilfered from the trade unions, democratic parties, church and charitable organizations. In April 1947, the Allied Control Council created that basis in legislation, issuing a directive valid for all four occupation zones.[17]

Although Americans and Germans had worked jointly on the law for restitution, the military government ultimately proclaimed the law on its own because there had been irreconcilable differences in regard to several points. Thus, the law was harsher on those acquiring property who had personally avoided exerting any pressure on persecuted victims, so-called *loyale Erwerber* ("loyal acquirers"), than the prime ministers of the German states thought was reasonable.[18] But the greatest degree of dissent was in respect to "assets without heirs." This pale legal phrase signified the inheritance of families that had been completely wiped out during the mass murder. The American military government was obliged by a promise it had made the Committee of American Jewish Organizations. According to that pledge, an international Jewish "successor organization" was to be created to take over assets and heirless property. Here the prime ministers and their advisors were apprehensive about the possible loss of larger amounts of assets that might be transferred abroad, despite the fact that they were urgently needed for reconstruction.

This point of dispute blocked any meeting of minds in the Control Council in hammering out a solution for all of occupied Germany. The British hesitated because they feared a successor organization would channel funds to the Jewish insurgency against the British mandate in Palestine. The French and Russian sides were more resolute in their opposition, arguing that assets without heirs had to be left to the disposition of the various German states.[19] Thus, the American initiative did not find sufficient support either in the Control Council or among the prime ministers in the American zone, which explains their unilateral decision. At the same time, the French introduced an ordinance that strongly differed, while the British military government chose in May 1949 to enact a simplified version of the law in the American zone. The regulation valid from July 1949 in West Berlin was based on this British version.[20]

It would appear that the prime ministers in the various occupied German states were quite relieved that the military administration had taken on full responsibility for the law on restitution, for this "extremely difficult matter"[21] was highly explosive, a veritable social time bomb. For several years, organized interest groups were up in arms agitating against the law, showcasing grave individual cases.[22] But that did not sway the Western Allies, and they adhered to a relatively speedy and strict implementation of restitution. Thus, already in the 1950s, most of the cases where private individuals and firms were required to restitute property were settled. Even after the establishment of the Federal Republic, the Western powers retained control on this matter. The laws issued by the military governments remained in force up until 1990; and into the mid-1950s, in the states of the earlier Bi-Zone, final judgments were reserved solely for Allied sitting judges. When occupation was formally terminated in 1955 with the Paris Accords, supreme judicial authority in this sphere was not transferred to the Federal Supreme Court (*Bundesgerichtshof*). Rather, a Supreme Restitution Court (*Oberstes Rückerstattungsgericht*) succeeded the Allied appellate courts. They were staffed by Allied and German judges on a parity basis, and chaired by neutral presidents from countries such as Sweden, Denmark, and Switzerland.[23] According to a contemporary critical observer, these courts were responsible for "the grand line of verdicts favorably disposed to reparations, in accordance with which the lower courts passed judgment, though not always willingly."[24]

What can be said about the quantitative side of these events? It is estimated that some 100,000 private individuals returned assets worth approximately DM 3.5 billion, in the main real estate, but also business enterprises and shares in firms. In today's prices, that is equivalent to some DM 10.5 billion.[25] What such dry figures mean in terms of social and economic history has to date been little researched, and remains an important field for future inquiry. Such research should be based in particular on perspectives grounded on life history and the history of experience of the persecuted and the beneficiaries of persecution, extending well beyond the year 1945.[26] What was the encounter like when original Jewish owners faced the "Aryan" owners of their former property in new roles as "plaintiff" and "accused"? How did that encounter develop and unfold? How great was the number of the so-called "righteous"—persons who had protected the interests of the former owner who had been forced to sell, perhaps even via secret trusteeship agreements regarding further business and income of the firm? Was there a corresponding social rise and decline of the "Aryanizers" congruent with the robbery and later restitution? Probably the fledgling economic miracle in the Federal Republic, coupled with readiness on the part of many victims to accept a settlement, often assured a soft landing, so to speak—as, for example, in the case of the department store chain Hertie.[27]

Those DM 3.5 billion of course represented only a fraction of what had been stolen from persecuted Jews. Aside from various estimates of unreported cases, and devaluation losses due to the currency reform, the figure does not include most of what the master expropriator, the German Reich, pilfered en masse. In its pillage and looting, mobile property was the principal target: precious metals, objects of art, stocks and equities, jewelry, quality furniture, and other valuables.[28] After the war, most of this was not accessible and thus could not be restituted. The Allied laws left open the question as to how claims against the German Reich for damages and indemnification should be settled. But the Western powers obligated the Federal Republic to settle this question in the framework of the accords that formally concluded occupation in 1955.[29] Bonn fulfilled that obligation in 1957 with the Federal Restitution Law (*Bundesrückerstattungsgesetz*), accepting responsibility for the "monetary obligations connected with restitution law" of the former Reich.[30]

The Federal Republic paid out some DM 4 billion in the framework of this law.[31] If the robbery had occurred abroad, however, damages were not always compensated; rather, the law stipulated that only if the said property had at the time been relocated to the territory of the later Federal Republic could a claim be made for restitution. Otherwise its restitution fell under the law of other states on whose territory the assets had been stolen from the owner. So it was incumbent on the claimant to prove the path that had been taken by the stolen objects or assets. That was often successful in the cases of robbery by the Reich in Western Europe, and thanks to a speed-up in collective actions before the courts, it also was a quick procedure. By contrast, owing to a lack of concrete evidence, claims relating to expropriation and robbery in Eastern Europe frequently proved unsuccessful.[32]

A provisional stock-taking on the topic "restitution in West Germany" thus shows three clear points. First, this segment of *Wiedergutmachung* can evidently be attributed only in a limited way to German self-determination and its imperatives. Rather, it is abundantly clear that the Allied occupying powers, especially the Americans, significantly influenced future directions. Secondly, already at this juncture one can see the beginnings of a distinctive *asymmetry* between East and West in the field of reparations. That asymmetry will emerge in ever more pronounced contours in the following section. Third, by the 1980s, even very knowledgeable and critical individuals were quite convinced that "on the whole ... in the field of restitution, everything that was humanly possibly has been achieved."[33] Since then, however, it has become very clear that various lacunae remain: by concentrating on the private or state beneficiary of an asset transfer, the restitution laws in postwar Germany paid too little attention to the involvement and monetary gains of middlemen. More recently, such persons have come under scrutiny, and have become a veritable media sensation within a discourse of "profiting from Aryanization" and "stolen gold." Yet there must be a clear distinction made here vis-a-vis Aryanization in the sense of one bank swallowing another. That doubtless long ago was the object of some restitution suit. Today what is of interest is a more shadowy domain: commissions and the like in the mediation and facilitation of Aryanization deals. That is also true in the case of "stolen gold." The most recent disputes involve commercial gain from trafficking in such gold. The gold itself, in so far as it was looted from the central banks of occupied countries, was immediately confiscated by the victorious powers and restituted in a proper procedure. If the gold had been robbed from private persons, claims could be filed in accordance with the Federal Restitution Law (*Bundesrückerstattungsgesetz*).[34]

In the case of the second pillar of *Wiedergutmachung*, compensation (*Entschädigung*), the foundations were also laid in the American zone. A uniform compensation law valid for all the states contains the basic concept that the federal laws later incorporated and which has not changed much since. That is especially true in the case of the definition of what constitutes a victim of persecution on the basis of political views, race, religion, or worldview, as well as the typology of "circumstances of injury sustained" that entitled individuals to particular forms of compensation.[35] The law was based almost exclusively on German drafts where the representatives of those who had suffered persecution for political reasons had an influential say in determining the law's specifics. The specific concern of the military government was to include displaced persons (DPs) in the group of those entitled to benefits in so far as they met the time requirement: presence on 1 January 1947 in a DP camp. In the main, these were liberated Jews from Eastern Europe who did not wish to return there, as well as Jews who had left Eastern Europe in 1946 fearful of new violence against them; many had sought asylum in the American zone.[36] With this change incorporated, the military government implemented the law in August 1949, just in time to provide the West German state with a prejudgment to accompany its first fledgling steps.[37]

But the first German Bundestag took its time in unifying the law on compensation to apply to all of the territory of the Federal Republic. Negotiations remained bogged down for years over questions of the distribution of costs and competencies between the federal government and the states. A special law for a specific group of persecuted persons was passed more quickly: the Law on Regulation of Wiedergutmachung for National Socialist Injustice for Members of the Civil Service. It was enacted in May 1951 and was followed a bit later by a supplementary law for members of the civil service living abroad. In substance the same, this variant was tailored to the situation of the emigrants and thus deserves the special scrutiny of scholars in exile and remigration research.[38] It is useful to examine the law of May 1951 in greater detail since it affords several significant historical insights into the period. This law embodies a "kind of yoking together" of two laws.[39] That same day, Law 131 went into effect. It regulated the claims of civil servants who had been expelled from the East, former professional soldiers and civil servants dismissed as a consequence of de-Nazification. This was quite generous in its provisions, so that a substantial number of persons tainted by a brown past were reinstated in influential posts or were granted very attractive pensions. Later generations may view this as scandalous, but that is not the way the first German Bundestag saw the matter.[40] On the contrary: it passed this law by unanimous vote, balancing it over against the law on

Wiedergutmachung, likewise passed unanimously. The linkage between the two is typical of the predominant spirit and mood of the early 1950s: people wanted less of a strict separation between perpetrators and victims and more bridge-building, domestic tranquility, and integration on the path toward to much-desired normalcy.[41]

In this connection, another aspect is of some interest, a certain tilt in preference. The thrust of this linkage assured that special compensation for the civil service ended up being more generous than the normal compensation allotted for the rest of the population. In the totality of *Wiedergutmachung*, there are serious disharmonies and imbalances, such as the fact that the persecuted civil servant received far better reparations than a non–civil servant who had likewise been persecuted. This discrepancy, intensifying over the years as a result of several new additions to the law, later contributed to one of the greatest scandals in the history of West Germany, namely, the brouhaha that led to the removal of the president of the Bundestag, Eugene Gerstenmaier, in January 1969. Since back in 1938 he had been denied the so-called *venia legendi* as a university lecturer for political reasons, thus blocking his road to a chance for a professorship, Gerstenmaier had applied for appropriate compensation. He was granted this including back payments, amounting to a sum of six figures. That decision was quite in keeping with the letter of the law: for example, Hannah Arendt and Herbert Marcuse had also been compensated, both based on the argument that normally they would have completed a habilitation and later become professors.[42] The public outcry that the president of the Bundestag had been compensated "in hard cash" for the fact that Nazi Germany had not allowed him to "become a professor and enjoy the dignity of the lectern,"[43] should have been directed against the law, not at Gerstenmaier. But the irascible Gerstenmaier made it easy for his opponents, provoking his adversaries with ill-considered pronouncements. This was compounded by the accusation, which could not be proved, that he had attempted, for his own benefit, to influence the revision of a law. The entire affair provided more an external occasion for his downfall than a genuine cause, during times that were itching for a changing of the political guard in Bonn.[44]

But let us return to the early 1950s. While the unified Federal Law on Compensation (*Bundesentschädigungsgesetz*) was bogged down, a new factor entered the equation: the state of Israel. After exploratory, secret contacts, a declaration by Adenauer in September 1951 initiated official talks with Israel. This led to triangular negotiations, since a third party was added at the table, the Conference on Jewish Material Claims against Germany (Claims Conference). It was a new umbrella association of the most important international Jewish organizations and represented the Jews living outside Israel in the negotiations.[45]

The negotiations in Wassenaar near The Hague, leading in September 1952 to the Luxembourg Agreement, form an especially moving chapter in the history of *Wiedergutmachung*. Indeed, the agreement with Israel was long considered in public awareness to be the "very essence of what *Wiedergutmachung* was."[46] And historical research to date has indeed largely concentrated on this partial area. For that reason, the state of research shows a complex picture.[47] (The present paper can comment only briefly on the Luxembourg Agreement.)

"What is the price per piece for our murdered grandparents?" This is what angry demonstrators on the streets of Israeli towns and cities shouted, where large segments of society reacted with disgust and outrage to the negotiations. The agreement took as its yardstick the cost for integrating surviving refugees and obligated the Federal Republic to providing material goods valued at some DM 3 billion to the state of Israel, spread over twelve years, as well as a payment of DM 450 million to the Claims Conference.[48] The timing and modalities of the goods, and less the total volume, were extremely important for Israel, since the country was at the time in a very desperate economic crisis.[49]

It has long been known that Adenauer made the agreement with Israel his own pet initiative and personal cause. He managed to have it passed against opposition in his own cabinet, in the government coalition,[50] the press,[51] and public opinion as measured by the pollsters.[52] The opponents who argued by pointing to the excessive costs were often bowing to the threats of sanctions by the Arab countries, or used them as an excuse to back down. No one dared to voice any anti-Semitic resentment, but here and there one could sense that such sentiments were still very much a part of the picture. The arguments regarding cost have to be taken seriously to a certain extent, not so much in view of this single agreement but rather in the context of the *totality of demands* that buffeted the federal government in the course of 1952. Thus, the Western Allies insisted that West Germany, as a state on the front lines in the Cold War, include rearmament costs of some DM 13 billion in its budget. In addition, simultaneous with negotiations with Israel, other negotiations were underway in London. There the Bonn government obligated itself to take over German foreign debt from the pre- and postwar period, to pay interest of DM 14.5 billion and then to pay it off.[53] That same year, the Bundestag passed a costly Law on Equalization of Burdens (*Lastenausgleichsgesetz*) for the expellees from the East. If one considers this and other factors, and the fact that the federal budget was DM 23 billion and economic upswing was not yet assured at that time, then one has to agree with the assessment by Adenauer's biographer Hans-Peter Schwarz: in 1952, the Adenauer government was on a "slippery slope" and had issued a risky bill of exchange for the future that could "only be redeemed under the most favorable circumstances."[54]

Adenauer would not have been able to push through the Israel agreement without the help of the Social Democrats in the Bundestag, who took into account a great distance to their own electorate over this issue,[55] and without the emphatic reference in the ranks of his own party that "the United States had a great interest in this."[56] Linking up with this perception, a controversy has developed over whether the Luxembourg Accords owe their existence to American pressure or to German voluntary readiness.[57] But, as is so often the case with analysis, such a coarse dichotomy does not get to the heart of the matter.[58] The truth is mixed here and can be best summarized as follows: in respect to the Israel agreement, the federal government had relatively large latitude for action, and Adenauer decided for reasons of morality, foreign policy, and trade to make a very strong statement here. The GDR propaganda hammered away at the agreement, denouncing it as a "dirty deal," a "business deal between West German and Israeli large capitalists" at the expense of the working masses in West Germany. But this barrage of propaganda provided the Federal Republic with additional credit in the competition over who could present the image of the better Germany to the international community.[59]

Though virtually unnoticed by the public, the Luxembourg Agreement contained a very important protocol that, likewise in its financial consequences, went far beyond the Israeli agreement that was then in the limelight. In the Hague Protocol No. 1, the Bonn government agreed with the Claims Conference on important principles and numerous details for the expansion and elaboration of the Federal Compensation Law.[60] The fact that a foreign NGO had achieved an influence regulated by a treaty on internal German law-making was called an "almost revolutionary event."[61] Connected with this was a consultative status that the Claims Conference utilized vigorously as the Federal Compensation Law and its amendments were worked out. Its status was thus far more than an interest group, since de facto it was given a kind of right of immediate access to the Federal chancellor. It is probably no exaggeration to call the Hague Protocol No. 1 the Magna Carta of the history of compensation.[62] In any case, the regulations agreed upon there went far beyond what the Western Allies wanted the German legislators to take note of when they signed the Bonn Convention (*Überleitungsvertrag*) in May 1952.[63] Inter alia, they obliged lawmakers in Germany to preserve the regulations of the Law on Compensation in the American zone as a minimal standard for the federal level. In order to grasp the formative phase of federal legislation on compensation, one must keep in mind both the internal German disputes and the pressure and influences impinging from abroad from the three Western occupational powers, plus the array of associations under the umbrella of the Claims Conference.

In July 1953, the time had come: the Bundestag passed the first Federal Law on Compensation by a large majority.[64] But, hammered together in the final weeks of the first legislative period, it harbored many deficiencies and a lack of clarity on a range of points. All those involved in its drafting regarded it as provisional, and many had made their acceptance conditional on its revision. Work on a major amendment began the following summer; it took almost two years to complete owing to a veritable mountain of unusually complicated individual questions.[65]

However, implementation of the 1953 law ran into some snags. That is the impression from Bundestag debates in which the champions of *Wiedergutmachung*, a small bipartisan group cooperating beyond party divisions, repeatedly criticized compensation practice in the years 1954–55 very vehemently. They spoke about an "alarming overall impression" (Franz Böhm/CDU), a "really shocking picture of the actual state of affairs" (Adolf Arndt/SPD), a "shameful practice" (Hans Reif/FDP).[66] Criticism focused on pitiful examples of poor legal judgment, delays in the issuing of necessary ordinances by the Federal Finance Ministry, the mazeway in the distribution of burdens and competencies, and the unsatisfactory performance of the administration at the level of the individual states. The Bundestag deputies accused the states of more or less serious deficiencies in organization in building up the offices for handling compensation claims. They saw a narrow-minded petty spirit at work among compensation officials, especially in those four states that had decided, in contradistinction to the other states, to place the compensation offices under the authority of the minister of finance.[67] As the heckling cry of "131!" shows, there were also suspicions that former bureaucrats of the Nazi state sat ensconced at the desks in these compensation offices, acting as a brake on the work of *Wiedergutmachung*.[68]

These sharp exchanges in the Bundestag, which were heavily reported on by the media,[69] have two important aspects. First, they broke through and dissipated a "certain hush" that reigned in the 1950s.[70] The debate over reparations directed attention back to the "unprecedented collective and mass crimes" of the Third Reich. These were not shrouded in silence but castigated, as were the "devastation of political morality" by the act of "having been a witness to these crimes" and the "years of hurrah for a criminal regime."[71] Second, these debates provide historians with an interesting indication of compensation practice at the time. Yet they are too narrow a basis for arriving at more general conclusions regarding the personnel and practice of the bureaucracy and the courts.[72] There is need for penetrating studies that would also have to examine the role of former victims of persecution in the spheres of administration and justice.[73]

A number of shocking cases are attributable more to deficiencies in the law than to its faulty interpretation and implementation, as illustrated by the following. In the spring of 1953, in the Jewish Home for the Elderly on Kaulbachstraße in Munich, an old man received a letter from the Bavarian Office for Compensation. It read: "The applicant emigrated in 1938 to Brazil, since he is a Jew. There is no further evidence that the applicant was persecuted for reasons of race. Rather, he emigrated abroad to avoid persecution. He returned to Germany in 1950 at the age of 70. According to Sec. 1 of the Law on Compensation, a person persecuted for reasons of political beliefs, race, religion or worldview is entitled to compensation. Since there is no evidence of persecution in the sense of Sec. 1 in this case, the request for compensation has been denied."[74]

When a history of experience of *Wiedergutmachung* is written in the future and its impact on the claimants is described, it will be necessary to read such sources against the grain, so to speak. What were the feelings of this old man as he read such absurd reasoning? If one goes to the bottom of this clumsily worded letter of rejection, you encounter the text verbatim of the existing law. It presupposed that the persecuting state was proactively involved in persecution of the individual victim. Otherwise, the lawmakers reasoned, anyone could claim that he or she had felt persecuted or had chose to forego certain advantages, such as a job in the civil service, for reasons of political opposition. It was not completely wrong to link the concept of persecution to features of a concrete act of persecution that could be investigated and established as having occurred. But it is very disturbing to note that even the best minds behind the project of reparations did not notice in due time the almost total disconnect here between legal-administrative decisions and reality in the case of collective persecution.

In a new version, this time thoroughly revised and unanimously adopted, the Federal Law on Compensation (*Bundesentschädigungsgesetz*, BEG) was published in 1956, but it was rendered retroactive to 1953 in order to repair these and other failings and mistakes in the law.[75] The BEG is the core legislation of West German reparations. Of the DM 103.8 billion distributed from public funds to date for purposes of *Wiedergutmachung* till March 1999, some 77 percent are attributable to this, if the version of 1953 and a later 1965 amendment are included. Roughly two million requests have been recognized in the framework of the BEG, and 1.2 million have been rejected.[76] The number of applications is known, but curiously, perhaps, there are no accurate statistics on the number of applicants. Roughly speaking, one can say that there are two approved requests for every claimant, since as a rule there were different types of damage for which compensation was claimed, most often to health and professional career.[77] So a reasonable estimate is that approximately one million persons received or will receive benefits based on the BEG. About 80 percent of the compensation funds flow abroad, some 50 percent to Israel. This reflects the fact that in many cases, former German citizens who emigrated are the recipients. Otherwise they would not have survived.

The BEG of 1956 brought a new kind of movement into the practice of compensation. In many respects the machinery was speeded up and claims were now handled quickly. The number of applications also rose markedly, especially from abroad. Formerly, many foreigners had had such a skeptical view of the readiness or ability of the Federal Republic to provide individual compensation that they did not even make an application.[78] This now changed, especially since probably the largest legal aid arrangement in legal history, the United Restitution Organization (URO), specialized in assisting Jewish victims of persecution, scattered across the planet, to their legal rights. At the peak of its activity, the URO had a staff of 1,000 and handled some 500,000 claims for about 300,000 claimants. Among its achievements was to clamp down on and limit the activity of attorneys in Germany and abroad who were demanding excessive and even exorbitant fees for their services.[79]

Unlike the agreement with Israel, the BEG was not in the public limelight. Contemporary observers even had the impression that this sphere lay "on a political and journalistic margin."[80] This assessment is untenable as a general characterization of the facts, since there are certainly counter-examples, such as the considerable echo of the critical debates in the Bundestag in 1954–55. There is a need in research for methodologically solid work on the resonance in the media. But the available indications suggest that the implementation of the law, like its genesis, on the whole did not spark much public interest. And news about related scandals, such as cases of fraud, excessive fees, the dishonorable departure of two chairs of the Committee on Compensation in the Bundestag, had a disproportionate impact. What the public could learn in the media about compensation probably strengthened resentment rather than diminished it.[81]

"We have to state quite openly that in our society, *Wiedergutmachung* has no popular appeal. That is the disconcerting feeling everyone has who deals with this question out of personal inclination, a sense of duty or for professional reasons," Franz Böhm noted in 1955, speaking in the Bundestag.[82] The political parties preferred to keep the topic of "compensation" as much as possible off the agendas of public debate. Otherwise, the scheme for compensation agreed upon with the Claims Conference would have encountered more opposition and less impetus.[83] Moreover, this did not garner any additional votes, since most of the compensation money went abroad. Thus the parties, or more accurately a handful of decisive politicians in the Bundestag Committee on Compensation, forged a kind of Grand Coalition (between the Christian Democrats and Social Democrats), acting without much consideration for public opinion.

So was *Wiedergutmachung* the enterprise of an elite cartel operating *against* the majority of the people?; or, to formulate it more correctly and cautiously: *without* a popular majority? Because a politically significant movement counter to compensation did not form, even if it would appear that leading politicians like Fritz Schäffer occasionally tried to instigate such a movement by means of demagogic pronouncements.[84] The lack of popular appeal of *Wiedergutmachung* apparently never reached proportions that were relevant for electoral behavior. The candidacy of Franz Böhm for the Bundestag is a good test case, since at the time he headed negotiations for the agreement with Israel and was an early highly visible champion of the laws on compensation, more in the public eye on this matter than almost anyone else. In 1952, he is said to have lamented: "What can you do when an entire people digs in its heels?"[85] But in 1953 and again in 1957, when he ran in a Frankfurt district where his party was in great danger, he won both times. There is still need for detailed studies on the echo of *Wiedergutmachung* in the German population. Such studies should carefully differentiate between milieus, generations, and time frames.[86]

Compensation lay shrouded in relative quiet or hush when in 1964–65 the sound of battle penetrated the stillness for a short time: an amendment to the BEG long in preparation had reached a decisive phase. The West German state had, with breathtaking speed, risen to join the ranks of the leading industrial economies. Its economy was booming. And thus ever more voices were heard that wanted to expand the compensation program, recognized as having been constrained by earlier conditions of scarcity.[87] Along with other organizations of former victims, it was the Claims Conference in particular that pressed for a new major amendment.[88] As a matter of principle, the Conference and its president Nahum Goldmann cultivated a diplomatic style of negotiation, bolstered by close and lasting contacts to the parliament, the government, and the administration. In addition, more means were now mustered to mobilize public opinion, both in the Federal Republic, where the Conference dispatched a PR expert, and in the United States, where a protest rally in May 1965, supported by a number of senators, caused a stir that also had its subsequent secondary effect on the German media.[89]

Controversial because of the costs it entailed, the amendment was published in September 1965 as the Federal Compensation Final Law (*Bundesentschädigungs-Schlußgesetz*).[90] The term "Final Law" (*Schlußgesetz*) may have absorbed something of the mentality of closure on the postwar era pervasive at the time in segments of the public, and echoed in a government declaration by Ludwig Erhard proclaiming the "end of the postwar period."[91] But the stamp of "finality" here also had a very specific function: addressed to the Claims Conference, it stated that its right to exercise influence derived from the Luxembourg Agreement had now reached a definitive final stage. Nahum Goldmann also let it be publicly known that this final law fulfilled all remaining wishes. That triggered substantial criticism of Goldmann from among groups of former victims.[92] He even called for the creation of a Jewish cultural foundation. After the end of *Wiedergutmachung*, it would keep alive the memory "of this unique body of law."[93]

Among the desiderata that the Claims Conference had stressed was an expansion of the circle of individuals entitled to compensation. Those former victims of persecution who had emigrated from Eastern Europe after the previous deadline day of 1 October 1953 were also to receive compensation. As a rule, these were East European Jews. For this end, the so-called "Post-Fifty-Three" claimants, the Final Law created a special fund of DM 1.2 billion.

The Final Law implemented far more than one hundred changes, all improvements. One of the changes was so badly necessary it is worth recalling. It was called "readjustment" (*Angleichung*) and made it possible to reopen cases that had been legally closed in order to eliminate false judgments. Once again it was necessary to amend mistaken developments. One was rooted in traditional psychiatric doctrine that had veritably infused law on insurance and maintenance since the 1920s. It stated that physically healthy individuals could, psychologically, withstand almost any burden. For that reason, leading psychiatrists did not wish to recognize the possibility that persecution by the Nazis could have caused psychological injury to health in victims of such persecution. Their practice of expert opinions led to a long series of rejections of such applications. At the end of the 1950s, a vehement dispute erupted among psychiatrists, and in 1963–64 another school came to the fore. It was able to effect path-breaking changes in the practice of expert opinion in compensation suits.[94] The Final Law reacted rapidly to these new standards in science. It stipulated that there should be a new decision if the entitled claimant filed a request for review of an already rejected claim.

Another erroneous development points to an especially deplorable chapter in the history of reparations. It involves the Sinti and Roma and other groups subsumed at the time under the term Gypsy. These groups of victims were actually not at a disadvantage due to the law but rather as a result of widespread justice practices and administrative bias. The Supreme Court had decided in 1956 that Roma and Sinti had not been persecuted for racial reasons until 1943, when Himmler ordered the deportation of large numbers of Gypsies to Auschwitz. Prior to 1943, according to this judgment, Roma and Sinti had been subjected not to racial persecution but rather to special police laws, and such laws were not open to demands for compensation.[95] This judgment points up the fact that the history of reparations has also been a history of distinction: distinguishing between what West German society saw as National Socialist injustice, and what it continued to practice as time-honored and accepted tradition, however riddled with bias. The judgment shows the continued presence of a mental disposition in which specific phases and forms of the oppression of the Gypsies appeared to be quite "normal"—and not any mode or manifestation of persecution.[96]

That was not the only high court decision of the 1950s and early 1960s in which a disastrous foundation in the history of mentality continued to have its pervasive effect. Another such decision was a Supreme Court ruling in 1961 whose interpretation was that the simple man on the street was not even permitted to resist the Nazi regime.[97] In the early and mid-1960s, a corrective shift became evident in the question of the persecution of the Gypsies as well, since the Supreme Court arrived at a reevaluation in 1963 and abandoned its earlier practice of mistaken judgment. Here, as in connection with other corrections, the section on "readjustment" in the Final Law was applied as a basis for change. Gypsies whose claims for compensation for persecution suffered before 1943 had been denied now had a new lease on litigation: they could now seek redress and appeal for a review. To turn the argument on its head, that means of course that over two decades after the war, the claims for compensation filed by Gypsies had been unjustly denied.

Finally, another basic pillar of West German compensation legislation must be mentioned. Since its original form in the American Zone, it had been the basis for all versions of compensation law and had also been reconfirmed in the Final Law. This was the highly consequential principle termed in legal language the "subjective-personal principle of territoriality." It made the circle of prospective claimants dependent on certain spatial relations to the territory of the Federal Republic or the earlier German Reich, linking regulations on residence and qualifying dates in a very complex fashion. In the version valid from 1956, it subsumed victims of persecution who were living on 31 December 1952 in the Federal Republic or West Berlin[98] as well as emigrants who during the time of their persecution had lived in the territory of the Reich in the borders of 1937 (the so-called Altreich)—in so far as up until the end of 1952, they had taken up residence in Israel or in some country in the West.[99] Victims of Nazi persecution among the Germans expelled from East-Central Europe were also included even if they did not come to West Germany until after 1952. At the request of the Claims Conference, the victims of persecution (as a rule Jews) were also included who had left the Eastern European areas of expulsion independently from the expulsions of Germans to the West. According to the BEG, this was up to the final qualifying date of 1 October 1953; according to the Final Law of 1965, it also subsumed the "Post-Fifty-Three." Here the principle of territoriality led to the requirement that these Jews were required to prove they had earlier belonged to the "German linguistic and cultural circle"—that is, that they were in effect ethnic Germans.

De facto, proof was reduced to a test of their knowledge of German. But can one imagine more embarrassing scenes than the ones created by the law in this connection? If immigrants from Eastern Europe, often forced by circumstances of deprivation, wished to file a claim for compensation, they gathered in the rooms of the Israeli ministry of finance or in a West German legation or consulate and endeavored to prove that they were proficient in the language of their persecutors.[100]

So even if the program of compensation was not conceived in terms of the laws of citizenship, it was basically aimed at the *German* victims of persecution, not foreign victims. A special regulation expanded the circle of entitlement to include stateless persons and refugees in the sense of the Geneva Convention. As a rule, these were Eastern Europeans who no longer were able or did not wish to return to their homeland, now under communist rule. On pressure from the Western powers, the gates to compensation were now opened for them too, but with a heavily reduced scope of claim. This was especially the case when they were not classified as victims of persecution for racial, political, or religious reasons but rather as "persons who suffered injury due to their nationality." The legal term "persons who suffered injury due to their nationality" was not clear in juridical terms and is historically questionable. Why? Because a special reason for persecution classified as "nationality" can hardly be separated and distinguished in a manner clearly demarcated from the racial and political contexts of National Socialist occupation in Eastern Europe.[101]

Global Agreements

But what was to be done with the foreign victims of National Socialist persecution, who were far more numerous? They were told to look to reparations that had to be worked out in terms of international law. This was certainly in keeping with the dominant doctrine in international law. The concept of reparations in the Versailles Treaty had expressly included civil injury to persons; injury to life and limb, health and freedom, deportation and forced labor—all that was enumerated there. The Potsdam Agreement related the concept generally to "losses and suffering." The Paris Reparations Agreement of January 1946 likewise did not distinguish between injury due to war and injury due to persecution. Rather, it bundled together all kinds of injury (with the exception of claims to social welfare insurance) in the concept of reparations.[102]

Basically it could also have been quite unimportant whether compensation for foreign victims of Nazi persecution was handled under the umbrella of *Wiedergutmachung* or reparations. But the London

Agreement on External German Debts (1953) created a very consequential difference. Article Five of the Agreement contained section 2, which for a long time was known only among experts.[103] In the meantime, it has become world famous, since it has been in the media limelight now for several years. It reads: "Consideration of claims arising out of the Second World War by countries which were at war with or were occupied by Germany during that war, and by nationals of such countries, against the Reich and agencies of the Reich, including costs of German occupation, credits acquired during occupation on clearing accounts and claims against the Reichskreditkassen shall be deferred until the final settlement of the problem of reparation." No statement is made about when a final regulation should occur, but the common understanding, and especially the view in Bonn, was that "final settlement" meant the signing of a peace treaty.[104] This stipulation agreed on at the London conference was controversial. The Dutch delegation in particular was vehemently and vociferously opposed, regarding it as unacceptable practice that individual claims to compensation by citizens of the Netherlands were blocked by this legislation. But in the end a powerful statement from the American delegation prevailed and the matter was closed.[105] Washington at the time did not wish to have the weak shoulders of the Federal Republic overburdened, and particularly did not want to see debt management endangered.

Thus, the claims of the foreign victims of Nazi persecution were in principle postponed until the signing of a peace treaty, and such a treaty retreated into the ever more distant future or, as people soon could imagine, would never come to pass. But influential associations of persecution victims in the Western neighbors of the Federal Republic were in no way prepared to countenance such an arrangement. With great public response, and in some cases with excellent contacts to the government, they represented the interests of citizens who had been confined in German concentration camps as resistance fighters or had been exploited as civilian forced laborers. For that reason, several Western European governments pressed for including the claims of the "victims from the West" (*Westverfolgte*), as they were called, under federal legislation on compensation. When it became clear with the passing of the BEG in 1956 that this had been unsuccessful, eight Western European countries submitted a joint démarche to the federal government in Bonn demanding compensation negotiations between Germany and individual countries.[106] In this they certainly departed from the basic line of the London Agreement on External German Debts, which they had accepted with open eyes, even including the exclusionary clause under Article 5, Sec. 2. But at that time they had followed the dictates of reason in foreign policy. Now domestic political pressure was the dominant factor shaping their position.

Subsequently there was a long tug-of-war in the question of whether and to what extent National Socialist acts of persecution came under the reparations clauses of the London Agreement on External German Debts. The Federal Republic believed it was in a dilemma. On the one hand, it wished to protect its legal position according to which the London Agreement relieved it of any obligation for reparations in international law until the signing of a peace treaty. On the other, it had a strong interest in eliminating any sources of friction in the process of Western integration, because that integration was the very elixir of life of the Federal Republic. The way out of the dilemma lay in proposing *voluntary* payments. On this basis, the Federal Republic concluded global agreements with eleven countries in Western, Northern and Southern Europe between 1959 and 1964, setting aside a total of DM 876 million earmarked for this purpose.[107]

Given scant attention by historical research to date, these eleven agreements made a major contribution to integrating the Federal Republic in the West.[108] Anticipating the peace treaty, that receded ever further into the distant and uncertain future, these agreements eliminated potential sources of friction by intermediate arrangements, and not only in regard to the controversial question of compensation. In a kind of piggy-back process, bilaterally, these agreements also eliminated a number of further impediments from the lingering legacy of the war. The conclusion of most of the negotiations, which initially were quite doggedly fought, came in the dramatic period of the second Berlin crisis. Now, as Bonn saw it, the most important thing was to "demonstrate to the East the unity of the West."[109] This was the same time frame in which the anti-Semitic incidents in West Germany (1959–60), and most especially the Eichmann trial in Jerusalem, made the topic of "mastering the past" a political issue of the first degree. The East German Socialist Unity Party (SED) in turn sought, organizing a veritable barrage of campaigns, to exploit this in a bid to discredit the Federal Republic, stylizing it as the Eldorado of Nazi criminals—and to enhance and refurbish if possible the image of the GDR as an "anti-fascist state."[110] These global agreements, in response to which the GDR had nothing it could place as a counterweight in the scales,[111] also served to a certain extent as a protective shield against "campaigns by the Eastern bloc to soften up the West."[112] The eleven agreements were recognized as gestures of good will.[113] Yet they remained within relatively modest proportions, so that several agreement partners expressly reserved the right, in a general review in accordance with Article 5, Sec. 2 of the London Agreement on German External Debts—that is, subsequent to conclusion of a peace treaty with Germany—to make further claims.

As the eleven agreements show, the Federal Republic could not and did not wish to leave the question of the "Western victims of persecution" unresolved in the context and deepening process of Western integration. But the situation was different when it came to the "Eastern victims of persecution." The East-West conflict and the division of Germany had also impacted on the entire structure of *Wiedergutmachung*. That will be touched on below in connection with the German-German settlement and in respect to the revival of questions of restitution and compensation as soon as the conflict was ended and Germany reunited. Here it is useful to note that the Cold War was given direct entry into West German law on compensation in the form of the so-called "diplomatic clause."[114] This clause excluded the possibility of compensation funds being channeled to countries with which the FRG had no diplomatic relations. Since Israel and Finland were excluded from this exception by means of a stipulation of de facto "as-if" relations, the exclusion in effect involved only those victims of persecution living in the countries of the Eastern bloc. Here the general tendency in the Cold War to seal oneself off from the other side almost hermetically played a key role. In individual cases, the logic of the Hallstein doctrine was a compounding actor of isolation, as in the case of Yugoslavia.[115] While residence in the Eastern bloc led to exclusion of possible claims, Bonn paid out, staggered over time, compensation on the order of DM 30 billion for the victims of persecution, mainly Jews, who emigrated from the East to the West.[116]

Among the few breakthroughs made by West German compensation law in the wall of the Iron Curtain were benefits for victims of pseudo-medical concentration camp experiments. In June 1960, the government in Bonn decided to pay such benefits regardless of the "diplomatic clause" and its blanket of restrictions. In this it was not motivated by its own wishes but rather was responding to pressure from across the Atlantic. A visit to the United States in the spring of 1960 by thirty-five Polish women, organized by the New York-based weekly *Saturday Review*, who had been victims of such experiments in the camp at Ravensbrück, caused a minor sensation in the American public, especially since the women also paid a visit to the Senate and were received in the White

House. Their exclusion from West German benefits met with such surprise and critique that the government in Bonn was advised over multiple channels to take care of this question and remove it from the stage of American public opinion. The Bundestag pressed ahead in May 1960 and passed a draft introduced as a bill by the SPD for the benefit of Polish victims of human experiments. In June 1960, the Cabinet in Bonn decided to introduce a new regulation for all of Eastern Europe, not just Poland.[117] Bonn initially utilized the assistance of the International Red Cross to handle the payments. In order to simplify the procedure, the Federal Republic later concluded relevant global agreements for a total of some DM 123 million with Yugoslavia (1961 und 1963), Czechoslovakia (1969), Hungary (1971), and Poland (1972).

Since Bonn and Moscow had had diplomatic relations since 1955, the exclusionary clause was not valid for the Soviet Union. But for its part, the Kremlin was not interested in negotiations over compensation with the Federal Republic. In order to help stabilize the GDR, which had been shaken by the popular uprising in June 1953, the Soviet Union decided in the fall of 1953 to forego any further reparations, without distinguishing between war damage in the more narrow sense and National Socialist persecution.[118] To compound matters back home, the millions of Soviet citizens who had been deported to Germany for forced labor found themselves after their return to the Soviet Union lumped together as suspected Nazi collaborators, and treated as such. The returning Soviet POWs suffered a similar fate. Many were imprisoned in Stalin's Gulag of camps and jails, and the others lived as second-class Soviet citizens, always fearful that their time in Germany would be regarded as an interlude of treason. The discrimination against the repatriated Soviet citizens remained part of Soviet life up until the era of Gorbachev. There was certainly no thought of demanding compensation for them! Then the first step would have had to be rehabilitation in their own country. Only the end of the East-West conflict has opened up new prospects for compensation for these double victims of dictatorship.[119]

Poland, along with western areas of the Soviet Union the country that had suffered the most in the Nazi war of expansion and destruction, chose in 1953 to forego any further German reparations. During the 1960s, however, it developed a legal conception that the individual claims for compensation by Poles who had suffered persecution at the hands of the Nazis, especially the concentration camp inmates and forced laborers, did not come under the concept of reparations. Apparently Poland held only the Federal Republic legally responsible for such claims, and not the GDR.[120] In the course of negotiations over the Warsaw Treaty as part of the new turn in Ostpolitik, this question was initially kept off the agenda. From the Polish perspective, other issues, especially the border question, were far more pressing, and the Brandt/ Scheel government did not wish any additional problems to burden the Eastern treaties, which were in any case hotly contested in domestic political discussion. But after conclusion of the negotiations in December 1970, the Poles raised the topic of compensation in an exploratory question, and also in official form after the 1972 ratification of the treaty.[121] The Bonn coalition stuck to the German position on the law, and Chancellor Willy Brandt drew an additional line of defense in internal talks with the head of the Polish CP, Wladyslaw Gomulka: it should be remembered, he noted, that Poland had received a third of former German state territory, and the German expellees had left behind assets and property of incalculable value.[122] This calculating way of approaching the question, a kind of weighing of the scales of acquisition and loss, still widespread today in popular (nonofficial) opinion, had a shaping impact at that time on public opinion. In terms of aggregate resulting facts, the argument was correct but ill conceived when it came to the individual victims of Nazi persecution and their compensation. After all, no material benefit had accrued to these persons as a result of the westward shift in Poland's national borders.

In contrast with other Western European countries, when it came to Poland, the Federal Republic did not voluntarily conclude any global agreement with Warsaw, aside from the special arrangement of assistance for the victims of pseudo-medical experiments.[123] But here it soon turned out that the Polish authorities were not passing the bulk of funds on to the victims. This hardly casts a favorable light on the perceived importance of individual compensation in communist Poland.[124] How minimal that was is revealed in a proposal made by the party chief Gomulka as early as 1970. He stated that he was contemplating "declaring the problem of compensation resolved" if Bonn was willing to grant Poland a substantial loan with attractive conditions.[125] At the height of détente, in connection with the Helsinki Conference 1975, Poland was indeed granted such a loan, as was given earlier to Yugoslavia. This can be viewed as a kind of indirect compensation, in some respects the Eastern European equivalent of the Western European global agreements. Here, though, the salient difference was that is was left entirely up to the government in Eastern Europe to decide whether the victims were given any individual benefits.[126] At the same time, a lump-sum agreement was reached on retirement pension claims by Polish forced laborers who had paid in social security to the German authorities during the war.[127] In this connection, it is useful to recall an especially sad chapter in Polish postwar history. In 1980, Bonn agreed with the Claims Conference on a small hardship fund for Jewish victims of Nazism who had since the mid-1960s been emigrating to the West and settling there. This also took into account the Jewish community in Poland. In 1968, under the pressure of the expulsion campaign, almost all remaining Jews had emigrated from Poland. The exodus in practical terms marked the end of Jewish history in Poland.[128]

Initiatives in the 1980s

In the early 1980s, experts generally believed that *Wiedergutmachung* was a closed chapter. For example, this was also the view of Walter Schwarz, one of the most knowledgeable experts on the matter. Schwarz had a quite extraordinary biography. He was born in Berlin in 1906, the son of Jewish-Polish immigrants. He studied law and shortly before the November 1938 pogrom, emigrated to Palestine. There under the British mandate he repeated his law exams. Schwarz then joined the RAF, serving four years in Africa. He was invited by the Jewish Agency to Munich and wrote a dissertation on restrictions on restitution and compensation, earning a doctorate from Heidelberg University.[129] Beginning in 1952, he built up an exemplary law practice in West Berlin specializing in *Wiedergutmachung*, of whose ramifications only few attorneys had a clear picture at the time. Among his clients were prominent personalities such as Max Reinhardt, Samuel Fischer, and Ernst Bloch.[130]

More and more Schwarz was regarded as a leading light, not merely a lawyer. He was the author of numerous memoranda, indefatigable in his efforts to spur new ideas in the development of law and jurisprudence, especially in dealing with reparations law. The law schools at the universities did not pay much attention to this neglected domain, so he decided to found and develop a special journal, *RzW*, and maintain it at a high level of excellence.[131] The periodical became to a certain extent the principal platform for discussion on *Wiedergutmachung*, an important forum of debate, critique, and documentation. In a number of cases, *RzW* also was the space where discussion was first initiated that led to an emendation of rulings by the higher and the highest courts, such as the past classification of Sinti and Roma as non-victims.[132] In addition, Walter Schwarz was the initiator and coeditor of the major semiofficial series on *Wiedergutmachung*, whose first volume, published in 1974, he authored.[133]

In 1981, the periodical stopped publication—due to a lack of new material. Schwarz sent his own personal copies to Tel Aviv University, which had forwarded him a special request, and wrote a newspaper article entitled "the construction workers leave the finished building."[134] In actual fact, the edifice of *Wiedergutmachung* had in the meantime become quite stable and solid, in many respects even impressive. Subsequent to the Final Law, though no further supplement had been worked out,[135] a number of improvements had been introduced, especially with the help of social insurance[136] and in the realm of better and more balanced basic rulings. Special funds had also made their appearance on the scene, such as the Fund for Compensation of Hardship in Individual Cases. In the main, this fund assisted Republican veterans of the Spanish Civil War, along with Sinti and Roma. In 1984, Schwarz commented that if he were to sum up his life's work, it could be encapsulated in the sentence: "Germans have a right to be *proud* of the whole program of *Wiedergutmachung*."[137]

But as the construction workers were leaving the building, a whole new and more cantankerous crew arrived at the site. They thought what had been accomplished was scandalous in the way it had gone wrong.[138] Schwarz faced a barrage of protest when he spoke again in April 1986 in the Berlin Parliament, invited as an expert consultant in consultations on an initiative of the Alternative Liste, and used the word "pride."[139] For his part, the grand old man admired, however ironically, the "nerve" of young Germans who had never themselves "experienced persecution or *Wiedergutmachung*." They were ignorant of the "ABCs of jurisprudence" but determined, all the more self-righteously, to pass judgment. In his view, the mounting criticism was guided more by the heart than by the head, fixated too much on "marginal problems and groups" instead of "what is really essential."[140] Here one may note that the generational change bound up with the shift in values since the mid-1960s also influenced *Wiedergutmachung*.[141] Schwarz had certainly retained a critical view of *Wiedergutmachung*. But as a pessimist who had learned from experience, he lowered the bar of expectation a bit, and as an attorney he paid more attention to the separation between the domains of law and morality and their distinctive characters. As a member of an older generation, he in part adhered to other criteria, especially when it came to marginal groups. And under the powerful impression of an unparalleled genocide, he himself a Jewish victim, he stuck to the dictum:

"All these vociferous little groups make up only a small proportion of the victims. The overwhelming majority are Jews."[142]

The critics stemmed primarily from the sphere of the Greens. They had two principal criticisms. First, they regarded the way in which compensation was undertaken as a scandalous episode. Expressions such as a "running battle against the victims," the "dark side of *Wiedergutmachung*," or even the "second round of persecution" became popular. As a matter of fact, as mentioned above, there are shocking examples, especially in the practice of medical expert opinions in the 1950s. But we lack a solid base of studies on implementation, so that there is still little clarity regarding the degree to which findings can be generalized on personnel selection, interpretation, implementation, and the impact of the legislation.[143]

On the other hand, the critics soon discovered the "forgotten victims," who had not originally been included in the concept of persecution of compensation law. This encompassed persons forcibly sterilized on the basis of the 1933 Hereditary Health Law, homosexuals, and the "asocials" or "professional criminals" interned in concentration camps, as well as deserters or "white rats" convicted of "undermining the morale of the Wehrmacht."[144] These groups actually had not been "forgotten" but rather had intentionally been bracketed out and excluded from the scope of the compensation scheme, a circle of entitlement reserved for victims of political, racial, or religious persecution. In large part, it had been representatives of the victims of political persecution who in the earlier years had insisted that no further categories be included under compensation legislation other than the familiar triad typology.[145] Different types of injustice, they argued, should be handled elsewhere, finding with this argument a sympathetic audience among all those who were for fiscal reasons seeking to hold down the costs for compensation. The fact that the "political" prisoners were more intent to exclude categories of prisoners such as "asocial elements" and "criminals" was due in part to their negative experiences with these groups in the prisoner society of the Nazi camps. In addition, the "political" victims believed they had yet to struggle for recognition themselves at a time when many Germans still had to learn a simple fact: that the resistance against National Socialism was not treason but rather, as the preamble to the Federal Law on Compensation stressed, a "contribution" deserving of merit.

Once again, the history of *Wiedergutmachung* turns out to be a history of distinction—here in the sense of the necessity to single out typical National Socialist injustice and to distinguish this from other types of injustice. In these groups mentioned, legislators rejected the alternative of yes or no, constructing a kind of compromise: accordingly, these groups were not the "victims of typical National Socialist law" in the sense of the Law on Compensation, because even in states based on the rule of constitutional law, there might have been penalties or sanctions for their "deviant" behavior. As in the case of forced sterilization, for example, which had also been practiced in Sweden and in a quite substantial number of states in the U.S.[146] On the other hand, the legislators recognized that the brutalizing intensification involved here, namely terror, was doubtless a form of gross injustice. For that reason, they included other groups in the collective category of "other forms of injustice by the state," for which the General Law on the Consequences of War (1957) constituted a kind of inclusive net. In the framework of this law, it was possible to file for compensation for hardship. But the hurdles were high and the valid time periods for application quite narrow, so that this legislation had little practical import for these groups.

There was much general consensus down into the early 1980s on the separation of "National Socialist injustice" and "other forms of injustice by the state." But then criticism waxed vehement and for the first time was also listened to. Indeed, this was an artificial distinction, because it separated out what belonged together in the ideological outlook of the Nazi regime—the health of the folk (the so-called *Volkskörper*) buttressed by an ideology of political and social biologism and advanced by means of war.[147] As in connection with the Sinti and Roma, for the "forgotten victims" as well: the history of *Wiedergutmachung* mirrors the "process of the changing perception of National Socialism and its crimes,"[148] as well as the very differential ability of various groups to effectively articulate and implement their own interests.

Thus, the heated controversy over the politics of historiography in the 1980s that peaked in the "Historians' Debate,"[149] was interwoven in part with discussion on an amplified concept of persecution. The speech by President Richard von Weizsäcker on 8 May 1985 should also be seen in this context, since he included some of the "forgotten victims" (though not all) in his words of memorialization. From the time the German Greens entered the Bundestag in 1983, one central focus in their initiatives in parliament had been to debate and draft possible changes to expand legislation on compensation.[150] The Bundestag successfully pressed the government to undertake a thoroughgoing review of the entire question and arranged public hearings, especially regarding the situation of the groups of victims previously on the margins of public awareness.[151]

The material result was a new fund for hardship cases established at the end of the 1980s in the framework of the Law on the Consequences of the War. But this also meant that these groups were not included in the scope of persecution as defined in the Law on Compensation.

If one looks at the final decade of the old Federal Republic up until the end point of reunification, when there was new interest in correcting the mistaken judgments handed down by National Socialist criminal courts,[152] what is striking is the discovery of the entire topic and complex of "forced labor." Up to the early 1980s, this had not been an important topic either in the public sphere, the media, or historical scholarship. All that changed within a few short years both in the media[153] and in an even more pronounced way in scholarship and in the schools.[154] This was in part due to the boom at the time in studies in the history of everyday life, *Alltagsgeschichte.* If one looked at everyday life under National Socialism, there was hardly a municipality or a firm, hardly even a small farmer, who did not have foreign workers. In the summer of 1944, there were 7.2 million in Germany. These were extremely heterogeneous groups of individuals with very different working and living conditions, ranging from employment as a kind of hired hand on the farm all the way to the terror of the program of "annihilation by work" (*Vernichtung durch Arbeit*). But those who had come to Germany more or less voluntarily were few and far between. Most were prisoners, living under compulsion. The local framework for this topic opened up a broad discussion in the public sphere, and in the history classroom as well. In the school competition for the President's Prize, whose topic in 1982–83 was "everyday life under National Socialism," 110 of the prize-winning essays dealt with POWs and foreign workers. At that time, the flood of historical interest was rarely linked with the question of compensation. But when this linkage became a major political topic at the end of the 1990s, many in the public were now prepared to listen. The groundwork had been laid: ten or fifteen years before they had dealt with that same complex in history classes in high schools across West Germany.

Germany's East: The Other Road Taken

The above sketch was centered on the West German history of *Wiedergutmachung.* But the East German history of reparations also belongs to the chronicle of a united Germany. Five characteristic differences spring to mind.[155]

One initial difference was anchored in the bifurcation in language, two worlds of discourse. In the GDR, *Wiedergutmachung* was the term used almost exclusively to designate reparations to the Soviet Union, especially in the form of the dismantling of factories, the channeling a portion of production to the Soviets, and the payment of costs for occupation. Up until the abandonment of further reparations, decided on in 1953, this constituted a very heavy burden indeed. In an estimate of total costs for dismantling, production allotments, and occupation payments for all four occupation zones, the Soviet zone accounted for some two thirds, while the other three zones together bore about a third of this burden.[156] That is why there is a popular and widespread view in the "new" federal states (former GDR) that the German Democratic Republic in effect paid off the costs of *Wiedergutmachung* on its own. Other burdens, such as the extraction of intellectual property, the loss of German property and assets abroad, and the labor of German POWs, cannot be clearly ascribed to the accounts of either Germany's East or West. But these categories in their entirety still do not encompass the concrete scope of the West German concept of *Wiedergutmachung*. It specifically includes restitution, compensation, and global agreements—all benefits that the GDR largely refused to provide. For that reason, one can read in the Western literature that for all practical purposes, the GDR really did not pay any *Wiedergutmachung*. The comparison points up a first difference here, where the divided language mirrors differing interests. The interest of the FRG was always to separate and distinguish between *Wiedergutmachung* and reparations. In contrast, the GDR was intent on fusing these two concepts in order to charge the huge amount of payments to the Soviet Union to the account of *Wiedergutmachung*, which in other respects was quite small.

A second difference was that the GDR restricted individual compensation for victims of National Socialist persecution strictly to bona fide citizens of the GDR. By contrast, some 80 percent of the compensation paid by West Germany flowed abroad, because most of those persecuted owed their survival to having emigrated. The restrictive practice of the GDR hit the persecuted Jews particularly hard, since only a small number had returned to settle in the Soviet zone. Most re-emigrated elsewhere when, at the beginning of the 1950s, a new wave of anti-Semitism surged across parts of Eastern Europe and penetrated into the GDR. Thus, only between one and two thousand Jews remained in East Germany, and over the course of the years, the community shrank, contracting into a tiny aggregate of several hundred members. Strict restriction of compensation to GDR citizens meant the de facto exclusion of the overwhelming proportion of the Jewish victims.

Third, the question of the composition of the circle of "recognized victims" in West Germany and East Germany led to a picture with powerful lines of contrast. West Germany attributed greatest importance to the persecution of the Jews; East Germany prioritized the persecuted communists. How did the FRG deal with this latter group? Since 1953, the Federal law on Compensation contained a political paragraph stipulating that individuals who "are opposed to the basic democratic and free system" forfeit their right to compensation. This was aimed primarily at the KPD (Communist Party) and the West Berlin branch of the Socialist Unity Party, the SED.[157] At the height of heated confrontation in the 1950s, the West German authorities and courts tended to interpret this clause very restrictively, so that apparently only very few from the communist resistance were awarded compensation.[158] In a 1961 ruling, the Federal Supreme Court (*Bundesverfassungsgericht*) declared the exclusion clause admissible, but it put a halt to restrictive practices and stipulated that an individual's behavior after the outlawing of the KPD in 1956 was important for the decision, not his or her behavior prior to this. In addition, the Final BEG Law of 1965 opened up access to hardship funds for such applicants. It is still impossible to say in a more general way how this easing affected compensation in practice, but it is evident that the communists in the West were in a precarious marginal position. By contrast, in the East they occupied positions high up the ladders of hierarchy, including the leadership echelon.

In the East, most of the "recognized victims" of Nazi persecution were cadres from the workers' movement who were now members of the SED. This was the product of having excluded the emigrated Jews, and, beginning in the 1950s, a veritable wave of revocations of the legal status of a victim. In this connection, political and ideological selection criteria also played a role, leading to a revival of persecution. That was especially manifest in the case of the Jehovah's Witnesses, who were earlier persecuted by the Nazis for religious reasons and were now outlawed once again by the GDR.[159] In the mid-1960s, a formal hierarchy was introduced that distinguished between the heroic "fighters against fascism" and the merely passive "victims of fascism." The "fighters," largely identical with earlier persecuted communists, received larger honorary pensions then the mere "victims."

The concept of persecution, defined and personified in this way, was closely bound up with the legitimacy and legitimation of the power monopoly of the SED. It constructed and presented its dictatorship as the fulfillment of the legacy of the German resistance, and the historical cult surrounding the "fighters against fascism" was designed to certify that resistance basically had been a communist affair, organized and developed by them. The transformation of a group of victims into a veritable icon of state propaganda had a high price affixed when viewed from the perspective of personal biography. Why? Because the politically stylized ritual was often far removed from personal reminiscences. It occupied one's own vital experience, colonized personal memory, filtering out the coarser grit and all that was contradictory to the dominant interpretation.[160] When it became clear that the VVN (Vereinigung der Verfolgten des Nazi-Regimes, Association of the Persecuted Victims of the Nazi Regime) was beginning to preserve a certain modicum of independence and was particularly against the integration of "patriotic Nazis" in the concept of the National Front, it was dissolved in 1953 and then replaced by an amenable and docile committee.[161]

The fourth point of comparison, again a strong node of contrast, involves restitution of property expropriated from the victims, especially the Jews. In Germany's West, a great deal was accomplished in this sphere—under Western Allied influence and congruent with the right of private property. In the East, a portion of Jewish communal property was restituted: several synagogues, communal buildings, and cemeteries. But the GDR adamantly refused, again and again, to consider restitution of Jewish private property or to pay indemnification for its loss. The reason for this lay initially in the priority assigned to Soviet demands for reparations. Then the temptation took hold to adjust and pave the path for socialist publicly owned property by special utilization of "Aryanized" Jewish property. The SED politburo came to an agreement that it should instrumentalize "Aryanization" as a doorway into nationalization in so far as "big capital" was concerned. But there was certainly controversy over the necessary extent of the refusal to return assets or indemnify them as a means to press ahead with the "construction of socialism." Paul Merker, who in his exile in Mexico had already championed reparations for the Jews, pleaded for a flexible concept which included the return of real estate and small-size factories. But like almost all emigrants to the West, in the early 1950s he was also swept up by the swirl of hysteria against Western "agents," and his engagement for the rights of the Jewish victims also contributed to his fate. When he was arrested in 1952, it was stated that Merker was an "agent of the U.S. finance oligarchy, who only demanded compensation for Jewish expropriated assets in order to facilitate the penetration of Germany by U.S. finance capital."[162]

Measured in terms of laws on private property, the way the SED chose to deal with "Aryanized" property was a glaring injustice. But even the "construction of socialism" did not exclude a less rigid approach to restitution and compensation, one that managed well without spiteful tirades, as the line pursued by Paul Merker shows.[163] Viewed in this way, there were thus two strata of the dead hand of the past lying one above the other in East Germany, until their removal in the wake of German unification. The Law on the Settlement of Open Questions on Property, a component of the Unification Treaty of September 1990, assured restitution to two groups: those who had been expropriated by the SED state since 1949 *and* those who had already lost their property as a result of persecution in the period 1933–45.[164] The government of de Maizière only agreed to this recourse to an earlier period with considerable misgivings. But the West German side regarded this step as extremely important, and there is talk that a letter (still in a closed archive) sent from President George Bush to Chancellor Helmut Kohl may have played a significant role in convincing Bonn to press for this.[165]

After a half century in a virtual state of suspension, tens of thousands of restitution proceedings are underway (or have been concluded) on the territory of the former GDR—though no longer involving the actual victims of Nazi injustice now but rather their heirs.[166] One such case can serve as an illustration, the family of the industrialist firm Simson Werke. Their firm, located in Suhl, produced cars in the 1920s, along with rifles for the Prussian police. In 1935, the family was robbed and chased off, so that Gauleiter Sauckel was able to transform the company into the Wilhelm-Gustloff-Werke. After 1945, the plant was incorporated into the state-owned Ernst Thälmann Combine, which manufactured millions of motorcycles under the stolen brand name of Simson. In 1993, sixty years after the beginning of this extended German saga of a factory's fate, the property in Suhl was restituted to the Simson heirs.[167]

Finally, the fifth point of comparison is likewise marked by striking contrast. It concerns the relations with Israel and the Claims Conference, which will be examined here only with respect to compensation. In West German history, these relations were marked by rapprochement; in East German history, they were marked largely by refusal. When in 1952 Israel and the Claims Conference concluded the Luxembourg Agreement with the Federal Republic, they also turned to the GDR, stating that it too bore responsibility for the Jewish victims of Nazism living in Israel or scattered around the world. But integrated into the anti-Israel and pro-Arab politics of the Soviet bloc, the GDR rejected this responsibility. While the FRG promoted "positive results in the foreign policy sphere with the aid of *Wiedergutmachung*," the GDR went in precisely the opposite direction, "conquering terrain in foreign policy by means of refraining from *Wiedergutmachung*," namely by currying favor among Arab countries in the Middle East.[168] Over the course of time, the shrill tone was modulated and disappeared, but right up until the end the SED maintained that the GDR was a new creation in international law, in its genesis imbued with the spirit of a higher plane of history. For that reason, the reasoning went, it bore no responsibility for the crimes of Hitlerian fascism. With this comfortable image of history in hand, the SED dictatorship managed to present its own existence as "the real *Wiedergutmachung*."[169]

In the meantime, things started moving again in the mid-1970s as the GDR began to gain ever greater international recognition and decided to embellish its ever more popular name and image a bit by means of a symbolic gesture. But the directors at the politburo only managed to stage one single and embarrassing act. Empowered by the politburo, the Committee of the Anti-Fascist Resistance Fighters of the GDR invited a representative of the Claims Conference to Berlin. In November 1976, a festive declaration was read to him. It stated that in the spirit of humanity, it had been decided to grant the Claims Conference a one-time payment of one million dollars. Instead of showing the expected pleasure and gratitude for this largesse, the representative excused himself and phoned New York. After a short discussion with the central office, he returned to decline the contribution. That did not dissuade the SED from publishing news of the contribution in the official paper *Neues Deutschland* and transferring the money to New York, from where it was returned immediately to Berlin. Alien worlds were here in diplomatic collision. The Claims Conference was used to a diplomatic style of negotiations and did not value such one-sided acts. Though the sum of one million dollars was quite substantial for an economy in notorious short supply of foreign currency, this was not enough in Manhattan even to buy a single house.[170] A further attempt followed in the 1980s, when the GDR, keen to achieve recognition under the most-favored-nation clause in trade with the United States, packed the question of compensation into a wider package for negotiation. This attempt proved abortive. Later, already in the maelstrom of its demise, the SED approached Israel and international Jewish organizations with offers motivated by a search for lifesavers to rescue GDR sovereignty from total immersion.[171]

In the end, the FRG took on the unpaid mortgage of the GDR vis-à-vis the Claims Conference in the process of unification and its consequences. In September 1990, an agreement by the two Germanys on implementing the Unification Treaty specifically stipulated such an obligation. As in the Luxembourg Agreement in 1952, here too there was an admixture of morality and rationality in foreign policy. A week prior to the agreement, a representative of the American embassy had held talks in the Chancellor's office. He let it be known that there was "considerable disquiet" at the Claims Conference due to the lack of clarification of the situation, noting that there was a "potential risk" here should the treaty on the Final Settlement with Germany (2 + 4) be presented to the Senate for ratification.[172]

New Movement after German Reunification

As has already become clear, the end of the Cold War and the reunification of Germany marked a watershed in the field of *Wiedergutmachung* as well. The formulation of old problems was now looked at anew under changed conditions, and fresh formulations were added to the dynamic picture.

Initially novel was the fact that unified Germany now also had to work through a whole new strand in the history of persecution: the victims of the SED dictatorship. It is indeed striking that compensation for injustices suffered in the GDR rarely generates any public interest. The laws on the rectification of SED injustices, their deficiencies and need for amendments did not stir the public.[173] How can we account for this sharp skewing in the distribution of interest in the two histories of persecution? There are various and diverse reasons, but one is especially important: the mass crimes of National Socialism and the violations of human rights in the GDR have quite different dimensions. In addition, the Nazi regime had directed the brunt of its aggression and terror against other peoples, while the SED dictatorship and the empire of Stasi chief Erich Mielke had violated human rights inside Germany, a domestic rather than foreign transgression.[174] That is one reason why there is such international interest in the one narrative of persecution and so little, indeed almost nothing, in the other. But human rights are not divisible. And in the biographies of the victims, some 200,000 individuals convicted in the GDR for political offenses, one injustice does not offset the other in the scales of right and wrong. For that reason, historiography and the public sphere in Germany would be well advised to show greater interest than before in the rehabilitation and compensation of the victims of the SED dictatorship.[175] What manner of timidity would it be if the view were to prevail that the victims of Nazism are accorded proper respect and their due while other (hi)stories of persecution are silenced or belittled?

In 1990, a new phase of movement and reconfiguration also began in the conjunct sphere of *Wiedergutmachung* for Nazi injustice. One of the factors for this new impetus has already been mentioned: united Germany took over settlement of restitution that the GDR had withheld from victims of National Socialist persecution, as well as obligations of the GDR to the Claims Conference.[176] Things also started to move on the West German paths of *Wiedergutmachung.* The so-called 2+4 Treaty of September 1990 marks a clear turning point. This treaty was not a peace treaty in the normal sense of international law. Rather, Kohl's government, with American support, did its best to avoid a peace treaty, and the files of the chancellor mention two precisely phrased reasons.[177] For one, a peace conference would have become a huge affair, wasteful of time. All countries that had been at war with the German Reich could have participated in it. Those were in toto about 60 nations. Helmut Kohl even sought to impress the American president by mentioning a colossal figure of 110 countries.[178] For another, Kohl wished to avoid a situation where a peace conference would begin to thaw out the question of reparations that had been put on ice with the London Agreement on External German Debts. It was impossible, "50 years after the end of the war, to start up again with reparations," that was "not feasible in terms of domestic internal politics." But a document contained in the chancellor's papers stated that in the absence of a formal peace treaty, the question of reparations "had de facto been concluded."[179]

In actual fact, the 2+4 Agreement totally excluded the question of reparations.[180] And from that juncture on, the government in Bonn/Berlin now considered it a closed chapter. By avoiding renewed mention of the question of reparations, Kohl wished to steer clear of a situation in which international demands—unpredictable in number and amount of compensation claimed—would begin to rain down on the Federal Republic. Instead Kohl sought a corner from which the German side could enter into agreements voluntarily, and thus from a more advantageous position. Thus, after the end of the East-West conflict, a series of similar global agreements were concluded to those signed around 1960 with the West. But this time the compass pointed eastward: 1991 with Poland, 1993 with the three successor states to the Soviet Union (Russian Federation, Ukraine, and White Russia), totaling some DM 1.5 billion.[181] Due to the truly huge number of victims of Nazi persecution in these areas, the center of the German war of conquest and destruction, and due to the correspondingly large divisor in distribution, a total sum of this magnitude sufficed for what is called in common parlance a humanitarian gesture. From 1995 to 1998, on a more modest scale, agreements were concluded with the Baltic states. The Czech Future Fund was also established. All these agreements were also suited in part to solicit in effect for the legal position of the Federal Republic, claiming that the question of reparations had, subsequent to the 2 + 4 Treaty, been closed. Very occasionally, a warning signal is sent from Washington—but up to now only to advance negotiations bogged down elsewhere.

Yet the strongest new turn, binding the history of *Wiedergutmachung* together with the great political events of our day, pertains to the involvement of German industry in the machinery of compensation, which to date has been financed largely by the state. Since the 1950s, German industry was repeatedly confronted with claims from former forced laborers. With a few exceptions, it had always managed to parry these demands, and found itself in a legally advantageous position.[182] Such claims were considered reparations, and thus came under the mechanism of the London Agreement on External German Debts. This referred solely to claims "against the Reich and agencies of the Reich," but it was widely believed that German industry had only acted "on behalf of agencies of the Reich" and on its instructions in employing forced laborers.

Since 1990, the foundations underpinning this defensive tactic eroded and then were washed away. Four factors were influential in this process and can be briefly summarized. First, the mechanism of effective blockage built into the London Agreement began to show cracks as some legal judgments started to view the 2+4 Treaty as the functional equivalent of a peace treaty. Second, historical inquiry has shown that the phrase "on behalf of the Reich" describes the scope for action, initiative, and thus the frame of accountability of the firms in the individual case, but not more broadly or on the average. Third, in 1996 the Federal Supreme Court rejected a tradition in international law according to which individual demands can be negotiated only as demands for reparations between individual states. It ruled that the individual can in a given case also defend his own claim.[183] Based on this decision, the field of possibilities for filing a complaint had suddenly been greatly expanded. Or, to phrase it differently and from a more comprehensive perspective, the newer development of expanded protections for human rights now entered the arena of *Wiedergutmachung*. Yet the path opened up by the decision of the high court presupposes that the foreign plaintiffs can refer to internal German law. And this law does not provide former forced laborers with concrete prospects that are clearly calculable.

The fourth factor links a general tendency of our era with the special topic of compensation: namely, globalization, here in the sense that many German firms have branches in the United States and thus come under the scope and jurisdiction of American law. It is well known that this was the lever for the wave of class-action suits against German firms. But quite aside from this legal means, potential loss of image or threats of boycott suffice to massively endanger the business interests in the important American market. One should not generalize too much, most especially in regard to firms that were previously quietly active in this matter. But on the whole it is justified to claim that the class-action suits in the United States were the single most important catalyzing factor that led in 1998 to the Foundation Initiative of the German Economy. This was followed by twelve difficult and thorny rounds of negotiations in which the amount of the funds to be provided by the foundation had to be negotiated, followed by discussions of the scheme for distribution and, finally, the securing of a "legal truce" (*Rechtsfrieden*) to protect the organization from litigation in the future. The Foundation Law was enacted in August 2000 after the signing of an international final declaration.[184]

Thus, after half a century, the point in time is rapidly approaching when material *Wiedergutmachung* will leave the sphere of political action and decision-making and enter the vaults of history. In the process, it will be transformed into an arena for probing historical research where much still remains to be done. This essay has pointed here and there to various desiderata. In closing I would like to stress several more overarching perspectives. First, the history of *Wiedergutmachung* offers specific probes and indicators for investigating the confrontation of German society with National Socialism. In this approach, four German pasts—under National Socialism, divided as East and West, and united since 1990—can be distinguished and linked in terms of several aspects. Second, it is necessary to explore more deeply the nexus between international concern and West German readiness to embark on *Wiedergutmachung* so that we can determine in the most precise possible way what was the effect of influences and impulses from abroad, and the extent of German latitude for action and independent initiatives. Third, needed are more detailed studies for East and West Germany on the question:

how did East-West tensions and competition between the two Germanys impact on the frame of orientation of *Wiedergutmachung*? Fourth, the implementation of the abstract idea of *Wiedergutmachung* on the plane of the concrete world of action was not only dependent on debates and laws, but also on what officials, expert witnesses, and judges did or failed to do. For this reason, we need painstaking studies on implementation of legislation. Finally, we still know too little about the importance of *Wiedergutmachung* in the lives of the victims, their expectations and experiences, individual and collective. This opens a broad terrain for biographical research and *Erfahrungsgeschichte*.

But the profession of history has no monopoly on the use of history. Whether and how *Wiedergutmachung* enters historical memory is ultimately dependent on the decision of us all. Doubtless there will be controversy. The very semantics of the word itself is controversial. And the well-meaning advice of Walter Schwarz—"Germans have a right to be *proud* of the whole program of *Wiedergutmachung*"—will divide the public into the customary triad of enthusiastic agreement, indignant rejection, and thoughtful reflection. Indeed: in the house of *Wiedergutmachung*, there are many mansions. In its chambers, light and shadow shift in accordance with the aspect chosen and the time at which it is observed. On the whole, it would be a mistake to deny that the Federal Republic has accomplished a great deal over the past several decades for *Wiedergutmachung*. Yet, if one takes into consideration the total amount of some DM 136 billion, this is less than for compensation distributed under the Equalization of Burdens Law (1952), which amounted to some DM 140 billion.[185] And far less than for the maintenance of war victims, with a total sum four times this size. Moreover, it is far larger not because maintenance law is more favorable but because the number of those entitled is far greater. And every aspect and facet in this shifting light, even those that signify success, remain referential. As signifiers, they point to something beyond, a stark background upon which large letters spell out: persecution, war of aggression, genocide.

Translated from the German by Bill Templer

Notes

1 Aleida Assmann and Ute Frevert, *Geschichtsvergessenheit, Geschichtsversessenheit. Vom Umgang mit deutschen Vergangenheiten nach 1945* (Stuttgart, 1999), 57. Hartmut Berghoff, "Zwischen Verdrängung und Aufarbeitung. Die bundesdeutsche Gesellschaft und ihre nationalsozialistische Vergangenheit in den Fünfziger Jahren," *Geschichte in Wissenschaft und Unterricht* 49 (1998): 103.—The original German version of this article appeared in *Vierteljahrshefte für Zeitgeschichte* 49 (2001): 167–214.

2. Lea Fleischmann, *Dies ist nicht mein Land. Eine Jüdin verläßt die Bundesrepublik* (Hamburg, 1980), 70.

3. The basic study by Constantin Goschler, *Wiedergutmachung. Westdeutschland und die Verfolgten des Nationalsozialismus (1945–1954)* (Munich, 1992), 25 signals in this direction. See *Deutsches Wörterbuch von Jacob und Wilhelm Grimm*, vol. 9 (Munich, 1984), 1469 f. (reprint of the edition Leipzig 1935).

4. An early example of this is the article published by Siegfried Moses in July 1943 in Tel Aviv: "Die Wiedergutmachungsforderungen der Juden." See on this: *In zwei Welten. Siegfried Moses zum 75. Geburtstag*, ed. Hans Tramer (Tel Aviv, 1962).

5. Franz Böhm, "Recht und Moral im Rahmen der Wiedergutmachung" (n.d., ms. of a speech, end of 1954, in his papers, Archiv für christlich-demokratische Politik, I-200, Nr. 006/2). Idem, "Wie besiegen wir die Trägheit des Herzens? Gedanken zur Wiedergutmachung," *Frankfurter Allgemeine Zeitung*, 13 January 1955, 2 and idem, "Die politische und soziale Bedeutung der Wiedergutmachung (1956)," in idem, *Reden und Schriften*, ed. Ernst-Joachim Mestmäcker (Karlsruhe, 1960), 193–215.

6. Heinrich v. Brentano, Christian Democratic parliamentary group, 17 March 1953. See *Die CDU/CSU-Fraktion im Deutschen Bundestag. Sitzungsprotokolle 1949–1953*, ed. Helge Heidemeyer (Düsseldorf, 1998), 693.

7. In respect to Adenauer's role in the agreement with Israel: Hans-Peter Schwarz, *Adenauer. Der Aufstieg 1876–1952* (Stuttgart, 1986), 899. From the large number of examples of a concept of *Wiedergutmachung* that was anything but trivializing, see Karl Jaspers, *Die Schuldfrage* (Heidelberg, 1946); Dieter Gosewinkel, *Adolf Arndt. Die Wiederbegründung des Rechtsstaats aus dem Geist der Sozialdemokratie 1945–1961* (Bonn, 1991), 225–246; Petra Weber, *Carlo Schmid 1896–1979. Eine Biographie* (Munich, 1996), 465–471. Among the guiding main ideas of Ernst Müller-Meiningen Jr., editor of the *Süddeutsche Zeitung* was that *Wiedergutmachung*, both material and moral, was something that had to be done "in the soul of every individual German" (*Süddeutsche Zeitung*, 5/6 April 1952, 2); the aspect of self-cleansing and purification—it was important "to make oneself good again"—was also emphasized by President Heuß, speech, "Week of Brotherhood," in *Bulletin des Presse- und Informationsamtes der Bundesregierung*, 6 March 1956, 401.

8. Bundesministerium der Finanzen, Entschädigung von NS-Unrecht. Regelungen zur Wiedergutmachung, Berlin 2001, 3, 48.

9. "*Schadensabwicklung*" is the term used here. It was introduced in the historians' debate by Max Horkheimer and Theodor W. Adorno, "Eine Art Schadensabwicklung—Die apologetischen Tendenzen in der deutschen Zeitgeschichtsschreibung," *Die Zeit*, 11 July 1986; the phrase was also used by Habermas the following year:

J. Habermas, *Eine Art Schadensabwicklung. Kleine Politische Schriften*, vol. VI (Frankfurt am Main, 1987).

10. Ludolf Herbst, "Einleitung," in *Wiedergutmachung in der Bundesrepublik Deutschland*, ed. Herbst and Constantin Goschler (Munich, 1989), 9.
11. Ralf Vogl, *Stückwerk und Verdrängung. Wiedergutmachung nationalsozialistischen Strafjustizunrechts in Deutschland* (Berlin/Baden-Baden, 1997).
12. Hans Georg Lehmann, "Wiedereinbürgerung, Rehabilitation und Wiedergutmachung nach 1945. Zur Staatsangehörigkeit ausgebürgerter Emigranten und Remigranten," *Exilforschung. Ein internationales Jahrbuch* 9 (1991): 90–103.
13. Such as the organizations Aktion Sühnezeichen and the Maximilian-Kolbe-Werk.
14. To date, it is primarily legal scholars who have looked at the entire field of this development. Of fundamental importance is a collective, semiofficial work written, with the exception of volume one, by the officials directly involved: *Die Wiedergutmachung nationalsozialistischen Unrechts durch die Bundesrepublik Deutschland*, ed. Bundesminister der Finanzen in cooperation with Walter Schwarz, vol. 1: Walter Schwarz, *Rückerstattung nach den Gesetzen der Alliierten Mächte* (Munich, 1974); vol. 2: Friedrich Biella et.al., *Das Bundesrückerstattungsgesetz* (Munich, 1981); vol. 3: Ernst Féaux de la Croix and Helmut Rumpf, *Der Werdegang des Entschädigungsrechts unter national- und völkerrechtlichem und politologischem Aspekt* (Munich, 1985); vol. 4: Walter Brunn et.al., *Das Bundesentschädigungsgesetz. Erster Teil (§§ 1 bis 50 BEG)* (Munich, 1981); vol. 5: Hans Giessler et.al., *Das Bundesentschädigungsgesetz. Zweiter Teil (§§ 51 bis 171 BEG)* (Munich, 1983); vol. 6: Hugo Finke et.al., *Entschädigungsverfahren und sondergesetzliche Entschädigungsregelungen* (Munich, 1982). An unbound supplement to vol. 1 is "Schlußbetrachtung" by Walter Schwarz; it is itself supplemented but not supplanted by idem, "Die Wiedergutmachung nationalsozialistischen Unrechts durch die Bundesrepublik Deutschland. Ein Überblick," in Herbst and Goschler, *Wiedergutmachung in der Bundesrepublik Deutschland*, 33–54. A useful perspective grounded on notions in the history of law and jurisprudence is Cornelius Pawlita, *"Wiedergutmachung" als Rechtsfrage? Die politische und juristische Auseinandersetzung um Entschädigung für die Opfer nationalsozialistischer Verfolgung 1945–1990* (Frankfurt a.M., 1993). The new survey by Hermann-Josef Brodesser et.al., *Wiedergutmachung und Kriegsfolgenliquidation. Geschichte—Regelungen—Zahlungen* (Munich, 2000) is based primarily on the semi-official collective work, the *Bundesgesetzblatt* and the periodical *RzW* (see fn. 130); the authors come from the sphere of the relevant administrative practice.
15. Schwarz, *Rückerstattung nach den Gesetzen der Alliierten Mächte*, 23–58; Goschler, *Wiedergutmachung*, 106–128.
16. See after the path-breaking study by Frank Bajohr, *"Arisierung" in Hamburg. Die Verdrängung der jüdischen Unternehmer 1933–1945* (Hamburg 1997), now also *"Arisierung" im Nationalsozialismus. Volksgemeinschaft, Raub und Gedächtnis*, ed. Irmtrud Wojak and Petes Hayes (Frankfurt a.M./New York, 2000), and Frank Bajohr, "Verfolgung aus gesellschaftsgeschichtlicher Perspektive. Die wirtschaftliche Existenzvernichtung der Juden und die deutsche Gesellschaft," *Geschichte und Gesellschaft* 26 (2000): 629–652.
17. Control Council Directive No. 50 was implemented in the four zones and Berlin with differing laws and ordinances. A summary overview is contained in Biella et.al., *Das Bundesrückerstattungsgesetz*, 14. The history of the restitution of "property of organizations" (termed in this way because such property was incorporated

into Nazi organizations) is almost a total terra incognita. Sparse data in Detlev Brunner, *50 Jahre Konzentration GmbH. Die Geschichte eines sozialdemokratischen Unternehmens 1946–1996* (Berlin, 1996), 47–51. Among the main tasks of the Konzentration GmbH, founded in 1946, was to regain expropriated party property for the SPD or to be compensated for this. As a first piece of choice real estate, the SPD regained the Karl Marx House in Trier in 1948; the SED had also made a claim for this property.

18. This involves, for example, the liability of private "buyers" for the portions of the price of sale retained by the Nazi regime and the degree of liability of second or third parties who later acquired the property or assets.
19. Rainer Hudemann, "Anfänge der Wiedergutmachung. Französische Besatzungszone 1945–50," *Geschichte und Gesellschaft* 13 (1987): 181–216.
20. The successor organizations established in 1947 in the U.S. Zone were the Jewish Restitution Successor Organisation (JRSO), and in 1950 in the British Zone the Jewish Trust Corporation for Germany (JTC); in 1951, the JTC acquired a French Branch when the French handling of the question of "property without heirs" adopted the American line. The share of the successor organizations in the value of restitution was apparently overestimated by contemporaries; Schwarz estimates it at 8 percent (*Rückerstattung nach den Gesetzen der Alliierten Mächte*, 377), rounding that off to 10 percent in his survey article in Herbst and Goschler, *Wiedergutmachung in der Bundesrepublik Deutschland*, 37.
21. As P.M. Ehard formulated it; see *Die Protokolle des Bayerischen Ministerrats 1945–1954*, ed. Historische Kommission bei der Bayerischen Akademie der Wissenschaften und der Generaldirektion der Staatlichen Archive Bayerns, vol. 1.: Das Kabinett Ehard: 21. Dezember 1946 bis 20. September 1947 (Munich, 2000), 265; on consultations on the law, see ibid., 111–116.
22. It is an undisputed fact that the law "in frequent cases led to severe consequences for the individual obligated to restitute property," but the proportion of such cases in the total picture is still unclear; quoted in Hans Strauss, "Die Rückerstattung entzogener und geraubter Vermögensgegenstände," in *Deutsche Wiedergutmachung 1957. Eine Serie von Vorträgen gehalten über den Sender WHOM, New York*, ed. Axis Victims League and American Association of Former European Jurists (Düsseldorf, 1957), 12–15, here 14. On its use for agitational purposes, see Constantin Goschler, "Die Auseinandersetzung um die Rückerstattung 'arisierten' jüdischen Eigentums nach 1945," in *Die Deutschen und die Judenverfolgung im Dritten Reich*, ed. Ursula Büttner (Hamburg, 1992), 339–356.
23. The by-laws of the Supreme Restitution Court (located in Herford) from an annex to part III ("*Innere Rückerstattung*") of the "*Vertrag zur Regelung aus Krieg und Besatzung entstandener Fragen*" (*Überleitungsvertrag*); signed in May 1952, this treaty became law in a revised version in March 1955 (BGBl. 1955 II, 181–194). Competence was not transferred to the Federal Supreme Court (Bundesgerichtshof) until 1990.
24. Strauss, *Die Rückerstattung entzogener und geraubter Vermögensgegenstände*, 14.
25. Schwarz, *Rückerstattung nach den Gesetzen der Alliierten Mächte*, 345–394. On the factor of recalculation, see *Fünfzig Jahre Deutsche Mark. Notenbank und Währung in Deutschland seit 1948*, ed. Deutsche Bundesbank (Munich, 1998), 311.
26. On this approach, see Ilse Birkwald, "Ein Opfer der Finanzverwaltung. Der ganz normale Fall Oppenheim vor und nach 1945," in *Verfolgung und Verwaltung. Die*

wirtschaftliche Ausplünderung der Juden und die westfälischen Finanzbehörden, ed. Alfons Kenkmann and Bernd-A. Rusinek (Münster, 1999), 102–121.

27. On this case, cf. Rolf Theis, *Wiedergutmachung zwischen Moral und Interesse. Eine kritische Bestandsaufnahme der deutsch-israelischen Regierungsverhandlungen* (Frankfurt a.M., 1989), 318–321; Franz Fichtl et.al., *"Bambergs Wirtschaft judenfrei." Die Verdrängung der jüdischen Geschäftsleute in den Jahren 1933 bis 1939* (Bamberg, 1998), 377–392.
28. Hans Umbreit, "Auf dem Weg zur Kontinentalherrschaft," in *Das Deutsche Reich und der Zweite Weltkrieg*, vol. 5/1 (Stuttgart, 1988), 3–345, here 309–320; Lynn H. Nicholas, *Der Raub der Europa. Das Schicksal europäischer Kunstwerke im Dritten Reich* (Munich, 1995); Anja Heuss, *Kunst- und Kulturgutraub. Eine vergleichende Studie zur Besatzungspolitik der Nationalsozialisten in Frankreich und der Sowjetunion* (Heidelberg, 2000).
29. In Part III ("Innere Rückerstattung") of the *Überleitungsvertrag* (see fn. 23).
30. See for details Biella, *Das Bundesrückerstattungsgesetz.*
31. *BMF. Dokumentation 3/99*, 38.
32. On this, see Biella, *Das Bundesrückerstattungsgesetz*, 269–275 (Eastern Europe), 531–583 (Western Europe). A distinction should be made between compensation for injury in monetary form, the concern here, and the return of still available goods which were illegally acquired in the occupied territories. On these restitution cases, see Gunther Mai, *Der Alliierte Kontrollrat in Deutschland 1945–1948* (Munich, 1995), 347–355.
33. Martin Hirsch, "Folgen der Verfolgung. Schädigung—Wiedergutmachung—Rehabilitierung," in *Die Bundesrepublik Deutschland und die Opfer des Nationalsozialismus. Tagung vom 25. bis 27. November 1983 in der Evangelischen Akademie Bad Boll*, ed. Protokolldienst 14/84 (Bad Boll, 1984), 19–32, here 21.
34. Johannes Bähr and Michael C. Schneider, *Der Goldhandel der Dresdner Bank im Zweiten Weltkrieg. Ein Bericht des Hannah-Arendt-Instituts* (Leipzig, 1999); Jonathan Steinberg, *Die Deutsche Bank und ihre Goldtransaktionen während des Zweiten Weltkrieges* (Munich, 1999); Gerald D. Feldman, "Unternehmensgeschichte im Dritten Reich und die Verantwortung der Historiker. Raubgold und Versicherungen, Arisierung und Zwangsarbeit," in *Geschichte vor Gericht. Historiker, Richter und die Suche nach Gerechtigkeit*, ed. Norbert Frei, Dirk van Laak and Michael Stolleis (Munich, 2000), 103–129.
35. The later even more differentiated basic pattern involved injury to life, limb, health, freedom, property, assets and economic advancement. The term "injury to life" in legal German signifies the killing of the breadwinner. Injury and damage to property and assets involved, for example, plunder, boycott and discriminatory special levies; this aspect in compensation law went together with the aspect in restitution law of the expropriation of property.
36. Angelika Königseder and Juliane Wetzel, *Lebensmut im Wartessal. Die jüdischen DPs (Displaced Persons) im Nachkriegsdeutschland* (Frankfurt a.M., 1994).
37. Goschler, *Wiedergutmachung*, 128–148. On the great variety of provisional arrangements after the war, often introduced by municipalities, counties and the autonomous organizations of liberated camp inmates, see for an overview Constantin Goschler, "Wiedergutmachung," in *Geschichte der Sozialpolitik in Deutschland seit 1945*, ed. Bundesministerium für Arbeit und Sozialordnung und

das Bundesarchiv, vol. 2: Die Besatzungszeit. Sozialpolitik zwischen Kriegsende und der Gründung zweier deutscher Staaten (Baden-Baden, 2000).

38. The "*Gesetz zur Regelung der Wiedergutmachung nationalsozialistischen Unrechts für die im Ausland lebenden Angehörige des öffentlichen Dienstes*" of 18 March 1952 provided a choice: return to the Federal Republic with a right to "preferential rehiring" or to remain in the land of emigration with a right to social welfare and maintenance payments. The law does not propose to provide "solely financial compensation and maintenance support," as assumed by Claus-Dieter Krohn, "Einleitung," in *Rückkehr und Aufbau nach 1945. Deutsche Remigranten im öffentlichen Lebens Nachkriegsdeutschlands*, ed. Krohn and Patrik von zur Mühlen (Marburg, 1997), 8–21, here 20; he then falsely concludes that the law contributed nothing to the topic of "re-integration of the emigrants." If the emigrants in question had built up a comfortable life for themselves (for example, as professors) abroad, then a return to Germany might have entailed substantial financial loss. If they remained abroad, they received German maintenance payments (where the modalities of payment in foreign exchange were not formally regulated until April 1954) in addition to their income there. If they chose to be reinstated in Germany, then they only had one income. This aspect encompasses only a portion of the generally quite multifaceted complex of motivation. But emigration research, as far as I can judge, has to date not considered this dimension at all, even in the otherwise very fruitful and informative case studies by Anikó Szabó, *Vertreibung, Rückkehr, Wiedergutmachung. Göttinger Hochschullehrer im Schatten des Nationalsozialismus* (Göttingen, 2000).
39. Basic here is the study by Udo Wengst, *Beamtentum zwischen Reform und Tradition. Beamtengesetzgebung in der Gründungsphase der Bundesrepublik Deutschland 1948–1953* (Düsseldorf, 1988), 233 f.; for further angles, see Goschler, *Wiedergutmachung*, quote 235.
40. See also fn. 68 below.
41. Norbert Frei, *Vergangenheitspolitik. Die Anfänge der Bundesrepublik und die NS-Vergangenheit* (Munich, 1996). The public symbolism also mitigated lines of separation with signs of bridging. Thus, in 1952, the Volkstrauertag (Memorial Day) was celebrated for the first time across all of West Germany uniformly. It was not only dedicated to the memory of the victims of the war but also absorbed the tradition of memorial days for the victims of Nazi persecution which had been established as a commemorative tradition everywhere in Germany after 1945.
42. Liliane Weissberg, "Introduction," in *Hannah Arendt, Rahel Varnhagen. The Life of a Jewess. First complete Edition*, ed. Liliane Weissberg (Baltimore/London, 1997), 38–41; Rolf Wiggershaus, *Die Frankfurter Schule. Geschichte, theoretische Entwicklung, politische Bedeutung* (Munich, 1988), 122.
43. Commentary in the *Frankfurter Rundschau*, 11 January 1969, 3. With this article and an editorial on the first page of the same issue, the paper spurred public interest in this case.
44. For a precise presentation of the legal facts and the preferential regulations of the law as well as the background to the amendment, which was the product of a decision by the Federal Supreme Court, see Otto Küster, "Die Rechtslage im Wiedergutmachungsfall Dr. Gerstenmaier," *Mitteilungsblatt der bayerischen Verfolgten und Widerstandskämpfer* 24 (1969): 1f. See also the detailed letter of explanation by Franz Böhm to the editors of the *Frankfurter Rundschau*, 13 January 1969, which the paper chose not to print (ACDP, I-200, Nr. 005/1).

45. Ronald W. Zweig, *German Reparations and the Jewish World: A History of the Claims Conference* (Boulder and London, 1987); Nana Sagi, *German Reparations: A History of the Negotiations* (New York, 1986).
46. Ludolf Herbst, "Einleitung," in Herbst and Goschler, *Wiedergutmachung in der Bundesrepublik Deutschland*, 13.
47. See the articles by Nana Sagi, Yeshayahu A. Jelinek, Rudolf Huhn, Michael Wolffsohn, Willy Albrecht, Norbert Frei in Herbst and Goschler, *Wiedergutmachung in der Bundesrepublik Deutschland*, with references to older literature and more recent studies such as: Axel Frohn, ed., *Holocaust and Shilumim: The Policy of Wiedergutmachung in the Early 1950s* (Washington, D.C., 1991); Peter L. Münch, "Zwischen 'Liquidation' und Wiederaufbau. Die deutschen Juden, der Staat Israel und die internationalen jüdischen Organisationen in der Phase der Wiedergutmachungsverhandlungen," *Historische Mitteilungen* 10 (1997): 81–111; Yechiam Weitz, "Ben Gurions Weg zum 'Anderen Deutschland' 1952–1963," *VfZ* 48 (2000): 255–279. An informative new edition is *Der Auswärtige Ausschuß des Deutschen Bundestages. Sitzungsprotokolle 1949–1953*, ed. Wolfgang Hölscher, 2 vols. (Düsseldorf, 1998), esp. the protocols of the sessions of 16 May 1952 and 12 March 1953, 783–805, 1495–1549.
48. Norman G. Finkelstein, *The Holocaust Industry: Reflections on the Exploitation of Jewish Suffering* (New York, 2000) accuses the Claims Conference of having used most of the DM 450 million for purposes other than intended. According to the Hague Protocol No. 2 the purpose of the funds was to "support, integrate and settle Jewish victims of National Socialist persecution according to the urgency of their needs as determined by the Claims Conference." The federal government was thinking here of individual assistance, especially in hardship cases not covered by federal compensation law. And it was indeed upset when the annual reports on utilization revealed other practices: in the main, the Claims Conference provided support to community institutions oriented to charity or cultural work. To justify this, it referred to its right to decide about the urgency of needs, underscoring the direct utility for former victims of persecution. If the limit of tolerance of the agreement had been violated, the government in Bonn could have turned to an arbitration court, as specifically stipulated in the protocol. It did not do this. Thus, in terms of the legal obligations, there was no use for purposes other than intended. Yet Finkelstein's critical analysis provides contemporary history with a welcome added reason to include the history of the recipient institutions of compensation (and the successor organizations in restitution) in the purview of their inquiry.
49. Israel chose the term *shilumim* (payments) as the equivalent for *Wiedergutmachung*, a word from biblical Hebrew. It had no connotation of the forgiving of guilt or guilt excused, exonerated. See Yeshayahu A. Jelinek, *Zwischen Moral und Realpolitik. Eine Dokumentensammlung* (Gerlingen, 1997), 22. On the economic effects, see Günter Könke, "Wiedergutmachung und Modernisierung. Der Beitrag des Luxemburger Abkommens von 1952 zur wirtschaftlichen Entwicklung Israels," *Vierteljahrschrift für Sozial- und Wirtschaftsgeschichte* 75 (1988): 503–548.
50. The CDU constituted one nucleus of opposition. A notoriously well-informed observer explained this by noting that the party "could not endorse the Israel proposal openly, given the mood of the Bavarian supporters of Christian Democracy." See "Parlamentarischer Bericht des Bundespresseamts, 18. März 1953," in *Die CDU/CSU-Fraktion im Deutschen Bundestag. Sitzungsprotokolle 1949–1953*, 688.

51. Critical of the agreement in particular were *Die Zeit*, *Der Spiegel* and *Stern*.
52. Werner Bergmann, *Antisemitismus in öffentlichen Konflikten. Kollektives Lernen in der politischen Kultur der Bundesrepublik 1949–1989* (Frankfurt a.M./New York, 1997), 174–185.
53. Christoph Buchheim, "Londoner Schuldenabkommen," in *Deutschland unter alliierter Besatzung 1945–1949/55*, ed. Wolfgang Benz (Berlin, 1999), 355–357. In the event, debt management proved to be an easy burden to carry since the West German balance of payments from 1953 on always showed a large foreign exchange surplus.
54. Schwarz, *Adenauer*, 904.
55. According to an Allensbach poll, in August 1952 more supporters of the SPD (44 percent) than the CDU (37 percent) regarded the agreement as superfluous. A further 27 percent of SPD supporters and 28 percent of CDU supporters were in favor of the agreement per se, but regarded the total amount agreed on as excessive. See Bergmann, *Antisemitismus*, 181.
56. Heinrich v. Brentano, in Christian Democrat parliamentary group on 17 March 1953; see *Die CDU/CSU-Fraktion im Deutschen Bundestag. Sitzungsprotokolle 1949–1953*, 693. From the large number of further statements that substantiate this: "The Chancellor believes the agreement is extremely important and wants it to be ratified before he leaves for the United States." See "Protokoll der Fraktionsvorstandssitzung vom 2. März 1953," ibid, 677.
57. Michael Wolffsohn has demonstrated that in the ensemble of negotiations in 1951/52, Washington's top priority was not the German-Israel Agreement. But the reverse conclusion that the reparations to Israel were provided "voluntarily and without American pressure" and "not due to opinion abroad, but despite what the *Ausland* thought" is exaggerated. See Michael Wolffsohn, *Ewige Schuld? 40 Jahre deutsch-jüdisch-israelische Beziehungen* (Munich/Zurich, 1988), 21 and idem, "Globalentschädigung für Israel und die Juden? Adenauer und die Opposition in der Bundesregierung," in Herbst and Goschler, *Wiedergutmachung in der Bundesrepublik Deutschland*, 172; idem likewise: "Das deutsch-israelische Wiedergutmachungsabkommen von 1952 im internationalen Zusammenhang," in *VfZ* 36 (1988): 691–731. Unproven is also the assertion that in the 1956 Suez crisis, Adenauer was asked by Dulles to freeze payments from Germany to Israel and refused, taking possible "difficulties with the most important ally" in the bargain (*Ewige Schuld*, 30f.); for a contrasting view, see Sven Olaf Bergötz, *Nahostpolitik in der Ära Adenauer. Möglichkeiten und Grenzen 1949–1963* (Düsseldorf, 1998), 393.
58. The assessment by Pross is faulty simply in terms of its chronology, see Christian Pross, *Wiedergutmachung. Der Kleinkrieg gegen die Opfer* (Frankfurt a.M., 1988), 292: "The Federal Republic bought Marshall Plan aid and integration into the Western alliance by means of the payment of reparations."
59. Angelika Timm, *Hammer, Zirkel, Davidstern. Das gestörte Verhältnis der DDR zu Zionismus und Staat Israel* (Bonn, 1997), 132,
60. "Protokoll Nr. 1," in *BGBl.* 1953 II, 85–94; "Protokoll Nr. 2," ibid., 94–97.
61. Ernst Katzenstein, "Jewish Claims Conference und die Wiedergutmachung nationalsozialistischen Unrechts," in *Die Freiheit des Anderen. Festschrift für Martin Hirsch*, ed. Hans Jochen Vogel (Baden-Baden, 1981), 219–226, here 224. Katzenstein, since 1956 director of the Claims Conference in the Federal Republic, participated intensively in work on the BEG in 1956, the Federal Restitution Law of

1957 and the Final Federal Compensation Law of 1965 with drafts, memoranda and other input.

62. Féaux de la Croix and Rumpf, *Der Werdegang des Entschädigungsrechts*, 198. However, studies based on archival materials on the genesis of the relevant laws, ordinances and amendments remain a desideratum for future research.
63. See Part IV ("Entschädigung") of the *Überleitungsvertrag* (see fn. 23).
64. Somewhat misleadingly termed Supplementary Federal Law on Compensation for the Victims of National Socialist Persecution (*Bundesergänzungsgesetz zur Entschädigung für Opfer der nationalsozialistischen Verfolgung*), the law came into force on 1 October 1953 (BGBl. 1953 I, p. 1387). The proposal by the minister of justice in the state of Baden-Württemberg Victor Renner to link its passage into law with a symbolic act of state in the former concentration camp Bergen-Belsen was not acted on (Parlamentsarchiv des Deutschen Bundestages, I 537, A 2, Nr. 22).
65. The amendment was prepared by a working group in which representatives of all the parliamentary groupings in the Bundestag as well as representatives of the states and several federal ministries took part. From the perspective of the finance ministry, see on this the report in Féaux de la Croix and Rumpf, *Der Werdegang des Entschädigungsrechts*, 83–92.
66. Debates on this took place on 10 December 1954, 23 February 1955 and 14 December 1955. The quotes are from the debate on 10 December 1954. See *Verhandlungen des Deutschen Bundestages. Stenographische Berichte*, Vol. 23, 3102, 3105, 3104.
67. The other states put the compensation offices under the control of the minister of the interior, the minister of labor, minister of social welfare, or minister of justice. See the overview in Finke, *Entschädigungsverfahren und sondergesetzliche Entschädigungsregelungen*, 9. It is necessary to examine whether, and if so how, these differences in administrative structure impacted on the practice of compensation.
68. *Verhandlungen des Deutschen Bundestages. Stenographische Berichte*, vol. 22, 3102 (10 December 1954), vol. 23, 3489 (23 February 1955). The heckler on both occasions was the CDU deputy Johannes Albers. He was referring to the law promulgated in May 1951 and dubbed the "*131er Gesetz*" (Law 131) that granted many former National Socialists a legal right to claim reinstatement in the civil service; see also fn. 39.
69. The Bavarian Radio broadcast a special program from which the *Süddeutsche Zeitung* printed excerpts in its edition on 11 November 1954 ("Der Skandal der Wiedergutmachung"); the *Frankfurter Allgemeine Zeitung* (14 December 1955) devoted a whole page to the debate.
70. In the meantime a topos, and less disputed in fact than in terms of its assessment, the terse phrase *gewisse Stille* ("a certain hush") first appears in Hermann Lübbe, "Der Nationalsozialismus im deutschen Nachkriegsbewußtsein," *Historische Zeitschrift* 236 (1983): 579–599. Lübbe interpreted it as a kind of therapeutic sleep, "a necessary political and social-psychological medium for the transformation of our postwar population into the citizenry of the Federal Republic of Germany."
71. Franz Böhm, 14 December 1955. See *Verhandlungen des Deutschen Bundestages. Stenographische Berichte*, vol. 27, 6328. Helmut Dubiel, *Niemand ist frei von der Geschichte. Die nationalsozialistische Herrschaft in den Debatten des Deutschen Bundestages* (Munich/Vienna, 1999) does not touch on this debate; but it could be regarded as among the Bundestag's finest hours in the 1950s.

72. Pross, *Wiedergutmachung*, 92–98 takes a different view. He leaves aside the praise that also mingled with the emotional critique. To "applause resounding from all corners," Franz Böhm on 14 December 1955 (6329) expressed "our thanks and respect for these magnificent thousands of individuals who, working in all kinds of offices, sometimes with too little training for the task, made tremendous efforts in the practical implementation of reparations."
73. BEG § 208, paragraph 3 stipulated that the chair or one of the assessors of the Compensation Chamber (in the regional courts) and of the Compensation Senate (in the higher regional courts and the appellate courts) should be drawn from the ranks of the "circle of persons persecuted." See the example of Platiel, head of the Kassel Regional Court, in Helga Haas-Rietschel and Sabine Hering, *Nora Platiel. Sozialistin—Emigrantin—Politikerin. Eine Biographie* (Cologne, 1990).
74. Letter from the Regional Compensation Office to Anton U., dated 9 April 1953 (Parlamentsarchiv des Deutschen Bundestags, I 537 B). The request referred to the Compensation Law of the U.S. Zone, retained in its essence in the Supplementary Federal Law on Compensation.
75. Federal Law on Compensation for the Victims of National Socialist Persecution (Bundesgesetz zur Entschädigung für Opfer der nationalsozialistischen Verfolgung), 29 June 1956 (*BGBl.* 1956 I, 559).
76. *BMF Dokumentation 3/99*, ed. Bundesministerium der Finanzen, 38f.
77. Karl Heßdörfer, "Die finanzielle Dimension," in Herbst and Goschler, *Wiedergutmachung in der Bundesrepublik Deutschland*, 55–59.
78. "Many potential beneficiaries had such little confidence in those laws that they did not even bother to register their claims," stated the *Report on URO's Activities 1954*, 1 February 1955.
79. Hans Günter Hockerts, "Anwälte der Verfolgten. Die United Restitution Organization," in Herbst and Goschler, *Wiedergutmachung in der Bundesrepublik Deutschland*, 249–271.
80. Work on *Wiedergutmachung* was being done "away from the focus of public interest, a lonely task devoid of any glamour," noted Otto Küster, "Umschau," *RzW* 9 (1958): 129. In retrospect, Walter Schwarz emphasized repeatedly that *Wiedergutmachung* lay "for almost four decades in a kind of space aside, on a political and journalistic margin"; that is the view, for example, of Schwarz, "Wiedergutmachung—Ein Überblick," in Herbst and Goschler, *Wiedergutmachung in der Bundesrepublik Deutschland*, 53.
81. Otto-Heinrich Greve was forced to resign because he had mixed his office with his private practice as an attorney; Alfred Frenzel resigned in 1960, after he had been arrested as a spy for the Czechoslovak Socialist Republic. Pointedly, Otto Küster, *Erfahrungen in der deutschen Wiedergutmachung* (Tübingen, 1967), 11, noted that along with the honoraria, deceit and fraud were the only thing that many Germans knew about the topic of *Wiedergutmachung*. Without questioning the role of the press in contributing to his assessment of the deplorable state of affairs, Rolf Zundel, "Dramaturgie eines Skandals," *Die Zeit*, 31 January 1969, 6, commented: "The reparations laws have never been popular. What became known of the practices here awakened suspicion and resentment."
82. *Verhandlungen des Deutschen Bundestages. Stenographische Berichte*, vol. 23, 3491 (23 February 1955).

83. The global agreements of the FRG with eleven West European countries, discussed below, likewise do not appear to have stirred much public interest.
84. Schäffer's contrary moves and pronouncements can only partially be explained by reference to his function as Federal Minister of Finance. The high point of his polemics came when he was no longer minister, in a speech at a function of the Christian Democrats in Plattling in December 1957, when he maintained inter alia that *Wiedergutmachung* was undermining the stability of the German mark. He caused quite a stir by this remark in the papers, but encountered a broad front of vehement rejection of his views. The Federal Cabinet also distanced itself, including his successor as finance minister, Franz Etzel. See "Schäffer auf Abwegen," *Süddeutsche Zeitung*, 18 December 1957; Kurt R. Grossmann, *Die Ehrenschuld. Kurzgeschichte der Wiedergutmachung* (Frankfurt a.M., 1967), 87; Michael Wolffsohn, "Von der verordneten zur freiwilligen 'Vergangenheitsbewältigung'? Eine Skizze der bundesdeutschen Entwicklung 1955/1965," *German Studies Review* 12, no. 1 (1989): 111–137.
85. Otto Küster, "Wiedergutmachung und Rehabilitierung," in: *Tagung vom 25. bis 27. November 1983 in der Evangelischen Akademie Bad Boll* (fn. 33), 86–89, here: 87.
86. In November 1957, the *Allgemeine Wochenzeitung der Juden in Deutschland* reported on a young plumber who had given the Jewish Community in Frankfurt a chandelier which he had made himself, saying: "I wanted contribute something to *Wiedergutmachung* myself and that's why I worked in my spare time on this chandelier, which is meant as a request for forgiveness." Quoted in Manfred Kittel, *Die Legende von der "Zweiten Schuld". Vergangenheitsbewältigung in der Ära Adenauer* (Berlin, 1993), 281.
87. The to date most detailed description of the genesis of the law, though totally from the perspective of the ministry involved, can be found in Féaux de la Croix and Rumpf, *Der Werdegang des Entschädigungsrechts*, 96–110.
88. In 1958, the Arbeitsgemeinschaft Deutscher Verfolgtenorganisationen (Consortium of German Organizations of Victims of Persecution) comprised the following: die Arbeitsgemeinschaft der Vertretungen politisch, rassisch und religiös Verfolgter, die Zentralstelle politisch verfolgter Sozialdemokraten, der Zentralrat der Juden in Deutschland, der Zentralverband demokratischer Widerstandskämpfer und Verfolgtenorganisationen (ZDWV) and der Zentralverband der durch die Nürnberger Gesetze Betroffenen nichtjüdischen Glaubens.
89. See the memoir report of this expert: Grossmann, *Ehrenschuld*, esp. 128–154. The head of the Press and Information Office of the Federal Government, Karl-Günther von Hase, spoke in this connection about a "campaign of world Jewry." See *Akten zur Auswärtigen Politik der Bundesrepublik Deutschland [AAPD]*, ed. Auswärtiges Amtes and Institut für Zeitgeschichte (Munich, 1965), vol. 1, 365 (22 February 1965).
90. *BGBl.* 1965 I, 1315.
91. In his official government declaration, 10 November 1965. See Klaus Hildebrand, *Von Erhard zur Großen Koalition 1963–1969* (Stuttgart/Wiesbaden, 1984), 160f. See also Ernst Ehrmann, "Wie lange noch und zu welchem Preis?," *Die Zeit*, 6 March 1964, 16: "Instead of perpetuating *Wiedergutmachung*, it should now really be laid to rest. It has performed its duty." It was time, he stressed, "to wrap it up so that we can begin a new chapter—without encumbrances from the past." The

FAZ commented on the law on 25 June 1964 with an editorial entitled "Ein Schlußstrich" (Final Stroke).

92. Grossmann, *Ehrenschuld*, 144. In order not to endanger the binding quality of Goldmann's acceptance and to avoid risking a remobilization of public opinion, ambassador Blankenhorn (London) emphatically warned about including benefits based on the Final Compensation Law within the Law on Securing of the Budget, which was being prepared after the federal election in the fall of 1965. See his letter to the Foreign Office, 2 December 1965 (*AAPD* 1965, vol. 3, 1833).
93. Goldmann gave President Heinrich Lübke a relevant memorandum on 22 January 1964 (*AAPD* 1964, vol. 1, Munich 1995, 198, note 35).
94. The breakthrough is marked by *Psychische Spätschäden nach politischer Verfolgung*, ed. Helmut Paul and Hans-Joachim Herberg (Basel/New York, 1963) and Walter v. Baeyer, Heinz Häfner and Karl Peter Kisker, *Psychiatrie der Verfolgten. Psychopathologische und gutachtliche Erfahrungen an Opfern der nationalsozialistischen Verfolgung und vergleichbarer Extrembelastungen* (Berlin, 1964); see also the excellent review by Ulrich Venzlaff, "Die Begutachtung psychischer Störungen Verfolgter," *Rechtsprechung zum Wiedergutmachungsrecht* 17 (1966): 196–200.
95. Arnold Spitta, "Entschädigung für Zigeuner? Geschichte eines Vorurteils," in Herbst and Goschler, *Wiedergutmachung in der Bundesrepublik Deutschland*, 385–401; Hockerts, *Anwälte*, 269–271.
96. See Gilad Margalit, "Die deutsche Zigeunerpolitik nach 1945," *VfZ* 45 (1997): 557–588, and the vivid research report: Michael Zimmermann, "Zigeunerbilder und Zigeunerpolitik in Deutschland. Eine Übersicht über neuere historische Studien," *Werkstatt Geschichte* 25 (2000): 35–58.
97. See Adolf Arndt, "Agraphoi nomoi (Widerstand und Aufstand)", *Neue Juristische Wochenschrift* 15 (1962): 430–433; Kittel, *Legende*, 209–212.
98. Or had lived before in the area of validity of the law in so far as claims by survivors were concerned.
99. In this way, emigrants from the territory of the later GDR and the German Eastern territories incorporated by Poland in 1945 were included under its umbrella. In the negotiations in the Hague, the Claims Conference had also called for inclusion of Jewish emigrants from Austria under West German compensation law, but this was proved impossible after Adenauer's emphatic rejection. On reparations in Austria, see "*Ich bin dafür, die Sache in die Länge zu ziehen.*" *Wortprotokolle der österreichischen Bundesregierung von 1945–52 über die Entschädigung der Juden*, ed. Robert Knight (Frankfurt a.M., 1988); Brigitte Bailer, *Wiedergutmachung kein Thema* (Vienna, 1993).
100. Uwe Johnson impressively described such a situation in his novel *Jahrestage* (3, April 1968 bis Juni 1968). Questionable practices in this connection are pointed out by Heinz Klee, "Die besonderen Gruppen von Verfolgten," in Giessler, *Das Bundesentschädigungsgesetz. Zweiter Teil*, 422–424.
101. Ulrich Herbert, "Nicht entschädigungsfähig? Die Wiedergutmachungsansprüche der Ausländer," in: Herbst and Goschler, *Wiedergutmachung in der Bundesrepublik Deutschland*, 273–302; Pawlita, "'Wiedergutmachung' als Rechtsfrage?," 352–372.
102. Burkhard Heß, "Völker- und zivilrechtliche Beurteilung der Entschädigung für Zwangsarbeit vor dem Hintergrund neuerer Entscheidungen deutscher Gerichte," in *Entschädigung für NS-Zwangsarbeit. Rechtliche, historische und politische Aspekte*,

ed. Klaus Barwig, Günther Saathoff and Nicole Weyde (Baden-Baden, 1998), 65–92; Pawlita, "'Wiedergutmachung' als Rechtsfrage?," 81–87, 119–124, 156–159; Uwe Kischel, "Wiedergutmachungsrecht und Reparationen. Zur Dogmatik der Kriegsfolgen," *Juristenzeitung* 3/1997: 126–131.

103. Herbert, "Nicht entschädigungsfähig?," 279 f.
104. Esp. Part VI (Reparations) of the *Überleitungsvertrag* (fn. 23), which stipulated: "The question of reparations will be settled by a peace treaty between Germany and its former adversaries, or before this by agreements relating to this question."
105. Peter Helmberger, "Der Versuch einer Generalbereinigung. Die Verhandlungen zwischen den Niederlanden und der Bundesrepublik um den Ausgleichsvertrag vom 8. April 1960," *Zentrum für Niederlande-Studien, Jahrbuch* 4 (1993): 71–98.
106. The countries were France, the Benelux states, Greece, Great Britain, Norway and Denmark.
107. The treaty partners were the eight countries of the 1956 démarche, with which the FRG negotiated up until the end of 1958 mulitlaterally, and from 1959 bilaterally, as well as Italy, Switzerland and Sweden. This was supplemented by the section on *Wiedergutmachung* in the German-Austrian Financial and Adjustment Treaty of October 1962.
108. To date, almost the only description available is that from the perspective of the ministry involved, by Féaux de la Croix and Rumpf, *Der Werdegang des Entschädigungsrechts*, 201–288. For the Netherlands see Helmberger, *Generalbereinigung*. Tobias Winstel (Munich) is now working on a study on the course of negotiations and horizon of significance of the agreements, based on the documents.
109. As noted by Rolf Lahr, the head of the German delegation in negotiations with the Netherlands, in April 1959, quoted in Helmberger, *Generalbereinigung*, 88. Agreement in the German-French negotiations was achieved shortly before the Paris summit of May 1960; the German ambassador in Paris, Blankenhorn, had sent an urgent telegram to the Foreign Ministry on 3 May 1960 and pressed for "as great a level of German cooperation as possible" in order to conclude matters before the summit. He was able to convince Adenauer of this urgency (*Politisches Archiv des Auswärtigen Amtes*, B81, vol. 201).
110. Michael Lemke, "Kampagnen gegen Bonn. Die Systemkrise der DDR und die West-Propaganda der SED 1960–1963," *VfZ* 41 (1993): 153–174.
111. On the demands for compensation which the GDR was confronted with as a result of the wave of recognition of the state in 1972/73, see Peter Jochen Winters, "Die Außenpolitik der DDR," in *Handbuch der deutschen Außenpolitik*, ed. Hans-Peter Schwarz, 2nd ed. (Munich/Zurich, 1976), 769–812, here 809f.
112. That is how van Scherpenberg, State Secretary in the Foreign Ministry, argued in a letter on 16 February 1960 to Hetlage, State Secretary in the federal ministry of finance, in order to underscore his demand that the negotiations on the German-Greek global agreement be concluded positively and as quickly as possible. Quoted in Susanne-Sophia Spiliotis, "Der Fall Merten, Athen 1959: Ein Kriegsverbrecherprozeß im Spannungsfeld von Wiedergutmachungs- und Wirtschaftspolitik" (M.A. thesis, Munich, 1991), 147. See also the document from the Political Archive of the Foreign Ministry "Öffentlichkeitsarbeit der Bundesregierung im Zusammenhang mit dem Eichmannprozeß", reprinted in Jelinek, *Zwischen Moral und Realpolitik*, 584–586.

113. Thus, the British foreign minister Butler, in discussion with State Secretary Carstens (Foreign Ministry), pointed on 15 July 1964 to the "good political effect which the agreement on reparations has had in the House of Commons," see *AAPD* 1964, vol. 2 (Munich, 1995), 840.
114. § 4, paragraph 1c BEG or § 238a BEG-Schlußgesetz.
115. When a Yugoslav delegation visited the Foreign Ministry in Bonn in September 1963 to explore the question of reparations, State Secretary Lahr was critical of their stance: "You can't just recognize one part of Germany and then demand that the other part of Germany fulfill obligations binding on the nation as a whole" (*AAPD* 1963, Vol. 2, Munich 1994, 1175). In the same matter, in June 1963, State Secretary Carstens had scribbled on the margin of a report: "The Soviet Occupation Zone ought to take care of that!" (ibid., 678).
116. This estimate in Brodesser et.al., *Wiedergutmachung und Kriegsfolgenliquidation*, 108 is in my view realistic.
117. See the M.A. thesis by Stephanie Baumann, "Entschädigung für Opfer von Humanexperimenten" (Munich, 1992), which is based on ministry documents. The decision by the Cabinet discounted a memo from the federal finance ministry of 25 May 1960 which warned against "abandoning, even in a single partial area, the exclusion of victims living in the Eastern bloc, which has up to now been firmly anchored in reparations law"; ibid., 95.
118. It is disputed whether this decision to forego compensation was related only to the GDR or to all of Germany. However, the Potsdam Agreement directed the reparations claims of the Soviet Union almost completely to their own occupation zone.
119. Pavel Poljan, "Die Endphase der Repatriierung sowjetischer Kriegsgefangener und die komplizierten Wege ihrer Rehabilitierung," in *Die Tragödie der Gefangenschaft in Deutschland und in der Sowjetunion 1941–1856*, ed. Klaus-Dieter Müller, Konstantin Nikitschin and Günther Wagenlehner (Cologne/Weimar, 1998), 365–394.
120. In any case, there is no relevant agreement between Poland and the GDR. It is still necessary to investigate, based on archival documents, whether there were internal explorations or abortive negotiations. According to Féaux de la Croix and Rumpf, *Der Werdegang des Entschädigungsrechts*, 340, the countries of the Eastern bloc made their demands for compensation exclusively to Bonn. In doing so, they accorded West Germany sole liability, while at the same time denying it the sole right to represent all of Germany. As a memo from State Secretary Carstens (note 113) there was of course also the reverse contradiction according to which the Soviet Zone, though not recognized internationally as a sovereign state, was to bear co-liability.
121. Krzysztof Miszczak, *Deklarationen und Realitäten. Die Beziehungen zwischen der Bundesrepublik Deutschland und der (Volks-)Republik Polen von der Unterzeichnung des Warschauer Vertrages bis zum Abkommen über gute Nachbarschaft und freundschaftliche Zusammenarbeit 1970 bis 1991* (Munich, 1993).
122. Willy Brandt, *Begegnungen und Einsichten. Die Jahre 1960–1975* (Hamburg, 1976), 538; Arnulf Baring and Manfred Görtemaker, *Machtwechsel. Die Ära Brandt-Scheel* (Stuttgart, 1982), 486f. After this manuscript was completed, *AAPD* 1970, vol. 3, Munich 2001 appeared, with relevant documents.
123. The relevant agreement for this compensation was that of 16 November 1972. It provided for 100 million DM (plus 3 million DM in administrative costs). Among its champions was Carlo Schmid, the ranks of its opponents included federal finance minister Alex Möller. On 3 December 1969, he wrote to Schmid: "If I

contemplate that some day we are going to reach an understanding in negotiations with countries of the Eastern bloc on a lump-sum general reparations agreement, then I can only imagine in horror what a role an agreement like this will have to play in such negotiations. An agreement that awarded the limited group of the Polish victims of pseudo-medical experiments DM 120 million, in addition to the roughly 20 million paid out since 1960, adding up to some 140 million." See Weber, *Carlo Schmid*, 737.

124. Miszczak, *Deklarationen und Realitäten*, 90f.
125. Brandt, *Begegnungen und Einsichten*, 538.
126. The pattern for this form of indirect compensation was based on two agreements with Yugoslavia in 1972 und 1974 covering more than DM 1 billion. See Féaux de la Croix and Rumpf, *Der Werdegang des Entschädigungsrechts*, 342. But already in 1963, Yugoslavia ad proposed granting credits as a way to "settle *Wiedergutmachung*" (*AAPD* 1963, vol. 2, Munich 1994, 758).
127. On the German-Polish treaty package of 1975 (credits in the amount of 1 billion DM, pension agreements, understanding on emigration), see vgl. Pawlita, "'Wiedergutmachung' als Rechtsfrage?," 435–436; Misczcak, *Deklarationen und Realitäten*, 153–169.
128. *Die Vertreibung der Juden aus Polen 1968. Antisemitismus und politisches Kalkül*, ed. Beate Kosmala (Berlin, 2000).
129. Dissertation published as Walter Schwarz, *Rückerstattung und Entschädigung. Eine Abgrenzung der Wiedergutmachungsformen* (Munich, 1952).
130. Walter Schwarz, *Späte Frucht. Bericht aus unsteten Jahren* (Hamburg, 1981).
131. The periodical *Rechtsprechung zum Wiedergutmachungsrecht* (Legal Judgments on Reparations Legislation, RzW) began publication in November 1949 in the Verlag C.H. Beck, Munich, initially as a compendium of court case decisions in the form of a supplement to the *Neue Juristische Wochenschrift*. Beginning in 1957, when Schwarz took over a editor, it added a section of essays, and from July 1961 appeared as an independent periodical. In its three decades of existence, only three German professors published in its pages. A selection of the critical commentaries by Walter Schwarz has also appeared in book form *In den Wind gesprochen? Glossen zur Wiedergutmachung des nationalsozialistischen Unrechts* (Munich, 1969).
132. Franz Calvelli-Adorno, "Die rassische Verfolgung der Zigeuner vor dem 1. März 1943," *RzW* 12 (1961): 529–537; this is how he introduced the new direction in incorrect high court rulings.
133. See note 14.
134. Walter Schwarz, "Zum letzten Kapitel der Wiedergutmachung," *Aufbau*, 14 January 1983.
135. In his declaration of 17 May 1974, Helmut Schmidt emphasized that the government considered *Wiedergutmachung* a "closed chapter." See *Die großen Regierungserklärungen der deutschen Bundeskanzler von Adenauer bis Schmidt*, ed. Klaus von Beyme (Munich, 1979), 333.
136. *Wiedergutmachung* in social insurance, especially in pensions, a topic to date little researched, is considered irreproachable. The relevant legislation began in the Bi-Zone and was substantially improved, particularly in 1971. Since social insurance does not list such costs separately, they are not contained in the customary cost accounts for *Wiedergutmachung*.
137. Letter to the editor, from Walter Schwarz, *Die Zeit*, 26 October 1984, 40.

138. Path-breaking was a conference of the Evangelische Akademie Bad Boll in November 1983 (see fn. 33) and a "Zeit-Dossier": Dörte v. Westernhagen, "Wiedergutgemacht?," *Die Zeit*, 5 October 1984, 33–36.
139. See Pross, *Wiedergutmachung*, S. 22.
140. See note 138.
141. The factor of generation in Mannheim's sense is instructive here, including the general rule that later generation units tend to choose certain leading figures from earlier generation units as mentors and sources of moral authentication. In the present context, Otto Küster became such a leading figure and mentor, see esp. Pross, *Wiedergutmachung*. Yet Pross overlooked the fact that is was precisely Küster who also had opposed including "asocial elements," victims of eugenic forced sterilization and Gypsies in the group of individuals entitled to compensation. On the question of generations, see Karl Mannheim, "Das Problem der Generationen," in: idem, *Wissenssoziologie. Auswahl aus dem Werk*, ed. Kurt H. Wolff (Berlin/Neuwied, 1964), 509–565 (first published in 1928).
142. See note 138. He was very hurt by the remark by Otto Küster recorded in the Bad Boll minutes (87): "The spokespersons for the Jews almost all are receiving this pension (occupational injury, H. G. H.), and to the extent their heart is not overflowing with sympathy for their fellow Jews who met a tragic fate, they might think they themselves were lacking in gratitude if they did not extoll our reparations (*Wiedergutmachung*)."
143. Kurt May, at that time an aging director of the Central Office of the URO, which all-told represented some 300,000 clients in matters of restitution and compensations, wrote me in 1988 regarding the book by Pross (subtitled "The Running Battle Against the Victims") that had just appeared. He had a very vehement negative opinion of the book and added that he would not permit staff at the URO to refer to the examples presented by Pross. More balanced than the title of the book, *Die Kehrseite der "Wiedergutmachung". Das Leiden von NS-Verfolgten in den Entschädigungsverfahren. Mit einem Vorwort von Hans Koschnick*, ed. Helga and Hermann Fischer-Hübner (Gerlingen, 1990), the authors note (24f.): Those "entitled have always spoken positively about the practice of compensation," especially persons who received benefits in the form of pensions. "It was precisely victims of persecution who, despite all the criticism, wished to see '*Wiedergutmachung*' evaluated as a whole. And in this sense regarded it positively as a lasting German achievement. On the other hand, it was impossible to overlook the fact that in far too many individual cases, there have been unjust and unsympathetic decisions."
144. The latter crime was termed in Nazi parlance "*Wehrkraftzersetzung*." Thus, for example, in 1983 a Projektgruppe für die vergessenen Opfer des NS-Regimes in Hamburg e.V. (Project Group for the Forgotten Victims of Nazism in Hamburg) was set up; it published the volume: *Verachtet—verfolgt—vernichtet. Zu den "vergessenen" Opfern des NS-Regimes* (Hamburg, 1986). On the echo of this topic in the press, see for example: "Die vergessenen Nazi-Opfer," *Frankfurter Rundschau*, 13 February 1986, 4; on its resonance in the church, see *Vergessene Opfer. Kirchliche Stimmen zu den unerledigten Fragen der Wiedergutmachung an nationalsozialistischen Opfern*, ed. Kirchenamt der Evangelischen Kirche in Deutschland (EKD) (Hannover, 1987). A Catholic Working Group published Laszlo Schirilla, *Wiedergutmachung für Nationalgeschädigte. Ein Bericht über die Benachteiligung von Opfern der nationalsozialistischen Gewaltherrschaft* (Munich, 1982) in its series.

145. Hans-Dieter Kreikamp, "Zur Entstehung des Entschädigungsgesetzes der amerikanischen Besatzungszone," in Herbst and Goschler, *Wiedergutmachung in der Bundesrepublik Deutschland*, 61–75; Goschler, *Wiedergutmachung*, 134f.; Hudemann, *Anfänge der Wiedergutmachung*; Regina Hennig, *Entschädigung und Interessenvertretung der NS-Verfolgten in Niedersachsen 1945–49* (Bielefeld, 1991), 36f.
146. Stefan Kühl, Die Internationale der Rassisten. Aufstieg und Niedergang der internationalen Bewegung für Eugenik und Rassenhygiene im 20. Jahrhundert (Frankfurt a.M., 1997). In the Reparations Committee of the Bundestag, Franz Böhm (CDU) had proposed to generally include victims of sterilization in the group of those entitled to benefits, because in the Third Reich a proper and legal sterilization procedure had been impossible. This view was opposed inter alia by the committee chair Greve (SPD); argument in such questions of inclusion and exclusion was at right angles to the party boundaries (Protokoll der 19. Sitzung des Ausschusses für Fragen der Wiedergutmachung vom 7. Februar 1956, 19/20; Parlamentsarchiv des Deutschen Bundestages, II 273) . On eugenic sterilization in the United States, see "Study Finds Similarities in U.S. and Nazi Eugenics Efforts," *Yale Bulletin and Calendar*, vol. 28:21, 18 February 2000. "By 1944, 30 states with sterilization laws had reported a total of more than 40,000 eugenical sterilizations—with those sterilized reported as insane or feebleminded. In the pre-Nazi period, German eugenicists expressed admiration for American leadership in instituting sterilization programs and communicated with their American colleagues about strategies.... Despite waning scientific and public support and the history of the human rights abuses of Nazi Germany, state-sponsored sterilizations in the U.S. continued long after the war, totaling approximately 22,000 in 27 states between 1943–63."
147. On the context of the history of persecution of these groups, see Gisela Bock, *Zwangssterilisation im Nationalsozialismus. Studien zur Rassenpolitik und Frauenpolitik* (Opladen, 1986); Wolfgang Ayaß, *"Asoziale" im Nationalsozialismus* (Stuttgart, 1995); Patrick Wagner, *Volksgemeinschaft ohne Verbrecher. Konzeptionen und Praxis der Kriminalpolizei in der Zeit der Weimarer Republik und des Nationalsozialismus* (Hamburg, 1996); Burckhard Jelloneck, *Homosexuelle unterm Hakenkreuz* (Paderborn, 1990).
148. Herbert, "Nicht entschädigungsfähig?," 294.
149. Ulrich von Hehl, *Nationalsozialistische Herrschaft* (Munich, 1996), 110–115.
150. *Anerkennung aller Opfer nationalsozialistischer Verfolgung*, ed. Die Grünen im Bundestag/Fraktion der Alternativen Liste Berlin (Bonn, 1986). The sudden spurt in parliamentary interest is reflected in the number of entries under "*Wiedergutmachung* of National Socialist injustice" in the index to the proceedings of the German Bundestag and Bundesrat: entries for the 8th legislative period (1976–80) fill two columns, for the 9th (1980–83) about a column and a half; for the 10th period (1983–87) there are, in marked contrast, eight and a half columns.
151. "Bericht der Bundesregierung über Wiedergutmachung und Entschädigung für nationalsozialistisches Unrecht sowie über die Lage der Sinti und Roma und verwandter Gruppen." Deutscher Bundestag, Drucksache 10/6287 vom 31. Oktober 1986; *Wiedergutmachung und Entschädigung für nationalsozialistisches Unrecht. Öffentliche Anhörung des Innenausschusses des Deutschen Bundestages am 24. Juni 1987*, ed. Deutscher Bundestag (Zur Sache; 87/3) (Bonn, 1987).
152. In the sense of the typology developed above: juridical rehabilitation. On this see Vogl, *Stückwerk und Verdrängung*. Symptomatic is the decision of the Bundestag,

25 January 1985, to the effect that the decisions of the National Socialist Volksgerichtshof had no legal validity.

153. A film version telecast by the ARD in1984 caused a sensation, see Benjamin B. Ferencz, *Lohn des Grauens. Die Entschädigung jüdischer Zwangsarbeiter. Ein offenes Kapitel deutscher Nachkriegsgeschichte* (Frankfurt a.M., 1981).

154. A survey of work in the 1980s: Hans-Ulrich Ludewig, "Zwangsarbeit im Zweiten Weltkrieg. Forschungsstand und Ergebnisse regionaler und lokaler Forschungen," *Archiv für Sozialgeschichte* 31 (1991): 558–577; a more recent overview of research in Mark Spoerer, "Zwangsarbeit im Dritten Reich, Verantwortung und Entschädigung," *GWU* 51 (2000): 508–527.

155. On the following, see Angelika Timm, *Jewish Claims against East Germany: Moral Obligations and Pragmatic Policy* (Budapest, 1997); idem, *Hammer, Zirkel, Davidstern*; Lothar Mertens, *Davidstern unter Hammer und Zirkel. Die Jüdischen Gemeinden in der SBZ/DDR und ihre Behandlung durch Partei und Staat 1945–1990* (Hildesheim, 1997); Jeffrey Herf, *Zweierlei Erinnerung. Die NS-Vergangenheit im geteilten Deutschland* (Berlin, 1998); Constantin Goschler, "Nicht bezahlt? Die Wiedergutmachung für Opfer der nationalsozialistischen Verfolgung in der SBZ/DDR," in *Wirtschaftliche Folgelasten des Krieges in der SBZ/DDR*, ed. Christoph Buchheim (Baden-Baden, 1995), 169–191; Constantin Goschler, "Wiedergutmachung als Vergangenheitsbewältigung," *Bohemia* 34 (1993): 295–304.

156. In summary form and with no illusions regarding the degree of accuracy that is methodologically achievable in terms of quantity and value: Christoph Buchheim, "Kriegsschäden, Demontagen und Reparationen. Deutschland nach dem Zweiten Weltkrieg," in *Materialien der Enquete-Kommission "Aufarbeitung von Geschichte und Folgen der SED-Diktatur in Deutschland"*, ed. Deutscher Bundestag, vol. II/2 (Baden-Baden, 1995), 1030–1069.

157. This direction is evidenced by the birth of that political clause from the spirit and matrix of the struggle in and for Berlin. It appears for the first time in the Berlin Law on Compensation of 8 January 1951, whose § 2, sec. 1 excluded individuals "who fight against the democratic form of government as adherents of a totalitarian system." The committee deliberations in the Bundestag on the Federal Supplementary Law (see inter alia "Sitzungsprotokoll des 23. Ausschusses am 7. Mai 1953," in *Parlamentsarchiv des Deutschen Bundestages*, I 537, A 2.) referred to this clause in the Berlin legislation.

158. See Gotthard Jasper, "Die disqualifizierten Opfer. Der Kalte Krieg und die Entschädigung für Kommunisten," in Herbst and Goschler, *Wiedergutmachung in der Bundesrepublik Deutschland*, 361–384. For a contrasting view, see Frank M. Bischoff and Hans-Jürgen Höötmann, "Wiedergutmachung. Erschließung von Entschädigungsakten im Staatsarchiv Münster," *Der Archivar* 51 (1998): 425–440, where the rulings of the Compensation Office in Arnsberg from 1954 to 1958 are evaluated: the requests of 2,416 persons who listed membership in the Communist Party (KPD) as the reason for their persecution were granted in 86 percent of the cases.

159. Ralf Kessler and Hartmut Rüdiger Peter, *Wiedergutmachung im Osten Deutschlands 1945–1953. Grundsätzliche Diskussionen und die Praxis in Sachsen-Anhalt* (Frankfurt a.M., 1996), 203–209; Gerald Hacke, *Zeugen Jehovas in der DDR. Verfolgung und Verhalten einer religiösen Minderheit* (Dresden, 2000).

160. Jürgen Danyel, "Die Opfer- und Verfolgtenperspektive als Gründungskonsens? Zum Umgang mit der Widerstandstradition und der Schuldfrage in der DDR,"

in *Die geteilte Vergangenheit. Zum Umgang mit Nationalsozialismus und Widerstand in beiden deutschen Staaten*, ed. Jürgen Danyel (Berlin, 1995), 31–46; Ralf Kessler and Hartmut Rüdiger Peter, "Antifaschisten in der SBZ. Zwischen elitärem Selbstverständnis und politischer Instrumentalisierung," *VfZ* 43 (1995): 611–633.

161. On the inclusion of the "patriots" among the "former Nazis" subsequent to an order from Stalin, see Wladimir K.Wolkow, "Die deutsche Frage aus Stalins Sicht (1947–1952)," *Zeitschrift für Geschichtswissenschaft* 48 (2000): 20–49. On the dissolution of the VVN, see Elke Reuter and Detlef Hansel, *Das kurze Leben der VVN von 1947 bis 1953. Die Geschichte der Vereinigung der Verfolgten des Naziregimes in der SBZ und in der DDR* (Berlin, 1997).
162. Decision by the CC of the SED, 25 November 1952, quoted in Timm, *Hammer, Zirkel, Davidstern*, 117. On Merker, see also Herf, *Zweierlei Erinnerung*, 138–193; on the relation between "Aryanization" and nationalization, see likewise Karen Hartewig, *Zurückgekehrt. Die Geschichte der jüdischen Kommunisten in der DDR* (Cologne, 2000).
163. The 1945 Law on *Wiedergutmachung* in Thuringia offered a further variant of restitution in the Soviet Zone. But it was soon eliminated by the SED and Soviet Military Administration in Germany (SMAD). See Thomas Schüler, "Das Wiedergutmachungsgesetz vom 14. September 1945 in Thüringen," *Jahrbuch für Antisemitismusforschung* 2 (1993): 118–138.
164. On the relevant § 1, sec. 6 of the Law on Property, its amendments and the later (1994) Law on Compensation and Equalization as an alternative to natural restitution, see Christina Eck, *Die Wiedergutmachung zwischen 1945 und 1989 und die Regelung der Ansprüche von Verfolgten des Nationalsozialismus in § 1 Absatz 6 VermG* (München, 1996); Fritz Ossenbühl, "Eigentumsfragen," in *Handbuch des Staatsrechts der Bundesrepublik Deutschland*, ed. Josef Isensee and Paul Kirchhof, vol. 9: Die Einheit Deutschlands: Festigung und Übergang (Heidelberg, 1997), 521–585, esp. 530f., 567, 573. See also the Hamburg dissertation by Philipp Spannuth, *Rückerstattung Ost: Der Umgang der DDR mit dem „arisierten" und enteigneten jüdischen Eigentum und die Gestaltung der Rückerstattung im wiedervereinigten Deutschland*, available online in full: Freiburger Dokumentenserver, http://www.freidok.uni-freiburg.de/volltexte/262 (18 September 2004).
165. Oral communication from an associate at the time in the Chancellor's office. The whole affair has not been included in the following volume, which points up the discreet style with which the Kohl government dealt with questions and matters Jewish: *Deutsche Einheit. Sonderedition aus den Akten des Bundeskanzleramtes 1989/90*, ed. Hanns Jürgen Küsters and Daniel Hofmann (München, 1998). That restitution relating to the Nazi period was part of the agenda of the George Bush (senior) administration is documented by Philip Zelikow and Condoleezza Rice, *Germany Unified and Europe Transformed: A Study in Statecraft* (Cambridge, 1995), 354f.
166. As the Federal Office on the Settlement of Open Questions on Property informed me on 24 May 2000, the proceedings in accordance with § 1 paragraph 6, Vermögensgesetz, are not listed separately.
167. See Fred David, "Die Krupps von Suhl," *Die Woche*, 4 March 1993, 13. On return of the assets of the SED, expropriated in 1933 and taken over by the SED in 1946, as well as the assets of the Social Democratic Workers' Sports Associations, see Brunner, *50 Jahre Konzentration*, 120–122.
168. Goschler, *Wiedergutmachung als Vergangenheitsbewältigung*, 301.

169. Ibid., 302.
170. This plastic comparison in value is made by Angelika Timm, *Alles umsonst? Verhandlungen zwischen der Claims Conference und der DDR über "Wiedergutmachung" und Entschädigung* (Berlin, 1996), 22.
171. Timm, *Jewish Claims against East Germany*; Patrick Moreau et.al., "Die Politik der letzten SED-Regierung und ihre Folgen," in *Materialien der Enquete-Kommission "Überwindung der Folgen der SED-Diktatur im Prozeß der deutschen Einheit"*, ed. Deutscher Bundestag, vol. 8/3 (Baden-Baden, 1999), 2008–2173, here 2147–2164.
172. Memo, Ministerialdirigent Duisberg, 13 September 1990, in Küsters and Hofmann, *Deutsche Einheit. Sonderedition aus den Akten des Bundeskanzleramtes 1989/90*, 1539–1541.
173. Wilhelm Tappert, *Die Wiedergutmachung von Staatsunrecht der SBZ/DDR durch die Bundesrepublik Deutschland nach der Wiedervereinigung* (Berlin, 1995); on the situation of the victims of the SED dictatorship and their rehabilitation, see *Materialien der Enquete-Kommission "Überwindung der Folgen der SED-Diktatur im Prozeß der deutschen Einheit,"* ed. Deutscher Bundestag, vol. II/2 (Baden-Baden, 1999), 101–390.
174. A convincing typology of the manifestations of SED injustice is provided by Klaus Marxen and Gerhard Werle, *Die strafrechtliche Aufarbeitung von DDR-Unrecht. Eine Bilanz* (Berlin/New York, 1999).
175. On their appropriate inclusion in the culture of memory, see vol. 6, *Materialien der Enquete-Kommission "Überwindung der Folgen der SED-Diktatur im Prozeß der deutschen Einheit"*, ed. Deutscher Bundestag (Baden-Baden, 1999) ("Gesamtdeutsche Formen der Erinnerung an die beiden deutschen Diktaturen und ihre Opfer—Archive"). On competition between the groups of victims and the changing phases in their public image, see Friedhelm Boll, "Beobachtungen aus lebensgeschichtlichen Interviews mit Verfolgten des Nationalsozialismus und mit Verfolgten der SBZ/DDR," in *Die Vergangenheit läßt uns nicht los*, ed. Klaus Dieter Müller and Annegret Stephan (Berlin, 1998), 153–172; see also Claus-Eberhard Boetzel, "Zur unterschiedlichen Behandlung von Verfolgten des Nationalsozialismus und des Stalinismus/Kommunismus," *Deutschland Archiv* 27 (1994): 1084–1096.
176. This is the form of the Article 2 Agreement that the federal government concluded on 29 October 1992 with the Claims Conference in accordance with Article 2 of the Supplementary Agreement of 18 September 1990 on the Unification Treaty. From 1993 to 1999, the Federal Republic paid out DM 1 billion in the framework of this agreement.
177. See especially the memo on the talk between the Chancellor and President George Bush at Camp David, 24 February 1990, in Küsters and Hofmann, *Deutsche Einheit. Sonderedition aus den Akten des Bundeskanzleramtes 1989/90*, 860–874. The following quotes taken from there.
178. It is not clear how Kohl arrived at such a high figure. Hermann Mosler and Karl Doehring, *Die Beendigung des Kriegszustands mit Deutschland nach dem zweiten Weltkrieg* (Cologne/Berlin, 1963), 443 and 452 enumerate "55 countries (without those in the Eastern bloc)," and there were eight countries counted in the East.
179. Submission by Ministerialdirektor Teltschik to Chancellor Kohl, 15 March 1990, in: Küsters and Hofmann, *Deutsche Einheit. Sonderedition aus den Akten des Bundeskanzleramtes 1989/90*, 955f.

180. By contrast, a clause on reunification in the London Agreement on External German Debts led in 1990 to a certain resurrection of debt management that will probably be continued up to 2010. See Philipp Heyde, *Das Ende der Reparationen. Deutschland, Frankreich und der Youngplan 1929–1932* (Paderborn, 1998), 455.
181. Herbert Küpper, "Die Wiedergutmachung nationalsozialistischen Unrechts in den Nachfolgestaaten der Sowjetunion," *Osteuropa* 7 (1996): 639–656; idem, "Die Wiedergutmachung nationalsozialistischen Unrechts in den Staaten Osteuropas," *Osteuropa* 7 (1996): 758–768. Experience with the administration of this fund is not completely positive. Thus, in the fall of 2000, a Ukrainian politician was arrested in Hanover under suspicion of having embezzled some 86 million DM. See "Millionenbetrug mit Fonds für Nazi-Opfer?," *Neue Zürcher Zeitung*, 17 October 2000.
182. See for details Ferencz, *Lohn des Grauens* and Barwig et.al., *Entschädigung für NS-Zwangsarbeit.*
183. The ruling of the Federal Supreme Court of 13 May 1996 is reprinted in Barwig et.al., *Entschädigung für NS-Zwangsarbeit*, 222–247.
184. The "Final Act" was signed on 17 July 2000 by representatives of the German economy, the federal government, the governments of the U.S., Israel, Poland, the Czech Republic, Belarus, the Ukraine and the Russian Federation, the Claims Conference and a number of attorneys for plaintiffs. The Law on the Establishment of a Foundation "Memory, Responsibility and the Future" of 2 August 2000 created a fund into which the German government and German business each contributed 5 billion DM.
185. On the Equalization of Burdens Law, see now the major study in English: Michael L. Hughes, *Shouldering the Burdens of Defeat: West Germany and the Reconstruction of Social Justice* (Chapel Hill, 1999).

Selected Bibliography

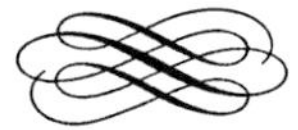

Abrams, Bradley F. "Morality, Wisdom and Revision: The Czech Opposition of the 1970s and the Expulsion of the Sudeten Germans." *East European Politics & Societies* 9 (1995): 234–255.

Adamovich, Ludwig. "Das Unbehagen in der Zweiten Republik." In *querela iuris. Gedächtnisschrift für Eduard Rabofsky.* Vienna and New York, 1996.

Adorno, Theodor, and Max Horkheimer. *Dialectic of Enlightenment.* New York, 1999 (first published in 1944).

Adunka, Evelyn. *Der Raub der Bücher—Plünderung in der NS-Zeit und Restitution nach 1945.* Vienna, 2002.

Alexander, Manfred. "Die tschechische Diskussion über die Vertreibung der Deutschen und deren Folgen." *Bohemia* 34 (1993): 390–409.

Altaras, Thea. *Synagogen in Hessen. Was geschah seit 1945? Eine Dokumentation und Analyse aus allen 221 hessischen Orten, deren Synagogenbauten die Pogromnacht 1938 und den 2. Weltkrieg überstanden. 223 architektonische Beschreibungen und Bauhistorien.* Königstein i. Taunus, 1988.

Anders, Günther. *Die Antiquiertheit des Menschen.* 2 vols. Munich, 2002.

Arendt, Hannah. *The Origins of Totalitarianism.* New York, 1951.

———. "Organized Guilt and Universal Responsibility." In *Collective Responsibility: Five Decades of Debate in Theoretical and Applied Ethics*, ed. Larry May and Stacey Hoffman. Savage, Maryland, 1991, 273–284.

Arning, Matthias. *Späte Abrechnung. Über Zwangsarbeiter, Schlussstriche und Berliner Verständigungen.* Frankfurt a.M., 2001.

Ashplant, T.G., Graham Dawson, and Michael Roper, ed. *The Politics of War Memory and Commemoration.* London and New York, 2000.

Assmann, Aleida, and Ute Frevert. *Geschichtsvergessenheit, Geschichtsversessenheit. Vom Umgang mit deutschen Vergangenheiten nach 1945.* Stuttgart, 1999.

Augustin, Milan. "Die Vertreibung der Deutschen aus tschechischer Sicht." *Sudetenland* 40 (1998): 206–241.

Authers, John, and Richard Wolffe. *The Victim's Fortune: Inside the Epic Battle over the Debts of the Holocaust.* New York, 2002.

Azaryahu, Maoz. "A Tale Of Two Cities: Commemorating The Israeli War Of Independence in Tel Aviv and Haifa." *Cathedra* 68 (1993): 98–125 (Hebrew).

Bachman, Gábor, László Rajk, and Miklós Peternák. *Ravatal. Catafalque.* [Laying Out.] Budapest, 1989.

Bachmann, Klaus, and Jerzy Kranz, ed. *Verlorene Heimat. Die Vertreibungsdebatte in Polen.* Bonn, 1998.

Baeyer, Walter v., Heinz Häfner, and Karl Peter Kisker. *Psychiatrie der Verfolgten. Psychopathologische und gutachtliche Erfahrungen an Opfern der nationalsozialistischen Verfolgung und vergleichbarer Extrembelastungen.* Berlin, 1964.

Bähr, Johannes, and Michael C. Schneider. *Der Goldhandel der Dresdner Bank im Zweiten Weltkrieg. Ein Bericht des Hannah-Arendt-Instituts.* Leipzig, 1999.

Bailer-Galanda, Brigitte. *Wiedergutmachung kein Thema. Österreich und die Opfer des Nationalsozialismus.* Vienna, 1993.

———. *Haider wörtlich. Führer in die Dritte Republik.* Vienna, 1995.

———. "Alle waren Opfer. Der selektive Umgang mit den Folgen des Nationalsozialismus." In *Inventur 45/55. Österreich im ersten Jahrzehnt der Zweiten Republik,* ed. Wolfgang Kos and Georg Rigele. Vienna, 1996, 181-200.

———, Eva Blimlinger, and Susanne Kowarc. *"Arisierung" und Rückstellung von Wohnungen in Wien. Die Vertreibung der jüdischen Mieter und Mieterinnen aus ihren Wohnungen und das verhinderte Wohnungsrückstellungsgesetz.* Vienna, 2000.

———. "Die Opfer des Nationalsozialismus und die so genannte Wiedergutmachung." In *NS-Herrschaft in Österreich. Ein Handbuch,* ed. Emmerich Tálos, Ernst Hanisch, Wolfgang Neugebauer, and Reinhard Sieder. Vienna, 2000, 892–894.

———. *Die Entstehung der Rückstellungs- und Entschädigungsgesetzgebung. Die Republik Österreich und das in der NS-Zeit entzogene Vermögen.* Vienna and Munich, 2003.

Bajohr, Frank. *"Arisierung" in Hamburg. Die Verdrängung der jüdischen Unternehmer 1933–1945.* Hamburg 1997.

———. "Verfolgung aus gesellschaftsgeschichtlicher Perspektive. Die wirtschaftliche Existenzvernichtung der Juden und die deutsche Gesellschaft." *Geschichte und Gesellschaft* 26 (2000): 629–652.

Balabkins, Nicholas. *West German Reparations to Israel.* New Brunswick, 1971.

Barkan, Elazar. *The Guilt of Nations: Restitution and Negotiating Historical Injustices.* New York, 2000.

Bárkány, Eugen, and Łudovít Dojč. *Židovské náboženské obce na Slovensku.* [The Jewish Religious Communities in Slovakia.] Bratislava, 1991.

Barta-Fliedl, Ilsebill, and Herbert Posch. *inventARISIERT. Enteignung von Möbeln aus jüdischem Besitz.* Vienna, 2000.

Barwig, Klaus, Günter Saathoff, and Nicole Weyde, ed. *Entschädigung für NS-Zwangsarbeit. Rechtliche, historische und politische Aspekte.* Baden-Baden, 1998.

Bauman, Zygmunt. *Holocaust and Modernity.* Cambridge, 1989.

Baumann, Ulrich. *Zerstörte Nachbarschaften. Christen und Juden in badischen Landgemeinden 1862–1940.* Hamburg, 2000.

Bazyler, Michael. "Holocaust Restitution Litigation in the United States: A Triumph of American Justice." Paper presented in conference "Confronting the Past: Memory, Identity, and Society," 4–5 February 2001, UCLA Center for Jewish Studies.

Bechtold-Comforty, Beate. "Jüdische Frauen auf dem Dorf—zwischen Eigenständigkeit und Integration." *Sozialwissenschaftliche Informationen* 18, no. 3 (1989): 157–169.

Becker, Franziska. *Gewalt und Gedächtnis. Erinnerungen an die nationalsozialistische Verfolgung einer jüdischen Landgemeinde.* Göttingen, 1994.

Ben-Artzi, Yossef. *Residential Patterns and Intra Urban Migration of Arabs in Haifa.* Haifa, 1980 (Hebrew).

———, and Tamir Goren. "Molding the Urban Space Of Haifa: Arabs in 1948." *Studies in the Geography Of Israel* 15 (1998): 7–27 (Hebrew).

Benjamin, Walter. "Capitalism as Religion." (1921) In *Selected Writings.* ed. Marcus Bullock and Michael W. Jennings. vol. 1, 1913–1926. Harvard, 1996.

Benvenisti, Miron. "The Hebrew Map." *Theory and Criticism* 11 (1997): 7–29 (Hebrew).

Benziman, Uzi, and Atallah Mansour. *Subtenants.* Jerusalem, 1992.

Berg, Nicolas. *Der Holocaust und die westdeutschen Historiker. Erforschung und Erinnerung.* Göttingen, 2003.

Berghoff, Hartmut. "Zwischen Verdrängung und Aufarbeitung. Die bundesdeutsche Gesellschaft und ihre nationalsozialistische Vergangenheit in den Fünfziger Jahren." *Vierteljahrshefte für Zeitgeschichte* 49 (2001): 167–214.

Bergmann, Werner. *Antisemitismus in öffentlichen Konflikten. Kollektives Lernen in der politischen Kultur der Bundesrepublik 1949–1989.* Frankfurt a.M. and New York, 1997.

Bergötz, Sven Olaf. *Nahostpolitik in der Ära Adenauer. Möglichkeiten und Grenzen 1949–1963.* Düsseldorf, 1998.

Bethke, Susann. "Die Entwicklung der tschechoslowakischen Diskussion um die Vertreibung der Deutschen." *Deutsche Ostkunde,* no. 3 (1992): 95–108.

Bibó, István. *Zur Judenfrage. Am Beispiel Ungarns nach 1944.* Frankfurt a.M., 1990.

Birkwald, Ilse. "Ein Opfer der Finanzverwaltung. Der ganz normale Fall Oppenheim vor und nach 1945." In *Verfolgung und Verwaltung. Die wirtschaftliche Ausplünderung der Juden und die westfälischen Finanzbehörden,* ed. Alfons Kenkmann and Bernd-A. Rusinek. Münster, 1999, 102–121.

Bischof, Günter. *Austria and the First Cold War, 1945–1955: The Leverage of the Weak.* Basingstoke, 1999.

Bischoff, Frank M., and Hans-Jürgen Höötmann. "Wiedergutmachung. Erschließung von Entschädigungsakten im Staatsarchiv Münster." *Der Archivar* 51 (1998): 425–440.

Blänsdorf, Agnes. "Zur Konfrontation mit der NS-Vergangenheit in der Bundesrepublik, der DDR und in Österreich: Entnazifizierung und Wiedergutmachungsleistungen." *Aus Politik und Zeitgeschichte*, no. 16/17 (1987): 3–18.

Boetzel, Claus-Eberhard. "Zur unterschiedlichen Behandlung von Verfolgten des Nationalsozialismus und des Stalinismus/Kommunismus." *Deutschland Archiv* 27 (1994): 1084–1096.

Böhm, Hans. *Reden und Schriften*, ed. Ernst-Joachim Mestmäcker. Karlsruhe, 1960.

Boll, Friedhelm. "Beobachtungen aus lebensgeschichtlichen Interviews mit Verfolgten des Nationalsozialismus und mit Verfolgten der SBZ/DDR." In *Die Vergangenheit läßt uns nicht los*, ed. Klaus Dieter Müller and Annegret Stephan. Berlin, 1998, 153–172.

Bömelburg, Hans-Jürgen, Renate Stößinger, and Robert Traba, ed. *Vertreibung aus dem Osten. Deutsche und Polen erinnern sich.* Olsztyn, 2000.

Borin, Jacqueline. "Embers of the Soul: The Destruction of Jewish Books and Libraries in Poland during World War II." *Libraries & Culture* 28, no. 4 (1993): 445–460.

Borneman, John. *After the Wall: East Meets West in the New Berlin.* New York, 1991.

———. *Belonging in the Two Berlins: Kin, State, Nation.* New York, 1992.

———. "Can Public Apologies Contribute to Peace? An Argument For Retribution." *The Anthropology of East Europe Review* 17 (1997): 7–20.

Borodziej, Włodzimierz. "'Każdemu należy się jego korona'. Wokół dyskusji o wysiedleniach Niemców z Polski." ["Each Deserves his Own Crown." Remarks on the Discussion Regarding the Expulsion of the Germans from Poland.] *Odra* 37, no. 1 (1997): 25–29.

———, and Artur Hajnicz. "Raport końcowy." [Final Report.] In *Kompleks wypędzenia.* [The Complex of Expulsion.] ed. Włodzimierz Borodziej. Kraków, 1998, 373–429.

———, and Hans Lemberg, ed. *'Unsere Heimat ist uns ein fremdes Land geworden...' Die Deutschen östlich von Oder und Neiße 1945–1950. Dokumente aus polnischen Archiven.* Marburg/Lahn, 2000.

Botz, Gerhard, and Gerald Sprengnagel, ed. *Kontroversen um Österreichs Zeitgeschichte. Verdrängte Vergangenheit, Österreich-Identität, Waldheim und die Historiker.* Frankfurt a.M. and New York, 1994.

Brandes, Detlef. *Der Weg zur Vertreibung 1938–1945. Pläne und Entscheidungen zum "Transfer" der Deutschen aus der Tschechoslowakei und Polen. Mit einem Vorwort von Hans Lemberg.* Munich, 2001.

Braun, Karl. "Die Bibliothek in Theresienstadt 1942–1945. Zur Rolle einer Leseinstitution in der 'Endlösung der Judenfrage'." *Bohemia* 40, no. 2 (1999): 367–386.

Brodesser, Hermann-Josef et. al. *Wiedergutmachung und Kriegsfolgenliquidation. Geschichte—Regelungen—Zahlungen.* Munich, 2000.

Brooks, Roy L., ed. *When Sorry Isn't Enough: The Controversy Over Apologies and Reparations for Human Injustice.* New York, 1999.

Brunner, Detlev. *50 Jahre Konzentration GmbH. Die Geschichte eines sozialdemokratischen Unternehmens 1946–1996*. Berlin, 1996.

Buchheim, Christoph. "Londoner Schuldenabkommen." In *Deutschland unter alliierter Besatzung 1945–1949/55*, ed. Wolfgang Benz. Berlin, 1999, 355–357.

Bundesministerium der Finanzen. *Entschädigung von NS-Unrecht. Regelungen zur Wiedergutmachung*. Berlin, 2001.

Buras, Piotr, and Piotr Majewski, ed. *Pamięć wypędzonych. Grass, Beneš i środkowoeuropejskie rozrachunki*. [The Memory of the Expellees. Grass, Beneš and Central European Statements.] Warsaw, 2003.

Burke, Peter. "Geschichte als soziales Gedächtnis." In *Mnemosyne. Formen und Funktionen der kulturellen Erinnerung*, ed. Aleida Assmann and Dietrich Harth. Frankfurt a.M., 1991, 289–304.

Carlyle, Thomas. "Chartism." In *Selected Writings*. Harmondsworth, 1971 (first published in 1839).

Carrillo, Elisa A. *Alcide de Gasperi: The Long Apprenticeship*. Notre Dame, 1965.

Cerný, Bohumil et al., ed. *Češi, Němci, Odsun. Diskuse nezávislých historiků*. [Czechs, Germans, Deportation. The Discussion among Independent Historians.] Prague, 1990.

Chaumont, Jean-Michel. *Die Konkurrenz der Opfer. Genozid, Identität und Anerkennung*. Lüneburg, 2001 (first published in Paris, 1997).

Chodakiewicz, Marek Jan. *Zydzi i Polacy 1918–1955. Wspólistnienie, Zaglada, Komunizm*. [Jews and Poles 1918–1955. Coexistence, Destruction, Communism.] Warsaw, 2000.

Craig, Gordon A. *Europe Since 1815*. New York, 1971.

Dahan-Kalev, Henriette. *"Self Organizing Systems: Wadi Salib and 'The Black Panthers'—Implications for Israeli Society."* Ph.D. diss., Hebrew University Jerusalem, 1991 (Hebrew).

Dahm, Volker. *Das Jüdische Buch im Dritten Reich*. 2nd rev. ed. Munich, 1993.

Danyel, Jürgen, ed. *Die geteilte Vergangenheit. Zum Umgang mit Nationalsozialismus und Widerstand in beiden deutschen Staaten*. Berlin, 1995.

Dawidowicz, Lucy S. *What is the Use of Jewish History?: Essays*, ed. Neal Kozodoy. New York, 1992.

De Zayas, Alfred-Maurice, and Charles M. Barber. *A Terrible Revenge: The Ethnic Cleansing of the East European Germans, 1944–1950*. New York, 1994.

Deák, István, Jan T. Gross, and Tony Judt, ed. *The Politics of Retribution in Europe: World War II and its Aftermath*. Princeton, 2003.

Dean, Martin. "The Plundering of Jewish Property in Europe. Five Recent Publications Documenting Property Seizure and Restitution in Germany, Belgium, Norway, and Belarus." *Holocaust and Genocide Studies* 15 (2001): 86–97.

Dehmlow, Raimund, ed. *Bücher und Bibliotheken in Ghettos und Lagern (1933–1945)*. Hannover, 1991.

Deutsche Bundesbank, ed. *Fünfzig Jahre Deutsche Mark. Notenbank und Währung in Deutschland seit 1948.* Munich, 1998.

Diner, Dan. *Der Krieg der Erinnerungen und die Ordnung der Welt.* Berlin, 1991.

———. "Kontraphobisch. Über Engführungen des Politischen." In ibid. *Kreisläufe. Nationalsozialismus und Gedächtnis.* Berlin, 1995, 95–111.

———. "Über Schulddiskurse und andere Narrative. Epistemologisches zum Holocaust." In *Bruchlinien. Tendenzen der Holocaustforschung,* ed. Gertrud Koch. Cologne, Weimar, and Vienna, 1999, 61–84.

———. *Das Jahrhundert verstehen. Eine universalhistorische Deutung.* Frankfurt a.M., 2000.

———. "Der Holocaust in den politischen Kulturen Europas. Erinnerung und Eigentum." In *Auschwitz. Sechs Essays zu Geschehen und Vergegenwärtigung,* ed. Klaus-Dietmar Henke. Dresden, 2001, 65–73.

Dmitrów, Edmund. *Niemcy i okupacja hitlerowska w oczach Polaków. Poglądy i opinie z lat 1945–1948.* [The Germans and the Hitler Occupation in the Eyes of the Poles. Views and Opinions from the Years 1945–1948.] Warsaw, 1987.

———, ed. *Der Beginn der Vernichtung. Zum Mord an den Juden in Jedwabne und Umgebung im Sommer 1941. Neue Forschungsergebnisse polnischer Historiker.* Osnabrück, 2004.

Dubiel, Helmut. *Niemand ist frei von der Geschichte. Die nationalsozialistische Herrschaft in den Debatten des Deutschen Bundestages.* Munich and Vienna, 1999.

Eck, Christina. *Die Wiedergutmachung zwischen 1945 und 1989 und die Regelung der Ansprüche von Verfolgten des Nationalsozialismus in § 1 Absatz 6 VermG.* Munich, 1996.

Eizenstat, Stuart E. *Imperfect Justice: Looted Assets, Slave Labor, and the Unfinished Business of World War II.* New York, 2003.

Embacher, Helga. *Die Restitutionsverhandlungen mit Österreich aus der Sicht jüdischer Organisationen und der Israelitischen Kultusgemeinde.* Vienna, 2002.

Emery, George. "István Bibó, 'The Jewish Question in Hungary'—A Review Essay." *Cross Currents* 4 (1985): 47–57.

Esch, Michael G. *"Gesunde Verhältnisse." Deutsche und polnische Bevölkerungspolitik in Ostmitteleuropa 1939–1950.* Marburg/Lahn, 1998.

Falah, Ghazi. "The 1948 Israeli-Palestinian War and its Aftermath: The Transformation and De-Signification of Palestine's Cultural Landscape." *Annals of the Association of American Geographers* 86, no. 2 (1996): 256–258.

———. "Living Together Apart. Residential Segregation in Mixed Arab-Jewish Cities in Israel." *Urban Studies* 33, no. 6 (1996): 823–857.

Falk, Richard. "The Holocaust and the Emergence of International Human Rights." Paper presented in conference "Confronting the Past: Memory, Identity, and Society," 4–5 February 2001, UCLA Center for Jewish Studies.

Feldman, Gerald D. "Unternehmensgeschichte im Dritten Reich und die Verantwortung der Historiker. Raubgold und Versicherungen, Arisierung und Zwangsarbeit." In *Geschichte vor Gericht. Historiker, Richter und die Suche nach Gerechtigkeit,* ed. Norbert Frei, Dirk van Laak, and Michael Stolleis. Munich, 2000, 103–129.

———. *Die Allianz und die deutsche Versicherungswirtschaft 1933–1945.* Munich, 2001.

———. "Reparations, Restitution, and Compensation in the Aftermath of National Socialism, 1945–2000." Paper presented in conference "Confronting the Past: Memory, Identity, and Society," 4–5 February 2001, UCLA Center for Jewish Studies.

Ferencz, Benjamin B. *Lohn des Grauens. Die Entschädigung jüdischer Zwangsarbeiter. Ein offenes Kapitel deutscher Nachkriegsgeschichte.* Frankfurt a.M., 1981.

Fichtl, Franz et.al. *"Bambergs Wirtschaft judenfrei." Die Verdrängung der jüdischen Geschäftsleute in den Jahren 1933 bis 1939.* Bamberg, 1998.

Finkelstein, Norman G. *The Holocaust Industry: Reflections on the Exploitation of Jewish Suffering.* New York, 2000.

Fischer-Hübner, Helga and Hermann, ed. *Die Kehrseite der "Wiedergutmachung". Das Leiden von NS-Verfolgten in den Entschädigungsverfahren. Mit einem Vorwort von Hans Koschnick.* Gerlingen, 1990.

Forster, David. *"Wiedergutmachung" in Österreich und in der BRD im Vergleich.* Innsbruck, Vienna, and Munich, 2001.

Frei, Norbert. *Adenauer's Germany and the Nazi Past: The Politics of Amnesty and Integration.* New York, 2002.

Friedländer, Saul. *Memory, History, and the Extermination of the Jews of Europe.* Bloomington, 1993.

Friedman, Philip. "The Fate of the Jewish Book during the Nazi Era." In *Essays on Jewish Booklore. Articles selected by Philip Goodman.* New York, 1972, 112–122.

Friedrich Ebert Foundation, ed. *The German Remembrance Fund and the Issue of Forced and Slave Labour: Contributions to a Seminar of the Washington Office of the Friedrich Ebert Foundation held in Washington, D.C. on November 1.* Washington, D.C., 1999.

Friedrich, Jörg. *Der Brand. Deutschland im Bombenkrieg 1940–1945.* Munich, 2002.

Frohn, Axel, ed. *Holocaust and Shilumim: The Policy of Wiedergutmachung in the Early 1950s.* Washington, D.C., 1991.

Frojimovics, Kinga, Géza Komoróczy, Viktória Pusztai, and Andrea Strbik, ed. *Jewish Budapest. Monuments, Rites, History.* Budapest, 1999.

Gaddis, John L. "Was the Truman Doctrine a Real Turning Point?" *Foreign Affairs* 52 (1974): 346–402.

———. *We Now Know: Rethinking Cold War History.* Oxford, 1997.

Gain, André. *La restauration et les biens des emigrés. La législation concernant les biens nationaux de seconde origine et son application dans l'Est de la France: 1814–1832.* Nancy, 1928.

Gerő, András. *Der Heldenplatz Budapest als Spiegel ungarischer Geschichte.* Budapest, 1990.

Géza, Boros. *Emlékművek '56-nak.* [Monuments for 1956.] Budapest, 1997.

Giesen, Bernhard. *Die Intellektuellen und die Nation. Eine deutsche Achsenzeit.* Frankfurt a.M., 1993.

Giordano, Ralph. *Die zweite Schuld oder Von der Last Deutscher zu sein.* Cologne, 1987.

Girard, Gene. *Das Heilige und die Gewalt.* Frankfurt a.M., 1992 (first published in 1972).

Glassheim, Eagle. "The Mechanics of Ethnic Cleansing: The Expulsion of Germans from Czechoslovakia, 1945–1947." In *Redrawing Nations: Ethnic Cleansing in East-Central Europe, 1944–1948*, ed. Philipp Ther and Ana Siljak. Lanham, 2001, 197–219.

Goldmann, Stefan. "Statt Totenklage Gedächtnis." *Poetica* 21 (1989): 43–66.

Goren, Tamir. "The History of the Disappearance of the 'Old City' from the Perspective of Haifa, 1948–1951." *Horizons in Geography* 40–41 (1994): 57–81 (Hebrew).

Goschler, Constantin. *Wiedergutmachung. Westdeutschland und die Verfolgten des Nationalsozialismus (1945–1954).* Munich, 1992.

———. "Die Auseinandersetzung um die Rückerstattung 'arisierten' jüdischen Eigentums nach 1945." In *Die Deutschen und die Judenverfolgung im Dritten Reich*, ed. Ursula Büttner. Hamburg, 1992, 339–356.

———. "Wiedergutmachung als Vergangenheitsbewältigung." *Bohemia* 34 (1993): 295–304.

———. "Nicht bezahlt? Die Wiedergutmachung für Opfer der nationalsozialistischen Verfolgung in der SBZ/DDR." In *Wirtschaftliche Folgelasten des Krieges in der SBZ/DDR*, ed. Christoph Buchheim. Baden-Baden, 1995, 169–191.

———. "Wiedergutmachung." In *Geschichte der Sozialpolitik in Deutschland seit 1945*, ed. Bundesministerium für Arbeit und Sozialordnung und das Bundesarchiv, vol. 2: Die Besatzungszeit. Sozialpolitik zwischen Kriegsende und der Gründung zweier deutscher Staaten. Baden-Baden, 2000.

———, and Jürgen Lillteicher, ed. *"Arisierung" und Restitution. Die Rückerstattung jüdischen Eigentums in Deutschland und Österreich nach 1945 und 1989.* Göttingen, 2002.

———. *Schuld und Schulden. Die Politik der Wiedergutmachung für NS-Verfolgte seit 1945.* Göttingen 2005.

Gosewinkel, Dieter. *Adolf Arndt. Die Wiederbegründung des Rechtsstaats aus dem Geist der Sozialdemokratie 1945–1961.* Bonn, 1991.

Götze, Andreas. "Verständnisprobleme auf dem Weg zur Partnerschaft nach 1989." In *Tschechen, Slowaken und Deutsche. Nachbarn in Europa.* ed. Niedersächsische Landeszentrale für politische Bildung. Hannover, 1995, 85–117.

Gotzmann, Andreas, Rainer Liedtke, and Till van Rahden, ed. *Juden, Bürger, Deutsche. Zur Geschichte von Vielfalt und Differenz 1800–1933.* Tübingen, 2001.

Gross, Jan T. "War as Revolution." In *The Establishment of Communist Regimes in Eastern Europe, 1944–1949*, ed. Leonid Gibianskii and Norman M. Naimark. Oxford, 1997, 17–42.

Gross, Jan T. *Neighbors: The Destruction of the Jewish Community in Jedwabne.* Princeton, 2001.

———. *Thou Shalt Not Kill: Poles on Jedwabne.* Warsaw, 2001.

———. *Wokól 'Sasiadów'. Polemiki i wyjasnienia.* [On 'Neighbors.' Polemics and Explanations.] Sejny, 2003.

Grossman, David. *Der geteilte Israeli. Über den Zwang, den Nachbarn nicht zu verstehen.* Munich, 1994.

Grossmann, Kurt R. *Die Ehrenschuld. Kurzgeschichte der Wiedergutmachung.* Frankfurt a.M., 1967.

Gur-Ze'ev, Ilan, and Ruth Linn. "Holocaust as Metaphor; Arab and Israeli Use of the Same Symbol." *Metaphor and Symbolic Activity* 11, no. 3 (1996): 195–206.

Gur-Ze'ev, Ilan. "The Morality of Acknowledging/not-Acknowledging the Other's Holocaust/Genocide." *Journal of Moral Education* 27, no. 2 (1998): 161–177.

———. "Defeating the Enemy Within: Exploring the Link between Holocaust Education and the Arab-Israeli Conflict." *Religious Education* 95, no. 4 (2000): 373–401.

———. "The Production of Self and the Destruction of the Other's Memory and Identity in Israeli-Palestinian Education on the Holocaust/'Nakbah'." *Studies in Philosophy and Education* 20, no. 3 (2001): 255–266.

Haas-Rietschel, Helga, and Sabine Hering. *Nora Platiel. Sozialistin—Emigrantin—Politikerin. Eine Biographie.* Cologne, 1990.

Habermas, Jürgen. *Eine Art Schadensabwicklung. Kleine Politische Schriften.* Frankfurt a.M., 1987.

———. *Strukturwandel der Öffentlichkeit. Untersuchungen zu einer Kategorie der bürgerlichen Gesellschaft.* Frankfurt a.M., 1990 (first published in 1962).

Hacke, Gerald. *Zeugen Jehovas in der DDR. Verfolgung und Verhalten einer religiösen Minderheit.* Dresden, 2000.

Hacking, Ian. "Memory Sciences, Memory Politics." In *Tense Past: Cultural Essays in Trauma and Memory,* ed. Paul Antze and Michael Lambek, New York, 1996, 67–88.

Hacohen, Dvora. *Immigrants in Turmoil: The Great Wave of Immigration to Israel and its Absorption, 1948–1953.* Jerusalem, 1994 (Hebrew).

Hahn, Eva, and Hans Henning Hahn. "Eine zerklüftete Erinnerungslandschaft wird planiert. Die Deutschen, 'ihre' Vertreibung und die sog. Beneš-Dekrete." *Transit. Europäische Revue,* no. 23 (2002): 103–116.

Hamburger Stiftung für Sozialgeschichte des 20. Jahrhunderts, ed. *Das Daimler-Benz-Buch. Ein Rüstungskonzern im "Tausendjährigen Reich".* Nördlingen, 1987.

Heimer, Carol A. *Reactive Risk and Rational Action: Managing Moral Hazard in Insurance Contracts.* Berkeley, 1985.

Heine, Heinrich. "Memoiren." In *Sämtliche Schriften,* ed. Klaus Briegleb, vol. 6/1. Munich, 1976.

Helmberger, Peter. "Der Versuch einer Generalbereinigung. Die Verhandlungen zwischen den Niederlanden und der Bundesrepublik um den Ausgleichsvertrag vom 8. April 1960." *Jahrbuch des Zentrums für Niederlande-Studien* 4 (1993): 71–98.

Henckaerts, Jean-Marie. *Mass Expulsions in Modern International Law and Practice.* The Hague, 1995.

Hennig, Regina. *Entschädigung und Interessenvertretung der NS-Verfolgten in Niedersachsen 1945–49.* Bielefeld, 1991.

Henry, Marilyn. *The Restitution of Jewish Property in Central and Eastern Europe.* New York, 1997.

Herbert, Ulrich. *A History of Foreign Labor in Germany, 1880–1980.* Ann Arbor, 1990.

———, ed. *Europa und der "Reichseinsatz". Ausländische Zivilarbeiter, Kriegsgefangene und KZ-Häftlinge in Deutschland 1938–1945.* Essen, 1991.

———, Karin Orth, and Christoph Dieckmann, ed. *Die nationalsozialistischen Konzentrationslager. Entwicklung und Struktur.* 2 vols. Göttingen, 1998.

———. *Best. Biographische Studien über Radikalismus. Weltanschauung und Vernunft 1903–1989,* 3rd ed., Bonn, 1996.

———. *Hitler's Foreign Workers: Enforced Foreign Labor in Germany under the Third Reich.* London, 1997.

———. *Geschichte der Ausländerpolitik in Deutschland. Saisonarbeiter, Zwangsarbeiter, Gastarbeiter, Flüchtlinge.* Munich, 2001.

Herbst, Ludolf, and Constantin Goschler, ed. *Wiedergutmachung in der Bundesrepublik Deutschland.* Munich, 1989.

Herf, Jeffrey. *Zweierlei Erinnerung. Die NS-Vergangenheit im geteilten Deutschland.* Berlin, 1998.

Heß, Burkhard. "Völker- und zivilrechtliche Beurteilung der Entschädigung für Zwangsarbeit vor dem Hintergrund neuerer Entscheidungen deutscher Gerichte." In *Entschädigung für NS-Zwangsarbeit. Rechtliche, historische und politische Aspekte,* ed. Klaus Barwig, Günther Saathoff, and Nicole Weyde. Baden-Baden, 1998, 65–92.

Heuss, Anja. *Kunst- und Kulturgutraub. Eine vergleichende Studie zur Besatzungspolitik der Nationalsozialisten in Frankreich und der Sowjetunion.* Heidelberg, 2000.

Hirsch, Martin. "Folgen der Verfolgung. Schädigung—Wiedergutmachung—Rehabilitierung." In *Die Bundesrepublik Deutschland und die Opfer des Nationalsozialismus. Tagung vom 25. bis 27. November 1983 in der Evangelischen Akademie Bad Boll,* ed. Protokolldienst 14/84. Bad Boll, 1984, 19–32.

Hobbes, Thomas. *Leviathan* [1651].

Hoffmann, Detlef. *Das Gedächtnis der Dinge. KZ-Relikte und KZ-Denkmäler 1945–1995.* Frankfurt a.M. and New York, 1998.

Hoogewoud, F. J. "The Nazi Looting of Books and its American 'Antithesis': Selected Pictures from the Offenbach Archival Depot's Photographic History and Its Supplement." *Studia Rosenthaliana* 26 (1992): 158–192.

Hopmann, Barbara, and Mark Spoerer. *Zwangsarbeit bei Daimler Benz.* Stuttgart, 1994.

Horel, Catherine. La restitution des biens juifs et le renouveau juif en Europe centrale (Hongrie, Slovaquie, République Tchèque). Bern, 2002.

Hörisch, Jochen. *Kopf und Zahl. Die Poesie des Geldes.* Frankfurt a.M., 1996.

Horváth, Zsolt K. "Önarcképcsarnok. A személyes emlékezés mint történeti probléma." [The Hall of Self-Portraits. Personal memory as a historical problem.] In *A történész szerszámosládája.* [The Tool-Kit of the Historian.] ed. András Szekeres. Budapest, 2002, 81–102.

Houžvička, Václav. *Reflexe sudetoněmecké otázky a postoje obyvatelstva ceského pohraničí k Německu.* [The Echo of the Sudeten German Question and Attitudes among the Czech Population in the Border Area Near Germany.] Prague, 1997.

Hovannisian, Robert, ed. *The Armenian Genocide in Perspective.* New Brunswick, N.J., 1986.

Hübl, Milan. "Glossen zu den Danubius-Thesen über die Aussiedlung der Deutschen." *Deutschland-Archiv* 12 (1979): 727–735.

Hudemann, Rainer. "Anfänge der Wiedergutmachung. Französische Besatzungszone 1945–1950." *Geschichte und Gesellschaft* 13 (1987): 181–216.

Hughes, Michael L. *Shouldering the Burdens of Defeat: West Germany and the Reconstruction of Social Justice.* Chapel Hill, 1999.

Irwin-Zarecka, Iwona. *Neutralizing Memory: The Jew in Contemporary Poland.* New Brunswick, 1990.

Jabloner, Clemens et al. *Schlussbericht der Historikerkommission der Republik Österreich. Vermögensentzug während der NS-Zeit sowie Rückstellungen und Entschädigungen seit 1945 in Österreich. Zusammenfassungen und Einschätzungen.* vol. 1. Vienna and Munich, 2003.

Jakubowska, Urszula. "Zygmunt Wojciechowski: O powrót Polski nad Odrę." [Zygmunt Wojciechowski: On Poland's Return to the Oder.] In *Polska-Kresy-Polacy. Studia Historyczne* [Poland—Border Areas—Poles. Historical Studies], ed. Stanisław Ciesielski, Teresa Kulak, and Krystyna Matwijowska. Wrocław, 1994, 215–223.

Jameson, Frederic. "Postmodernism, or The Cultural Logic of Late Capitalism." *New Left Review* 146 (1984): 53–92.

Jankowski, Robert, ed. *Jedwabne. Spór historyków wokól ksiazki Jana T. Grossa "Sasiedzi".* [Jedwabne. The Historians' Debate on the Book by Jan Tomasz Gross "Neighbors".] Warsaw 2002.

Jaspers, Karl. *The Question of German Guilt.* New York, 1947.

Jedermann, František [pseudonym]. *Verlorene Geschichte. Bilder und Texte aus dem heutigen Sudetenland.* Cologne, 1985.

Jeggle, Utz. *Judendörfer in Württemberg.* Tübingen, 1969.

———, and Albert Ilien. "Die Dorfgemeinschaft als Not- und Terrorzusammenhang. Ein Beitrag zur Sozialgeschichte des Dorfes und zur Sozialpsychologie seiner Bewohner." In *Dorfpolitik. Sozialwissenschaftliche Analyse. Didaktische Hilfen,* ed. Hans Georg Wehling. Opladen, 1980, 38–53.

Jelinek, Yeshayahu A. *Zwischen Moral und Realpolitik. Eine Dokumentensammlung.* Gerlingen, 1997.

Jonca, Karol, ed. *Wysiedlenia Niemców i osadnictwo ludności polskiej na obszarze Krzyżowa-Świdnica (Kreisau-Schweidnitz) w latach 1945–1948. Wybór dokumentów.* [The Expulsion of the Germans and Resettlement of the Poles in the Area Krzyzowa-Swidnica (Kreisau-Schweidnitz) 1945–1948. Documentation.] Wrocław, 1997.

Jones, Howard. *A New Kind of War: America's Global Strategy and the Truman Doctrine in Greece.* New York, 1989.

Judt, Tony. "The Past is Another Country: Myth and Memory in Postwar Europe." *Daedalus* 4 (1992): 83–118.

Kallus, Rachel, and Hubert Law-Yone. "National Home/Personal Home. The Role of Public Housing in the Shaping of Space." *Theory and Criticism* 16 (2000): 153–180 (Hebrew).

Kamen, Charles S. "After the Catastrophe II: The Arabs in Israel, 1948–51." *Middle Eastern Studies* 24 (1988): 68–109.

Kanafani, Ghassan. *Palestine's Children: Returning to Haifa and Other Stories.* London, 2000.

Kaplan, Marion. *Jüdisches Bürgertum. Frau, Familie, Identität im Kaiserreich.* Hamburg, 1991.

Katzenstein, Ernst. "Jewish Claims Conference und die Wiedergutmachung nationalsozialistischen Unrechts." In *Die Freiheit des Anderen. Festschrift für Martin Hirsch,* ed. Hans Jochen Vogel. Baden-Baden, 1981, 219–226.

Kedar, Alexandre. *"Israeli Law and the Redemption of Arab Land, 1948–1969."* Ph.D. diss., Harvard University, 1996.

———. "The Legal Transformation of Ethnic Geography: Israeli Law and the Palestinian Landholder 1948–1967." *New York University Journal of International Law and Politics* 33, no. 4 (2001): 923–1000.

———. "On the Legal Geography of Ethnocratic Settler States: Notes Towards A Research Agenda." *Current Legal Issues* 5 (2003): 401–441.

Kemp, Adriana. "Borders, Space and National Identity in Israel." *Theory and Criticism* 16 (2000): 13–43 (Hebrew).

———. "State Control Resistance in the Israeli Borderlands." In *Mizrachim in Israel: A Critical Observation into Israel's Ethnicity,* ed. Hannan Hever, Yehouda Shenhav, and Pnina Motzafi-Haller. Tel Aviv, 2002, 36–67 (Hebrew).

Kessler, Ralf, and Hartmut Rüdiger Peter. "Antifaschisten in der SBZ. Zwischen elitärem Selbstverständnis und politischer Instrumentalisierung." *Vierteljahreshefte für Zeitgeschichte* 43 (1995): 611–633.

———. *Wiedergutmachung im Osten Deutschlands 1945–1953. Grundsätzliche Diskussionen und die Praxis in Sachsen-Anhalt.* Frankfurt a.M., 1996.

Kesting, Hanno. *Geschichtsphilosophie und Weltbürgerkrieg.* Heidelberg, 1959.

Keyserlingk, Robert H. *Austria in World War II: An Anglo-American Dilemma.* Kingston and Montreal, 1988.

Kirchhoff, Markus. *Häuser des Buches. Bilder jüdischer Bibliotheken.* Leipzig, 2002.

Kittel, Manfred. *Die Legende von der "Zweiten Schuld". Vergangenheitsbewältigung in der Ära Adenauer.* Berlin, 1993.

Klimó, Árpád von. *Nation, Konfession, Geschichte. Zur nationalen Geschichtskultur Ungarns im europäischen Kontext (1860–1948).* Munich, 2003.

Knight, Robert. "Restitution and Legitimacy in Post-war Austria: 1945–1953," *Leo Baeck Institute Yearbook* 36 (1991): 413–441.

———, ed. *"Ich bin dafür, die Sache in die Länge zu ziehen:" Die Wortprotokolle der österreichischen Bundesregierung von 1945 bis 1952 über die Entschädigung der Juden.* Cologne and Weimar, 2000.

Kochański, Aleksander, ed. *Protokół obrad KC PPR w maju 1945 roku.* [Minutes of the Central Commission of the Polish Workers Party, May 1945.] Warsaw, 1992.

Kocka, Jürgen. "Eine durchherrschte Gesellschaft," In *Sozialgeschichte der DDR*, ed. Hartmut Kaelble et. al. Stuttgart, 1994.

Kogon, Eugen. *The Theory and Practice of Hell: The German Concentration Camps and the System behind Them.* London and New York, 1950.

Kohler, Lotte, and Hans Saner, ed. *Hannah Arendt. Karl Jaspers: Correspondence, 1926–1969.* New York, 1992.

Königseder, Angelika, and Juliane Wetzel. *Lebensmut im Wartessal. Die jüdischen DPs (Displaced Persons) im Nachkriegsdeutschland.* Frankfurt a.M., 1994.

Könke, Günter. "Wiedergutmachung und Modernisierung. Der Beitrag des Luxemburger Abkommens von 1952 zur wirtschaftlichen Entwicklung Israels." *Vierteljahrschrift für Sozial- und Wirtschaftsgeschichte* 75 (1988): 503–548.

Koselleck, Reinhart. *Critique and Crisis: Enlightenment and the Pathogenesis of Modern Society.* Oxford, 1988.

———. "Formen und Traditionen des negativen Gedächtnisses." In *Verbrechen erinnern. Die Auseinandersetzung mit Holocaust und Völkermord*, ed. Volkhard Knigge and Norbert Frei. Munich, 2002, 21–32.

Kosmala, Beate, ed. *Die Vertreibung der Juden aus Polen 1968. Antisemitismus und politisches Kalkül.* Berlin, 2000.

Kovács, Éva. "Mythen und Rituale des ungarischen Systemwechsels." *Österreichische Zeitschrift für Geschichtswissenschaften* 10, no. 2 (1999): 210–237.

Král, Václav, ed. *Die Deutschen in der Tschechoslowakei 1933–1947. Dokumentensammlung.* Prague, 1964.

Křen, Jan. "Odsun Němců ve světle nových pramenů." [The Deportation of the Germans in the Light of New Sources.] *Dialog. Měsíčník pro politiku, hospodářství a kultury* [Dialogue. Monthly for Politics, the Economy and Culture], no. 4–6 (1967): 1–10.

———. "Tschechen und Deutsche. Kritische Bemerkungen." In *Zur Geschichte der deutsch-tschechischen Beziehungen. Eine Sammelschrift tschechischer Historiker aus dem Jahr 1980.* Berlin, 1985, 5–57.

———, Václav Kural, and Detlef Brandes. *Integration oder Ausgrenzung. Deutsche und Tschechen 1890–1945.* Bremen, 1986.

———. *Konfliktní společenství. Češi a Němci 1780–1918.* [Communities in Conflict. Czechs and Germans 1780–1918.] Prague, 1990.

Kretzmer, David. *The Legal Status of the Arabs in Israel.* Boulder, 1990.

Krzoska, Markus. *Für ein Polen an Oder und Ostsee. Zygmunt Wojciechowski als Historiker und Publizist.* Osnabrück, 2003.

Kučera, Jaroslav. "Das Auseinandergehen mit den Deutschen. Ein Blick von tschechischer Seite." In *Böhmen,* ed. Peter Becher and Hubert Ettl. Vietach, 1992, 99–108.

———. "Die Vertreibung. Die Debatte um die Aussiedlung der deutschen Bevölkerung in der Tschechoslowakei und ihre politische Bedeutung." *Österreichische Zeitschrift für Geschichtswissenschaft* 3 (1992): 238–248.

———. "Zwischen Geschichte und Politik. Die aktuelle Diskussion über die Vertreibung der Deutschen in der tschechischen Gesellschaft und Politik." In *Flucht und Vertreibung. Zwischen Aufrechnung und Verdrängung,* ed. Robert Streibel. Vienna, 1994, 174–187.

Kühn-Ludewig, Maria, ed. *Displaced Books. Bücherrückgabe aus zweierlei Sicht. Beiträge und Materialien in Zusammenhang von NS-Zeit und Krieg.* 2nd ed. Hannover, 1999.

———. *Johannes Pohl (1904–1960). Judaist und Bibliothekar im Dienste Rosenbergs. Eine biographische Dokumentation.* Hannover, 2000.

Kunštat, Miroslav. "Deutsch-tschechische Beziehungen—deutsch-tschechischer Dialog?" *Transodra* 12/13 (1996): 20–29.

Küpper, Herbert. "Die Wiedergutmachung nationalsozialistischen Unrechts in den Nachfolgestaaten der Sowjetunion." *Osteuropa* 7 (1996): 639–656, 758–768.

Kurkowska-Budzan, Marta. "My Jedwabne." *Polin* 15 (2002): 401–407.

Kurnitzky, Horst. *Ödipus. Ein Held der westlichen Welt. Über die zerstörerischen Grundlagen der Zivilisation.* Berlin, 1978.

Kurtz, Michael J. *Nazi Contraband: American Policy on the Return of European Cultural Treasures, 1945–1955.* New York and London, 1985.

Küster, Otto. *Erfahrungen in der deutschen Wiedergutmachung.* Tübingen, 1967.

Łach, Stanisław, ed. *Władze komunistyczne wobec Ziem Odzyskanych po II wojnie światowej.* [The Communist Authorities vis-à-vis the Territories Recovered after WWII.] Słupsk, 1997.

Lehmann, Hans Georg. "Wiedereinbürgerung, Rehabilitation und Wiedergutmachung nach 1945. Zur Staatsangehörigkeit ausgebürgerter Emigranten und Remigranten." *Exilforschung. Ein internationales Jahrbuch* 9 (1991): 90–103.

Lemberg, Hans. "'Ethnische Säuberungen':Ein Mittel zur Lösung von Nationalitätenproblemen?" *Aus Politik und Zeitgeschichte*, no. 46 (1992): 27–38.

Lepsius, M. Rainer. "Das Erbe des Nationalsozialismus und die politische Kultur der Nachfolgestaaten des 'Großdeutschen Reiches'." In *Kultur und Gesellschaft. Verhandlungen des 24. Deutschen Soziologentags, des 11. Österreichischen Soziologentags und des 8. Kongresses der Schweizerischen Gesellschaft für Soziologie in Zürich 1988*, ed. Max Haller, Hans-Joachim Hoffmann-Nowotny, and Wolfgang Zapf. Frankfurt a.M. and New York, 1989, 247–264.

Lessing, Hannah M. "Der Nationalfonds. Die Arbeit des Nationalfonds der Republik Österreich und Österreichs Umgang mit der Vergangenheit." In *Nationalfonds der Republik Österreich für Opfer des Nationalsozialismus*, ed. Nationalfonds der Republik Österreich für Opfer des Nationalsozialismus. 2nd ed. Vienna, 2003, 54.

Levy, Daniel, and Natan Sznaider. *Erinnerung im globalen Zeitalter. Der Holocaust.* Frankfurt a.M., 2001.

———. "Memory Unbound. The Holocaust and the Formation of Cosmopolitan Memory." *European Journal of Social Theory* 5, no. 1 (2002): 87–106.

Lillie, Sophie. *Was einmal war. Handbuch der enteigneten Kunstsammlungen Wiens.* Vienna, 2003.

Lippóczy, Piotr, and Tadeusz Walichnowski. *Przesiedlenie ludności niemieckiej z Polski po II wojnie światowej w świetle dokumentów.* [The Resettlement of the German Population from Poland after WWII in the Light of Documentation.] Warsaw and Łódź, 1982.

Liskovsky, Aharon. "The 'present absentees' in Israel." *The New Orient* 6 (1960): 186–192 (Hebrew).

Lotfi, Gabriele. *KZ der Gestapo. Arbeitserziehungslager im Dritten Reich.* Stuttgart and Munich, 2000.

Loth, Wilfried. *The Division of the World: 1941–1955.* London, 1988.

Löwenthal, Leo. "Calibans Erbe. Bücherverbrennungen und kulturelle Verdrängungsmechanismen." In *Kanon und Zensur. Archäologie der literarischen Kommunikation II*, ed. Aleida and Jan Assmann. Munich, 1987, 227–236.

Lübbe, Hermann. "Der Nationalsozialismus im deutschen Nachkriegsbewußtsein." *Historische Zeitschrift* 236 (1983): 579–599.

Ludewig, Hans-Ulrich. "Zwangsarbeit im Zweiten Weltkrieg. Forschungsstand und Ergebnisse regionaler und lokaler Forschungen" *Archiv für Sozialgeschichte* 31 (1991): 558–577.

Machcewicz, Paweł, and Krzysztof Persak, ed. *Wokół Jedwabnego.* [Around Jedwabne.] 2 vols. Warsaw, 2002.

Maier, Charles. *Dissolution: The Crisis of Communism and the End of East Germany.* Princeton, 1997.

Margalit, Gilad. "Die deutsche Zigeunerpolitik nach 1945." *Vierteljahreshefte für Zeitgeschichte* 45 (1997): 557–588.

Markowski, Mieczysław, ed. *Trudne dni. Wrocław 1945 r. we wspomnieniach pionierów.* [Difficult Days. Wrocław 1945 in the Memories of Pioneers.] 3 vols. Wrocław, 1960–1962.

Marrus, Michael R. *The Unwanted: European Refugees in the Twentieth Century.* Oxford, 1985.

Marx, Karl. *Das Kapital.* vol. 3 Marx-Engels-Werke 25. Berlin, 1971.

Marxen, Klaus, and Gerhard Werle. *Die strafrechtliche Aufarbeitung von DDR-Unrecht. Eine Bilanz.* Berlin and New York, 1999.

Mattl, Siegfried, and Karl Stuhlpfarrer. "Auf deinem Altar ist Österreich. Österreichische Selbstbespiegelungen und Opferphantasien seit 1945." *Zukunft,* no. 4 (1985): 19–23.

Mauss, Marcel. *The Gift: The Form and Reason for Exchange in Archaic Societies.* New York, 2000 (originally published in 1925).

Melloni, Sandra. "Die Geschichte des Klaviers. Warum ich über das Klavier schreibe, und was dieses Klavier schon hinter sich hat." In *Dokumentationsarchiv des österreichischen Widerstandes. Jahrbuch 1989.* Vienna, 1989, 173–177.

Mertens, Lothar. *Davidstern unter Hammer und Zirkel. Die Jüdischen Gemeinden in der SBZ/DDR und ihre Behandlung durch Partei und Staat 1945–1990.* Hildesheim, 1997.

Minow, Martha. *Between Vengeance and Forgiveness: Facing History after Genocide and Mass Violence.* Boston, 1998.

Mochocki, Władysław. "Polnisch-sowjetische Freundschaft 'auf Banditentum und Raub reduziert?' Die Rote Armee in Polens wiedergewonnenen Gebieten 1945–1947." *Osteuropa* 48 (1998): 286–299.

Mommsen, Hans, and Manfred Grieger. *Das Volkswagenwerk und seine Arbeiter im Dritten Reich.* Düsseldorf, 1996.

Morris, Benny. *1948 And After: Israel And The Palestinians.* Oxford, 1990.

———. *The Birth of the Palestinian Refugee Problem Revisited.* Cambridge 2004.

Mosler, Hermann, and Karl Doehring. *Die Beendigung des Kriegszustands mit Deutschland nach dem zweiten Weltkrieg.* Cologne and Berlin, 1963.

Müller, Ingo. *Hitler's Justice. The Courts of the Third Reich.* Cambridge, 1991.

Münch, Peter L. "Zwischen 'Liquidation' und Wiederaufbau. Die deutschen Juden, der Staat Israel und die internationalen jüdischen Organisationen in der Phase der Wiedergutmachungsverhandlungen." *Historische Mitteilungen* 10 (1997): 81–111.

Muszyński, Mariusz. *Przejęcie majątków niemieckich przez Polskę po II wojnie światowej. Studium prawnomiędzynarodowe i porównawcze.* [Poles Take Possession of German Property after WWII. A Study in International and Comparative Law.] Bielsko-Biała, 2003.

Naimark, Norman M. *Fires of Hatred: Ethnic Cleansing in Twentieth Century Europe.* Cambridge, 2001.

Nicholas, Lynn H. *Der Raub der Europa. Das Schicksal europäischer Kunstwerke im Dritten Reich.* Munich, 1995.

Niekrasz, Lech Zdzislaw, ed. *Operacja "Jedwabne": mity i fakty.* [Operation 'Jedwabne'. Myths and Facts.] Wroclaw, 2001.

Niethammer, Lutz. "Schuld und Schulden," *Zeitschrift für KulturAustausch* 49, no. 4 (1999): 48–52.

———. *Kollektive Identität. Heimliche Quellen einer unheimlichen Konjunktur.* Reinbek b. Hamburg, 2000.

———. "Klärung und Aufklärung. Aufgaben und Lücken der Zwangsarbeiterforschung." In *Zwangsarbeiterforschung als gesellschaftlicher Auftrag,* ed. Klaus Tenfelde. Bochum, 2001, 13–22.

———. *Ego-Histoire? Und andere Erinnerungs-Versuche.* Vienna, 2002.

Nitschke, Bernadetta. "Polacy wobec Niemców—odpowiedzialność Niemców za zbrodnie wojenne." [The Germans vis-à-vis the Poles. German Responsibility for War Crimes.] *Zeszyty Historyczne* 1998, no. 123: 3–26.

———. *Wysiedlenie czy wypędzenie? Ludność niemiecka w Polsce 1945–1949.* [Resettlement or Expulsion? The German Population in Poland 1945–1949.] Toruń, 2001.

Nolywaika, Joachim. *Flucht und Vertreibung der Deutschen. Die Tragödie im Osten und im Sudetenland.* Kiel, 1996.

Nora, Pierre. "General Introduction: Between Memory and History." In idem., *Realms of Memory: Rethinking the French Past.* vol. 1. New York, 1996, 1–23.

Novick, Peter. *The Holocaust in American Life.* Boston and New York, 1999.

Nowak, Jerzy Robert. *Sto klamstw J. T. Grossa o Jedwabnem i zydowskich sasiadach.* [The 100 Lies of Jan Tomasz Gross about Jedwabne and the Jewish Neighbors.] Warsaw, 2001.

Opalski, Magdalena, and Israel Bartal. *Poles and Jews: A Failed Brotherhood.* Hanover and London, 1992.

Orłowski, Hubert, and Andrzej Sakson, ed. *Utracona ojczyzna. Przymusowe wysiedlenia, deportacje i przesiedlenia jako wspólne doświadczenie.* [Lost Homeland. Forced Expulsions, Deportation and Resettlement as a Shared Experience.] Poznan, 1997.

Österreichischer Bundespressedienst, ed. *Maßnahmen der Republik Österreich zugunsten bestimmter politisch, religiös oder abstammungsmäßig Verfolgter seit 1945.* Vienna, 1988.

Pappe, Ilan. "The Tantura Case in Israel; the Katz Research and Trial." *Journal of Palestine Studies* 30, no. 3 (2001): 19–39.

———. "The Katz and the Tantura Affairs: History, Historiography, the Court and the Israeli Academia." *Theory and Criticism* 20 (2002): 191–218 (Hebrew).

Pasák, Tomáš. "Přemysl Pitters Initiative bei der Rettung deutscher Kinder im Jahre 1945 und seine ablehnende Haltung gegenüber der inhumanen Behandlung der Deutschen in tschechischen Internierungslagern." In *Der Weg in die Katastrophe.*

Deutsch-tschechoslowakische Beziehungen 1938–1947, ed. Detlef Brandes and Václav Kural. Essen, 1994, 201–213.

Paul, Helmut, and Hans-Joachim Herberg, ed. *Psychische Spätschäden nach politischer Verfolgung*. Basel and New York, 1963.

Pawlita, Cornelius. *"Wiedergutmachung" als Rechtsfrage? Die politische und juristische Auseinandersetzung um Entschädigung für die Opfer nationalsozialistischer Verfolgung 1945–1990*. Frankfurt a.M., 1993.

Pelinka, Anton. "Die geänderte Funktionalität von Vergangenheit und Vergangenheitspolitik. Das Ende der Konkordanzdemokratie und die Verschiebung der Feindbilder." *Österreichische Zeitschrift für Politikwissenschaft* 30, no. 1 (2001): 44–56.

Péter, György. *Néma Hagyomány. Kollektív felejtés és a kései múltértelmezés 1956 1989-ben. A régmúltól az örökségig*. [Silent Tradition. Collective Forgetting and Belated Interpretation of the 1956 Revolution in 1989. From the Past to Heritage.] Budapest, 2000.

Petri, Edit. *Kárpótlás és kárrendezés Magyarországon 1989–1998*. [Compensation and Compensative Legislation in Hungary 1989–1988.] Budapest, 1998.

Podlasek, Maria. *Wypędzenie Niemców z terenów na wschód od Odry i Nysy Łużyckiej. Relacje świadków*. [The Expulsion of the Germans from the Areas East of the Oder and Lausitz Neisse. Reports by Eyewitnesses.] Warsaw, 1995.

Poggi, Gianfranco. *Money and the Modern Mind: Georg Simmel's Philosophy of Money*. Berkeley, 1993.

Polonsky, Antony, ed. *My Brother's Keeper?: Recent Polish Debates on the Holocaust*. London, 1990.

———, and Joanna Michlic, ed. *The Neighbors Respond: The Controversy over the Jedwabne Massacre in Poland*. Princeton, 2004.

Pross, Christian. *Paying for the Past: The Struggle Over Reparations for Surviving Victims of Nazi Terror*. Baltimore, 1998.

Rásky, Béla, and Karin Liebhart. "Hösök áldozatok, vértanúk / Helden, Opfer, Märtyrer. Versuch einer Genealogie in ungarischen und österreichischen nationalen Mythen und historischen Erzählungen." In *Zeitreise Heldenberg. Lauter Helden. Katalog zur Niederösterreichischen Landesausstellung 2005*, ed. Wolfgang Müller Funk and Georg Kugler. Vienna, 2005, 77–84.

Rathkolb, Oliver, ed. *Revisiting the National Socialist Legacy: Coming to Terms with Forced Labor, Expropriation, Compensation, and Restitution*. Innsbruck, 2002.

———. "NS-Kunstraub und Diversion in den Erinnerungen über den Holocaust in Europa." In *Kunst—Kommunikation—Macht. 6. Österreichischer Zeitgeschichtetag 2003*, ed. Ingrid Bauer et al. Innsbruck, 2004, 443–448.

Ratner, Steven, and Jason Abrams. *Accountability for Human Rights Atrocities in International Law: Beyond the Nuremberg Legacy*. New York, 1997.

Raz-Krakotzkin, Amnon. "A Few Comments on Orientalism, Jewish Studies and Israeli Society." *Jama'a* 3, no. 2 (1998): 34–61.

Redecker, Niels v. *Die polnischen Vertreibungsdekrete und die offenen Vermögensfragen zwischen Deutschland und Polen.* Frankfurt a.M., 2003.

Reichel, Peter. *Vergangenheitsbewältigung in Deutschland. Die Auseinandersetzung mit der NS-Diktatur von 1945 bis heute.* Munich, 2001.

Reichling, Gerhard. *Die deutschen Vertriebenen in Zahlen. Teil 1: Umsiedler, Verschleppte, Vertriebene, Aussiedler 1940–1985.* Bonn, 1986.

Reuter, Elke, and Detlef Hansel. *Das kurze Leben der VVN von 1947 bis 1953. Die Geschichte der Vereinigung der Verfolgten des Naziregimes in der SBZ und in der DDR.* Berlin, 1997.

Richarz, Monika. "Viehhandel und Landjuden im 19. Jahrhundert. Eine symbiotische Wirtschaftsbeziehung in Südwestdeutschland." *Menora. Jahrbuch für deutsch-jüdische Geschichte* 1 (1990): 66–88.

———, and Reinhard Rürup, ed. *Jüdisches Leben auf dem Lande. Studien zur deutsch-jüdischen Geschichte.* Tübingen, 1997.

Robinson, Nehemiah. *Indemnification and Reparations.* New York, 1944.

Roth, Michael S., and Charkles G. Salas, ed. *Disturbing Remains: Memory, History, and Crisis in the Twentieth Century.* Los Angeles, 2001.

Roth, Stephen J. "Indemnification of Hungarian Victims of Nazism." In *The Holocaust in Hungary Fifty Years Later,* ed. Randolph Braham and Attila Pók. New York, 1997.

Rupnow, Dirk. *Täter, Opfer, Gedächtnis. Das "jüdische Zentralmuseum" in Prag 1942–1945.* Vienna, 2000.

Šabata, Jaroslav. "Tschechen und die (sudeten-)deutsche Frage oder die Beneš-Dekrete und die europäische Frage." *Transodra* 12/13 (1996): 36–39.

Safrian, Hans, and Hans Witek. *Und keiner war dabei. Dokumente des alltäglichen Antisemitismus in Wien 1938.* Vienna, 1988.

Sagi, Nana. *German Reparations: A History of the Negotiations.* Jerusalem 1980.

Sandner, Günther. "Hegemonie und Erinnerung. Zur Konzeption von Geschichts- und Vergangenheitspolitik." *Österreichische Zeitschrift für Politikwissenschaft* 30, no. 1 (2001): 5–19.

Scharsach, Hans-Henning, and Kurt Kuch. *Haider. Schatten über Europa.* Cologne, 2000.

Schechtman, Joseph B. *Postwar Population Transfers in Europe 1945–1955.* Philadelphia, 1962.

Schidorsky, Dov. "Das Schicksal jüdischer Bibliotheken im Dritten Reich." In *Bibliotheken während des Nationalsozialismus,* ed. Peter Vodosek and Manfred Komorowsky, part II. Wiesbaden, 1992, 189–222.

———. "Confiscation of Libraries and Assignments to Forced Labour. Two Documents of the Holocaust." *Libraries & Culture* 33 (1998): 347–388.

———. "Germany in the Holy Land. Its Involvement and Impact on Library Development in Palestine and Israel." *Libri* 49 (1999): 26–42.

Schieder, Theodor, ed. *Documents on the Expulsion of the Germans from Eastern-Central-Europe: A Selection and Translation from Dokumentation der Vertreibung der Deutschen aus Ost-Mitteleuropa.* Bonn, 1960–1961.

Schiefelbein, Dieter. *Das "Institut zur Erforschung der Judenfrage Frankfurt am Main." Vorgeschichte und Gründung 1935–1939.* Frankfurt a.M., 1993.

———. "Das 'Institut zur Erforschung der Judenfrage Frankfurt am Main.' Antisemitismus als Karrieresprungbrett im NS-Staat." In *Jahrbuch 1998/99 zur Geschichte und Wirkung des Holocaust*, ed. Fritz-Bauer-Institut. Frankfurt a.M. and New York, 1999, 43–71.

Schlichting, Günter. "Eine Fachbibliothek zur Judenfrage. Die Münchener Bibliothek des Reichsinstituts für Geschichte des Neuen Deutschlands." *Historische Zeitschrift* 162 (1940): 567–572.

Schmidt-Hartmann, Eva. "Menschen oder Nationen? Die Vertreibung der Deutschen aus tschechischer Sicht." In *Die Vertreibung der Deutschen aus dem Osten*, ed. Wolfgang Benz. Frankfurt a.M., 1995, 178–198.

Schmitt, Carl. "Das Zeitalter der Neutralisierung und Entpolitisierungen." In idem., *Der Begriff des Politischen.* Berlin, 1987 [1932], 79–95.

Scholem, Gershom. *Briefe I, 1914–1947*, ed. Itta Shedletzky. Munich, 1994.

Schüler, Thomas. "Das Wiedergutmachungsgesetz vom 14. September 1945 in Thüringen." *Jahrbuch für Antisemitismusforschung* 2 (1993): 118–138.

Schulz, Gerhard. Das *Zeitalter der Gesellschaft. Aufsätze zur politischen Sozialgeschichte der Neuzeit.* Munich, 1969.

Schulz, Helga, ed. *Bevölkerungstransfer und Systemwandel. Ostmitteleuropäische Grenzen nach dem Zweiten Weltkrieg.* Berlin, 1998.

Schwarz, Hans-Peter. *Konrad Adenauer: A German Politician and Statesman in an Age of War, Revolution, and Reconstruction.* Providence, 1995.

Schwarz, Walter. *Rückerstattung und Entschädigung. Eine Abgrenzung der Wiedergutmachungsformen.* Munich, 1952.

———. *In den Wind gesprochen? Glossen zur Wiedergutmachung des nationalsozialistischen Unrechts.* Munich, 1969.

———. *Späte Frucht. Bericht aus unsteten Jahren.* Hamburg, 1981.

Seikaly, May. *Haifa—Transformation of an Arab Society, 1918–1939.* New York, 1995.

Shamir, Ronen. "Suspended in Space: Bedouins Under the Law of Israel." *Law and Society Review* 30, no. 2 (1996): 231–257.

Shavit, David. "The Emergence of Jewish Public Libraries in Tsarist Russia." *Journal of Library History* 20, no. 3 (1985): 239–252.

———. *Hunger for the Printed Word: Books and Libraries in the Jewish Ghettos of Nazi-Occupied Europe.* Jefferson, NC and London, 1997.

Shenhav, Yehouda. "What Palestinians and Jews from Arab Lands Have in Common?: Nationalism and Ethnicity Examined Through the Compensation Question." *Hagar International Social Science Review* 1, no. 1 (2000): 71–110.

Shohat, Ella. "Sepharadim in Israel: Zionism from the Standpoint of its Jewish Victims." *Social Text* 19/20 (1988): 1–35.

Siegrist, Hannes, and David Sugarman, ed. *Eigentum im internationalen Vergleich, 18.–20. Jahrhundert.* Göttingen, 1999.

Simmel, Georg. *Philosophie des Geldes.* Berlin, 1900.

Simon, Dieter. "Verordnetes Vergessen." In *Amnestie oder die Politik der Erinnerung in der Demokratie,* ed. Gary Smith and Avishai Margalit. Frankfurt a.M., 1997, 21–36.

Skąpska, Grażyna. "Zwischen Kollektivismus und Individualismus. Staatsbürgerschaft in der polnischen Verfassungsgeschichte." In *Staatsbürgerschaft in Europa. Historische Erfahrungen und aktuelle Debatten,* ed. Christoph Conrad and Jürgen Kocka. Hamburg, 2001, 255–278.

Slapnicka, Helmut. "Die rechtlichen Grundlagen für die Behandlung der Deutschen und der Magyaren in der Tschechoslowakei 1945–1948." In *Nationale Frage und Vertreibung in der Tschechoslowakei und Ungarn 1938–1948,* ed. Richard G. Plaschka, Horst Haselsteiner, Arnold Suppan, and Anna M. Drabek. Vienna, 1997, 153–192.

Smith, Helmut Walser. "The Discourse of Usury: Relations Between Christians and Jews in the German Countryside, 1880–1914." *Central European History* 32, no. 3 (1999): 255–276.

Sofsky, Wolfgang. *The Order of Terror: A Sociology of the Concentration Camp.* Princeton, 1997.

Spannuth, Philipp. *"Rückerstattung Ost: Der Umgang der DDR mit dem „arisierten" und enteigneten jüdischen Eigentum und die Gestaltung der Rückerstattung im wiedervereinigten Deutschland."* Ph.D. diss., Hamburg University, 2004.

Spiliotis, Susanne-Sophia. *Verantwortung und Rechtsfrieden. Die Stiftungsinitiative der deutschen Wirtschaft.* Frankfurt a.M., 2003.

Spoerer, Mark. *Zwangsarbeit unter dem Hakenkreuz. Ausländische Zivilarbeiter, Kriegsgefangene und Häftlinge im Deutschen Reich und im besetzten Europa 1939–1945.* Stuttgart and Munich, 2001.

Staněk, Tomáš. "Politischer Hintergrund und Organisation der Aussiedlung der Deutschen aus den böhmischen Ländern von Mai bis August 1945." In *Odsun. Die Vertreibung der Sudetendeutschen. Begleitband zur Ausstellung.* Munich, 1995, 113–152.

———. *Perzekuce 1945. Perzekuce tzv. státně nespolehlivého obyvatelstva v českiých zemích (mimo tábory a věznice) v květnu—srpnu 1945.* [Persecution 1945. The Persecution of the So-Called Politically Unreliable Population in the Bohemian Lands (except in Camps and Jails) from May to August 1945.] Prague, 1996.

———. "1945—Das Jahr der Verfolgung. Zur Problematik der außergerichtlichen Nachkriegsverfolgung in den böhmischen Ländern." In *Erzwungene Trennung. Vertreibungen und Aussiedlungen in und aus der Tschechoslowakei 1938–1947 im Vergleich mit Polen, Ungarn und Jugoslawien,* ed. Detlef Brandes, Edita Ivaničková, and Jiří Pešek. Essen, 1999, 123–152.

Starr, Joshua. "Jewish Cultural Property under Nazi Control." *Jewish Social Studies* 12 (1950): 27–48.

Steinberg, Jonathan. *Die Deutsche Bank und ihre Goldtransaktionen während des Zweiten Weltkrieges.* Munich, 1999.

Steiner, Maria. *(Un)gebrochene Kontinuitäten. Paula Wessely—Eine "österreichische Institution".* Vienna and Innsbruck, 2000.

Steinlauf, Michael. *Bondage to the Dead: Poland and the Memory of the Holocaust.* Syracuse, NY, 1995.

———. "Poland." In *The World Reacts to the Holocaust,* ed. David S. Wyman and Charles H. Rosenzweig. Baltimore and London, 1996.

Stiefel, Dieter, ed. *Die politische Ökonomie des Holocaust. Zur wirtschaftlichen Logik von Verfolgung und 'Wiedergutmachung'.* Vienna and Munich, 2001.

Stobiecki, Rafał. "Between Continuity and Discontinuity: A Few Comments on the Post-War Development of Polish Historical Research." *Zeitschrift für Ostmitteleuropa-Forschung* 50, no. 21 (2001): 214–229.

Stourzh, Gerald. *Um Einheit und Freiheit. Staatsvertrag, Neutralität und das Ende der Ost-West-Besetzung Österreichs 1945–1955.* Vienna, 1998.

Strauss, Hans. "Die Rückerstattung entzogener und geraubter Vermögensgegenstände." In *Deutsche Wiedergutmachung 1957. Eine Serie von Vorträgen gehalten über den Sender WHOM, New York,* ed. Axis Victims League and American Association of Former European Jurists. Düsseldorf, 1957, 12–15.

Streit, Christian. *Keine Kameraden. Die Wehrmacht und die sowjetischen Kriegsgefangenen 1941–1945.* Stuttgart, 1978.

Stuhlpfarrer, Karl. "Österreich, das erste Opfer Hitlerdeutschlands. Die Geschichte einer Sage und ihre Bedeutung." In *Die Mauern der Geschichte. Historiographie in Europa zwischen Diktatur und Demokratie,* ed. Gustavo Corni and Martin Sabrow. Leipzig, 1996, 233–244.

Šutaj, Štefan. "Ungarische Minderheit in der Slowakei während der Nachkriegsentwicklung." In *Nationale Frage und Vertreibung in der Tschechoslowakei und Ungarn 1938–1945. Aktuelle Forschungen,* ed. Richard G. Plaschka. Vienna, 1997.

Szabó, Anikó. *Vertreibung, Rückkehr, Wiedergutmachung. Göttinger Hochschullehrer im Schatten des Nationalsozialismus.* Göttingen, 2000.

Szczegóła, Hieronim. "Przedpoczdamskie wysiedlenia Niemców z Polski (czerwiec-lipiec 1945)." [The Expulsion of the Germans from Poland Before Potsdam (June–July 1945).] In *Ludność niemiecka na ziemiach polskich w latach 1939–1945 i jej powojenne losy.* [The German Population on Polish Territory 1939–1945 and Their Post-War Fate.] ed. Włodzimierz Jastrzębski. Bydgoszcz, 1995, 47–55.

Sznaider, Natan. "Consumerism as Civilizing Process: Israel and Judaism in the Second Age of Modernity." In *International Journal for Politics, Culture and Society* 14, no. 2 (2000): 297–314.

———. *The Compassionate Temperament: Care and Cruelty in Modern Society.* Boulder, Co., 2000.

Szücs, György. "A 'zsarnokság' szoborparkja." ["The Monument Meadow of Tyranny."] *budapesti negyed* 2, no. 1 (1994): 151–165.

Tanner, Jakob. "Geschichtswissenschaft und moralische Ökonomie der Restitution: Die Schweiz im internationalen Kontext," *Zeitgeschichte* 30, no. 5 (2003): 268–280.

Taylor, Charles. *The Politics of Recognition*. Princeton, 1992.

The Research Staff of the Commission on European Jewish Cultural Reconstruction. "Tentative List of Jewish Cultural Treasures in Axis-Occupied Countries." *Jewish Social Studies* 8 (1946), Supplement: 1–103.

Theis, Rolf. *Wiedergutmachung zwischen Moral und Interesse. Eine kritische Bestandsaufnahme der deutsch-israelischen Regierungsverhandlungen*. Frankfurt a.M., 1989.

Ther, Philipp. *Deutsche und polnische Vertriebene. Gesellschaft und Vertriebenenpolitik in der SBZ/DDR und Polen 1945–1956*. Göttingen, 1998.

———, and Ana Siljak. *Redrawing Nations: Ethnic Cleansing in East-Cenrral Europe, 1944–1948*. Lanham, 2001.

Timm, Angelika. *Alles umsonst? Verhandlungen zwischen der Claims Conference und der DDR über "Wiedergutmachung" und Entschädigung*. Berlin, 1996.

———. *Hammer, Zirkel, Davidstern. Das gestörte Verhältnis der DDR zu Zionismus und Staat Israel*. Bonn, 1997.

———. *Jewish Claims against East Germany: Moral Obligations and Pragmatic Policy*. Budapest, 1997.

Torpey, John. "'Making Whole What Has Been Smashed': Reflections on Reparations." *Journal of Modern History* 73, no. 2 (2001): 333–358.

Traba, Robert. *Kraina tysiąca granic. Szkice o historii i pamięci*. [Country of the Thousand Borders. Studies on History and Memory.] Olsztyn, 2003.

Tramer, Hans, ed. *In zwei Welten. Siegfried Moses zum 75. Geburtstag*. Tel Aviv, 1962.

Trausch, Gilbert. *Robert Schuman, Les racines et l'oeuvre d'un grand Européen*. Luxembourg, 1986.

Uhl, Heidemarie. *Zwischen Versöhnung und Verstörung. Eine Kontroverse um Österreichs historische Identität fünfzig Jahre nach dem "Anschluß"*. Cologne and Weimar, 1992.

———. "Gedächtnisraum Graz. Zeitgeschichtliche Erinnerungszeichen im öffentlichen Raum von 1945 bis zur Gegenwart." In *Erinnerung als Gegenwart. Jüdische Gedenkkulturen*, ed. Sabine Hödl and Eleonore Lappin. Berlin and Vienna, 2000, 211–232.

———. "Transformationen des österreichischen Gedächtnisses. Geschichtspolitik und Denkmalkultur in der Zweiten Republik." *Tel Aviver Jahrbuch für deutsche Geschichte* 29 (2000): 317–341.

———. "Das 'erste Opfer.' Der österreichische Opfermythos und seine Transformation in der Zweiten Republik," *Österreichische Zeitschrift für Politikwissenschaft*, no. 1 (2001): 19–34.

Unabhängige Expertenkommission Schweiz-Zweiter Weltkrieg, ed. *Die Schweiz, der Nationalsozialismus und der Zweite Weltkrieg. Schlussbericht*. Zurich, 2002.

Unfried, Berthold. "Restitution und Entschädigung von entzogenem Vermögen im internationalen Vergleich. Entschädigungsdebatte als Problem der Geschichtswissenschaft." *Zeitgeschichte* 30, no. 5 (2003): 243–267.

Venzlaff, Ulrich. "Die Begutachtung psychischer Störungen Verfolgter." *Rechtsprechung zum Wiedergutmachungsrecht* 17 (1966): 196–200.

Vogl, Ralf. *Stückwerk und Verdrängung. Wiedergutmachung nationalsozialistischen Strafjustizunrechts in Deutschland.* Berlin and Baden-Baden, 1997.

Volnhalls, Clemens, ed. *Entnazifizierung. Politische Säuberung und Rehabilitierung in den vier Besatzungszonen, 1945–1949.* Munich, 1991.

Walzer, Tina, and Stephan Templ. *Unser Wien. "Arisierung" auf österreichisch.* Berlin, 2001.

Washitz, Joseph. *"Social Changes in Haifa's Arab Society Under the British Mandate."* Ph.D. diss., Hebrew University Jerusalem, 1993 (Hebrew).

Weber, Petra. *Carlo Schmid 1896–1979. Eine Biographie.* Munich, 1996.

Weigel, Sigrid. "Shylocks Wiederkehr. Die Verwandlung von Schuld in Schulden oder: Zum symbolischen Tausch der Wiedermachung." In *Fünfzig Jahre danach. Zur Nachgeschichte des Nationalsozialismus,* ed. idem. and Birgit Erdle. Zurich, 1996, 165–192.

———. *Literatur als Voraussetzung der Kulturgeschichte. Schauplätze von Shakespeare bis Benjamin.* Munich, 2004.

Weinbaum, Laurence. "Defrosting History: The Restitution of Jewish Property in Eastern Europe." In *The Plunder of Jewish Property during the Holocaust,* ed. Avi Beker. Basingstoke, 2001, 83–110.

Weinberg, Gerhard L. *A World at Arms: A Global History of World War II.* New York, 1994.

Weiss, George, ed. *Einige Dokumente zur Rechtsstellung der Juden und zur Entziehung ihres Vermögens 1933–1945.* Berlin, 1954.

Weiss, Hilde, and Christoph Reinprecht. *Demokratischer Patriotismus oder ethnischer Nationalismus in Ostmitteleuropa. Empirische Analysen zur nationalen Identität in Ungarn, Tschechien, Slowakei und Polen.* Vienna, 1998.

Weitz, Yechiam. "Ben Gurions Weg zum 'Anderen Deutschland' 1952–1963." *Vierteljahreshefte für Zeitgeschichte* 48 (2000): 255–279.

Wengst, Udo. *Beamtentum zwischen Reform und Tradition. Beamtengesetzgebung in der Gründungsphase der Bundesrepublik Deutschland 1948–1953.* Düsseldorf, 1988.

Wiggershaus, Rolf. *Die Frankfurter Schule. Geschichte, theoretische Entwicklung, politische Bedeutung.* Munich, 1988.

Wilkiewicz, Zbigniew R. "Die großen nationalen Mythen Polens." In *Nationale Mythen und Rituale in Deutschland, Frankreich und Polen,* ed. Yves Bizeul. Berlin, 2000, 59–72.

Wojak, Irmtrud, and Petes Hayes, ed. *"Arisierung" im Nationalsozialismus. Volksgemeinschaft, Raub und Gedächtnis.* Frankfurt a.M. and New York, 2000.

Wolffsohn, Michael. "Das deutsch-israelische Wiedergutmachungsabkommen von 1952 im internationalen Zusammenhang." *Vierteljahreshefte für Zeitgeschichte* 36 (1988): 691–731.

———. *Ewige Schuld? 40 Jahre deutsch-jüdisch-israelische Beziehungen.* Munich and Zurich, 1988.

———. "Von der verordneten zur freiwilligen 'Vergangenheitsbewältigung'? Eine Skizze der bundesdeutschen Entwicklung 1955–1965." *German Studies Review* 12, no. 1 (1989): 111–137.

Woodward, Susan. *Balkan Tragedy: Chaos and Dissolution after the Cold War.* Washington, D.C., 1995.

Wronge, Wanja. *Und dann mußten wir raus. I wtedy nas wywieźli. Wanderungen durch das Gedächtnis. Von Vertreibungen der Polen und Deutschen 1939–1949. Wędrówki po obszarze pamięci. O wypędzeniach Polaków i Niemców.* Berlin, 2000.

Yablonka, Hanna. *Foreign Brethren: Holocaust Survivors in the State of Israel 1948–1952.* Jerusalem, 1994 (Hebrew).

Yazbak, Mahmoud. "Ha-Hagira ha-Arawit le-Haifa bein ha-Shanim 1933–1948." ["The Arab Immigration to Haifa Between the Years 1933–1948".] *Cathedra* 45 (1987): 131–146.

Young, James E. *Writing and Rewriting the Holocaust: Narrative and Consequences of Interpretation.* Bloomington, 1988.

Young-Bruehl, Elisabeth. *Hannah Arendt: For Love of the World.* New Haven and London, 1982.

Zelikow, Philip, and Condoleezza Rice. *Germany Unified and Europe Transformed: A Study in Statecraft.* Cambridge, 1995.

Zelizer, Vivienne. *Morals and Markets: The Development of Life Insurance in the United States.* New York, 1979.

———. "The Social Meaning of Money: 'Special Monies'." *American Journal of Sociology* 95 (1989): 342–77.

Zimmerman, Joshua D., ed. *Contested Memories: Poles and Jews during the Holocaust and its Aftermath.* New Brunswick, 2003.

Zimmermann, Michael. "Zigeunerbilder und Zigeunerpolitik in Deutschland. Eine Übersicht über neuere historische Studien." *Werkstatt Geschichte* 25 (2000): 35–58.

Zumbansen, Peer, ed. *Zwangsarbeit im Dritten Reich. Erinnerung und Verantwortung. Juristische und zeithistorische Betrachtungen.* Baden-Baden, 2002.

Zweig, Ronald W. *German Reparations and the Jewish World: A History of the Claims Conference.* London, 2001.

———. *The Gold Train—The Destruction of Jews and the Looting of Hungary.* New York, 2002.

CONTRIBUTORS

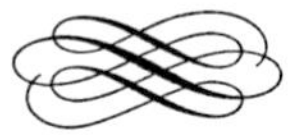

Elazar Barkan is professor of international and public affairs at Columbia University. He is the co-director of the human rights concentration at the School of International and Public Affairs (SIPA) at Columbia. He is the author of *The Guilt of Nations: Restitution and Negotiating Historical Injustices* (New York, 2000).

Ulrich Baumann is a research associate at the Foundation of the Memorial to the Murdered Jews of Europe, Berlin. He is the author of *Zerstörte Nachbarschaften. Christen und Juden in badischen Landgemeinden 1862–1940* (Hamburg, 2000).

John Borneman is professor of anthropology at Princeton University. He is the author of *Subversions of International Order. Toward a Political Anthropology of Culture* (New York, 1997) and editor of *Death of the Father: An Anthropology of the End in Political Authority* (New York, 2003).

Dan Diner is professor at the Hebrew University of Jerusalem and director of the Simon Dubnow Institute for Jewish History and Culture at Leipzig University. He is the author of *Beyond the Conceivable: Studies on Germany, Nazism, and the Holocaust* (Berkeley, 2000). His latest publication is *Versiegelte Zeit. Über den Stillstand der islamischen Welt* (Munich, 2005).

François Guesnet is an associated fellow at the Simon Dubnow Institute for Jewish History and Culture at Leipzig University and visiting professor of historical social sciences at Potsdam University. He is the author of *Polnische Juden im 19. Jahrhundert. Lebensbedingungen, Rechtsnormen und Organisation im Wandel* (Cologne, 1998).

Hans Günter Hockerts is professor of modern history at the Ludwig-Maximillians-Universität München. He is editor of *Koordinaten deutscher Geschichte in der Epoche des Ost-West-Konflikts* (Munich, 2004).

Catherine Horel is a research fellow at the Centre National de la Recherche Scientifique, Paris, and associate professor at the Institute of European Studies at the University of Louvain, Belgium. She is the author of *La restitution des biens juifs et le renouveau juif en Europe centrale (Hongrie, Slovaquie, République Tchèque)* (Bern, 2002).

Clemens Jabloner is president of the Higher Administrative Court Wien, Austria. He served as head of the Austrian Historical Commission from 1998 to 2003. He is coeditor of the *Schlussbericht der Historikerkommission der Republik Österreich* (Oldenburg, 2003).

Markus Kirchhoff is a research fellow at the Simon Dubnow Institute for Jewish History and Culture at Leipzig University. He is the author of *Häuser des Buches. Bilder jüdischer Bibliotheken* (Leipzig, 2002) and *Von Text zu Land. Palästina im wissenschaftlichen Diskurs 1865–1920* (Göttingen 2005).

Claudia Kraft is professor of East European history at Erfurt University. She is the author of *Europa im Blick der polnischen Juristen. Rechtsordnung und juristische Profession im Spannungsfeld zwischen Nation und Europa 1918–1939* (Frankfurt a.M., 2002).

Lutz Niethammer has been professor of modern history at the historical department of the Friedrich Schiller University Jena. He is the author of *Posthistoire—Ist die Geschichte zu Ende?* (Reinbek, 1989) and *Ego-Histoire? Und andere Erinnerungs-Versuche* (Vienna, 2002). From 1998 to 1999 he served as scientific advisor to the German Federal Chancellery on the question of compensation for Nazi forced laborers.

Béla Rásky has been a research fellow at the Austrian Science and Research Liaison Office, Vienna. He is the author of *Kulturpolitik und Kulturadministration in Europa. 42 Einblicke* (Vienna, 1995).

Natan Sznaider is professor of sociology at the Academic College of Tel Aviv-Jafo and the author of *The Compassionate Temperament: Care and Cruelty in Modern Society* (Lanham, 2001). Together with Daniel Levy, he published *Erinnerung im globalen Zeitalter. Der Holocaust* (Frankfurt a.M., 2001).

Heidemarie Uhl is a research fellow at the Commission for Cultural Studies and Performing Arts of the Austrian Academy of Sciences, Vienna. She is editor of *Zivilisationsbruch und Gedächtniskultur. Das 20. Jahrhundert in der Erinnerung des beginnenden 21. Jahrhunderts* (Innsbruck, 2003).

Sigrid Weigel is professor of literature at Technische Universität Berlin and director of the Zentrum für Literaturforschung Berlin. She is the author of *Literatur als Voraussetzung der Kulturgeschichte. Schauplätze von Shakespeare bis Benjamin* (Munich, 2004).

Yfaat Weiss is a research fellow in the department of Jewish history at the University of Haifa and director of the Bucerius Institute for Contemporary German History and Society, Haifa. She is the author of *Staatsbürgerschaft und Ethnizität. Deutsche und polnische Juden am Vorabend des Holocaust* (Munich, 2000).

Gotthart Wunberg has been professor of modern German literature at the University of Tübingen and served as director of Internationales Forschungszentrum Kulturwissenschaften Wien (IFK), Austria. He is the author of *Jahrhundertwende. Studien zur Literatur der Moderne* (Tübingen, 2001).

Index

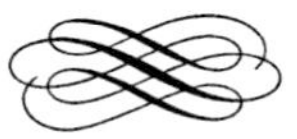